peng

GLOBAL STRATEGIC MANAGEMENT

Mike W. Peng is the Provost's Distinguished Professor of Global Strategy at the University of Texas at Dallas. He holds a bachelor's degree from Winona State University, Minnesota, and a PhD degree from the University of Washington, Seattle. Prior to joining UT Dallas, Professor Peng had been on the faculty at the Ohio State University, Chinese University of Hong Kong, and University of Hawaii. In addition, he has held visiting or courtesy appointments in Australia (University of Sydney and Queensland University of Technology), Britain (University of Nottingham), China (Xi'an Jiaotong University, Sun Yat-sen University, and Cheung Kong Graduate School of Business), Denmark (Copenhagen Business School), Hong Kong (Chinese University of Hong Kong, Hong Kong Polytechnic University, and University of Hong Kong), Vietnam (Foreign Trade University), and the United States (University of Memphis, University of Michigan, Seattle Pacific University, and Western Washington University).

Professor Peng is widely regarded as one of the most prolific and most influential scholars in global strategy—both the United Nations and the World Bank have cited his work in major publications. Truly global in scope, his research focuses on firm strategies in regions such as Asia, Central and Eastern Europe, and North America, covering countries such as China, Egypt, Hong Kong, India, Japan, Russia, South Africa, South Korea, Thailand, the United States, and Vietnam. He has published approximately 60 articles in leading journals and authored four books. The first two are *Behind the Success and Failure of US Export Intermediaries* (Quorum, 1998) and *Business Strategies in Transition Economies* (Sage, 2000). His *Global Business* (South-Western Cengage Learning, 2009) has recently been launched. The first edition of *Global Strategic Management* (South-Western Thomson, 2006) has been successfully used in over 20 countries, and has been translated into Chinese (published by Posts and Telecom Press, Beijing, 2007) and into Portuguese (published by Thomson Brasil, São Paolo, 2008).

Professor Peng is active in leadership positions in his field. At the Strategic Management Society (SMS), he was the first elected officer of the Global Strategy Interest Group (2005–2008), now serving as its Chair. He also co-chaired the first SMS conference on China strategy in Shanghai (2007). At the Academy of International Business (ABI), he was a Co-Program Chair for the Research Frontiers Conference in San Diego (2006) and is currently guest-editing a *Journal of International Business Studies* special issue on "Asia and global business." At the Academy of Management, (AOM) he was in charge of the Junior Faculty Consortium for the International Management Division for the Atlanta meetings (2006). Professor Peng has served on the editorial boards of the *Academy of Management Journal, Academy of Management Review, Journal of International Business Studies, Journal of World Business*, and *Strategic Management Journal*. He has also guest-edited the *Journal of Management Studies*. At present, he is Editor-in-Chief of the *Asia Pacific Journal of Management*.

On a worldwide basis, Professor Peng has taught students at all levels—undergraduate, MBA, PhD, EMBA, executive, and faculty training programs. Some of his former PhD students are now professors at California State University, Chinese University of Hong Kong, Georgia State University, Hong Kong University of Science and Technology, Lehigh University, Northeastern University, Oregon State University, Southern Methodist University, St. John's University, University of Colorado at Boulder, University of Missouri at St. Louis, and University of Texas at Dallas.

Professor Peng is also an active faculty trainer and consultant. He has provided on-the-job training to over 200 professors around the world. Every year since 1999, he has conducted faculty training workshops on how to teach international business at the University of Memphis with faculty participants from around the country. He has consulted for organizations such as BankOne, Berlitz International, Chinese Chamber of Commerce, Greater Dallas Asian American Chamber of Commerce, Hong Kong Research Grants Council, Manufacturers Alliance/MAPI, National Science Foundation, Nationwide Insurance, Ohio Polymer Association, SAFRAN, US-China Business Council, and The World Bank. His practitioner-oriented research has appeared in *Harvard Business Review, Academy of Management Executive,* and *China Business Review.*

Professor Peng has received numerous awards and recognitions. He has been recognized as a Foreign Expert by the Chinese government. One of his *Academy of Management Review* papers has been found to be a "new hot paper" (based on citations) representing the *entire* field of Economics and Business by the Institute for Scientific Information (ISI), which publishes the Social Sciences Citation Index (SSCI). One of his Babson conference papers won a Small Business Administration (SBA) Award for the best paper exploring the importance of small businesses to the US economy. Professor Peng is a recipient of the Scholarly Contribution Award from the International Association for Chinese Management Research (IACMR). He has also been quoted in *Newsweek, The Exporter Magazine, Business Times* (Singapore), and Voice of America.

In addition, Professor Peng's high-impact, high-visibility research has also attracted significant external funding, totaling more than half a million dollars from sources such as the (US) National Science Foundation, Hong Kong Research Grants Council, and Chinese National Natural Science Foundation.

To Agnes, Grace, and James

brief contents

contents

Five Force. (ads & disads).

chapter 4   Institutions, Cultures, and Ethics   90

Informal.

Institutions as perspective.

Formal.

chapter 8   Global Competitive Dynamics   248

The first edition of *Global Strategic Management* intended to set a new standard for strategic management and international business textbooks in general and for global strategy textbooks in particular. This book serves the needs of three types of undergraduate or MBA courses: (1) global or international strategy courses, (2) strategic management courses (especially those taught by internationally oriented instructors), and (3) international business courses (especially those taught by strategically oriented instructors). Based on enthusiastic support from students and professors in Australia, Austria, Brazil, Britain, Canada, China, France, Germany, Hong Kong, India, Macau, the Netherlands, New Zealand, Norway, Portugal, Romania, South Korea, Sweden, Taiwan, Thailand, and the United States, the first edition achieved unprecedented success, and was already translated into Chinese and Portuguese.

The second edition of *Global Strategic Management* aspires to do even better. It continues the market-winning framework centered on the "strategy tripod" pioneered in the first edition, and has been thoroughly updated to capture the rapidly moving research and events of the past several years. Its most strategic features include (1) a broadened definition of "global strategy," (2) a comprehensive and innovative coverage, (3) an in-depth and consistent explanation of cutting-edge research, and (4) an interesting and accessible way to engage students.

A Broadened Definition of "Global Strategy"

In this book, "global strategy" is defined not as a particular multinational enterprise (MNE) strategy, but as "strategy around the globe." While emphasizing international strategy, we do not exclusively focus on it. Just like "international business" is about "business" (in addition to being "international"), "global strategy" is most fundamentally about "strategy" before being "global." Most global strategy and international business textbooks take the perspective of the foreign entrant, typically the MNE, often dealing with issues such as how to enter foreign markets and how to look for local partners. Important as these issues are, they cover only one side of international business—namely, the foreign side. The other side, naturally, is how domestic firms strategize by competing against each other and against foreign entrants. Failing to understand the "other side," at best, covers only one side of the coin.

A Comprehensive and Innovative Coverage

With a broadened definition of "global strategy," this book covers the strategies of both large MNEs and small entrepreneurial firms, both foreign entrants and domestic firms, and both firms from developed economies and companies from emerging economies. As a result, this text offers the most comprehensive and innovative coverage of global strategy topics available on the market. In short, it is the world's first *global,* global-strategy book. Its unique features include:

- A chapter on institutions, cultures, and ethics (Chapter 4) and a focus on the emerging institution-based view of strategy (in addition to the traditional industry- and resource-based views) throughout the book.

- A chapter on entrepreneurship (Chapter 6), especially its internationalization aspects.

- A chapter on global competitive dynamics (Chapter 8), including substantial discussions on cartel, antitrust, and antidumping issues typically ignored by other textbooks.

- A chapter on both product and geographic diversification (Chapter 9), which is the first time these crucial aspects of corporate strategies appear in the *same* textbook chapter.

- A chapter on corporate governance around the world (Chapter 11). This is the first time in a major textbook both the principal-agent conflicts and principal-principal conflicts are given *equal* "air time."

- A chapter on corporate social responsibility (Chapter 12), an increasingly important area of interest.

- Geographically comprehensive coverage, not only covering firms from the developed economies of the Triad (North America, Western Europe, and Japan), but also those from emerging economies of the world (including Africa, Asia, and Latin America).

- A consistent theme on ethics, which is not only highlighted in Chapters 4 and 12 but also throughout all chapters in the form of Ethical Challenge features and ethics-based critical discussion questions.

An In-depth and Consistent Explanation

The breadth of the field poses a challenge to textbook authors. My respect and admiration for the diversity of the field has increased tremendously as research for the book progresses. To provide an in-depth and evidence-based explanation, I have systematically drawn on the latest research, including some of my own work. Specifically, *every* article in each issue published in the last ten years in leading journals such as the *Academy of Management Journal, Academy of Management Review, Journal of International Business Studies,* and *Strategic Management Journal* has been consulted. Much other related work has also been cited. Consequently, the Endnotes after each chapter are lengthy and comprehensive. While not every work in the literature is cited, I am confident that I have left no major streams of research untouched. Readers, especially contributors to the literature, should feel free to check the Index of Names to verify this claim.

Given the breadth of the field, it is easy to lose focus. To combat this tendency, I have endeavored to provide a consistent set of frameworks in *all* chapters. This is done in three ways. First, I have focused on the four most fundamental questions in strategic management raised by Richard Rumelt, David Teece, and Dan Schendel.[1] These are (1) Why do firms differ? (2) How do firms behave? (3) What determines the scope of the firm? and (4) What determines the success and failure of firms around the globe? I have emphasized the fourth question about firms' performance, which has also been argued to be the leading question guiding global strategy and international business research today.[2]

Another way to combat the tendency to lose sight of the "forest" while scrutinizing various "trees" is to consistently draw on the "strategy tripod"—the three leading perspectives on strategy, namely, the industry-, resource-, and institution-based views. An innovative feature is the development of the institution-based view.[3] In *every* chapter, these three views are integrated to develop a comprehensive model.[4]

Finally, I have written a "Debates and Extensions" section for *every* chapter except Chapter 1 (which is a debate in itself). Virtually all textbooks uncritically present knowledge "as is" and ignore the fact that the field is alive with numerous debates. Because debates drive practice and research ahead, it is imperative that students be exposed to various cutting-edge debates.

An Interesting and Accessible Way to Engage Students

If you fear this book might be very boring because it draws so heavily on current research, you would be wrong. I have used a clear, engaging, conversational style to tell the "story." Relative to rival books, my chapters are generally livelier and shorter. In fact, most chapters in the second edition have been downsized relative to their length in the first edition. In addition, I have developed a number of tactics to engage students:

- Every chapter starts with an Opening Case, which draws students into the plot.

- I have woven a large number of interesting anecdotes into the text. In addition to examples from the business world, nontraditional examples range from ancient Chinese military writings to the Roman Empire's import quotas, from quotes from *Anna Karenina* to the mutually assured destruction (MAD) strategy during the Cold War.

- Every chapter contains a number of Strategy in Action boxes, which single out interesting examples as "mini-cases" to enhance learning.

- Every chapter ends with a Closing Case with case discussion questions.

---

[1] R. Rumelt, D. Teece, & D. Schendel (eds.), 1994, *Fundamental Issues in Strategy: A Research Agenda,* Boston: Harvard Business School Press.

[2] M. W. Peng, 2004, Identifying the big question in international business research, *Journal of International Business Studies,* 35 (2): 99–108.

[3] M. W. Peng, D. Wang, & Y. Jiang, 2008, An institution-based view of international business strategy: A focus on emerging economies, *Journal of International Business Studies,*39 (5): 920-936.

[4] K. E. Meyer, S. Estrin, S. Bhaumik, & M. W. Peng, 2008, Institutions, resources, and entry strategies in emerging economies, *Strategic Management Journal* (in press).

- Every chapter also contains ethics-based critical discussion questions to facilitate discussions, driving home the point that ethics is a theme that cuts across all the chapters, not just Chapters 4 and 12.

- A number of shorter Video Cases (drawn from 50 Lessons) and longer Integrative Cases.

What's New in the Second Edition?

Thoroughly revised, every chapter has numerous updates, each containing a new "Ethical Challenge" feature and an added "The Savvy Strategist" section. All Video Cases have been replaced, eight new Integrative Cases have been introduced, and six Integrative Cases used in the first edition have all been updated by the original authors. Some highlights of the changes include:

- Chapter 1 Opening Case: How did *Global Strategy* enter and compete in China?

- Chapter 1: The idea of "semiglobalization"

- Strategy in Action 3.2. ANA: Refreshing the parts other airlines can't reach

- Strategy in Action 4.1. Kenya's flower industry copes with recent riots

- Chapter 6 Opening Case: An American chasing the China dream

- Chapter 7 Opening Case: Danone versus Wahaha: From alliance to divorce

- Chapter 8 Closing Case: Fighting the online video game wars in China

- Strategy in Action 8.1: Cisco versus Huawei: War and peace

- Strategy in Action 8.2: Publish or perish in patent race

- Strategy in Action 9.3. Making M&As fly in China (based on a *Harvard Business Review* article I published)

- Chapter 10 Closing Case: Moving headquarters overseas

- Chapter 11 Opening Case: The private equity challenge

- Strategy in Action 11.2. Sarbanes-Oxley and New York

- Chapter 12 Closing Case: Which side is Toyota on?

- Strategy in Action 12.1: Is Icelandic Glacial really "carbon neutral"?

Again, these are mere highlights of the changes throughout the chapters. In terms of cases outside of the chapters, a completely new set of Video Cases, which are interviews of global strategists coming from a dedicated video provider (50 Lessons) has been assembled. They are available to help instructors enhance the effectiveness of their teaching. Leading organizations featured in the Video Cases include:

- Body Shop International

- Boston Scientific

- Halifax Bank of Scotland

- Ford Motor Company

- Marriott International

- Publicis Groupe

- Rio Tinto

- Royal Bank of Scotland

In terms of Integrative Cases, the "incumbents" used in the first edition have all been thoroughly revised and updated. The majority of Integrative Cases are new ones:

- AGRANA

- Mattel and the toy recalls

- How Chinese toymakers respond to recalls

- Unilever's "Fair & Lovely" whitening cream—a reprint of a complete article from the field's leading journal, *Strategic Management Journal* (a first among all strategy textbooks)

- 3i's private equity investment in China's Little Sheep

- Have you offset your own carbon emissions?

- Building a better rat trap for the Irula in rural India

Overall, the second edition of *Global Strategy* has packed its pages with relevance, timeliness, and excitement, not to mention the strategic with the practical. To see how this book, itself a global product, competes around the world, check out the Chapter 1 Opening Case.

Support Materials

A full set of supplements is available for students and adopting instructors, all designed to facilitate ease of learning, teaching, and testing.

INSTRUCTOR'S RESOURCE DVD-ROM. Instructors will find at their fingertips all of the teaching resources they need to plan, teach, grade, and assess student understanding and progress with this all-in-one resource for *Global Strategic Management*. The IR-DVD-ROM contains:

- Instructor's Manual—This valuable time-saving Instructor's Manual includes comprehensive resources to streamline course preparation, such as teaching suggestions, lecture notes, and answers to all chapter questions. Also included are discussion guidelines and answers for the Integrative Cases found at the end of each part.

- Testbank—The *Global Strategic Management* Testbank in ExamView® software allows instructors to create customized tests by choosing from true/false, multiple choice, and short answer/essay questions for each of the 12 chapters. Ranging in difficulty, all questions have been tagged to the text's Learning Objectives and AASCB standards to ensure students are meeting the course criteria.

- PowerPoint® Slides—A comprehensive set of PowerPoint® slides assists instructors in the presentation of the chapter material, enabling students to synthesize key concepts.

- Video Cases—Perhaps one of the most exciting and compelling bonus features of this edition, these 17 short and powerful video clips, produced by 50 Lessons, provide additional guidance on strategies around the globe. The video clips offer real-world business acumen and valuable learning experiences from an array of internationally known business leaders.

PRODUCT SUPPORT WEBSITE. We offer a *Global Strategic Management* product support website at international.cengage.com, where instructors can download files for the Instructor's Manual, Testbank, and PowerPoint slides.

As *Global Strategic Management* launches its second edition, I first want to thank all our customers—professors, instructors, and students—around the world who have made the book's success possible. At UT Dallas, I thank my colleagues Tev Dalgic, Dave Deeds, Anne Ferrante, Dave Ford, John Fowler, Richard Harrison, Jonathan Hochberg, Marilyn Kaplan, Seung-Hyun Lee, John Lin, Livia Markoczy, Kumar Nair, Joe Picken, Orlando Richard, Jane Salk, Eric Tsang, Habte Woldu, Laurie Ziegler, and the leadership team—Hasan Pirkul (dean), Varghese Jacob (associate dean), and Greg Dess (area coordinator)—for creating and nurturing a supportive intellectual environment. I also thank my two PhD students, Erin Pleggenkuhle-Miles and Yasuhiro Yamakawa, who not only helped me with the revisions for the second edition, but also authored excellent case materials. Rachel Pinkham, Managing Editor of the *Asia Pacific Journal of Management* where I serve as Editor-in-Chief, also graciously helped with proofreading. In addition, this research has been generously supported by a National Science Foundation Faculty Career Grant (SES 0552089) and a Provost's Distinguished Research Professorship, to which I am grateful.

At Cengage Learning/South-Western (formerly South-Western Thomson), I thank the "Peng team" that not only publishes *Global Strategic Management* but also *Global Business*: Melissa Acuna, Editor-in-Chief; Michele Rhoades, Senior Acquisitions Editor; Jennifer King, Developmental Editor; Kimberly Kanakes, Executive Marketing Manager; Clint Kernen, Marketing Manager; Sarah Rose, Marketing Coordinator; Tippy McIntosh, Senior Art Director; and Terri Coats, Executive Director, International.

In the academic community, I would like to thank the reviewers for this edition:

- Sara B. Kimmel, Belhaven College

- Ted W. Legatski, Texas Christian University

In addition, I thank colleagues who provided informal feedback to me on the book (if you wrote me but I failed to mention your name here, my apologies—blame this on the volume of such e-mails):

- David Ahlstrom (Chinese University of Hong Kong, China)

- J. C. Cuervo (University of Macau, China)

- Charles Dhanaraj (Indiana University, USA)

- Joyce Falkenberg (Norwegian School of Economics and Business Administration, Norway)

- Myles Gartland (Rockhurst University, USA)

- John Gerace (Chestnut Hill College, USA)

- Katalin Haynes (Texas A&M University, USA)

- Fernanda Ilhéu (ISEG/Technical University of Lisbon, Portugal)

- Basil Janavaras (Minnesota State University, USA)
- Marshall Shibing Jiang (Brock University, Canada)
- Bob Hoskisson (Arizona State University, USA)
- Ben Kedia (University of Memphis, USA)
- Seung-Hyun Lee (University of Texas at Dallas, USA)
- Mark Lowenstein (Newburry College, USA)
- Anoop Madhok (York University, Canada)
- Charles Mambula (Suffolk University, USA)
- Alfredo Mauri (Saint Joseph's University, USA)
- Klaus Meyer (University of Bath, UK)
- Susan Michie (University of Evansville, USA)
- Paul Miesing (State University of New York at Albany, USA)
- Deb Mukherjee (University of Akron, USA)
- David Pritchard (Rochester Institute of Technology, USA)
- Mike Pustay (Texas A&M University, USA)
- Gongming Qiun (Chinese University of Hong Kong, China)
- Wonchan Ra (Hankuk University of Foreign Studies, South Korea)
- Pradeep Kanta Ray (University of New South Wales, Australia)
- Trond Randøy (Agder University College, Norway)
- Alan Rugman (Indiana University, USA)
- Prashant Salwan (Indian Institute of Management, India)
- Hyung-Deok Shin (Hongik University, South Korea)
- Anne Smith (University of Tennessee, USA)
- Martin Stack (Rockhurst University, USA)
- Yu-Shan Su (Chang Jung Christian University, Taiwan)
- Siri Terjesen (Texas Christian University, USA and Queensland University of Technology, Australia)
- Mark Wellman (University of Maryland, USA)
- En Xie (Xi'an Jiaotong University, China)
- Gracy Yang (University of Sydney, Australia)
- Haibin Yang (City University of Hong Kong, China)
- Xiaohua Yang (Queensland University of Technology, Australia)
- Michael Young (Hong Kong Baptist University, China)

- Wu Zhan (University of Sydney, Australia)

- Shujun Zhang (Sun Yat-sen University, China)

- Jessie Qi Zhou (Southern Methodist University, USA)

- Alan Zimmerman (City University of New York, College of Staten Island, USA)

I also want to thank four very special colleagues: Sun Wei and Lui Xinmei (Xi'an Jiaotong University) in China, Joaquim Carlos Racy (Pontifícia Universidade Católica de São Paulo), and George Bedinelli Rossi (Universidade de São Paulo) in Brazil. They loved the book so much that they were willing to endure the pain of translating the first edition into Chinese and Portuguese. Their hard work has enabled *Global Strategic Management* to reach wider audiences globally, living up to its self-proclaimed tagline as a "*global,* global-strategy book." In comparison, most translated textbooks are later editions issued after the "bugs" have been worked out of previous editions.

For the second edition, a total of 20 colleagues from Australia, Canada, China, Singapore, and the United States have kindly contributed case materials. They are:

- Hari Bapuji (University of Manitoba, Canada)

- Paul Beamish (University of Western Ontario, Canada)

- Liz Bogard (University of Texas at Dallas, USA)

- Hao Chen (University of Texas at Dallas, USA)—two cases

- Jeremy DeLaCruz (University of Texas at Dallas, USA)

- Guillermo Estrada (University of Texas at Dallas, USA)

- Lily Fang (INSEAD, Singapore)

- Yi Jiang (California State University, East Bay, USA)

- Aneel Karnani (University of Michigan, USA)

- Aldas Pranas Krianciunas (Purdue University, USA)

- Roger Leeds (Johns Hopkins University, USA)

- Yuan Lu (Chinese University of Hong Kong, China)

- Cathy Partin (University of Texas at Dallas, USA)

- Erin Pleggenkuhle-Miles (University of Texas at Dallas, USA)

- Robert Satterfield (University of Texas at Dallas, USA)

- Charles Stevens (The Ohio State University, USA)

- Sunny Li Sun (University of Texas at Dallas, USA)—two cases

- Qingjiu (Tom) Tao (Lehigh University, USA)

- Siri Terjesen (Texas Christian University, USA and Queensland University of Technology, Australia)

- Yasuhiro Yamakawa (University of Texas at Dallas, USA)

Last, but by no means least, I thank my wife Agnes, my daughter Grace, and my son James—to whom this book is dedicated. I have been blessed with such a beautiful family. I have named Agnes CEO, CFO, COO, CIO, CTO, and CPO for our family, the last of which is coined by me, which stands for "chief parenting officer." When the first edition was finished in late 2004, Grace, age two at that time, was getting into "princess mania" big time and James was a chubby newborn. Now, my six-year-old Grace has lost her first teeth, reads voraciously (two of the first words she can recognize from a book are "global" and "strategy"), and wants to be a serious writer (she can write paragraphs and short stories now!). My four-year-old James has conceptually (and correctly) answered his preschool teacher's question "What's special about daddy?" "Daddy works all the time!" As a third-generation professor in my family, I can't help but wonder whether one (or both) of them will become a fourth-generation professor someday. To all of you, my thanks and my love.

MWP
September 30, 2008

Strategy Around the Globe

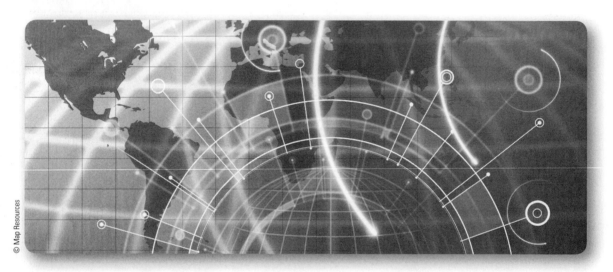

© Map Resources

Knowledge Objectives

After studying this chapter, you should be able to

1. Offer a basic critique of the traditional, narrowly defined "global strategy"

2. Articulate the rationale behind studying global strategy

3. Define what is strategy and what is global strategy

4. Outline the four fundamental questions in strategy

5. Participate in the debate on globalization with a reasonably balanced view and a keen awareness of your likely bias

OPENING CASE: HOW DID *GLOBAL STRATEGY* ENTER AND COMPETE IN CHINA?

Every reader naturally expects this book to talk about the global strategy of *other* companies. However, how many of you thought that this book would also be a global product, published by a multinational enterprise (MNE) that competes around the world? Our publisher, known as Cengage Learning since 2007, is an MNE that operates in 39 countries. Cengage Learning emphasizes its brands, such as our own South-Western brand that specializes in business and economics college textbooks. The history of South-Western Cengage Learning is interesting. Founded in 1902, South-Western, based in Cincinnati, Ohio, was an independent US publisher. In 1986, Canada's Thomson Corporation bought South-Western, which then became a division known as South-Western Thomson Learning. In early 2007, Thomson Corporation, in order to raise funds to acquire Reuters, sold Thomson Learning for $7.75 billion to two private equity groups in Britain and Canada. In July 2007, Thomson Learning, under new British and Canadian ownership, changed its name to Cengage Learning. The name was based on being at the "center of engagement" for learning.

In business and economics textbooks, South-Western Cengage Learning is number one in the world in terms of market share, followed by McGraw-Hill Irwin and Pearson Prentice Hall.

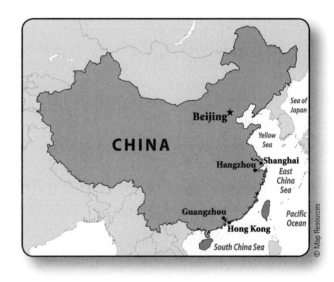

While competition historically focused on the United States and other English-speaking countries, it is now worldwide. Launched in January 2005 and copyrighted in 2006, *Global Strategic Management* targeted courses in strategic management and international business. While there was no shortage of textbooks in these two areas, *Global Strategic Management* broke new ground by being the first to specifically address their *intersection*. Thanks to enthusiastic students and professors in Australia, Austria, Brazil, Britain, Canada, China, France, Germany, Hong Kong, India, Macau, the Netherlands, New Zealand, Norway, Portugal, Romania, South Korea, Sweden, Taiwan, Thailand, and the United States, *Global Strategic Management* achieved unprecedented success. The first edition was already translated into two foreign languages (Chinese and Portuguese)—in contrast, most translated textbooks are later editions, published after the "bugs" have been worked out of earlier editions.

Although competition, in theory, is global, in practice Cengage Learning needs to win one market after another. How the first edition of *Global Strategic Management* entered and competed in China is a case in point. China's rising appetite for high-quality business education has attracted most Western textbook publishers. Many leading English-language textbooks you study have translated versions in Chinese.

To stand out among the crowd, valuable, rare, and hard-to-imitate capabilities are a must. *Global Strategic Management* is packed with value. (Who doesn't want to strategize around the globe?) To enhance the value added for different customers, *Global Strategic Management* is available in three versions in China: (1) a paperback form known as the International Student Edition (ISE), (2) a Chinese–English bilingual edition (select Chinese passages are translated and printed on the margin of the ISE), and (3) a Chinese-only translation. *Global Strategic Management* is also rare because (as noted earlier) no previous textbook successfully merged "global" with "strategy." Furthermore, not only is the Chinese translation of *Global Strategic Management* hard to imitate, it is *impossible* to imitate. This is because your author, born in China, is the only Chinese-speaking author of a leading Western textbook, and I offered direct help when translators encountered difficulties. Because of jargon, translating textbooks is always challenging, and most translated textbooks contain translation errors. Because none of the authors of other translated textbooks speaks or reads Chinese, it is impossible for them to lend a helping hand in translation. It is not surprising that the Chinese

version of *Global Strategic Management* offers the highest quality and smoothest translation among all translated textbooks in China. (In comparison, the Portuguese translation of *Global Strategic Management* published in Brazil has no such unique advantage because I could not help with it.) Finally, the time and execution of the launch were also impeccable. Since I co-chaired the first Strategic Management Society conference in China in Shanghai in May 2007, the launch team included a copy of the Chinese translation as part of the conference materials for *all* 150 attendees (professors and PhD students), who would most likely be interested in this book.

A foreign entrant also needs to know the rules of the game—both formal and informal. The formal rules in China stated that foreign companies could not publish books on their own. Cengage Learning thus licensed the translation of *Global Strategic Management* to a leading Chinese publisher: Posts and Telecom Press. (In comparison, Brazil allowed Cengage Learning's wholly owned subsidiary to publish the Portuguese translation.) A thorough understanding of the informal rules is also a must. Experienced editors at Posts and Telecom Press advised that the title be changed to *Global Business Strategy* (*Quanqiu Qiye Zhanlue*). Since books in China need to clear censorship, censors might dislike "global strategy," fearing it could be seen as a reference to "global military strategy." Throughout the book, when "China, Hong Kong, and Taiwan" were mentioned, the politically correct translated version would read "China, Hong Kong, China, and Taiwan, China." Finally, one entire case was preemptively taken out by Chinese editors. That case was titled "Dealing with Counterfeiting" (see pages 137 and 138 in the first edition).

Overall, behind *Global Strategic Management*'s launch in China was a combination of a capable global publisher and its experienced Chinese partner, a winning product, excellent country-specific knowledge, and a meticulous attention to detail. Not surprisingly, most leading universities in China, such as Peking, Shanghai Jiaotong, Sun Yat-sen, Tsinghua, and Xi'an Jiaotong Universities, have embraced this book, quickly making it a market leader.

Sources: I thank Michele Rhoades and Terri Coats (both at South-Western Cengage Learning) for their assistance. Based on (1) Author's interviews with executives at South-Western Cengage Learning and Posts and Telecom Press, 2005–08; (2) M. W. Peng, 2006, *Global Strategy*, Cincinnati: South-Western Cengage Learning; (3) M. W. Peng, 2007, *Quanqiu Qiye Zhanlue*, translated by W. Sun & X. Lui, Beijing, China: Posts & Telecom Press; (4) M. W. Peng, 2008, *Estratégia Global*, translated by J. C. Racy & G. B. Rossi, São Paulo, Brazil: South-Western Cengage Learning.

A *Global* Global-Strategy Book

How do firms, such as Cengage Learning, McGraw-Hill, and Pearson, compete around the globe? In the publishing industry in China, how do various foreign entrants and local firms interact, compete, and/or sometimes collaborate? What determines their success and failure? Since strategy is about competing and winning, this book on global strategy will help current and would-be strategists answer these and other important questions. Setting an example by itself, the book you are reading is a real global product that leverages its strengths, engages rivals, and competes around the world (see Opening Case).

However, this book does *not* focus on a particular form of international (cross-border) strategy, which is characterized by the production and distribution of standardized products and services on a worldwide basis. For over two decades, this strategy, commonly referred to as "global strategy" for lack of a better word, has often been advocated by traditional global strategy books.[1] However, there is now a great deal of rumbling and soul-searching among managers frustrated by the inability of their "world car," "world drink," or "world commercial" to conquer the world.

In reality, **multinational enterprises (MNEs),** defined as firms that engage in **foreign direct investment (FDI)** by directly controlling and managing value-adding activities in other countries,[2] often have to adapt their strategies, products, and services for local markets. For example, the Opening Case clearly shows that in the publishing industry, one size does not fit all. In the automobile industry, there is no "world car." Cars popular in one region are often rejected by customers elsewhere. (The Toyota Camry is America's best-selling car but a poor seller in Japan.) The Volkswagen Golf and the Ford Mondeo (marketed as the Contour in the United States), which have dominated Europe, have little visibility in the streets of Asia and North America.[3] The so-called "world drink," Coke Classic, actually tastes different around the world (with varying sugar content). The Coca-Cola Company's effort in pushing for a set of "world commercials" centered on the polar bear cartoon character presumably appealing to some worldwide values and interests has been undermined by uncooperative TV viewers around the world. Viewers in warmer weather countries had a hard time relating to the furry polar bear. In response, Coca-Cola switched to more costly but more effective country-specific advertisements. For instance, the Indian subsidiary launched an advertising campaign that equated Coke with "thanda," the Hindi word for "cold."

multinational enterprise (MNE)

A firm that engages in foreign direct investment (FDI) by directly controlling and managing value-adding activities in other countries.

foreign direct investment (FDI)

A firm's direct investment in production and/or service activities abroad.

The German subsidiary has developed a series of commercials that show a "hidden" kind of eroticism (!).[4]

It is evident that the narrow notion of "global strategy" in vogue over the past two decades (in other words, the "one-size-fits-all" strategy), while useful for some firms in certain industries, is often incomplete and unbalanced. This is reflected in at least three manifestations:

- Too often, the quest for worldwide cost reduction, consolidation, and restructuring in the name of "global strategy" has sacrificed local responsiveness and global learning. The results have been unsatisfactory in many cases and disastrous in others. Many MNEs have now decided to pull back from such a strategy. MTV has switched from standardized (American) English-language programming to a variety of local languages. With over 5,000 branches in 79 countries, HSBC is one of the world's largest and most global banks. Yet, instead of highlighting its "global" power, HSBC brags about being "the world's *local* bank."

- Almost by definition, the narrow notion of "global strategy" focuses on how to compete internationally, especially on how global rivals, such as Coca-Cola and Pepsi, Toyota and Honda, and Boeing and Airbus, meet each other in one country after another. As a result, the issue of how domestic companies compete with each other and with foreign entrants seems to be ignored. Does anyone know the nationalities and industries of the following companies: Cemex, Embraer, Huawei, Hutchison Whampoa, and Ranbaxy? Based in Mexico, Brazil, China, Hong Kong, and India, these five firms are world-class competitors in, respectively, cement, aerospace, telecommunications equipment, ports and telecommunications services, and pharmaceutical industries. They represent some of the top MNEs from emerging economies. If such firms are outside the radar screen of global strategists, then perhaps the radar has too many blind spots.[5]

- The current brand of "global strategy" seems relevant only for MNEs from developed economies, primarily North America, Europe, and Japan—commonly referred to as the **Triad**—to compete in other developed economies, whereby income levels and consumer preferences may be similar. **Emerging economies** (or **emerging markets**), a term that has gradually replaced the term developing economies since the 1990s, now command a full one-third of the worldwide FDI flow and half of the global gross domestic product (GDP) measured at purchasing power parity.[6] Brazil, Russia, India, and China—now known as **BRIC** in the new jargon—command more attention. Many local firms rise to the challenge, not only effectively competing at home but also launching offensives abroad, thus creating serious ramifications for Triad-based MNEs.[7] (see Strategy in Action 1.1)

As a result, modifying (or even abandoning) the traditional "global strategy" has increasingly been entertained.[8] The Closing Case illustrates how to strategically focus on the base of the global economic pyramid (or, in short, **base of the pyramid**), which has been ignored by traditional "global strategy." Overall, this book can be considered as part of this broad movement in search of a better understanding of how to effectively strategize and compete around the globe, not being merely about "global strategy" per se. This book differentiates itself from existing global strategy

Triad

Three primary regions of developed economies: North America, Europe, and Japan.

emerging economies (emerging markets)

A label that describes fast-growing developing economies since the 1990s.

BRIC

Brazil, Russia, India, and China

base of the pyramid

The vast majority of humanity, about four billion people, who make less than $2,000 a year.

Strategy in Action 1.1 - Li Ning Goes Global

Li Ning is China's leading sporting goods company. It was founded in 1989 by Li Ning, who captured three gold medals in gymnastics in the 1984 Los Angeles Olympic Games. Li Ning thus became a national hero in China at the age of 21, and he enjoys almost 100% recognition of his name in the country. On August 8, 2008, Li Ning lighted the flame for the games at the opening ceremony of the Beijing Olympics.

Li Ning (hereafter referring to the company, not the founder) positioned itself at an intermediate price/value range between international and local brands. In China, Nike and Adidas focus on the high end with footwear retail prices of $75 to $125 per pair, and most local rivals target the low end at $7 to $25 per pair. Li Ning is the only player with the midrange pricing of $25 to $60 per pair. There are more than 200 sporting goods brands in China. The top-three players—Nike, Adidas, and Li Ning (in that order)—have approximate market shares of 10%, 9.3%, and 8.7%, respectively. Li Ning thus is well within striking distance to surge ahead. It remains well ahead of local competitors (its closest local peer, Anta, has a 3% market share).

Li Ning intensely benchmarks itself against the industry leader, Nike. Over time, as Li Ning grows, it has gained more self-confidence with a clearer identity. Li Ning has become a genuine upgrade, rather than a cheaper alternative, for China's emerging middle class.

Li Ning embarked on internationalization in 2001 by sponsoring Spain's men's and women's basketball teams. In 2005, it forged a strategic partnership with the (US) National Basketball Association (NBA), as part of its "Anything is Possible" marketing campaign. Since then, Li Ning signed agreements with three NBA stars: Shaq O'Neal of the Miami Heat, Damon Jones of the Cleveland Cavaliers, and Chuck Hayes of the Houston Rockets. Over the last few years, Li Ning has undergone visible brand-image and product quality upgrades. It now brags about its global credentials as a sponsor of NBA superstars and the 2006 men's basketball world championship team, Spain.

All eyes are now on the 2008 Beijing Olympics. Although Li Ning has lost out to Adidas to be the official sponsor of the games, Li Ning has instead sponsored four Chinese teams with gold medal potential (gymnastics, diving, table tennis, and shooting), the Spanish men's and women's basketball teams, the Sudanese track and field team, the Argentinean basketball team, as well as the entire Swedish Olympic delegation. Li Ning hopes that the Beijing Olympics will mark its coming of age as one of the top-five global sporting goods brands.

Sources: This case was written by **Sunny Li Sun** (University of Texas at Dallas) under the supervision of Professor Mike W. Peng. It was based on (1) D. Chai & K. So, 2007, Li Ning Co. Ltd.: New NBA coup to strengthen brand appeal, Merrill Lynch Research, December 12; (2) A. Jenwipakul & P. McKenzie, 2006, CLSA Research on Li Ning, December 14; (3) Li Ning Company IPO and Annual Reports, 2004, 2005, 2006; (4) Y. Liu, 2006, Li Ning rebounding with Shaq? *Beijing Review,* December 21; (5) M. W. Peng, 2006, Li Ning: From Olympic gold medalist to star entrepreneur, in M. W. Peng, *Global Strategy* (pp. 205–206), Cincinnati, OH: South-Western Cengage Learning.

books by providing a more balanced coverage, not only in terms of the traditional "global strategy" and "non-global strategy," but also in terms of both MNEs' and local firms' perspectives. Furthermore, in addition to developed economies, this book has also devoted extensive space to competitive battles waged in emerging economies (see both Opening Case and Closing Case). In a nutshell, this is truly a *global* global-strategy book.

Why Study Global Strategy?

Global strategy is one of the most exciting and challenging subjects offered by business schools. Why study it? There are three compelling reasons. First, the most sought-after and highest-paid business school graduates (both MBAs and undergraduates) are typically management consultants with expertise in global strategy. You can be one of them. Outside the consulting industry, if you aspire to join the top ranks of many large firms, expertise in global strategy is often a prerequisite. While eventually international experience, not merely knowledge, may be required,[9] mastery of the knowledge of, and demonstration of interest in, global strategy during your education will eventually make you a more ideal candidate to be selected as an expatriate (expat) manager to gain such an experience.[10] So, don't forget to add a line on your resume that you have studied this strategically important course.

Second, even for graduates at large companies with no interest in working for the consulting industry and no aspiration to compete for the top job, as well as those individuals who work at small firms or are self-employed, you may find yourself dealing with foreign-owned suppliers and buyers, competing with foreign-invested firms in your home market, and perhaps even selling and investing overseas. Or alternatively, you may find yourself working for a foreign-owned corporation, your previously domestic employer acquired by a foreign player, or your unit ordered to shut down for global consolidation. Approximately 80 million people worldwide, including six million Americans, one million British, and 18 million Chinese, are directly employed by foreign-owned firms. Understanding how strategic decisions are made may facilitate your own career in such organizations.[11] If there is a strategic rationale to downsize your unit, you would want to be able to figure this out as soon as possible and be the first to post your resume on Monster.com, instead of being the first to receive a pink slip. In other words, you want to be more *strategic*. After all, it is your career that is at stake. Don't be the last in the know!

Overall, in this age of globalization, "how do you keep from being Bangalored? Or Shanghaied?"[12] (That is, have your job outsourced to India or China.) To do this, you must first understand what strategy is, which is discussed next.

What Is Strategy?

Origin

strategic management

A way of managing the firm from a strategic, "big picture" perspective.

Derived from the ancient Greek word *strategos*, the word "strategy" originally referred to the "art of the general." Strategy has very strong military roots, the word itself dating back to around 500 BC with the work of Sun Tzu, a Chinese military strategist.[13] Sun Tzu's most famous teaching is "Know yourself, know your opponents; encounter a hundred battles, win a hundred victories." The application of the principles of military strategy to business competition, known as **strategic management** (or strategy in short), is a more recent phenomenon, developed since the 1960s.[14]

Plan versus Action

strategy as plan

A perspective that suggests that strategy is most fundamentally embodied in explicit, rigorous formal planning as in the military.

Because business strategy is a relatively young field (despite the long roots of military strategy), what defines strategy has been a subject of intense debate.[15] Three schools of thought have emerged (shown in Table 1.1). The first, **"strategy as plan"** school is the oldest. Drawing on the work of Carl von Clausewitz, a Prussian (German) military

TABLE 1.1   What is Strategy?

STRATEGY AS PLAN

- "Concerned with drafting the plan of war and shaping the individual campaigns and, within these, deciding on the individual engagements" (von Clausewitz, 1976)[1]
- "A set of concrete plans to help the organization accomplish its goal" (Oster, 1994)[2]

STRATEGY AS ACTION

- "The art of distributing and applying military means to fulfill the ends of policy" (Liddel Hart, 1967)[3]
- "A pattern in a stream of actions or decisions" (Mintzberg, 1978)[4]
- "The creation of a unique and valuable position, involving a different set of activities...making trade-offs in competing...creating fit among a company's activities" (Porter, 1996)[5]

STRATEGY AS INTEGRATION

- "The determination of the basic long-term goals and objectives of an enterprise, and the adoption of courses of action and the allocation of resources necessary for carrying out these goals" (Chandler, 1962)[6]
- "An integrated and coordinated set of commitments and actions designed to exploit core competencies and gain a competitive advantage" (Hitt, Ireland, and Hoskisson, 2003)[7]
- "The analyses, decisions, and actions an organization undertakes in order to create and sustain competitive advantages" (Dess, Lumpkin, and Eisner, 2008)[8]

Sources: Based on (1) C. von Clausewitz, 1976, *On War*, vol. 1 (p. 177), London: Kegan Paul; (2) S. Oster, 1994, *Modern Competitive Analysis*, 2nd ed. (p. 4), New York: Oxford University Press; (3) B. Liddell Hart, 1967, *Strategy*, 2nd rev. ed. (p. 321), New York: Meridian; (4) H. Mintzberg, 1978, Patterns in strategy formulation (p. 934), *Management Science*, 24: 934–948; (5) M. Porter, 1996, What is strategy? (pp. 68, 70, 75), *Harvard Business Review*, 74 (6): 61–78; (6) A. Chandler, 1962, *Strategy and Structure* (p. 13), Cambridge, MA: MIT Press; (7) M. Hitt, D. Ireland, & R. Hoskisson, 2003, *Strategic Management*, 5th ed. (p. 9), Cincinnati: South-Western Cengage Learning; (8) G. Dess, G. T. Lumpkin, & A. Eisner, 2008, *Strategic Management*, 4th ed. (p. 8), Chicago: McGraw-Hill Irwin.

strategist of the 19th century,[16] this school suggests that strategy is embodied in the same explicit rigorous formal planning as in the military. The most extreme long-range planning can probably be found in Matsushita's 250-year plan (see Strategy in Action 1.2).

However, the planning school has been challenged by the likes of Liddell Hart, a British military strategist of the early 20th century, who argued that the key to strategy is a set of flexible goal-oriented actions.[17] Hart favored an indirect approach, which seeks rapid flexible actions to avoid clashing with opponents head-on. Within the field of business strategy, this **"strategy as action"** school has been advocated by Henry Mintzberg, a Canadian scholar. Mintzberg posited that in addition to the **intended strategy** that the planning school emphasizes, there can be an **emergent strategy** that is not the result of "top-down" planning, but that is the outcome of a stream of smaller decisions from the "bottom up."[18] For example, Meg Whitman, eBay's CEO, shared:

> This is a completely new business, so there's only so much analysis you can do . . . It's better to put something out there and see the reaction and fix it on the fly. You could spend six months getting it perfect in the lab . . . But we're better off spending six days putting it out there, getting feedback, and then evolving it.[19]

strategy as action

A perspective that suggests that strategy is most fundamentally reflected by firms' pattern of actions.

intended strategy

A strategy that is deliberately planned for.

emerging strategy

A strategy based on the outcome of a stream of smaller decisions from the "bottom up."

Strategy in Action 1.2 - A 250-Year Plan at Matsushita

Konosuke Matsushita is universally referred to as KM at Matsushita, the company he established in Japan. The electronics giant Matsushita is now known for its world-class brands such as Panasonic, Pioneer, and JVC. On May 5, 1932, the fourteenth anniversary of the company's founding, KM announced his business philosophy and a 250-year plan for the company, broken up into ten 25-year segments. The business philosophy, which has become institutionalized through training programs worldwide, defines fundamental goals and primary means of achieving them. The philosophy proposes that "the purpose of an enterprise is to contribute to society by supplying goods of high quality at low prices in ample quantity," and that "profit comes in compensation for contribution to society." It is encapsulated in the Seven Spirits of Matsushita: (1) service through industry, (2) fairness, (3) harmony and cooperation, (4) struggle for progress, (5) courtesy and humility, (6) adjustment and assimilation, and (7) gratitude.

To sarcastic outsiders, this plan may sound like a joke, because it is hardly a "plan" and cannot be very precise. However, serious strategists would argue that this plan is defined by actions, thus leading to an integration of both the "strategy as plan" and "strategy as action" schools of thought. Within Matsushita, managers still refer to these obviously flexible principles constantly and have used them to guide strategic thinking long after the death of KM.

Sources: Based on (1) C. Bartlett & S. Ghoshal, 1989, *Managing Across Borders: The Transnational Solution* (p. 41), Boston: Harvard Business School Press; (2) www.panasonic.co.jp.

Each of these two schools of thought has merits and drawbacks. Strategy in Action 1.3 compares and contrasts them by drawing on real strategies used by the German and French militaries in 1914.

Strategy as Theory

strategy as integration

A perspective that suggests that strategy is neither solely about plan nor action and that strategy integrates elements of both schools of thought.

strategy

A firm's theory about how to compete successfully.

Although the debate between the planning school and action school is difficult to resolve, many scholars and managers have realized that, in reality, the essence of strategy is likely to be a *combination* of both planned deliberate actions and unplanned emergent activities, thus leading to a **"strategy as integration"** school.[20] First advocated by Alfred Chandler,[21] an American business historian, this more balanced, "strategy as integration" school of thought has been adopted in many strategy textbooks, and is the perspective we embrace here. Specifically, we extend the "strategy as integration" school by defining **strategy** as *a firm's theory about how to compete successfully*.[22] In other words, if we have to define strategy with one word, our choice is neither plan nor action—it is *theory*.

Strategy in Action 1.3 - German and French Military Strategy, 1914

Although Germany and France are now the best of friends within the European Union (EU), they had fought for hundreds of years (World War II was the last war in which they butted heads). Prior to the commencement of hostilities that led to World War I in August 1914, both sides had planned for a major military confrontation.

Known as the Schlieffen Plan, the German plan was meticulous. Focusing on the right wing, German forces would smash through Belgium. Every day's schedule of march was fixed in advance: Brussels would be taken by the 19th day, the French frontier crossed on the 22nd, and Paris conquered and a decisive victory attained by the 39th. Heeding Carl von Clausewitz's warning that military plans that left no room for the unexpected could result in disaster, the Germans with infinite care had endeavored to plan for every contingency except one—flexibility.

Known as Plan 17, the French plan was a radical contrast to the German plan. Humiliated in the 1870 Franco–Prussian War, during which France lost two provinces (Alsace and Lorraine), the French were determined to regain their lost territories. However, the French had a smaller population and thus a smaller army. Since the French army could not match the German army man for man, the French military emphasized the individual initiatives, actions, and bravery (known as *élan vital,* the all-conquering will).

© Map Resources

A total of five sentences from Plan 17 was all that was shown to the generals who would lead a million soldiers into battle. As a strategy exercise, we can speculate that Sentence 1 would be "Target Berlin," Sentence 2 "Recover Alsace and Lorraine," and the last sentence "Good luck!" Now, fill in the blanks for the two other sentences—it won't be too hard.

Sources: Based on (1) B. Tuchman, 1962, *The Guns of August,* New York: Macmillan; (2) US Military Academy, 2008, *Map: Northwest Europe 1914,* Department of History, www.dean.usma.edu.

Table 1.2 outlines the four advantages associated with our "strategy as theory" definition. First, it capitalizes on the insights of both planning and action schools. This is because a firm's theory of how to compete will simply remain an idea until it has been translated into action. Thus, formulating a theory (advocated by the planning school as **strategy formulation**) is merely a first step; implementing it through a series of actions (noted by the action school as **strategy implementation**) is a necessary second part. Graphically (Figure 1.1), a strategy entails a firm's assessment at point A of its own strengths (S) and weaknesses (W), its desired performance levels at point B, and the opportunities (O) and threats (T) in the environment. Such a **SWOT analysis** resonates very well with Sun Tzu's teachings on the importance of knowing "yourself" and "your opponents." After such an assessment, the firm formulates its theory on how to best connect points A and B. In other words, the broad arrow becomes its intended

strategy formulation
The crafting of a firm's strategy.

strategy implementation
The actions undertaken to carry out a firm's strategy.

TABLE 1.2   **Four Advantages of the "Strategy as Theory" Definition**

- Integrating both planning and action schools
- Leveraging the concept of "theory," which serves two purposes (explanation and prediction)
- Requiring replications and experimentations
- Understanding the difficulty of strategic change

Sources: Adapted from (1) World Bank, 2004, World Development Indicators database (www.worldbank.org, accessed July 25, 2004), and (2) *Fortune,* 2004, The Fortune Global 500, July 26: F1–F2.

strategy. However, given so many uncertainties, not all intended strategies may prove successful, and some may become unrealized strategies. On the other hand, other unintended actions may become emergent strategies with a thrust toward point B. Overall, this definition of strategy enables us to retain the elegance of the planning school with its more orthodox logical approach and to entertain the flexibility of the action school with its more dynamic experimental character.

Second, this new definition rests on a simple but powerful idea, the concept of "theory." The word "theory" often frightens students and managers because it seems to imply "abstract" and "impractical."[23] But it shouldn't. A theory is merely a statement describing relationships between a set of phenomena. At its core, a theory serves two powerful purposes: to *explain* the past and to *predict* the future. If a theory is too complicated, nobody can understand, test, or use it. For example, the theory of gravity explains why many people committing suicide were successful by jumping off a cliff, and predicts that should you (hypothetically) harbor such a dangerous tendency, you will be equally successful by doing the same. Likewise, Wal-Mart's theory, "everyday low prices," captures the essence of all the activities performed by its 1.8 million employees in 6,000 stores in 15 countries. This theory explains why Wal-Mart has been successful in the past. Even many people who don't like Wal-Mart often shop there. After all, who doesn't like "everyday low prices"? It also predicts that Wal-Mart will continue to do well by focusing on low prices.

FIGURE 1.1   **The Essence of Strategy**

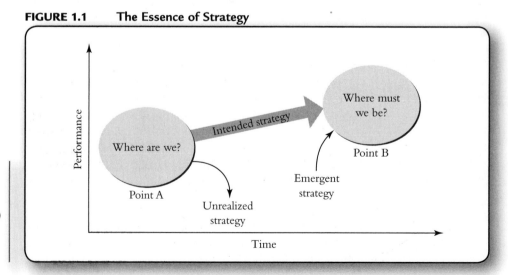

SWOT analysis

A strategic analysis of a firm's internal strengths (S) and weaknesses (W) and the opportunities (O) and threats (T) in the environment.

Third, a theory proven successful in one context during one time period does not necessarily mean it will be successful elsewhere. As a result, a hallmark of theory building and development is **replication**—that is, repeated testing of theory under a variety of conditions to establish its applicable boundaries. For instance, after several decades of experiments in outer space, we now know that the theory of gravity is Earth bound and that it does not apply in outer space. This seems to be the essence of business strategy.[24] Firms successful in one product or country market—that is, having proven the merit of their theory once—constantly seek to expand into newer markets and replicate their previous success. In new markets, firms sometimes succeed, and other times fail. As a result, these firms are able to gradually establish the *limits* of their particular theory about how to compete successfully. For instance, Wal-Mart's theory failed in both Germany and South Korea and the retail giant had to pull out from those markets recently.

Finally, the "strategy as theory" perspective helps us understand why it is often difficult to change strategy.[25] Imagine how hard it is to change an established theory. The reason certain theories are widely accepted is because of their past success. However, past success does not guarantee future success. Although scientists are supposed to be objective, they are also human and many of them may be unwilling to concede the failure of their favorite theories even in the face of repeatedly failed tests. Think about how much resistance from the scientific establishment that Galileo, Copernicus, and Einstein had to face initially. The same holds true for strategists. Bosses were promoted to current positions because of their past success in developing and implementing "old" theories. National heritage, organizational politics, and personal career considerations may prevent many bosses from admitting the evident failure of an existing strategy. Yet, the history of scientific progress suggests that although difficult, it is possible to change established theories. If enough failures in testing are reported and enough researchers raise doubts about certain theories, their views, which may be marginal initially, gradually drive out failed theories and introduce better ones. The painful process of strategic change in many companies is similar. Usually a group of managers, backed by performance data, challenge the current strategy. They propose a new theory on how to best compete, which initially is often marginalized by top management. But eventually, the momentum of the new theory may outweigh the resistance of the old strategy, thus leading to some strategic change. For example, Wal-Mart recently changed its strategy from "everyday low prices" to "save money, live better," in order to soften its reputation as a ruthless cost cutter, an image that had attracted much criticism.

Overall, strategy is not a rulebook, a blueprint, or a set of programmed instructions. Rather, it is a firm's theory about how to compete successfully, a unifying theme that gives coherence to its various actions. Because every firm—just like every individual—is different, one firm's successful theory (strategy) will not necessarily work for other firms. Just as military strategies and generals have to be studied simultaneously, an understanding of business strategies around the globe would be incomplete without an appreciation of the role top managers play as strategists. Although mid- and lower-level managers need to understand strategy, they typically lack the perspective and confidence to craft and execute a *firm-level* strategy. Top management must exercise leadership by making strategic choices.[26] Since the directions and operations of a firm typically are a reflection of its top managers, their personal preferences, based on their own culture, background, and experience, may affect firm strategy.[27] Therefore, although this book focuses on firm strategies, it is also about strategists who lead their firms.

replication

Repeated testing of theory under a variety of conditions to establish its applicable boundaries.

Fundamental Questions in Strategy

Although strategy around the globe is a vast area, we will focus our attention only on the *most fundamental* issues, which act to define a field and to orient the attention of students, practitioners, and scholars in a certain direction. Specifically, we will address the following four fundamental questions:[28]

- Why do firms differ?

- How do firms behave?

- What determines the scope of the firm?

- What determines the success and failure of firms around the globe?

Why Do Firms Differ?

In every modern economy, firms, just like individuals, differ. This question thus seems obvious and hardly generates any debate. However, much of our knowledge about "the firm" is from research on firms in the United States and to a lesser extent the United Kingdom, both of which are embedded in what is known as Anglo-American capitalism. A smaller literature deals with other Western countries such as Germany, France, and Italy, collectively known as continental European capitalism.[29] While some differences between Anglo-American and continental European firms have been reported (such as a shorter and a longer investment horizon, respectively),[30] the contrast between these Western firms and their Japanese counterparts is more striking.[31] For example, instead of using costly acquisitions typically found in the West, Japanese firms extensively employ a network form of supplier management, giving rise to the term *keiretsu* (interfirm network). The word *keiretsu* is now frequently used in English-language publications without the explanation given in the parentheses—an educated reader of *Business Week, The Economist,* or *The Wall Street Journal* is presumed to already understand it.[32]

More recently, as the strategy radar screen scans the business landscape in emerging economies, more puzzles emerge. For example, it is long established that economic growth can hardly occur in poorly regulated economies. Yet, given China's strong economic growth and its underdeveloped formal institutional structures (such as a lack of effective courts), how can China achieve rapid rates of economic growth?[33] Among many answers to this intriguing puzzle, a partial answer suggests that interpersonal networks (*guanxi*), cultivated by managers, may serve as informal substitutes for formal institutional support. In other words, interpersonal relationships among managers are translated into an interfirm strategy of relying on networks and alliances to grow the firm, which, in the aggregate, contributes to the growth of the economy.[34] As a result, the word *guanxi* has now become the most famous Chinese business word to appear in English-language media, again often without the explanation provided in parentheses.[35] Similarly, the Korean word *chaebol* (large business group) and the Russian word *blat* (relationships) have also entered the English vocabulary.[36] Behind each of these deceptively simple words lies some fundamental differences on how to compete around the world.

FIGURE 1.2   The "Strategy Tripod": Three Leading Perspectives on Strategy

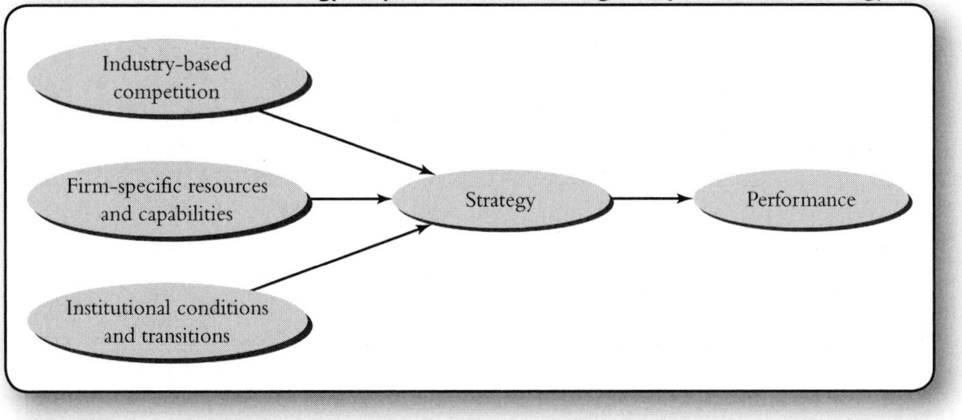

How Do Firms Behave?

This question focuses on what determines firms' theories about how to compete. Figure 1.2 identifies three leading perspectives that collectively lead to a **strategy tripod**. The first, the industry-based view, suggests that the strategic task is mainly to examine the five competitive forces affecting an industry (interfirm rivalry, threat of potential entry, bargaining power of suppliers, bargaining power of buyers, and threat of substitutes), and stake out a position that is less vulnerable relative to these five forces. While the industry-based view primarily focuses on the *external* opportunities and threats (the O and T in a SWOT analysis), the second, the resource-based view, largely concentrates on the *internal* strengths and weaknesses (S and W) of the firm. This view posits that it is firm-specific capabilities that differentiate successful firms from failing ones.

Recently, an institution-based view has emerged to account for differences in firm strategy.[37] This view argues that in addition to industry- and firm-level conditions, firms also need to take into account the influences of formal and informal rules of the game. Shown in our Opening Case, an understanding of the formal and informal rules of the game explains a great deal about how South-Western Cengage Learning launched the first edition of *Global Strategic Management* in China.

Collectively viewed as a strategy tripod, these three views form the backbone of the first part of this book, "Foundations of Global Strategy" (Chapters 2, 3, and 4). They shed considerable light on the question "How do firms behave?"

What Determines the Scope of the Firm?

This question first focuses on the growth of the firm. Most companies in the world seem to have a lingering love affair with growth. The motivation to grow is fueled by the excitement associated with a growing organization. For publicly listed firms, without growth, the share price will not grow. However, there is a limit, beyond which further growth may backfire. As a result, downsizing, downscoping, and withdrawals are often necessary. In other words, answers to the question, "What determines the scope of the firm?" pertain not only to the growth of the firm, but also to the contraction of the firm.

strategy tripod

A framework that suggests that strategy as a discipline has three "legs" or key perspectives: industry-, resource-, and institution-based views.

In developed economies, a conglomeration strategy featuring unrelated product diversification, which was in vogue in the 1960s and 1970s, was found to destroy value and was largely discredited by the 1980s and 1990s—witness how many firms are still trying to divest and downsize in the West. However, this strategy seems to be alive and well in many emerging economies.[38] Although puzzled Western media and consultants often suggest that conglomerates destroy value and should be dismantled in emerging economies, empirical evidence suggests otherwise. Recent research in China, India, Indonesia, Israel, Peru, South Africa, South Korea, and Taiwan reports that some (but not all) units affiliated with conglomerates may enjoy higher profitability than independent firms, suggesting that there are some discernible performance *benefits* associated with conglomeration in emerging economies.[39] One reason behind such a contrast lies in the institutional differences between developed and emerging economies. Viewed through an institutional lens, conglomeration may make sense (at least to some extent) in emerging economies, because this strategy and its relatively positive link with performance may be a function of the level of institutional (under)development in these countries.[40]

In addition to product scope, careful deliberation of the geographic scope is important. On the one hand, for companies aspiring to become global leaders, a strong position in *each* of the three Triad markets is often necessary. Expanding market position in key emerging economies, such as Brazil, Russia, India, and China (known as BRIC), may also be desirable. But on the other hand, it is not realistic that all companies can, or should, "go global." Given the recent hype to "go global," many companies may have entered too many countries too quickly and may be subsequently forced to withdraw.

What Determines the Success and Failure of Firms around the Globe?

This focus on performance, more than anything else, defines the field of strategic management and international business.[41] We are not only interested in *acquiring* and *leveraging* competitive advantage, but also in *sustaining* such advantages over time and across regions. All three major perspectives that form the "strategy tripod" ultimately seek to answer this question.

The industry-based view posits that the degree of competitiveness in an industry largely determines firm performance. Shown in the Opening Case, the structure of the college textbook publishing industry, such as stable brands and high entry barriers, explains a great deal behind the dominance of the top three incumbents in business and economics college textbook publishing around the world.

The resource-based view suggests that firm-specific capabilities drive performance differences. Within the same industry, while some firms win, others struggle. Winning firms such as South-Western Cengage Learning tend to have valuable, unique, and hard-to-imitate capabilities, such as having a "Mr. Global" born in China to author *Global Strategy,* which will inherently have a more global flavor. Rival publishers have a hard time competing with *Global Strategy,* because a majority of other textbook authors were born in the United States, who, despite their best efforts, will naturally exhibit a US-centric tendency.

The institution-based view argues that institutional forces also provide an answer to differences in firm performance. As illustrated by Cengage Learning's penetration of the China market with *Global Strategy* (Opening Case), firms must "think global" and "act local" *simultaneously*. It is difficult to imagine firms not doing their "homework" by getting to know the various formal and informal rules of the game in overseas markets will emerge as winners in the global marketplace.

Overall, although there are many debates among the different schools of thought, the true determinants of firm performance probably involve a *combination* of these three-pronged forces (see Figure 1.2).[42] While these three views present relatively straightforward answers, the reality of global competition often makes these answers more complex and murky. If you survey ten managers from ten countries on what performance exactly is, you are likely to get ten different answers. Long-term or short-term performance? Financial returns or market shares? Profits maximized for shareholders or benefits maximized for stakeholders (individuals and organizations that are affected by a firm's actions and thus have a stake in how a firm is managed)? It is difficult to find an easy uncontroversial answer, and generalizations based on stereotypes may not hold up. For example, it is widely believed that relative to Western firms, Asian firms tend to be willing to sacrifice short-term financial performance for long-term market gains.[43] Yet, when actually working side-by-side with Asian counterparts in joint ventures, many Western managers are surprised that some of their Asian colleagues actually have a much *shorter* horizon, being eager to "harvest" for a quick buck (or yen, yuan, or won).[44] The reasons behind the differences between such myths and realities remain to be explored.

In summary, these four questions represent some of the most fundamental puzzles in strategy. While other questions can be raised, they all relate in one way or another to these four. Thus, answering these four questions will be the primary focus of this book and will be addressed in *every* chapter.

What Is Global Strategy?

"Global strategy" has at least two meanings. First, as noted earlier, the traditional and narrowly defined notion of "global strategy" refers to a particular theory on how to compete, and is centered on offering standardized products and services on a worldwide basis.[45] This strategy obviously is only relevant for large Triad-based MNEs active in many countries. Smaller firms in developed economies and most firms in emerging economies operating in only one or a few countries may find little use for this definition.

Second, "global strategy" can also refer to any strategy outside one's home country. Americans seem especially likely to use the word "global" this way, which essentially becomes the same as "international." For example, Wal-Mart's first foray outside the United States in 1991 was widely hailed as evidence that Wal-Mart had "gone global." In fact, Wal-Mart had only expanded into Mexico at that time. While this was an admirable first step for Wal-Mart, the action was similar to Hong Kong firms doing business in mainland China or German companies investing in Austria. To many Asians and Europeans familiar with international business, there is nothing significantly "global" about these activities in neighboring countries. After all, Mexico is not even an "overseas" market when viewed from the United States, because the word "overseas," by definition, indicates the crossing of a large body of water. So, why the hype about the word "global," especially among Americans? This is because historically, the vast US domestic markets made it unnecessary for many firms to seek overseas markets.

As a result, when many US companies do venture abroad, even in countries as close as Mexico, they are likely to be fascinated about their "discovery of global markets." In part because of such traditional US-centric mentality, calling non-US (or non-domestic) markets "global" markets becomes a cliché.[46] Since everyone seems to want a more exciting "global" strategy rather than a plain-vanilla "international" one, we may lose the ability to differentiate types of cross-border strategy (such as the traditional "global strategy" discussed earlier).[47]

So what do we mean by "global strategy" in *this* book? *Neither* of the preceding definitions will do. Here, **global strategy** is defined as *strategy of firms around the globe*—essentially various firms' theories about how to compete successfully. Seeking to break out of the US-centric straightjacket, this book deals with both the strategy of MNEs (some of which may fit into the traditional narrow global strategy definition) and the strategy of smaller firms (some of which may have an international presence, while others may be purely domestic). These firms compete in both developed and emerging economies. We do *not* exclusively concentrate on firms doing business abroad, which is the traditional domain of global strategy books. To the extent that international business involves two sides, namely, domestic firms and foreign entrants, an exclusive focus on foreign entrants covers only one side and, thus, paints a partial picture. The strategy of domestic firms is equally important. As a result, a truly *global* global-strategy book needs to provide a balanced coverage. This is the challenge we will take on throughout this book.

What Is Globalization?

The rather abstract five-syllable word **globalization** is now frequently heard and debated.[48] Those who approve of globalization count its contributions to include higher economic growth and standards of living, increased sharing of technologies, and more extensive cultural integration. Critics argue that globalization undermines wages in rich countries, exploits workers in poor countries, and gives MNEs too much power. So what exactly is globalization? This section (1) outlines three views on it, (2) recommends the "pendulum" view, and (3) introduces the idea of "semiglobalization."

Three Views on Globalization

global strategy

(1) Strategy of firms around the globe. (2) A particular form of international strategy, characterized by the production and distribution of standardized products and services on a worldwide basis.

globalization

The close integration of countries and peoples of the world.

Depending on what sources you read, globalization could be:

- A new force sweeping through the world in recent times

- A long-run historical evolution since the dawn of human history

- A pendulum that swings from one extreme to another from time to time

An understanding of these views helps put things in perspective. First, opponents of globalization suggest that globalization is a new phenomenon since the late 20th century, driven by both the recent technological innovations and Western hypocrisy designed for MNEs to exploit and dominate the world. While presenting few clearly worked-out alternatives to the present economic order, other than an ideal world free of environmental stress, social injustice, and branded sportswear (allegedly made by "sweatshops"), pundits of this view nevertheless often argue that globalization needs to be slowed down if not stopped.[49] Most antiglobalization protesters seem to share this view.

A second view contends that globalization has always been part and parcel of human history.[50] Historians are debating whether globalization started 2,000 or 8,000 years ago. MNEs existed for more than two millennia, with their earliest traces discovered in the Assyrian, Phoenician, and Roman empires.[51] International competition from low-cost countries is nothing new. In the first century AD, so concerned was the Roman emperor Tiberius about the massive quantity of low-cost Chinese silk imports that he imposed the world's first known import quota of textiles.[52] Today's most successful MNEs do not come close to wielding the historical clout of some MNEs such as Britain's East India Company during colonial times. In a nutshell, globalization is nothing new and will always march on.

A third view suggests that globalization is the "closer integration of the countries and peoples of the world, which has been brought about by the enormous reduction of the costs of transportation and communication, and the breaking down of artificial barriers to the flows of goods, services, capital, knowledge, and (to a lesser extent) people across borders."[53] Globalization is neither recent nor one-directional. It is, more accurately, a process similar to the swing of a pendulum.

The Pendulum View on Globalization

The third notion of globalization, the pendulum view, probably makes the most sense because it helps us understand the ups and downs of globalization. The current era of globalization originated in the aftermath of World War II, when major Western nations committed to global trade and investment. However, between the 1950s and the 1970s, this view was not widely shared. Communist countries, such as China and the (former) Soviet Union, sought to develop self-sufficiency. Many non-communist developing countries, such as Argentina, Brazil, India, and Mexico, focused on protecting domestic industries. However, refusing to participate in global trade and investment ended up breeding uncompetitive industries. In contrast, four developing economies in Asia, namely, Hong Kong, Singapore, South Korea, and Taiwan, earned their stripes as the "Four Tigers" by participating in the global economy.

Inspired by the "Four Tigers," more and more countries, such as China in the late 1970s, Latin America in the mid-1980s, Central and Eastern Europe in the late 1980s, and India in the 1990s, realized that joining the world economy was a must. As these countries started to emerge as new players in the world economy, they became collectively known as "emerging economies."[54] As a result, globalization rapidly accelerated. For example, between 1990 and 2000, while world output grew by 23%, global trade expanded by 80% and the total flow of FDI increased fivefold.[55]

However, being a pendulum, globalization is unable to keep going in one direction. The 1990s saw some significant backlash against it. First, the rapid growth of globalization led to the historically inaccurate view that globalization is new. Second, it created fear among many people in developed economies, because emerging economies not only seem to compete away many low-end manufacturing jobs, but also increasingly appear to threaten some high-end jobs. Finally, some factions in emerging economies complained against the onslaught of MNEs, which allegedly not only destroy local companies, but also local cultures and values as well as the environment.

While small-scale acts of vandalizing McDonald's restaurants are reported in a variety of countries, the December 1999 antiglobalization protests in Seattle and the September 2001 terrorist attacks in New York and Washington are undoubtedly the most extreme acts of antiglobalization forces at work. As a result, international travel was curtailed, and global trade and investment flows slowed in the early 2000s.[56]

More recently, worldwide economic growth has again been humming on all cylinders. World GDP, cross-border trade, and per capita GDP have all soared to historically high levels. More than half of the world GDP growth now comes from emerging economies, whose per capita GDP grew 4.6% annually in the decade ending 2007. BRIC has become a new buzzword. Developed economies are also doing well, averaging 2% per capita GDP growth in the same period. *Fortune* in 2007 declared that "for your average globetrotting *Fortune* 500 CEO, right now is about as good as it gets."[57] Yet, the same article cautioned that "Assuming history at some point proves yet again unkind . . . it pays to be vigilant." As the US economy threatens to enter recession and the rest of the world is bracing for such a slowdown (as of this writing, April 2008), being strategically vigilant is certainly wise.

Overall, like the proverbial elephant, globalization is seen by everyone and rarely comprehended. All of us felt sorry when we read the story of a bunch of blind men trying to figure out the shape and form of the elephant. Although we are not blind, our task is more challenging than blind men studying a standing animal. This is because we (1) try to live with, (2) try to avoid being crushed by, and (3) even attempt to profit from the rapidly moving (back and forth!) beast called globalization. We believe that the view of globalization as a pendulum is a more balanced and realistic perspective. Like the two-faced Janus (a Roman god), globalization has both rosy and dark sides.[58]

Semiglobalization

Most measures of market integration (such as trade and FDI) have recently scaled new heights but still fall far short of complete globalization. In other words, what we have may be labeled **semiglobalization**, which is more complex than extremes of total isolation and total globalization. Semiglobalization suggests that barriers to market integration at borders are high, but not high enough to completely insulate countries from each other.[59] Semiglobalization calls for more than one way of doing business around the globe. Total isolation on a nation-state basis would suggest a localization strategy (treating each country as a unique market), and total globalization would lead to a standardization strategy (treating the entire world as one market—"one size fits all"). However, there is no single right strategy in the world of semiglobalization, resulting in a wide variety of experimentations. Overall, (semi)globalization is neither to be opposed as a menace nor to be celebrated as a panacea; it is to be *engaged*.[60]

Global Strategy and Globalization at a Crossroads

semiglobalization

A perspective that suggests that barriers to market integration at borders are high but not high enough to completely insulate countries from each other.

The challenge confronting strategists around the globe in the 21st century is enormous. The world of semiglobalization calls for a variety of strategic experimentations.[61] This book is designed to help you make informed strategic choices. As a backdrop for the remainder of this book, this section first offers a basic overview of three fundamental events at the dawn of the 21st century that define the global landscape today. Second, as Sun Tzu taught us a long time ago, knowing yourself and your opponents is imperative.

Three Defining Events

At the dawn of the 21st century, three sets of sudden high-profile events have occurred that have significant ramifications for companies and strategists around the world: (1) antiglobalization protests, (2) terrorist attacks, and (3) corporate governance crises.

First, large-scale antiglobalization protests began in December 1999, when more than 50,000 protesters blocked downtown Seattle to derail a World Trade Organization (WTO) meeting. The demonstrators were protesting against a wide range of issues, including job losses resulting from foreign competition, downward pressure on unskilled wages, and environmental destruction. Since Seattle, antiglobalization protesters have turned up at just about every major globalization meeting, and some protests have become violent. It is obvious that numerous individuals in many countries believe that globalization has detrimental effects on living standards and the environment. The debate on globalization has numerous dimensions, and neither the proglobalization forces nor the antiglobalization forces have won the debate.[62]

A second set of events center on the terrorist attacks in New York and Washington, DC, on September 11, 2001, and the resultant war on terror in Afghanistan, Iraq, and elsewhere. Since then, terrorists have struck Indonesia, Spain, and Britain. Terrorism, which used to be "a random political risk of relatively insignificant proportions,"[63] is now a leading concern for business leaders around the globe.[64] Heightened risk of terrorism has (1) reduced freedom of international movement as various countries curtail visas and immigration, (2) enhanced security checks at airports, seaports, and land border crossing points, and (3) cancelled or scaled down trade and FDI deals, especially in high-risk regions such as the Middle East.

Finally, the world has been engulfed in a corporate governance crisis. Although many believe that Enron's implosion in 2001 triggered this crisis, globally, the corporate governance crisis probably erupted in 1997 with the Asian financial crisis. At its core, the Asian financial crisis was a corporate governance crisis, because majority shareholders in many Asian firms, who were often family owners, abused minority shareholders.[65] Fast forward to America circa 2001, where corporate scandals on such a large scale had been unthinkable. Yet, the scandals of Enron and WorldCom sent shockwaves throughout the world. Since then, there has been no shortage of high-profile corporate scandals. Citigroup's private bank was forced to shut down because of blatant violation of Japanese regulations. Siemens, as of this writing (April 2008), is under investigation by authorities in over 20 countries for bribery and corruption charges. As a result, social responsibility, ethics, and governance, long regarded as "backburners," have now increasingly become central topics for strategy discussions.[66]

Future historians will no doubt suggest that these three are crucial events that have changed our world. In a nutshell, current and would-be strategists now have to live with a great deal of uncertainties in the *post-Seattle, post-9/11, post-Enron* world.

Know Yourself, Know Your Opponents

A fundamental reason that many executives, policymakers, and scholars were caught off guard by the antiglobalization protests and the terrorist attacks is that they have failed to heed Sun Tzu's most famous maxim: Strategists need to both know themselves and their opponents. To know yourself calls for a thorough understanding of not only your strengths, but also your limitations. Many individuals fail to understand their limitations, or simply choose to ignore them. Although relative to the general public, executives, policymakers, and scholars tend to be better educated and more cosmopolitan, they, just like everybody else, are likely to be biased too. Most of them, in both developed and emerging economies in the last two decades, are biased toward acknowledging the benefits of globalization.[67]

Although it has long been known that globalization carries both benefits and costs (see Strategy in Action 1.4), many executives, policymakers, and scholars have failed to take into sufficient account the social, political, and environmental costs associated with globalization. However, that these elites share certain perspectives on globalization does *not* mean that most other members of society share the same views. Unfortunately, many elites mistakenly assume that the rest of the world either is, or should be, more like "us." To the extent that powerful economic and political institutions are largely controlled by these elites, it is not surprising that some powerless and voiceless antiglobalization groups end up resorting to unconventional tactics, such as protests, to make their point.

It is certainly interesting and perhaps alarming to note that as would-be strategists who will shape the world economy in the future, current business school students already exhibit values and beliefs favoring globalization that are similar to those held by executives, policymakers, and scholars, and that are different from those held by the general public. Shown in Table 1.3, American business students, relative to the general public, have significantly more positive (almost one-sided) views toward globalization.[68] My teaching and lectures around the world reveal that most business students worldwide—regardless of nationality—seem to share such positive views on globalization. This is not surprising, given that both self-selection to study business and socialization within the curriculum, in which free trade is widely regarded as positive, may lead to certain attitudes in favor of globalization. Consequently, business students may focus more on the economic gains of globalization, and be less concerned with its darker sides.

Current and would-be strategists need to be aware of their own bias embodied in such one-sided views toward globalization. Since business schools aspire to train future business leaders by indoctrinating them with the dominant values managers hold, these results suggest that business schools may have largely succeeded in this mission. However, to the extent that there are strategic blind spots in the views of the current managers (and professors), these findings are potentially alarming. They reveal that at a relatively young age (average 22 years of age in the study reported in Table 1.3), business students already share these blind spots. Despite possible self-selection in choosing to major in business, there is no denying that student values are shaped, at least in part, by the educational experience business schools provide. Knowing such limitations, business school professors and students need to work especially hard to break out of the straitjacket of the narrow views almost exclusively in favor of globalization.

nongovernmental organization (NGO)

Organization advocating causes such as the environment, human rights, and consumer rights that are not affiliated with government.

Other than knowing "yourself," a second part of Sun Tzu's most famous teaching is to "know your opponents." While competitor analysis (including buyers, suppliers, and substitutes) is always discussed in strategy books, such analysis appears to be too narrow. A lot of opponents of globalization are **nongovernmental organizations (NGOs)**, such as environmentalists and consumer groups. Ignoring them will be a grave failure in due diligence when doing business around the globe.[69] Instead of viewing NGOs as

Strategy in Action 1.4 - **Are US Multinationals Good for America?**

Ethical Challenge

Most debates on MNEs around the world focus on the impact of foreign MNEs on domestic economies. Recent debates have highlighted the role of home-grown MNEs in the US economy itself. On the positive side, US MNEs are productive, innovative, hiring more skilled workers, and paying higher wages (at least 6% more than non-MNEs in the United States). As a group, their financial performance is enviable: among Standard & Poor's (S&P) 1,500 companies, the top 150 nonfinancial multinationals, such as HP, Pfizer, and eBay, have commanded 60% pretax income and revenues and employed close to 50% of the workforce. By the end of 2007, the top 150 were flush with more than $500 billion in cash. In contrast, smaller domestically oriented firms have a weaker profit outlook and have a harder time borrowing in the middle of the subprime mess.

However, on the not-so-positive side, in the past decade, US MNEs have been decoupling from the US economy. They still have headquarters in the United States, are still listed in US stock exchanges, and most of their shareholders are still American (foreigners own 13% of US equities). But their expansion has been mostly overseas. Between 2000 and 2005, US MNEs cut more than two million jobs at home and added approximately the same number of jobs overseas. In 2007, US exports, historically fueled by large multinationals, commanded only 12% of the GDP, roughly where they were in 1997—meaning, essentially, that no real growth occurred. However, sales by foreign subsidiaries of US MNEs grew from 20% of the US GDP in 1997 to 25% in 2007.

American executives are not shy about articulating their strategy. "Our employee base will continue to shift, with the number of jobs in high-quality, lower-cost areas outside the US growing," announced chairman and CEO of Electronic Data Systems (EDS). In 2007, EDS granted early retirement to 2,400 US employees, and expected its non-US employees to grow from 14,000 at the end of 2005 to 45,000 at the end of 2008. In 2006, Delphi filed for Chapter 11 (bankruptcy) protection in order to slash its US

employees from 32,000 to 7,000. Delphi's bankruptcy filing was careful to exclude its 115,000-worker foreign operations, which were destined to grow.

In the middle of a subprime mess, the American economy—and the Federal Reserve—needs the multinationals to help out. Will they lend a helping hand to lift their home economy out of a downturn? Since 2003, the value of the dollar has fallen by 20% against the currencies of major US trading partners (including a 15% drop against the Chinese yuan). Labor costs in China and other low-wage countries have grown. Thanks to skyrocketing oil prices, transportation costs to ship goods from China and elsewhere have grown, making it more attractive to invest and produce in the United States.

However, US MNEs do not make investment location decisions on short-term economic outlooks alone. One of their leading concerns is one of the world's highest corporate income tax rates imposed by Uncle Sam, while many other countries lure them away with low taxes. In response, proposals are floating to offer tax incentives for US multinationals to keep investments and jobs at home. However, critics question why these financially healthy MNEs need to be subsidized, while many other sectors and individuals in the country are hurting.

Sources: Based on (1) *Business Week,* 2006, Go bankrupt, then go overseas, April 24: 52-53; (2) *Business Week,* 2008, Multinationals: Are they good for America? March 10: 41-46; (3) M. W. Peng, 2009, *Global Business,* Cincinnati: South-Western Cengage Learning.

TABLE 1.3   **Views on Globalization: American General Public versus Business Students**

Percentage Answering "Good" For the Question: Overall, Do You Think Globalization is *Good* or *Bad* for	General Public[1] (N = 1,024)	Business Students (Average Age 22)[2] (N = 494)
• US consumers like you	68%	96%
• US companies	63%	77%
• The US economy	64%	88%
• Strengthening poor countries' economies	75%	82%

Sources: Based on (1) A. Bernstein, 2000, Backlash against globalization, *Business Week*, April 24: 43; (2) M. W. Peng & H. Shin, 2008, How do future business leaders view globalization? *Thunderbird International Business Review* (p. 179), 50 (3): 175–182. All differences are statistically significant.

opponents, many firms view them as partners.[70] NGOs do raise a valid point on the necessity of firms, especially MNEs, to have a broader concern for various stakeholders affected by their actions.[71]

In summary, in the *post-Seattle, post-9/11, post-Enron* era, global strategy and globalization are at a crossroads. There is a growing recognition that the traditionally defined narrow notion of "global strategy" may not work, and that globalization as we know it in the last two decades may have passed its high-water mark. Thus, new thinking is called for. This book represents an answer to such calls.

Organization of the Book

This book has three parts. The first part concerns *foundations*. Following this chapter, Chapters 2, 3, and 4 introduce the "strategy tripod," consisting of the three leading perspectives on strategy: industry-, resource-, and institution-based views. Students will be systematically trained to use this "tripod" to analyze a variety of strategy problems. The second part covers *business-level strategies*. In contrast to most global strategy books' focus on large MNEs, we start with the internationalization of small entrepreneurial firms (Chapter 5), followed by ways to enter foreign markets (Chapter 5), to leverage alliances and networks (Chapter 7), and to manage global competitive dynamics (Chapter 8). Finally, the third part deals with *corporate-level strategies*. Chapter 9 on diversifying, acquiring, and restructuring starts this part, followed by strategies to structure, learn, and innovate (Chapter 10), to govern the corporation around the world (Chapter 11), and to profit from corporate social responsibility (Chapter 12).

A unique organizing principle is a consistent focus on the "strategy tripod" and on the four fundamental questions regarding strategy in *all* chapters. Following this chapter (which contains numerous debates), every chapter has a substantial "Debates and Extensions" section. Virtually all textbooks uncritically present knowledge "as is." The reality is that our field has no shortage of debates.[72] Since debates drive practice and research ahead, it is imperative that students be exposed to cutting-edge debates and encouraged to form your own views when engaging in these debates.[73]

CHAPTER SUMMARY

1. *Offer a basic critique of the traditional, narrowly defined "global strategy"*

   • The traditional and narrowly defined notion of "Global strategy" is characterized by the production and distribution of standardized products and services on a worldwide basis—in short, a "one size fits all" approach. This strategy has often backfired in practice.

   • As a *global* global-strategy book, this book provides a more balanced coverage, not only in terms of the traditional "global strategy" and "non-global strategy" but also in terms of both MNEs' and local firms' perspectives. Moreover, this book has devoted extensive space to emerging economies.

2. *Articulate the rationale behind studying global strategy*

   • To better compete in the corporate world that will appreciate expertise in global strategy.

3. *Define what is strategy and what is global strategy*

   • There is a debate between two schools of thought: "strategy as plan" and "strategy as action." This book, together with other leading textbooks, instead follows the "strategy as integration" school.

   • In this book, strategy is defined as a firm's theory about how to compete successfully, while global strategy is defined as strategy of firms around the globe.

4. *Outline the four fundamental questions in strategy*

   • The four fundamental questions are (1) Why do firms differ? (2) How do firms behave? (3) What determines the scope of the firm? and (4) What determines the success and failure of firms around the globe?

   • The three leading perspectives guiding our exploration are industry-, resource-, and institution-based views, which collectively form a "strategy tripod."

5. *Participate in the debate on globalization with a reasonably balanced view and a keen awareness of your likely bias*

   • Some view globalization as a recent phenomenon, while others believe that it has been evolving since the dawn of human history.

   • We suggest that globalization is best viewed as a process similar to the swing of a pendulum.

   • Strategists, according to Sun Tzu, need to know themselves and know their opponents. In light of the fact that globalization has its dark side, current and would-be strategists need to know themselves, especially their hidden proglobalization bias.

KEY TERMS

Base of the pyramid	Intended strategy	Strategy as action
BRIC	Multinational enterprise (MNE)	Strategy as integration
Emergent strategy		Strategy as plan
Emerging economies (emerging markets)	Nongovernmental organization (NGO)	Strategy formulation
Foreign direct investment (FDI)	Replication	Strategy implementation
Global strategy	Semiglobalization	Strategy tripod
	Strategic management	SWOT analysis
Globalization	Strategy	Triad

CRITICAL DISCUSSION QUESTIONS

1. A skeptical classmate says: "Global strategy is relevant for top executives such as CEOs in large companies. I am just a lowly student who will struggle to gain an entry-level job, probably in a small company. Why should I care about it?" How do you convince her that she should care about global strategy?

2. **ON ETHICS:** Some argue that globalization benefits citizens of rich countries. Others argue that globalization benefits citizens of poor countries. What are the ethical dilemmas here? What do you think?

3. **ON ETHICS:** Critics argue that MNEs, through FDI, allegedly both exploit the poor in poor countries and take jobs away from rich countries. If you were the CEO of an MNE from a developed economy or from an emerging economy, how would you defend your firm?

4. **ON ETHICS:** What are some of the darker sides (in other words, costs) associated with globalization? How can strategists make sure that the benefits of their various actions outweigh their drawbacks (such as job losses in developed economies and environmental damage in emerging economies)?

CLOSING CASE

Ethical Challenge

Strategy for the Base of the Pyramid

For Triad-based MNEs, even their traditional "global strategy" is not very global. It often focuses on affluent customers in North America, Europe, and Japan. Even when they enter emerging economies, they often concentrate on high-income customers there. Thus, this strategy only deals with the approximately one billion people at the top of the global economic pyramid and virtually ignores the vast numbers at the

FIGURE 1.3   The Global Economic Pyramid

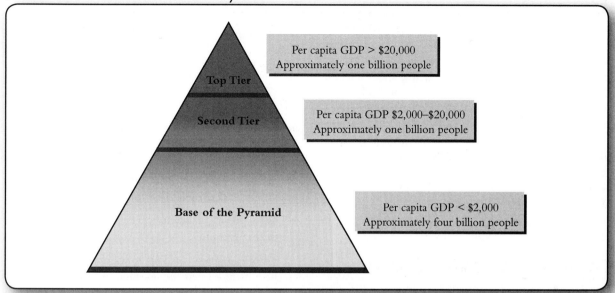

Top Tier
Per capita GDP > $20,000
Approximately one billion people

Second Tier
Per capita GDP $2,000–$20,000
Approximately one billion people

Base of the Pyramid
Per capita GDP < $2,000
Approximately four billion people

Sources: Adapted from (1) C. K. Prahalad & S. Hart, 2002, The fortune at the bottom of the pyramid, *Strategy+Business*, 26: 54–67; (2) S. Hart, 2005, *Capitalism at the Crossroads* (p. 111), Philadelphia: Wharton School Publishing.

bottom. The second tier of the pyramid consists of over one billion people making $2,000–$20,000 each year. Four billion people in the world at the base of the pyramid earn less than $2,000 each per year (see Figure 1.3) and are typically ignored.

The MNEs' strategy is easy to understand. They assume that the poor have no money and that there are no profitable opportunities. However, despite low individual income, the poor's collective buying power is substantial. The poor in Rio de Janeiro, Brazil, for instance, have a total purchasing power of $1.2 billion. While existing business models on how to serve affluent customers would indeed have a hard time at the base of the pyramid, entrepreneurial opportunities exist and are being exploited mostly by local firms and a small number of far-sighted MNEs. In India, for example, Arvind Mills introduced Ruf and Tuf jeans, a ready-to-make kit priced at $6, which is now the market leader in India, beating global brands such as Levi's that sell for $20–$40 a pair. In rural Bangladesh, where the per capita income was only $300, few could afford cell phones. So Grameen Telecom innovatively provided a $175 "micro loan" with a cellular phone to entrepreneurs, who would then sell phone usage on a per-call basis to locals and make $300 a year. Grameen's founder Muhammad Yunus won a Nobel Peace Prize in 2006.

Given that developed markets are well saturated, the base of the pyramid may indeed provide strong growth engines, not only for emerging economies but also for developed markets. For example, Unilever, based on the success of its Indian subsidiary, Hindustan Lever, in rural India, has now focused on the base of the pyramid as a strategic priority at the *corporate* level. More than 44% of Unilever's sales worldwide now come from emerging economies. However, adaptation will be crucial. In India, Unilever sells 70% of its shampoo in one-use sachets for a couple of cents. While the big bottle that Western consumers take for granted has better value, most Indian consumers at the base of the pyramid can afford only small sachets. At present, automakers such as GM and Honda are racing to develop $5,000 car models for the emerging Chinese middle class. Given these automakers' inability to profitably produce such models in the United States and Japan, imagine the profit potential these developed-in-China models may have back home where entry-level cars now sell for close to $10,000.

To the extent Western MNEs often find it tough going in these unfamiliar territories, it is not surprising that some new MNEs from emerging economies—called Third World multinationals or "dragon multinationals"—well versed in such an alternative business model are capturing the hearts, minds, and wallets of customers in emerging economies. In the Philippines, Jollibee beats the mighty McDonald's and is now venturing out to Southeast Asia and the Middle East. Out of China, Lenovo aspires to become "king of the hill" in the PC battle. In January 2008, India's Tata Motors unleashed a "one lakh" car (one lakh is 100,000 rupees, roughly $2,500), sending shockwaves throughout Western automakers. For now, Tata Motors is happy serving the Indian market, but what if it decides to export this super-low-cost car to other countries?

Overall, discovering creative ways to configure products and services to tackle the base of the pyramid has great ethical and moral benefits because they improve the standards of living for many people and facilitate economic development. However, firms do not have to do this for charitable purposes. There is money to be made by such a strategy of *great leap downward*. The million (or billion) dollar question is: How?

Sources: Based on (1) P. Aulakh, 2007, Emerging multinationals from developing economies, *Journal of International Management,* 13: 235-240; (2) L. Brouthers, E. O'Donnell, & J. Hadjimarcou, 2005, Generic product strategies for emerging market exports into Triad nation markets, *Journal of Management Studies,* 42: 225-245; (3) N. Dawar & A. Chattopadhyay, 2002, Rethinking marketing programs for emerging markets, *Long Range Planning,* 35: 457-474; (4) *The Economist,* 2008, No lakh of daring, January 12: 59; (5) *The Economist,* 2008, The legacy that got left on the shelf, February 2: 77-79; (6) T. London &

S. Hart, 2004, Reinventing strategies for emerging markets, *Journal of International Business Studies,* 35: 350-370; (7) J. Mathews, 2006, Dragon multinationals as new features of globalization in the 21st century, *Asia Pacific Journal of Management,* 23: 5-27; (8) M. W. Peng, D. Wang, & Y. Jiang, 2008, An institution-based view of international business strategy, *Journal of International Business Studies,* 39 (in press); (9) C. K. Prahalad & A. Hammond, 2002, Serving the world's poor, profitably, *Harvard Business Review,* September: 48-57; (10) M. Wright, I. Filatotchev, R. Hoskisson, & M. W. Peng, 2005, Strategy research in emerging economies, *Journal of Management Studies,* 42: 1-33; (11) Y. Yamakawa, M. W. Peng, & D. Deeds, 2008, What drives new ventures to internationalize from emerging to developed economies, *Entrepreneurship Theory and Practice,* 32: 59-82.

Case Discussion Questions

1. What are the more attractive industries for the base of the pyramid?

2. From a resource-based view, what determines firm performance in emerging economies?

3. From an institution-based view, what are the crucial differences in formal and informal rules of the game between developed and emerging economies?

4. Some argue that aggressively investing in emerging economies is not only economically beneficial but also highly ethical, because it may potentially lift many people out of poverty. However, others caution that in the absence of reasonable hopes of decent profits (the base of the pyramid is notoriously turbulent due to political and economic uncertainties), rushing to emerging economies is reckless. How would you participate in this debate?

NOTES

Journal acronyms *AME*–*Academy of Management Executive;* *AMJ*–*Academy of Management Journal;* *AMLE*–*Academy of Management Learning and Education;* *AMR*–*Academy of Management Review;* *APJM*–*Asia Pacific Journal of Management;* *ASQ*–*Administrative Science Quarterly;* *BW*–*Business Week;* *EMJ*–*European Management Journal;* *ETP*–*Entrepreneurship Theory and Practice;* *HBR*–*Harvard Business Review;* *IJMR*–*International Journal of Management Reviews;* *JIBS*–*Journal of International Business Studies;* *JIM*–*Journal of International Management;* *JMS*–*Journal of Management Studies;* *JWB*–*Journal of World Business;* *MIR*–*Management*

International Review; *OSc*–*Organization Science;* *SMJ*–*Strategic Management Journal;* *TIBR*–*Thunderbird International Business Review*

1. V. Govindarajan & A. Gupta, 2001, *The Quest for Global Dominance,* San Francisco: Jossey-Bass; G. Yip, 2003, *Total Global Strategy II,* Upper Saddle River, NJ: Prentice Hall.

2. This definition of the MNE can be found in R. Caves, 1996, *Multinational Enterprise and Economic Analysis,* 2nd ed. (p. 1), New York: Cambridge University Press;

J. Dunning, 1993, *Multinational Enterprises and the Global Economy* (p. 30), Reading, MA: Addison-Wesley. Other terms are multinational corporation (MNC) and transnational corporation (TNC), which are often used interchangeably with MNE. To avoid confusion, we will use MNE throughout this book.

3. A. Rugman & R. Hodgetts, 2001, The end of global strategy, *EMJ*, 19: 333-343.

4. K. Macharzina, 2001, The end of pure global strategies? (p. 106), *MIR*, 41: 105–108.

5. *The Economist*, 2008, The challengers, January 12: 62–64.

6. *The Economist*, 2006, Climbing back, January 21: 69–70.

7. J. Mathews, 2006, Dragon multinationals as new features of globalization in the 21st century, *APJM*, 23: 5–27; M. W. Peng, 2000, *Business Strategies in Transition Economies*, Thousand Oaks, CA: Sage; Y. Yamakawa, M. W. Peng, & D. Deeds, 2008, What drives new ventures to internationalize from emerging to developed economies, *ETP*, 32: 59–82.

8. "Transnational" and "metanational" have been proposed to extend the traditional notion of "global strategy." See C. Bartlett & S. Ghoshal, 1989, *Managing Across Borders*, Boston: Harvard Business School Press; Y. Doz, J. Santos, & P. Williamson, 2001, *From Global to Metanational*, Boston: Harvard Business School Press. A more radical idea is to abandon "global strategy." See A. Rugman, 2001, *The End of Globalization*, New York: AMACOM; A. Rugman, 2005, *The Regional Multinationals*, Cambridge, UK: Cambridge University Press.

9. C. Daily, S. T. Certo, & D. Dalton, 2000, International experience in the executive suite, *SMJ*, 21: 515–523; A. Yan, G. Zhu, & D. Hall, 2002, International assignments for career building, *AMR*, 27: 373–391.

10. Expatriate managers often command significant premium in compensation. In US firms, their average total compensation package is $250,000–$300,000. See M. W. Peng, 2009, *Global Business*, Cincinnati: South-Western Cengage Learning.

11. W. Newburry, 2001, MNC interdependence and local embeddedness influences on perceptions of career benefits from global integration, *JIBS*, 32: 497–508.

12. *BW*, 2007, The changing talent game (p. 68), August 20: 68–71.

13. Sun Tzu, 1963, *The Art of War*, translation by S. Griffith, Oxford: Oxford University Press.

14. I. Ansoff, 1965, *Corporate Strategy*, New York: McGraw-Hill; D. Schendel, & C. Hofer, 1979, *Strategic Management*, Boston: Little, Brown.

15. M. de Rond & R. Thietart, 2007, Choice, chance, and inevitability in strategy, *SMJ*, 28: 535–551; T. Hafsi & H. Thomas, 2005, The field of strategy, *EMJ*, 23: 507–519; D. Hambrick & J. Fredrickson, 2005, Are you sure you have a strategy? *AME*, 19: 51–62; S. Julian & J. Ofori-Dankwa, 2008, Toward an integrative cartography of two strategic issue diagnosis frameworks, *SMJ*, 29: 93–114; R. Nag, D. Hambrick, & M. Chen, 2007, What is strategic management, really? *SMJ*, 28: 935–955.

16. C. von Clausewitz, 1976, *On War*, London: Kegan Paul.

17. B. Liddell Hart, 1967, *Strategy*, New York: Meridian.

18. H. Mintzberg, 1994, *The Rise and Fall of Strategic Planning*, New York: Free Press. See also J. Bower & C. Gilbert, 2007, How managers' everyday decisions create or destroy your company's strategy, *HBR*, February: 72–79; K. Shimizu & M. Hitt, 2004, Strategic flexibility, *AME*, 18: 44–58.

19. Quoted in J. Pfeffer & R. Sutton, 2006, Evidence-based management (p. 72), *HBR*, January: 63–74.

20. M. Farjourn, 2002, Towards an organic perspective on strategy, *SMJ*, 23: 561–594; J. Mahoney, 2005, *Economic Foundation of Strategy*, Thousand Oaks, CA: Sage.

21. A. Chandler, 1962, *Strategy and Structure*, Cambridge, MA: MIT Press.

22. J. Barney, 2002, *Gaining and Sustaining Competitive Advantage*, 2nd ed. (p. 6), Upper Saddle River, NJ: Prentice Hall; P. Drucker, 1994, The theory of business, *HBR*, September–October: 95–105.

23. C. Christensen & M. Raynor, 2003, Why hard-nosed executives should care about management theory, *HBR*, September: 67–74.

24. G. Gavetti & J. Rivkin, 2005, How strategists really think, *HBR*, April: 54–63; S. Winter & G. Szulanski, 2001, Replication as strategy, *OSc*, 12: 730–743.

25. W. Boeker, 1997, Strategic change, *AMJ*, 40: 152–170; A. Pettigrew, R. Woodman, & K. Cameron, 2001, Studying organizational change and development, *AMJ*, 44: 697–713; T. Reay, K. Golden-Biddle, & K. Germann, 2006, Legitimizing a new role, *AMJ*, 49: 977–998.

26. J. Child, 1972, Organizational structure, environment, and performance: The role of strategic choice, *Sociology*, 6: 1–22; R. Kaplan & D. Norton, 2005, The office of strategy management, *HBR*, October: 72–80.

27. J. Guntz & R. M. Jalland, 1996, Managerial careers and business strategies, *AMR*, 21: 718–756; D. Hambrick & P. Mason, 1984, Upper echelons, *AMR*, 9: 193–206; M. Porter, J. Lorsch, & N. Nohria, 2004, Seven surprises for new CEOs, *HBR*, October: 62–72.

28. R. Rumelt, D. Schendel, & D. Teece (eds.), 1994, *Fundamental Issues in Strategy* (p. 564), Boston: Harvard Business School Press.

29. R. Whittington & M. Mayer, 2000, *The European Corporation*, Oxford, UK: Oxford University Press.

30. C. Carr, 2005, Are German, Japanese, and Anglo-Saxon strategic decision styles still divergent in the context of globalization? *JMS*, 42: 1155–1188.

31. E. Gedajlovic & D. Shapiro, 1998, Management and ownership effects, *SMJ*, 19: 533–553; L. Thomas & G. Waring, 1999, Competing capitalisms, *SMJ*, 20: 729–748.

32. K. Banerji & R. Sambharya, 1996, Vertical *keiretsu* and international market entry, *JIBS*, 27: 89–113; J. Dyer, 1996, Does governance matter? *Keiretsu* alliances and asset specificity as sources of Japanese competitive advantage, *OSc*, 7: 649–666; M. W. Peng, S. Lee, & J. Tan, 2001, The *keiretsu* in Asia, *JIM*, 7: 253–276.

33. M. Boisot & J. Child, 1996, From fiefs to clans and network capitalism, *ASQ*, 41: 600–628; M. W. Peng & P. Heath, 1996, The growth of the firm in planned economies in transition, *AMR*, 21: 492–528.

34. M. W. Peng & Y. Luo, 2000, Managerial ties and firm performance in a transition economy, *AMJ*, 43: 486–501.

35. S. Park & Y. Luo, 2001, *Guanxi* and organizational dynamics, *SMJ*, 22: 455–477; E. Tsang, 1998, Can *guanxi* be a source of sustained competitive advantage for doing business in China, *AME*, 12: 64–73.

36. An example of scholarly work with the word *chaebol* in the title is H. Kim, R. Hoskisson, L. Tihanyi, & J. Hong, 2004, The evolution and restructuring of diversified business groups in emerging markets: The lessons from *chaebols* in Korea, *APJM*, 21: 25–48. An example with the word *blat* in the title is S. Michailova & V. Worm, 2003, Personal networking in Russia and China: *Blat* and *guanxi*, *EMJ*, 21: 509–519.

37. M. W. Peng, D. Wang, & Y. Jiang, 2008, An institution-based view of international business strategy, *JIBS* (in press).

38. M. W. Peng & A. Delios, 2006, What determines the scope of the firm over time and around the world? *APJM*, 23: 385–405.

39. S. Chang & J. Hong, 2002, How much does the business group matter in Korea? *SMJ*, 23: 265–274; M. Guillen, 2000, Business groups in emerging economies, *AMJ*, 43: 362–380; T. Khanna & J. Rivkin, 2001, Estimating the performance effects of business groups in emerging markets, *SMJ*, 22: 45–74; M. Li & Y. Wong, 2003, Diversification and economic performance, *APJM*, 20: 243–265; Y. Lu & J. Yao, 2006, Impact of state ownership and control mechanisms on the performance of group affiliated companies in China, *APJM*, 23: 485–503; L. Nachum, 2004, Geographic and industrial diversification of developing country firms, *JMS*, 41: 273–294; D. Yiu, G. Bruton, & Y. Lu, 2005, Understanding business group performance in an emerging economy, *JMS*, 42: 183–206.

40. M. W. Peng, S. Lee, & D. Wang, 2005, What determines the scope of the firm over time? *AMR*, 30: 622–633. See also K. B. Lee, M. W. Peng, & K. Lee, 2008, From diversification premium to diversification discount during institutional transitions, *JWB*, 43: 47–65.

41. M. W. Peng, 2004, Identifying the big question in international business research, *JIBS*, 25: 99–108; M. W. Peng, D. Wang, S. Sun, & E. Pleggenkuhle-Miles, 2008, A unified framework for international business, Working paper, University of Texas at Dallas. See also M. Mankins & R. Steele, 2005, Turning great strategy into great performance, *HBR*, July–August: 65–72.

42. J. Doh, H. Teegen, & R. Mudambi, 2004, Balancing private and state ownership in emerging markets' telecommunications infrastructure, *JIBS*, 35: 233–250.

43. K. Laverty, 1996, Economic "short-termism," *AMR*, 21: 825–860.

44. R. Peterson, C. Dibrell, & T. Pett, 2002, Long- versus short-term performance perspectives of Western European, Japanese, and US companies, *JWB*, 37: 245–255.

45. T. Levitt, 1983, The globalization of markets, *HBR*, May–June: 92–102.

46. There is evidence that US companies, on average, are less "global" relative to their Asian and European rivals. See J. Johansson & G. Yip, 1994, Exploiting globalization potential, *SMJ*, 15: 579–601.

47. Yip, 2003, *Total Global Strategy II* (p. 7).

48. T. Clark & L. Knowles, 2003, Global myopia, *JIM*, 9: 361–372.

49. A. Giddens, 1999, *Runaway World,* London: Profile; A. Prakash & J. Hart, 2000, *Coping with Globalization,* London: Routledge; S. Strange, 1996, *The Retreat of the State,* Cambridge, UK: Cambridge University Press.

50. B. Husted, 2003, Globalization and cultural change in international business research, *JIM,* 9: 427–433.

51. K. Moore & D. Lewis, 1999, *Birth of the Multinational,* Copenhagen: Copenhagen Business School Press.

52. D. Yergin & J. Stanislaw, 2002, *The Commanding Heights* (p. 385), New York: Simon & Schuster.

53. J. Stiglitz, 2002, *Globalization and Its Discontents* (p. 9), New York: Norton.

54. The term, "emerging economies," was probably coined in the 1980s by Antonie van Agtmael, a Dutch officer at the World Bank's International Finance Corporation (IFC). See Yergin & Stanislaw, 2002, *The Commanding Heights* (p. 134).

55. United Nations, 2000, *World Investment Report 2000,* New York and Geneva: United Nations.

56. J. Oxley & K. Schnietz, 2001, Globalization derailed? *JIBS,* 32: 479–496.

57. All quotes in this paragraph are from *Fortune,* 2007, The greatest economic boom ever, July 23: 75–80.

58. L. Eden & S. Lenway, 2001, Multinationals: The Janus face of globalization, *JIBS,* 32: 383–400.

59. P. Ghemawat, 2007, *Redefining Global Strategy,* Boston: Harvard Business School Press.

60. M. Guillen, 2001, *The Limits of Convergence* (p. 232), Princeton, NJ: Princeton University Press; W. Stanbury & I. Vertinsky, 2004, Economics, demography and cultural implications of globalization, *MIR,* 44: 131–151.

61. J. Ricart, M. Enright, P. Ghemawat, S. Hart, & T. Khanna, 2004, New frontiers in international strategy, *JIBS,* 35: 175–200.

62. J. Bhagwati, 2004, *In Defense of Globalization,* New York: Oxford University Press; R. Rajan & L. Zingales, 2003, *Saving Capitalism from the Capitalists,* New York: Crown.

63. M. Kotabe, 2005, Global security risks and international competitiveness (p. 453), *JIM,* 11: 453–455.

64. P. Barnes & R. Oloruntoba, 2005, Assurance of security in maritime supply chains, *JIM,* 11: 519–540;

M. Czinkota, G. Knight, P. Liesch, & J. Steen, 2005, Positioning terrorism in management and marketing, *JIM,* 11: 581–604; N. Kshetri, 2005, Pattern of global cyber war and crime, *JIM,* 11: 541–562; S. Li, S. Tallman, & M. Ferreira, 2005, Developing the eclectic paradigm as a model of global strategy, *JIM,* 11: 479–496; R. Spich & R. Grosse, 2005, How does homeland security affect US firms' international competitiveness? *JIM,* 11: 457–478.

65. M. Young, M. W. Peng, D. Ahlstrom, G. Bruton, & Y. Jiang, 2008, Corporate governance in emerging economies, *JMS,* 45: 196–220.

66. K. Schnatterly, 2003, Increasing firm value through detection and prevention of white-collar crime, *SMJ,* 24: 587–614.

67. A. Bird & M. Stevens, 2003, Toward an emergent global culture and the effects of globalization on obsolescing national cultures, *JIM,* 9: 395–407.

68. M. W. Peng & H. Shin, 2008, How do future business leaders view globalization? *TIBR,* 50: 175-182.

69. H. Teegen, J. Doh, & S. Vachani, 2004, The importance of nongovernmental organizations (NGOs) in global governance and value creation, *JIBS,* 35: 463–483.

70. D. Rondinelli & T. London, 2003, How corporations and environmental groups cooperate, *AME,* 17: 61–76; S. Hart & M. Milstein, 2003, Creating sustainable value, *AME,* 17: 56–67.

71. A. Peredo & J. Chrisman, 2006, Toward a theory of community-based enterprise, *AMR,* 31: 309–328; C. Robertson & W. Crittenden, 2003, Mapping moral philosophies, *SMJ,* 24: 385–392.

72. J. Barney, 2005, Should strategic management research engage public policy debates? *AMJ,* 48: 945–948; L. Donaldson, 2005, For positive management theories, *AMLE,* 4: 109–113; S. Ghoshal, 2005, Bad management theories are destroying good management practices, *AMLE,* 4: 75–91; D. Hambrick, 2005, Venturing outside the monastery, *AMJ,* 48: 961–962; M. Hitt, 2005, Management theory and research, *AMJ,* 48: 963–966; D. Ricks, 2003, Globalization and the role of the global corporation, *JIM,* 9: 355–359.

73. M. W. Peng & E. Pleggenkuhle-Miles, 2009, Current debates in global strategy, *IJMR* (in press).

chapter 2

Industry Competition

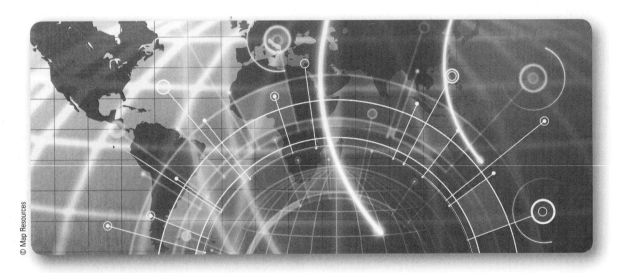

© Map Resources

KNOWLEDGE OBJECTIVES

After studying this chapter, you should be able to

1. Define industry competition

2. Analyze an industry using the five forces framework

3. Articulate the three generic strategies

4. Understand the seven leading debates concerning the industry-based view

5. Draw strategic implications for action

Opening Case: The Automobile Industry: From Good Life to Bloodbath at the Top

Plagued with overcapacity, the automobile industry is intensely competitive. However, life is not equally stressful for companies in the three broad segments within the industry: mass market, luxury, and ultra-luxury. The number of mass market players, such as Chrysler, Ford, General Motors (GM), Honda, Hyundai, Nissan, Renault, Toyota, and Volkswagen (VW), is numerous, and competition is intense. For example, it takes an average of $3,400 of incentives per vehicle for the American Big Three to move their cars. This is not the worst: Saab broke a record by spending $6,200 on incentives per vehicle sold in 2007. These incentives crush industrywide profit margins, which on average stand at a low 5%. The luxury market has fewer players, such as Audi, BMW, Lexus, Mercedes, and Porsche. They use fewer gimmicks such as fat rebates or 0% financing, and their margins are at a relatively healthy 10%. Life in the ultra-luxury market seems to be most tranquil. Competition is more "gentlemanly," and changes come at a glacial pace. The handful of players, such as Ferrari, Lamborghini, and Rolls-Royce, produce a small number of cars each year for the world's most discriminating customers: approximately 10,000 a year for cars priced above $150,000. Profits per car may exceed $20,000. This a world apart from the mass market profits, which sometimes can be as low as $150 per car thanks to incentives. Overall, in the ultra-luxury group, margins are comfortable, indicating a good life at the top.

However, such a good life may be a thing of the past. It seems that every self-respecting carmaker is rushing to invade the lucrative ultra-luxury market, thus prompting a high-stakes drama never seen before. In 2003, three German carmakers launched three new entrants for the ultra-luxury market. Mercedes offered a $320,000 Maybach, which traces its roots to the gull-winged legendary 1952 SLR model. BMW, which took over Rolls-Royce in 1998, launched a $360,000 Rolls-Royce Phantom. VW, having bought Britain's Bentley, stormed into this high-end market with a $160,000 Bentley Continental GT. Positioned as the "driver's car," the Bentley Continental GT outsold the Phantom and the Maybach by a 4-to-1 ratio (4,000 versus 1,000 cars) in its first year. Other players such as Acura, Cadillac, Jaguar, and Lexus are all looking forward to entering the fray. Facing such gathering storms, "old timers," such as Aston Martin and Maserati, also rush to add new models.

With 40%–50% growth of supply in the ultra-luxury market projected for the next decade, the million dollar question is whether so many new entrants will glut the market, repeating what is happening in the mass market. Carmakers emphasize that their ultra-luxury products are "not about transportation." They are more like jewelry, horses, and other items that are part of the affluent lifestyle. BMW, Mercedes, and VW's Bentley are confident that they can grow the market by offering wealthy buyers more choices.

Carmakers are also eyeing virgin territory. In China, while overall growth is strong, the mass market already has a huge glut, forcing average vehicle prices to *fall* by 7% in 2007. Not surprisingly, the most lucrative cut is the ultra-luxury segment, where automakers enjoy the greatest pricing power. In China, sales of premium marques, the fastest growing segment, have tripled in the past five years. In 2002, Bentley opened a dealership in Beijing. Now it has seven dealerships around the country. Mercedes was encouraged by the fact that so many Chinese Mercedes buyers were in their 40s, considerably younger than the typical 50s-plus customers back in Europe and North America. But still, the United States remains the largest and most competitive luxury market that can make or break a carmaker. Overall, it seems that a bloodbath is in the making at the top of the global automobile industry.

Sources: Based on (1) *Auto Observer,* 2008, January incentives more generous than year ago, February 1 (www.autoobserver.com); (2) *Business Week,* 2004, Stealing a lead in luxury, December 6: 134–136; (3) *Business Week,* 2007, Luxury cars in China, April 19; (4) *Business Week,* 2008, Big China plans for Japan's big three, January 18; (5) *The Economist,* 2003, Is one Rolls-Royce enough, January 24: 49–50.

Why is the ultra-luxury car market turning from relative peace and tranquility to more head-on competition? Why are firms that previously weren't competing in this market now entering? What are the responses of existing players (incumbents)? How do components suppliers and car buyers react? Finally, are there any substitutes for these cars? This chapter addresses these and other strategic questions. We accomplish this by introducing the industry-based view, which is one of the three leading perspectives on strategy. (The other two, resource- and institution-based views, will be covered in Chapters 3 and 4, respectively.)

As noted in Chapter 1, a basic strategy tool is SWOT analysis, dealing with internal strengths (S), weaknesses (W), environmental opportunities (O), and threats (T). The focus of this chapter is O and T from the industry environment (S and W will be discussed later). We start by defining industry competition. Then, the five forces framework will be introduced, followed by a discussion of three generic strategies. Finally, we spell out seven leading debates.

industry

A group of firms producing products (goods and/or services) that are similar to each other.

perfect competition

A competitive situation in which price is set by the "market," all firms are price takers, and entries and exits are relatively easy.

industrial organization (IO) economics

A branch of economics that seeks to better understand how firms in an industry compete and then how to regulate them.

Defining Industry Competition

An **industry** is a group of firms producing products (goods and/or services) that are similar to each other. The traditional understanding is based on Adam Smith's (1776) model of **perfect competition,** in which price is set by the invisible hand known as the "market," where all firms are price takers, and entries and exits are relatively easy. However, such perfect competition is rarely observed in the real world. Consequently, since the late 1930s, a more realistic branch of economics, called **industrial organization (IO) economics** (or **industrial economics**), has emerged. Its primary contribution is a **structure-conduct-performance (SCP) model. Structure** refers to the structural attributes of an industry (such as the costs of entry/exit). **Conduct** is firm actions (such as product differentiation). **Performance** is the result of firm conduct in response to industry structure, which can be classified as (1) average (normal), (2) below-average, and (3) above-average. The model suggests that industry structure determines firm conduct (or strategy), which, in turn, determines firm performance.[1]

However, the goal of IO economics is *not* to help firms compete; instead, it is to help policymakers better understand how firms compete in order to properly regulate them. In terms of the number of firms in one industry, there is a continuum ranging from thousands of small firms in perfect competition to only one firm in a **monopoly** (in between, can exist an **oligopoly** with only a few players or a **duopoly** with two competitors). The numerous small firms can only hope to earn average returns at best, whereas the monopolist may earn above-average returns. Economists and policymakers are usually alarmed by above-average returns, which they label "excess profits." Monopoly is usually outlawed and oligopoly scrutinized.

Such an intense focus on above-average firm performance is shared by IO economics and strategy. However, IO economists and policymakers are concerned with the *minimization* rather than the maximization of above-average profits. The name of the game, from the perspective of strategists in charge of the profit-maximizing firm, is exactly the opposite—to try to earn above-average returns (of course, within legal and ethical boundaries). Therefore, strategists have turned the SCP model upside down, by drawing on its insights to help firms perform better.[2] This transformation comprises the heart of this chapter.

The Five Forces Framework

The industry-based view of strategy is underpinned by the **five forces framework**, first advocated by Michael Porter (a Harvard strategy professor who is an IO economist by training), and later extended and strengthened by numerous others. This section introduces this framework.

From Economics to Strategy

In 1980, Porter "translated" and extended the SCP model for strategy audiences.[3] The result is the well-known five forces framework, which forms the backbone of the industry-based view of strategy. Shown in Figure 2.1, these five forces are (1) the intensity of rivalry among competitors, (2) the threat of potential entry, (3) the bargaining power of suppliers, (4) the bargaining power of buyers, and (5) the threat of substitutes. A key proposition is that firm performance critically depends on the degree of competitiveness of these five forces within an industry. The stronger and more competitive these forces are, the less likely the focal firm will be able to earn above-average returns, and vice versa (Table 2.1).

Actions indicative of a high degree of rivalry include (1) frequent price wars, (2) proliferation of new products, (3) intense advertising campaigns, and (4) high-cost competitive actions and reactions (such as honoring all *competitors'* coupons). Such intense rivalry threatens firms by reducing profits.[4] The key question is: What conditions have led to it?

At least six sets of conditions emerge (Table 2.1). First, the number of competitors is crucial. The more concentrated an industry is, the fewer competitors there will be, and the more likely those competitors will recognize their mutual interdependence and

structure
Structural attributes of an industry such as the costs of entry/exit.

conduct
Firm actions such as product differentiation.

performance
The result of firm conduct.

structure-conduct-performance (SCP) model
An industrial organization economics model that suggests industry structure determines firm conduct (strategy), which in turn determines firm performance

monopoly
A situation whereby only one firm provides the goods and/or services for an industry.

oligopoly
A situation whereby a few firms control an industry.

duopoly
A special case of oligopoly that only has two players.

FIGURE 2.1   The Five Forces Framework

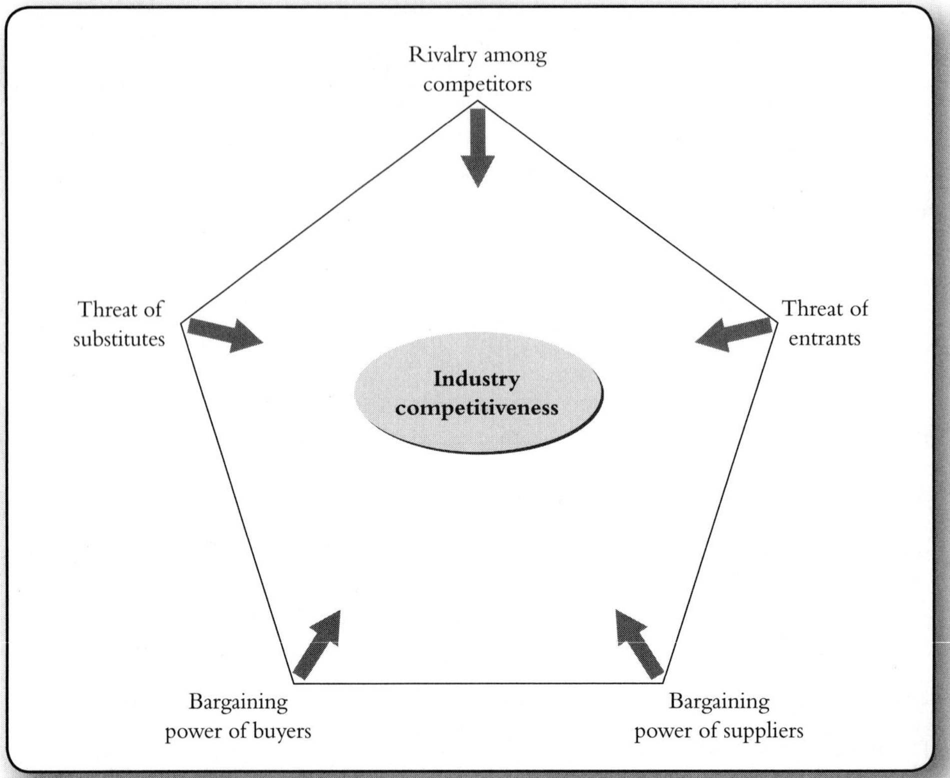

five forces framework

A framework governing
the competitiveness of
an industry proposed
by Michael Porter. The
five forces are (1) the
intensity of rivalry among
competitors, (2) the
threat of potential entry,
(3) the bargaining power
of suppliers, (4) the bargaining power of buyers,
and (5) the threat of
substitutes.

dominance

A situation whereby the
market leader has a very
large market share.

thus restrain their rivalry. As shown in the Opening Case, the few luxury car competitors historically do not engage in intense competitive actions (such as deep discounts)
typically found among mass market competitors.

Second, competitors of similar size, market influence, and product offerings often
vigorously compete with each other. This is especially true for firms unable to differentiate their products, such as airlines. How many airlines have flown into the skies of
bankruptcy lately? In contrast, the presence of a dominant player lessens rivalry because
it can set industrywide prices and discipline behaviors deviating too much from the
prices norm. De Beers in the diamond industry is one such example.

Third, in industries whose products are "big tickets" and purchased infrequently
(such as mattresses and motorcycles), it may be difficult to establish **dominance**—the
market leader has a very large market share. The upshot is more intense rivalry.[5] In
contrast, it may be relatively easier for leading firms to dominate in "staple goods"
industries with low-price, more frequently purchased products. Examples include beers
and facial tissues, dominated by Anheuser Busch (Budweiser) and Kimberly-Clark
(Kleenex), respectively (see Table 2.2). This is because consumers for "staple goods"
are not likely to spend much time on their purchase decisions and find it convenient
to stick with well-known brands. On the other hand, consumers for "big ticket" items
are more interested in searching for a good deal every time they buy, and may not
automatically rely on the reputation of leading firms. For instance, how often do you

TABLE 2.1   Threats of the Five Forces

FIVE FORCES	THREATS INDICATIVE OF STRONG COMPETITIVE FORCES THAT CAN DEPRESS INDUSTRY PROFITABILITY
Rivalry among competitors	• A large number of competing firms • Rivals are similar in size, influence, and product offerings • High-price low-frequency purchases • Capacity is added in large increments • Industry slow growth or decline • High exit costs
Threat of potential entry	• Little scale-based advantages (economies of scale) • Little non-scale-based advantages • Inadequate product proliferation • Insufficient product differentiation • Little fear of retaliation due to the focal firm's lack of excess capacity • No government policy banning or discouraging entry
Bargaining power of suppliers	• A small number of suppliers • Suppliers provide unique differentiated products • Focal firm is not an important customer of suppliers • Suppliers are willing and able to vertically integrate forward
Bargaining power of buyers	• A small number of buyers • Products provide little cost savings or quality-of-life enhancement • Buyers purchase standard undifferentiated products from focal firm • Buyers are willing and able to vertically integrate backward
Threat of substitutes	• Substitutes superior to existing products in quality and function • Switching costs to use substitutes are low

buy a car? Chances are that the next time you buy a car, you would do some research again. Therefore, the current producer that sold you a car several years ago runs the risk of losing you as a customer.

Fourth, in some industries, new capacity must be added in large increments, thus fueling intense rivalry.[6] If the route between two seaports is currently served by two shipping companies (each with one ship of equal size), any existing company's (or new entrant's) new addition of merely one ship will increase the new capacity by 50%. Thus, the two existing shipping companies are often compelled to cut prices. In addition to shipping, industries such as hotels, petrochemicals, semiconductors, and steel often periodically experience overcapacity, leading to price-cutting as a primary coping mechanism.[7]

TABLE 2.2   **Big Tickets versus Staple Goods**

PRODUCT	US MARKET LEADER	LEADER'S MARKET SHARE	LEADER'S SHARE AMONG TOP-4 FIRMS
BIG TICKETS: HIGH-PRICE LESS-FREQUENTLY PURCHASED PRODUCTS			
Athletic footwear	Reebok	25%	40%
Automobile	General Motors	35%	46%
Mattresses	Sealy	25%	46%
Men's jeans	VF Corporation	26%	40%
Motorcycles	Honda	33%	42%
Refrigerators	General Electric	34%	38%
STAPLE GOODS: LOW-PRICE MORE-FREQUENTLY PURCHASED PRODUCTS			
Beer	Anheuser Busch (Budweiser)	44%	52%
Facial tissues	Kimberly-Clark (Kleenex)	47%	56%
Laundry detergents	Procter & Gamble	53%	59%
Lightbulb	General Electric	59%	62%
Photographic film	Kodak	76%	81%
Processed cheese	Kraft	54%	71%

Source: Adapted from J. Shamsie, 2003, The context of dominance: An industry-driven framework for exploiting reputation (pp. 214–215), *Strategic* Management Journal, 24: 199–215. All data are average US market share data during 1987–1994.

Fifth, slow industry growth or decline makes competitors more desperate, often unleashing actions not used previously (see Strategy in Action 2.1). For instance, when facing declining consumer interest in fast food, McDonald's launched its $1 menu featuring the Big N'Tasty burger, which cost $1.07 to *make* in some restaurants. This action, designed to wear out McDonald's chief rivals, Burger King and Wendy's, squeezed industrywide margins.[8]

Finally, industries experiencing high exit costs are likely to see firms continue to operate at a loss.[9] Specialized equipment and facilities that are of little or no alternative use, or that cannot be sold off, pose as exit barriers. In addition, emotional, personal, and career costs, especially on the part of executives admitting failure, may be high. In Japan and Germany, managers may be legally prosecuted if their firms file for bankruptcy.[10] Thus, it is not surprising that these executives will try everything before admitting failure and taking their firms to exit the industry.

Overall, if there are only a small number of rivals led by a few dominant firms, new capacity is added incrementally, industry growth is strong, and exit costs are reasonable, the degree of rivalry is likely to be moderate and industry profits more stable. Conditions opposite from those may unleash intense rivalry. Chapter 8 will discuss more details of interfirm rivalry.

Threat of Potential Entry

incumbents

Current members of an industry that compete against each other.

In addition to keeping an eye on existing rivals, established firms in an industry, which are called **incumbents,** also have a vested interest in keeping out potential new entrants. New entrants are motivated to enter an industry because of the lucrative

Strategy in Action 2.1 - Fighting in the Small Arms Industry

Ethical Challenge

Producing rifles, handguns, and ammunition, the small arms industry is not small. With sales of $7.5 billion a year, over 1,200 companies based in about 100 countries fight for a piece of the action. Good for mankind but bad for the industry, small arms sales have remained flat since the end of the Cold War. While there is no shortage of armed conflicts, the over 600 million items of small arms in circulation create a thriving market for *used* pieces that producers of new weapons hate. Perhaps the most enduring icon is the AK-47 assault rifle sold by Soviet and now Russian exporters as well as licensed producers in Eastern Europe and China. The estimated 100 million copies of AK-47s in circulation have created a permanent glut. In 2004, retired Russian general Mikhail Kalashnikov who designed the AK-47 (which stands for "automatic Kalashnikov first made in 1947") and the Russian firm Izhmash that made the weapon accused the United States of buying *pirate* AK-47s for the Iraqi military.

In the United States, gunmakers such as Alliant, Colt, and Smith & Wesson face a steadily dropping crime rate—historically a killer for handgun sales—and the rise of cheap competition from Brazil and Israel. Three coping strategies are used. First: Exit. Romanian gunmaker Romarm recently began producing sewing and washing machines. Izhmash now hawks machine tools. Second: Collaborate. Germany's Heckler & Koch (H&K), Belgium's FN Herstal, France's GIAT, and the United States' Alliant have begun working together. Third: Differentiate. In 2005, Smith & Wesson unleashed a supersize .50-caliber handgun, the Five Hundred, that sold for $1,000. One of the leading collaborative projects among incumbents, like Alliant and H&K mentioned earlier, is to pack more lethality into the Objective Individual Combat Weapon (OICW). Combining the function of a rifle (like the M-16) and a 20mm grenade, the OICW can send out a barrage of shells to spray shrapnel at the enemy. Even before the OICW enters production, it has already received a barrage of criticisms on the ethicality of this weapon. According to one critic, this weapon relieves "the soldier of the need to take careful or steady aim" and is likely to result in indiscriminate killing. However, desperate times call for desperate measures, and the ethical problems associated with this weapon seem unlikely to deter it from entering Western militaries.

Sources: Based on (1) Arms Trade Resource Center, 2008, Profiling the small arms industry (www.worldpolicy.org); (2) J. Ness, 2004, Swords into vodka, *Newsweek*, November 22: 46; (3) Wikipedia, 2008, Arms industry (en.wikipedia.org).

---

above-average returns some incumbents earn.[11] For example, EMC dominated the data-storage industry during the 1990s. One competitor joked that EMC stood for "Excessive Margin Company." As a result, a powerful pack of heavyweights, led by IBM, HP, and Cisco, entered this industry to "eat EMC's lunch."[12]

Incumbents' primary weapons are **entry barriers,** which refer to industry structures increasing the costs of entry. For instance, Airbus's new A380 burned $12 billion and Boeing's new 787 consumed $10 billion before their maiden flights. Facing such sky-high entry barriers, all potential entrants, including those backed by the Japanese, Korean, and Chinese governments, have quit. The key question is: What conditions have created such high entry barriers?

Shown in Table 2.1, at least six structural attributes are associated with high entry barriers. The first is whether incumbents enjoy **scale-based advantages.** The key concept is **economies of scale,** which refer to reductions in *per unit* costs by increasing the scale of production.[13] For example, Galanz, a Chinese microwave producer, produced

entry barriers

The industry structures that increase the costs of entry.

scale-based advantages

Advantages derived from economies of scale (the more a firm produces some products, the lower the unit costs become).

200,000 units in 1999. In 2002, it manufactured 13 million microwave ovens for more than 200 brands. Such a high output has enabled Galanz to rapidly reap benefits from its economies of scale. Today, Galanz is the undisputed "king of the hill," making approximately 22 million units every year that represent about one-third of the world's microwave production.[14]

Another set of advantages that incumbents may enjoy is independent of scale—**non-scale-based advantages.** For example, proprietary technology (such as patents) is helpful. Entrants have to "invent around," the outcome of which is costly and uncertain. Entrants can also directly copy proprietary technology, which may trigger lawsuits by incumbents for patent violations. This happened to Nexgen, a computer chip maker, when Intel filed such lawsuits. Nexgen paid a heavy price by being forced out of the industry.[15] Another source of such advantages is know-how, the intricate knowledge of how to make products and serve customers that takes years, sometimes decades, to accumulate. It is often difficult for new entrants to duplicate such know-how.

In addition to scale- and non-scale-based low-cost advantages, another entry barrier is **product proliferation,** which refers to efforts to fill product space in a manner that leaves little "unmet demand" for potential entrants.[16] For example, South-Western Cengage Learning, our multibillion dollar multinational publisher (see Chapter 1 Opening Case), has teamed with your author (whose nickname is "Mr. Global") to not only publish this market-leading text, *Global Strategy,* but also *Global Business* and *Global Business Express* around the world. For non-English readers who are dying to arm themselves with the wisdom contained in *Global Strategy,* there are *Quanqiu Qiye Zhanlue* (the Chinese translation) and *Estratégia Global* (the Portuguese translation).

Also important is **product differentiation,** which refers to the uniqueness of the incumbents' products that customers value. Its two underlying sources are (1) brand identification and (2) customer loyalty. Incumbents, often through intense advertising, would like customers to identify their brands with some unique attributes. BMW brags about its cars being the "ultimate driving machines." Champagne makers in the French region of Champagne argue that competing products made elsewhere are not really worthy of the name, Champagne.

A second source of product differentiation is customer loyalty, especially when switching costs for new products are substantial. Many high-technology industries are characterized by **network externalities,** whereby the value a user derives from a product increases with the number (or the network) of other users of the same product.[17] These industries have a "winner take all" property, whereby winners (incumbents) whose technology standard is embraced by the market (such as Microsoft Word, Excel, and PowerPoint) are essentially locking out potential entrants. In other words, these industries have an interesting "*increasing* returns" characteristic, as opposed to "*diminishing* returns" taught in basic economics.

Another entry barrier is possible retaliation by incumbents. Incumbents often maintain some **excess capacity,** designed to punish new entrants. To think slightly outside the box, perhaps the best example is the armed forces. They cost taxpayers huge sums of money and clearly represent excess capacity in peace time. But they exist for one reason—to deter foreign invasion. No country has ever unilaterally disbanded its armed forces, and the worst punishment for defeated countries (such as Germany and Japan in 1945 and Iraq in 2003) is to have their military dismantled. In general, the more credible and predictable the retaliation, the more likely new entrants may be deterred.

---

economies of scale

Reduction in per unit costs by increasing the scale of production.

non-scale-based advantages

Low-cost advantages that are not derived from the economies of scale.

product proliferation

Efforts to fill product space in a manner that leaves little "unmet demand" for potential entrants.

product differentiation

The uniqueness of products that customers value.

network externalities

The value a user derives from a product increases with the number (or the network) of other users of the same product.

excess capacity

Additional production capacity currently underutilized or not utilized.

Coca-Cola has been known to retaliate by slashing prices if any competitor (other than Pepsi) crosses the threshold of 10% share in any market. As a result, potential entrants often think twice before proceeding.

Finally, government policy banning or discouraging entries can serve as another entry barrier.[18] For example, the US government does not allow foreign entrants to invest in the defense industry and only allows up to 25% equity injection from foreign carriers in the airline industry. The Indian government bans large-scale entry by foreign retailers such as Wal-Mart. In almost every case, the lowering of government-imposed entry barriers leads to a proliferation of new entrants, threatening the profit margins of incumbents. This, of course, is exactly why Indian retail incumbents lobby so hard to prevent the onslaught of foreign entrants.

Overall, if incumbents can leverage scale- and/or non-scale-based advantages, offer numerous products, provide sufficient differentiation, maintain a credible threat of retaliation, and/or enjoy regulatory protection, the threat of potential entry becomes weak. Thus, incumbents can enjoy higher profits.

Bargaining Power of Suppliers

Suppliers are organizations that provide inputs, such as materials, services, and manpower, to firms in the focal industry. The **bargaining power of suppliers** refers to their ability to raise prices and/or reduce the quality of goods and services. Four conditions may lead to suppliers' strong bargaining power (Table 2.1). First, if the supplier industry is dominated by a few firms, they may gain an upper hand. For example, in the PC industry, the most profitable players are not Dell and Lenovo, but their two suppliers, Microsoft (operating systems) and Intel (microprocessors), which possess stronger bargaining power. Conversely, numerous individual coffee growers in Africa and Latin America possess little bargaining power when dealing with multinationals such as Nestle and Starbucks.

Second, the bargaining power of suppliers can become substantial if they provide unique, differentiated products with few or no substitutes.[19] For instance, for Coca-Cola bottlers, there is only one supplier for Coke syrup. If Coca-Cola hikes up the syrup price, bottlers, which actually bottle, market, and distribute the soda, will have to swallow these increases, even if they are unable to pass the price increases on to consumers. It is hardly surprising that Coca-Cola's return on equity is substantially higher than that of its bottlers (38% versus 6% in the mid-2000s).[20]

Third, suppliers may exercise strong bargaining power if the focal firm is *not* an important customer. Boeing and Airbus, for example, are not too concerned with losing the business of small airlines, which may only purchase one to two aircraft at a time. Consequently, they often refuse to lower prices. In contrast, they are intensely concerned about losing large airlines, such as American, Japan, and Singapore Airlines. As a result, lower prices are often offered.

Finally, suppliers may enhance their bargaining power if they are willing and able to enter the focal industry by **forward integration**.[21] In other words, suppliers may threaten to become both suppliers *and* rivals. For example, in addition to supplying shoes to traditional department and footwear stores, Nike has established a number of Nike Towns in major cities.

In summary, powerful suppliers can squeeze profitability out of firms in the focal industry. Firms in the focal industry, thus, have an incentive to strengthen their own bargaining power by reducing their dependence on certain suppliers. For example,

bargaining power of suppliers

The ability of suppliers to raise prices and/or reduce the quality of goods and services.

forward integration

Acquiring and owning downstream assets.

Wal-Mart has implemented a policy of not having any supplier account for more than 3% of its purchases.

The Bargaining Power of Buyers

From the perspective of buyers (individual or corporate), firms in the focal industry are essentially suppliers. Therefore, our previous discussion on suppliers is relevant here (Table 2.1). Four conditions lead to the strong bargaining power of buyers. First, a small number of buyers leads to strong bargaining power. For example, hundreds of automobile component suppliers try to sell to a small number of automakers, such as BMW, GM, and Honda. These buyers frequently extract price concessions and quality improvements by playing off suppliers against each other. When these automakers invest abroad, they often encourage or coerce suppliers to invest with them and demand that supplier factories be sited next to the assembly plants—at suppliers' own expenses. Not surprisingly, many suppliers comply.[22] This is how Toyota cloned Toyota City in Guangzhou, China, whose main Toyota-owned factory is surrounded by 30 supplier factories.

Second, buyers may enhance their bargaining power if products of an industry do not clearly produce cost savings or enhance the quality of life for buyers. For example, repeated and frequent upgrades in software packages are causing buyer fatigue. Heads of information technology (IT) departments are increasingly suspicious about whether the costly new "gadgets" are really able to help their companies save money. The upshot is that reluctant buyers can either refuse to buy or extract significant discounts.

Third, buyers may have strong bargaining power if they purchase standard, undifferentiated commodity products from suppliers. Although automobile components suppliers as a group possess less bargaining power relative to automakers, suppliers are *not* equally powerless. There are usually several tiers.[23] The top tier suppliers are the most crucial, often supplying nonstandard, differentiated key components such as electric systems, steering wheels, and car seats. The bottom tier consists of suppliers making standard, undifferentiated commodity products such as seat belt buckles, cup holders, or simply nuts and bolts. Not surprisingly, top tier suppliers possess more bargaining power than bottom tier suppliers.

Finally, like suppliers, buyers may enhance their bargaining power by entering the focal industry through **backward integration.** Buyers such as COSTCO, Tesco, and Marks & Spencer now directly compete with their own suppliers such as Procter & Gamble (P&G) and Johnson & Johnson by procuring store-brand products. Store brands (also known as private labels), such as Kirkland (for COSTCO), Kenmore (for Sears), Kroger, and Safeway brands, compete side-by-side with national brands on the shelf space. At present, store-brand grocery products command approximately 40% of sales in Britain, 20% in France, and 15% in the United States.[24]

In summary, powerful or desperate buyers may enhance their bargaining power. Buyers' bargaining power may be minimized if firms can sell to numerous buyers, identify clear value added, provide differentiated products, and enhance entry barriers.

Threat of Substitutes

Substitutes are products of different industries that satisfy customer needs currently met by the focal industry. For instance, while Pepsi is *not* a substitute for Coke (Pepsi is a rival

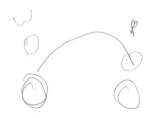

backward integration

Acquiring and owning upstream assets.

substitutes

Products of different industries that satisfy customer needs currently met by the focal industry.

in the same industry), tea, coffee, juice, and water are—that is, they are still beverages but are in a different product category. Two areas of substitutes are particularly threatening (Table 2.1). First, if substitutes are superior to existing products in quality and function, they may rapidly emerge to attract a large number of customers. For example, music downloads (both legal and illegal kinds) are now rapidly eating into CD sales. In India, Tata's "one lakh" car may become a viable substitute for motorcycles and rickshaws (see Chapter 1 Closing Case).

Second, substitutes may pose significant threats if switching costs are low. For example, consumers incur virtually no costs when switching from sugar to a sugar substitute such as NutraSweet. Both are readily available in restaurants and grocery stores. On the other hand, no substitutes exist for large passenger jets, especially for transoceanic transportation. The only other way to go to Hawaii or New Zealand seems to be swimming (!). As a result, Boeing and Airbus can charge higher prices than would be the case if there were substitutes for their products.

Overall, the possible threat of substitutes requires firms to vigilantly scan the larger environment, as opposed to the narrowly defined focal industry. Enhancing customer value (such as price, quality, utility, and location) may reduce the attractiveness of substitutes.

Lessons from the Five Forces Framework

Taken together, the five forces framework offers three significant lessons (Table 2.3):

- The framework reinforces the important point that not all industries are equal in terms of their potential profitability. The upshot is that when firms have the luxury to choose (such as diversified companies contemplating entry to new industries or entrepreneurial start-ups scanning new opportunities), they will be better off if they choose an industry whose five forces are weak. Michael Dell confessed that he probably would have avoided the PC industry had he known how competitive the industry would become.

- The task is to assess the opportunities (O) and threats (T) underlying each competitive force affecting an industry, and then estimate the likely profit potential of the industry.

- The challenge, according to Porter, is "to stake out a position that is less vulnerable to attack from head-to-head opponents, whether established or new, and less vulnerable to erosion from the direction of buyers, suppliers, and substitutes."[25] In other words, the key is to *position* your firm well within an industry and defend its position. Consequently, the five forces framework also becomes known as the **industry positioning** school.

TABLE 2.3   Lessons from the Five Forces Framework
• Not all industries are equal in terms of potential profitability.
• The task for strategists is to assess the opportunities (O) and threats (T) underlying each of the five competitive forces affecting an industry.
• The challenge is to stake out a position that is strong and defensible relative to the five forces.

industry positioning
Ways to position a firm within an industry in order to minimize the threats presented by the five forces.

TABLE 2.4   The Five Forces and the Internet

Five Forces	Threats Represented by the Internet
Rivalry among competitors	• Reduces differentiation among competitors • Drives the basis of competition to price • Increases the number of competitors that, despite having some online presence, may be outside the region/country
Threat of potential entry	• Reduces entry barriers such as the need for sales forces and brick-and-mortar channels • Internet applications are difficult to keep proprietary from new entrants • Incumbents do not have sufficient advantage to deter entry
Bargaining power of suppliers	• It is more convenient for suppliers to reach end users, reducing the leverage of the focal firm • Internet procurement and digital marketplaces may give all companies equal access to suppliers, reducing the value of "special relationships"
Bargaining power of buyers	• Buyers possess greater information on products of the focal firm and competitors, facilitating comparison shopping • Buyers can reach producers (suppliers) more easily, reducing the bargaining power of the focal firm in distribution industries
Threat of substitutes	• The proliferation of Internet applications may create new substitutes, making the focal firm's products (goods and services) obsolete

Source: Adapted from R. Hamilton, E. Eskin, & M. Michaels, 1998, "Assessing competitors: The gap between strategic intent and core capability" (p. 413 and p. 415), *Long Range Planning*, 31: 406–417. Copyright © 1998. Reprinted with permission from Elsevier.

Although the thrust of this framework was put forward by Porter nearly 30 years ago, it has continued to assert strong influence on strategy practice and research today. While it has been debated and modified (introduced later), its core features remain remarkably insightful when analyzing new phenomena such as e-commerce. Table 2.4 suggests that despite the myth that the Internet may completely rewrite the rules of competition, quite the contrary may be true. The so-called "New Economy" appears more "like an old economy that has access to a new technology."[26] Unfortunately, from the perspective of the five forces, the very benefits of the Internet, such as making information widely available and linking buyers and sellers together, may threaten profit margins of the focal firms that try to capture these benefits.[27]

generic strategies

Strategies intended to strengthen the focal firm's position relative to the five competitive forces, including (1) cost leadership, (2) differentiation, and (3) focus.

Three Generic Strategies

Having identified the five forces underlying industry competition, the next challenge is how to make strategic choices. Porter suggested three **generic strategies**, (1) cost leadership, (2) differentiation, and (3) focus, all of which are intended to strengthen the focal firm's position relative to the five competitive forces (see Table 2.5).[28]

TABLE 2.5 **Three Generic Competitive Strategies**

	PRODUCT DIFFERENTIATION	MARKET SEGMENTATION	KEY FUNCTIONAL AREAS
Cost leadership	Low (mainly by price)	Low (mass market)	Manufacturing, materials, and logistics management
Differentiation	High (mainly by uniqueness)	High (many market segments)	Research and development, marketing, and sales
Focus	Low (mainly by price) or high (mainly by uniqueness)	Low (one or a few segments)	Any kind of functional area

Source: Adapted from M. W. Peng, J. Tan & T. Tong, 2004, "Ownership types and strategic groups in an emerging economy" from *Journal of Management Studies.* Reprinted by permission of Blackwell Publishing.

Cost Leadership

Recall that our definition of strategy (see Chapter 1) is a firm's theory about how to compete successfully. A **cost leadership** strategy basically indicates that a firm's theory about how to compete successfully centers on low costs and prices. Offering the same value of a product at a lower price—in other words, better value—tends to attract many more customers. A cost leader often positions its products to target the "average" customers for the mass market with little differentiation. The key functional areas of cost leaders are manufacturing, materials, and logistics management. The hallmark of this strategy is a *high-volume low-margin* approach.

A cost leader, such as Wal-Mart, can minimize the threats from the five forces. First, it is able to charge lower prices and make better profits compared with higher cost rivals. Second, its low-cost advantage is a significant entry barrier. Third, the cost leader typically buys a large volume from suppliers, whose bargaining power is reduced. Even Wal-Mart's largest supplier, P&G, is afraid of Wal-Mart's size. In response, P&G recently acquired Gillette to enhance its size and, hence, its bargaining power. Fourth, the cost leader would be less negatively affected if strong suppliers increase prices or powerful buyers force prices down. Finally, the cost leader challenges substitutes to not only outcompete the utility of its products, but also its prices, a very difficult proposition. Thus, a true cost leader is relatively safe from these threats.

However, a cost leadership strategy has at least two drawbacks. First, there is always the danger of being outcompeted on costs. This forces the leader to *continuously* search for lower costs. All the mass-market automakers in the world are now nervously watching India's "one lakh" car, the Tata Nano, sold for under $3,000 (see Chapter 1 Closing Case). If the Tata Nano were successfully exported, the impact on the profit margins of existing low-cost leaders whose entry-level cars now sell for $8,000 to $10,000 would be devastating. Second, in the relentless drive to cut costs, a cost leader may cut corners that upset customers. A case in point is Toyota's attempt to market a car in Japan with unpainted bumpers. Consumers quickly noticed and rebelled, forcing this model to be withdrawn.

Overall, a cost leadership strategy is pursued by most companies, which find little alternative basis for distinction. However, a number of other firms have decided to be different, by embracing the second generic strategy discussed next.

Differentiation

A **differentiation** strategy focuses on how to deliver products that customers perceive to be valuable and different (Table 2.5). While cost leaders serve "typical" customers,

cost leadership

A competitive strategy that centers on competing on low cost and prices.

differentiation

A strategy that focuses on how to deliver products that customers perceive as valuable and different.

differentiators target customers in smaller well-defined segments who are willing to pay premium prices. The key is a *low-volume high-margin* approach. The ability to charge higher prices enables differentiators to outperform competitors unable to do so. A Lexus car is not significantly more expensive to produce than a Chrysler car. Yet, customers always pay more to get a Lexus. To attract customers willing to pay premiums, differentiated products must have some truly (or perceived) unique attributes, such as quality, sophistication, prestige, and luxury. The challenge is to identify these attributes and deliver value centered on them for *each* market segment.[29] Therefore, in addition to maintaining a strong lineup for its 3-, 5-, and 7-series, BMW is now filling in the "gaps" by adding the new 1- and 6-series.[30] For differentiators, research and development (R&D) is an important functional area through which new features can be experimented with and introduced. Another key function is marketing and sales, focusing on both capturing customers' psychological desires that lure them to buy and satisfying their needs after the sales through excellent services.

According to the five forces framework, the less a differentiator resembles its rivals, the more protected its products are. For instance, Disney theme parks advertise the unique experience associated with Disney movie characters, whereas Kings Island and Six Flags theme parks brag about how fast and tall their roller coasters are. In lingerie, Victoria's Secret emphasizes her—I mean "its"—seductive secret. The bargaining power of suppliers is relatively less of a problem because differentiators may be better able to pass on some (but not unlimited) price increases to customers than cost leaders can. Similarly, the bargaining power of buyers is less problematic because differentiators tend to enjoy relatively strong brand loyalty.

On the other hand, a differentiation strategy has two drawbacks. First, the differentiator may have difficulty sustaining the basis of differentiation in the long run. There is always the danger that customers may decide that the price differential between the differentiator's and cost leader's products is not worth paying for. Second, the differentiator has to confront relentless efforts of imitation. As the overall quality of the industry goes up, brand loyalty in favor of the leading differentiators may decline. For example, IBM's PCs used to command a premium in the 1980s, but not any more. By 2004, IBM was forced to sell its money-losing PC division to a Chinese rival, Lenovo. The upshot is that differentiators must watch out for imitators and avoid pricing their products out of the market.

Overall, a differentiation strategy requires more creativity and capability than a single-minded drive to lower costs. Successful differentiators are able to earn healthy returns.

Focus

A **focus** strategy serves the needs of a particular segment or niche of an industry (Table 2.5). The segment can be defined by (1) geographical market, (2) type of customer, or (3) product line. While the breadth of the focus is a matter of degree, focused firms usually serve the needs of a segment so unique that broad-based competitors choose not to serve it. As shown in the Opening Case, a small number of focused competitors, such as Bentley and Lamborghini, dominate the ultra-luxury car market.

In essence, a focused firm is a specialized differentiator or a specialized cost leader. Although it sounds like a tongue twister, a specialized differentiator (such as Bentley) is basically more differentiated than the large differentiator (such as BMW). This approach

focus

A strategy that serves the needs of a particular segment or niche of an industry.

may be successful when a focused firm possesses intimate knowledge about a particular segment. The logic of how a traditional differentiator can dominate the five forces, discussed before, applies here, the only exception being a much smaller and narrower, but sharper, focus. The two drawbacks, namely, the difficulty to sustain such expensive differentiation and the challenge of defending against ambitious imitation, also apply here.

A focused firm can also be a specialized cost leader. For example, India's focused IT firms, such as Infosys, Wipro, and TCS, have successfully competed with US giants many times their size, such as Accenture, EDS, and IBM. Indian firms have developed an excellent reputation of providing high-quality services at low costs. Again, the same rationale for a traditional cost leader to dominate the five forces, described earlier, applies here. The key difference is that a focused cost leader deals with a narrower segment. The two drawbacks, the danger of being outcompeted on costs and of cutting too many corners, are also relevant here.

Lessons from the Three Generic Strategies

The essence of the three strategic choices is whether to *perform activities differently* or to *perform different activities* relative to competitors.[31] Two lessons emerge. First, cost and differentiation are two fundamental strategic dimensions. The key is to choose one dimension and focus on it consistently. Second, companies that are stuck in the middle—that is, neither having the lowest cost nor sufficient differentiation (or focus)—may be indicative of having either no or drifting strategy. Their performance may suffer as a consequence. However, the second point is subject to debate, as outlined next.

Debates and Extensions

Although the industry-based view is a powerful strategic tool, it is not without its controversies. Therefore, a new generation of strategists needs to understand some of these debates and thus avoid uncritical acceptance of the traditional view. This section introduces seven leading debates: (1) clear versus blurred boundaries of industry, (2) threats versus opportunities, (3) five forces versus a sixth force, (4) stuck in the middle versus all rounder, (5) industry rivalry versus strategic groups, (6) integration versus outsourcing, and (7) industry- versus firm- and institution-specific determinants of firm performance.

Clear versus Blurred Boundaries of Industry

The heart of the industry-based view is the identification of a clearly demarcated industry. However, this concept of an industry may be increasingly elusive. For example, consider the television broadcasting industry. The emergence of cable, satellite, and telecommunications technologies has blurred the industry's boundaries. A television in the future may be able to control household security systems, play interactive games, and place online orders—essentially blending with the functions of a computer. To jockey for advantageous positions in preparation for such a future, there have been a large number of mergers and alliances between television, telecommunications, cable, software, and movie companies in recent years. In other words, the competitors of ABC not only include CBS, NBC, CNN, and Fox, but also AT&T, SkyTV, Microsoft, Apple, Sony, and others. So what exactly is this "industry"? A new concept is to view all the players involved as an "ecosystem."[32] However, it will be challenging to specify the boundaries of such an ecosystem.

Threats versus Opportunities

Even assuming that industry boundaries can be clearly identified, the assumption that all five forces are (at least potential) threats seems too simplistic. This view has been challenged on two accounts. First, strategic alliances are on the rise, and even competitors are increasingly exploring opportunities to collaborate. GM and Toyota manufacture cars together. Samsung provides computer chips to Sony. In other words, if these rivals do not love each other, they do not hate each other either. Compared with the traditional black-and-white view, this more complicated and realistic view requires a more sophisticated understanding of today's competition *and* collaboration (see Chapters 7 and 8 for more details).

Second, even if firms do not directly collaborate with competitors, intense rivalry within an industry, long considered a "no-no," may become an opportunity instead of a threat. In the IT industry, a number of ambitious companies from India, Israel, Singapore, and South Korea, instead of staying at home and enjoying the relative tranquility as suggested by the five forces framework, have come to Silicon Valley to seek out the most competitive environment. Their rationale is that only by being closer to where the action is, can they hope to become globally competitive.[33] In other words, the new strategic motto seems to be: "Love thy competitors! They make you stronger." Overall, it seems that the five forces model may have overemphasized the threat (T) part of the SWOT analysis. A more balanced view needs to highlight both O and T.

Five Forces versus a Sixth Force

The five forces Porter identified in the 1980s are not necessarily exhaustive. In 1990, Porter added related and supporting industries as an important force that affects the competitiveness of an industry.[34] This is endorsed by Andrew Grove, the former CEO of Intel, who suggested the term, **complementors.**[35] Basically, complementors are firms that sell products that add value to the products of a focal industry.[36] The complementors to the PC industry are firms that produce software applications. When complementors produce exciting products (such as new games), the demand for PCs grows, and vice versa. Therefore, it may be helpful to add complementors as a possible sixth force.[37] This is especially important for high-technology industries with "increasing returns" (in other words, "winner-take-all" markets) discussed earlier.

Stuck in the Middle versus All Rounder

A key proposition in the industry-based view is that firms must choose either cost leadership or differentiation. Pursuing both may make firms "stuck in the middle" with poor performance prospects.[38] However, examples of highly successful firms abound, such as Toyota, which stand out as both cost leaders *and* differentiators. As a result, a debate has emerged. First, critics argue that holding technology constant, for firms already operating at the maximum efficiency scale, further cost savings are not possible and differentiation is a must.[39] This can be illustrated by the instant-noodle war erupting in Asia, in which all rivals try to be both cost leaders and differentiators (Strategy in Action 2.2).

complementors

A firm that sells products that add value to the products of a focal industry.

flexible manufacturing technology

Modern manufacturing technology that enables firms to produce differentiated products at low costs (usually on a smaller batch basis than the large batch typically produced by cost leaders).

Strategy in Action 2.2 - Our Instant Noodles Are Better than Yours!

Instant noodles, invented in Japan in 1957, have been voted by the Japanese as their most important 20th century innovation. When these pre-cooked noodles first came out, they cost six times as much as the fresh noodles. Now after 50 years, the technology is mature, enabling a number of firms to become low-cost producers. As a result, an instant-noodle war is erupting in Asia.

Consumers in low-income countries such as Indonesia and Vietnam are price-sensitive, forcing firms to compete on price. The next phase of competition seems to be differentiation, as firms launch a proliferation of new flavors. In one year, Indofood of Indonesia, the world's largest manufacturer of instant noodles, launched 12 regional flavors to appeal to resurgent local pride sparked by recent political decentralization of the country. Indofood has been forced to do so because it is under attack by new players such as Alhami, which undercuts Indofood on price. In addition, Alhami embraces an Islamic image and boasts that its noodles are *halal*, or permissible for Muslims, a message that resonates very well in Indonesia, the world's most populous Muslim country.

Similar drama is unfolding in Vietnam, whereby three big state-owned companies, 40 private firms, and two foreign multinationals, the Anglo-Dutch giant Unilever and Taiwan's Uni-President Enterprises, are all scrambling for a piece of the action. One private firm launched 20 new flavors in one year, including several Korean-flavored noodles, one of which was a *kimchi* flavor, a quintessential Korean delicacy—anything Korean, ranging from TV shows to

makeup, was considered hip among the Vietnamese lately. Not to be outdone, a usually sleepy state-owned firm launched 10 new flavors at the same time, including its own *kimchi* noodles. Interestingly, managers at Unilever and Uni-President, who are not Koreans, are scratching their heads trying to decide whether they want their products to be "Korean" or not.

Source: Based on (1) *The Economist*, 2007, Momofuku Ando, January 20: 94; (2) *Far Eastern Economic Review*, 2003, The instant-noodle war, January 9: 42–43.

Second, critics suggest that technology may not be constant. The idea that differentiators cannot be cost competitive is influenced by manufacturing technology in the 1970s, whereas more recently, **flexible manufacturing technology** has enabled firms to produce differentiated products at a low cost (usually on a smaller batch basis than the large batch typically produced by cost leaders). Thus, the name of the game may become **mass customization**, pursuing cost leadership and differentiation *simultaneously*.[40]

mass customization

Mass produced but customized products.

A review of 17 studies finds that instead of being underdogs, some (but not all) firms "stuck in the middle" may have potential to be "all rounders," being both cost competitive and differentiated.[41] Another study finds that for exporters in Brazil, Chile, and Mexico, a cost leadership strategy bodes well for developed economies, whereas a differentiation strategy succeeds in other emerging economies.[42] Thus, internationally ambitious firms from these countries may need to deploy both strategies simultaneously when entering different markets. While not conclusive, these findings do raise questions and enrich the substance of the debate.

Industry Rivalry versus Strategic Groups

While the five forces framework focuses on the industry level, how meaningful it is depends on how an "industry" is defined. In a broadly defined industry, such as the automobile industry, obviously not every firm is competing against each other. However, some groups of firms within a broad industry *do* compete against each other, such as the mass market, luxury, and ultra-luxury groups in the Opening Case (Figure 2.2). These different groups of firms are thus known as **strategic groups.** It is argued that strategy within one group tends to be similar: Within the automobile industry, the mass market group pursues cost leadership, the luxury group differentiation, and the ultra-luxury group focus. It is also believed that members within a strategic group tend to have similar performance.[43]

While this intuitive idea seems uncontroversial, a debate has erupted on two issues. First, how stable are strategic groups?[44] In other words, how easy or difficult is it for firms to change from one strategic group to another? As illustrated by our Opening Case, strong incentives exist for firms in the mass market group to charge into the luxury group. Can they do it? The launch of Lexus, Acura, and Infiniti by Toyota, Honda, and Nissan, respectively, suggests that despite the challenges, it is possible. However, Mazda entertained the idea of launching its own luxury brand but decided to quit. The root cause is **mobility barriers,** which are within-industry differences that inhibit the movement between strategic groups.[45] Clearly, Mazda was not confident

strategic groups

Groups of firms within a broad industry

mobility barriers

Within-industry difference that inhibits the movement between strategic groups.

FIGURE 2.2   Strategic Groups in the Auto Industry

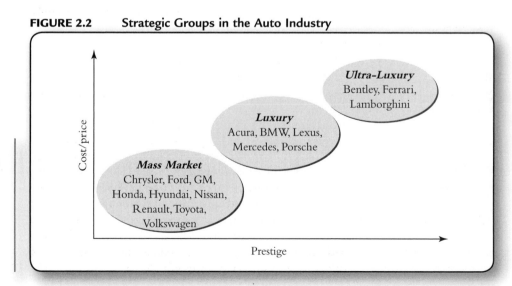

Strategy in Action 2.3 - Can Hyundai Go Upmarket?

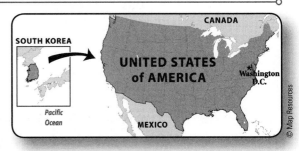

Would you believe that South Korea's Hyundai has better quality than Toyota and Honda? The automobile industry's authoritative J. D. Power survey in 2006 found that Hyundai indeed had the third highest quality in the industry (behind only Lexus and Porsche). Trouble is, just like you, most car buyers don't buy it. Only 23% of all new-car buyers in the United States bother to consider buying a Hyundai. This compares with 65% and 50% for Toyota and Honda, respectively.

Make no mistake: Hyundai is very capable. It was the fastest growing automaker in the US market in the 2000s. Elbowing its way into the entry-level market, Hyundai captured many value-conscious buyers, who appreciated the more *tangible* equipment and performance at lower prices (6%–10% lower than those of rivals). However, with the Korean won appreciating 25% against the dollar over the past three years, the price gap was narrowing between imports of entry-level Hyundai cars from South Korea and more highly regarded brands. Hyundai thus was forced to go after the higher margin high-end market. To offset the won appreciation, Hyundai's $1 billion plant in Montgomery, Alabama,

beefed up production. Yet, it turned out cars twice as fast as dealers ordered them. The problem? "When we don't have a price story," said David Zuchowski, Hyundai's vice president for sales, "we have no story." For high-end buyers, it is the *intangible* reputation and mystique that count. In 2007, Hyundai launched its upscale Genesis sedan (in the $30,000–$35,000 price range) and audaciously compared it with both the BMW 5 series and the Lexus ES350. Does Hyundai have what it takes to win the hearts, minds, and wallets of high-end car buyers?

Sources: Based on (1) *Business Week,* 2007, Hyundai still gets no respect, May 21: 68–70; (2) www.jdpower.com.

---

about its ability to overcome mobility barriers. Recently, Hyundai has fought a similar uphill battle (Strategy in Action 2.3). Will Hyundai succeed or fail?

A second issue centers on the data that classify strategic group memberships. Since strategic group analysis usually requires large quantities of objective data,[46] how useful is it when there is a paucity of data, especially when entering new markets such as emerging economies? Research suggests that while objective data are hard to find, subjective measures tapping into executives' cognitive inclusion and exclusion of certain firms as competitors may provide more reliable clues.[47] This is because executives, when confronting the complexity and chaos of industry competition, are likely to use some *simplifying* schemes to better organize their strategic understanding around some identifiable reference points.[48] In the Chinese electronics industry, executives use ownership type, a simple and easily identifiable reference point, to mentally organize strategic groups.[49] In other words, state-owned enterprises tend to compete with each other, private-owned firms watch each other closely, and foreign entrants view other foreign entrants as a strategic group (Table 2.6). Interviews with these executives find that members within the same self-identified strategic group benchmark intensely against each other, but care less about what is going on in other groups.

TABLE 2.6   **Strategic Groups and Ownership Types in the Chinese Electronics Industry**

STRATEGIC GROUP	DEFENDER	ANALYZER	REACTOR
Ownership type	State ownership	Foreign ownership	Private ownership
Customer base	Stable	Mixed	Unstable
Product mix	Stable	Mixed	Changing
Growth strategy	Cautious	Mixed	Aggressive
Managers	Older, more conservative	Mixed	Younger, more aggressive

Source: Adapted from M. W. Peng, J. Tan, & T. Tong, 2004, Ownership types and strategic groups in an emerging economy (p. 1110), *Journal of Management Studies*, 41 (7): 1105–1129.

Overall, strategic groups have become a useful but somewhat controversial middle ground between industry- and firm-level analyses. Regardless of whether "real" strategic groups exist, if the idea of strategic groups helps managers simplify the complexity they confront when analyzing an industry, then the strategic group concept seems to have some value.

Integration versus Outsourcing

How to determine the scope of a firm is one of the four most fundamental questions in strategy.[50] As noted earlier, the industry-based view advises the focal firm to consider integrating *backward* (to compete with suppliers) or *forward* (to compete with buyers)—or at least threaten to do so. This strategy is especially recommended when market uncertainty is high, coordination with suppliers/buyers requires tight control, and the number of suppliers/buyers is small.[51] (What if they hold us up, if we don't buy them out?) However, this strategy is very expensive, because it takes huge sums of capital to acquire independent suppliers/buyers and most acquisitions end up in failure (see Chapter 9).

In the last two decades, a great debate has erupted challenging the wisdom of integration. Critics make two points. First, they argue that under conditions of uncertainty, *less* integration is advisable.[52] When demand is uncertain, a focal firm with no internal components units can simply reduce output by discontinuing or not renewing supply contracts, whereas a firm stuck with its own internal supplier units may keep producing simply to keep these supplier units employed. In other words, integration may reduce strategic *flexibility*.[53] Second, internal suppliers, which had to work hard for contracts if they were independent suppliers, may lose high-powered market incentives, simply because their business is now taken care of by the "family."[54] Over time, these internal suppliers may become less competitive relative to outside suppliers. The focal firm thus faces a dilemma: To go with outside suppliers will keep internal suppliers idle, but to choose internal suppliers will sacrifice cost and quality. In the last two decades, integration is out of fashion and outsourcing (turning over an activity to an outside supplier) is in vogue.

The outsourcing movement has been influenced by the Japanese challenge in the 1980s and 1990s. Given that the five forces framework is a product of prevailing Western strategic practices of the 1970s, the Japanese way of managing suppliers, through what is called a *keiretsu* (interfirm network), seems radically different. For example, in the 1990s, GM, which had 700,000 employees, downsized 90,000 employees, whereas

Toyota's *total* headcount was only about 65,000, less than the number of people GM reduced. A lot of activities performed by GM, such as those in internal supplier units, are undertaken by Toyota's *keiretsu* member firms using non-Toyota employees.

At the same time, Toyota has far fewer suppliers than GM. They tend to be "cherry picked," trusted members of the *keiretsu*. Instead of treating suppliers as adversaries who should be kept at arm's length, Toyota treats its suppliers (mostly first-tier ones) as collaboration partners by codeveloping proprietary technology with them, relying on them to deliver directly to the assembly line just in time, and helping them when they are in financial difficulty. However, Toyota does not only rely on trust and goodwill. To minimize the potential loss of high-powered market incentive on the part of *keiretsu* members, a dual sourcing strategy—namely, splitting the contract between a *keiretsu* member and a nonmember (often a local company when Toyota moves abroad)—is often practiced.[55] This makes sure that both the internal (*keiretsu*) and external suppliers are motivated to do their best.

Healthy relationships with suppliers may have direct benefits.[56] Overall, the Japanese approach, exemplified by Toyota, has been widely admired and imitated by firms throughout the world.[57] Overall, similar to the idea discussed earlier that rivalry may represent opportunities instead of threats, solid value-adding relationships with suppliers (and buyers and other partners) are now widely regarded as a source of competitive advantage.[58]

However, this is not the end of the debate. In a curious turn of events, while many US firms have become more "Japanese-like," Japanese companies are increasingly under pressure to become more "American-like" (!) after coping with over a decade of recession in the 1990s and beyond. This is because some outsourced activities, crucial to the core business, should not have been outsourced; otherwise, the firm risks becoming a "hollow corporation."[59] Supplier relations that are too close may introduce rigidities, resulting in a loss of much-needed flexibility.[60] In Japan, previously rock-solid buyer-supplier links have started to fray. There is now less willingness to help troubled suppliers improve. Even *keiretsu* members, previously discouraged (if not outright forbidden) to seek contracts outside the network, are now encouraged to look for work elsewhere, because it is believed that the benefits of learning from dealing with other customers may eventually accrue to the lead firm (such as Toyota).[61] Overall, the rise and fall of these two perspectives in the last two decades suggest very careful analysis is needed when making decisions on the optimal scope of the firm.[62]

Industry- versus Firm- and Institution-Specific Determinants of Performance

The industry-based view argues that firm performance is most fundamentally determined by industry-specific attributes.[63] This view has recently been challenged, from two directions. The first is the resource-based view. Although the five forces framework suggests that particular industries (such as airlines) are highly unattractive, certain firms, such as JetBlue in the United States and Ryanair in Europe, not only enter but also succeed. What is going on? A short answer is that there must be firm-specific resources and capabilities that determine firm performance.

A second challenge comes from the critique that the industry-based view "ignores industry history and institutions."[64] Porter's work, first published in 1980, may have carried some hidden, taken-for-granted assumptions underpinning the way competition was structured in the United States in the 1970s. As "rules of the game" in a society, institutions obviously affect firm strategies. For example, cost leadership as a strategy is *banned* by law in the Japanese bookselling industry. All bookstores have to sell new books at the same price without discount. Thus, Amazon, whose primary weapon was low price, had a hard time elbowing its way into Japan (see Integrative Case on the Japanese bookselling industry). Clearly, strategists need to understand how institutions affect competition. This view has become known as the institution-based view. Overall, these two views complement the industry-based view,[65] and we will introduce them in Chapters 3 and 4.

Making Sense of the Debates

The seven debates suggest that the industry-based view—and in fact the strategy field as a whole—is dynamic, exciting, and yet unsettling. All these debates direct their attention to Porter's work, which has become an *incumbent* in the field. When describing his work, Porter deliberately chose the word "framework" rather than the more formal "model." In his own words, "frameworks identify the relevant variables and the questions that the user must answer in order to develop conclusions tailored to a particular industry and company."[66] In this sense, Porter's frameworks have succeeded in identifying variables and raising questions, while not necessarily providing definitive answers. Although the degree of contentiousness among these debates is not the same, it is evident that the last word has not been written on any of them.

The Savvy Strategist

The savvy strategist can draw at least three important implications for action (Table 2.7). (1) You need to understand your industry inside and out by focusing on the five forces.[67] The industry-based view provides a systematic *foundation* for industry analysis and competitor analysis, upon which more detailed examination, introduced in later chapters, can be added. (2) Be aware that additional forces, some of which are discussed in the "Debates and Extensions" section, may influence the competitive dynamics of your industry. The five forces framework should be a start, but not the end of your strategic analysis. (3) Realize that industry is not destiny. While the industry-based view is a powerful framework to understand the behavior and performance of the "average" firm, you need to be aware that certain firms may do well in a structurally unattractive industry. Your job is to lead your firm to become a high-flying outlier despite the pull of gravity of some unattractive attributes of your industry.

In conclusion, we suggest that the industry-based view directly answers the four fundamental questions discussed in Chapter 1. First, why do firms differ? The industry-based view suggests that the five forces in different industries lead to diversity in firm behavior. The answer to the second question, "How do firms behave?" boils down to how they maximize opportunities and minimize threats presented by the five forces.

TABLE 2.7   Strategic Implications for Action

- Establish an intimate understanding of your industry by focusing on the five forces.
- Be aware that additional forces may influence the competitive dynamics of your industry.
- Realize that industry is not destiny. Certain firms may do well in a structurally unattractive industry.

Third, what determines the scope of the firm? A traditional answer is to examine the relative bargaining power of the focal firm relative to that of suppliers and buyers. Integration would result in an expanded scope of the firm. However, more recent work suggests caution. Firms are advised to leverage opportunities of outsourcing, remain focused on core activities, and be willing to collaborate not only with suppliers and buyers but also possibly their competitors. Finally, what determines the international success and failure of firms around the globe? The answer, again, is that industry-specific conditions must have played an important role in determining firm performance around the world.

CHAPTER SUMMARY

1. *Define industry competition*

   - An industry is a group of firms producing similar goods and/or services.

   - The industry-based view of strategy grows out of industrial organization (IO) economics, which helps policymakers better understand how firms compete so policymakers can properly regulate them.

   - Pioneered by Michael Porter, the five forces framework forms the backbone of the industry-based view of strategy, which draws on the insights of IO economics to help firms better compete.

2. *Analyze an industry using the five forces framework*

   - The stronger and more competitive the five forces are, the less likely that firms in an industry are able to earn above-average returns, and vice versa.

   - The five forces are (1) rivalry within an industry, (2) threat of potential entry, (3) bargaining power of suppliers, (4) bargaining power of buyers, and (5) threat of substitutes.

3. *Articulate the three generic strategies*

   - The three generic strategies are: (1) cost leadership, (2) differentiation, and (3) focus.

4. *Understand the seven leading debates concerning the industry-based view*

   - These are (1) clear versus blurred boundaries of industry, (2) threats versus opportunities, (3) five forces versus a sixth force, (4) stuck in the middle versus all rounder, (5) integration versus outsourcing, (6) industry rivalry versus strategic groups, and (7) industry- versus firm- and institution-specific determinants of firm performance.

5. *Draw strategic implications for action*

   - Establish an intimate understanding of your industry by focusing on the five forces.

   - Be aware that additional forces may influence the competitive dynamics of your industry.

   - Realize that industry is not destiny. Certain firms may do well in an unattractive industry.

KEY TERMS

Backward integration	Flexible manufacturing technology	Non-scale-based advantages
Bargaining power of suppliers	Focus	Oligopoly
Complementor	Forward integration	Perfect competition
Conduct	Generic strategies	Performance
Cost leadership	Incumbent	Product differentiation
Differentiation	Industrial organization (IO) economics	Product proliferation
Dominance	Industry	Scale-based advantages
Duopoly	Industry positioning	Strategic group
Economies of scale	Mass customization	Structure
Entry barrier	Mobility barrier	Structure-conduct-performance (SCP) model
Excess capacity	Monopoly	
Five forces framework	Network externalities	Substitutes

CRITICAL DISCUSSION QUESTIONS

1. Why do price wars often erupt in certain industries (such as the automobile industry), but less frequently in other industries (such as the diamond industry)? What can a firm do to discourage price wars or be better prepared for price wars?

2. Compare and contrast the five forces affecting the airline industry, the fast food industry, the beauty products industry, and the pharmaceutical industry (1) on a *worldwide* basis and (2) in *your* country. Which industry holds more promise for earning higher returns? Why?

3. Conduct a five forces analysis of the "business school" industry or the "higher education" industry. Identify the "strategic group" to which your home institution belongs. Then, use this analysis to explain why your home institution is doing well (or poorly) in the competition for better students, professors, donors, and ultimately rankings.

4. ***ON ETHICS:*** "Excessive profits" coming out of monopoly, duopoly, or any kind of strong market power are targets for government investigation and prosecution (for example, Microsoft was charged by both US and EU competition authorities). Yet, strategists openly pursue above-average profits, which are argued to be "fair profits." Do you see an ethical dilemma here? Make your case either as an antitrust official or as a firm strategist (such as Bill Gates).

Five Forces in the Beauty Products Industry

As a $160 billion-a-year global industry, the beauty products industry encompasses makeup, skin and hair care, perfumes, cosmetic surgery, health clubs, and diet pills. Incumbents have remarkably long staying power in this industry. L'Oreal of France, today's industry leader, was founded in 1909. In 1911, both Nivea of Germany and Shiseido of Japan were established. In America, Elizabeth Arden and Max Factor were founded at about the same time. All these brands are still around, although not necessarily as independent companies.

Recently, the industry has been growing at approximately 7% a year, more than twice the rate of the developed world's GDP. Two groups around the world underpin such strong growth: (1) richer, aging baby-boomers in developed economies and (2) an increasingly more affluent middle class in emerging economies such as Brazil, China, India, Russia, and South Korea. Brazil, for example, has a larger army of Avon Ladies (900,000 strong) than its men and women in the army and navy *combined* (!).

Three major changes affect this industry. First, a number of new entrants have emerged. Most luxury goods firms, such as Chanel, Dior, Ralph Lauren, and Yves St Laurent, now have beauty products. Two consumer goods giants, Procter & Gamble (P&G) and Unilever, pose probably the most significant threats. As their traditional products such as diapers and soaps mature, they are increasingly pouring resources into their beauty divisions. Second, changes in consumer behavior help no-frills retail chains such as Wal-Mart gain bargaining power, at the expense of fashionable department stores, whose selling costs are high and whose sales are declining. Wal-Mart, for example, only wants to deal with a handful of big suppliers, which plays into the strength of L'Oreal and P&G. Smaller players, such as Estee Lauder and Revlon, which depend more on department stores, are hurting as a result. Finally, incumbents increasingly fight back, by emphasizing how unique their products are. L'Oreal, for example, advertised how many patents it has filed. Shiseido claimed that its Body Creator skin gel can melt 1.1 kilograms (2.4 pounds) of body fat a month without any need to diet or exercise.

While the market for traditional beauty products becomes increasingly competitive, the industry's real growth may come from areas outside the "radar screen" of the main players: cosmetic surgery and well-being products. First, cosmetic surgery is no longer the exclusive territory of actresses and celebrities. In the United States, it used to cost $12,000 to reconstruct a woman's breasts ten years ago—now it can be done for $600. More than 70% of such customers now earn less than $50,000 a year. The US market for cosmetic surgery, a $20 billion business, has grown 220% since 1997. The second area for growth is well-being products, consisting of spas, salons, and clubs linking beauty with natural solutions such as exercise and diet, as opposed to chemicals. The market has been fragmented with numerous entrepreneurs operating a few spas, salons, and clubs here and there. It seems that sooner or later, traditional beauty products companies will turn their attention to these new areas.

Sources: Based on (1) Duke University Libraries Digital Collections, 2008, Brief history of beauty and hygiene products (library.duke.edu); (2) *The Economist*, 2003, Pots of promise, May 24: 69–71; (3) *The Economist*, 2003, The right to be beautiful, May 24: 9; (4) N. Shute, 2004, Makeover nation, *US News & World Report*, May 31: 53–63.

Case Discussion Questions

1. Why do incumbents have long staying power in this industry?

2. How do new entrants overcome entry barriers? How do incumbents react to new entries?

3. Why do retail chains gain bargaining power as buyers at the expense of department stores?

4. Should traditional competitors focus on expanding new country markets in emerging economies, or on entering hot new growth product markets in developed economies?

NOTES

Journal acronyms *AJS–American Journal of Sociology;*
AME–Academy of Management Executive; **AMJ**–*Academy*
of Management Journal; **AMP**–*Academy of Management*
Perspectives; **AMR**–*Academy of Management Review;* **APJM**–
Asia Pacific Journal of Management; **ASQ**–*Administrative Science*
Quarterly; **BW**–*Business Week;* **HBR**–*Harvard Business Review;*
JIBS–*Journal of International Business Studies;* **JIM**–*Journal*
of International Management; **JMS**–*Journal of Management*
Studies; **LRP**–*Long Range Planning;* **OSc**–*Organization Science;*
QJE–*Quarterly Journal of Economics;* **SMJ**–*Strategic Management*
Journal; **SMR**–*Sloan Management Review*

1. F. Scherer, 1980, *Industrial Market Structure and
   Economic Performance,* Boston: Houghton Mifflin.

2. M. Porter, 1981, The contribution of industrial organization to strategic management, *AMR,* 6: 609–620;
   C. Zott & R. Amit, 2008, The fit between product
   market strategy and business model, *SMJ,* 29: 1–26.

3. M. Porter, 1980, *Competitive Strategy,* New York:
   Free Press.

4. K. Cool, L. Roller, & B. Leleux, 1999, The relative
   impact of actual and potential rivalry on firm profitability in the pharmaceutical industry, *SMJ,* 20: 1–14.

5. J. Shamsie, 2003, The context of dominance, *SMJ,* 24:
   199–215.

6. D. Simon, 2005, Incumbent pricing responses to entry,
   SMJ, 26: 1229–1248.

7. J. Henderson & K. Cool, 2003, Learning to time
   capacity expansions, *SMJ,* 24: 393–413.

8. *BW,* 2003, Hamburger hell, March 3: 104–108.

9. C. Decker & T. Mellewigt, 2007, Thirty years after
   Michael E. Porter, *AMP,* 21: 41–55.

10. S. Lee, M. W. Peng, & J. Barney, 2007, Bankruptcy
    law and entrepreneurship development: A real
    options perspective, *AMR,* 32: 257–272.

11. G. Dowell, 2006, Product line strategies of new
    entrants in an established industry, *SMJ,* 27: 959–979.

12. *BW,* 2002, Everybody wants to eat EMC's lunch,
    September 2: 76–77; *BW,* 2005, From the brink to
    the big leagues, August 15: 60–61.

13. F. Katrishen & N. Scordis, 1998, Economics of scale
    in services, *JIBS,* 29: 305–324; R. Makadok, 1999,
    Interfirm differences in scale economics and the evolu-
    tion of market shares, *SMJ,* 20: 935–952.

14. G. Ge & D. Ding, 2008, A strategic analysis of surging
    Chinese manufacturers, *APJM,* 25 (in press).

15. M. Schilling, 1998, Technological lockout, *AMR,* 23:
    267–284.

16. T. Cottrell & B. Nault, 2004, Product variety and
    firm survival in the microcomputer software industry,
    SMJ, 25: 1005–1025; A. Mainkar, M. Lubatkin, &
    W. Schulze, 2006, Toward a product-proliferation
    theory of entry barriers, *AMR,* 31: 1062–1075.

17. C. Hill, 1997, Establishing a standard, *AME,* 11 (2):
    7–26; M. Schilling, 2002, Technology success and
    failure in winner-take-all markets, *AMJ,* 45: 387–398;
    V. Shankar & B. Bayus, 2003, Network effects and
    competition, *SMJ,* 24: 375–384.

18. M. Delmas & Y. Tokat, 2005, Deregulation, gover-
    nance structures, and efficiency, *SMJ,* 26: 441–460;
    P. Ingram & H. Rao, 2004, Store wars, *AJS,* 110:
    446–487.

19. M. Bensaou & E. Anderson, 1999, Buyer-supplier
    relations in industrial markets, *OSc,* 10: 460–481;
    S. Michael, 2000, Investments to create bargaining
    power, *SMJ,* 21: 497–514.

20. *BW,* 2002, Coke: The cost of babying bottlers,
    December 9: 93–94.

21. R. Gulati, P. Lawrence, & P. Puranam, 2005,
    Adaptation in vertical relationships, *SMJ,* 26: 415–440.

22. M. W. Peng, S. Lee, & J. Tan, 2001, The *keiretsu* in
    Asia, *JIM,* 7: 253–276.

23. A. Kaufman, C. Wood, & G. Theyel, 2000, Collaboration
    and technology linkages, *SMJ,* 21: 649–663.

24. *The Economist,* 2003, A survey of food (p. 7),
    December 13: 1–16.

25. M. Porter, 1998, *On Competition* (p. 38), Boston:
    Harvard Business School Press.

26. M. Porter, 2001, Strategy and the Internet (p. 78),
    HBR, March: 63–78; S. Rangan & R. Adner, 2001,
    Profits and the Internet, *SMR,* summer: 44–53.

27. Porter, 2001, Strategy and the Internet (p. 66);
    S. Zaheer & A. Zaheer, 2001, Market microstructure
    in a global B2B network, *SMJ,* 22: 859–873.

28. M. Porter, 1985, *Competitive Advantage,* New York:
    Free Press.

29. W. Desarbo, K. Jedidi, & I. Sinha, 2001, Customer value analysis in a heterogeneous market, *SMJ*, 22: 845–857; M. Kroll, P. Wright, & R. Heiens, 1999, The contribution of product quality to competitive advantage, *SMJ*, 20: 375–384; O. Sorenson, 2000, Letting the market work for you, *SMJ*, 21: 577–592.

30. *BW*, 2003, BMW: Will Panke's high-speed approach hurt the brand? June 9: 57–60.

31. M. Porter, 1996, What is strategy? *HBR*, 74 (6): 61–78.

32. D. Teece, 2007, Explicating dynamic capabilities, *SMJ*, 28: 1319–1350.

33. L. Nachum, 2000, Economic geography and the location of TNCs, *JIBS*, 31: 367–385; R. Pouder & C. St. John, 1996, Hot spots and blind spots, *AMR*, 21: 1192–1225.

34. M. Porter, 1990, *The Competitive Advantage of Nations*, New York: Free Press.

35. A. Grove, 1996, *Only the Paranoid Survive*, New York: Doubleday.

36. J. Bonardi & R. Durand, 2003, Managing network effects in high-tech markets, *AME*, 17 (4): 40–52.

37. D. Yoffie & M. Kwak, 2006, With friends like these, *HBR*, September: 89–98.

38. S. Thornhill & R. White, 2007, Strategic purity, *SMJ*, 28: 553–561.

39. C. Hill, 1988, Differentiation versus low cost or differentiation and low cost, *AMR*, 13: 401–412.

40. N. Warren, K. Moore, & P. Cardona, 2002, Modularity, strategic flexibility, and firm performance, *SMJ*, 23: 1123–1140.

41. C. Campbell-Hunt, 2000, What have we learned about generic competitive strategy? *SMJ*, 21: 127–154.

42. P. Aulakh, M. Kotabe, & H. Teegen, 2000, Export strategies and performance of firms from emerging economies, *AMJ*, 43: 342–361.

43. G. Leask & D. Parker, 2007, Strategic groups, competitive groups, and performance within the UK pharmaceutical industry, *SMJ*, 28: 723–745; F. Mas-Ruiz, J. Nocolau-Gonzalbez, & F. Ruiz-Moreno, 2005, Asymmetric rivalry between strategic groups, *SMJ*, 26: 713–745; A. Nair & S. Kotha, 2001, Does group membership matter? *SMJ*, 22: 221–235; J. Short, D. Ketchen, T. Palmer, & G. T. Hult, 2007, Firm, strategic group, and industry influences on performance, *SMJ*, 28: 147–167.

44. D. Dranove, M. Peteraf, & M. Shanley, 1998, Do strategic groups exist? *SMJ*, 19: 1029–1044.

45. R. Caves & M. Porter, 1977, From entry barriers to mobility barriers, *QJE*, 91: 241–261; J. Lee, K. Lee, & S. Rho, 2002, An evolutionary perspective on strategic group emergence, *SMJ*, 23: 727–746.

46. R. Hamilton, E. Eskin, & M. Michaels, 1998, Assessing competitors, *LRP*, 31: 406–417; J. D. Osborne, C. Stubbart, & A. Ramaprasad, 2001, Strategic groups and competitive enactment, *SMJ*, 22: 435–454.

47. D. Johnson & D. Hoopes, 2003, Managerial cognition, sunk costs, and the evolution of industry structure, *SMJ*, 24: 1057–1068; J. Porac, H. Thomas, F. Wilson, D. Paton, & A. Kanfer, 1995, Rivalry and the industry model of Scottish knitwear producers, *ASQ*, 40: 203–227; M. Peteraf & M. Shanley, 1997, Getting to know you, *SMJ*, 18: 165–186.

48. G. McNamara, R. Luce, & G. Tompson, 2002, Examining the effect of complexity in strategic group knowledge structures on firm performance, *SMJ*, 23: 151–170.

49. M. W. Peng, J. Tan, & T. Tong, 2004, Ownership types and strategic groups in an emerging economy, *JMS*, 41: 1105–1129.

50. A. Afuah, 2003, Redefining firm boundaries in the face of the Internet, *AMR*, 28: 34–53; M. Jacobides, 2005, Industry change through vertical disintegration, *AMJ*, 48: 465–498.

51. O. Williamson, 1985, *The Economic Institutions of Capitalism*, New York: Free Press.

52. N. Argyres & J. Liebeskind, 1999, Contractual commitments, bargaining power, and government inseparability, *AMR*, 24: 49–63.

53. R. D'Aveni & A. Ilinitch, 1992, Complex patterns of vertical integration in the forest products industry, *AMJ*, 35: 596–625; S. Nadkarni & V. Narayanan, 2007, Strategic schemas, strategic flexibility, and firm performance, *SMJ*, 28: 243–270.

54. J. Mahoney, 1992, The choice of organizational form, *SMJ*, 13: 559–584; A. Vining, 2003, Internal market failure, *JMS*, 40: 431–457.

55. J. Richardson, 1993, Parallel sourcing and supplier performance in the Japanese automobile industry, *SMJ*, 14: 339–350.

56. J. Dyer, 1997, Specialized supplier networks as a source of competitive advantage, *SMJ*, 17: 271–292;

D. Griffith & M. Myers, 2005, The performance implications of strategic fit of relational norm governance strategies in global supply chain relationships, *JIBS,* 36: 254–269.

57. K. Banerji & R. Sambharya, 1996, Vertical *keiretsu* and international market entry, *JIBS,* 27: 89–113; X. Martin, W. Mitchell, & A. Swaminathan, 1995, Recreating and extending Japanese automobile buyer-supplier links in North America, *SMJ,* 16: 589–619; J. Womack, D. Jones, & D. Roos, 1990, *The Machine that Changed the World,* New York: Harper & Row.

58. J. Dyer & H. Singh, 1998, The relational view, *AMR,* 23: 660–679.

59. J. Barthelemy, 2003, The seven deadly sins of outsourcing, *AME,* 17 (2): 87–98; A. Takeishi, 2001, Bridging inter- and intra-firm boundaries, *SMJ,* 22: 403–433.

60. M. Kotabe, X. Martin, & H. Domoto, 2003, Gaining from vertical partnerships, *SMJ,* 24: 293–316.

61. C. Ahmadjian & J. Lincoln, 2001, *Keiretsu,* governance, and learning, *OSc,* 12: 683–701; R. Lamming, 2000, Japanese supply chain relationships in recession,

LRP, 33: 757–778; J. McGuire & S. Dow, 2009, Japanese keiretsu: Past, present, future, *APJM* (in press).

62. M. Leiblein, J. Reuer, & F. Dalsace, 2002, Do make or buy decisions matter? *SMJ,* 23: 817–833; C. Nicholls-Nixon & C. Woo, 2003, Technology sourcing and output of established firms, *SMJ,* 24: 651–666.

63. A. McGahan & M. Porter, 1997, How much does industry matter, really? *SMJ,* 18: 15–30.

64. S. Oster, 1994, *Modern Competitive Analysis,* 2nd ed. (p. 46), New York: Oxford University Press.

65. J. Bou & A. Satorra, 2007, The persistence of abnormal returns at industry and firm levels, *SMJ,* 28: 707–722; A. van Witteloostujin & C. Boone, 2006, A resource-based theory of market structure and organizational form, *AMR,* 31: 409–426.

66. M. Porter, 1994, Toward a dynamic theory of strategy, in R. Rumelt, D. Schendel, & D. Teece (eds.), *Fundamental Issues in Strategy* (p. 427), Boston: Harvard Business School Press.

67. X. Lecocq & B. Demil, 2006, Strategizing industry structure, *SMJ,* 27: 891–898.

chapter 3

Resources and Capabilities

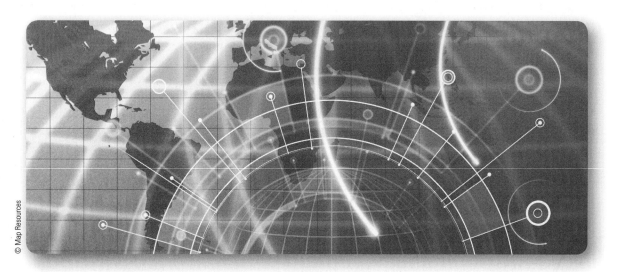

© Map Resources

KNOWLEDGE OBJECTIVES

After studying this chapter, you should be able to

1. Explain what firm resources and capabilities are

2. Undertake a basic SWOT analysis along the value chain

3. Decide whether to keep an activity in-house or outsource it

4. Analyze the value, rarity, imitability, and organizational aspects of resources and capabilities

5. Participate in four leading debates on the resource-based view

6. Draw strategic implications for action

Opening Case: Zara Breaks Industry Rules

Zara is one of the hottest fashion chains of the 21st century. Founded in 1975, Zara's parent, Inditex, has become one of the leading global apparel retailers. Since its initial public offering (IPO) in 2001, Inditex tripled its sales and profits and doubled the number of stores for its eight brands, of which Zara contributes two-thirds of total sales. Headquartered in Spain, Zara is active not only throughout Europe, but also in Asia and North America. As of 2008, the total number of stores was over 3,100 in 64 countries (the three newest countries entered were China, Serbia, and Tunisia). Zara stores occupy some of the priciest top locations: Paris' Champs-Elysées, Tokyo's Ginza, New York's Fifth Avenue, and Dallas' Galleria. Zara's formidable rise around the globe has generated significant profits. In terms of sales, Gap is still bigger ($16 billion) than Inditex ($12 billion), but Zara's 16.5% margins beat Gap's 11%. Overall, Zara succeeds by breaking and then rewriting a number of rules about competition in the fashion retail industry.

Rule number one: Avoid stock-outs (a store running out of items in demand). Zara's answer? Occasional shortages contribute to an urge to buy now. With new items arriving at stores *twice* a week, experienced Zara shoppers know that "If you see something and don't buy it, you can forget about coming back for it because it will be gone." The small batch of merchandise during a short window of opportunity for purchasing motivates shoppers to visit Zara stores more frequently. In London, shoppers visit the average store four times a year, but frequent Zara 17 times annually. There is a good reason to do so: Zara makes about 20,000 items a year, about triple what Gap does. As a result, "At Gap, everything is the same," according to a Zara fan, "and buying from Zara, you'll never end up looking like someone else."

Rule number two: Bombarding shoppers with ads is a must. Gap and H&M spend, on average, 3%–4% of their sales on ads. Zara begs to differ: It devotes just 0.3% of its sales to ads. The high traffic in the stores alleviates some need for advertising in the media, most of which only serves as a reminder to visit the stores.

Rule number three: Outsource. Gap and H&M do not own any production facilities. However, outsourcing production (mostly to Asia) requires a long lead time, usually several months ahead. Again, Zara has decisively deviated from the norm. By concentrating (most, but not all, of) its production in-house and in Spain, Zara has developed a super-responsive supply chain. It designs, produces, and delivers a new garment to its stores in a mere 15 *days,* a pace that is unheard of in the industry. The best speed the rivals can achieve is two *months*. Outsourcing is not necessarily "low cost" because errors in prediction can easily lead to unsold inventory, forcing retailers to offer steep discounts. The industry average is to offer 40% discounts across all merchandise. In contrast, Zara sells more at full price, and when it discounts, it averages only 15%.

Rule number four: Strive for efficiency through large batches. In contrast, Zara intentionally deals with small batches. Because of its flexibility, Zara does not worry about "missing the boat" for a season. When new trends emerge, Zara can react quickly. More interestingly, Zara runs its supply chain like clockwork with a fast but predictable rhythm: Every store places orders twice a week. Trucks and cargo flights run on established schedules—like a bus service. From Spain, shipments reach most European stores in 24 hours, US stores in 48 hours, and Asian stores in 72 hours. Not only do store staff know exactly when shipments will arrive, regular customers know that too, thus motivating them to check out the new merchandise more frequently on those days, which are known as "Z days" in some cities.

Sources: Based on (1) *Business Week,* 2006, Fashion conquistador, September 4: 38–39; (2) K. Ferdows, M. Lewis, & J. Machuca, 2004, Rapid-fire fulfillment, *Harvard Business Review,* November: 104–110; (3) www.zara.com.

Why is Zara able to stand out in a very crowded and competitive industry? Why does it break a number of industry norms, such as avoiding stock-outs, running numerous ads, outsourcing production, and producing in large batches? More important, how can Zara design, produce, and deliver a new garment in a mere 15 *days,* when it takes its rivals several *months* to get this done? Why do its rivals fail to match Zara's super-responsive supply chain? The answer is that there must be certain resources and capabilities specific to Zara that are not shared by rivals. This insight has been developed into a **resource-based view,** which has emerged as one of the three leading perspectives on strategy (the third one will be introduced in Chapter 4).[1]

While the industry-based view focuses on how "average" firms within one industry (such as Zara's rivals) compete, the resource-based view sheds considerable light on how individual firms (such as Zara) differ from each other within one industry. In SWOT analysis, the industry-based view deals with the *external* O and T, and the resource-based view concentrates on the *internal* S and W.[2] A key question is: How can high-flyers such as Zara defy gravity and sustain competitive advantage?[3] In this chapter, we first define resources and capabilities, and then discuss the value chain analysis. Afterward, we focus on value (V), rarity (R), imitability (I), and organization (O) through a VRIO framework. Debates and extensions follow.

Understanding Resources and Capabilities

A basic proposition of the resource-based view is that a firm consists of a bundle of productive resources and capabilities.[4] **Resources** are defined as "the tangible and intangible assets a firm uses to choose and implement its strategies."[5] There is some debate regarding the definition of capabilities. Some argue that capabilities are a firm's capacity to dynamically deploy resources. They suggest a crucial distinction between resources and capabilities, and advocate a "dynamic capabilities" view.[6]

While scholars may debate the fine distinctions between resources and capabilities, these distinctions are likely to "become badly blurred" in practice.[7] For example, is

resource-based view

A leading perspective of strategy which suggests that differences in firm performance are most fundamentally driven by differences in firm resources and capabilities.

resources

The tangible and intangible assets a firm uses to choose and implement its strategies.

TABLE 3.1 Examples of Resources and Capabilities

Tangible Resources and Capabilities	Examples
Financial	• Ability to generate internal funds • Ability to raise external capital
Physical	• Location of plants, offices, and equipment • Access to raw materials and distribution channels
Technological	• Possession of patents, trademarks, copyrights, and trade secrets
Organizational	• Formal planning, command, and control systems • Integrated management information systems
Intangible Resources and Capabilities	**Examples**
Human	• Managerial talents • Organizational culture
Innovation	• Research and development capabilities • Capacities for organizational innovation and change
Reputation	• Perceptions of product quality, durability, and reliability among customers • Reputation as a good employer • Reputation as a socially responsible corporate citizen

Sources: Adapted from (1) J. Barney, 1991, Firm resources and sustained competitive advantage, *Journal of Management,* 17: 101; (2) R. Hall, 1992, The strategic analysis of intangible resources, *Strategic Management Journal,* 13: 135–144.

Zara's store location a resource or capability? How about its ability to quickly turn around merchandise? For current and would-be strategists, the key is to understand how these attributes help improve firm performance, as opposed to figuring out whether they should be labeled as resources or capabilities. Therefore, in this book, we will use the terms "resources" and "capabilities" *interchangeably* and often in *parallel*. In other words, **capabilities** are defined here the same way as resources.

All firms, including the smallest ones, possess a variety of resources and capabilities. How do we meaningfully classify such diversity? A useful way is to separate them into two categories: tangible and intangible ones (Table 3.1). **Tangible resources and capabilities** are assets that are observable and more easily quantified. They can be broadly divided into four categories:

- **Financial resources and capabilities.** Zara's ability to fund its ambitious overseas expansion is an example.

- **Physical resources and capabilities.** For example, while many people attribute the success of Amazon to its online savvy (which makes sense), a crucial reason Amazon has emerged as the largest bookseller is because it has built some of the largest physical, *brick-and-mortar* book warehouses in key locations.

capabilities

The tangible and intangible assets a firm uses to choose and implement its strategies.

tangible resources and capabilities

Assets that are observable and more easily quantified.

- **Technological resources and capabilities.**[8] For instance, over 60% of Canon's products on the market today, including popular digital cameras, have been introduced during the past two years.

- **Organizational resources and capabilities.** One example is Zara's super-responsive supply chain, which runs like clockwork with a fast but predictable rhythm.

Intangible resources and capabilities, by definition, are harder to observe and more difficult (or sometimes impossible) to quantify (see Table 3.1). Yet, it is widely acknowledged that they must be "there," because no firm is likely to generate competitive advantage by solely relying on tangible resources and capabilities alone.[9] Examples of intangible assets include:

- **Human resources and capabilities.**[10] The Closing Case has an example on how the Portman Ritz-Carlton Hotel in Shanghai, China, manages and leverages its human resources (HR).

- **Innovation resources and capabilities.**[11] Some firms are renowned for innovations. For instance, Samsung Electronics has recently emerged as a new powerhouse for cool designs and great gadgets.

- **Reputation resources and capabilities.** Reputation can be regarded as an outcome of a competitive process in which firms signal their attributes to constituents.[12] While firms do not become reputable overnight, it makes sense to leverage reputation after acquiring it.[13] That is why Toyota, Honda, and Nissan launched three luxury brands—Lexus, Acura, and Infiniti, respectively. Conversely, ambitious Chinese firms such as Haier and TCL are handicapped by their lack of reputation outside China.

It is important to note that all resources and capabilities discussed here are merely *examples,* and that they do not represent an exhaustive list. As firms forge ahead, discovery and leveraging of new resources and capabilities are likely.

Resources, Capabilities, and the Value Chain

If a firm is a bundle of resources and capabilities, how do they come together to add value? A value chain analysis allows us to answer this question. Shown in Panel A of Figure 3.1, most goods and services are produced through a chain of vertical activities (from upstream to downstream) that add value—in short, a **value chain.** The value chain typically consists of two areas: primary activities and support activities.[14]

Each activity requires a number of resources and capabilities. Value chain analysis forces managers to think about firm resources and capabilities at a very micro, activity-based level.[15] Given that no firm is likely to have enough resources and capabilities to be good at all primary and support activities, the key is to examine whether the firm has resources and capabilities to perform a *particular* activity in a manner superior to competitors—a process known as **benchmarking** in SWOT analysis.

If managers find that their firm's particular activity is unsatisfactory, a decision model (shown in Figure 3.2) can remedy the situation. In the first stage, managers ask: "Do we really need to perform this activity in-house?" Figure 3.3 introduces a framework to take a hard look at this question, whose answer boils down to (1) whether an activity is industry-specific or common across industries, and (2) whether this activity is proprietary

intangible resources and capabilities

Hard-to-observe and difficult-to-codify resources and capabilities.

value chain

Goods and services produced through a chain of vertical activities that add value.

benchmarking

Examination as to whether a firm has resources and capabilities to perform a particular activity in a manner superior to competitors.

FIGURE 3.1   The Value Chain

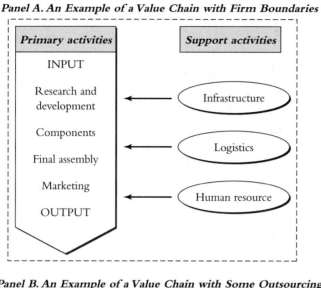

Panel A. An Example of a Value Chain with Firm Boundaries

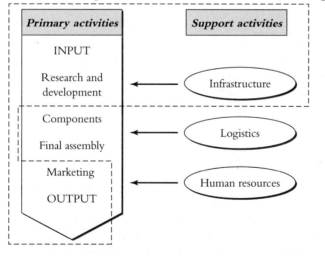

Panel B. An Example of a Value Chain with Some Outsourcing

(firm-specific) or not. The answer is "No" when the activity is found in Cell 2 in Figure 3.3 with a great deal of commonality across industries and little need for keeping it proprietary—known in the recent jargon as a high degree of **commoditization.** The answer may also be "No" if the activity is in Cell 1 in Figure 3.3, which is industry-specific but also with a high level of commoditization. Then, the firm may want to outsource this activity, sell the unit involved, or lease the unit's services to other firms (see Figure 3.2). This is because operating multiple stages of uncompetitive activities in the value chain may be cumbersome and costly.

commoditization

A process of market competition through which unique products that command high prices and high margins generally lose their ability to do so—these products thus become "commodities."

FIGURE 3.2   A Decision Model in a Value Chain Analysis

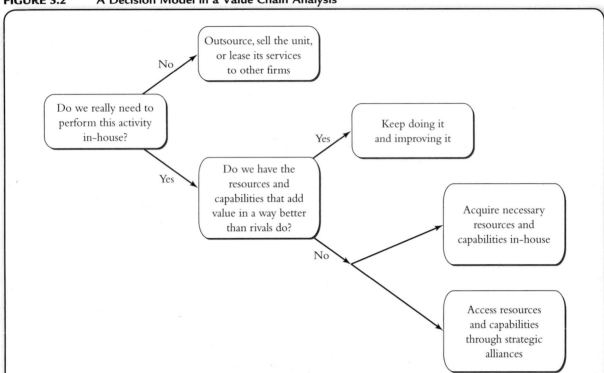

Think about steel, definitely a crucial component for automobiles. But the question for automakers is: "Do we need to make steel ourselves?" The requirements for steel are common across end-user industries—that is, the steel for automakers is essentially the same for construction, defense, and other steel-consuming end users (ignoring minor technical differences for the sake of our discussion). For automakers, while it is imperative to keep the auto making activity (especially engine and final assembly) proprietary (Cell 3 in Figure 3.3), there is no need to keep steel making in-house. Therefore, although many automakers such as Ford and GM historically were involved in steel making, none of them does it now. In other words, steel making is outsourced and steel commoditized. In a similar fashion, Ford and GM no longer make glass, seats, and tires as they did before.

Outsourcing is defined as turning over an organizational activity to an outside supplier that will perform it on behalf of the focal firm. For example, many consumer products companies (such as Nike), which possess strong capabilities in upstream activities (such as design) and downstream activities (such as marketing), have outsourced manufacturing to suppliers in low-cost countries. A total of 80% of the value of Boeing's new 787 Dreamliner is provided by outside suppliers. This compares with 51% for existing Boeing aircraft.[16] Recently, not only is manufacturing often outsourced, a number of service activities, such as information technology (IT), HR, and

outsourcing

Turning over all or part of an activity to an outside supplier to improve the performance of the focal firm.

FIGURE 3.3   **In-House versus Outsource**

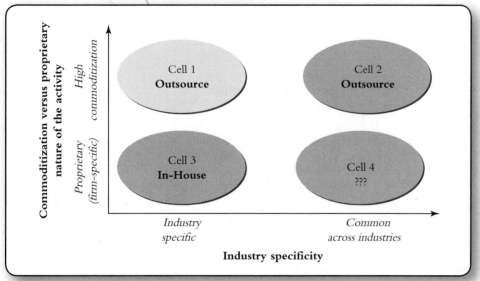

Note: At present, no clear guidelines exist for cell 4, where firms either choose to perform activities in-house or outsource.

logistics, are also outsourced. The driving force is that many firms, which used to view certain activities as a very special part of their industries (such as airline reservations and bank call centers), now believe that these activities have relatively generic attributes that can be shared across industries. Of course, this changing mentality is fueled by the rise of service providers, such as EDS and Infosys in IT, Hewitt Associates and Manpower in HR, Flextronics and Hon Hai in contract manufacturing, and DHL and UPS in logistics. These specialist firms argue that such activities can be broken off from the various client firms (just as steel making was broken off from automakers decades ago) and leveraged to serve multiple clients with greater economies of scale.[17] For client firms, such outsourcing results in "leaner and meaner" organizations, which can better focus on core activities (see Figure 3.1 Panel B).

If the answer to the question, "Do we really need to perform this activity in-house?" is "Yes" (Cell 3 in Figure 3.3), but the firm's current resources and capabilities are not up to the task, then there are two choices (see Figure 3.2). First, the firm may want to acquire and develop capabilities in-house so that it can perform this particular activity better.[18] Microsoft's 1980 acquisition of the QDOS operating system (the precursor of the once ubiquitous MS-DOS system) from Seattle Computer Products for only $50,000 is a famous example of how to acquire a useful resource upon which to add more value.[19] Second, if a firm does not have enough skills to develop these capabilities in-house, it may want to access them through alliances. For example, neither Sony nor Ericsson was strong enough to elbow into the mobile handset market. They thus formed a joint venture named Sony Ericsson to penetrate it.

Conspicuously lacking in both Figures 3.2 and 3.3 is the *geographic* dimension— domestic versus foreign locations. Because the two terms, "outsourcing" and "offshoring," have emerged rather recently, there is a great deal of confusion, especially among some journalists, who often casually equate them as the same. So to minimize confusion, we

FIGURE 3.4   Location, Location, Location

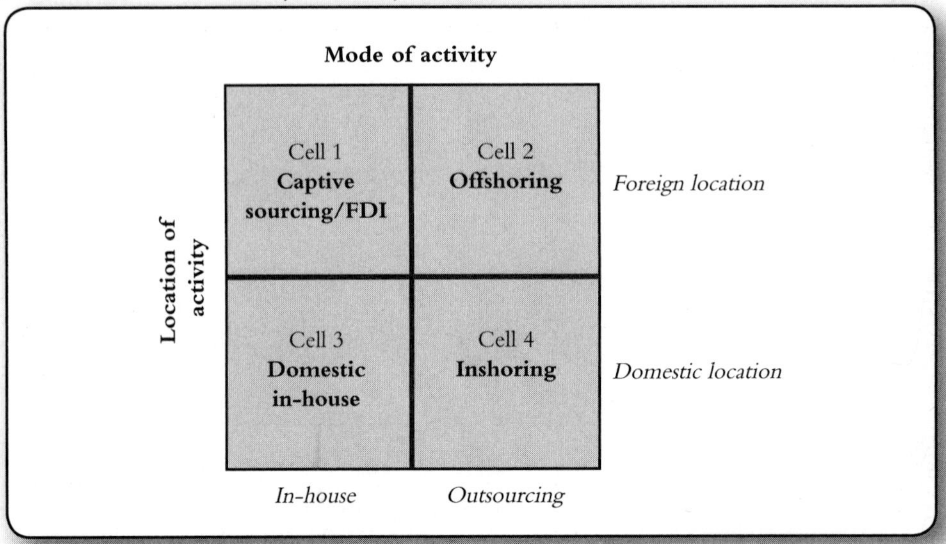

go from two terms to four terms in Figure 3.4, based on locations and modes (in-house versus outsource):

- **Offshoring**—international/foreign outsourcing

- **Inshoring**—domestic outsourcing

- **Captive sourcing**—setting up subsidiaries to perform in-house work in foreign locations

- **Domestic in-house activity**

Despite this set of new labels, we need to clearly be aware that **offshoring** and **inshoring** are simply international and domestic variants of outsourcing, respectively, and that **captive sourcing** is conceptually identical to foreign direct investment (FDI), which is nothing new in the world of global strategy (see Chapters 1 and 6 for details). One interesting lesson we can take away from Figure 3.4 is that even for a single firm, value-adding activities may be geographically dispersed around the world, taking advantage of the best locations and modes to perform certain activities. For instance, a Dell laptop may be designed in the United States (domestic in-house activity), its components may be produced in Taiwan (offshoring) as well as the United States (inshoring), and its final assembly may be in China (captive sourcing/FDI). When customers call for help, the call center may be in India, Ireland, Jamaica, or the Philippines, manned by an outside service provider—Dell may have outsourced the service activities through offshoring.

Overall, a value chain analysis engages managers to ascertain a firm's strengths and weaknesses on an activity-by-activity basis, *relative to rivals,* in a SWOT analysis (see Strategy in Action 3.1 for an example in making luxury cars). The recent proliferation of new labels is intimidating, causing some gurus to claim that "21st-century offshoring

offshoring

International/foreign outsourcing.

inshoring

Domestic outsourcing.

captive sourcing

Setting up subsidiaries to perform in-house work in foreign location. Conceptually identical to foreign direct investment (FDI).

Strategy in Action 3.1 - **Outsourcing Luxury Car Production**

The term "make-or-buy decisions" is a jargon that refers to decisions on whether to produce in-house ("make") or outsource ("buy"). In manufacturing, firms would want to "make" if (1) the product contains a high level of proprietary technology, (2) the product requires close coordination in the supply chain, and (3) suppliers are less capable. On the other hand, firms prefer to "buy" (or outsource) when (1) strategic flexibility is necessary, (2) suppliers lower cost, and (3) several capable suppliers vigorously compete.

In luxury car production, believe it or not, Porsche, Mercedes, and BMW have all used contract manufacturers to make *entire* cars (not just components). How they do it is interesting. Porsche has used Finland's Valmet. However, such outsourcing does not involve Porsche's high-end 911, Cayenne, and Carrera models. Valmet makes the Boxster, a luxury car in the eyes of many but which is nevertheless Porsche's *low*-end model. In another example, Austria's Magna Steyr has assembled the Mercedes-Benz M-class SUV and the BMW X3. This is similar

to one electronics contract manufacturer making products for Philips and Sony side-by-side, except in the case of luxury car making, a lot more proprietary technology is involved. Given the sensitive nature of such outsourcing, BMW's contract with Magna Steyr ran to more than 5,000 pages (!). Conflicts are still inevitable with contract manufacturers. To avoid overdependence on one contract manufacturer, Porsche has recently reclaimed one-third of the Boxster's production back to Germany.

Sources: Based on (1) B. Arrunada & X. Vazquez, 2006, When your contract manufacturer becomes your competitor, *Harvard Business Review,* September: 135–145; (2) M. Kotabe, R. Parente, & J. Murray, 2007, Antecedents and outcomes of modular production in the Brazilian automobile industry, *Journal of International Business Studies,* 38: 84–106; (3) A. Parmigiani, 2007, Why do firms both make and buy? *Strategic Management Journal,* 28: 285–311; (4) M. W. Peng, Y. Zhou, & A. York, 2006, Behind the make or buy decisions in export strategy, *Journal of World Business,* 41: 289–300; (5) F. Rothaermel, M. Hitt, & L. Jobe, 2006, Balancing vertical integration and strategic outsourcing, *Strategic Management Journal,* 27: 1033–1056.

really is different."[20] In reality, under the skin of the new vocabulary, we still see the time-honored SWOT analysis at work. The next section introduces a framework on how to do this.

A VRIO Framework[21]

The resource-based view focuses on the value (V), rarity (R), imitability (I), and organizational (O) aspects of resources and capabilities, leading to a **VRIO framework.** Summarized in Table 3.2, addressing these four important questions has a number of ramifications for competitive advantage.

The Question of Value

Do firm resources and capabilities add value? The preceding value chain analysis suggests that this is the most fundamental question with which to start.[22] Only value-adding resources can possibly lead to competitive advantage, whereas non-value-adding capabilities may lead to competitive *disadvantage*. With changes in the competitive landscape, previous value-adding resources and capabilities may become obsolete. The evolution of IBM is a case in point. IBM historically excelled in making hardware, including

VRIO framework

A resource-based framework that focuses on the value (V), rarity (R), imitability (I), and organizational (O) aspects of resources and capabilities.

TABLE 3.2   **The VRIO Framework: Is a Resource or Capability . . .**

Valuable?	Rare?	Costly to Imitate?	Exploited by Organization?	Competitive Implications	Firm Performance
No	—	—	No	Competitive disadvantage	Below average
Yes	No	—	Yes	Competitive parity	Average
Yes	Yes	No	Yes	Temporary competitive advantage	Above average
Yes	Yes	Yes	Yes	Sustained competitive advantage	Consistently above average

Sources: Adapted from (1) J. Barney, 2002, *Gaining and Sustaining Competitive Advantage*, 2nd ed. (p. 173), Upper Saddle River, NJ: Prentice Hall; (2) R. Hoskisson, M. Hitt, & R. D. Ireland, 2004, *Competing for Advantage* (p. 118), Cincinnati: Cengage Learning South-Western.

tabulating machines in the 1930s, mainframes in the 1960s, and personal computers (PCs) in the 1980s. However, as competition for hardware heated up, IBM's capabilities in hardware not only added little value, but also increasingly became core rigidities that stood in the way of the firm moving into new areas.[23] Since the 1990s, under two new CEOs, IBM has been transformed into focusing on more lucrative software and services, where it has developed new value-adding capabilities, aiming to become an on-demand computing *service* provider for corporations. As part of this new strategy, IBM sold its PC division to China's Lenovo in 2004.

The relationship between valuable resources and capabilities and firm performance is straightforward. Instead of becoming strengths, non–value-adding resources and capabilities, such as IBM's historical expertise in hardware, may become weaknesses. If firms are unable to get rid of non–value-adding resources and capabilities, they are likely to suffer below-average performance.[24] In the worst case, they may become extinct, a fate IBM narrowly skirted during the early 1990s. Similarly, Nintendo exited its earlier lines of business (toys and playing cards) and developed new value-adding capabilities first in arcade games and more recently in video games. "Continuous strategic renewal," in the words of Gary Hamel, a strategy guru, "is the only insurance against irrelevance."[25]

The Question of Rarity

Simply possessing valuable resources and capabilities may not be enough. The next question asks: How rare are valuable resources and capabilities? At best, valuable but common resources and capabilities will lead to competitive parity but not an advantage. Consider the identical aircraft made by Boeing and Airbus used by Southwest, JetBlue, Ryanair, and most other airlines. They are certainly valuable, yet it is difficult to derive competitive advantage from these aircraft alone. Airlines have to work hard on how to use these same aircraft *differently* (see Strategy in Action 3.2 for an example). The same is true for bar codes, enterprise resource planning (ERP) software, and radio frequency identification (RFID) tags. Their developers are too willing to sell them everywhere, thus undermining their novelty (rarity) value.

Only valuable and rare resources and capabilities have the potential to provide some temporary competitive advantage. Overall, the question of rarity is a reminder of the cliché: If everyone has it, you can't make money from it. For example, the quality of the American Big Three automakers is now comparable with the best Asian

---

Strategy in Action 3.2 - ANA: Refreshing the Parts Other Airlines Can't Reach

The new Boeing 787 Dreamliner is the first plane to introduce a game-changing technology—lightweight plastic composites. As a result, this midsize long-haul jet is regarded as a technological wonder that is 20% more fuel efficient than similar-sized planes. Not surprisingly, airlines around the world love it. In the four years (2004–2007) before the 787 took to the air, it became the fastest selling airliner in history, winning 700 orders. Its launch customer is All Nippon Airways (ANA), Japan's second largest international airline (after Japan Airlines) and its largest domestic airline. ANA plans to start flying the Dreamliner in 2008.

The Dreamliner will certainly be valuable to the first airline to fly it. However, its novelty will soon disappear, as 650 planes will follow ANA's first 50 to enter service. In other words, the Dreamliner is valuable, not necessarily rare, and relatively easy to imitate—Boeing is happy to produce for any airline that is willing to cough up $160 million for a copy. What is ANA's response to hold on to its competitive advantage associated with the 787? It plans to install bidet-toilets as standard in its fleet of Dreamliners, in a bid to attract more fastidious passengers from Japan where the washlet is commonplace. Approximately 60% of Japanese households have a bidet. On July 10, 2007, when the Dreamliner was unveiled at Boeing's plant in Everett, Washington, ANA chief executive Mineo Yamamoto proudly announced at the ceremony that the bidet-toilets onboard the 787 will be a key source of differentiation by "refreshing the parts other airlines cannot reach."

Sources: Based on (1) *The Economist,* 2005, Air war, June 25: 12; (2) *South China Morning Post,* 2007, Boeing unveils new, green 787 jetliner, July 10: A8; (3) Wikipedia, 2008, All Nippon Airways (en.wikipedia.org).

---

and European rivals. However, even in their home country, the Big Three's quality improvements have not translated into stronger sales. Instead, their US market share has declined from 80% in 1975 to just over 50% recently. The point is simple: Flawless high quality is now expected among car buyers, is no longer rare, and thus provides no advantage.

The Question of Imitability

Valuable and rare resources and capabilities can be a source of competitive advantage only if competitors have a difficult time imitating them. While it is relatively easier to imitate a firm's *tangible* resources (such as plants), it is a lot more challenging and often impossible to imitate *intangible* capabilities (such as tacit knowledge, superior motivation, and managerial talents).[26] In an effort to maintain a high-quality manufacturing edge, many Japanese firms intentionally employ "super technicians" (or *supaa ginosha*)—an honor designated by the Japanese government. They handle mission-critical work, such as mounting tiny chips onto circuit boards for laptops at Sharp, and their quality is better than that of robots.[27] While robots can be purchased by rivals, no robots, and few humans elsewhere, can imitate the skills and dedication of the "super technicians" in Japan.

Imitation is difficult. Why? Because of two words: **causal ambiguity,** which refers to the difficulty of identifying the causal determinants of successful firm performance.[28] For three decades, Toyota has been meticulously studied by all automakers and numerous non-automakers around the world, yet none has figured out what exactly leads to its prominence, and thus none has been able to challenge it. If anything, Toyota has *widened* the performance gap between itself and the rest of the pack, rising to (almost)

causal ambiguity
The difficulty of identifying the causal determinants of successful firm performance.

become the number one automaker by volume in the world. Market capitalization says it all: Toyota is now worth more than the American Big Three *combined,* and more than Honda and Nissan put together. Its net profits are far bigger than the combined total of the American Big Three. Over the past 30 years, during which every auto-maker has been allegedly "learning from Toyota," Toyota's productivity has grown sevenfold, twice as much as Detroit's finest despite their serious efforts to keep up.[29]

A natural question is: How does Toyota do it? Usually a number of resources and capabilities will be nominated, including its legendary "Toyota production system," its aggressive ambition, and its mystical organizational culture—now codified as the "Toyota Way" by itself.[30] While all of these resources and capabilities are plausible, what *exactly* is it? This truly is a million dollar question, because knowing the answer to this question is not only intriguing to scholars and students, it can also be hugely profitable for Toyota's rivals. Unfortunately, outsiders usually have a hard time under-standing what a firm does inside its boundaries. We can try, as many rivals have, to identify Toyota's recipe for success by drawing up a long list of possible reasons, labeled as "resources and capabilities" in our classroom discussion. But in the final analysis, as outsiders we are not sure.[31]

What is even more fascinating for scholars and students and more frustrating for rivals is that often managers of a focal firm such as Toyota do not know exactly what contributes to their firm's success. When interviewed, they can usually generate a long list of what they do well, such as a strong organizational culture, a relentless drive, and many other attributes. To make matters worse, different managers of the same firm may have a different list. When probed as to which resource or capability is "it," they usually suggest that it is all of the above in *combination.* This is probably one of the most interesting and paradoxical aspects of the resource-based view: If insiders have a hard time figuring out what unambiguously contributes to their firm's performance, it is not surprising that outsiders' efforts in understanding and imitating these capabilities are usually flawed and often fail.[32]

Overall, valuable and rare but imitable resources and capabilities may give firms some temporary competitive advantage, leading to above-average performance for some period of time. However, such advantage is not likely to be sustainable. Shown by the example of Toyota, only valuable, rare, and *hard-to-imitate* resources and capa-bilities may potentially lead to sustained competitive advantage.

The Question of Organization

Even valuable, rare, and hard-to-imitate resources and capabilities may not give a firm a sustained competitive advantage if it is not properly organized. Although movie stars represent some of the most valuable, rare, and hard-to-imitate as well as highest-paid resources, *most* movies flop. More generally, the question of organization asks: How can a firm (such as a movie studio) be organized to develop and leverage the full poten-tial of its resources and capabilities?

complementary assets

Numerous noncore assets that comple-ment and support the value-adding activities of core assets.

Numerous components within a firm are relevant to the question of organization.[33] In a movie studio, these components include talents in "smelling" good ideas, photogra-phy crews, musicians, singers, makeup specialists, animation artists, and managers on the business side who deal with sponsors, distributors, and local sites. These compo-nents are often called **complementary assets,**[34] because by themselves they are difficult to generate box office hits. For the favorite movie you saw most recently, do you still remember the names of its makeup artists? Of course, not—you probably only remember the stars. However, stars alone cannot generate hit movies either. It is the *combination* of star resources and complementary assets that creates hit movies. "It may be that not just a few resources and capabilities enable a firm to gain a competitive advantage but that literally thousands of these organizational attributes, bundled together, generate such advantage."[35]

Another idea is **social complexity,** which refers to the socially complex ways of organizing typical of many firms. Many multinationals consist of thousands of people scattered in many different countries. How they overcome cultural differences and are organized as one corporate entity and achieve organizational goals is profoundly complex.[36] Oftentimes, it is their invisible relationships that add value.[37] Such organizationally embedded capabilities are thus very difficult for rivals to imitate (see the Closing Case for an example). This emphasis on social complexity refutes what is half-jokingly called the "Lego" view of the firm, in which a firm can be assembled (and disassembled) from modules of technology and people (a la Lego toy blocks). By treating employees as identical and replaceable blocks, the "Lego" view fails to realize that social capital associated with complex relationships and knowledge permeating many firms can be a source of competitive advantage.

Overall, only valuable, rare, and hard-to-imitate capabilities that are organizationally embedded and exploited can possibly lead to sustained competitive advantage and persistently above-average performance.[38] Because capabilities cannot be evaluated in isolation, the VRIO framework presents four interconnected and increasingly difficult hurdles for them to become a source of sustainable competitive advantage (Table 3.2). In other words, these four aspects come together as one "package"—as illustrated by Strategy in Action 3.3 using private military companies as an example.

Debates and Extensions

Like the industry-based view outlined in Chapter 2, the resource-based view has its fair share of controversies and debates. Here, we introduce four leading debates: (1) firm- versus industry-specific determinants of performance, (2) static resources versus dynamic capabilities, (3) offshoring versus non-offshoring, and (4) domestic resources versus international capabilities.

Firm- versus Industry-Specific Determinants of Performance

At the heart of the resource-based view is the proposition that firm performance is most fundamentally determined by firm-specific resources and capabilities, whereas the industry-based view argues that firm performance is ultimately a function of industry-specific attributes. The industry-based view points out persistently different average profit rates of different industries, such as pharmaceutical versus grocery industries.[39] The resource-based view, on the other hand, has documented persistently different performance levels among firms within the same industry, such as Zara versus other fashion retailers.[40] A number of studies find industry-specific effects to be more significant.[41] However, a *larger* number of studies are supportive of the resource-based view—firm-specific capabilities are stronger determinants of firm performance than industry-specific effects.[42]

social complexity

The socially complex ways of organizing typical of many firms.

Strategy in Action 3.3 - Capabilities of Private Military Companies

Ethical Challenge

Private military companies (PMCs) form a $100 billion global industry. Although often stereotyped as "mercenaries," modern PMCs are professional firms that offer valuable, unique, and hard-to-imitate capabilities in an environment that most individuals, firms, and governments, as well as national militaries, would prefer to avoid. To PMCs, the war in Iraq has been a pot of gold. As US allies withdraw, PMCs rush in. PMCs have now grown into the second largest military contingent in Iraq (about 20,000 to 30,000 personnel) after the US (national) forces. Although not every PMC directly engages in the battlefield, this line of work is certainly dangerous. Approximately 700 PMC personnel have died in Iraq. An ethical challenge confronting PMCs is how to *responsively* deploy their lethal capabilities while getting the job done.

In October 2007, a furious US Congress held hearings on Blackwater, a PMC that, according to the Iraqi government, allegedly killed 17 innocent civilians in Baghdad. Blackwater's staunchest defenders tended to be US officials protected by its private soldiers. US officials preferred PMCs because PMC personnel were regarded as more highly trained than (national) military guards. Blackwater's founder, Erik Prince, told the

Congressional committee that "no individual protected by Blackwater has ever been killed or seriously injured," while 30 of its private soldiers died on the job.

Sources: Based on (1) *The Economist*, 2007, Blackwater in hot water, October 13: 51; (2) M. W. Peng, 2009, Private military companies: Dogs of war or pussycats of peace? in *Global Business* (pp. 118–120), Cincinnati: South-Western Cengage Learning.

While the debate goes on, it is important to caution against an interest in declaring one side of the debate to be "winning." There are two reasons for such caution—methodological and practical. First, while industry-based studies have used more observable proxies such as entry barriers and concentration ratios, resource-based studies have to confront the challenge of how to measure *unobservable* firm-specific capabilities, such as organizational learning, knowledge management, and managerial talents. While resource-based scholars have created many innovative measures to "get at" these capabilities, these measures at best are "observable consequences of unobservable resources" and can be subject to methodological criticisms. Critics contend that the resource-based view seems to follow the logic that "show me a success story and I will show you a core competence [resource] (or show me a failure and I will show you a missing competence)."[44] Resource-based theorists readily admit that "the source of sustainable competitive advantage is likely to be found in different places at different points in time in different industries."[45] While such reasoning can insightfully *explain* what happened in the past, it is difficult to *predict* what will happen in the future. For instance, are we going to do better than rivals if we match, say, their equipment and locations?

Second and perhaps more important, there is a good practical reason to believe that it is the *combination* of both industry- and firm-specific attributes that collectively drives firm performance. They have in fact been argued to be the two sides of the same "coin" of strategic analysis from the very beginning of the development of the resource-based view.[46] It seems to make better sense when viewing both perspectives as *complementary* to each other. This point has been underscored by several recent studies.[47] One study reports (1) that for industry leaders and losers, firm-specific factors matter significantly more than industry-specific factors, and (2) that for most other firms, the industry effect turns out to be more important for performance than firm-specific factors.[48] Overall, it seems evident that blending these two insightful frameworks may generate more insight.

Static Resources versus Dynamic Capabilities

Another debate stems from the relatively static nature of the resource-based logic, which essentially suggests "Let's identify S and W in a SWOT analysis and go from there." Such a snapshot of the competitive situation may be adequate for slow-moving industries (such as meat packing), but it may be less satisfactory for dynamically fast-moving industries (such as IT). Critics, therefore, posit that the resource-based view needs to be strengthened by a heavier emphasis on dynamic capabilities.[49]

More recently, as we advance into a "knowledge economy," a number of scholars argue for a "knowledge-based" view of the firm.[50] Tacit knowledge, probably the most valuable, unique, hard-to-imitate, and organizationally complex resource, may represent the ultimate dynamic capability a firm can have in its quest for competitive advantage.[51] Such invisible assets range from knowledge about customers through years (and sometimes decades) of interaction, to knowledge about product development processes and political connections.

Focusing on knowledge-based dynamic capabilities, recent research suggests some interesting, counter-intuitive findings. Summarized in Table 3.3, while the hallmark for resources in relatively slow-moving industries (such as hotels and railways) is complexity that is difficult to observe and results in causal ambiguity, capabilities in very dynamic high-velocity industries (such as IT) take on a different character. They are "simple (not complicated), experiential (not analytic), and iterative (not linear processes)."[52] In other words, while traditional resource-based analysis urges firms to rigorously analyze their strengths and weaknesses and then plot some linear application of their resources ("learning before doing"), firms in high-velocity industries have to engage in "learning by doing." The imperative for strategic flexibility calls for simple (as opposed to complicated) routines, which help managers stay focused on broadly important issues without locking them into specific details or the use of inappropriate past experience (see the quote from eBay's CEO Meg Whitman in Chapter 1 on p. 9). For instance, Yahoo!'s successful strategic alliance process is largely unstructured, consisting of two simple rules: (1) no exclusive deals and (2) the basic service provided by the alliance (such as party planning and online greeting cards) must be free. These simple rules afford Yahoo! managers wide latitude for experimenting with a variety of alliance deals and formats.[53]

TABLE 3.3   Dynamic Capabilities in Slow- and Fast-Moving Industries

	SLOW-MOVING INDUSTRIES	FAST-MOVING (HIGH-VELOCITY) INDUSTRIES
Market environment	Stable industry structure, defined boundaries, clear business models, identifiable players, linear and predictable change	Ambiguous industry structure, blurred boundaries, fluid business models, ambiguous and shifting players, nonlinear and unpredictable change
Attributes of dynamic capabilities	Complex, detailed, analytic routines that rely extensively on existing knowledge ("learning before doing")	Simple, experiential routines that rely on newly created knowledge specific to the situation ("learning by doing")
Focus	Leverage existing resources and capabilities	Develop new resources and capabilities
Execution	Linear	Iterative
Organization	A tightly bundled collection of resources with relative stability	A loosely bundled collection of resources, which are frequently added, recombined, and dropped
Outcome	Predictable	Unpredictable
Strategic goal	Sustainable competitive advantage (hopefully for the long term)	A series of short-term (temporal) competitive advantage

Sources: Adapted from (1) K. Eisenhardt & J. Martin, 2000, Dynamic capabilities: What are they? *Strategic Management Journal,* 21: 1105–1121; (2) G. Pisano, 1994, Knowledge, integration, and the locus of learning, *Strategic Management Journal,* 15: 85–100.

Not all fast-moving industries are high-tech ones. As the pace of competition accelerates, more industries, including many traditional low-tech ones, are becoming fast moving—for example, think of the fashion retail industry (Opening Case). The end result is **hypercompetition,** whose hallmark is a shortened window during which a firm may command competitive advantage.[54] In hypercompetition, firms undertake dynamic maneuvering intended to unleash a series of small, unpredictable, but powerful actions to erode rivals' competitive advantage.

Overall, recent research on dynamic capabilities suggests that the current resource-based view may have overemphasized the role of leveraging existing resources and capabilities and underemphasized the role of developing new ones. The assumption that a firm is a tightly bundled collection of resources may break down in high-velocity environments, whereby resources are added, recombined, and dropped with regularity.[55] For example, in the chaotic and fickle world of e-commerce, being tightly bundled may be a liability rather than an asset. In such a world of hypercompetition whereby sustainable competitive advantage may be unrealistic, a series of short-term unpredictable advantage seems to be the best a firm can hope for.[56]

Offshoring versus Non-Offshoring

As noted earlier, offshoring—or more specifically, international (offshore) outsourcing—has emerged as a leading corporate movement in the 21st century.[57] While outsourcing

hypercompetition

A way of competition centered on dynamic maneuvering intended to unleash a series of small, unpredictable but powerful, actions to erode the rival's competitive advantage.

TABLE 3.4   Benefit of $1 US Spending on Offshoring to India

BENEFIT TO THE UNITED STATES	$	BENEFIT TO INDIA	$
Savings accruing to US investors/customers	0.58	Labor	0.10
Exports of US goods/services to providers in India	0.05	Profits retained in India	0.10
Profit transfer by US-owned operations in India back to the US	0.04	Suppliers	0.09
Net direct benefit retained in the United States	*0.67*	*Central government taxes*	*0.03*
Value from US labor reemployed	0.46	State government taxes	0.01
Net benefit to the United States	*1.13*	*Net benefit to India*	*0.33*

Source: Based on text in D. Farrell, 2005, Offshoring: Value creation through economic change, *Journal of Management Studies,* 42: 675–683. Farrell is director of the McKinsey Global Institute, and she refers to a McKinsey study.

manufacturing to countries such as China and Mexico is now largely accepted, what has become very controversial recently is the outsourcing of increasingly high-end services, starting with IT now encompassing all sorts of "business process outsourcing" (BPO) to countries led by India. Because digitization and commoditization of service work is only enabled by the very recent rise of the Internet and the reduction of international communication costs, whether such offshoring proves to be a long-term benefit or hindrance to Western firms and economies is debatable.[58]

Proponents argue that offshoring creates enormous value for firms and economies. Western firms are able to tap into low-cost and high-quality labor that translates into significant cost savings. They can also focus on their core capabilities, which may add more value than dealing with noncore (and often uncompetitive) activities. In turn, offshoring service providers, such as Infosys and Wipro, develop *their* core competencies in IT/BPO. Focusing on offshoring between the United States and India, a McKinsey study reports that for every dollar of spending by US firms on India, US firms save 58 cents (Table 3.4). Overall, $1.46 of new wealth is created, of which the US economy captures $1.13 and India captures the other 33 cents.[59] While acknowledging that some US employees may lose their jobs, offshoring proponents suggest that, on balance, offshoring is a win-win solution for both US and Indian firms and economies.

Critics of offshoring make three points on strategic, economic, and political grounds. Strategically, if, according to some outsourcing gurus, "even core functions like engineering, R&D, manufacturing, and marketing can—and often should—be moved outside,"[60] what is left of the firm? In manufacturing, US firms have gone down this path before, with disastrous results. For example, Radio Corporation of America (RCA), having invented the color TV, outsourced its production to Japan in the 1960s, a *low*-cost country at that time. Fast forward to the 2000s, the United States no longer has any US-owned color TV producers left, and the nationality of RCA itself, after being bought and sold several times, is now *Chinese* (France's Thomson sold RCA to China's TCL in 2003). Critics argue such offshoring nurtures rivals.[61] Why after 2000 are Indian IT/BPO firms emerging as strong rivals challenging EDS and IBM? It is in part because Indian firms built up their capabilities doing work for EDS and IBM in the 1990s—remember Y2K (the IT industry's race before the year 2000 to fix the "millennium bug" problem)?

Economically, critics contend that in addition to Western firms reducing their firm-level capabilities and competitiveness, they are not sure whether developed economies, as a whole, actually gain more. While shareholders and corporate high-flyers embrace offshoring (see Chapter 1), offshoring increasingly results in job losses in high-end areas such as design, R&D, and IT/BPO. While white-collar individuals who lose jobs will naturally hate it, the net impact (consolidating all economic gains and losses including job losses) on developed economies may still be negative.

Finally, critics make political arguments, arguing that many large US firms claim that they are "global companies" and that they are not bound by "American values" any more. All these firms are interested in the "cheapest and most exploitable" labor. Not only is work commoditized, people (such as IT programmers) are degraded as "tradable commodities" that can be jettisoned. As a result, large firms that outsource work to emerging economies are often accused of being unethical, destroying jobs at home, ignoring corporate social responsibility, violating customer privacy (for example, by sending tax returns and credit card numbers to be processed overseas), and in some cases undermining national security. Not surprisingly, the debate often becomes political, emotional, and explosive when such accusations are made.

Domestic Resources versus International (Cross-Border) Capabilities

Do firms that are successful domestically have what it takes to win internationally? If you ask managers at The Limited Brands, their answer would be "No." The Limited Brands is the number one US fashion retailer, which has a successful retail empire of 4,000 stores throughout the country with brands such as The Limited, Victoria's Secret, and Bath & Body Works. Yet, it has refused to go abroad—not even to Canada. On the other hand, the ubiquitous retail outlets of Zara, LVMH, Gucci, and United Colors of Benetton in major cities around the world suggest that their answer would be "Yes!"

Some domestically successful firms continue to succeed overseas. For example, IKEA has found that its Scandinavian style of furniture combined with do-it-yourself flat packaging is very popular around the globe. IKEA thus has become a global cult brand. However, many other domestically formidable firms are burned badly overseas. Wal-Mart withdrew from Germany and South Korea recently. Similarly, Wal-Mart's leading global rival, France's Carrefour, had to exit the Czech Republic, Japan, Mexico, Slovakia, and South Korea recently. Starbucks' bitter brew has also failed to turn into sweet profits overseas.

Are domestic resources and cross-border capabilities essentially the same? The answer can be either "Yes" or "No."[62] This debate is an extension of the larger debate on whether international business is different from domestic business. Answering "Yes" to this question is an excellent argument for having stand-alone international business courses (and for having a global strategy textbook like this one). Answering "No" to this question argues that "international business" fundamentally is about "business," which is well covered by strategy, finance, and other courses (most textbooks in these areas have at least one chapter on "international topics"). This question is obviously very important for companies and business schools. However, there is no right or wrong answer. It is important to emphasize the advice: *think global, act local.* In practice, this means that despite grand global strategic designs, companies have to concretely win one local market (country) after another.

The Savvy Stategist

The savvy strategist can draw at least three important implications for action (Table 3.5). First, there is nothing very novel in the proposition that firms "compete on resources and capabilities." The subtlety comes when managers attempt, via the VRIO framework, to distinguish resources and capabilities that are valuable, rare, hard-to-imitate, and organizationally embedded from those that do not share these attributes. In other words, the VRIO framework can greatly aid the time-honored SWOT analysis, especially the S and W part. Managers, who cannot pay attention to every capability, must have some sense of what *really* matters. A common mistake that managers often make when evaluating their firms' capabilities is failing to assess them relative to rivals', thus resulting in a mixed bag of both good and mediocre capabilities. Using the VRIO framework, a value chain analysis helps managers make decisions on what capabilities to focus on in-house and what to outsource. Increasingly, what really matters is not tangible resources that are relatively easy to imitate, but intangible capabilities that are harder for rivals to lay their arms around. Capabilities not meeting these criteria need to be jettisoned or outsourced.

Second, relentless imitation or benchmarking, while important, is not likely to be a successful strategy. Follower firms have a tendency to mimic the most visible, the most obvious, and, consequently, the *least* important practices of winning firms. At best, follower firms that meticulously replicate every resource possessed by winning firms can hope to attain competitive parity. Firms so well endowed with resources to imitate others may be better off by developing their own unique capabilities. The best performing firms, such as Zara, often create new ways of adding value.

Third, a competitive advantage that is sustained does not imply that it will last forever, which is not realistic in today's global competition. All a firm can hope for is a competitive advantage that can be sustained for as long as possible. However, over time, all advantages may erode. As noted earlier, each of IBM's product-related advantages associated with tabulating machines, mainframes, and PCs was sustained for a period of time. But eventually, these advantages disappeared. Therefore, the lesson for

TABLE 3.5	Strategic Implications for Action
• Managers need to build firm strengths based on the VRIO framework.	
• Relentless imitation or benchmarking, while important, is not likely to be a successful strategy.	
• Managers need to build up resources and capabilities for future competition.	

[handwritten: value, rarity, inimitation, organization]

all firms, including current market leaders, is to develop strategic *foresight*—"over-the-horizon radar" is a good metaphor. Such strategic foresight enables firms to anticipate future needs and move early to identify, develop, and leverage resources and capabilities for future competition.[63]

Finally, how does the resource-based view answer the four fundamental questions in strategy? The idea that each firm is a unique bundle of resources and capabilities directly addresses the first question: Why do firms differ? The answer to the second question—How do firms behave?—boils down to how they take advantage of their strengths embodied in resources and capabilities and overcome their weaknesses. Third, what determines the scope of the firm? The value chain analysis suggests that the scope of the firm is determined by how a firm performs different value-adding activities relative to rivals. Lastly, what determines the success and failure of firms around the globe? Are winning firms lucky or are they smart? The answer from the resource-based view, again, boils down to firm-specific resources and capabilities, although a stroke of luck certainly helps.

CHAPTER SUMMARY

1. *Explain what firm resources and capabilities are*

   - "Resources" and "capabilities" are tangible and intangible assets a firm uses to choose and implement its strategies.

2. *Undertake a basic SWOT analysis along the value chain*

   - A value chain consists of a stream of activities from upstream to downstream that add value.

   - A SWOT analysis engages managers to ascertain a firm's strengths and weaknesses on an activity-by-activity basis relative to rivals.

3. *Decide whether to keep an activity in-house or outsource it*

   - Outsourcing is defined as turning over all or part of an organizational activity to an outside supplier.

   - An activity with a high degree of industry commonality and a high degree of commoditization can be outsourced, and an industry-specific and firm-specific (proprietary) activity is better performed in-house.

   - On any given activity, the four choices for managers in terms of modes and locations are (1) offshoring, (2) inshoring, (3) captive sourcing/FDI, and (4) domestic in-house activity.

4. *Analyze the value, rarity, imitability, and organizational aspects of resources and capabilities*

   - A VRIO framework suggests that only resources and capabilities that are valuable, rare, inimitable, and organizationally embedded will generate sustainable competitive advantage.

5. *Participate in four leading debates on the resource-based view*

- They are (1) firm- versus industry-specific determinants of performance, (2) static resources versus dynamic capabilities, (3) offshoring versus non-offshoring, and (4) domestic resources versus international capabilities.

6. *Draw strategic implications for action*

- Managers need to build firm strengths based on the VRIO framework.

- Relentless imitation or benchmarking, while important, is not likely to be a successful strategy.

- Managers need to build up resources and capabilities for future competition.

KEY TERMS

Benchmarking	Hypercompetition	Resource-based view
Capability	Inshoring	Social complexity
Captive sourcing	Intangible resources and capabilities	Tangible resources and capabilities
Causal ambiguity	Offshoring	Value chain
Commoditization	Outsourcing	VRIO framework
Complementary assets	Resource	

CRITICAL DISCUSSION QUESTIONS

1. Pick any pair of rivals (such as Samsung/Sony, Nokia/Motorola, and Boeing/ Airbus), and explain why one outperforms another.

2. Conduct a VRIO analysis of your business school in terms of (1) perceived reputation (such as rankings), (2) faculty strength, (3) student quality, (4) administrative efficiency, (5) IT, and (6) building maintenance, relative to the top three rival schools. If you were the dean with a limited budget, where would you invest precious financial resources to make your school number one among its rivals? Why?

3. **ON ETHICS:** Ethical dilemmas associated with offshoring are plenty. Pick one of these dilemmas, make a case to either defend your firm's offshoring activities or argue against such activities (assuming you are employed at a firm headquartered in a developed economy).

4. **ON ETHICS:** Since firms read information posted on competitors' websites, is it ethical to provide false information on resources and capabilities on corporate websites? Do the benefits outweigh the costs?

CLOSING CASE
The Portman Ritz-Carlton, Shanghai

How does a five-star hotel differ from its lower-tier competitors? How does the best five-star hotel stand out among its five-star peers? The answer is "People," according to Mark DeCocinis, general manager of the five-star Portman Ritz-Carlton Hotel in Shanghai, China, which has been named the "Best Employer in Asia" by Hewitt Associates three times.

"Our priority is taking care of our people," said DeCocinis in an interview. "We're in the service business, and service comes only from people. It's about keeping our promise to our employees and making that an everyday priority. Our promise is to take care of them, trust them, develop them, and provide a happy place for them to work. The key is everyday execution."

One of the "secrets" behind the Portman Ritz-Carlton's success is that the general manager interviews every prospective employee. This process of course is time-consuming on the part of the busy general manager. Yet, by doing that, the general manager is able to get a "feel" of the intangible nature of employee attitudes. In terms of the questions that the general manager asks, DeCocinis shared: "I usually ask them about themselves and try to make a connection. But the important question is: Why do you want to join? Whatever they say, the most important notion needs to be 'I *enjoy working with* people,' not just using the phrase 'I *like* people' . . . I really want to find out what motivates them. If the person smiles naturally, that's very important to us, because this is something you can't force." In a culture featuring more reserved expressions, service personnel who smile naturally will indeed become valuable and rare resources appreciated by hotel guests.

The Portman Ritz-Carlton's employee satisfaction rate is 98%, and its guest satisfaction is between 92% and 95%. To translate excellent HR management to better firm performance, the hotel's performance goals are aligned with Ritz-Carlton's corporate goal—from the company to the hotel, and from the hotel to each division. This means that everyone is part of

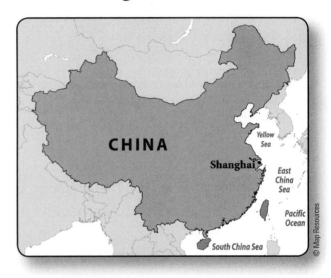

the whole. Every employee comes up with a plan to reach the goal for the next year, measured by guest satisfaction, financial performance, and employee satisfaction. The bonus at the end of the year is based on improvements.

In China, many multinationals face a constant shortage of talent and high employee turnover. Yet, the Portman Ritz-Carlton has not only been able to attract, but also to retain high-quality talent to deliver excellent customer service and ensure profitable growth. What are its "secrets" behind its ability to *retain* such individuals? Among many secrets, DeCocinis pointed to one incident:

During the 2003 SARS crisis, business started to deteriorate. By April, our occupancy rate, which should have been at 95%, dropped to 35% . . . The first step was for me and the executive team to take a 30% pay cut . . . Then it got worse. In May, the occupancy rate was 17%–18%. We reduced the workweek to four days, and people were asked to take their outstanding paid leave days. And then, when these reserves were getting used up, that's when everyone really pulled together. Employees who were single gave their shifts to colleagues who had families to support. Some employees were worried that their contracts would not be renewed given the low occupancy rates, we renewed them without a second thought . . . Our employee satisfaction rate that year was 99.9% . . . This was one of those negative things that turned out to be extremely positive.

Such a willingness to go the extra mile to ensure employee satisfaction is reciprocated by a loyal, dedicated, and hard-working work force that radiates the precious and rare smile in China. Within the Ritz-Carlton family of 59 hotels worldwide, the Portman Ritz-Carlton has been rated the highest in employee satisfaction for five consecutive years. It has also won the prestigious Platinum Five-Star Award by the China National Tourism Administration. It is one of three hotels in China, and the only Shanghai hotel,

to receive this inaugural award, which is the highest hospitality award in China.

Source: Based on (1) A. Yeung, 2006, Setting the people up for success: How the Portman Ritz-Carlton Hotel gets the best from its people, *Human Resource Management,* 45 (2): 267–275. (2) www.ritzcarlton.com/en/Properties/Shanghai/Default.htm

Case Discussion Questions

1. What is the main source behind the Portman Ritz-Carlton's performance?

2. How valuable, rare, and hard-to-imitate are its human resources?

3. How organizationally embedded are its capabilities?

4. If you were the general manager of a rival hotel, how would you respond?

NOTES

Journal acronyms *AER–American Economic Review; AME–Academy of Management Executive; AMJ–Academy of Management Journal; AMR–Academy of Management Review; BW–Business Week; HBR–Harvard Business Review; JIBS–Journal of International Business Studies; JM–Journal of Management; JMS–Journal of Management Studies; JWB–Journal of World Business; LRP–Long Range Planning; MIR–Management International Review; OSc–Organization Science; SMJ–Strategic Management Journal*

1. J. Barney, 1991, Firm resources and sustained competitive advantage, *JM,* 17: 99–120; M. W. Peng, 2001, The resource-based view and international business, *JM,* 27: 803–829.

2. G. Dess, T. Lumpkin, & M. Eisner, 2007, *Strategic Management,* 3rd ed. (p. 78), Chicago: McGraw-Hill.

3. F. Acedo, C. Barroso, & J. Galan, 2006, The resource-based theory, *SMJ,* 27: 621–636; C. Armstrong & K. Shimizu, 2007, A review of approaches to empirical research on the resource-based view of the firm, *JM,* 33: 959–986; S. Newbert, 2007, Empirical research on the resource-based view of the firm, *SMJ,* 28: 121–146; D. Sirmon, M. Hitt, & R. D. Ireland, 2007, Managing firm resources in dynamic environments to create value, *AMR,* 32: 273–292.

4. M. W. Peng & P. Heath, 1996, The growth of the firm in planned economies in transition, *AMR,* 21: 492–528; E. Penrose, 1959, *The Theory of the Growth of the Firm,* London: Blackwell. See also A. Goerzen & P. Beamish, 2007, The Penrose effect, *MIR,* 47: 221–239; M. Pettus, 2001, The resource-based view as a developmental growth process, *AMJ,* 44: 878–896; J. Steen & P. Liesch, 2007, A note on Penrosian growth, resource bundles, and the Upssala model of internationalization, *MIR,* 47: 193–206; D. Tan & J. Mahoney, 2007, The dynamics of Japanese firm growth in US industries, *MIR,* 47: 259–279.

5. J. Barney, 2001, Is the resource-based view a useful perspective for strategic management research? (p. 54), *AMR,* 26: 41–56.

6. C. Helfat & M. Peteraf, 2003, The dynamic resource-based view, *SMJ,* 24: 997–1010; D. Sirmon, M. Hitt, & R. D. Ireland, 2007, Managing firm resources in dynamic environments to create value, *AMR,* 32: 273–292; G. Schreyogg & M. Kliesch-Eberl, 2007, How dynamic can organizational capabilities be? *SMJ,* 28: 913–933; D. Teece, 2007, Explicating dynamic capabilities, *SMJ,* 28: 1319–1350; D. Teece, G. Pisano, & A. Shuen, 1997, Dynamic capabilities and strategic management, *SMJ,* 18: 509–533.

7. J. Barney, 2002, *Gaining and Sustaining Competitive Advantage,* 2nd ed. (p. 157), Upper Saddle River, NJ: Prentice Hall.

8. E. Danneels, 2007, The process of technological competence leveraging, *SMJ,* 28: 511–533; A. Phene, K. Fladmoe-Lindquist, & L. Marsh, 2006, Breakthrough innovations in the US biotechnology industry, *SMJ,* 27: 369–388.

9. A. Carmeli & A. Tishler, 2004, The relationships between intangible organizational elements and organizational performance, *SMJ,* 25: 1257–1278; S. Dutta, O. Narasimhan, & S. Rajiv, 2005, Conceptualizing and measuring capabilities, *SMJ,* 26: 277–285.

10. N. Hatch & J. Dyer, 2004, Human capital and learning as a source of competitive advantage, *SMJ,* 25: 1155–1178.

11. B. Allred & H. K. Steensma, 2005, The influence of industry and home country characteristics on firms' pursuit of innovation, *MIR,* 45: 383–412; J. Birkinshaw, R. Nobel, & J. Ridderstrale, 2002, Knowledge as a contingency variable, *OSc,* 13: 274–289; H. Cho & V. Pucik, 2005, Relationship among innovativeness, quality, growth, profitability, and market value, *SMJ,* 26: 555–575; S. McEvily, K. Eisenhardt, & J. Prescott, 2004, The global acquisition, leverage, and protection of technologies competencies, *SMJ,* 25: 713–722; K. Smith, C. Collins, & K. Clark, 2005, Existing knowledge, knowledge creation capability, and the rate of new product introduction in high-technology firms, *AMJ,* 48: 346–357; M. Subramaniam & M. Youndt, 2005, The influence of intellectual capital on the types of innovative capabilities, *AMJ,* 48: 450–463.

12. N. Gardberg & C. Fombrun, 2006, Corporate citizenship, *AMR,* 31: 329–346; K. Mayer, 2006, Spillovers and governance, *AMJ,* 49: 69–84; V. Rindova, T. Pollock, & M. Hayward, 2006, Celebrity firms, *AMR,* 31: 50–71; M. Washington & E. Zajac, 2005, Status evolution and competition, *AMJ,* 48: 282–296.

13. P. Lee, 2001, What's in a name.com? *SMJ,* 22: 793–804; P. Roberts & G. Dowling, 2002, Corporate reputation and sustained superior financial performance, *SMJ,* 23: 1077–1093.

14. M. Porter, 1985, *Competitive Advantage,* New York: Free Press; A. Hinterhuber, 2002, Value chain orchestration in action and the case of the global agrochemical industry, *LRP,* 35: 615–635.

15. A. Parmigiani, 2007, Why do firms both make and buy? *SMJ,* 28: 285–311.

16. *BW,* 2006, The 787 encounters turbulence, June 19: 38–40.

17. M. Jacobides & S. Winter, 2005, The co-evolution of capabilities and transaction costs (p. 404), *SMJ,* 26: 395–413; M. H. Safizadeh, J. Field, & L. Ritzman, 2008, Sourcing practices and boundaries of the firm in the financial services industry, *SMJ,* 29: 79–91.

18. A. Ranft & M. Lord, 2002, Acquiring new technologies and capabilities, *OSc,* 13: 420–441.

19. R. Makadok, 2001, Toward a synthesis of the resource-based and dynamic capability views of rent creation (p. 388), *SMJ,* 22: 387–401.

20. D. Levy, 2005, Offshoring in the new global political economy (p. 687), *JMS,* 42: 685–693.

21. This section draws heavily from Barney, 2002, *Gaining and Sustaining* (pp. 159–174).

22. R. Adner & P. Zemsky, 2006, A demand-based perspective on sustainable competitive advantage, *SMJ,* 27: 215–239; S. Lippman & R. Rumelt, 2003, A bargaining perspective on resource advantage, *SMJ,* 24: 1069–1086; J. Morrow, D. Sirmon, M. Hitt, & T. Holcomb, 2007, Creating value in the face of declining performance, *SMJ,* 28: 271–283.

23. D. Leonard-Barton, 1992, Core capabilities and core rigidities, *SMJ,* 13: 111–125.

24. D. Lavie, 2006, Capability reconfiguration, *AMR,* 31: 153–174; N. Siggelkow, 2001, Change in the presence of fit, *AMJ,* 44: 838–857; G. P. West & J. DeCastro, 2001, The Archilles heel of firm strategy, *JMS,* 38: 417–442.

25. G. Hamel, 2006, Management innovation (p. 78), *HBR,* February: 72–84.

26. S. Ethiraj, P. Kale, M. Krishnan, & J. Singh, 2005, Where do capabilities come from and how do they matter? *SMJ,* 26: 25–45; A. Knott, D. Bryce, & H. Posen, 2003, On the strategic accumulation of intangible assets, *OSc,* 14: 192–208; D. Miller, 2003, An asymmetry-based view of advantage, *SMJ,* 24: 961–976; G. Ray, J. Barney, & W. Muhanna, 2004, Capabilities, business processes, and competitive advantage, *SMJ,* 25: 23–37; R. Schroeder, K. Bates, & M. Junttila, 2002, A resource-based view of manufacturing strategy, *SMJ,* 23: 105–118; B. Skaggs & M. Youndt, 2004, Strategic positioning, human capital, and performance in service organizations, *SMJ,* 25: 85–99.

27. *BW,* 2005, Better than robots, December 26: 46–47.

28. A. King, 2007, Disentangling interfirm and intrafirm causal ambiguity, *AMR,* 32: 156–178; T. Powell, D. Lovallo, & C. Caringal, 2006, Causal ambiguity, management perception, and firm performance, *AMR,* 31: 175–196.

29. *The Economist,* 2005, The quick and the dead, January 29: 10–11.

30. K. Watanabe, 2007, Lessons from Toyota's long drive, *HBR,* July–August: 74–83.

31. S. Dobrev, 2007, Competition in the looking-glass market, *SMJ,* 28: 1267–1289; M. Lieberman & S. Asaba, 2006, Why do firms imitate each other? *AMR,* 31: 366–385.

32. A. Lado, N. Boyd, P. Wright, & M Kroll, 2006, Paradox and theorizing within the resource-based view, *AMR,* 31: 115–131.

33. G. Hoetker, 2006, Do modular products lead to modular organizations? *SMJ,* 27: 501–518; M. Kotabe, R. Parente, & J. Murray, 2007, Antecedents and outcomes of modular production in the Brazilian automobile industry, *JIBS,* 38: 84–106.

34. N. Stieglitz & K. Heine, 2007, Innovations and the role of complementarities in a strategic theory of the firm, *SMJ,* 28: 1–15.

35. J. Barney, 1997, *Gaining and Sustaining Competitive Advantage* (p. 155), Reading, MA: Addison-Wesley. See also J. Jansen, F. Van den Bosch, & H. Volberda, 2005, Managerial potential and related absorptive capacity, *AMJ,* 48: 999–1015; Y. Kor & J. Mahoney, 2005, How dynamics, management, and governance of resource deployments influence firm-level performance, *SMJ,* 26: 489–496; Y. Mishina, T. Pollock, & J. Porac, 2004, Are more resources always better for growth? *SMJ,* 25: 1179–1197; S. Thomke & W. Kuemmerle, 2002, Asset accumulation, interdependence, and technological change, *SMJ,* 23: 619–635; P. Yeoh & K. Roth, 1999, An empirical analysis of sustained advantage, *SMJ,* 20: 637–653.

36. J. Birkinshaw & N. Hood, 1998, Multinational subsidiary evolution, *AMR,* 23: 773–795; A. Delios & P. Beamish, 2001, Survival and profitability, *AMJ,* 44: 1028–1038.

37. T. Kostova & K. Roth, 2003, Social capital in multinational corporations and a micro-macro model of its formation, *AMR,* 28: 297–317; P. Moran, 2005, Structural vs. relational embeddedness, *SMJ,* 26: 1129–1151.

38. J. Fahy, G. Hooley, J. Beracs, K. Fonfara, & V. Gabrijan, 2003, Privatization and sustainable advantage in the emerging economies of Central Europe, *MIR,* 43: 407–428.

39. R. Schmalensee, 1985, Do markets differ much? *AER,* 75: 341–351.

40. C. Zott, 2003, Dynamic capabilities and the emergence of intraindustry differential firm performance, *SMJ,* 24: 97–125.

41. A. McGahan & M. Porter, 1997, How much does industry matter, really? *SMJ,* 18: 15–30; G. Waring, 1996, Industry differences in the persistence of firm-specific returns, *AER,* 86: 1253–1265.

42. J. Hough, 2006, Business segment performance redux, *SMJ,* 27: 45–61; A. Mauri & M. Michaels, 1998, Firm and industry effects within strategic management, *SMJ,* 19: 211–219; T. Ruefli & R. Wiggins, 2003, Industry, corporate, and segment effects and business performance, *SMJ,* 24: 861–879; R. Rumelt, 1991, How much does industry matter? *SMJ,* 12: 167–185; Y. Spanos, G. Zaralis, & S. Lioukas, 2004, Strategy and industry effects on profitability, *SMJ,* 25: 139–165.

43. P. Godfrey & C. Hill, 1995, The problem of unobservables in strategic management research (p. 530), *SMJ,* 16: 519–533.

44. O. Williamson, 1999, Strategy research (p. 1093), *SMJ,* 20: 1087–1108. See also R. Priem & J. Butler, 2001, Is the resource-based "view" a useful perspective for strategic management research? *AMR,* 26: 22–40; T. Powell, 2003, Strategy without ontology, *SMJ,* 24: 285–291.

45. D. Collis, 1994, How valuable are organizational capabilities (p. 151), *SMJ,* 15: 143–152.

46. B. Wernerfelt, 1984, A resource-based view of the firm (p. 171), *SMJ,* 5: 171–180; C. Lengnick & J. Wolff, 1999, Similarities and contradictions in the core logics of three strategy research streams, *SMJ,* 20: 1109–1132.

47. S. Chang & H. Singh, 2000, Corporate and industry effects on business unit competitive position, *SMJ,* 21: 739–752; J. Child, L. Chung, & H. Davis, 2003, The performance of cross-border units in China, *JIBS,* 34: 242–254; D. Griffith & M. Harvey, 2001, A resource perspective of global dynamic capabilities, *JIBS,* 32: 597–606.

48. G. Hawawini, V. Subramanian, & P. Verdin, 2003, Is performance driven by industry- or firm-specific factors? *SMJ,* 24: 1–16.

49. R. Adner & C. Helfat, 2003, Corporate effects and dynamic managerial capabilities, *SMJ,* 24: 1011–1026; S. Winter, 2003, Understanding dynamic capabilities, *SMJ,* 24: 991–998; M. Zollo & S. Winter, 2002, Deliberate learning and the evolution of dynamic capabilities, *OSc,* 13: 339–351.

50. J. Birkinshaw, R. Nobel, & J. Ridderstrale, 2002, Knowledge as a contingency variable, *OSc,* 13: 274–289; D. DeCarolis & D. Deeds, 1999, The impact of stocks and flows of organizational knowledge on firm performance, *SMJ,* 20: 953–968; A. Grandori & B. Kogut, 2002, Dialogue on organization and knowledge, *OSc,* 13: 224–231.

51. J. Barney, M. Wright, & D. Ketchen, 2001, The resource-based view of the firm: Ten years after 1991, *JM,* 27: 625–641; S. Berman, J. Down, & C. Hill, 2002, Tacit knowledge as a source of competitive advantage in the National Basketball Association, *AMJ,* 45: 13–32.

52. K. Eisenhardt & J. Martin, 2000, Dynamic capabilities: What are they? (p. 1113), *SMJ,* 21: 1105–1121.

53. Eisenhardt & Martin, 2000, Dynamic capabilities (p. 1112).

54. R. D'Aveni, 1994, *Hypercompetition,* New York: Free Press; A. Ilinitch, R. D'Aveni, & A. Lewin, 1996, New organizational forms and strategies for managing in hypercompetitive environments, *OSc,* 7: 211–220.

55. S. Brown & K. Eisenhardt, 1998, *Competing on the Edge,* Boston: Harvard Business School Press; T. Moliterno & M. Wiersema, 2007, Firm performance, rent appropriation, and the strategic resource divestment capability, *SMJ,* 28: 1065–1087.

56. R. Wiggins & T. Ruefli, 2005, Schumpeter's ghost, *SMJ,* 26: 887–911.

57. B. Kedia & D. Mukherjee, 2008, Understanding offshoring, *JWB* (in press).

58. J. Doh, 2005, Offshore outsourcing, *JMS,* 42: 695–704.

59. D. Farrell, 2005, Offshoring: Value creation through economic change, *JMS,* 42: 675–683.

60. M. Gottfredson, R. Puryear, & S. Phillips, 2005, Strategic sourcing (p. 132), *HBR,* February: 132–139.

61. C. Rossetti & T. Choi, 2005, On the dark side of strategic sourcing, *AME,* 19 (1): 46–60.

62. J. Boddewyn, B. Toyne, & Z. Martinez, 2004, The meanings of "international management," *MIR,* 44: 195–212; L. Nachum, 2003, International business in a world of increasing returns, *MIR,* 43: 219–245.

63. G. Hamel & C. K. Prahalad, 1994, *Competing for the Future,* Boston: Harvard Business School Press.

chapter 4

Institutions, Cultures, and Ethics

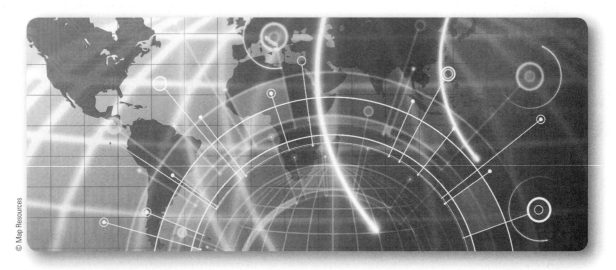

© Map Resources

KNOWLEDGE OBJECTIVES

After studying this chapter, you should be able to

1. Explain the concept of institutions

2. Understand the two primary ways of exchange transactions that reduce uncertainty

3. Articulate the two propositions underpinning an institution-based view of strategy

4. Appreciate the strategic role of cultures

5. Identify the strategic role of ethics culminating in a strategic response framework

6. Participate in three leading debates on institutions, cultures, and ethics

7. Draw strategic implications for action

OPENING CASE: BEHIND THE PROFITABILITY OF BIG PHARMA

The pharmaceutical industry is dominated by large multinational enterprises (MNEs) collectively known as the Big Pharma. They include Merck, Eli Lilly, Bristol-Myers, and Pfizer of the United States; GlaxoSmithKline (GSK) and Wellcome of Britain; and Hoffman La Roche, Ciba Geigy, Novartis, and Sandoz of Switzerland. Characterized by a relentless drive for research and development (R&D), the industry typically ranks among the most profitable in the world.

While industry structure and firm resources can certainly shed light on what is behind Big Pharma's enviable performance, what seems equally important is the role of institutional frameworks. For example, the US government helps make sure that Big Pharma reap huge profits. The world's most stringent drug approval requirements imposed by the Food and Drug Administration (FDA) significantly heighten the entry barriers, since only the "big boys" can afford to play such a game. Since cheaper drugs are not allowed to be imported, Americans often pay more than twice what Canadians and Europeans pay for the *same* drugs developed in the United States (Table 4.1). As a result, Americans spend approximately $240 billion a year on drugs, more than Britain, Canada, France, Germany, Italy, and Japan *combined*. Elderly and poor people not covered by insurance, approximately 15% of the US population, suffer disproportionately more from the high prices.

Elsewhere in the world, the visible hand of governments is also evident. In Canada, drug companies do not have to pay for expensive advertising because drugs are distributed by the nationwide insurance program that covers every resident. In Britain, the Ministry of Health directly negotiates with drugmakers, each with a different profit margin. British and foreign firms with intensive R&D in the country are able to negotiate higher margins relative to foreign firms that simply export to the country.

According to *Business Week,* "today, most drug prices are determined not by markets but by clout." This business model is currently under siege. Virtually every American retirement community is reportedly importing cheaper drugs from Canada, mostly through the Internet. Even if Americans are allowed to import drugs only from Canada, the savings may be up to $38 billion a year—at the expense of Big Pharma.

At the same time, Big Pharma is also challenged by poor countries infested by diseases such as AIDS, malaria, and tuberculosis. These countries demand that their drugmakers be licensed to manufacture cheaper generic versions of currently patented drugs regardless of the wishes of the patent holders—the so-called "compulsory licensing" scheme. The largely symbolic royalties Big Pharma will receive hardly compensate for the lucrative profits these firms stand to lose. For instance, since generic AIDS drugs

91

TABLE 4.1   Prices of the Same US Developed Drugs Around the World

US DEVELOPED DRUGS	LIPITOR	ZOLOFT	NEXIUM
Per prescription	20 mg; 30 tablets	50 mg, 30 tablets	20 mg, 28 capsules
US prices	$93.99	$69.99	$112.00
Canadian prices	$70.74	$55.30	$74.87
Mexican prices	$88.74	Not sold	$63.46
French prices	$54.45	$28.96	$44.35
Indian prices (generics)	$7.50	$2.24	$2.09

were introduced in Brazil in 1997, Big Pharma has had to drop prices by as much as 65%. In India, local companies not only manufacture a variety of generic drugs but also export them. Recently, Mexico has threatened to do the same.

Big Pharma is fighting these threats at every turn. Firms argue that their wellspring of innovation will run dry if their patents are not protected. In addition, they suggest that the legalization of drug imports in the United States will add to the growing threat of counterfeit drugs that may put patients at risk. Drug companies also worry that the cheap drugs they sell in poor countries may make their way back to rich countries. In addition, such globally differential pricing may give their home governments some added ammunition to cut drug prices at home. Fundamentally, consumers in rich countries, especially the United States, subsidize consumers elsewhere. While American consumers are increasingly sick of doing this, poor countries are essentially demanding that their consumers be subsidized *more*. From an ethical standpoint, Big Pharma is often challenged for failing to deploy their R&D prowess to combat tropical diseases, the solution of which will have little (or no) profit potential in rich countries. In response, GSK and Novartis have recently established new units to develop drugs for tropical diseases, and have announced that other than earning kudos for corporate social responsibility, they do not expect to profit from these new ventures.

Sources: Based on (1) *Business Week,* 2003, Rethinking the drug business, August 11: 108; (2) *Business Week,* 2003, Why do we pay more? August 11: 26–28; (3) *Business Week,* 2007, The rush to test drugs in China, May 28: 60–61; (4) *The Economist,* 2005, Prescription for change, June 18: 1–20.

What determines the strategies and performance of firms in the pharmaceutical industry? What is behind its historically high profitability? What about its future? It is evident that the industry- and resource-based perspectives introduced in the previous two chapters, while certainly insightful, are not enough to answer these intriguing questions. It is difficult to imagine how Big Pharma could become so profitable without government-imposed entry barriers. It is equally plausible to hypothesize that Big Pharma's historically fat profit margins may become thinner in the face of heightened competition allowed by domestic and foreign governments. Overall, firm strategies and performance are, to a large degree, determined by institutions, popularly known as "the rules of the game" in a society. In other words, how firms play the game and win (or lose), at least in part, depends on how the rules are made and enforced. Popularized since the 1990s, this **institution-based view,** covering institutions, cultures, and ethics, has emerged as one of the three leading perspectives on strategy. This chapter first introduces the institution-based view. Then we discuss the strategic role of cultures and ethics, followed by a strategic response framework. Debates and implications follow.

Understanding Institutions

Definitions

Building on the "rules of the game" metaphor, Douglass North, a Nobel laureate in economics, more formally defines **institutions** as "the humanly devised constraints that structure human interaction."[1] An **institutional framework** is made up of formal and informal institutions governing individual and firm behavior. These institutions are supported by three "pillars" identified by Richard Scott, a leading sociologist. They are (1) regulatory, (2) normative, and (3) cognitive pillars.[2]

Shown in Table 4.2, **formal institutions** include laws, regulations, and rules. Their primary supportive pillar, the **regulatory pillar,** is the coercive power of governments. For example, while many individuals and companies may pay taxes out of their patriotic duty, a larger number of them pay taxes in fear of the coercive power of the government if they are caught not paying taxes.

On the other hand, **informal institutions** include norms, cultures, and ethics. The two main supportive pillars are normative and cognitive. The **normative pillar** refers to how the values, beliefs, and actions of other relevant players—collectively known as **norms**—influence the behavior of focal individuals and firms. For instance, the recent norms centered on rushing to invest in China and India have prompted many Western firms to imitate each other without a clear understanding of how to make such moves work.[3] Cautious managers resisting such "herding" are often confronted by board members and investors: "Why are we not in China and India?"

Also supporting informal institutions, the **cognitive pillar** refers to the internalized, taken-for-granted values and beliefs that guide individual and firm behavior. For example, what triggered "whistle blowers" to report Enron's wrongdoing was their belief in what's right and wrong. While the norms are not to "rock the boat," "whistle blowers" choose to follow their internalized personal beliefs on what's right by overcoming the norms that encourage silence.

TABLE 4.2   Dimensions of Institutions

Degree of Formality	Examples	Supportive Pillars
Formal institutions	• Laws • Regulations • Rules	• Regulatory (coercive)
Informal institutions	• Norms • Cultures • Ethics	• Normative • Cognitive

institution-based view

A leading perspective of strategy that argues that in addition to industry- and firm-level conditions, firms also need to take into account wider influences from sources such as the state and society when crafting strategy.

institution

Humanly devised constraints that structure human interaction—informally known as the "rules of the game."

institutional framework

A framework of formal and informal institutions governing individual and firm behavior.

formal institutions

Institutions represented by laws, regulations, and rules.

regulatory pillar

How formal rules, laws, and regulations influence the behavior of individuals and firms.

informal institutions

Institutions represented by norms, cultures, and ethics.

normative pillar

How the values, beliefs, and norms of other relevant players influence the behavior of individuals and firms.

What Do Institutions Do?

While institutions do many things, their key role, in two words, is to *reduce uncertainty*.[4] By signaling which conduct is legitimate and which is not, institutions constrain the range of acceptable actions. In short, institutions reduce uncertainty, which can be potentially devastating.[5] Political uncertainty such as ethnic riots may render long-range planning obsolete. Economic uncertainty such as failure to carry out contractual obligations may result in economic losses. A recent case of political and economic uncertainty can be seen in Kenya (Strategy in Action 4.1).

Uncertainty surrounding economic transactions can lead to **transaction costs,** which are defined as costs associated with economic transactions—or more broadly, the costs of doing business. A leading transaction cost theorist, Oliver Williamson, refers to frictions in mechanical systems: "Do the gears mesh, are the parts lubricated, is there needless slippage or other loss of energy?" He goes on to suggest that transaction costs can be regarded as "the economic counterpart of frictions: Do the parties to exchange operate harmoniously, or are there frequent misunderstandings and conflicts?"[6]

An important source of transaction costs is **opportunism,** defined as self-interest seeking with guile. Examples include misleading, cheating, and confusing other parties in transactions that will increase transaction costs. Attempting to reduce such transaction costs, institutional frameworks increase certainty by spelling out the rules of the game so that violations (such as failure to fulfill a contract) can be mitigated with relative ease (such as through formal arbitration and courts).

Without stable institutional frameworks, transaction costs may become prohibitively high, to the extent that certain transactions simply would not take place. In the absence of credible institutional frameworks that protect investors, investors may choose to put their money abroad. Rich Russians often choose to purchase a soccer club in London or a seaside villa in Cyprus, instead of investing in Russia—in other words, the transaction costs for doing business in Russia may be too high.

How Do Institutions Reduce Uncertainty?

Throughout the world, two primary kinds of institutions—informal and formal—reduce uncertainty. Often called **relational contracting,** the first kind of economic transaction is known as an **informal, relationship-based, personalized exchange.** In many parts of the world, there is no need to write an IOU note when you borrow money from your friends. Insisting on such a note, either by you or, worse, by your friends, may be regarded as an insulting lack of trust. While you are committed to paying your friends back, they also *believe* you will—thus, your transaction is governed by informal norms and cognitive beliefs based on what friendship is about. In case you opportunistically take the money and run, your reputation will be ruined and you will not only lose these friends but also, through their word of mouth, lose other friends who may loan you money in the future.

However, in addition to the benefits of friendship, there are costs—remember how much time you have spent with friends and how many gifts you have given them? Plotted graphically (Figure 4.1), initially, at time T1, the costs to engage in relational contracting are high (at point A) and the benefits low (at point B), because parties need to build strong social networks through a time- and resource-consuming process to check each other out (such as going to school together). If relationships stand the test of

---

norm

The prevailing practice of relevant players that affect the focal individuals and firms.

cognitive pillar

The internalized, taken-for-granted values and beliefs that guide individual and firm behavior.

transaction costs

Costs associated with economic transaction—or more broadly, costs of doing business.

opportunism

Self-interest seeking with guile.

relational contracting

Contracting based on informal relationships (*see also* informal, relationship-based, personalized exchange).

informal, relationship-based, personalized exchange

A way of economic exchange based on informal relationships among transaction parties. Also known as relational contracting.

Strategy in Action 4.1 - Kenya's Flower Industry Copes with Uncertainty

Some 25% of Europe's cut flowers come from Kenya. After a tentative start in the 1980s, the industry is now the country's third-largest foreign-currency earner, bringing in $120 million a year. The top two earners, tourism and tea, have been wrecked by spasms of bloodletting and ethnic cleansing since December 2007's disputed election. Safari lodges are mostly closed, and package tourism on the coast is ruined for the rest of the year. Lost exports are costing the tea industry $2 million a *day*, and violence on the big tea estates around Kericho has destroyed machinery, warehouses, and housing.

The flower farms are hanging on, but the violence could not have come at a worse time. Although they grow button-hole carnations in every shade of cream, the real money is in red roses. The Lake Naivasha Growers' Group, an alliance of owners, says Valentine's Day accounts for one-third of their annual production. Oserian, one of the largest farms, hoped to sell 6 million roses in the week surrounding February 14, 2008. Its 5,000 workers live on the farm, and nearly all have been reporting for work. The story is very different on the smaller farms, where workers live off-site in their own, often squalid and insecure housing.

Several days of work were lost when violence reached Lake Naivasha (90 kilometers/56 miles northwest of Nairobi) on January 26, 2008. Killings elsewhere in the country led to an explosion of anger and a systematic campaign to drive out workers belonging to the Luo group. A local trade union says 3,000 of the 30,000 workers employed in Naivasha's flower farms have abandoned their jobs, most of them Luos. The growers are trying to limit further trouble by housing displaced workers in a temporary camp. Hiring replacements will not be difficult, since the average monthly salary of $80 plus benefits is considered a good wage.

Roses need labor-intensive watering, pruning, and treating before they can be clipped and flown daily to buyers in Amsterdam and London. The best are sold through (Dutch) auctions to florists; those of lesser quality end up in European supermarkets. Kenya emerged as a flower power when Israel scaled down its own industry. Since then, Kenya has lost business to neighboring Ethiopia, which offers tax breaks and better security, but Naivasha's perfect intensity of sunlight and days of near-constant length should keep it on top. In any case, the owners are stoical. "We are committed privateers," says one. "We'll just pick up and move somewhere else in Africa."

Source: The Economist, 2008, "Roses are Red," February 9: 71. Copyright © 2008 by the Economist Group. Reprinted by permission of the Economist Group via Copyright Clearance Center.

time, then benefits may outweigh costs. Over time, when the scale and scope of informal transactions expand, the costs per transaction move down (from A to C and then E) and benefits move up (from B to C and then D), since the threat of opportunism is limited by the extent to which informal sanctions may be imposed against opportunists

FIGURE 4.1   Informal Relationship-Based Personalized Exchange

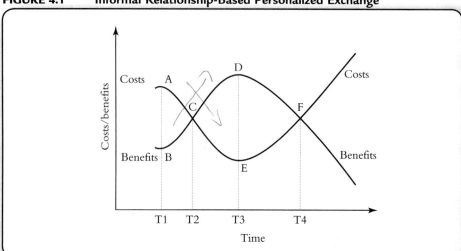

Source: M. W. Peng (2003), Institutional transitions and strategic choices (p. 279), *Academy of Management Review,* 28 (2): 275–296.

if necessary.[7] There is little demand for costly formal third-party enforcement (such as an IOU note scrutinized by lawyers and notarized by governments). Thus, between T2 and T3, you and your friends—and the economy collectively—are likely to benefit from relational contracting.[8]

Past time T3, however, the costs of such a mode may gradually outweigh its benefits, because "the greater the variety and numbers of exchange, the more complex the kinds of agreements that have to be made, and so the more difficult it is to do so" informally.[9] Specifically, there is a limit as to the number and strength of network ties an individual or firm can possess. In other words, how many good friends can each person (or firm) have? Nobody can claim to have 100 *good* friends (regardless of how one defines "good friends"). When the informal enforcement regime is weak, trust can be easily exploited and abused. What are you going to do if your (so-called) friends who borrow money from you refuse to pay you back or simply disappear? As a result, the limit of relational contracting is likely to be reached at time T3. Past T4, the costs are likely to gradually outweigh the benefits.

Often termed **arm's-length transaction,** the second institutional mode to govern relationships is a **formal, rule-based, impersonal exchange** with third-party enforcement. As the economy expands, the scale and scope of transactions rise (you want to borrow more money to start up a firm and there are many entrepreneurs like you), calling for the emergence of third-party enforcement through formal market-supporting institutions. Shown in Figure 4.2, the initial costs per transaction are high, because of the high costs of formal institutions. Credit bureaus, courts, police, and lawyers are expensive (Strategy in Action 4.2 shows that India cannot afford a large number of judges). Small villages usually cannot afford (and do not need) them. Over time, however, third-party enforcement is likely to facilitate the widening of markets, because unfamiliar parties, people who are not your friends and who would have been deterred to transact with you before, are now confident enough to trade with you (and others).

arm's-length transactions

Transactions in which parties keep a distance (*see also* formal, rule-based, impersonal exchange).

formal, rule-based, impersonal exchange

A way of economic exchange based on formal transactions in which parties keep a distance (*see also* arm's-length transactions).

FIGURE 4.2   Formal Rule-Based Impersonal Exchange

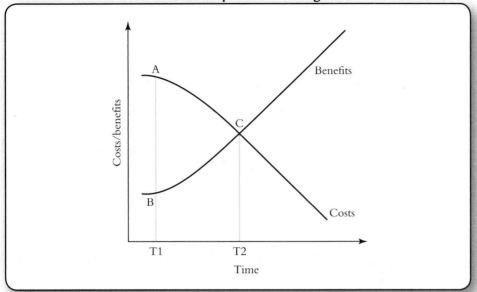

Source: M. W. Peng (2003), Institutional transitions and strategic choices (p. 280), *Academy of Management Review*, 28 (2): 275–296.

In other words, with an adequate formal institutional framework, you (or your firm) can now borrow from local banks, out-of-state banks, or even foreign banks. Thus, formal market-supporting institutions facilitate more new entries (such as all the new start-ups you and your fellow entrepreneurs can found and all these banks that provide financing) by lowering transaction costs. Consequently, firms are able to grow, and economies to expand.

There is no presumption that formal institutions are inherently better than informal ones, because in many situations the demand for formal institutions is not evident. Both forms complement each other. Relational contracting has an advantage when the size of the economy is limited—imagine a small village where everybody knows each other. Its disadvantage is that it may cause firms to stick with established relationships rather than working with new untried players, thus creating barriers to entry. As transaction complexity rises, informal dealings within the group may become difficult—imagine a city or national economy whereby it would be too difficult to impose informal sanctions against opportunists. Arm's-length transactions, on the other hand, help overcome these barriers, by bringing together formerly distant groups (firms, communities, and even countries) to enjoy the gains from complicated long-distance trade. These rule-based transactions thus become increasingly attractive as more new players enter the game. A global economy simply cannot operate on informal institutions alone. This explains the proliferation of formal international institutions such as the International Monetary Fund and the World Trade Organization in the postwar era.

Overall, interactions between institutions and firms that reduce transaction costs shape economic activity. In addition, institutions are not static.[10] **Institutional transitions,** defined as "fundamental and comprehensive changes introduced to the formal and

institutional transitions

Fundamental and comprehensive changes introduced to the formal and informal rules of the game that affect organizations as players.

Strategy in Action 4.2 - Resolving Commercial Disputes in India

In July 2006, the government reported that the number of civil and criminal cases pending before India's courts exceeded 30 million, up from 20 million in 1997. Among the reasons are a shortage of judges—just 11 for every one million people, compared with 51 in Britain and 107 in America. There is also what Nick Archer, a lawyer with a British firm, Slaughter and May, calls a "frightening lack of case management." Cases are not assigned to a particular judge for their duration and are often adjourned.

A few foreign firms figure in the staggering judicial backlog. Scott Wilson Kirkpatrick, a British firm of consulting engineers, has been waiting more than five *years* for an award of more than $1 million that an arbitration panel made in its favor against the government of the state of Jharkhand. The state government appealed to an Indian court, and eventually to the Supreme Court, which has yet to hear the case.

In his book *Courts and Their Judgments,* written in 2001, Arun Shourie, a journalist and a former minister, described a similar case involving one of the world's big manufacturers of compressors. Eight *years* into the dispute, it was, he noted, "nowhere near resolution." "Is a person or firm that is put through the mill like this liable to be eager to do business with India?" he asked. Mr. Shourie also noted that the delays have made foreign firms loathe to signing contracts

under which awards set by arbitration panels can be challenged in Indian courts. Does this help India, he wondered—or even its lawyers?

Source: Excerpts from *The Economist,* 2006, The Long Arms of the Law, July 1:40. © The Economist Group, as conveyed through Copyright Clearance Center, Inc.

informal rules of the game that affect organizations as players,"[11] are widespread in the world, especially in emerging economies (see Chapter 1). It is evident that managers making strategic choices during such transitions must take into account the nature of institutional frameworks and their transitions, a perspective introduced next.

An Institution-Based View of Business Strategy

Overview

Historically, much of the strategy literature, as exemplified by the industry- and resource-based views, does not discuss the specific relationship between strategic choices and institutional frameworks. To be sure, the influence of the "environment" has been noted. However, what has dominated much of the existing work is a "task environment" view that focuses on economic variables such as market demand and technological change.[12]

FIGURE 4.3   The Porter Diamond: Determinants of National Competitive Advantage

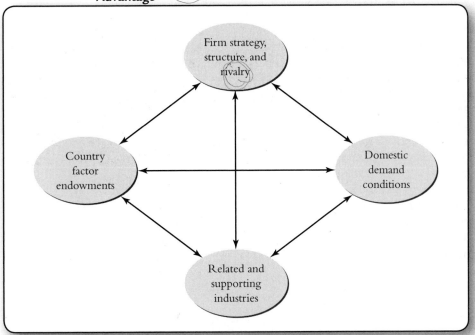

A case in point is Porter's influential "diamond" model (Figure 4.3) that argues that competitive advantage of different industries in different nations depends on four factors.[13] According to this model, first, **firm strategy, structure, and rivalry** within one country are essentially the same industry-based view covered in Chapter 2. Second, **factor endowments** refer to the natural and human resource repertoires. Third, **related and supporting industries** provide the foundation upon which key industries can excel. Switzerland's global excellence in pharmaceuticals goes hand-in-hand with its dye industry. Finally, tough **domestic demand** propels firms to scale new heights to satisfy such demand. Why is the American movie industry so competitive worldwide? One reason is that American moviegoers demand the very best "sex and violence" (two themes that sell universally if artfully packaged). Endeavoring to satisfy such domestic demand, movie studios unleash *High School Musical 2* after *High School Musical* and *Spiderman 3* after *Spiderman 1* and *Spiderman 2*—each time packing more excitement to go beyond the previous production. Overall, Porter argues that the combination of these four factors explains what is behind the competitive advantage of globally leading industries in different countries.

Interesting as the "diamond" model is, it has been criticized for ignoring histories and institutions, such as what is *behind* firm rivalry.[14] Among strategists, Porter is not alone. Given that most research focuses on market economies, a market-based institutional framework has been taken for granted—in fact, no other strategy textbook has devoted a full chapter to institutions like this one.

firm strategy, structure, and rivalry

How industry structure and firm strategy interact to affect interfirm rivalry.

factor endowments

The endowments of production factors such as land, water, and people in one country.

related and supporting industries

Industries that are related to and/or support the focal industry.

domestic demand

Demand for products and services within a domestic economy.

FIGURE 4.4   Institutions, Firms, and Strategic Choices

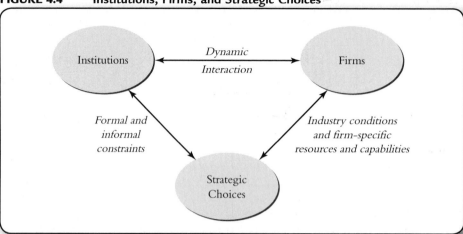

Sources: Adapted from (1) M. W. Peng, 2000, *Business Strategies in Transition Economies* (p. 45), Thousand Oaks, CA: Sage; (2) M. W. Peng, 2002, Towards an institution-based view of business strategy (p. 253), *Asia Pacific Journal of Management,* 19 (2): 251–267.

Such an omission is unfortunate, because, as practitioners have known for a long time, strategic choices, such as those made by Big Pharma, are selected within, and constrained by, institutional frameworks in developed economies (see Opening Case). Today, this insight becomes more important as more firms do business abroad, especially in emerging economies. The striking institutional differences between developed and emerging economies have propelled the institution-based view to the forefront of strategy discussions.[15] Shown in Figure 4.4, the institution-based view focuses on the dynamic interaction between institutions and firms, and considers strategic choices as the outcome of such an interaction. Specifically, strategic choices are not only driven by industry structure and firm-specific resources and capabilities emphasized by traditional strategic thinking, but are also a reflection of the formal and informal constraints of a particular institutional framework.[16]

Overall, it is increasingly acknowledged that institutions are more than background conditions, and that "institutions *directly* determine what arrows a firm has in its quiver as it struggles to formulate and implement strategy and to create competitive advantage."[17] At present, the idea that "institutions matter" is no longer novel or controversial. What needs to be better understood is *how* they matter.[18]

Two Core Propositions

The institution-based view suggests two core propositions on how institutions matter (Table 4.3). First, managers and firms *rationally* make strategic choices within institutional constraints.[19] In the pharmaceutical industry (Opening Case), while the institutional framework in the United States fosters innovations that command premiums, the institutional framework in Japan *discourages* innovations that may make old drugs obsolete—old drugs often are the most profitable ones there (Strategy in Action 4.3). Both strategies are perfectly rational within their own institutional frameworks.

TABLE 4.3   **Two Core Propositions of the Institution-Based View**

Proposition 1	Managers and firms *rationally* pursue their interests and make choices within the formal and informal constraints in a given institutional framework.
Proposition 2	While formal and informal institutions combine to govern firm behavior, in situations where formal constraints are unclear or fail, informal constraints will play a *larger* role in reducing uncertainty and providing constancy to managers and firms.

In another example, hundreds of firms and thousands of individuals around the world are involved with counterfeiting. Close to 10% of all world trade is reportedly in counterfeits. Remember this is not slavery, and everyone involved has voluntarily entered this business. However, none of the high school graduates around the world, when filling out a career form in terms of what career they would pursue after graduation, has ever declared an interest in joining counterfeiting. So what happened? Why are so many individuals and firms involved? The key to understanding this strategy is the realization that managers and entrepreneurs who make such a strategic choice are not immoral monsters but just ordinary people. They have made a *rational* decision (from their standpoint at least) given an institutional environment of weak intellectual protection and the availability of moderately capable manufacturing and distribution skills.[20] Of course, to suggest that a strategy of counterfeiting may be rational does not deny the fact that it is unethical and illegal. However, without an understanding of its institutional basis, it is difficult to devise effective countermeasures.

The second proposition is that while formal and informal institutions combine to govern firm behavior, in situations where formal constraints fail, informal constraints will play a *larger* role in reducing uncertainty and providing constancy to managers and

Strategy in Action 4.3 - Why Are Japanese Pharmaceutical Firms Not World-Class?

Most enthusiastic consumers of Toyota and Sony in the West would have a hard time naming a single Japanese pharmaceutical firm that is world-famous. This is not surprising because there is none. Why? The health care system in Japan does not reward innovative new drugs. The Ministry of Health, Labor, and Welfare (*korosho*) negotiates drug prices with firms. However, once fixed, prices are not allowed to rise. If prices remain the same but manufacturing costs decrease because of economies of scale, then the *oldest* drugs, not the newest, command the highest margins in Japan. Drug prices sometimes do change. However, they *fall*—thanks to mandatory price cuts imposed by *korosho* to curtail health care costs. Thus, there is little incentive for Japanese pharmaceutical firms to aggressively invest in R&D to bring out breakthrough medicines that require high R&D expenditures and premium prices. Instead, Japanese firms have relied on licensing Western drugs. However, this strategy is now becoming harder because Western firms like to sell more drugs on their own in Japan. In the $58 billion pharmaceutical market (the world's second largest), foreign firms now account for a third of sales, and Pfizer has unseated Takeda as "king of the hill." To better defend their home market, Japanese pharmaceutical firms now have to beef up R&D.

Sources: Based on (1) *The Economist,* 2005, Looking east, June 18: 8; (2) J. Mahlich, 2008, Patents and performance in the Japanese pharmaceutical industry, Working paper, Austrian Economic Chamber, Vienna.

firms. For example, when the formal institutional regime collapsed with the disappearance of the former Soviet Union, it is largely the informal constraints, based on personal relationships and connections (called *blat* in Russian) among managers and officials, that have facilitated the growth of many entrepreneurial firms.[21]

Many observers have the impression that relying on informal connections is a strategy relevant only to firms in emerging economies and that firms in developed economies pursue only "market-based" strategies. This is far from the truth. Even in developed economies, formal rules make up only a small (although important) part of institutional constraints, and informal constraints are pervasive. Just as firms compete in product markets, firms also fiercely compete in the political marketplace characterized by informal relationships.[22] The best connected firms are able to reap huge benefits. For every dollar on lobbying spent by US defense firms, they reap $28, on average, in earmarks from Uncle Sam, and more than 20 firms grab $100 or more.[23] This kind of enviable return on investment (ROI) compares favorably to capital expenditure (where $1 spent brings in $17 in revenues) or direct marketing (where $1 spent barely generates $5 in sales). Basically, if a firm cannot be a cost, differentiation, or focus leader, it may still beat the competition on other grounds—namely, the nonmarket political environment featuring informal relationships.[24] To use the resource-based language, political assets may be very valuable, rare, and hard-to-imitate. Note that lobbying is not necessarily indicative of "corruption"—just a demonstration of certain firms' mastery of the rules of the game.

The Strategic Role of Cultures

The Definition of Culture

Although hundreds of definitions of culture have appeared, we will use the one proposed by the world's foremost cross-cultural expert, Geert Hofstede, a Dutch professor. He defines **culture** as "the collective programming of the mind which distinguishes the members of one group or category of people from another."[25] Although most international business textbooks and trade books talk about culture (often presenting numerous details such as how to present business cards in Japan and how to drink vodka in Russia), virtually all strategy books ignore culture because culture is regarded as "too soft." Unfortunately, this belief is narrow-minded in today's global economy.[26] While not touching on the numerous "how-to" aspects (which are certainly important but can be found elsewhere), here we will focus on the *strategic* role of culture.

Before proceeding, it is important to make two points to minimize confusion. First, although it is customary to talk about American culture or Brazilian culture, there is no strict one-to-one correspondence between cultures and nation-states. Within the United States, there are numerous sub-cultures such as the Asian American and African American culture. The same is true for multiethnic countries such as Belgium, China, India, Indonesia, Russia, South Africa, and Switzerland.[27] Second, there are many layers of culture, such as regional, ethnic, and religious cultures. Within a firm, one will find a specific organizational culture (such as the Toyota culture). Having acknowledged the validity of these two points, we will follow Hofstede by using the term "culture" when discussing *national* culture—unless otherwise noted. While this is a matter of expediency, it is also a reflection of the institutional realities of the world, which consists of over 200 nation-states imposing different institutional frameworks.

culture

The collective programming of the mind that distinguishes the members of one group or category of people from another.

The Five Dimensions of Culture

While many ways exist to identify dimensions of culture,[28] the work of Hofstede has become by far the most influential. He and his colleagues have proposed five dimensions (Table 4.4). First, **power distance** is the extent to which less powerful members within a country expect and accept that power is distributed unequally. For example, in high power distance Brazil, the richest 10% of the population receives approximately 50% of the national income, and everybody accepts this as "the way it is." In low power distance Sweden, the richest 10% gets only 22% of the national income.[29] In the United States, subordinates often address their bosses on a first-name basis, a reflection of a relatively low power distance. While this boss, Mary or Joe, still has the power to fire you, the distance appears to be shorter than if you have to address this person as Mrs. Y or Dr. Z. In low power distance American universities, all faculty members, including the lowest ranked assistant professors, are commonly addressed as "Professor A." In high power distance British universities, only full professors are allowed to be called "Professor B" (everybody else is called "Dr. C" or "Ms. D" [if D does not have a PhD]). German universities are perhaps more extreme: Full professors with PhDs need to be honored as "Prof. Dr. X" (your author would be "Prof. Dr. Peng" if I were to work at a German university).

Second, **individualism** refers to the perspective that the identity of an individual is fundamentally his or her own, whereas **collectivism** refers to the idea that the identity of an individual is primarily based on the identity of his or her collective group (such as family, village, or company). In individualistic societies (led by the United States), ties between individuals are relatively loose and individual achievement and freedom are highly valued. In contrast, in collectivist societies (such as many countries in Africa, Asia, and Latin America), ties between individuals are relatively close and collective accomplishments are often sought after.

Third, the **masculinity** versus **femininity** dimension refers to sex role *differentiation*. In every traditional society, men tend to have occupations that reward assertiveness, such as politicians, soldiers, and executives. Women, on the other hand, usually work in caring professions such as teachers and nurses in addition to being homemakers. High masculinity societies (led by Japan) continue to maintain such a sharp role differentiation along gender lines. In low masculinity societies (led by Sweden), women increasingly become politicians, scientists, and soldiers (think about the movie *GI Jane*), and men frequently assume the role of nurses, teachers, and *househusbands*.

Fourth, **uncertainty avoidance** refers to the extent to which members in different cultures accept ambiguous situations and tolerate uncertainty. Members of high uncertainty avoidance cultures (led by Greece) place a premium on job security, career patterns, and retirement benefits. They also tend to resist change, which, by definition, is uncertain. Low uncertainty avoidance cultures (led by Singapore) are characterized by a greater willingness to take risk and less resistance to change.

Finally, **long-term orientation** emphasizes perseverance and savings for future betterment. China, which has the world's longest continuous written history of approximately 5,000 years and the highest contemporary savings rate, leads the pack. On the other hand, members of short-term orientation societies (led by Pakistan) prefer quick results and instant gratification.

Overall, Hofstede's dimensions are interesting and informative. They are also largely supported by subsequent work.[30] It is important to note that Hofstede's dimensions are

---

power distance

The degree of social inequality.

individualism

The perspective that the identity of an individual is most fundamentally based on his or her own individual attributes (rather than the attributes of a group).

collectivism

The perspective that the identity of an individual is most fundamentally based on the identity of his or her collective group (such as family, village, or company).

masculinity

A relatively strong form of societal-level sex role differentiation whereby men tend to have occupations that reward assertiveness and women tend to work in caring professions.

femininity

A relatively weak form of societal-level sex role differentiation whereby more women occupy positions that reward assertiveness and more men work in caring professions.

uncertainty avoidance

The extent to which members in different cultures accept ambiguous situations and tolerate uncertainty.

TABLE 4.4   **Hofstede Dimensions of Culture**[a]

POWER DISTANCE	INDIVIDUALISM	MASCULINITY	UNCERTAINTY AVOIDANCE	LONG-TERM ORIENTATION
Malaysia (104)	USA (91)	Japan (95)	Greece (112)	China (118)
Guatemala (95)	Australia (90)	Austria (79)	Portugal (104)	Hong Kong (96)
Panama (95)	UK (89)	Venezuela (73)	Guatemala (101)	Taiwan (87)
Philippines (94)	Canada (80)	Italy (70)	Uruguay (100)	Japan (80)
Mexico (81)	Netherlands (80)	Switzerland (70)	Belgium (94)	South Korea (75)
Venezuela (81)	New Zealand (79)	Mexico (69)	El Salvador (94)	Brazil (65)
Arab countries (80)	Italy (76)	Ireland (68)	Japan (92)	India (61)
Ecuador (78)	Belgium (75)	Jamaica (68)	Yugoslavia (88)	Thailand (56)
Indonesia (78)	Denmark (74)	UK (66)	Peru (87)	Singapore (48)
India (77)	Sweden (71)	Germany (66)	France (86)	Netherlands (44)
West Africa (77)	France (71)	Philippines (64)	Chile (86)	Bangladesh (40)
Yugoslavia (76)	Ireland (70)	Colombia (64)	Spain (86)	Sweden (33)
Singapore (74)	Norway (69)	South Africa (63)	Costa Rica (86)	Poland (32)
Brazil (69)	Switzerland (68)	Ecuador (63)	Panama (86)	Germany (31)
France (68)	Germany (67)	USA (62)	Argentina (86)	Australia (31)
Hong Kong (68)	South Africa (65)	Australia (61)	Turkey (85)	New Zealand (30)
Colombia (67)	Finland (63)	New Zealand (58)	South Korea (85)	USA (29)
El Salvador (66)	Austria (55)	Greece (57)	Mexico (82)	Great Britain (25)
Turkey (66)	Israel (54)	Hong Kong (57)	Israel (81)	Zimbabwe (25)
Belgium (65)	Spain (51)	Argentina (56)	Colombia (80)	Canada (23)
East Africa (64)	India (48)	India (56)	Venezuela (76)	Philippines (19)
Peru (64)	Japan (46)	Belgium (54)	Brazil (76)	Nigeria (16)
Thailand (64)	Argentina (46)	Arab block (53)	Italy (75)	Pakistan (0)
Chile (63)	Iran (41)	Canada (52)	Pakistan (70)	
Portugal (63)	Jamaica (39)	Malaysia (50)	Austria (70)	
Uruguay (61)	Brazil (38)	Pakistan (50)	Taiwan (69)	
Greece (60)	Arab countries (38)	Brazil (49)	Arab countries (68)	
South Korea (60)	Turkey (37)	Singapore (48)	Ecuador (67)	
Iran (58)	Uruguay (36)	Israel (47)	Germany (65)	
Taiwan (58)	Greece (35)	Indonesia (46)	Thailand (64)	
Spain (57)	Philippines (32)	West Africa (46)	Iran (59)	
Pakistan (55)	Mexico (30)	Turkey (45)	Finland (59)	
Japan (54)	East Africa (27)	Taiwan (45)	Switzerland (58)	
Italy (50)	Yugoslavia (27)	Panama (44)	West Africa (54)	
Argentina (49)	Puerto Rico (27)	Iran (43)	Netherlands (53)	
South Africa (49)	Malaysia (26)	France (43)	East Africa (52)	
Jamaica (45)	Hong Kong (25)	Spain (42)	Australia (51)	
USA (40)	Chile (23)	Peru (42)	Norway (50)	

TABLE 4.4   *(continued)*

POWER DISTANCE	INDIVIDUALISM	MASCULINITY	UNCERTAINTY AVOIDANCE	LONG-TERM ORIENTATION
Canada (39)	West Africa (20)	East Africa (41)	South Africa (49)	
Netherlands (38)	Singapore (20)	El Salvador (40)	New Zealand (49)	
Australia (36)	Thailand (20)	South Korea (39)	Indonesia (48)	
Costa Rica (35)	El Salvador (19)	Uruguay (38)	Canada (48)	
Germany (35)	South Korea (18)	Guatemala (37)	USA (46)	
UK (35)	Taiwan (17)	Thailand (34)	Philippines (44)	
Switzerland (34)	Peru (16)	Portugal (31)	India (40)	
Finland (33)	Costa Rica (15)	Chile (28)	Malaysia (36)	
Norway (31)	Pakistan (14)	Finland (26)	UK (35)	
Sweden (31)	Indonesia (14)	Yugoslavia (21)	Ireland (35)	
Ireland (28)	Colombia (13)	Costa Rica (21)	Hong Kong (29)	
New Zealand (22)	Venezuela (12)	Denmark (16)	Sweden (29)	
Denmark (18)	Panama (11)	Netherlands (14)	Denmark (23)	
Israel (13)	Ecuador (8)	Norway (8)	Jamaica (13)	
Austria (11)	Guatemala (6)	Sweden (8)	Singapore (8)	

a. Arab, East Africa, and West Africa are clusters of multiple countries. Germany and Yugoslavia refer to the former West Germany and the former Yugoslavia, respectively.

Source: Adapted from G. Hofstede, 1997, *Cultures and Organizations: Software of the Mind* (pp. 26, 53, 84, 113, 166), New York: McGraw-Hill. Data on the first four dimensions are based on surveys of IBM employees during 1968–72, first published in G. Hofstede, 1980, *Culture's Consequences,* Beverly Hills, CA: Sage. Data on the fifth dimension are based on surveys of students during the 1980s, first published in The Chinese Culture Connections, 1987, Chinese values and the search for culture-free dimensions of culture, *Journal of Cross-Cultural Psychology,* 18: 143–164.

not perfect, and have attracted some criticisms.[31] However, it is fair to suggest that these dimensions represent a *starting point* for us in trying to figure out the role of culture in global strategy.

Cultures and Strategic Choices

A great deal of strategic choices is consistent with Hofstede's cultural dimensions. For example, solicitation of subordinate feedback and participation, widely practiced in low power distance Western countries, is regarded as a sign of weak leadership and low integrity in high power distance countries such as Egypt, India, Mexico, and Russia.[32]

Individualism and collectivism also affect strategic choices. Individualist US firms may often try to differentiate themselves, whereas collectivist Japanese firms tend to converge on some defensible positions.[33] Because entrepreneurs are usually willing to take more risk, individualistic societies tend to foster relatively more entrepreneurship, whereas collectivism may result in relatively lower levels of entrepreneurship.[34]

Likewise, masculinity and femininity may have strategic implications. The stereotypical manager in masculine societies is "assertive, decisive, and 'aggressive' (only in masculine societies does this word carry a positive connotation)," whereas the stylized manager in feminine societies is "less visible, intuitive rather than decisive, and accustomed to seeking consensus."[35] At the economy level, masculine countries (such as Japan) may

long-term orientation

A perspective that emphasizes perseverance and savings for future betterment.

have a relative advantage in mass manufacturing, making products efficiently, well, and fast. Feminine countries (such as Denmark) may have a relative advantage in small-scale customized manufacturing.[36]

Uncertainty avoidance also has a bearing on strategic behavior. Managers in low uncertainty avoidance countries (such as Great Britain) rely more on experience and training, whereas managers in high uncertainty avoidance countries (such as China) rely more on rules and procedures.

In addition, cultures with a long-term orientation are likely to nurture firms with long horizons in strategic planning. Strategy in Action 1.1 discusses Matsushita's 250-year plan. While this is certainly an extreme case, Japanese and Korean firms in general are known to be relatively more willing to forego short-term profits and focus more on market share, which, in the long term, may translate into financial gains.[37] In comparison, Western firms focus on relatively short-term profits.[38]

Overall, there is strong evidence pointing out the strategic importance of culture.[39] Sensitivity to cultural differences can not only help strategists better understand what is going on in other parts of the world, but can also avoid strategic blunders (see Table 4.5 for examples). In addition, while "what is different" cross-culturally can be interesting, it can also be unethical and illegal—all depending on the institutional frameworks in which firms are embedded. Thus, it is imperative that current and would-be strategists be aware of the importance of business ethics, as introduced next.

TABLE 4.5   Some Cross-Cultural Blunders

- Electrolux, a major European home appliance maker, advertised its powerful vacuum machines in the United States using the slogan "Nothing sucks like an Electrolux!"

- In Mexico, a US firm, Perdue Chicken, translated its slogan, "It takes a tough man to make a tender chicken," into Spanish. The translation read: "It takes a hard man to make a chicken aroused."

- A Spanish company sent a team of expatriates to Saudi Arabia that included a number of young intelligent women dressed in the height of current style. Upon arrival, the Saudi police took a look at their miniskirts and immediately sent the entire team back on the next flight to Spain. The expatriate team and the company belatedly learned that despite the heat, women in Saudi Arabia never show their bare legs.

- A Japanese subsidiary CEO in New York, at a staff meeting consisting of all American employees, informed everyone of the firm's grave financial losses and passed on a request from headquarters in Japan that everyone redouble efforts. The staff immediately redoubled their efforts—by sending their resumes out to other employers.

- In Malaysia, an American expatriate was introduced to an important potential client he thought was named "Roger." He proceeded to call this person "Rog." Unfortunately, this person was a "Rajah," which is an important title of nobility in high power distance Malaysia. Upset, the Rajah walked away from the deal.

- In the United States, some Brazilian and Japanese expatriates treated American secretaries as personal servants, insisting that they serve coffee. Shortly after arrival, a British expatriate angered minority employees by firing several black middle managers (including the head of the firm's affirmative action program). They were all sued by the offended employees.

Sources: Based on text in (1) P. Dowling & D. Welch, 2005, *International Human Resource Management,* 4th ed., Cincinnati: South-Western Cengage Learning; (2) M. Gannon, 2008, *Paradoxes of Culture and Globalization,* Thousand Oaks, CA: Sage; (3) D. Ricks, 1999, *Blunders in International Business,* 3rd. ed., Oxford, UK: Blackwell.

The Strategic Role of Ethics

The Definition and Impact of Ethics

Ethics refers to the norms, principles, and standards of conduct governing individual and firm behavior.[40] Ethics is not only an important part of *informal* institutions, but is also deeply reflected in *formal* laws and regulations. Recent corporate scandals (such as Enron) have pushed ethics to the forefront of global strategy discussions, with numerous firms introducing a **code of conduct**—a set of guidelines for making ethical decisions.[41] There is a debate on what motivates firms to become ethical.

- A *negative* view suggests that some firms may simply jump onto the ethics "bandwagon" under social pressures to appear more legitimate without necessarily becoming more ethical.

- A *positive* view maintains that some (although not all) firms may be self-motivated to "do it right" regardless of social pressures.[42]

- An *instrumental* view believes that good ethics may simply represent a useful instrument to help make good profits.[43]

All sides of the debate, however, agree that it is increasingly clear that ethics can make or break a firm. Firms with an ethical, trustworthy reputation will not only earn kudos, but may gain significant competitive advantage by attracting more investors, customers, and employees. Perhaps the best way to appreciate the strategic value of ethics is to examine what happens after some crisis. As a "reservoir of goodwill," the value of an ethical reputation is *magnified* during crisis. One study finds that all US firms engulfed in crises (such as the tampering of Johnson & Johnson's Tylenol and the *Exxon Valdez* oil spill) took an average hit of 8% of their market value in the first week. However, after ten weeks, the stock of firms with ethical reputations actually *rose* 5%, whereas those without such reputations dropped 15%.[44] Paradoxically, catastrophes may allow more ethical firms to shine. The upshot seems to be that ethics pays (see Figure 4.5).

Managing Ethics Overseas

Managing ethics overseas is challenging, because what is ethical in one country may be unethical elsewhere.[45] When dealing with underperforming employees who are the primary breadwinners of their families, Korean and American managers are likely to view that keeping them is ethical and unethical, respectively.[46] Facing such differences, how can managers prepare themselves?

Two schools of thought exist.[47] First, **ethical relativism** refers to an extension of the cliché, "When in Rome, do as the Romans do." If women in Muslim countries are discriminated against, so what? Likewise, if industry rivals in China can fix prices, who cares? Isn't that what "Romans" do in "Rome"? Second, **ethical imperialism** refers to the absolute belief that "There is only one set of Ethics (with the big E), and we have it." Americans are especially renowned for believing that their ethical values should be applied universally.[48] For example, since sexual discrimination and price fixing are wrong in the United States, they must be wrong everywhere else. In practice, however, neither of these schools of thought is realistic. At the extreme,

---

ethics

The norms, principles, and standards of conduct governing individual and firm behavior.

code of conduct (code of ethics)

Written policies and standards for corporate conduct and ethics.

ethical relativism

The relative thinking that ethical standards vary significantly around the world and that there are no universally agreed upon ethical and unethical behaviors.

ethical imperialism

The imperialistic thinking that one's own ethical standards should be applied universally around the world.

FIGURE 4.5   Integrity Can Command a Premium

"Jenny, can we charge the client extra because of our reputation for integrity?"

Source: Business Review, 2006, June (volume 84 number 6): 94. © 2006 by Nick Hobart.

ethical relativism would have to accept any local practice, whereas ethical imperialism may cause resentment and backlash among locals.

Three "middle-of-the-road" guiding principles have been proposed by Thomas Donaldson, a business ethicist (Table 4.6). First, respect for human dignity and basic rights (such as those concerning health, safety, and the needs for education instead of working at a young age) should determine the absolute minimal ethical thresholds for *all* operations around the world.

Second, respect for local traditions suggests cultural sensitivity. If gifts are banned, foreign firms can forget about doing business in China and Japan. While hiring employees' children and relatives instead of more qualified applicants is illegal according to US equal opportunity laws, Indian companies routinely practice such nepotism, which would strengthen employee loyalty. What should US companies setting up subsidiaries in India do? Donaldson advises that such nepotism is not necessarily wrong—at least in India.

TABLE 4.6   Managing Ethics Overseas: Three "Middle-of-the-Road" Approaches

- Respect for human dignity and basic rights
- Respect for local traditions
- Respect for institutional context

Sources: Based on text in (1) T. Donaldson, 1996, Values in tension: Ethics away from home, *Harvard Business Review*, September-October: 4–11; (2) J. Weiss, 2006, *Business Ethics*, 4th ed., Cincinnati: South-Western Cengage Learning.

Finally, respect for institutional context calls for a careful understanding of local institutions. Codes of conduct banning bribery are not very useful unless accompanied by guidelines for the scale of appropriate gift giving/receiving. Citigroup allows employees to accept noncash gifts whose nominal value is less than $100. *The Economist* lets its journalists accept any noncash gift that can be consumed in a single day—thus, a bottle of wine is acceptable but a *case* of wine is not. Overall, these three principles, although far from perfect, can help managers make decisions about which they and their firms may feel relatively comfortable.[49]

Ethics and Corruption

Ethics helps to combat **corruption,** often defined as the abuse of public power for private benefits usually in the form of bribery (in cash or in kind).[50] Corruption distorts the basis for competition that should be based on products and services, thus causing misallocation of resources and slowing economic development.[51] Some evidence reveals that corruption discourages foreign direct investment (FDI).[52] If the level of corruption in Singapore (very low) increases to the level in Mexico (in the middle range), it reportedly would have the same negative effect on FDI inflows as raising the tax rate by 50%.[53]

However, there are exceptions. China is an obvious case, where corruption is often reported. Another exception seems to be Indonesia, whose former president Suharto was known as "Mr. Ten Percent," which refers to the well-known (and transparent!) amount of bribes foreign firms were expected to pay him or members of his family. Why are these two countries popular FDI destinations? For two reasons. First, the vast potential of these two economies may outweigh the drawbacks of corruption. Second, overseas Chinese (mainly from Hong Kong and Taiwan) and Japanese firms are leading investors in mainland China and Indonesia, respectively. While Hong Kong, Taiwan, and Japan may be relatively "cleaner," they are not among the "cleanest" countries. It is possible that "acquiring skills in managing corruption [at home] helps develop a certain competitive advantage [in managing corruption overseas]."[54]

If that is indeed the case, it is not surprising that many US firms complained that they were unfairly restricted by the Foreign Corrupt Practices Act (FCPA), a law enacted in 1977 that bans bribery to foreign officials. They also pointed out that overseas bribery expenses were often tax-deductible (!) in many EU countries such as Austria, France, Germany, and the Netherlands—at least until the late 1990s. However, even with the FCPA, there is no evidence that US firms are inherently more ethical than others. The FCPA itself was triggered by investigations in the 1970s of many corrupt US firms. Even the FCPA makes exceptions for small "grease" payments to get goods through customs abroad. Most alarmingly, a recent World Bank study reports that despite over two decades of FCPA enforcement, US firms actually "exhibit systematically *higher* levels of corruption" than other OECD firms (original italics).[55]

Overall, the FCPA can be regarded as an institutional weapon in the global fight against corruption. Recall that every institution has three supportive pillars: regulatory, normative, and cognitive (Table 4.2). Despite the FCPA's formal *regulatory* "teeth," for a long time, there was neither a *normative* pillar nor a *cognitive* pillar. The norms among other OECD firms used to be to pay bribes first and get a tax deduction later (!)—a clear sign of ethical relativism (see Closing Case on Seimens). Only in 1997 did the OECD Convention on Combating Bribery of Foreign Public Officials commit all

corruption

The abuse of public power for private benefit usually in the form of bribery.

30 member countries (essentially all developed economies) to criminalize bribery. It went into force in 1999. A more ambitious campaign is the UN Convention against Corruption, signed by 106 countries in 2003 and activated in 2005. If every country criminalizes bribery and every investor resists corruption, their combined power will eradicate it. However, this will not happen unless FCPA-type legislation is institutionalized *and* enforced in every country (see Closing Case on Siemens).

A Strategic Response Framework for Ethical Challenges

At its core, the institution-based view focuses on how certain strategic choices, under institutional influences, are diffused from a few firms to many.[56] In other words, the attention is on how certain practices (such as from paying bribes to refusing to pay) become *institutionalized*. Such forces of institutionalization are driven by a combination of regulatory, normative, and cognitive pillars. How firms strategically respond to ethical challenges, thus, leads to a strategic response framework. It features four strategic choices: (1) reactive, (2) defensive, (3) accommodative, and (4) proactive strategies (Table 4.7).

A reactive strategy is passive. Even when problems arise, firms do not feel compelled to act, and denying is usually the first line of defense. The need to take necessary action is neither internalized through cognitive beliefs, nor becoming any norm in practice. That leaves only formal regulatory pressures to compel firms to act. For example, Ford Motor Company marketed the Pinto car in the early 1970s, knowing that its gas tank had a fatal design flaw that could make the car susceptible to exploding in rear-end collisions. Citing high costs, Ford decided not to add an $11-per-car improvement. Sure enough, accidents happened and people were killed and burned in Pintos. Still, for several years Ford refused to recall the Pinto, and more lives were lost. Only in 1978, under intense formal pressures from the government and court cases and informal pressures from the media and consumer groups, did Ford belatedly recall all 1.5 million Pintos.[57]

A defensive strategy focuses on regulatory compliance. In the absence of regulatory pressures, firms often fight informal pressures coming from the media and activists. In the early 1990s, Nike was charged for running "sweatshops," while these incidents

TABLE 4.7   Strategic Responses to Ethical Challenges

Strategic Responses	Strategic Behaviors	Examples in the Text
Reactive	Deny responsibility; do less than required	Ford Pinto fire (the 1970s)
Defensive	Admit responsibility but fight it; do the least that is required	Nike (the 1990s)
Accommodative	Accept responsibility; do all that is required	Ford Explorer rollovers (the 2000s)
Proactive	Anticipate responsibility; do more than is required	BMW (the 1990s)

took place in its contractors' factories in Indonesia and Vietnam. Although Nike did not own these factories, its initial statement, "We don't make shoes," failed to convey any ethical responsibility. Only when several senators began to suggest legislative solutions did Nike become more serious.

An accommodative strategy features emerging organizational norms to accept responsibility and a set of increasingly internalized cognitive beliefs and values toward making certain changes. These normative and cognitive values may be shared by a number of firms, thus leading to new industry norms. In other words, it becomes legitimate to accept a higher level of ethical and moral responsibility beyond what is minimally required legally. In this fashion, Nike and the entire sportswear industry became more accommodative toward the late 1990s.

In another example, in 2000, when Ford Explorer vehicles equipped with Firestone tires had a large number of fatal rollover accidents, Ford evidently took the painful lesson from its Pinto fire fiasco in the 1970s. It aggressively initiated a speedy recall, launched a media campaign featuring its CEO, and discontinued the 100-year-old relationship with Firestone. While critics argue that Ford's accommodative strategy was to place blame squarely on Firestone, the institution-based view (especially Proposition 1) suggests that such highly rational actions are to be expected. Even if Ford's public relations campaign was only "window dressing," publicizing a set of ethical criteria against which it can be judged opens doors for more scrutiny by concerned stakeholders. It probably is fair to say that Ford became a better corporate citizen in 2000 than what it was in 1975.

Finally, proactive firms anticipate institutional changes and do more than is required. In 1990, BMW anticipated its emerging responsibility associated with the German government's proposed "take-back" policy, requiring automakers to design cars whose components can be taken back by the same manufacturers for recycling. BMW not only designed easier-to-disassemble cars, but also signed up the few high-quality dismantler firms as part of an exclusive recycling infrastructure. Further, BMW actively participated in public discussions and succeeded in establishing its approach as the German national standard for automobile disassembly. Other automakers were thus required to follow BMW's lead. However, they had to fight over smaller lower-quality dismantlers or develop in-house dismantling infrastructure from scratch.[58] Through such a proactive strategy, BMW has facilitated the emergence of new environmentally friendly norms in both car design and recycling. In brief, proactive firms go beyond the current regulatory requirements to do the "right thing."[59]

Overall, these four strategic responses are not mutually exclusive. As shown by the Nike example, one firm may adopt different strategic responses as the ethical challenges it faces progress. While there is probably a certain element of "window dressing," the fact that proactive firms are going beyond the current regulatory requirements is indicative of the normative and cognitive beliefs held by many managers on the importance of doing the "right thing."

Debates and Extensions

Relative to the industry- and resource-based views, the institution-based view is the newest leading perspective on strategy. Not surprisingly, some significant debates emerge, including (1) opportunism versus individualism/collectivism, (2) cultural distance versus institutional distance, and (3) "bad apples" versus "bad barrels."

Opportunism versus Individualism/Collectivism[60]

Opportunism is a major source of uncertainty, and transaction cost theorists maintain that institutions emerge to combat opportunism. However, critics argue that emphasizing opportunism as "human nature" may backfire in practice.[61] This is because if a firm assumes that employees will steal and thus places surveillance cameras everywhere, then employees who otherwise would not steal may feel alienated enough to do exactly that. If firm A insists on specifying minute details in an alliance contract in order to prevent firm B from behaving opportunistically *in the future*, A is likely to be regarded by B as being not trustworthy and being opportunistic *now*. This is especially the case if B is from a collectivist society.[62] Thus, attempts to combat opportunism may beget opportunism.

Transaction cost theorists acknowledge that opportunists are a minority in any population. However, theorists contend that because of the difficulty to identify such a minority of opportunists *before* they cause any damage, it is imperative to place safeguards that, unfortunately, treat everybody as a potential opportunist. For example, thanks to the work of only 19 terrorists, millions of air travelers around the world since September 11, 2001, now have to go through heightened security. Everybody hates it, but nobody argues that it is unnecessary. This debate, therefore, seems deadlocked.

One cultural dimension, individualism/collectivism, may hold the key to an improved understanding of opportunism. A common stereotype is that players from collectivist societies (such as China) are more collaborative and trustworthy, and that those from individualist societies (such as America) are more competitive and opportunistic.[63] However, this superficial understanding is *not* necessarily the case. Collectivists are more collaborative *only* when dealing with **in-group** members—individuals and firms regarded as a part of their own collective. The flip side is that collectivists discriminate more harshly against **out-group** members—individuals and firms not regarded as a part of "us." On the other hand, individualists, who believe that every person (firm) is on his/her (its) own, make less distinction between in-group and out-group. Therefore, while individualists may indeed be more opportunistic than collectivists when dealing with in-group members (this fits the stereotype), collectivists may be *more* opportunistic when dealing with out-group members. Thus, on balance, the average Chinese is not inherently more trustworthy than the average American. The Chinese motto regarding out-group members is: "Watch out for strangers. They will screw you!"

This helps explain why the United States, the leading individualist country, is among societies with a higher level of spontaneous trust, whereas there is greater interpersonal and interfirm *distrust* in the large society in China than in the United States.[64] This also explains why it is important to establish *guanxi* for individuals and firms in China; otherwise, life can be very challenging in a sea of strangers.

While this insight is not likely to help improve airport security screening, it can help managers and firms better deal with each other. Only through repeated social interactions can collectivists assess whether to accept newcomers as in-group members. If foreigners who, by definition, are from an out-group refuse to show any interest in joining the in-group, then it is fair to take advantage of them. For example, don't ever refuse the friendly offer of a cup of coffee from a Saudi business man, which is considered an affront. Most of us do not realize that to "feel free to say no when offered food or drink" reflects the cultural underpinning of individualism, and folks in collectivist societies do

in-group

Individuals and firms regarded as part of "us."

out-group

Individuals and firms not regarded as part of "us."

not view this as an option (unless one wants to offend the host). This misunderstanding, in part, explains why many cross-culturally naïve Western managers and firms often cry out loud for being taken advantage of in collectivist societies—they are simply being treated as "deserving" out-group members.

Cultural Distance versus Institutional Distance

Given cross-cultural differences and conflicts, it is not surprising that, for instance, Japanese–US joint ventures are shorter lived than Japanese–Japanese joint ventures.[65] Basically, when disputes and misunderstandings arise, it is difficult to ascertain whether the other side is deliberately being opportunistic or is simply being (culturally) different. Firms in general may prefer to do business with culturally close countries, because of the shorter **cultural distance.**[66]

However, critics make three arguments.[67] First, they point out a number of findings inconsistent with the cultural distance hypothesis.[68] In China, one study reports that joint ventures between local and Western firms outperform those between local and Asian firms.[69] In Italy, one study finds a positive association between cultural distance and cross-border acquisition performance.[70]

Second, critics contend that given the complexity of foreign entry decisions, cultural distance, while important, is but one of many factors to consider. For instance, relative to national culture, organizational (firm-specific) culture may be equally important in affecting alliance performance.[71]

Finally, some argue that perhaps cultural distance can be complemented (but not replaced) by the **institutional distance** concept, which is "the extent of similarity or dissimilarity between the regulatory, normative, and cognitive institutions of two countries."[72] For example, the cultural distance between Canada and China is virtually as huge as the cultural distance between Canada and Hong Kong (where 98% of the population is ethnic Chinese). However, the institutional distance between Canada and Hong Kong is much *shorter:* Both use common law, speak English as an official language, and share a common heritage of being former British colonies. Therefore, before entering mainland China, Canadian firms may have a preference to enter Hong Kong first.

This emerging idea is gathering some momentum, as scholars start to look beyond the cultural dimensions and investigate the intricacies of other institutional differences around the world.[73] For instance, if favorite sports can be regarded as "national institutions," the world can be roughly divided into three regions: baseball, cricket, and soccer. This logic suggests that in countries where baseball is the national favorite sport, such as Japan and Mexico (except Cuba), US firms are likely to lead in the multinational sector—presumably because of the shorter institutional distance between these countries crazy about baseball. In countries where cricket captures people's hearts, like Australia and India, British multinationals may take the lead. Finally, in countries where people are crazy about soccer, continental European MNEs are likely to beat their global rivals.[74]

Bad Apples versus Bad Barrels

This debate focuses on the root cause of unethical business behavior. One argument suggests that people may have ethical or unethical predispositions *before* joining firms.

cultural distance

The difference between two cultures along some identifiable dimensions.

institutional distance

The extent of similarity or dissimilarity between the regulatory, normative, and cognitive institutions of two countries.

Another side of the debate argues that while there are indeed some opportunistic "bad apples," many times people commit unethical behavior not because they are "bad apples" but because they are spoiled by "bad barrels." Some firms not only condone but may even expect unethical behavior. For example, at the now-defunct Arthur Andersen, the norms were to "make the numbers" no matter what. Similarly, Siemens has recently been criticized for breeding a "bad barrel" (see Closing Case).

The debate on "bad apples" versus "bad barrels" is an extension of the broader debate on "nature versus nurture." Are we who we are because of our genes (nature) or our environments (nurture)? Most studies report that human behavior is the result of both nature *and* nurture. Although individuals and firms (staffed by people) do have some ethical or unethical predispositions that influence their behavior, the institutional environment (such as organizational norms and national institutions) can also have a profound impact. In a nutshell, even "good apples" may turn bad in "bad barrels."

The Savvy Strategist

Strategy is about choices. When seeking to understand how these choices are made, practitioners and scholars usually "round up the usual suspects," namely, industry structures and firm-specific resources and capabilities. While these views are very insightful, they usually do not pay adequate attention to the underlying *context*. A contribution of the institution-based view is to emphasize the importance of institutions, cultures, and ethics as the bedrock propelling or constraining strategic choices. Overall, if strategy is about the "big picture," then the institution-based view reminds current and would-be strategists not to forget the "bigger picture."

By focusing on institutions, cultures, and ethics, the savvy strategist draws at least three important implications for action (Table 4.8). First, when entering a new country, do your homework by having a thorough understanding of the formal and informal institutions governing firm behavior. While you don't necessarily have to do "as the Romans do" when in "Rome," you need to understand *why* Romans do things in a certain way. In countries that emphasize informal relational exchanges, insisting on formalizing the contract right away may backfire.

Second, strengthen cross-cultural intelligence by building awareness, expanding knowledge, and leveraging skills.[75] In cross-cultural encounters, while you may not share (or may disagree) with the values held by others, you will need to at least obtain a roadmap of the informal institutions governing their behavior. Of course, culture is not everything. It is advisable not to read too much into culture, which is one of many variables affecting global strategy. But it is imprudent to ignore culture.

TABLE 4.8   Strategic Implications for Action

- When entering a new country, do your homework by having a thorough understanding of the formal and informal institutions governing firm behavior.
- Strengthen cross-cultural intelligence by building awareness, expanding knowledge, and leveraging skills.
- Integrate ethical decision making as part of the core strategy processes of the firm—faking it does not last very long.

Third and finally, integrate ethical decision making as part of the core strategy processes of the firm—faking it does not last very long. You need to be aware of the prevailing norms. The norms around the globe in the 2000s are more culturally sensitive and ethically demanding than, say, those in the 1970s. This is not to suggest that every local norm needs to be followed. However, failing to understand and adapt to the changing norms by "sticking one's neck out" in an insensitive and unethical way may lead to unsatisfactory or disastrous results, as Siemens found out recently (see Closing Case). The best managers expect norms to shift over time by constantly deciphering the changes in the informal "rules of the game" and by taking advantage of new opportunities—how BMW managers proactively shaped the automobile recycling norms serves as a case in point.

We conclude this chapter by revisiting the four fundamental questions. First, why do firms differ? The institution-based view points out the institutional frameworks that shape firm differences. Second, how do firms behave? The answer also boils down to institutional differences. Third, what determines the scope of the firm? Chapter 9 will have more details on how institutions have shaped the evolution of the scope of the firm. Finally, what determines the success and failure of firms around the globe? The institution-based view argues that firm performance is, at least in part, determined by the institutional frameworks governing strategic choices.

CHAPTER SUMMARY

1. *Explain the concept of institutions*

   - Commonly known as "the rules of the game," institutions have formal and informal components, each with different supportive pillars (the regulatory, normative, and cognitive pillars).

2. *Understand the two primary ways of exchange transactions that reduce uncertainty*

   - Institutions reduce uncertainty in two primary ways: (1) informal relationship-based personalized exchanges (known as relational contracting), and (2) formal rule-based impersonal exchanges with third-party enforcement (known as arm's-length transaction).

3. *Articulate the two propositions underpinning an institution-based view of strategy*

   - Proposition 1: Managers and firms rationally pursue their interests and make strategic choices within formal and informal institutional constraints.

   - Proposition 2: In situations where formal constraints fail, informal constraints will play a *larger* role.

4. *Appreciate the strategic role of cultures*

   - According to Hofstede, national culture has five dimensions: (1) power distance, (2) individualism/collectivism, (3) masculinity/femininity, (4) uncertainty avoidance, and (5) long-term orientation. Each has some significant bearing on strategic choices.

5. *Identify the strategic role of ethics culminating in a strategic response framework*

- When managing overseas, two schools of thought are (1) ethical relativism and (2) ethical imperialism.

- Three "middle-of-the-road" principles focus on respect for (1) human dignity and basic rights, (2) local traditions, and (3) institutional context.

- When confronting ethical challenges, a strategic framework suggests four strategic choices: (1) reactive, (2) defensive, (3) accommodative, and (4) proactive strategies.

6. *Participate in three leading debates on institutions, cultures, and ethics*

- The key debates focus on (1) opportunism versus individualism/collectivism, (2) cultural distance versus institutional distance, and (3) "bad apples" versus "bad barrels."

7. *Draw strategic implications for action*

- When entering a new country, do your homework by having a thorough understanding of the formal and informal institutions governing firm behavior.

- Strengthen cross-cultural intelligence.

- Integrate ethical decision making as part of the core strategy processes of the firm.

Key Terms

arm's-length transactions	firm strategy, structure, and rivalry	institution-based view
code of conduct (code of ethics)	formal institutions	long-term orientation
cognitive pillar	formal, rule-based, impersonal exchange	masculinity
collectivism		norm
corruption	individualism	normative pillar
cultural distance	informal institutions	out-group
culture	informal, relationship-based, personalized exchange	opportunism
domestic demand		power distance
ethical imperialism	in-group	regulatory pillar
ethical relativism	institution	related and supporting industries
ethics	institutional distance	relational contracting
factor endowments	institutional framework	transaction costs
femininity	institutional transitions	uncertainty avoidance

CRITICAL DISCUSSION QUESTIONS

1. If you were the CEO of a leading domestic company in Kenya, what would be your responses during and after the violent turmoil in 2007–2008 (see Strategy in Action 4.1)? If you were the CEO of a foreign company operating in Kenya, what would be your course of action?

2. Some argue that *guanxi* (relationships and connections) is a unique Chinese-only phenomenon embedded in the Chinese culture. As evidence, they point out that this word, *guanxi*, has now entered the English language and is often used in main-stream media (such as the *Wall Street Journal*) without explanations provided in brackets when describing relationship-based strategies in China. Others disagree, arguing that every culture has a word or two describing what the Chinese call *guanxi,* such as *blat* in Russia, *guan he* in Vietnam, and "old boys' network" in the English-speaking world. They suggest that the intensive use of *guanxi* in China (and elsewhere) is a reflection of the lack of formal institutional frameworks. Which side of the debate would you join? Why?

3. **ON ETHICS:** Assume you work for a New Zealand company exporting a container of kiwis to Haiti. The customs official informs you that there is a delay in clearing your container through customs and it may last a month. However, if you are willing to pay an "expediting fee" of US$200, he will try to make it happen in one day. What are you going to do?

CLOSING CASE

Ethical Challenge

Siemens in a Sea of Scandals

Founded in 1847, Siemens, headquartered in Munich and Berlin, is an engineering conglomerate that produces power generation equipment, transportation systems, medical devices, and numerous other industrial products. Approximately 80% of sales, 70% of factories, and 66% of its 475,000 work force are outside Germany. In 2006, Siemens had revenues of €87 billion from 190 countries.

Recently, Siemens found itself engulfed in a sea of scandals around the globe. In November 2007, Siemens, whose shares are listed on the New York Stock Exchange, disclosed in its SEC Form 6-K to the US Securities and Exchange Commission (SEC): Authorities around the world were conducting investigations of Siemens and certain of its current and former employees "regarding allegations of public corruption, including criminal breaches of fiduciary duty including embezzlement, as well as bribery, money laundering,

and tax evasion, among others." According to the report, authorities from the following countries/regions were involved:

- Brazil
- China
- Czech Republic
- European Union/ European Commission
- Germany
- Greece
- Hungary
- Indonesia
- Italy
- Japan
- Mexico
- New Zealand
- Norway
- Poland
- Slovakia
- South Africa
- Switzerland
- Turkey
- United States

In the same report, Siemens disclosed that its internal investigation uncovered $1.9 billion in questionable payments made to outsiders by the company from 2000 to 2006. In its own words:

> These payments raise concerns in particular under the Foreign Corrupt Practices Act (FCPA) of the United States, anti-corruption legislation in Germany, and similar legislation in other countries. The payments identified were recorded as deductible business expenses in prior periods [2000–06] in determining income tax provisions . . . the Company's investigation determined that certain of these payments were non-deductible under tax regulations of Germany and other jurisdictions.

Of these numerous cases, German prosecutors already uncovered evidence that Siemens used bribes to land contracts around the globe, and extracted $290 million in fines. While authorities in other countries were probing deeper, Siemens was bracing for probably the nastiest bite from the US Department of Justice and the SEC, which were interested in making an example of it. Washington wants to hold foreign firms to the same standards as their US rivals. Armed with the FCPA, US authorities often deliberately

punished companies caught in wrongdoing harder than foreign governments. For example, when the Norwegian government imposed a $3 million fine on energy producer Statoil for paying bribes in Iran, US authorities hit it with an additional $18 million fine. As of this writing (February 2008), no concrete fines were announced by the US authorities, but experts suggested that the fines might be three times the size of the illegal payments identified by Siemens.

Siemens cooperated with the investigations. In response to the scandals, the company undertook a number of measures: Its Supervisory Board established a Compliance Committee, its Managing Board engaged an external attorney to provide a protected communication channel for employees and third parties, the company appointed a Chief Compliance Officer, marketed a Compliance hotline to employees, and adopted a Global Amnesty Program for employees who voluntarily provided useful information regarding their wrongdoing. Talk is cheap, according to critics. Many critics are suspicious of whether these measures would transform such a "bad barrel."

Sources: Based on (1) *Business Week,* 2007, Siemens braces for a slap from Uncle Sam, November 6: 78–79; (2) FCPA Blog, 2008, How much will Siemens pay? January 22 (fcpablog.bogspot.com); (3) Siemens AG, 2007, Form 6-K Report of Foreign Private Issuer (Legal Proceedings), November 8, New York: SEC.

Case Discussion Questions

1. What are the costs and benefits of bribery?

2. Is the FCPA unnecessarily harsh or do its provisions dispense the appropriate level of punishment?

3. In your view, how heavy should Siemens be fined? In addition to fines, what else can be done?

4. Are some of Siemens employees "bad apples" or is Siemens a "bad barrel"?

Notes

Journal acronyms *AME–Academy of Management Executive;* **AMJ–***Academy of Management Journal;* **AMLE–** *Academy of Management Learning and Education;* **AMR–** *Academy of Management Review;* **APJM–***Asia Pacific Journal of Management;* **ASQ–***Administrative Science Quarterly;* **BW–***Business Week;* **CMR–***California Management Review;* **HBR–***Harvard Business Review;* **IJCCM–***International Journal of Cross-Cultural Management;* **JIBS–***Journal of International Business Studies;* **JIM–***Journal of International Management;* **JM–***Journal of Management;* **JMS–***Journal of Management Studies;* **JWB–***Journal of World Business;* **LRP–***Long Range Planning;* **MIR–***Management International Review;* **OSc–** *Organization Science;* **RES–***Review of Economics and Statistics;* **SMJ–***Strategic Management Journal.*

1. D. North, 1990, *Institutions, Institutional Change, and Economic Performance* (p. 3), New York: Norton.

2. W. R. Scott, 1995, *Institutions and Organizations,* Thousand Oaks, CA: Sage.

3. M. Guillen, 2003, Experience, imitation, and the sequence of foreign entry, *JIBS,* 34: 185–198; J. Lu, 2002, Intra- and inter-organizational imitative behavior, *JIBS,* 33: 19–37.

4. M. W. Peng, 2000, *Business Strategies in Transition Economies* (pp. 42–44), Thousand Oaks, CA: Sage.

5. R. Click, 2005, Financial and political risks in US direct foreign investment, *JIBS,* 36: 559–575; S. Elbanna & J. Child, 2007, Influences on strategic decision making, *SMJ,* 28: 431–453; D. Elenkov, 1997, Strategic uncertainty and environmental scanning, *SMJ,* 18: 287–302.

6. O. Williamson, 1985, *The Economic Institutions of Capitalism* (pp. 1–2), New York: Free Press.

7. J. Hagen & S. Choe, 1998, Trust in Japanese interfirm relations, *AMR,* 23: 589–600.

8. M. W. Peng, 2003, Institutional transitions and strategic choices, *AMR,* 28: 275–296. See also S. Li, 1999, The benefits and costs of relation-based governance, Unpublished working paper, Hong Kong: City University of Hong Kong.

9. North, 1990, *Institutions* (p. 34).

10. S. Puffer & D. McCarthy, 2007, Can Russia's state-managed, network capitalism be competitive? *JWB,* 42: 1–13.

11. Peng, 2003, Institutional transitions and strategic choices (p. 275). See also E. George, P. Chattopadhyay, S. Sitkin, & J. Barden, 2006, Cognitive underpinning of institutional persistence and change, *AMR,* 31: 347–365.

12. L. Brouthers, S. Werner, & E. Matulich, 2000, The influence of Triad nations' environments on price-quality product strategies and MNC performance, *JIBS,* 31: 39–62; S. Kotha & A. Nair, 1995, Strategy and environment as determinants of performance, *SMJ,* 16: 497–518; V. Rindova & C. Fombrun, 1999, Constructing competitive advantage, *SMJ,* 20: 691–710.

13. M. Porter, 1990, *Competitive Advantage of Nations,* New York: Free Press.

14. H. Davies & P. Ellis, 2001, Porter's *Competitive Advantage of Nations, JMS,* 37: 1189–1215.

15. M. Wright, I. Filatotchev, R. Hoskisson, & M. W. Peng, 2005, Strategy research in emerging economies, *JMS,* 42: 1–33.

16. N. Biggart & R. Delbridge, 2004, Systems of exchange, *AMR,* 29: 28–49; C. Oliver, 1997, Sustainable competitive advantage, *SMJ,* 18: 679–713.

17. P. Ingram & B. Silverman, 2002, Introduction (p. 20, added italics), in P. Ingram & B. Silverman (eds.), *The New Institutionalism in Strategic Management:* 1–30. Amsterdam: Elsevier. See also M. Kotabe & R. Mudambi, 2003, Institutions and international business, *JIM,* 9: 215–217; A. Parkhe, 2003, Institutional environments, institutional change, and international alliances, *JIM,* 9: 305–216.

18. S. Makino, T. Isobe, & C. Chan, 2004, Does country matter? *SMJ,* 25: 1027–1043; T. Tong, T. Alessandri, J. Reuer, & A. Chintakananda, 2008, How much does country matter? *JIBS* (in press).

19. S. Elbanna & J. Child, 2007, The influence of decision, environmental, and firm characteristics on the rationality of strategic decision-making, *JMS,* 44: 561–590; M. Peteraf & R. Reed, 2007, Managerial discretion and internal alignment under regulatory constraints and change, *SMJ,* 28: 1089–1112.

20. K. Gillespie, 2003, Smuggling and the global firm, *JIM,* 9: 317–333.

21. M. W. Peng, 2001, How entrepreneurs create wealth in transition economies, *AME,* 15 (1): 95–108.

22. M. Lord, 2003, Constituency building as the foundation for corporate political strategy, *AME*, 17: 112–124; R. Schuler, K. Rehbein, & R. Cramer, 2002, Pursuing strategic advantage through political means, *AMJ*, 45: 659–672.

23. *BW*, 2007, Inside the hidden world of earmarks, September 17: 56–59.

24. J. Boddewyn & T. Brewer, 1994, International-business political behavior, *AMR*, 19: 119–143; J. Bonardi, G. Holburn, & R. Bergh, 2006, Nonmarket strategy performance, *AMJ*, 49: 1209–1228.

25. G. Hofstede, 1997, *Cultures and Organizations: Software of the Mind* (p. 5), New York: McGraw-Hill; G. Hofstede, 2007, Asian management in the 21st century, *APJM*, 24: 421–428.

26. P. C. Earley & R. Peterson, 2004, The elusive cultural chameleon, *AMLE*, 3: 100–115.

27. K. Au, 1999, Intra-cultural variation, *JIBS*, 30: 799–813.

28. E. Hall & M. Hall, 1987, *Hidden Differences*, Garden City, New York: Doubleday; S. Ronen & O. Shenkar, 1985, Clustering countries on attitudinal dimensions, *AMR*, 10: 435–454.

29. World Bank, 2004, World Development Indicators (www.worldbank.org).

30. B. Kirkman, K. Lowe, & C. Gibson, 2006, A quarter century of *Culture's Consequences, JIBS*, 37: 285–320; K. Leung, R. Bhagat, N. Buchan, M. Erez, & C. Gibson, 2005, Culture and international business, *JIBS*, 36: 357–378.

31. T. Fang, 2003, A critique of Hofstede's fifth national culture dimension, *IJCCM*, 3: 347–368; R. House, P. Hanges, M. Javidan, P. Dorfman, & V. Gupta, 2004, *Culture, Leadership, and Organizations*, Thousand Oaks, CA: Sage.

32. C. Fey & I. Bjorkman, 2001, The effect of HRM practices on MNC subsidiary performance in Russia, *JIBS*, 32: 59–75; S. Michailova, 2002, When common sense becomes uncommon, *JWB*, 37: 180–187.

33. S. Kotha, R. Dunbar, & A. Bird, 1995, Strategic action generation, *SMJ*, 16: 195–220.

34. T. Begley & W. Tian, 2001, The socio-cultural environment for entrepreneurship, *JIBS*, 32: 537–553.

35. Hofstede, 1997, *Cultures and Organizations* (p. 94).

36. Ibid., (p. 95).

37. R. Peterson, C. Dibrell, & T. Pett, 2002, Long- vs. short-term performance perspectives of Western European, Japanese, and US companies, *JWB*, 37: 245–255; L. Thomas & G. Waring, 1999, Competing capitalism, *SMJ*, 20: 729–748.

38. K. Laverty, 1996, Economic "short-termism," *AMR*, 21: 825–860.

39. A. Bhardwaj, J. Dietz, & P. Beamish, 2007, Host country cultural influences on foreign direct investment, *MIR*, 47: 29–50; J. Hennart & J. Larimo, 1998, The impact of culture on the strategy of MNEs, *JIBS*, 29: 515–538; K. Lee, G. Yang, & J. Graham, 2006, Tension and trust in international business negotiations, *JIBS*, 37: 623–641; S. Makino & K. Neupert, 2000, National culture, transaction costs, and the choice between joint venture and wholly owned subsidiary, *JIBS*, 31: 705–713; J. Salk & M. Brannen, 2000, National culture, networks, and individual influence in a multinational management team, *AMJ*, 43: 191–202.

40. L. Trevino, G. Weaver, & S. Reynolds, 2006, Behavioral ethics in organizations, *JM*, 33: 951–990.

41. R. Durand, H. Rao, & P. Monin, 2007, Code and conduct in French cuisine, *SMJ*, 28: 455–472; J. Stevens, H. K. Steensma, D. Harrison, & P. Cochran, 2005, Symbolic or substantive document?, *SMJ*, 26: 181–195.

42. D. Quinn & T. Jones, 1995, An agent morality view of business policy, *AMR*, 20: 22–42.

43. R. E. Freeman, 1984, *Strategic Management: A Stakeholder Approach*, Boston: Pitnam.

44. C. Fombrun, 2001, Corporate reputations as economic assets, in M. Hitt, R. E. Freeman, & J. Harrison (eds.), *The Blackwell Handbook of Strategic Management* (pp. 289–312), Cambridge, UK: Blackwell.

45. W. Bailey & A. Spicer, 2007, When does national identity matter? *AMJ*, 50: 1462–1480; D. McCarthy & S. Puffer, 2008, Interpreting the ethicality of corporate governance decisions in Russia, *AMR*, 33: 11–31.

46. T. Jackson, 2000, Making ethical judgments, *APJM*, 17: 443–472.

47. This section draws heavily from T. Donaldson, 1996, Values in tension, *HBR*, September–October: 4–11.

48. D. Vogel, 1992, The globalization of business ethics, *CMR*, Fall: 30–49.

49. K. Lee, G. Qian, J. Yu, & Y. Ho, 2005, Trading favors for marketing advantage, *JIM*, 13: 1–35;

A. Spicer, T. Dunfee, & W. Bailey, 2004, Does national context matter in ethical decision making? *AMJ,* 47: 610–620.

50. N. Khatri, E. Tsang, & T. Begley, 2006, Cronyism, *JIBS,* 37: 61–75; K. Martin, J. Cullen, J. Johnson, & K. Parboteeah, 2007, Deciding to bribe, *AMJ,* 50: 1401–1422; P. Rodriguez, K. Uhlenbruck, & L. Eden, 2004, Government corruption and the entry strategies of multinationals, *AMR,* 30: 383–396.

51. C. Robertson & A. Watson, 2004, Corruption and change, *SMJ,* 25: 385–396; J. H. Zhao, S. Kim, & J. Du, 2003, The impact of corruption and transparency on foreign direct investment, *MIR,* 43: 41–62.

52. J. Doh & R. Ramamurti, 2003, Reassessing risk in developing country infrastructure, *LRP,* 36: 337–354; S. Globerman & D. Shapiro, 2003, Governance infrastructure and US foreign direct investment, *JIBS,* 34: 19–39.

53. S. Wei, 2000, How taxing is corruption on international investors? *RES,* 82: 1–11.

54. M. Habib & L. Zurawicki, 2002, Corruption and foreign direct investment (p. 295), *JIBS,* 33: 291–307.

55. J. Hellman, G. Jones, & D. Kaufmann, 2002, Far from home: Do foreign investors import higher standards of governance in transition economies (p. 20), Working paper, Washington: World Bank (www.worldbank.org).

56. M. Lounsbury, 2007, A tale of two cities, *AMJ,* 50: 289–307.

57. L. Trevino & K. Nelson, 2004, *Managing Business Ethics,* 3rd ed. (p. 13), New York: Wiley.

58. S. Hart, 2005, *Capitalism at the Crossroads,* Philadelphia, PA: Wharton School Publishing.

59. I. Guler, M. Guillen, & J. Macpherson, 2002, Global competition, institutions and the diffusion of organizational practices, *ASQ,* 47: 207–232.

60. This section draws heavily from C. Chen, M. W. Peng, & P. Saparito, 2002, Individualism, collectivism, and opportunism, *JM,* 28: 567–583.

61. S. Ghoshal & P. Moran, 1996, Bad for practice, *AMR,* 21: 13–47.

62. R. Bhagat, B. Kedia, P. Herveston, & H. Triandis, 2002, Cultural variations in the cross-border transfer of organizational knowledge, *AMR,* 27: 204–221; P. Doney, J. Cannon, & M. Mullen, 1998, Understanding the influence of national culture on the development of trust, *AMR,* 23: 601–620.

63. J. Cullen, K. P. Parboteeah, & M. Hoegl, 2004, Cross-national differences in managers' willingness to justify ethically suspect behaviors, *AMJ,* 47: 411–421.

64. F. Fukuyama, 1995, *Trust,* New York: Free Press; G. Redding, 1993, *The Spirit of Chinese Capitalism,* NY: Gruyter.

65. J. Hennart & M. Zeng, 2002, Cross-cultural differences and joint venture longevity, *JIBS,* 33: 699–716.

66. B. Kogut & H. Singh, 1988, The effect of national culture on the choice of entry mode, *JIBS,* 19: 411–432; J. West & J. Graham, 2004, A linguistic-based measure of cultural distance and its relationship to managerial values, *MIR,* 44: 239–260.

67. K. Singh, 2007, The limited relevance of culture to strategy, *APJM,* 24: 421–428.

68. J. Evans & F. Mavondo, 2002, Psychic distance and organizational performance, *JIBS,* 33: 515–532; S. O'Grady & H. Lane, 1996, The psychic distance paradox, *JIBS,* 27: 309–333; O. Shenkar, 2001, Cultural distance revisited, *JIBS,* 32: 519–535; L. Tihanyi, D. Griffith, & C. Russell, 2005, The effect of cultural distance on entry mode choice, international diversification, and MNE performance, *JIBS,* 36: 270–283.

69. J. Li, K. Lam, & G. Qian, 2001, Does culture affect behavior and performance of firms? *JIBS,* 32: 115–131.

70. P. Morosini, S. Shane, & H. Singh, 1998, National cultural distance and cross-border acquisition, *JIBS,* 29: 137–158.

71. V. Pothukuchi, F. Damanpour, J. Choi, C. Chen, & S. Park, 2002, National and organizational culture differences and international joint venture performance, *JIBS,* 33: 243–265.

72. D. Xu & O. Shenkar, 2002, Institutional distance and the multinational enterprise (p. 608), *AMR,* 27: 608–618. See also L. Busenitz, C. Gomez, & J. Spencer, 2000, Country institutional profiles, *AMJ,* 43: 994–1003; D. Dow & A. Karunaratna, 2006, Developing a multidimensional instrument to measure psychic distance stimuli, *JIBS,* 37: 578–602; T. Kostova & S. Zaheer, 1999, Organizational legitimacy under conditions of complexity, *AMR,* 24: 64–81; D. Xu, Y. Pan, & P. Beamish, 2004, The effect of regulative and normative

distances on MNE ownership and expatriate strategies, *MIR,* 44: 285–307.

73. K. Brouthers & L. Brouthers, 2001, Explaining the national cultural distance paradox, *JIBS,* 32: 177–189; A. Delios & W. Henisz, 2003, Policy uncertainty and the sequence of entry by Japanese firms, 1980–98, *JIBS,* 34: 227–242.

74. S. Rangan & A. Drummond, 2002, Explaining outcomes in competition among foreign multinationals in a focal host market, *SMJ,* 25: 285–293.

75. J. Johnson, T. Lenartowicz, & S. Apud, 2006, Cross-cultural competence in international business, *JIBS,* 37: 525–543; A. Tsui, S. Nifadkar, & A. Ou, 2007, Cross-national, cross-cultural organizational behavior research, *JM,* 33: 426–478.

The Japanese Bookselling Industry[1]

Charles E. Stevens

Fisher College of Business, The Ohio State University

In the Japanese retail bookselling industry, where discounting is banned by a cartel formed by incumbents, two new entrants, Bookoff and Amazon Japan, have successfully established themselves recently.

The Japanese are voracious readers. With annual sales approaching $10 billion, the Japanese retail bookselling industry is approximately as large as the US bookselling industry on a per-capita basis as of 2008.[2] Despite the fact that the population of Japan is only half that of the United States, Japan has approximately 17,000 retail book stores compared to the 11,000 book stores in the United States.[3] Most of the largest book stores in Japan have been in existence since the World War II era, if not earlier—Maruzen (www.maruzen.co.jp [Japanese] or www.maruzen.co.jp/corp/en [English]), one of the largest booksellers in Japan, has been in business since 1869.

However, the competitive environment in the Japanese retail bookselling industry differs in many respects from its US counterpart. First, whereas the United States is dominated by a small number of large retail chains (principally Amazon, Barnes & Noble, and Borders), Japan is characterized by a large number of relatively small stores. For example, while Maruzen's 2006–2007 sales of $850 million are impressive by Japanese standards, they pale in comparison to the sales figures of Amazon ($14.84 billion), Barnes & Noble ($5.44 billion), and Borders ($4.24 billion) in the same period (see Exhibit 1).[4] Likewise, Maruzen's 30 stores

and 1,000 employees are greatly overshadowed by Barnes & Noble's 800 stores and 51,000 employees. Additionally, while the American book market has shown steady growth in the past decade, the Japanese market has shrunk—industry sales have *dropped* by 20% over the last decade.[5] As a result, several thousand booksellers, mostly small "mom and pop" operations, have been forced out of business.

---

[1] This case was written by Charles E. Stevens (Fisher College of Business, The Ohio State University). © Charles E. Stevens. Reprinted with permission. Yen has been converted at a rate of US$1 = 117 Yen (based on the average exchange rate from 2006-2007).

[2] The Japan Times: "Why have Japan's bookworms turned?" (January 6, 2008).

[3] JETRO: *Nihon no Shuppan Sangyo no Dōkō 2006,* US Census.

[4] Yahoo! Finance, Yahoo! Japan Finance.

[5] JETRO: *Nihon no Shuppan Sangyo no Dōkō 2006.*

EXHIBIT 1   Net Sales of American and Japanese Bookstores ($ millions)

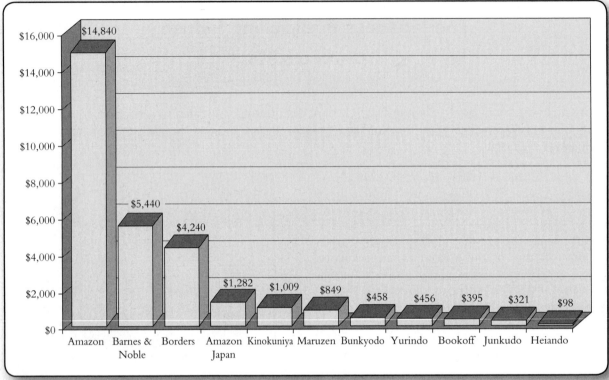

Sources: Yahoo! Finance, Yahoo! Japan Finance, Company web pages and annual reports. Sales figures are for 2006–2007.

This case introduces the competitive forces shaping the Japanese retail bookselling industry, with an emphasis on interfirm rivalry and two new entrants, Bookoff (www.bookoff.co.jp) and Amazon Japan (www.amazon.co.jp), both of which successfully created unique strategies to succeed in an otherwise stagnant industry.

Industry Dynamics

Suppliers

Book retailers usually buy their books from wholesalers and sometimes directly from publishers. Competition in the area of book distribution is very low. Nippon Shuppan Hanbai (www.nippan.co.jp) and Tohan (www.tohan.jp), both founded immediately after World War II, traditionally control between 70% and 90% of the book wholesale market.[6] Also, there is a system called the *Itaku Hanbai Seido* ("Consignment Sale System") in place that allows retailers and wholesalers to return unsold books to the publisher free of charge, reducing risk and inventory levels for wholesalers and especially retailers. Because retailers can return unsold books free of charge, they carry book inventories larger than what would normally be considered efficient. As shown in Exhibit 2, many publications end up being returned (the return rate for books is nearly 40%).[7] Consequently, publishers and wholesalers prefer to supply larger retailers first—the large sales volumes

[6] Hoover's Online: http://hoovers.com/.

[7] JETRO: *Nihon no Shuppan Sangyo no Dōkō 2006.*

EXHIBIT 2   Percentage of Published Materials Returned to Publishers

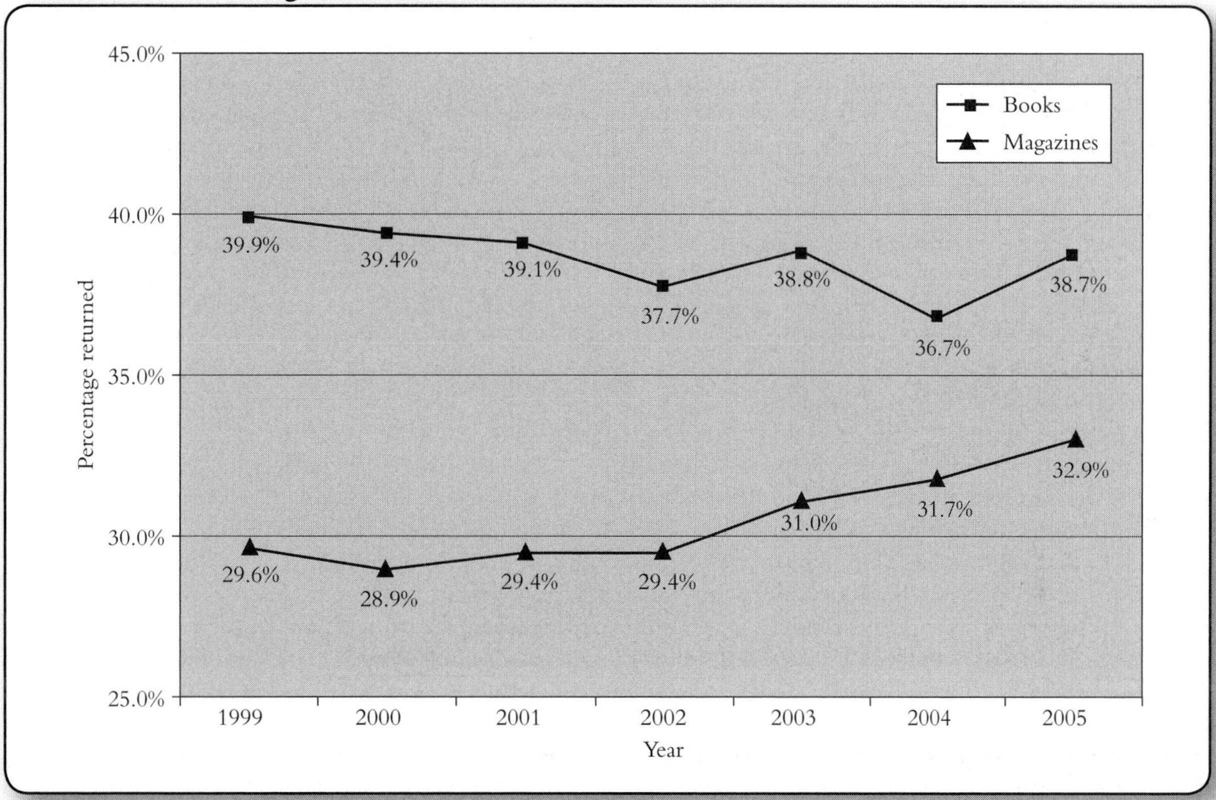

Source: JETRO: *Nihon no Shuppan Sangyo no Dōkō 2006.*

at the larger stores result in fewer books returned to publishers, leading to higher profits for the large retailers (because they have preferential access to the newest and most popular books) and publishers (because they do not have to worry as much about returned books by supplying larger retailers first) alike.

Although the publishers' policy of supplying large retailers first has helped the bottom lines of the large retailers and the publishers, small retailers are increasingly going out of business because they are unable to stock their stores with the newest bestsellers.[8] Customers, in turn, must go to larger retailers since customers are unable to find the books they want at their neighborhood book stores. Thus, small retailers are confronted with the following paradox: Publishers will not supply them with the most lucrative bestsellers because of the small retailers' declining sales and the risk of returned books, but the small retailers' declining sales are due in large part to the fact that publishers will not supply them with the most lucrative bestsellers (!).

Buyers

The rise of the Internet has had a profound effect on the bookselling industry in Japan. While the Japanese used to lag behind other developed economies in terms of Internet penetration several years ago, they have now closed the gap. In 2002, 40% of Japanese were Internet users compared to 60% of Americans. In 2007, the figures were 68% and 70%, respectively, for

---

[8] The Japan Times: "Why have Japan's bookworms turned?" (January 6, 2008).

Japanese and Americans—a virtual tie.[9] The Internet as a substitute form of entertainment has been cited as a cause for the overall drop in book sales in Japan, but others note that despite similar Internet use in the United States, the American publishing industry remains strong.[10] One advantage of the rise of the Internet, however, has been the accompanying increase in online book sales. Whereas few Japanese booksellers had websites for e-commerce at the beginning of the decade, most now have websites where customers can order books. In 2005, over $80 million in book sales were conducted over the Internet in Japan—a 50% increase from 2004 (!).[11]

Several aspects of Internet usage are relatively unique to Japan. First, the use of mobile phones to access the Internet is much higher in Japan than the United States. Japanese users not only purchase books using their phones, they also read books on their phone. This has even given rise to a new book genre created to take advantage of this unique medium—the so-called "cell phone novel" that tends to be shorter in length and also incorporates graphics and animations.[12] Also, while Internet usage has increased in Japan, e-commerce continues to lag behind relative to the United States. This is due to the aversion of many Japanese to credit card use and fears of identity theft—Japan is still largely a "cash society" despite the recent increase in the use of credit cards and even cell phones to make purchases. Given that credit cards are the primary payment method for online transactions, this mentality has understandably hampered e-commerce in Japan.

Interfirm Rivalry

As noted earlier, interfirm rivalry in this industry is characterized by large numbers of relatively small booksellers. While the American bookselling industry is dominated by the triumvirate of Amazon, Barnes & Noble, and Borders, the Japanese market has no dominant bookseller or booksellers that have cornered the market (see Exhibit 1). One of the key reasons that no significant industry consolidation has occurred is the unique price-fixing system that makes it illegal for larger and potentially more efficient booksellers to use price competition to drive out small competitors. Since 1980, laws have allowed publishers to fix the price of new books, music, and newspapers in the bookselling industry. In other words, if the publisher sets the price of a book at 5,000 yen (approximately $45), all retailers are obligated to sell that book to the consumer for exactly 5,000 yen. The fixed price means that retailers are unable to compete on price.

These price-fixing laws are known as the *Saihanbai Kakaku Iji Seido* ("Resale Price Maintenance System," commonly known as the "*Saihan* system"). Despite anti-monopolistic legislature in Japan, cartels are illegal only if they substantially restrain competition "contrary to the public interest."[13] Supporters of the *Saihan* system have successfully argued to the Japanese government that cartels in the book publishing and retail industry neither run contrary to the public interest nor substantially restrain competition. They argue that the *Saihan* system increases the number of publishers and booksellers, giving consumers a greater choice of reading materials and booksellers. Combined with the ability of retailers to return unsold books, this encourages booksellers to take a chance on giving shelf space to the works of lesser known authors. Thus, even though book sales have been decreasing over the past decade, the number of new titles has indeed been on the rise (see Exhibit 3).

While it is true that the number of booksellers, publishers, and book titles are comparatively higher in Japan since the introduction of the *Saihan* system, this has not translated into higher sales. Stagnation in

---

[9] Internet World Stats: http://www.internetworldstats.com/.

[10] The Japan Times: "Why have Japan's bookworms turned?" (January 6, 2008).

[11] JETRO: *Nihon no Shuppan Sangyo no Dōkō 2006.*

[12] JETRO: *Nihon no Shuppan Sangyo no Dōkō 2006.*

[13] M. Kotabe & K.W. Wheiler, 1996, *Anticompetitive Practices in Japan* (p.86), New York: Praeger.

EXHIBIT 3 **Japanese Bookselling Industry: Declining Sales, Increasing New Titles**

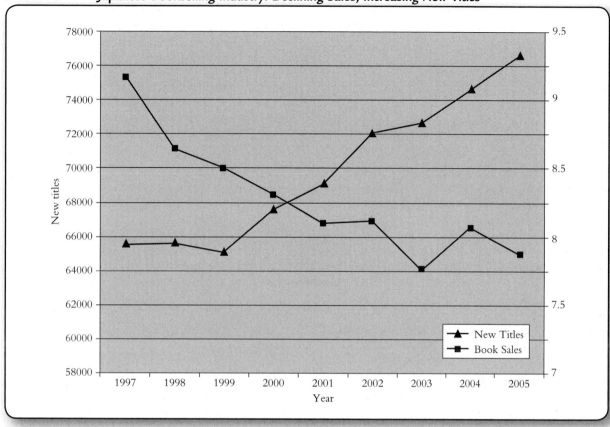

Source: JETRO: *Nihon no Shuppan Sangyo no Dōkō 2006.*

sales along with the steady increase of costs over time has reduced the profitability of both large chains and small stores. This has led industry analysts to predict a coming wave of mergers and consolidations.[14]

A book available in multiple book stores is an undifferentiated commodity. Consequently, competing on price would be a normal competitive strategy for new entrants. However, because of the *Saihan* system, which makes discounting illegal, it would appear that the already oversaturated Japanese retail bookselling industry would be an inhospitable host for new entrants. Nevertheless, there have been two recent entrants, Bookoff (founded in 1991) and Amazon (which entered Japan in 2000). Both have threatened

to revolutionize the bookselling industry in Japan in a surprisingly short time (see Exhibits 4 and 5). Despite the difficulty of entering a saturated and largely undifferentiated industry, Bookoff and Amazon each used dramatically different strategies to succeed. The next sections will consider each company separately, and chronicle their successes and setbacks.

Bookoff

Over the years, Bookoff has been accused of unfair competition, cheating authors out of royalties, representing a threat to Japanese culture, single-handedly

[14] The Japan Times: "Why have Japan's bookworms turned?" (January 6, 2008).

EXHIBIT 4   Sales Trends in Japan

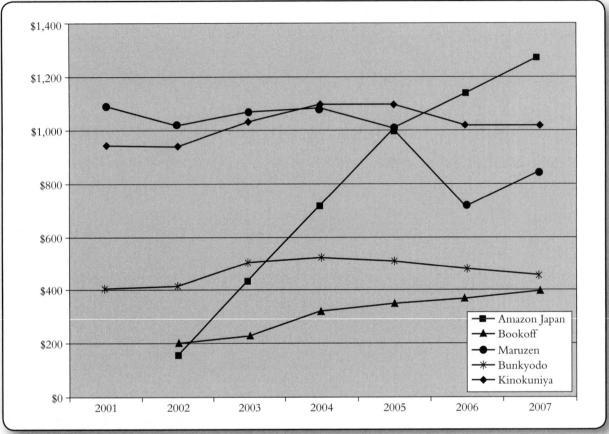

destroying the nation's book industry, and corrupting Japanese youth.[15] However, Bookoff is not a "foreign invader." It is entirely Japanese owned. The reason why competitors spit venom when they hear founder Takashi Sakamoto's name, and the reason why Bookoff has grown from one store to become one of Japan's largest retailers (with almost 900 stores as of 2008) in only a decade is simple: Bookoff uses a loophole in the *Saihan* system that enables it to be the only major bookseller that can lower the prices on their merchandise. The same *Saihan* system that supported the bookselling cartel for decades is the same system that is now handcuffing the industry leaders.

Bookoff has taken advantage of the situation, seeing its sales soar to almost $400 million in the 2006–2007 fiscal year—doubling its performance in five years.

The reason Bookoff can lower prices is due entirely to the fact that it is a *used*-book store. Used books are a major exemption to the *Saihan* system, as are books published outside of Japan (such as English language titles imported from the United States). It should be noted that Sakamoto prefers to call Bookoff a "new-used" book store. Due to several new technologies that Sakamoto has championed, Bookoff is able to "rehabilitate" used books, using techniques that clean book covers and grind down dog-eared pages to make

---

[15] TIME Asia Online: http://www.time.com/time/asia/magazine/article/0,13673,501030217-421071,00.html.

EXHIBIT 5   **Financial Performance of Three Japanese Industry Leaders and Amazon**

	BOOKOFF	MARUZEN	BUNKYODO	AMAZON
Stock Price	$4.42	$0.91	$3.93	$72.96
EPS	$0.90	$0.39	-$0.75	$1.12
Price/Earnings	4.96	2.46	-5.22	64.97
ROE	19.76%	73.92%	-25.89%	58.48%
ROA	8.00%	9.49%	-1.96%	7.55%

Source: Yahoo! Finance, Yahoo! Japan Finance, data from February 18, 2008.

a used book look practically new. In other words, Bookoff is able to sell books at new book quality and used book prices—and because of the *Saihan* system there is nothing competitors can do about it! Additionally, Bookoff stores are as large, clean, and bright as the stores of large retailers like Kinokuniya or Maruzen. The only visual difference between Bookoff and its competitors is the price tag (!).

Another difference between Bookoff and its competitors is the organization of the company. Unlike most bureaucracy-laden Japanese companies, Bookoff stores are all franchised, and owners and employees are encouraged to act like entrepreneurs. Additionally, unlike traditional used-book stores, Bookoff has a simple buy-back policy: it buys books from the customers at 10% of its list price and sells them at 50% of their list price (the list price is the price "fixed" by the publisher that the other booksellers must sell new books at). In other words, Bookoff would buy a 5,000 yen book for 500 yen and then sell that book, once it has been cleaned, for 2,500 yen.

At first glance, it may seem miraculous that a used-book store has had such great success in Japan, a country that is traditionally image-conscious. However, Japan has been in and out of recessions since the early 1990s, and consumer buying trends are reflecting financial hardships. Economic realities are reshaping values, and

attitudes toward used goods are becoming favorable. Consumers are becoming more focused on the efficient use of a good instead of simply the possession of it.[16] A "new-used" book store such as Bookoff is an acceptable compromise for the still image-conscious, but increasingly thrifty, Japanese consumer.

Young people in particular are getting on the Bookoff bandwagon. Forty percent of students in Japan now prefer these new-used stores to new stores.[17] The entire used-goods industry in Japan is increasingly being referred to as the "recycle industry" by its members, emphasizing the environmental benefits of "recycling" older goods, such as books and CDs, instead of simply throwing them away. As Japan moves away from its bubble economy and *kaisute* (buy-and-throw-away) mindset of the 1980s and 1990s, and as Japanese youth grow increasingly vocal in voicing their discontent toward the low priority the environment is given by the government, this has become a smooth marketing move that has paid off for the self-styled "recycle stores." People can make a few yen selling back their old books, save a few by buying new-used ones, and come out feeling frugal and environmentally conscious without suffering a drop-off in the quality of their books. It appears to be a win-win situation for consumers and for stores like Bookoff.

---

[16] Ion Global – Japan Internet Report: http://www.jir.net/jir9_02.html.

[17] The Book & the Computer: http://www.honco.net/os/index_0302.html. "Student" is defined as students from elementary school through college.

Amazon Japan

By the end of 2000, Amazon had already established itself as one of the three main booksellers in its domestic market, along with the much older Barnes & Noble and Borders. Amazon's success in the United States was based on its price advantage and wide selection, as it was able to offer a greater variety of books at a lower price than its bricks-and-mortar competitors. The less concentrated Japanese bookselling industry—the largest Japanese bookseller, Maruzen, was only one-fifth the size of Amazon's largest American competitor, Barnes & Noble—seemed ripe for the taking. When Amazon opened the "virtual doors" on its Japanese subsidiary on November 11, 2000, it appeared to be in a position to exploit a first-mover advantage and feast on a Japanese bookselling industry characterized by a large market but small competitors. However, optimism soured quickly when Amazon Japan's 2001 sales were a disappointing $150 million—a drop in the bucket compared to Amazon's worldwide sales of $4 billion. Amazon's struggles were puzzling given its great success in the United States.

Not surprisingly, the primary source of Amazon's troubles lay with the unique *Saihan* system of Japan. For Amazon, whose primary competitive advantage rested on its ability to offer the lowest prices, the *Saihan* system was a critical roadblock. While this could have spelled doom for Amazon, by the end of 2007 Amazon stood on top of its Japanese competitors, raking in approximately $1.3 billion in sales (almost ten times the sales volume of 2001). In 2001, Amazon's sales in Japan made up only 4% of its global sales. By 2007, Amazon's Japan operations accounted for over 10%.[18]

How did Amazon do this? First, even though Amazon was not the first online bookseller in Japan, it was the first to sell a wide variety of products besides books. Seven months after opening its Japanese store, Amazon added music, DVDs, and videos to its selection of books. In October 2001, Amazon began selling computer software and video games. By 2005, the software and gaming division was Amazon's second-largest source of sales after books. Games are not regulated by the *Saihan* system, which allows Amazon to give its customary 20%–30% discounts for these products. Between 2001 and 2008, many more products were added, including electronics, kitchen appliances, toys, sporting goods, and health and beauty products. By 2005, book sales made up less than half of Amazon Japan's total sales, a clear indication of the growing breadth of Amazon's product lineup. By this time, Amazon's online sales presence was nearly as large as that of Yahoo!'s Japanese site and Rakuten, the Japanese equivalent of eBay. Unlike books and music, many of these products are not under *Saihan* regulations, allowing Amazon to offer a large variety of products at discount prices. Even though Amazon was unable to sell books, music, and a few other core products at discount prices, it was able to differentiate itself by offering a larger selection of products than its competitors.

Second, Amazon adjusted to the unique cultural environment of Japan. As mentioned earlier, a fear of fraud has made the Japanese comparatively more hesitant to make Internet credit card purchases. In response, Amazon Japan started a service in April 2006 that allowed its customers to make payments at any of over 70,000 convenience stores and ATMs throughout the country, enabling customers to avoid the risk of online fraud (as of 2007, Amazon Japan is the only Amazon subsidiary to offer this service). Also, in Japanese book stores there is a long tradition of *tachi-yomi* (standing-and-reading), where customers will pick up a book or magazine and stand to read it for as much as an hour or two. Following in the footsteps of its US online store, in November 2005 Amazon Japan began to offer the "look inside" option for many of its books, allowing customers to read excerpts and passages from books before they purchase them.

Finally, Amazon used clever methods to bypass the *Saihan* system to indirectly offer products at lower prices. First, Amazon offered free shipping on purchases over 5,000 yen (approximately $45). Later, the minimum amount was lowered to 1,500 yen (about $13)—lower than the $25 minimum offered by its US online store (as of 2008). Free shipping put Amazon on par with its bricks-and-mortar competitors, but gave it an advantage over other online stores that by and large did not (or could not) offer this service. Late

---

[18] Amazon does not separate its international sales by country, so sales figures here are from estimates by industry experts (for example, CNET Japan: http://japan.cnet.com/news/media/story/0,2000056023,20089876,00.htm).

in 2003, Amazon Japan opened a Japanese version of its highly successful "Amazon Marketplace," where third-party users sell both new and used products to each other. This allowed Amazon to indirectly sell books and music at prices below *Saihan*-mandated prices as third-party users. These third-party users, who are not bound by *Saihan* laws, officially made the transaction, not Amazon. Finally, Amazon started using a points system that allowed customers to accumulate points based on the price of items purchased that could be redeemed for a gift certificate. Even though Amazon could not discount the prices on each item directly, the one-to-one correspondence between the price of items purchased and redeemable gift certificates created a nearly identical result. Several Japanese publishers have vehemently protested the use of this point system as a violation of the *Saihan* system of price fixing, but other retailers have followed suit, making the point system a common practice in the Japanese bookselling industry.[19] Despite a slow start, once Amazon adjusted its strategy to the unique institutional environment of Japan, its sales took off and allowed the company to enjoy the same success it had gained in its home US market.

Future Trends

The main defining characteristic of the Japanese retail bookselling industry is the unique institutional context. The *Itaku Hanbai* system that allows retailers to return books to publishers free of charge and the *Saihan* system that allows publishers to fix the price at which retailers can sell their books to the end consumer have been in place since 1980, and have dramatically affected the competitive dynamics of this industry. Although there have been several attempts at reform, the government has not been able to garner enough support or motivation to pass anything yet. However, Japanese antitrust laws are currently in a state of flux, and with the "unfair" success of Bookoff and Amazon Japan in getting around aspects of the *Saihan* system, the clamor for reform (if not outright repeal) of the system has dramatically increased both within and outside the industry.[20] Although the Japanese government has historically been slow to act, given the general malaise of the Japanese economy and the government's desperation to jump-start it, many see open competition as inevitable. Booksellers worldwide eyeing Japan must continue to focus on this situation. Any change that occurs in Japan will radically alter how domestic and foreign booksellers approach this large and potentially lucrative market.

Case Discussion Questions

1. Why is the profitability of large Japanese retail booksellers relatively poor and their scale relatively small?

2. The *Saihan* system serves as a price-fixing cartel to deter entry. This practice, often labeled "collusive" and "anticompetitive," would be illegal in many countries such as the United States. What are the benefits for individual companies and the industry to participate in this system? What are the costs?

3. Draw on the industry-, resource-, and institution-based views to explain the success of Bookoff and Amazon Japan.

4. What is going to happen if the *Saihan* system dissolves?

5. If you were a board member of Barnes & Noble or Borders, would you approve a proposal to open a series of book stores in Japan now? Would you change your mind if the *Saihan* system dissolves?

---

[19] JETRO: *Nihon no Shuppan Sangyo no Dōkō 2006*.

[20] Japan Entrepreneur Report: http://www.japanentrepreneur.com/200302.html.

AGRANA[1]

Erin Pleggenkuhle-Miles
University of Texas at Dallas

How does the Vienna-based AGRANA grow from having five factories in Austria in 1988 to operating 55 factories around the world in 2007?

Although most readers of this book probably have never heard of AGRANA, virtually everyone has heard of Nestlé, Coca-Cola, Danone, PepsiCo, Archer Daniels Midland (ADM), Tyson Foods, and Hershey Foods. Headquartered and listed in Vienna, Austria, AGRANA is one of the leading suppliers to these multinational brands around the world. With revenues of US$2.6 billion and capitalization of $1.4 billion, AGRANA is the world's leader in fruit preparations and one of Central Europe's leading sugar and starch companies.

AGRANA was formed in 1988 as a holding company for three sugar factories and two starch factories in Austria. In the last two decades, it has become a global player with 55 production plants in 26 countries with three strategic pillars: sugar, starch, and fruit. AGRANA supplies most of its fruit preparations and fruit juice concentrates to the dairy, baked products, ice cream, and soft drink industries. In other words, you may not know AGRANA, but you have probably enjoyed many AGRANA products. How did AGRANA grow from a local supplier serving primarily the small Austrian market to a global player?

From Central and Eastern Europe to the World

In many ways, the growth of AGRANA mirrors the challenges associated with regional integration in Europe and then with global integration of multinational production in the last two decades. European integration has two components. First, EU integration accelerated throughout Western Europe in the 1990s. This means that firms such as AGRANA, based in a relatively smaller country, Austria (with a population of 8.2 million), needed to grow its economies of scale to fend off the larger rivals from other European countries blessed with larger home country markets and hence larger economies of scale. Second, since 1989, Central and Eastern European (CEE)[2] countries, formerly off limits to Western European firms, have opened their markets. For Austrian firms such as AGRANA, the timing of the CEE countries'

---

[1] This case was written by Erin Pleggenkuhle-Miles (University of Texas at Dallas) under the supervision of Professor Mike Peng. © Erin Pleggenkuhle-Miles. Reprinted with permission.

[2] Central and Eastern Europe (CEE) typically refers to (1) Central Europe (former Soviet bloc countries such as the Czech Republic, Hungary, Poland, and Romania and three Baltic states of the former Soviet Union) and (2) Eastern Europe (the European portion of the 12 post-Soviet republics such as Belarus, Russia, and Ukraine).

arrival as potential investment sites was fortunate. Facing powerful rivals from larger Western European countries but being constrained by its smaller home market, AGRANA has aggressively expanded its foreign direct investment (FDI) throughout CEE. Most CEE countries have since become EU members. As a result, CEE provides a much larger playground for AGRANA, allowing it to enhance its scale, scope, and thus its competitiveness.

At the same time, multinational production by global giants such as Nestlé, ConAgra, Coca-Cola, PepsiCo, and Danone has been growing by leaps and bounds, reaching more parts of the world. Emerging as a strong player not only in Austria and CEE but also in the EU, AGRANA has further "chased" its corporate buyers by investing in and locating supplier operations around the world. This strategy has allowed AGRANA to better cater to the expanding needs of its corporate buyers.

Until 1918, Vienna had been the capital of the Austro-Hungarian Empire, whose territory not only included today's Austria and Hungary but also numerous CEE regions. Although formal ties were lost (and in fact cut during the Cold War), informal ties through cultural, linguistic, and historical links never disappeared. These ties have been reactivated since the end of the Cold War, thus fueling a rising interest among Austrian firms to enter CEE.

Overall, from an institution-based view, it seems natural that Austrian firms would be pushed by pressures arising from the EU integration and pulled by the attractiveness of CEE. However, among hundreds of Austrian firms that have invested in CEE, not all are successful and some have failed miserably. So, how can AGRANA emerge as a winner from its forays into CEE? The answer boils down to AGRANA's firm-specific resources and capabilities, a topic that we turn to next.

EXHIBIT 1   **AGRANA Plants in Different Divisions**

SEGMENT	1988–1989	2002–2003	2006–2007
Sugar	4	15	13
Starch	2	5	5
Fruit	0	0	37
Total	6	20	55

Source: AGRANA company presentation, June 2007, http://www.agrana.com.

Product-Related Diversification

AGRANA has long been associated with sugar and starch production in CEE. Until 2003, AGRANA's focus on the sugar and starch industries worked well. However, the reorganization of the European sugar market by the European Union (EU) Commission in recent years motivated AGRANA to look in new directions for future growth opportunities.[3] This new direction—fruit—has since become the third and largest division at AGRANA (see Exhibit 1).

How to diversify? As a well-known processor in the sugar and starch industries, AGRANA wanted to capitalize on its core competence—the refining and processing of agricultural raw materials (sugar beets, cereals, and potatoes). To capitalize on its accumulated knowledge of the refinement process, AGRANA decided to diversify into the fruit-processing sector (Exhibit 2 gives a brief description of each of the three current divisions). First, entry into the fruit sector ensured additional growth and complemented AGRANA's position in the starch sector. Since the Starch Division was already a supplier to the food and beverage industry, this allowed AGRANA to benefit from those relationships previously developed when

---

[3] One component of the Common Agricultural Policy (CAP) of the EU is the common organization of the markets in the sugar sector (CMO Sugar). CMO Sugar regulates both the total EU quantity of sugar production and the quantity of sugar production in each sugar-producing country. It also controls the range of sugar prices, essentially limiting competition by assigning quotas to incumbent firms, such as AGRANA. In 2006, the EU passed sugar reforms reducing subsidies and price regulation, influencing the competition in the marketplace. These reforms included a reduction of sugar production by six million tons over a four-year transition period. Sugar reforms such as these have forced some of AGRANA's competitors to close a number of sugar facilities. However, AGRANA's executives are optimistic about AGRANA's future due to its investments in the fruit and starch markets.

EXHIBIT 2　　　**AGRANA Divisions**

Sugar:	AGRANA Sugar maintains nine sugar factories in five EU countries (Austria, Czech Republic, Slovakia, Hungary, and Romania) and is one of the leading sugar companies in Central Europe. The sugar AGRANA processes is sold to both consumers (via the food trade) and manufacturers in the food and beverage industries. Within this sector, AGRANA maintains customer loyalty by playing off its competitive strengths, which include high product quality, matching product to customer needs, customer service, and just-in-time logistics.
Starch:	AGRANA operates four starch factories in three countries (Austria, Hungary, and Romania). The products are sold to the food and beverage, paper, textile, construction chemicals, pharmaceutical, and cosmetic industries. To maintain long-term client relationships, AGRANA works in close collaboration with its customers and develops "made-to-measure solutions" for its products. As a certified manufacturer of organic products, AGRANA is Europe's leading supplier of organic starch.
Fruit:	This third segment was added to the core sugar and starch segments to ensure continued growth during a time when AGRANA reached the limits allowed by competition law in the sugar segment. The Fruit Division operates 39 production plants across every continent. Like the Starch Division, the Fruit Division does not make any consumer products, limiting itself to supplying manufacturers of brand-name food products. Its principal focus is on fruit preparations and the manufacturing of fruit juice concentrates. Fruit preparations are special customized products made from a combination of high-grade fruits and sold in liquid or lump form. Manufacturing is done in the immediate vicinity of AGRANA customers to ensure a fresh product. Fruit juice concentrates are used as the basis for fruit juice drinks and are supplied globally to fruit juice and beverage bottlers and fillers.

Source: AGRANA International website, http://www.agrana.com.

it entered the fruit sector. Second, because the fruit sector is closely related to AGRANA's existing core sugar and starch businesses, AGRANA could employ the expertise and market knowledge it has accumulated over time, thus benefiting its new Fruit Division. AGRANA's core competence of the refinement process allowed it to diversify into this new segment smoothly.

AGRANA's CEO, Johann Marihart, believes that growth is an essential requirement for the manufacturing of high-grade products at competitive prices. Economies of scale have become a decisive factor for manufacturers in an increasingly competitive environment. In both the sugar and starch segments, AGRANA grew from a locally active company to one of Central Europe's major manufacturers in a very short span of time. Extensive restructuring in the Sugar and Starch divisions has allowed AGRANA to continue to operate efficiently and competitively in the European marketplace. Since its decision to diversify into the fruit-processing industry in 2003, Marihart has pursued a consistent acquisitions policy to exploit strategic opportunities in the fruit preparations and fruit juice concentrates sectors.

Acquisitions

How does AGRANA implement its expansion strategy? In a word: acquisitions. Between 1990 and 2001, AGRANA focused on dynamic expansion into CEE sugar and starch markets by expanding from five plants to 13 and almost tripling its capacity. As the Sugar Division reached a ceiling to its growth potential due to EU sugar reforms, AGRANA began searching for a new opportunity for growth. Diversifying into the fruit industry aligned with AGRANA's goal to be a leader in the industrial refinement of agricultural raw materials. AGRANA began its diversification into the fruit segment in 2003 with the acquisitions of Denmark's Vallø Saft and Austria's Steirerobst. By July 2006, AGRANA's Fruit Division had acquired three additional holding firms and was reorganized so all subsidiaries were operating under the AGRANA brand.

AGRANA diversified into the fruit segment in 2003 through the acquisition of five firms. With the acquisition of Denmark's Vallø Saft Group (fruit juice concentrates) in April 2003, AGRANA gained a presence in Denmark and Poland. The acquisition of an interest (33%) in Austria's Steirerobst (fruit preparations and fruit juice concentrates) in June 2003 gave AGRANA an increased presence in Austria, Hungary, and Poland, while also establishing a presence in Romania, Ukraine, and Russia. AGRANA fully acquired Steirerobst in February 2006, and it first began acquiring France's Atys Group (fruit preparations) in July 2004 (25%). The acquisition of Atys Group was complete in December 2005 (100%) and was AGRANA's largest acquisition, since Atys had 20 plants spread across every continent. In November 2004, AGRANA acquired Belgium's Dirafrost (fruit preparations) under the Atys Group, and two months later (January 2005) acquired Germany's Wink Group (fruit juice concentrates) under the Vallø Saft Group. AGRANA's most recent expansion was a 50-50 joint venture under the Vallø Saft Group with Xianyang Andre Juice Co. Ltd. (fruit juice concentrates) in China. These acquisitions allowed AGRANA to quickly (within two years!) become a global player in the fruit segment. Exhibit 3 provides an overview of AGRANA's present locations around the globe.

The strategy of AGRANA is clearly laid out in its 2006–2007 annual report: "AGRANA intends to continue to strengthen its market position and profitability in its core business segments . . . and to achieve a sustainable increase in enterprise value. This will be done by concentrating on growth and efficiency, by means of investments and acquisitions that add value, with the help of systematic cost control and through sustainable enterprise management." AGRANA's growth strategy, consistent improvement in productivity, and value-added approach have enabled it to provide continual increases in its enterprise value and dividend distributions to shareholders. The key to AGRANA's global presence in the fruit segment is not only its many acquisitions but its ability to quickly integrate those acquired into the group to realize synergistic effects.

In Exhibit 4, the annual revenue is given for each sector. Although the Sugar Division was the leader in 2005–2006, contributing 50% of the revenue, AGRANA's 2006–2007 annual report announced the Fruit Division as the new revenue leader (48%), surpassing projected expectations. AGRANA attributes its growth in the fruit sector to increases in dietary awareness and per capita income, two trends that are forecasted to continue to rise in the future.

Diversifying Into Biofuel

In light of further EU sugar reforms, AGRANA has continually looked for new growth opportunities. On May 12, 2005, the supervisory board of AGRANA gave the go-ahead for the construction of an ethanol facility in Pichelsdorf, Austria. Construction was complete in October 2007. However, due to the surge in prices for wheat and corn international commodity markets, it was shut down and is scheduled to commence operation in the spring of 2008. AGRANA first began making alcohol in 2005, in addition to starch and isoglucose, at its Hungrana, Hungary, plant in a preemptive move to accommodate forthcoming EU biofuel guidelines. This move into ethanol was seen as a logical step by CEO Marihart. Similar to its move into the fruit sector, the production of ethanol allows AGRANA to combine its extensive know-how of processing agricultural raw materials with its technological expertise and opens the door for further growth.

Sources: Based on media publications and company documents. The following sources were particularly helpful: (1) AGRANA investor information provided by managing director, Christian Medved, to Professor Mike Peng at the Strategic Management Society Conference, Vienna, October 2006; (2) AGRANA Company Profile 2007; (3) AGRANA Annual Report 2005–2006 and 2006–2007, http://www.agrana.com (accessed August 1, 2007); (4) Sugar Traders Association, http://www.sugartraders.co.uk/ (accessed May 4, 2007); (5) N. Merret, 2007, Fruit segment drives Agrana growth, Food Navigator.com Europe, January 12; (6) N. Merret, 2006, Agrana looks east for competitive EU sugar markets, Confectionery News.com, November 29; (7) AGRANA Preliminary Results for Financial Year 2006–2007, press release, May 7, 2007; (8) AGRANA Semi-Annual Report 2007–2008 (accessed February 14, 2008); (9) C. Blume, N. Strang, & E. Farnstrand, *Sweet Fifteen: The Competition on the EU Sugar Markets,* Swedish Competition Authority Report, December 2002.

EXHIBIT 3   AGRANA Plant Locations as of 2007

	SUGAR	STARCH	FRUIT	ETHANOL
Argentina			1	
Australia			1	
Austria	4	3	2	1
Belgium			1	
Bosnia Herzegovina	1 (50%)*			
Brazil			1	
Bulgaria			1 (50%)	
China			2	
Czech Republic	2		1	
Denmark			1	
Fiji			1	
France			2	
Germany			1	
Hungary	3	1 (50%)	3	X**
Mexico			1	
Morocco			2	
Poland			4	
Romania	2	1	1	
Russia			1	
Serbia			1	
Slovakia	1			
South Africa			1	
South Korea			1	
Turkey			1	
Ukraine			2	
USA			4	
Total Plants	13	5	37	1

* AGRANA's holding is given in parentheses when not 100%.
** The Hungrana, Hungary, plant also produces some ethanol.
Source: AGRANA 2006–2007 Annual Report.

EXHIBIT 4   AGRANA by Division

	SUGAR	STARCH	FRUIT	TOTAL
Staff	2723	776	4724	8223
2005–2006 Revenue*	1040.04** (50%)	314.01 (15%)	730.62 (35%)	2084.67
2006–2007 Revenue	1059.34 (41%)	292.27 (11%)	1234.71 (48%)	2586.33

* Reported in USD, May 17, 2007, exchange rate used in calculation (US $1 = €0.74).
** Figures are reported in millions.
Source AGRANA 2006–2007 Annual Report.

Case Discussion Questions

1. From an industry-based view, how would you characterize competition in this industry?

2. From an resource-based view, what is behind AGRANA's impressive growth?

3. From an institution-based view, what opportunities and challenges have been brought by the integration of EU markets in both Western Europe and CEE?

4. From an international perspective, what challenges do you foresee AGRANA facing as it continues its expansion into other regions, such as East Asia?

Mattel and the Toy Recalls (B)[1]

Hari Bapuji
University of Manitoba

Paul Beamish
Ivey School of Business, University of Western Ontario

Mattel recalls thousands of toys made in China due to quality issues.

"China is now issuing two types of toys: leaded and un-leaded."

– Jay Leno, U.S. Talk Show Host

On August 14, 2007, the U.S. Consumer Product Safety Commission (CPSC) in cooperation with Mattel announced five different recalls of Mattel's toys. See Exhibit 1 for excerpts of the CPSC recall notices. On the same day, Mattel issued a press release (see Exhibit 2) and held a press conference. Bob Eckert, CEO of Mattel, made a five minute briefing and answered the questions posed by the reporters. Following are some excerpts from Eckert's address.[2]

As you know today Mattel announced in cooperation with the U.S. Consumer Product Safety Commission voluntary recalls on two issues, a product recalled for impermissible levels of lead and an expansion of the November 2006 magnet recall. We've already put measures in place to

address these issues, and I will talk about those in a moment. Obviously we don't wanna have recalls, but in acting responsibly we won't hesitate to take action to correct issues to assure the safety of our products and the safety of children. I want to underscore that Mattel has extremely rigorous testing and quality procedures in place and we will continue to be vigilant in enforcing quality and safety. First Mattel has voluntarily recalled one toy from the Cars die cast vehicle line, manufactured between May 2007 and July 2007 containing impermissible levels of lead. The recall of the 'Sarge Toy' results from Mattel's on going testing procedures. The Cars toy was produced by Early Light Industrial Company, one of Mattel's contract manufacturing

---

[1] This case was written on the basis of published sources. Consequently, the interpretations and perspectives presented are not necessarily those of Mattel and other organizations represented in this case or any of their employees.

[2] Transcript of Eckert's address to reporters.

facilities in China, which subcontracted the painting of parts of the toy to another vendor named Hong Li Da, also in China. While the painting subcontractor was required to utilize certified paint supplied directly from Early Light, he had instead violated Mattel standards and utilized paint from a non-authorized third party supplier. To address this issue we have immediately implemented a strengthened three point check system . . . . (details of the system)

Additionally Mattel is voluntarily recalling certain toys with magnets manufactured between January 2002 and January 31st, 2007 that may release small powerful magnets. The recall expands upon Mattel's voluntary recall of 8 toys in November 2006 and is based on a thorough internal review of all of our brands that have toys with magnets and analyzed the ways in which magnets may come loose. Since January, 2007 all magnets used in our toys have been locked into the toy with sturdy material holding in the edges around the exposed face of the magnet or completely covering the magnet. We now believe it is prudent to recall our older toys with magnets that do not meet our latest retention system requirements. This means we are recalling 72 toys that were distributed in prior years. The safety of children is our main concern and we're confident that our new requirements work based on our continued testing and consumer experience. The risk of magnets are swallowed is serious and we believe that all our toys with magnets should have the safety benefit of our new standards.

The news of the recall spread like wildfire all over the world. The media coverage it received was unprecedented, with TV channels running the story through the day. Several analysts pointed to the previous recalls of Chinese-made goods and demanded that the U.S. and Chinese governments must act. The recall of Mattel toys was quickly followed by several other recalls of Chinese-made goods. About 40 different products, most made in China, were recalled for excess lead. Mattel announced three more recalls on September 4 in which an additional 773,900 toys made in China were recalled for excess lead.

The spate of recalls severely eroded consumer confidence. In a poll conducted by Reuters/Zogby,[3] the majority of people (close to 80 per cent) reported that they were apprehensive about buying goods made in China. Nearly two-thirds (63 per cent) of the respondents reported that they were likely to participate in a boycott of Chinese goods until the Chinese government improved the regulations governing the safety of the goods exported to the United States. Several other opinion polls conducted by news agencies and market research firms revealed similar sentiments.

The governments in the West quickly responded to the crisis of confidence. At a summit of North American political leaders in Canada, the heads of governments of Canada, the United States, and Mexico decided to crack down on unsafe goods, particularly those designed for children. Using the Mattel recalls case, EU Consumer Commissioner Meglena Kuneva, initiated an extensive review of the strengths and weaknesses of the consumer product safety mechanisms in Europe. The review had involved extensive work with national surveillance authorities, the Chinese authorities, the U.S. authorities, the European toy industry, retailers, as well as consultations with the European Parliament. The government of Brazil decided to halt the import of toys by Mattel until the lead issue was resolved.

The U.S. Senate as well as the House of Commons held hearings on the safety of imported products and Bob Eckert was summoned to testify in both the hearings. In those hearings, Eckert asserted:[4] "a few vendors, either deliberately or out of carelessness, circumvented our long-established safety standards and procedures."

The recalls catapulted consumer product safety to the center of debate. Questions were raised about whether the CPSC had enough resources to ensure

---

[3] http://www.signonsandiego.com/news/nation/20070919-0400-usa-foodsafety-poll.html

[4] Testimony of Robert Eckert, CEO, Mattel, to the Sub-committee on Commerce, Trade, and Consumer Protection of the Committee on Energy and Commerce. September 19, 2007.

product safety. Consumer advocates and some politicians pointed to the steady budget and staffing cuts the CPSC faced; with 420 employees in 2007, the CPSC was half its size of the 1980s. Many wondered if that number was adequate to monitor 15,000 consumer products in a market valued at US$614 billion. It was pointed out that CPSC had only one employee devoted to testing the safety of toys. Also, only 15 CPSC inspectors were available to check all the U.S. ports where import shipments were received.[5]

Given the limited resources of the CPSC, it was easy for unscrupulous companies to "play truant." And, the CPSC "lacked the teeth" to check it. For example, the maximum penalty the CPSC could impose on companies for violations was $1.8 million. Imposing penalties was never easy because the burden of proof rested with the CPSC. Additionally, the CPSC could not even make public its concerns or investigations about companies. It was required by law to take prior approval of the companies whose names were being divulged.[6]

The role of Mattel in ensuring product safety was also under scrutiny. Some observers pointed that Mattel had not informed the CPSC within the stipulated time. In the past, Mattel was fined twice by the CPSC for not informing the latter about product hazards in a timely manner. If the alleged delay by managers was indeed true, then it was possible that shareholders might sue the directors and senior executives of the company for the delays and exposing the company to risk.

In an interview with the *Wall Street Journal,* Eckert felt that the CPSC requirement of immediately reporting the incidents was unreasonable and that Mattel had the freedom to investigate the incidents before providing the information to the CPSC. When asked by the media about the time Mattel took to recall, Eckert said that the company asked the CPSC to initiate a fast-track recall and they acted as fast as they could. Some observers criticized Mattel for being unapologetic about the recalls. Efforts by several reporters to reach Mattel after August 14 were in vain.

Mattel's customers were livid about the recalls and wondered if the company had any control and monitoring systems at all because they were recalling toys sold over the previous three years. Some wondered if Mattel had any quality systems to test the manufactured toys for safety. As the recalls were announced, parents found it difficult to empty the toy baskets of their children without "breaking their hearts." Some families filed class-action lawsuits, asking Mattel to pay for tests to determine if children were exposed to lead. More lawsuits were expected to follow.

The recalls made the licensors of brands to Mattel, such as Disney and Sesame Workshop, very nervous. They feared the erosion of their brand value because of the lead paint issue. Disney announced independent testing of the toys it made with Disney brand names. One of the largest toy retailers, Toys 'R' Us also began to conduct its own lead testing of toys on its shelves.[7]

The continued attention to the issue of recall and particularly Mattel's role began to affect the image of all toys sold in the United States. The toys made by every company were being scrutinized and consumers were looking more carefully at the toys to find out where they were made. Many consumers rushed in search of toys made in the United States or other developed countries, but they were hard to find. Not to be discouraged, some enthusiasts set up websites to inform shoppers about where to buy American toys (www.howtobuyamerican.com) and others set up businesses that sold toys not made in China, aptly named NMC Toys (Not Made in China Toys www.nmctoys.com). A few companies, such as Little Tykes, which manufactured some of their toys in the United States began to prominently display Made in USA labels on their toys.

Some analysts argued that the suppliers in China and elsewhere were compromising on safety to meet the ever increasing pressure of the Western toy companies to supply toys and other products at a cheaper cost, even in the face of increasing raw material and wage costs. This resulted in a double-squeeze for the toy suppliers. Some consumer advocates asserted

---

[5] Stephen Labaton. Bigger budget? No, responds safety agency. *New York Times,* Oct. 30, 2007.

[6] Felcher M. 2001. *It's No Accident: How Corporations Sell Dangerous Baby Products.* Common Courage Press: Monroe, ME

[7] http://www.reuters.com/article/domesticNews/idUSN1040588720070910

that companies like Mattel which brought the toys into the United States had the primary responsibility for ensuring the safety of products — that no matter where in the global supply chain, the problem might have occurred.

The suppliers in China faced pressures from large toy companies, who in turn faced pressures from large retailers, to cut down costs. Additionally, the economic growth enjoyed by China resulted in rising wages, and a general increase in the cost of doing business. Within China, toy-making is clustered in Guangdong province. The Nominal Wage Rate Index (NWRI) in Guangdong increased to 545 in 2003 from a base of 100 in 1991. The increase was much higher than the national average of 450 in 2003, and was fifth largest within China. The average Consumer Price Index (CPI) in China rose from 100 in 1992 to 202 in 2004. The rise in CPI was less stark for Guangdong province, reaching 189.[8]

The suppliers in China faced another problem: the rising value of the yuan when compared to other Asian currencies. For example, since 1997 the Chinese yuan has appreciated nearly four fold against the Indonesian rupiah, doubled in value against the Philippine peso, and increased in value by at least 1.5 times against the South Korean won, the Malaysian ringgit and the Thai baht. As a result, these destinations were becoming increasingly attractive for manufacturing and the advantage of operating in China was eroding.[9]

As a result of the increased wages, cost of living and the value of the yuan, the pattern of economic activity in China underwent a rapid change. Industrial activity had shifted to higher-value industries which could absorb the rising costs. Exhibit 3 presents the changes in industry concentration by region in China. From being dominant in only one region in 1990, electronic equipment was the most dominant industrial activity in four regions in 2006.[10] The shift in industrial activity was best captured in the words of the Mattel CEO:

> Wage rates are going up in southern China, and it's harder for us to find employees in southern China. You know, next to a toy factory 20 years ago, there was empty land. Today next to every toy factory, I think you can look to your left and see a cell phone plant or some sort of electronics plant. You might be able to look to your right and see an auto manufacturer.

The effect of recalls began to take a toll on the already besieged toy suppliers in China. On August 11, 2007, Cheung Shu-hung, who directly managed the operations of Lee Der, committed suicide. He was 48, single, and lived in a 250 square foot room in one of Lee Der's offices. He was considered to be kind to the factory workers and was credited with the better working conditions that prevailed in the three factories of Lee Der. Shop floor salaries for a 10-hour, six-day week in Lee Der factories ranged between US$120 and 180 a month, higher than the local average of $130 a month for seven-day week schedules that often ran 14-hours a day. Also, employees received overtime pay when the shift exceeded 10 hours. One of the last things Cheng Shu-hung did was to sell his factories and pay wages to his employees.[11]

Following the recalls, Chinese employees in Lee Der and other factories became jobless. The conditions of workers became an issue of discussion. Some observers wondered what the effect of lead was on the employees who painted lead on the toys, and thus ingested it, every day of the week.

The recalls began to severely erode "Brand China" and the Chinese government quickly set up a taskforce under the leadership of Chinese Vice Premier Wu Yi to ensure product safety. This taskforce intensified the inspection of Chinese plants and suspended or revoked the export licenses of hundreds of companies. Some suppliers named in the recalls were jailed.

---

[8] Delios A, Beamish P, Zhao X. 2008. The evolution of Japanese investment in China: From toys to textiles to business process outsourcing. *Asia Pacific Business Review* (forthcoming).

[9] Ibid.

[10] Ibid.

[11] http://www.ckgsb.edu.cn:8080/article/600/3051.aspx

Faced with intense pressure from all quarters, the Chinese authorities asserted that the majority of products made in China were safe and that Western companies were unduly blaming China. Several suppliers who worked with big companies and were forced to close factories or lay off workers asserted that Mattel and other large companies were making them scapegoats.

In what appeared to be a counter-offensive, China rejected North American imports such as frozen pig kidneys imported from the United States and frozen pork spareribs from Canada. These products were found to contain residues of ractopamine, forbidden for use as veterinary medicine in China.[12] Also, China rejected shipments of U.S.-made orange pulp and dried apricots containing high levels of bacteria and preservatives.[13]

In an effort aimed at enhancing product safety, the CPSC and its Chinese-counterpart AQSIQ met in Washington on September 11-12, 2007. This meeting culminated in agreement to ban the use of lead in toys made in China. At the meeting, in his address, the AQSIQ chief asserted that the West was blaming China for the problems created by its toy companies. In support of his assertion, he mentioned a recent Canadian study which found that the majority of toy recalls in the U.S. were due to design flaws.

According to a report in the *New York Times* on September 12, 2007, two Canadian business school researchers, after analyzing the toy recalls in the United States over the previous 20 years, found that 76 per cent of the recalls were due to design flaws such as sharp edges, easily detachable small parts, and long strings. In contrast, only 10 per cent were due to manufacturing flaws such as using poor material, incorrect assembly, and use of unacceptable material like lead paint. The researchers argued that China should not be blamed for most of the recalls, when a vast majority of the problems were because of the designs made in the corporate headquarters of toy companies.

Mattel had considerable interests in China. Five of its factories were located in China and a very large number of factories made toys for Mattel, directly or indirectly. The Chinese news agencies began to report that Chinese suppliers were being made a scapegoat by Mattel, despite the fact that 90 per cent of the toys recalled on August 14 were due to magnets detaching, which was a design problem for which Mattel was responsible. The loss of reputation for China as a result of the recalls was huge and Mattel seemed like the floodgate that had opened it.

Case Discussion Questions

1. What went wrong with Mattel's recall strategy?

2. Who are Mattel's stakeholders? Who did Mattel cater to in the recall?

3. What values did Mattel exhibit during the recall? How did they affect Mattel?

4. What should Mattel do right now and in the future?

---

[12] http://www.cbc.ca/consumer/story/2007/09/17/china-trade.html

[13] http://www.cbc.ca/consumer/story/2007/06/26/china-trade.html

EXHIBIT 1

CPSC RECALL NOTICES

FOR IMMEDIATE RELEASE
August 14, 2007
Release #07-273

Firm's Recall Hotline: (888) 597-6597
CPSC Recall Hotline: (800) 638-2772
CPSC Media Contact: (301) 504-7908

Additional Reports of Magnets Detaching from Polly Pocket Play Sets Prompts Expanded Recall by Mattel

WASHINGTON, D.C. - The U.S. Consumer Product Safety Commission, in cooperation with the firm named below, today announced a voluntary recall of the following consumer product. Consumers should stop using recalled products immediately unless otherwise instructed.

Name of Products: Various Polly Pocket dolls and accessories with magnets

Units: About 7.3 million play sets (about 2.4 million play sets were recalled on November 21, 2006)

Importer: Mattel Inc., of El Segundo, Calif.

Hazard: Small magnets inside the dolls and accessories can come loose. The magnets can be found by young children and swallowed or aspirated. If more than one magnet is swallowed, the magnets can attract each other and cause intestinal perforation or blockage, which can be fatal.

Incidents/Injuries: Since the previous recall announcement, Mattel has received more than 400 additional reports of magnets coming loose. CPSC was aware in the first recall announcement of 170 reports of the magnets coming out of the recalled toys. There had been three reports of serious injuries to children who swallowed more than one magnet. All three suffered intestinal perforations that required surgery.

Description: The recalled Polly Pocket play sets contain plastic dolls and accessories that have small magnets. The magnets measure 1/8 inch in diameter and are embedded in the hands and feet of some dolls, and in the plastic clothing, hairpieces and other accessories to help the pieces attach to the doll or to the doll's house. The model number is printed on the bottom of the largest pieces on some of the play sets. Products manufactured after November 1, 2006 and are currently on store shelves are not included in this recall. Contact Mattel if you cannot find a model number on your product to determine if it is part of the recall.

Sold at: Toy stores and various other retailers from May 2003 through November 2006 for between $15 and $30.

Manufactured in: China

Remedy: Consumers should immediately take these recalled toys away from children and contact Mattel to receive a voucher for a replacement toy of the customer's choice, up to the value of the returned product.

~~~~~~~~~~~~~~

Mattel Recalls Doggie Day Care™ Magnetic Toys Due to Magnets Coming Loose

Name of Product: Doggie Day Care™ play sets

Units: About 1 million

Importer: Mattel Inc., of El Segundo, Calif.

Hazard: Small magnets inside the toys can fall out. Magnets found by young children can be swallowed or aspirated. If more than one magnet is swallowed, the magnets can attract each other and cause intestinal perforation or blockage, which can be fatal.

Incidents/Injuries: The firm has received two reports of magnets coming loose. No injuries have been reported.

Description: The recalled Doggie Day Care play sets have various figures and accessories that contain small magnets.

Sold at: Toy stores and various other retailers nationwide from July 2004 to August 2007 for between $4 and $20.

Manufactured in: China

Remedy: Consumers should immediately take the recalled toys away from children and contact Mattel to receive a free replacement toy.

~~~~~~~~~~~~~~~~~~~~~

Mattel Recalls Barbie and Tanner™ Magnetic Toys Due to Magnets Coming Loose

Name of Product: Barbie and Tanner™ play sets

Units: About 683,000

Importer: Mattel Inc., of El Segundo, Calif.

Hazard: A small magnet inside the "scooper" accessory can come loose. Magnets found by young children can be swallowed or aspirated. If more than one magnet is swallowed, the magnets can attract each other and cause intestinal perforation or blockage, which can be fatal.

Incidents/Injuries: The firm has received three reports of magnets coming loose. No injuries have been reported.

EXHIBIT 1 *(continued)*

Description: The recall involves Barbie and Tanner™ play sets -- model numbers J9472 and J9560. The toys include a "scooper" accessory with a magnetic end. Recalled scoopers have a visible, silver-colored, disc-shaped magnet on the end of the scooper. Scoopers with a white material covering the magnet and products manufactured after January 31, 2007 are not recalled.
Sold at: Toy stores and various other retailers nationwide May 2006 to August 2007 for about $16.
Manufactured in: China
Remedy: Consumers should immediately take the recalled toys away from children and contact Mattel to receive a free replacement toy.
~~~~~~~~~~~~~~~~~~~~~

Mattel Recalls "Sarge" Die Cast Toy Cars Due To Violation of Lead Safety Standard
Name of Product: "Sarge" die cast toy cars
Units: About 253,000
Importer: Mattel Inc., of El Segundo, Calif.
Hazard: Surface paints on the toys could contain lead levels in excess of federal standards. Lead is toxic if ingested by young children and can cause adverse health effects.
Incidents/Injuries: None reported.
Description: The recall involves die cast "Sarge" 2 ½ inch toy cars. The toy looks like a military jeep and measures about 2 ½ inches long by 1 inch high by 1 inch wide. The recalled toy has the markings "7EA" and "China" on the bottom. The "Sarge" toy car is sold alone or in a package of two, and may have the product number M1253 (for single cars) and K5925 (for cars sold as a set) printed on the packaging. The cars marked "Thailand" are not included in this recall.
Sold at: Retail stores nationwide from May 2007 through August 2007 for between $7 and $20 (depending on whether they were sold individually or in sets).
Manufactured in: China
Remedy: Consumers should immediately take the recalled toys away from children and contact Mattel. Consumers will need to return the product to receive a replacement toy.
~~~~~~~~~~~~~~~~~~~~~

Mattel Recalls Batman™ and One Piece™ Magnetic Action Figure Sets Due To Magnets Coming Loose
Name of Product: Batman™ and One Piece™ magnetic action figure sets
Units: About 345,000
Importer: Mattel Inc., of El Segundo, Calif.
Hazard: Small, powerful magnets inside the accessories of the toy figures can fall out and be swallowed or aspirated by young children. If more than one magnet is swallowed, they can attract inside the body and cause intestinal perforation, infection or blockage which can be fatal.
Incidents/Injuries: The firm is aware of 21 incidents where a magnet fell out of the toy figure, including a case of a 3-year-old boy who was found with a magnet in his mouth. The boy did not swallow the magnet and no injuries have been reported to Mattel and CPSC.
Description: The recalled Batman™ toys include:

- The Batman™ Magna Battle Armor™ Batman™ figure with model number J1944,

- The Batman™ Magna Fight Wing™ Batman™ figure with model number J1946,

- The Batman™ Secret ID™ figure with model number J5114, and

- The Batman™ Flying Fox™ figure with model number J5115. The seven inch tall action figures include the Batman logo on the front and include magnetic accessories. The model number is located on the lower right corner of the tag which is sewn to the figure.

The recalled One Piece™ toy is:

- One Piece™ Triple Slash Zolo Roronoa™ figure with model number J4142. The 5 ½ inch tall action figure has green hair, black pants, and has magnets in his hands which connect to magnets on various swords that the figure can hold. The model number is printed on the back of the action figure's left leg.

Sold at: Discount department stores and toy stores nationwide from June 2006 through June 2007 for about $11.
Manufactured in: China
Remedy: Consumers should immediately stop using the toy and contact Mattel for instructions on how to return it to receive a free replacement toy.

EXHIBIT 2

MATTEL PRESS RELEASE - MATTEL ANNOUNCES EXPANDED RECALL OF TOYS

One product recalled for impermissible levels of lead
November 2006 magnet recall expanded

EL SEGUNDO, Calif., August 14, 2007 – Mattel, Inc. announced today that the company has voluntarily recalled one toy from the "CARS" die-cast vehicle line ("Sarge" character), manufactured between May 2007 and July 2007, containing impermissible levels of lead. The recalled vehicles include 436,000 total toys, including 253,000 in the U.S. and 183,000 outside of the U.S.

The recall of the Sarge toy results from Mattel's increased investigation and ongoing testing procedures following the recall of select Fisher-Price toys on August 1, 2007. The toy was produced by Early Light Industrial Co., Ltd (Early Light), one of Mattel's contract manufacturing facilities in China, which subcontracted the painting of parts of the toy to another vendor, Hong Li Da (HLD), also in China. While the painting subcontractor, HLD, was required to utilize paint supplied directly from Early Light, it instead violated Mattel's standards and utilized paint from a non-authorized third-party supplier.

"We have immediately implemented a strengthened three-point check system: First, we're requiring that only paint from certified suppliers be used and requiring every single batch of paint at every single vendor to be tested. If it doesn't pass, it doesn't get used. Second, we are tightening controls throughout the production process at vendor facilities and increasing unannounced random inspections. Third, we're testing every production run of finished toys to ensure compliance before they reach our customers. We've met with vendors to ensure they understand our tightened procedures and our absolute requirement of strict adherence to them," said Jim Walter, senior vice president of Worldwide Quality Assurance, Mattel.

Additionally, Mattel announced the voluntary recall of magnetic toys manufactured between January 2002 and January 31, 2007, including certain dolls, figures, play sets and accessories that may release small, powerful magnets. The recall expands upon Mattel's voluntary recall of eight toys in November 2006 and is based on a thorough internal review of all Mattel's brands. Mattel is recalling 18.2 million magnetic toys globally (9.5 million in the U.S.); however, the majority of the toys are no longer at retail. Beginning in January 2007, Mattel implemented enhanced magnet retention systems in its toys across all brands.

"Since our November 2006 magnet-related recall, we have implemented more robust magnet retention systems and more rigorous testing. We are exercising caution and have expanded the list of recalled magnetic toys due to potential safety risks associated with toys that might have loose magnets," said Walter.

"The safety of children is our primary concern, and we are deeply apologetic to everyone affected," said Robert A. Eckert, chairman and chief executive officer, Mattel. "Mattel has rigorous procedures, and we will continue to be vigilant and unforgiving in enforcing quality and safety. We don't want to have recalls, but we don't hesitate to take quick and effective action to correct issues as soon as we've identified them to ensure the safety of our products and the safety of children."

Issues Safety Alert to Consumers

Mattel is working in cooperation with the U.S. Consumer Product Safety Commission and other regulatory agencies worldwide. Mattel is also working with retailers worldwide to identify and remove affected products from retail shelves.

Details of the recall are as follows

Mattel voluntarily recalled 63 magnetic toys sold at retail prior to January 2007. Magnetic toys recalled within the U.S. include 44 Polly Pocket™ toys, 11 Doggie Day Care® toys, 4 Batman™ toys, 1 One Piece™ toy, and the accessory part of 2 Barbie® toys. For additional information regarding the magnetic toy recall, contact Mattel at (888) 597-6597, or visit the company's Web site at www.service.mattel.com.

The Sarge toy from the "CARS" die-cast vehicle line was manufactured between May 2007 and August 2007. For additional information regarding the Sarge toy recall, contact Mattel at (800) 916-4997, or visit the company's Web site at www.service.mattel.com.

A full list of products is published on the company's Web site at www.mattel.com, as well as by the Consumer Products Safety Commission. Consumers should immediately take these products away from children and contact Mattel to arrange return and to receive a voucher for a replacement toy of the consumer's choice, up to the value of the returned product.

Source: Mattel Website

EXHIBIT 3 **Industry Concentration by Region in China (1990–2006)**

REGION	INDUSTRY (1990)	CONC.	INDUSTRY (2000)	CONC.	INDUSTRY (2006)	CONC.
North	Industrial Machinery	16%	Industrial Machinery	17%	Electronic Equipment	17%
Northeast	Apparel	20%	Industrial Machinery	17%	Electronic Equipment	19%
East	Apparel	27%	Apparel	16%	Electronic Equipment	19%
Mid-South	Electronic Equipment	26%	Electronic Equipment	28%	Electronic Equipment	30%
Southwest	Food Products	50%	Transportation Equipment	49%	Transportation Equipment	47%
Northwest	Food Products	25%	Industrial Machinery	41%	Industrial Machinery	32%

Note: North = Beijing, Tianjin, Hebei, Shanxi, Inner Mongolia
Northeast = Liaoning, Jilin, Heilongjiang
East = Shanghai, Jiangsu, Zhejiang, Anhui, Fujian, Jiangxi, Shandong
Mid-South = Henan, Hubei, Hunan, Guangdong, Guangxi, Hainan
Southwest = Chongqing, Sichuan, Guizhou, Yunnan, Tibet
Northwest = Shaanxi, Gansu, Qinghai, Ningxia, Xinjiang

Source: Delios A, Beamish P, Zhao X. 2008. The evolution of Japanese investment in China: From toys to textiles to business process outsourcing. Asia Pacific Business Review (forthcoming).

How Chinese Toymakers Respond to Recalls[1]

Hao Chen

University of Texas at Dallas

Facing a sudden onslaught of product recalls, Chinese toymakers responded differently.

According to China Central Television, in 2008, 75% of the toys in the world were made in China, 70% of which were made in Guangdong Province. In total, approximately 10,000 factories in China export toys. Although Chinese toymakers dominate the world market, they are still vulnerable because they do not "call the shots." Instead, they depend on their partners, especially leading Western toy companies such as Mattel, for survival. In fact, most Chinese toymakers are original equipment manufacturers (OEM), which do not have their own brands and mainly produce toys or toy parts for their buyers such as Mattel.

In 2007, Chinese toymakers caught everyone's eyes with the large-scale toy recalls released by the Consumer Product Safety Commission (CPSC), a US government agency, in collaboration with Mattel. According to the CPSC database, the first toy recall in the United States was issued in 1974 by a US manufacturer. It was not until 1988 that the first recall announcement on toys made in China was issued. As the number of Made-in-China toys has increased, the number of recall announcements has grown over the years (Exhibit 1). While toy recalls have been made before, the scale and scope of such recalls during 2007 were unprecedented. Exhibit 2 shows the results of online searches using keywords "toy recall in the US + year" in Google (English) and "*wan ju zhao hui* ("toy recall" in Chinese) + year" in Baidu (China's most popular search engine). Clearly, media scrutiny, from both Chinese and foreign sources, dramatically intensified during 2007.

Under such pressures, how have Chinese toymakers responded? While much of the Western media has focused on the behavior of Western toy companies such as Mattel, and treated suppliers of Mattel's toys as one monolithic bloc of "Chinese toymakers," in reality, tremendous diversity exists among various Chinese toymakers, and so each will respond differently.

We can broadly classify Chinese toymakers into three categories. (1) The first type adopts a *passive* strategy. They pay little attention to the formal and informal requirements at home and abroad governing the necessity of paying attention to product quality, and tend to act after recalls. Thus, they are most likely to be eliminated by the market. (2) The second group of toymakers is *defensive:* they accept responsibility but do the least required. (3) The third kind of firms adopts a *proactive* strategy and seeks to act before recalls. Each of these types can be illustrated by the following case studies based on three different firms in Guangdong Province.

Lee Der Toy Company

Lee Der was founded in 1993 in Foshan, Guangdong. The company is a joint venture by Fenjiang Industrial Company from Chancheng District, Foshan, and Lee Der Industrial Company, Ltd., from Hong Kong. Both parent companies owned 50% of the stakes of Lee Der. For more than ten years, Lee Der had been producing toys and toy parts for Mattel's leading toys such as

---

[1] This case was written by Hao Chen (University of Texas at Dallas) under the supervision of Professor Mike Peng. It was based on published sources. The views expressed are those of the author and not necessarily those of the individuals and organizations mentioned. © Hao Chen. Reprinted with permission.

EXHIBIT 1   Number of Toy Recall Announcements in the United States (1988–2007)

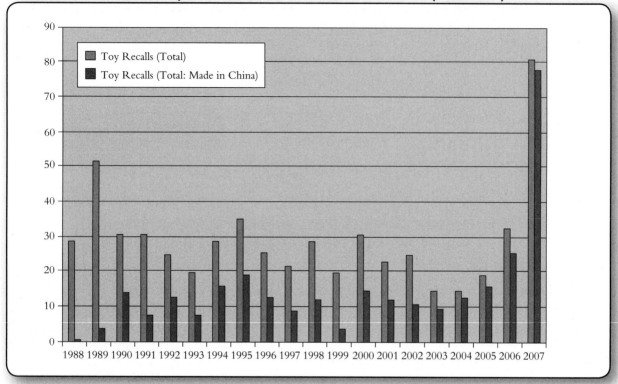

Source: www.cpsc.gov.

EXHIBIT 2   Recall Related News in Both Chinese and English Media (2002–2007)

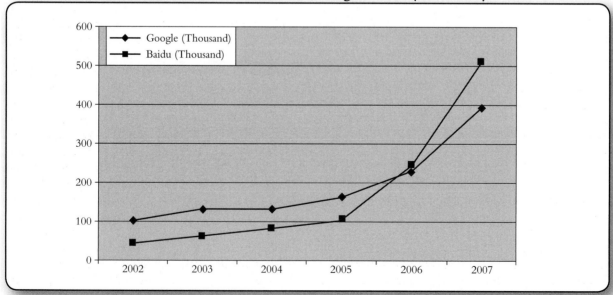

Sources: www.google.com (English) and www.baidu.com (Chinese).

Barbie and Fisher-Price toys. Before the recalls, Lee Der was the second largest toy manufacturer in Foshan.

On August 2, 2007, Fisher-Price, a subsidiary of Mattel, reported the recall of 967,000 pieces of plastic preschool toys made by Lee Der to CPSC. These toys were reported to contain an excessive amount of lead in the paint. Due to pressures from the public, Fisher-Price revealed the name of Lee Der, its Chinese contract manufacturer, to the press. It was the first time a US company involved in a recall released its Chinese supplier's information directly to the press.

The reason Lee Der's toys contained an excessive amount of lead was that Lee Der's paint supplier, Dongxing New Energy Limited (Dongxing), supplied Lee Der with "fake paint." Mattel had been requesting that its Chinese suppliers use paint from its contract paint suppliers or test each batch of paint purchased from a non-certified supplier. Lee Der apparently violated these contractual requirements. Dongxing was not on Mattel's contract paint supplier list, and the paint from Dongxing was not tested by Lee Der. In fact, the boss of Dongxing is a friend of Shu-hung Cheung, vice chairman of the board of Lee Der. According to company records, Cheung owned one-fourth of Lee Der. He was also the primary strategic decision maker in the company.

After the recall, Lee Der found itself in a difficult position, facing criticism from both the US and Chinese sides. While the US government and consumers were understandably upset, the Chinese government was also upset because the irresponsible behavior of Lee Der (and other toymakers) undermined the quality image of potentially *all* goods made in China. After the recall, Chinese officials temporarily banned Lee Der from exporting products. In total, the recall cost Lee Der US$30 million. Lee Der tried to make some amendments after the recall. For example, it produced new toys, which it claimed had passed quality tests and met US standards. However, all was in vain. Two weeks later, Cheung committed suicide in his factory warehouse due to the pressure, bringing a tragic end to Lee Der.

In this case, Lee Der represented a firm that chose a passive strategy to deal with institutional pressures. It denied its responsibility as a supplier and contract manufacturer and violated the rules of the game. It also acted reluctantly after recalls, which made it more passive under increasing institutional pressures. Once a firm ignores the existing problems or mistakes it makes, it overlooks the possible negative outcome from those mistakes. When institutional pressures intensify, such as announced recalls, it may not have time to respond strategically, nor have the resources to pool to help it through.

Le Qu Toys

Le Qu Toys was a family-owned company established in 1987 in Dongguan, Guangdong. Gam-gwan Dang, owner of the company, built Le Qu from scratch. By producing toys for foreign companies and developing its own brands, Le Qu became the third largest toy manufacturer in Dongguan. Different from Lee Der, Le Qu had its own design team and was able to produce its own brands, such as Di Qu intellectual toys. However, most of its profit came from its foreign importers. Also different from Lee Der, Le Qu had been carefully following domestic requirements for manufacturing quality. Le Qu exported toys to the United States, Europe, and Africa, and enjoyed a good reputation among partners and competitors since the beginning of its establishment.

Dang was overwhelmed by the success of Le Qu. As a successful entrepreneur, he became a billionaire. But he failed to anticipate the serious consequences that the recalls could bring to him and to Le Qu. In fact, he did not do much to prevent recalls from happening. In 2007, Le Qu also received recalls from Mattel. Le Qu was so vulnerable that it did not survive the recall due to a lack of experience, preparation, and sufficient working capital. In early 2008, Le Qu filed for bankruptcy and afterwards Dang sold all his Le Qu properties.

Like many other toymakers in China, Le Qu failed to pay attention to the rules of the game overseas. Although it had a long history of relationships with companies from around the world, it did not learn much from them. Only after the recall arrived did Le Qu realize the importance of complying with foreign regulations. Unfortunately, Le Qu's late response led to fatal consequences. Companies that adopt a defensive strategy such as Le Qu face the possibility of losing legitimacy in the eyes of their stakeholders (such as foreign importers), consumers, and governments. They may also become vulnerable after foreign institutional pressures begin asserting their influence.

Early Light Industrial Co., Ltd. (ELI)

ELI is a private company owned by Francis Choi, an entrepreneur in Hong Kong. Choi started the company in 1972. In 1983, he became one of the earliest entrepreneurs to establish factories in mainland China. After two decades of development, ELI became one of the largest toy manufacturers in the world, producing leading toy products such as those associated with Snoopy.

ELI faced the same problem of excessive lead levels in their paint that Lee Der experienced. Also in 2007, ELI received a recall from Mattel to withdraw 436,000 pieces of "Sarge" toy cars from the US market. However, this did not become a disaster for ELI. In fact, the toys involved in this recall were not manufactured in ELI's factories. Instead, they were made by ELI's subcontractors.

Before the recall was announced, ELI had already found that problems might arise due to the unstable quality of its paint suppliers. Different from Lee Der and Le Qu, ELI did not tolerate this problem. It made several moves to avoid future issues. First, it built new factories to integrate each process of its toy manufacturing in 2005, far earlier than the 2007 recall. Then, it signed contracts with several subcontractors to deal with the increasing demand in the market to support its expansion. Only those that had good quality and high productivity were considered. In addition, ELI built its own inspection team to test any hazardous elements of its products and control the quality of its toys.

Nevertheless, ELI could not control certain problems, given its limited resources—for instance, its subcontractors made mistakes, too. This was the main reason ELI received recalls in 2007. After the recalls, ELI realized it needed to make itself less dependent on subcontractors in the future. As for its next move, ELI plans to reduce the percentage of product made by its subcontractors to 10% in 2008 and aims to soon use no subcontractors.

Companies such as ELI, which take their responsibility seriously and continuously improve themselves, often proactively act before recalls happen and so avoid possible losses. As a result, these companies have a higher chance of maintaining their legitimacy under institutional pressures.

The Road Ahead

Of course, this is not just a toy problem. The strategic choices a company makes when facing institutional pressures from home and abroad are crucial. Chinese regulations for manufacturing exist, but they are not vigorously enforced until an outcry erupts from overseas recalls. To simply gamble, as many Chinese toymakers have done—hoping they can "get by" without devoting serious effort to meeting quality standards—is no longer viable in today's global marketplace. For Chinese toy exporters that have survived this crisis but more generally for concerned companies around the globe, the lesson is that a more proactive strategy is the best safeguard against possible negative consequences down the road.

Sources: Based on (1) H. Bapuji & P. W. Beamish, 2008, Mattel and the Toy Recalls (A) and (B), Ivey Case Study, University of Western Ontario; (2) China Central Television (CCTV) reports; (3) CNN reports online; (4) M. W. Peng & H. Chen, 2008, Strategic responses to global institutional pressures in the Chinese toy industry, Working paper, University of Texas at Dallas; (5) Southern Metropolis Daily; (6) www.lequ.com; (7) www.cpsc.gov.

Case Discussion Questions

1. What are the pros and cons of each of these strategic choices?

2. If you were a toy company executive and you were aware that the problem behind the recall was due to design flaws and not manufacturing flaws, what would be your reaction?

3. If your company's products were cited as unsafe, what strategy would you choose to deal with the crisis?

Business-Level Strategies

Foreign Markets Entries

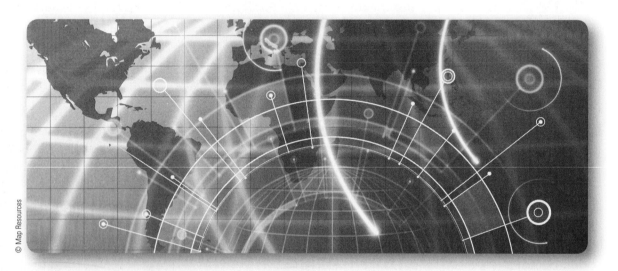

KNOWLEDGE OBJECTIVES

After studying this chapter, you should be able to

1. Understand the necessity to overcome the liability of foreignness

2. Articulate a comprehensive model of foreign market entries

3. Match the quest for location-specific advantages with strategic goals (*where* to enter)

4. Compare and contrast first and late mover advantages (*when* to enter)

5. Follow a decision model that outlines specific steps for foreign market entries (*how* to enter)

6. Participate in three leading debates on foreign market entries

7. Draw strategic implications for action

Opening Case: Wal-Mart in Germany

Wal-Mart is the world's largest company ranked by sales. Its sales are as big as its main US rivals—Costco, Home Depot, Kmart, Kroger, Sears, and Target—*combined*. In 2007, it operated 3,900 stores in the United States and 2,700 stores in Argentina, Brazil, Britain, Canada, China, Japan, Mexico, and Puerto Rico. Conspicuously missing from this list is Germany, from which Wal-Mart pulled out in humiliation in 2006 after ten years of struggle.

Wal-Mart went to Germany in 1997, after acquiring two German store chains, Wertkauf and Interspar. Competitors naturally trembled, given Wal-Mart's fearsome reputation as a super low-cost competitor. Soon, Competitors found that they could breathe more easily, because Wal-Mart seemed to get nearly everything wrong in what experts called "a textbook case of how not to enter a foreign market."

Although the $370 billion German retail market was huge and lucrative, it was populated by formidable competitors, such as Metro, Aldi, and Lidl. As incumbents, they had been around for a long time and knew the needs and wants of German shoppers inside and out. Wal-Mart, having never competed in continental Europe prior to its 1997 entry into Germany, had to learn from scratch.

Strategically, Wal-Mart found it difficult to flex its muscles. German shopping hours are short, so Wal-Mart had to forget about offering 24-hour shopping. Stores had to close on Sundays. What was worse, Wal-Mart had fierce competition from Aldi and Lidl, two aggressive discount chains. Wal-Mart was unable to undercut its rivals' prices because Wal-Mart's infrastructure in Germany, which for a while supported two costly headquarters, piled up too much cost without achieving economies of scale.

On the people side, Wal-Mart also made a mistake by first appointing an American boss for Germany who spoke no German. In addition, he insisted that his German managers speak English. The next head, an Englishman, tried to run the show from Britain. These foreign bosses failed to connect with the German customers and employees. The insistence that staff smile at customers as brightly as possible and help them pack their shopping bags was a mistake in Germany since many Germans regarded such behavior from shop personnel with deep suspicion and felt uncomfortable. German employees felt equally uncomfortable and awkward when being told to follow a simple "American" wish: smile at customers.

Wal-Mart did not give up without putting up a strong fight, though. After installing a German chief, Wal-Mart was savvier about the local market by catering to local tastes better—for example, offering a special on fresh carp, an Easter specialty. However, in Germany, Wal-Mart's 95 stores failed to match Aldi's 4,000 in terms of convenience. In terms of prices, even when Wal-Mart could selectively undercut Aldi, the price differences were often too little to motivate shoppers to travel the extra distance to a less conveniently located Wal-Mart store. While Wal-Mart enjoyed a scale advantage on globally sourced products, its bargaining power did not translate to regional brands of bratwurst and beer. Wal-Mart tried to improve distribution and build relationships with local suppliers, but it was stuck in the middle between improving existing store sales and building more new ones, which would be time-consuming and costly.

In the grocery market in Germany, Wal-Mart commanded only a 2% market share ($3.2 billion a year), whereas Aldi boasted a 19% share. In its ten years in Germany, only once did Wal-Mart publish its financial results: It lost $550 million in 2003. By the time Wal-Mart sold its stores to Metro, another German rival, for an undisclosed amount in 2006, it declared that it would take a one-time charge of €1 billion on completion. Therefore, it is safe to assume that the mighty Wal-Mart never made a tiny profit in Germany.

Sources: Based on (1) *Business Week,* 2005, Wal-Mart, April 11: 54; (2) *The Economist,* 2006, Heading for the exit, August 5: 54; (3) *The Economist,* 2006, Trouble at till, November 4: 18; (4) Wikipedia, 2008, Wal-Mart (en.wikipedia.org).

How do companies such as Wal-Mart enter foreign markets? Why do they enter certain countries but not others? In Germany, why did Wal-Mart fail to translate its success at home and in other countries? These are some of the key questions addressed in this chapter. Entering foreign markets is crucial for global strategy. Focusing on the necessity to overcome the liability of foreignness, this chapter develops a comprehensive model based on the "strategy tripod"—namely, industry-, resource-, and institution-based views. Then we focus on three crucial dimensions: *w*here, *w*hen, and *how*—known as the 2W1H dimensions. Debates and extensions follow.

Overcoming the Liability of Foreignness

Although globalization gurus such as Thomas Friedman and Theodore Levitt claim that the world is "flat,"[1] the reality is that the world is still full of bumps. Far from full globalization, our world, at best, can be seen as undergoing "semiglobalization" according to Pankaj Ghemawat (as first discussed in Chapter 1).[2] Consequently, even highly capable companies such as Wal-Mart cannot guarantee successful foreign market entries. Wal-Mart's experience in Germany is far from an isolated event; in 2006, it also withdrew from South Korea. And it is not alone. Numerous other firms have been burned overseas.

Why is it so challenging to succeed overseas? This is primarily because of the **liability of foreignness,** which is the *inherent* disadvantage foreign firms experience in host countries because of their non-native status.[3] Such a liability is manifested in at least two dimensions. First, numerous differences exist in formal and informal institutions governing the rules of the game (such as regulatory, language, and cultural differences). While local firms are already well versed in these rules, foreign firms have to quickly learn them. As Wal-Mart painfully found out in Germany, failure to learn these rules may have costly consequences.

liability of foreignness

The inherent disadvantage foreign firms experience in host countries because of their nonnative status.

Strategy in Action 5.1 - A Warship Named *Joint Venture*

With a military budget larger than that of the next five powers combined, the United States is the world's largest defense market. For non-US firms, however, this is also the toughest nut to crack because the US military is famously protective of US firms. It is, therefore, remarkable that one Australian shipbuilder, Incat, has overcome a substantial liability of foreignness by whetting the appetite of *all* branches of the US military (except the Air Force). Its secret? A world-leading technology in high-speed wave-piercing catamarans that allows it to have an approximately 50% global market share of high-speed commercial ferries. With relatively slight modifications, this technology can be adapted for military sealift and amphibious operations. In 2001, Incat produced a 96-meter ship, appropriately named *Joint Venture* (HSV-X1), as an evaluation platform for the joint forces of the US Navy, Marine Corps, Army, and Coast Guard. In 2003, *Joint Venture* successfully acted as a command, control, and staging platform for the special operations forces that took the Iraqi port of Umm Qasr. Its sister ship, *Spearhead* (TSV-1X), left Australia and sailed straight to the Persian Gulf in 2002. *Spearhead* also excelled in Iraq in 2003. The overwhelming interest from US forces has led Incat to set up a (real) joint venture (JV) with Bollinger, a builder of US Navy and Coast Guard patrol boats,

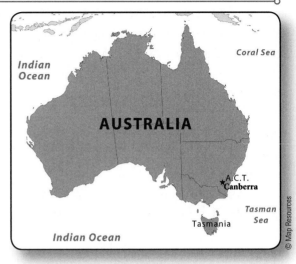

to capitalize on such opportunities. In 2005, the two ships distinguished themselves in the Hurricane Katrina relief efforts because they were able to deliver a large payload directly to the beach when port facilities were damaged. There is no doubt more ships built by Incat and its JV partner will be operated by US forces in the future.

Sources: Based on (1) www.bollinger-incatusa.com and (2) www. incat.com.au.

Second, although customers in this age of globalization *supposedly* no longer discriminate against foreign firms, the reality is that foreign firms are often still discriminated against, sometimes formally and other times informally. For example, in government procurement, most governments prefer to "buy national" (such as "Buy American"). In consumer products, the discrimination against foreign firms is less, but is still far from disappearing. For years, American rice and beef, suspected (although never proven) to contain long-term health hazards because of genetic modification, have been informally resisted by individual consumers in Japan and Europe, even *after* formal discriminatory policies imposed by their governments were removed.

Against such significant odds, the primary weapon foreign firms use is to deploy overwhelming resources and capabilities in the hope of offsetting the liability of foreignness, while still leaving them some competitive advantage.[4] Strategy in Action 5.1 outlines how an Australian shipbuilder charged into the intensely competitive US defense market by developing overwhelming capabilities that four branches of the US military craved.

Understanding the Propensity to Internationalize

Despite recent preaching by some gurus that every firm should go abroad, the reality is that not every firm is ready for it. Prematurely venturing overseas may be detrimental to overall firm performance, especially for smaller firms whose margin for error is very small. Even for large firms such as Wal-Mart, burning cash in Germany with no hope in sight does not make sense either (Opening Case). Therefore, strategists need to carefully decide whether doing business abroad is warranted. So what motivates some firms to go abroad, while others are happy to stay at home?

At the risk of oversimplification, we can identify two underlying factors: (1) size of the firm and (2) size of the domestic market, which lead to a 2 × 2 framework (Figure 5.1). In Cell 1, large firms in a small domestic market are likely to be very enthusiastic internationalizers, because they can quickly exhaust opportunities in a small country. Consider ABB of Switzerland, which specializes in large power-generation equipment (and many other products). The demand for such equipment in Switzerland is rather limited. As a result, 97% of ABB's sales and 95% of its employees are outside of Switzerland.

In Cell 2, many small firms in a small domestic market are labeled "follower internationalizers," because they often follow their larger counterparts to go abroad as suppliers.[5] Even small firms that do not directly supply large firms may similarly venture abroad, because of the inherently limited size of the domestic market. A considerable number of small firms from small countries such as Austria, Finland, Hong Kong, New Zealand, and Singapore are active overseas.

In Cell 3, large firms in a large domestic market are labeled "slow internationalizers," because their overseas activities are usually (but not always) slower than those of enthusiastic internationalizers in Cell 1. For example, Wal-Mart's pace of internationalization is slower when compared with its two global rivals based in relatively smaller countries, Carrefour of France and Metro of Germany.

FIGURE 5.1   Firm Size, Domestic Market Size, and Propensity to Internationalize

	Size of the Firm		
Size of the Domestic Market	(Cell 1) Enthusiastic internationalizer	(Cell 2) Follower internationalizer	*Small Domestic Market*
	(Cell 3) Slow internationalizer	(Cell 4) Occasional internationalizer	*Large Domestic Market*
	Large Firm	*Small Firm*	

FIGURE 5.2   A Comprehensive Model of Foreign Market Entries

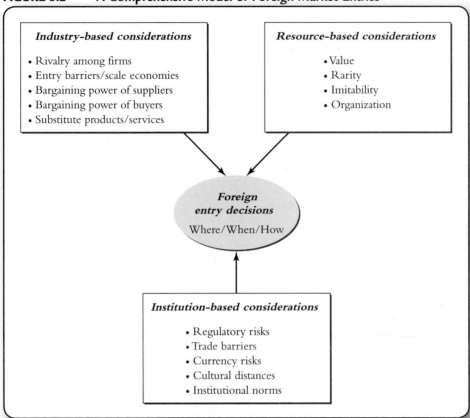

Finally, in Cell 4, most small firms in a large domestic market confront a "double whammy" on the road to internationalization, both because of their relatively poor resource base and the size of their domestic market. Many small firms in the United States do not feel compelled to go abroad. Overall, small firms in a large domestic market can be labeled "occasional internationalizers" (that is, if they have any international business at all). One joke is that if the United States were divided into 50 independent countries, then the number of US multinational enterprises (MNEs) would skyrocket.[6]

A Comprehensive Model of Foreign Market Entries

Assuming the decision to internationalize is a "go," strategists must make a series of decisions regarding the location, timing, and mode of entry, collectively known as the *w*here, *w*hen, and *h*ow ("2W1H") aspects, respectively.[7] Underlying each decision is a set of strategic considerations drawn from the three leading perspectives discussed earlier, which form a comprehensive model (Figure 5.2).

Industry-Based Considerations

Industry-based considerations are primarily drawn from the five forces framework first introduced in Chapter 2. First, rivalry among established firms may prompt certain moves. Firms, especially those in oligopolistic industries, often match each other in foreign entries.[8] If Komatsu and FedEx enter a new country—let's say Afghanistan—Caterpillar and DHL, respectively, probably would feel compelled to follow. Sometimes, firms may enter foreign markets to retaliate. For example, Texas Instruments (TI) entered Japan not to make money but to *lose* money. The reason was that TI faced the low price Japanese challenge in many markets, whereas rivals such as NEC and Toshiba were able to charge high prices in Japan and use domestic profits to cross-subsidize their overseas expansion. By entering Japan and slashing prices there, TI retaliated by incurring a loss. This forced the Japanese firms to defend their profit sanctuary at home, whereby they had more to lose.

Second, the higher the entry barriers, the more intense firms will be in attempting to compete abroad. A strong presence overseas in itself can be seen as a major entry barrier. By tapping into wider and bigger markets, international sales can increase scale economies and deter entry. It would be mind-boggling to imagine how high the costs of Boeing and Airbus aircraft would be in the absence of international sales.

Third, the bargaining power of suppliers may prompt certain foreign market entries, often called backward vertical integration because they involve multiple stages of the value chain. Many extractive industries feature extensive backward integration overseas (such as bauxite mining), in order to provide a steady supply of raw materials to late stage production (such as aluminum smelting). Since natural resources are not always found in politically stable countries, many firms have no choice but to enter politically uncertain countries. Still remember the 1998 James Bond movie, *The World Is Not Enough*? It features the Caspian Sea oil intrigue involving Western MNEs, former Soviet republics, and Middle Eastern countries, and the plot thickens with an attempted nuclear explosion in Istanbul, Turkey. While the movie is fictitious, the real world of oil exploration is perhaps no less risky (or exciting). At present, Western oil exploration vessels are surveying the South China Sea. Each boat is escorted by naval warships of China, Indonesia, Malaysia, Philippines, and Vietnam—all armed to the teeth with real guns and missiles aimed at each other (!). Why do these Western MNEs go through such troubles to secure oil supplies? Evidently, the costs of going through such troubles are still less than the costs of having to deal with strong, unfriendly suppliers such as OPEC.

Fourth, the bargaining power of buyers may lead to certain foreign market entries, often called forward vertical integration.[9] Sony, for example, has entered downstream activities abroad through the acquisition of Columbia Pictures and Sony Music. Despite the huge financial costs, it is often believed that the benefits outweigh the costs under certain circumstances.

Finally, the market potential of substitute products may encourage firms to bring them abroad. If the third-generation (3G) wireless technology, in addition to being a cell phone, can indeed substitute for videoconferencing, cameras, camcorders, e-mails, and game machines, people in a variety of countries may demand it. It is based on this belief that Hutchison Whampoa, a Hong Kong–based conglomerate, has embarked on an ambitious but risky campaign to bring 3G to nine countries.

Overall, how an industry is structured and how its five forces are played out significantly affect foreign entry decisions.[10] Next, we examine the influence of resource-based considerations.

Resource-Based Considerations

The VRIO framework introduced in Chapter 3 sheds considerable light on entry decisions, with a focus on their *v*alue, *r*arity, *i*mitability, and *o*rganization aspects (Figure 5.2).[11] First, the value of firm-specific resources and capabilities plays a key role behind decisions to internationalize.[12] It is often the superb value of firm-specific assets that allows foreign entrants to overcome the liability of foreignness. Sadly, Wal-Mart failed to provide much value to shoppers in Germany (Opening Case).

Second, the rarity of firm-specific assets encourages firms that possess them to leverage such assets overseas. Patents, brands, and trademarks legally protect the rarity of certain product features. It is not surprising that patented and branded products, such as cars and DVDs, are often aggressively marketed overseas. However, here is a paradox: Given the uneven protection of intellectual property rights, the more countries these products are sold in (becoming less rare), the more likely counterfeits will pop up somewhere around the globe. The question of rarity, therefore, directly leads to the next issue of imitability.

Third, if firms are concerned that their imitable assets might be expropriated in certain countries, they may choose *not* to enter. In other words, the transaction costs may be too high. This is primarily because of **dissemination risks,** defined as the risks associated with the unauthorized imitation and diffusion of firm-specific assets. If a foreign company grants a license to a local firm to manufacture or market a product, "it runs the risk of the licensee, or an employee of the licensee, disseminating the know-how or using it for purposes other than those originally intended."[13] The worst nightmare is to have nurtured a competitor, as Pizza Hut found out in Thailand. Pizza Hut's long-time franchise operator in Thailand disseminated Pizza Hut's know-how and established a direct competitor, The Pizza Company, which recently controlled 70% of the market in Thailand.[14]

Finally, the organization of firm-specific resources and capabilities as a *bundle* favors firms with strong complementary assets integrated as a system and encourages them to utilize these assets overseas. Many MNEs are organized in a way that protects them against entry and favors them as entrants into other markets—consider the near total vertical integration at ExxonMobil and BP.

In summary, the resource-based view suggests an important set of underlying considerations underpinning entry decisions. In the case of imitability and dissemination risk, it is obvious that these issues are related to property rights protection, which leads to our next topic.

Institution-Based Considerations

dissemination risks

The risks associated with the unauthorized diffusion of firm-specific assets.

Since Chapter 4 has already illustrated a number of *informal* institutional differences such as cultural differences, here we focus on the *formal* institutional constraints confronting foreign entrants: (1) regulatory risks, (2) trade barriers, and (3) currency risks (Figure 5.2).

Strategy in Action 5.2 - Chinese Banks Eye US Assets: Tough Road Ahead

The subprime mess has crushed US bank stocks but has stimulated interest among Chinese banks eyeing the US market. Hot domestic growth and active trading pushed China's top three banks, Industrial and Commercial Bank of China, China Construction Bank, and Bank of China, to be the top three banks in the *world* (in the order shown here) by market value, overtaking HSBC (4th), Bank of America (5th), Citigroup (6th), and JP Morgan Chase (7th). In early 2008, of the 14 banks listed in Shanghai, the average price-to-earnings ratio was 41.3. This gave them plenty of buying power, especially when compared with US rivals' average ratio of 10.6.

However, plenty of Chinese cash and desperate US banks in need of cash injections may not be good enough for the deals to work. Roadblock number one is US regulators. The Federal Reserve System (or the "Fed" in short) must sign off on any deal in which a foreign investor takes more than 5% of equity in a US bank. When evaluating Chinese banks' applications, the Fed lacks experience because they operate in a very different regulatory environment. All three top banks are state owned with a history of lax oversight and corruption—Bank of China was engulfed in a scandal when, in 2002, its New York branch made improper loans and was fined by both US and Chinese regulators for $20 million. However, blatant discrimination against Chinese banks would not only violate US and WTO regulations for free market access, but would also jeopardize US banks' own expansion in China. China limits foreign equity in its banks to 25%, but China's regulators have hinted that if US counterparts approve more applications of Chinese banks to open US branches, China may raise these caps.

As of this writing (February 2008), only one mainland Chinese bank was approved to make a strategic investment in a US bank. In November 2007, Mingsheng Bank, China's eighth-largest (with $111 billion assets), bought a 10% stake in the San Francisco–based UCBH Holdings (NASDAQ: UCBH—with $10 billion assets). Mingsheng's victory was intriguing, as UCBH, in need of cash, had considered several state-owned Chinese partners. However, in the end UCBH opted to team up with Mingsheng because Mingsheng was one of the few privately owned banks that had limited ties to the Chinese government and therefore had the best chance of clearing the Fed's regulatory hurdle.

Despite its victory as a first mover, Mingsheng cannot laugh too hard because the road ahead will be tough. Foreign banks have a history of charging into the United States with mega-spending and then getting burned big time. In 2003, the highly capable HSBC spent $14 billion to buy Household to enter the US subprime mortgage market and burned an $11 billion hole on its balance sheet in 2007. Given the real estate meltdown, "you would have to be extremely brave," said one expert, "or extremely stupid to buy a US bank."

Sources: Based on (1) *Business Week,* 2007, Chinese banks head for the US, November 5: 28–29; (2) *Business Week,* Deals gone bad, December 17: 11; (3) M. W. Peng, 2006, Making M&As fly in China, *Harvard Business Review,* March: 26–27; (4) *www.cmbc.com.cn;* (5) www.ucbh.com.

REGULATORY RISKS

These are defined as those risks associated with unfavorable government policies (see Strategy in Action 5.2). Some governments may demand that foreign entrants share technology with local firms, essentially *increasing* the dissemination risk. Even as a WTO member, the Chinese government has continued its historical practice of approving only joint ventures for foreign automakers and has banned their attempt to set up wholly-owned subsidiaries. The government's openly proclaimed goal has been to "encourage" local automakers to learn from their foreign partners.

A well-known regulatory risk is the **obsolescing bargain,** referring to the deal struck by MNEs and host governments, which change their requirements *after* the entry of MNEs.[15] It typically unfolds in three rounds:

- In Round One, the MNE and the government negotiate a deal. The MNE usually is not willing to enter in the absence of some reasonable government assurance of property rights, earnings, and even some incentives (such as tax holidays).

- In Round Two, the MNE enters and, if all goes well, earns profits that may become visible.

- In Round Three, the government, often pressured by domestic political groups, may demand renegotiations of the deal that seems to yield "excessive" profits to the foreign firm (which, of course, regards these as "fair" and "normal" profits). The previous deal, therefore, becomes obsolete.

The government's tactics include removing incentives, demanding a higher share of profits and taxes, and even confiscating foreign assets—in other words, **expropriation.** The Indian government in the 1970s, for example, demanded that Coca-Cola share its secret formula, something that the MNE did not even share with the US government. At this time, the MNE has already invested substantial sums of resources (called **sunk costs**) and often has to accommodate some new demands; otherwise, it may face expropriation or exit at a huge loss (as Coca-Cola did in India). Coca-Cola's experience in India, unfortunately, was not alone. Numerous governments in Africa, Asia, and Latin America in the 1950s, 1960s, and 1970s expropriated MNE assets through nationalization by turning them over to state-owned enterprises (SOEs). It is not surprising that foreign firms do not appreciate the risk associated with such obsolescing bargains.[16]

Recently, some decisive changes have occurred around the world in favor of foreign entries (see Chapter 1). Many governments increasingly realize that nationalization of foreign MNE assets does not necessarily maximize their national interests. While expropriation drives MNEs away, SOEs are often unable to run the operations as effectively as did MNEs and so most SOEs end up losing money and destroying value. Therefore, the global trend since the 1980s and 1990s has been privatization, which, being the opposite of nationalization, turns state-owned assets into private firms (see Chapter 11). Interestingly, many private bidders are MNEs.[17] Understandably, MNEs often push for the transparency and predictability in host-government decision making *before* committing to new deals. Coca-Cola, for example, agreed to return to India in the 1990s with an explicit commitment from the government that its secret formula would be untouchable.

Overall, there is a global competition among host governments (especially those in the developing world) to transform their relationship with MNEs from a confrontational to a cooperative one.[18] While regulatory risks, especially those associated with expropriation, have decreased significantly around the world, individual countries still vary considerably, thus calling for very careful analysis of such risks.[19] As recently as in 2006, Venezuela, Bolivia, and Ecuador expropriated the oil fields run by some Western MNEs.

TRADE BARRIERS.

Trade barriers include (1) tariff and nontariff barriers, (2) local content requirements, and (3) restrictions on certain entry modes. **Tariff barriers,** taxes levied on imports, are

obsolescing bargain
The deals struck by MNEs and host governments, which change their requirements after the entry of MNEs.

expropriation
Confiscation of foreign assets invested in one country.

sunk costs
Irrevocable costs occurred and investments made.

trade barriers
Barriers blocking international trade.

tariff barriers
Taxes levied on imports.

government-imposed entry barriers. **Nontariff barriers** are more subtle. For example, the Japanese customs inspectors, in the name of detecting unwanted bacteria from abroad, often insist on cutting *every* tulip bulb exported from the Netherlands vertically down the middle. The Dutch argument that their tulips have been safely exported to just about every other country in the world has not been persuasive in Japan. These barriers effectively encourage foreign entrants to produce locally and discourage them from exporting.

However, even after foreign entrants set up factories locally, they can still export completely knocked down (CKD) kits to be assembled in host countries. Such factories are nicknamed "screw-driver plants"—only screw drivers plus local labor would be needed. In response, many governments have imposed **local content requirements,** mandating that a "domestically produced" product can still be subject to tariff and nontariff barriers unless a certain fraction of its value (such as 51% in the United States) is truly produced domestically.

Certain entry modes also have restrictions. Many countries limit or even ban wholly foreign-owned subsidiaries. For example, in the United States, foreign airlines are not allowed to operate wholly owned subsidiaries or acquire US airlines. They are only allowed to control no more than 25% equity of any US airline (a ceiling reached by KLM Royal Dutch Airlines in Northwest Airlines).

CURRENCY RISKS

Currency risks stem from unfavorable movements of the currencies to which firms are exposed. For instance, Nestle's sales volume in Brazil grew by 10% during 2002. But because of currency deterioration, its Brazil revenues in Swiss francs actually went *down* by 30% during the same period.[20] Honda is similarly hurt by the strong yen, which appreciated against the dollar since 2000. Since Honda made 80% of its profits in the United States, their value, when translated into the Japanese yen, became much lower.[21] If the Chinese yuan appreciates (as demanded by the US government), domestic and foreign firms producing there may lose a significant chunk of their low-cost advantage.

In response, firms can speculate or hedge.[22] **Speculation** involves commitments to stable currencies. However, this is risky in case of wrong bets of currency movements. For example, Japan Airlines (JAL) needed US dollars to purchase Boeing aircraft but its revenues were mostly in yen. In 1985, it entered a 10-year contract with foreign exchange traders at a rate of $1 to 185 yen. This looked like a great deal given the 1985 exchange rate of $1 to 240 yen. However, by 1994, the yen had surged against the dollar to $1 to 99 yen. Because JAL was bound by the contract to purchase dollars at the rate of $1 to 185 yen, it was paying 86% (!) more than it needed to for every Boeing aircraft it bought.[23] **Hedging** means spreading out activities in a number of countries in different currency zones in order to offset the currency losses in certain regions through gains in other regions. This was one of the key motivations behind Toyota's 1998 decision to set up a new factory in France, instead of expanding its existing British operations (which would cost less in the short run)—France is in the Euro zone that the British refused to join.

In addition to *formal* institutional constraints, firms also need to develop a sophisticated understanding of numerous *informal* aspects such as cultural distances and institutional norms. Since Chapter 4 has already discussed these issues at length, we will not repeat them here other than to stress their importance. We will, however, revisit some of them in the next section.

---

nontariff barriers

Trade and investment barriers which do not entail tariffs.

local content requirements

Government requirements that certain products be subject to higher import tariffs and taxes unless a given percentage of their value is produced domestically.

currency risks

Risks stemming from exposure to unfavorable movements of the currencies.

speculation

Making bets on currency movements by committing to stable currencies.

hedging

Spreading out activities in a number of countries in different currency zones to offset the currency losses in certain regions through gains in other regions.

Overall, the value of the core proposition of the institution-based perspective on strategy, "Institutions matter," is *magnified* in foreign entry decisions.[24] Rushing abroad without a solid understanding of institutional differences can be hazardous and even disastrous.

Where to Enter?

Like real estate, the motto for international business is "Location, location, location." In fact, such a *spatial* perspective (that is, doing business outside of one's home country) is a defining feature of international business.[25] Two sets of considerations drive the location of foreign entries: (1) strategic goals and (2) cultural and institutional distances. Each is discussed next.

Location-Specific Advantages and Strategic Goals

Favorable locations in certain countries may give firms operating there what are called **location-specific advantages.** We may regard the continuous expansion of international business as an unending saga in search of location-specific advantages. Certain locations simply possess geographical features that are difficult to match by others. Singapore, for instance, is an ideal stopping point for sea and air traffic connecting Europe and the Middle East on the one hand, and East Asia and Australia on the other. Vienna is an attractive site as MNE regional headquarters for Central and Eastern Europe. Miami, which advertises itself as the "Gateway of the Americas," is an ideal location both for North American firms looking south and Latin American companies coming north.

Beyond geographical advantages, location-specific advantages also arise from the clustering of economic activities in certain locations, usually referred to as **agglomeration.** The basic idea dates back at least to Alfred Marshall, a British economist who first published it in 1890. Essentially, location-specific advantages stem from (1) knowledge spillovers among closely located firms that attempt to hire individuals from competitors, (2) industry demand that creates a skilled labor force whose members may work for different firms without having to move out of the region, and (3) industry demand that facilitates a pool of specialized suppliers and buyers to also locate in the region.[26] Because, due to agglomeration, certain cities and regions can develop a cluster of related businesses in the *absence* of obvious geographic advantages, this idea has great appeal to policymakers. Inspired by Silicon Valley, in the United States we now have Silicon Forest (Portland, Oregon), Silicon Mountain (Colorado Springs), and Silicon Alley (Manhattan). Around the world, we can find Silicon Island (Singapore), Silicon Bog (Ireland), Silicon Glen (Scotland), Silicon North (Ottawa), and Silicon Wadi (Israel).

Given that different locations offer different benefits, it is imperative that strategic goals be matched with locations (Table 5.1).

- Firms interested in **seeking natural resources** have to go after certain resources that are tied to particular foreign locations, such as oil in the Middle East, Russia, and Venezuela. Although the Venezuelan government has become more hostile now, Western oil firms have to put up with it.

location-specific advantages

Advantages associated with operating in a specific location.

agglomeration

Clustering economic activities in certain locations.

natural resource seeking

Firms entering foreign markets in search of natural resources.

TABLE 5.1   Matching Strategic Goals with Locations

STRATEGIC GOALS	LOCATION-SPECIFIC ADVANTAGES	ILLUSTRATIVE LOCATIONS MENTIONED IN THE TEXT
Natural resource seeking	Possession of natural resources and related transport and communication infrastructure	Oil in the Middle East, Russia, and Venezuela
Market seeking	Abundance of strong market demand and customers willing to pay	Seafood in Japan
Efficiency seeking	Economies of scale and abundance of low-cost factors	Manufacturing in China; copper refining in Texas
Innovation seeking	Abundance of innovative individuals, firms, and universities	IT in Silicon Valley and Bangalore; financial services in New York and London; aerospace in Russia

- **Market seeking** firms go after countries that offer strong demand for their products and services. For example, the Japanese appetite and willingness to pay for seafood has motivated seafood exporters around the world—ranging from the nearby China and Korea to the distant Norway and Peru—to ship their catch to Japan in order to fetch top dollar (or yen).

- **Efficiency seeking** firms often single out the most efficient locations featuring a combination of scale economies and low-cost factors.[27] Numerous MNEs have entered China, which now manufactures two-thirds of the world's photocopiers, shoes, toys, and microwave ovens; half of its DVD players, digital cameras, and textiles; one-third of its desktop computers; and a quarter of its mobile phones, TV sets, and steel.[28] Shanghai alone reportedly has a cluster of over 300 of the *Fortune* Global 500 firms there. It is important to note that China does not present the absolutely lowest labor costs in the world, and Shanghai is the *highest* cost city in China. However, its attractiveness lies in its ability to enhance foreign entrants' efficiency by lowering *total* costs. Since the key efficiency concern is lowest total costs, it is also not surprising that some nominally "high cost" countries (such as the United States) continue to attract significant FDI. For instance, Grupo Mexico, the world's third largest copper producer, has moved some of its energy-thirsty refining operations from "high cost" Mexico to "low cost" Texas, where electricity costs 4 cents per kilowatt hour as opposed to 8.5 cents in Mexico.[29]

- **Innovation seeking** firms target countries and regions renowned for generating world-class innovations, such as Silicon Valley and Bangalore (IT), New York and London (financial services), and Russia (aerospace). Such entries can be viewed as "an option to maintain access to innovations resident in the host country, thus generating information spillovers that may lead to opportunities for future organizational learning and growth"[30] (see Chapter 10 for details).

Overall, these four strategic goals, while analytically distinct, are not mutually exclusive. Also, location-specific advantages may grow, evolve, and/or decline. If policymakers fail to maintain the institutional attractiveness (for example, by raising taxes) and if companies overcrowd and bid up factor costs such as land and talents, some firms may move out of locations previously considered advantageous.[31] For instance, Mercedes and BMW had proudly projected a 100% "Made in Germany"

market seeking

Firms going after the most lucrative markets for their products and services.

efficiency seeking

Firms going after certain locations in search of efficiency gains.

innovation seeking

Firms targeting countries and regions renowned for generating world-class.

image until the early 1990s. Both are now replacing it with "Made by Mercedes" and "Made by BMW" products manufactured in countries such as Brazil, China, Mexico, South Africa, and the United States. Such an emphasis on firm-specific (as opposed to location-specific) advantages illustrates both the relative decline of Germany's location-specific advantages and the rise of other countries' advantages.

Cultural/Institutional Distances and Foreign Entry Locations

In addition to strategic goals, another set of considerations centers on cultural/institutional distances (see also Chapter 4). **Cultural distance** is the difference between two cultures along some identifiable dimensions (such as individualism).[32] Considering culture as an informal part of institutional frameworks governing a particular country, **institutional distance** is "the extent of similarity or dissimilarity between the regulatory, normative, and cognitive institutions of two countries."[33] Many Western consumer products firms have shied away from Saudi Arabia citing its stricter rules of personal behavior—in essence, its cultural and institutional distance being too large.

Two schools of thought have emerged. The first is associated with **stage models,** arguing that firms will enter culturally similar countries during their first stage of internationalization, and that they may gain more confidence to enter culturally distant countries in later stages.[34] This idea is intuitively appealing: It makes sense for Belgium firms to first enter France, taking advantage of common cultural and language traditions. Business between countries that share a language on average is three times greater than between countries without a common language. Firms from common-law countries (English-speaking countries and Britain's former colonies) are more likely to be interested in other common-law countries. Colony-colonizer links (such as Britain's ties with the Commonwealth and Spain's with Latin America) boost trade significantly. In general, MNEs from emerging economies perform better in other developing countries, presumably because of their closer institutional distance and similar stages of economic development.[35] There is some evidence documenting certain performance benefits of competing in culturally and institutionally adjacent countries.[36]

Citing numerous counter-examples, a second school of thought argues that considerations of strategic goals such as market and efficiency are more important than cultural/institutional considerations.[37] For instance, natural resource seeking firms have some compelling reasons to enter culturally and institutionally distant countries (such as Papua New Guinea for bauxite, Zambia for copper, and Nigeria for oil). On Sakhalin Island, a very remote part of the Russian Far East, which is rich in energy reserves, Western oil majors have to live with Russia's unfriendly strong-arm tactics to grab more shares and profits that are recently described as "thuggish ways" by *The Economist*.[38] Because Western oil majors have few alternatives elsewhere, cultural, institutional, and geographic distance in this case does not seem relevant—they simply have to be there and let the Russians dictate the terms. Further, there is some counter-intuitive (although inconclusive) evidence that in a particular host country, firms from distant countries do not necessarily underperform those from neighboring countries.[39] Overall, in the complex calculus underpinning entry decisions, locations represent but one of several important sets of considerations. As shown next, entry timing and modes are also crucial.

cultural distance

The difference between two cultures along some identifiable dimensions.

institutional distance

The extent of similarity or dissimilarity between the regulatory, normative, and cognitive institutions of two countries.

stage models

Models which suggest firms internationalize by going through predictable stages from simple steps to complex operations.

When to Enter?

Unless a firm is approached by unsolicited foreign customers that may lead to "passive" entries, conscientious entry timing considerations center on whether there are compelling reasons to be early or late entrants in certain countries. There is often a quest for **first mover advantages,** defined as the advantages that first movers obtain and that later movers do not enjoy.[40] However, first movers may also encounter significant disadvantages, which in turn become **late mover advantages.** Table 5.2 shows a number of first mover advantages.

- First movers may gain advantage through proprietary technology. They also ride down the learning curve in pursuit of scale and scope economies in new countries.

- First movers may make preemptive investments. A number of Japanese MNEs have "cherry picked" leading local suppliers and distributors as new members of the expanded *keiretsu* networks in Southeast Asia, and blocked access to them by late entrants from the West.[41]

- First movers may erect significant entry barriers for late entrants, such as customer switching costs. Parents, having bought one brand of disposable diapers (such as Huggies or Pampers) for their first child, often stick with this brand for their other children.

- Intense domestic competition may drive some non-dominant firms to seek fortunes abroad in order to avoid clashing with dominant firms head-on in their home market. Among Japanese MNEs active in the United States, Sony, Honda, and Epson all entered ahead of their domestic industry leaders, Matsushita, Toyota, and NEC, respectively.

- First movers may build precious relationships with key stakeholders such as customers and governments. Motorola, for example, entered China in the early 1980s. Later, China adopted Motorola's technology as its national paging standard, locking out other rivals (at least for the initial period).

On the other hand, the potential advantages of first movers may be counterbalanced by various disadvantages (see Table 5.2). Examples abound where first mover firms have instead lost, such as EMI in CT scanners, de Haviland in jet airliners, and Netscape in Internet browsers. Learning from others' mistakes, late mover firms such as GE, Boeing, and Microsoft (Explorer), respectively, win. Specifically, late mover advantages are manifested in three ways.

first mover advantages

The advantages that first movers enjoy and later movers do not.

late mover advantages

Advantages associated with being a later mover (also known as first mover disadvantages).

TABLE 5.2   First Mover Advantages and Late Mover Advantages

First Mover Advantages	Late Mover Advantages (or First Mover Disadvantages)
• Proprietary, technological leadership	• Opportunity to free ride on first mover investments
• Preemption of scarce resources	• Resolution of technological and market uncertainty
• Establishment of entry barriers for late entrants	• First mover's difficulty to adapt to market changes
• Avoidance of clash with dominant firms at home	
• Relationships and connections with key stakeholders such as customers and governments	

- Late movers may be able to free ride on first movers' pioneering investments. For example, a first mover in 3G technology, such as Hong Kong's Hutchison Whampoa that is trying to introduce 3G in nine countries simultaneously, needs to incur huge advertising expenses to educate customers on *both* what 3G technology is and why its offering is the best. A late mover can free ride on such customer education by only focusing on why its particular product is the best.

- First movers face greater technological and market uncertainties. After some of these uncertainties are removed, late movers may join the game with massive firepower. Some MNEs such as IBM and Matsushita are known to have such a tendency.

- As incumbents, first movers may be locked into a given set of fixed assets or be reluctant to cannibalize existing product lines in favor of new ones. Late movers may be able to take advantage of first movers' inflexibility by leapfrogging first movers.

Overall, while there is some evidence pointing out first mover advantages,[42] there is also evidence supporting a late mover strategy.[43] Unfortunately, a mountain of research is still unable to conclusively recommend a particular entry timing strategy. Although first movers may have an *opportunity* to win, their pioneering status is not a birthright for success.[44] For example, among all three first movers that entered the Chinese automobile industry in the early 1980s, Volkswagen has captured significant advantages, Chrysler has had very moderate success, and Peugeot failed and had to exit. Among late movers that entered in the late 1990s, while many are struggling, GM, Honda, and Hyundai have gained significant market shares. It is obvious that entry timing cannot be viewed in isolation and entry timing per se is not the sole determinant of success and failure of foreign entries. It is through *interaction* with other strategic variables that entry timing has an impact on performance.[45]

How to Enter?

This section first focuses on the large- versus small-scale entry. Then, it introduces a decision model. The first step is to determine whether to pursue equity or non-equity modes of entry. This crucial decision differentiates MNEs (involving equity modes) from non-MNEs (relying on non-equity modes). Finally, we outline the pros and cons of various equity and non-equity modes.

Scale of Entry: Commitment and Experience

One key dimension in foreign entry decisions is the **scale of entry.** A number of European financial services firms, such as ABN Amro, HSBC, and ING Group, have recently spent several billion dollars to enter the United States by making a series of acquisitions. The benefits of these large-scale entries are a demonstration of strategic commitment to certain markets. This both helps assure local customers and suppliers ("We are here for the long haul!") and deters potential entrants. The drawbacks are (1) limited strategic flexibility elsewhere and (2) huge losses if these large-scale "bets" turn out to be wrong—this is the case in the current US subprime mess.

Small-scale entries are less costly. They focus on organizational learning by getting firms' "feet" wet—"learning by doing"—while limiting the downside risk.[46] For example, to enter the market of Islamic finance whereby no interest can be charged (per teaching of the Koran), Citibank set up a subsidiary Citibank Islamic Bank, HSBC

scale of entry
The amount of resources committed to foreign market entry.

established Amanah, and UBS launched Noriba. They were all designed to experiment with different interpretations of the Koran on how to make money while not committing religious sins. It is simply not possible to acquire such an ability outside the Islamic world. Overall, there is evidence that the longer foreign firms stay in host countries, the less liability of foreignness they experience.[47] The drawbacks of small-scale entries are a lack of strong commitment, which may lead to difficulties in building market share and in capturing first mover advantages.

Modes of Entry: The First Step on Equity versus Non-equity Modes

Among numerous modes of entry, managers are unlikely to consider all of them simultaneously. Given the complexity of entry decisions, it is imperative that managers *prioritize,* by considering only a few manageable key variables first and then contemplating other variables later. Therefore, a decision model (shown in Figure 5.3 and explained in Table 5.3) is helpful.[48]

FIGURE 5.3   The Choice of Entry Modes: A Decision Model

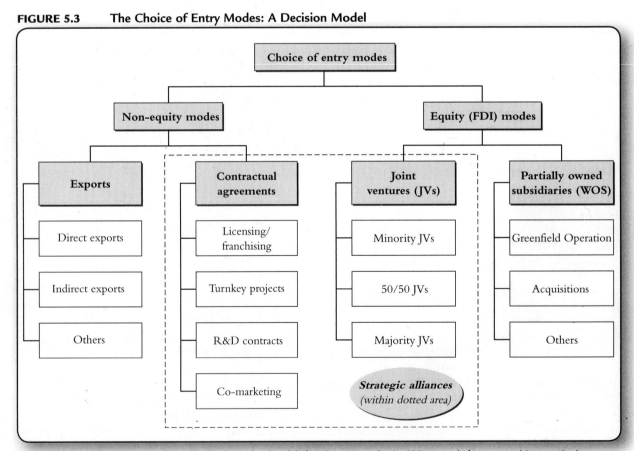

Sources: Adapted from Y. Pan & D. Tse, 2000, The hierarchical model of market entry modes (p. 538), *Journal of International Business Studies,* 31: 535–554. The dotted area labeled "strategic alliances," including both non-equity modes (contractual agreements) and equity modes (JVs), is added by the present author. See Chapter 7 for more details on strategic alliances.

TABLE 5.3   Modes of Entry: Advantages and Disadvantages

ENTRY MODES	ADVANTAGES	DISADVANTAGES
1. NON-EQUITY MODES: EXPORTS		
Direct exports	• Economies of scale in production concentrated in home country • Better control over distribution	• High transportation costs for bulky products • Marketing distance from customers • Trade barriers and protectionism
Indirect exports	• Concentration of resources on production • No need to directly handle export processes	• Less control over distribution (relative to direct exports) • Inability to learn how to operate overseas
2. NON-EQUITY MODES: CONTRACTUAL AGREEMENTS		
Licensing/franchising	• Low development costs • Low risk in overseas expansion	• Little control over technology and marketing • May create competitors • Inability to engage in global coordination
Turnkey projects	• Ability to earn returns from process technology in countries where FDI is restricted	• May create efficient competitors • Lack of long-term presence
R&D contracts	• Ability to tap into the best locations for certain innovations at low costs	• Difficult to negotiate and enforce contracts • May nurture innovative competitors • May lose core innovation capabilities
Co-marketing	• Ability to reach more customers	• Limited coordination
3. EQUITY MODES: JOINT VENTURES		
Joint Ventures	• Sharing costs, risks, and profits • Access to partners' knowledge and assets • Politically acceptable	• Divergent goals and interests of partners • Limited equity and operational control • Difficult to coordinate globally
4. EQUITY MODES: WHOLLY OWNED SUBSIDIARIES		
Greenfield operations	• Complete equity and operational control • Protection of know-how • Ability to coordinate globally	• Potential political problems and risks • High development costs • Add new capacity to industry • Slow entry speed (relative to acquisitions)
Acquisitions	• Same as greenfield (above) • Do not add new capacity • Fast entry speed	• Same as greenfield (above), except adding new capacity and slow speed • Post-acquisition integration problems

In the first step, considerations for small- versus large-scale entries usually boil down to the equity (ownership) issue. **Non-equity modes** (exports and contractual agreements) tend to reflect relatively smaller commitments to overseas markets, whereas **equity modes** (joint ventures and wholly owned subsidiaries) are indicative of relatively larger and harder-to-reverse commitments. Equity modes call for the establishment of independent organizations overseas (partially or wholly controlled), while non-equity modes do not require such independent establishments.

non-equity modes
Modes of foreign market entries which do not involve the use of equity.

The distinction between equity and non-equity modes is not trivial. In fact, it is what defines an MNE: An MNE enters foreign markets via equity modes through foreign direct investment (FDI). A firm that merely exports/imports with no FDI is usually not regarded as an MNE. Why would a firm, say, an oil importer, want to become an MNE by directly investing in the oil-producing country, instead of relying on the market mechanism by purchasing oil from an exporter in that country?

Relative to a non-MNE, an MNE has three principal advantages, ownership (O), location (L), and internalization (I)—Since we already discussed location already, we focus on ownership and internalization here. By owning assets in both oil-importing and oil-producing countries, the MNE is better able to manage and coordinate cross-border activities, such as delivering crude oil to the oil refinery in the importing country right at the moment its processing capacity becomes available (just-in-time delivery), instead of letting crude oil sit in expensive ships or storage tanks for a long time. This advantage is therefore called **ownership advantage.**

Another advantage stems from the removal of the market relationship between an importer and an exporter, which may suffer from high transaction costs. Using the market, deals have to be negotiated, prices agreed upon, and deliveries verified, all of which entail significant costs. What is more costly is the possibility of opportunism on both sides. For instance, the oil importer may refuse to accept a shipment *after* its arrival citing unsatisfactory quality, but the real reason could be the importer's inability to sell refined oil downstream (people may drive less due to high oil prices). The exporter is thus forced to find a new buyer for a boatload of crude oil on a last-minute "fire sale" basis. On the other hand, the oil exporter may demand higher-than-agreed-upon prices, citing a variety of reasons ranging from inflation to natural disasters. The importer thus has to either (1) pay more or (2) refuse to pay and suffer from the huge costs of keeping expensive refinery facilities idle. These transaction costs increase international market inefficiencies and imperfections. By replacing such a market relationship with a single organization spanning both countries (a process called **internalization,** basically transforming external markets with in-house links), the MNE thus reduces cross-border transaction costs and increases efficiencies.[49] This advantage is called **internalization advantage.**

Relative to a non-MNE, an MNE, which operates in certain desirable locations, enjoys a combination of ownership (O), location (L—discussed earlier), and internalization (I) advantages (Figure 5.4). These are collectively labeled as the **OLI advantages** by John Dunning, a leading MNE scholar.[50] Overall, the first step in entry mode considerations is extremely critical. A strategic decision must be made in terms of whether to undertake FDI and become an MNE by selecting equity modes.

Modes of Entry: The Second Step on Making Actual Selections

During the second step, managers consider variables within *each* group of non-equity and equity modes.[51] If the decision is to export, then next on the agenda would be direct exports or indirect exports. **Direct exports** represent the most basic mode, capitalizing on economies of scale in production concentrated in the home country and affording better control over distribution. While direct exports may work if the export volume is small, it is not optimal when the firm has a large number of foreign buyers. "Marketing 101" suggests that the firm needs to be closer, both physically and psychologically, to its customers, prompting the firm to consider more intimate overseas

---

equity modes

Modes of foreign market entry which involve the use of equity.

ownership resource **advantage**

Advantage associated with directly owning assets overseas, which is one of the three key advantages of being a multinational enterprise (the other two are location and internalization advantages).

internalization

The process of replacing a market relationship with a single multinational organization spanning both countries.

internalization advantage

The advantage associated with internalization, which is one of the three key advantages of being a multinational enterprise (the other two are ownership and location advantages).

OLI advantages

Ownership, location, and internalization advantages which are typically associated with MNEs.

direct exports

Directly selling products made in the home country to customers in other countries.

FIGURE 5.4   The OLI Advantages Associated with Being an MNE through FDI

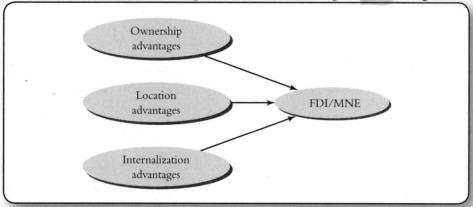

involvement such as FDI. In addition, direct exports may provoke protectionism. In 1981, the success of direct automobile exports from Japan led the US government to impose a voluntary export restraint (VER) agreement on Japanese cars—never mind that, in the absence of protectionist threats, the Japanese would not have voluntarily agreed to do so.

Another export strategy is **indirect exports** through export intermediaries.[53] This strategy not only enjoys the economies of scale in domestic production (similar to direct exports), it is also relatively worry-free. A significant amount of export trade in commodities (such as textiles, woods, and meats), which compete primarily on price, is indirect through intermediaries.[54] Indirect exports have some drawbacks because of the introduction of third parties, such as export trading companies with their own agendas and objectives that are not necessarily the same as the exporter's.[55] The primary reason the exporter chooses intermediaries is because of information asymmetries concerning risks and uncertainties associated with foreign markets. Intermediaries with international contacts and knowledge essentially make a living by taking advantage of such information asymmetries. They may have a vested interest in making sure that such asymmetries are not reduced. Intermediaries, for example, may repackage the products under their own brand and insist on monopolizing the communication with overseas customers. If the exporter is interested in learning more about overseas markets, indirect exports will not provide great opportunities for such learning.[56]

The next group of non-equity entry modes is contractual agreements consisting of (1) licensing/franchising, (2) turnkey projects, (3) R&D contracts, and (4) co-marketing. First, in **licensing/franchising agreements,** the licensor/franchisor sells the rights to intellectual property such as patents and know-how to the licensee/franchisee for a royalty fee. The licensor/franchisor, thus, does not have to bear the full costs and risks associated with foreign expansion. On the other hand, the licensor/franchisor does not have tight control over production and marketing.[57] Its worst fear is to have nurtured a competitor, as Pizza Hut found out in Thailand (discussed earlier in this chapter).

Turnkey projects refer to projects in which clients pay contractors to design and construct new facilities and train personnel. At project completion, contractors will

indirect exports

Exporting indirectly through domestic-based export intermediaries.

licensing/franchising agreements

Agreements according to which the licensor/franchiser sells the rights to intellectual property, such as patents and know-how, to the licensee/franchisee for a royalty fee.

turnkey projects

Projects in which clients pay contractors to design and construct new facilities and train personnel.

build-operate-transfer (BOT) agreements

A special kind of turn-key project in which contractors first build facilities, then operate them for a period of time, and then transfer back to clients. These BOT-type turnkey projects have a longer duration than tradi-tional build-transfer type turnkey projects.

R&D contracts

Outsourcing agreements in R&D between firms (that is, firm A agrees to perform certain R&D work for firm B).

co-marketing

Agreements among a number of firms to jointly market their products and services.

equity modes

Modes of foreign market entry which involve the use of equity.

joint venture (JV)

A "corporate child" that is a new entity given birth and jointly owned by two or more parent companies.

wholly owned subsidiaries (WOS)

Subsidiaries located in foreign countries which are entirely owned by the MNE.

hand clients the proverbial "key" to facilities ready for operations—hence the term "turnkey." The advantages entail the ability to earn returns from process technology in countries where FDI is restricted (such as power generation). The drawbacks are two-fold. First, if foreign clients are competitors, selling them state-of-the-art technology through turnkey projects may boost their competitiveness. Second, turnkey projects do not allow for a long-term presence after the "key" is handed to clients. To obtain a longer-term presence, **build-operate-transfer (BOT) agreements** are now often used, instead of the traditional "build-transfer" type of turnkey projects.

R&D contracts refer to outsourcing agreements in R&D between firms (firm A agrees to perform certain R&D work for firm B). They allow firms to tap into the best locations for certain innovations at relatively low costs, such as aerospace research in Russia. However, three drawbacks may emerge. First, given the uncertain and multi-dimensional nature of R&D, these contracts are often difficult to negotiate and enforce. While delivery time and costs are relatively easy to negotiate, quality is often difficult to assess. Second, such contracts may nurture competitors. A number of Indian IT firms, nurtured by such work, are now on a global offensive to eat the lunch of Western rivals. Finally, firms that rely on outsiders to perform R&D may, in the long run, lose some of their core R&D capabilities.

Co-marketing refers to efforts among a number of firms to jointly market their products and services. Fast-food chains such as McDonald's often launch co-marketing campaigns with movie studios and toy makers to hawk toys based on certain movie characters. Through code sharing, airline alliances such as One World and Star Alliance extensively engage in co-marketing. The advantages are the ability to reach more cus-tomers. The drawbacks center on limited control and coordination.

The next group is equity modes, all of which entail some FDI, transforming the firm to become an MNE.[58] A **joint venture (JV)** is a "corporate child"—that is, a new entity given birth and jointly owned by two or more parent companies. It has three principal forms: Minority JV (less than 50% equity), 50/50 JV, and majority JV (more than 50% equity). JVs have three advantages. (1) An MNE shares costs, risks, and profits with a local partner, possessing a certain degree of control while limiting risk exposure. (2) The MNE gains access to knowledge about the host country; the local firm, in turn, benefits from the MNE's capabilities. (3) JVs may be politically more acceptable.

In terms of disadvantages, first, JVs often involve partners from different backgrounds and goals—so conflicts are natural. Second, effective equity and operational control may be difficult to achieve since everything has to be negotiated (and, in some cases, fought over). Finally, the nature of the JV does not give an MNE the tight control over a for-eign subsidiary that it may need for global coordination (such as simultaneously launch-ing new products around the world). Overall, all sorts of non–equity-based contractual agreements and equity-based JVs can be broadly considered as strategic alliances (within the dotted area in Figure 5.3). Chapter 7 will discuss strategic alliances in detail.

The last group of entry modes refers to **wholly owned subsidiaries (WOSs).** A WOS can be set up in two primary ways.[59] The first is to establish **"greenfield" operations** from scratch (on a proverbial piece of "greenfield" formerly used for agricultural purposes). This has three advantages. First, a greenfield WOS gives an MNE complete control, thus eliminating the headaches associated with JVs. Second, this undivided control leads to better protection of proprietary technology. Third, a WOS allows for centrally coordinated global actions.[60] Sometimes, a subsidiary (such as TI's in Japan, discussed earlier) will be ordered to launch actions that by design will *lose* money. Local licensees/franchisees or JV partners are unlikely to accept such a subservient role—being ordered to lose money (!). In terms of drawbacks, a greenfield WOS tends to be expensive and risky, not only financially but also politically. The conspicuous foreignness embodied in such a WOS may become a target for nationalistic sentiments. Another drawback is that greenfield operations add new capacity to an industry, which will make a competitive industry more crowded—think of all the greenfield Japanese automobile transplants built in the United States. Finally, greenfield operations suffer from a slow entry speed (relative to acquisitions).

The second way to establish a WOS is through an **acquisition.** Although this is the last mode we discuss here, it is probably the most important mode in terms of the amount of capital involved (representing approximately 70% of worldwide FDI). In addition to sharing all the benefits of greenfield WOS, acquisitions also enjoy two additional advantages, namely, (1) adding no new capacity and (2) faster entry speed (see Opening Case). For example, in less than a decade (the 1990s), two leading banks in Spain with little prior international experience, Santander and Bilbao Vizcaya, became the largest foreign banks in Latin America through some 20 acquisitions. In terms of drawbacks, acquisitions share all the disadvantages of greenfield WOS, except adding new capacity and slow entry speed. In addition, acquisitions have to confront a unique and potentially devastating disadvantage—post-acquisition integration problems (see Chapter 9).

Debates and Extensions

This chapter has already covered some crucial debates, such as first versus late mover advantages. Here we discuss three heated *recent* debates: (1) liability versus asset of foreignness, (2) global versus regional geographic diversification, and (3) cyberspace versus conventional entries.

Liability versus Asset of Foreignness

Instead of the "liability of foreignness," one contrasting view argues that under certain circumstances, being foreign can be an *asset* (that is, a competitive advantage). Japanese and German cars are viewed as of higher quality in the United States. Many American movies rake in more money overseas than at home. American cigarettes are "cool" among smokers in Central and Eastern Europe. Anything Korean—ranging from handsets and TV shows to *kimchi* (pickled cabbage)-flavored instant noodles—is considered hip in Southeast Asia. Conceptually, this is known as the **country-of-origin effect,** which refers to the positive or negative perception of firms and products from a certain country.[61] However, whether foreignness is indeed an asset or a liability remains tricky. Disneyland Tokyo became wildly popular in Japan, because it played up its American image. But Disneyland Paris received relentless negative press coverage in France, because it insisted on its "wholesome American look." To play it safe, Hong Kong Disneyland has endeavored to strike the elusive balance between American image and Chinese flavor.

Over time, the country-of-origin effect may shift. A number of UK firms used to proudly sport names such as British Telecom and British Petroleum. Recently, they

---

greenfield operations

Building factories and offices from scratch (on a proverbial piece of "greenfield" formerly used for agricultural purposes).

acquisition

The transfer of control of assets, operations, and management from one firm (target) to another (acquirer); the former becoming a unit of the latter.

country-of-origin effect

The positive or negative perception of firms and products from a certain country.

have shied away from being "British" and rebranded themselves simply as BT and BP. In Britain, these changes are collectively known as the "B phenomenon." These costly rebranding campaigns are not casual changes. They reflect less confidence in Britain's positive country-of-origin effect. Recently, BAE Systems, formerly British Aerospace, has complained that its British origin is pulling its legs in its largest market, the US defense market. Only US citizens are allowed to know the details of its most sensitive US contracts, and even its British CEO cannot know such details. This is untenable now that two-fifths of its sales are in the United States. Thus, BAE Systems is seriously considering becoming "American." However, in an interesting twist, an "Americanized" BAE Systems may encounter liability of foreignness in Britain.[62] Not surprisingly, the "B phenomenon" is controversial in Britain. One lesson we can draw is that foreignness can either be a liability or an asset, and that changes are possible.[63]

Global versus Regional Geographic Diversification

In this age of globalization, debate continues on the optimal geographic scope for MNEs.[64] Despite the widely held belief (and frequently voiced criticism from anti-globalization activists) that MNEs are expanding "globally," Alan Rugman and Alain Verbeke report that, surprisingly, even among the largest *Fortune* Global 500 MNEs, few are truly "global."[65] Using some reasonable criteria (at least 20% of sales in *each* of the three regions of the Triad consisting of Asia, Europe, and North America but less than 50% in any one region), they find a total of only *nine* MNEs to be "global" (Column 1 of Table 5.4). Next to "global" MNEs, 25 firms are "bi-regional" MNEs that have at least 20% of sales in each of the two regions of the Triad but less than 50% in any one. Interestingly, 11 MNEs are "host-region-based," with at least 50% of sales in one of the Triad regions other than their home region. The majority of the remaining *Fortune* Global 500 (over 450) are "home-region-oriented" MNEs—in other words, they may be labeled regional, but *not* global, firms.

Should most MNEs further "globalize"? There are two answers. First, most MNEs know what they are doing and their current geographic scope is the maximum they can manage. Some of them may have already over-diversified and will need to downscope. Second, these data only capture a snapshot (in 2000s) and some MNEs may become more "globalized" over time. While the debate goes on, it has at least taught us one important reason: Be careful when using the word "global."[66] The *majority* of the largest MNEs are not necessarily very "global" in their geographic scope.

Cyberspace versus Conventional Entries

From an institution-based view, the arrival of the Internet has sparked a new debate: Whose rules of the game should e-commerce follow? While pundits argue that globalization is undermining the power of national governments, there is little evidence that the modern nation-state system, in existence since the 1648 Treaty of Westphalia, is retreating. Legally, one can argue that a *multinational* enterprise is a total fiction that does not exist. Since incorporation is only possible under national law, every MNE is essentially a bunch of *national* companies (subsidiaries) registered in various countries.[67]

Although some suggest that geographic jurisdiction may be meaningless in cyberspace, others argue that the Internet is "no more a borderless medium than the telephone, the telegraph, postal service, facsimile, or smoke signal [of the ancient times]."[68] According to this view, the Chinese authorities could legitimately demand that Yahoo!

TABLE 5.4   **Geographic Diversification of the Largest Multinational Enterprises (MNEs) by Sales**

"GLOBAL" MNEs[1]	"BI-REGIONAL" MNEs[2]	"HOST-REGION-BASED" MNEs[3]
1 BM	1 BP Amoco	1 DaimlerChrysler
2 Sony	2 Toyota	2 ING Group
3 Philips	3 Nissan	3 Royal Ahold
4 Nokia	4 Unilever	4 Honda
5 Intel	5 Motorola	5 Santander
6 Canon	6 GlaxoSmithKline	6 Delhaize 'Le Lion'
7 Coca-Cola	7 EADS	7 AstraZeneca
8 Flextronics	8 Bayer	8 News Corporation
9 LVMH	9 Ericsson	9 Sodexho Alliance
	10 Alstom	10 Manpower
	11 Aventis	11 Wolseley
	12 Diageo	
	13 Sun Microsystems	
	14 Bridgestone	
	15 Roche	
	16 3M	
	17 Skanska	
	18 McDonald's	
	19 Michelin	
	20 Kodak	
	21 Eletrolux	
	22 BAE Systems	
	23 Alcan	
	24 L'Oreal	
	25 Lafarge	

1. "Global" MNEs have at least 20% of sales in each of the three regions of the Triad (Asia, Europe, and North America), but less than 50% in any one region.
2. "Bi-regional MNEs" have at least 20% of sales in each of the two regions of the Triad, but less than 50% in any one region.
3. "Host-region-based" MNEs have more than 50% of sales in one of the Triad regions other than their home region.

Source: Adapted from A. Rugman & A. Verbeke, 2004, A perspective on regional and global strategies of multinational enterprises (pp. 8–10), *Journal of International Business Studies,* 35: 3–18.

China provide information on a dissident journalist who allegedly threatened China's national security by leaking "state secrets" and who was eventually jailed. However, by complying with the Chinese request, Yahoo! found itself being labeled "unethical" in the United States, with its CEO and general counsel being dragged to a Congressional hearing in 2007. Unfortunately, this was not the first time Yahoo! found itself squeezed

Strategy in Action 5.3 - Did Yahoo! Really Enter France?

Ethical Challenge

In the late 1990s, Yahoo! hosted third-party auctions, some of which sold Nazi memorabilia. Although perfectly legal, and indeed protected under the First Amendment of the Constitution in the United States, sales of Nazi items are illegal in France. Yahoo! was thus challenged in a French court. During the process, Yahoo! removed Nazi materials from its French language portal to comply with the French law. However, in November 2000, the French court ruled that Yahoo! must prevent French computer users from accessing any Yahoo! site—*in any language*—on which such items were sold or face a fine of 100,000 French Francs (US$17,877) per day. Yahoo! first asked a US court to declare that this decision could not be enforced in the United States because it violated the First Amendment and that American firms were not obliged to follow French rules outside France. A US court supported this argument. However, by early 2001, Yahoo! changed its mind and decided to self-censor, removing all items that "promote or glorify violence or hatred" from its site.

At the heart of this case is the controversy of whether France has the legal or ethical right to assert its law to order Yahoo!, which apparently only had a virtual presence in France, to change behavior that was in full compliance with US law. The fundamental question is whether national territorial jurisdiction applies to cyberspace. Some analysts see the French

decision as a dangerous one, because taken to the extreme, it would imply that every jurisdiction on the planet regulates everything on the Internet. Others contend that cyberspace entries into foreign markets, just like brick-and-mortar entries, must follow local rules.

Sources: Based on (1) S. Kobrin, 2001, Territoriality and the governance of cyberspace, *Journal of International Business Studies,* 32: 687–704; (2) P. Lasserre, 2003, *Global Strategic Management* (p. 390), London: Palgrave.

between a rock and a hard place when authorities in different countries clashed (see Strategy in Action 5.3). In the absence of harmonization among formal national regulations and informal norms (to cooperate with versus to resist local security authorities demanding sensitive information) concerning cyberspace, such clashes seem inevitable.

The Savvy Strategist

Foreign market entries are crucial in global strategy. Without these first steps, firms will remain domestic players. The challenges associated with internationalization are daunting, the complexities enormous, and the stakes high. Consequently, the

TABLE 5.5   **Strategic Implications for Action**

- Grasp the dynamism underlying the industry in a host country that you are looking into.
- Develop overwhelming resources and capabilities to offset the liability of foreignness.
- Understand the rules of the game—both formal and informal—governing competition in foreign markets.
- Match efforts in market entry and geographic diversification with strategic goals.

savvy strategist can draw four implications for action (Table 5.5). First, from an industry-based view, you need to thoroughly understand the dynamism underlying the industry in a foreign market you are looking into. For strategists in Chinese banks eyeing US banking assets, a legitimate question is whether this is an attractive market. Remember a quote from an expert: "In the current environment, you would have to be extremely brave or extremely stupid to buy a US bank" (see Strategy in Action 5.2).

Second, from a resource-based view, you and your firm need to develop overwhelming capabilities to offset the liability of foreignness. Perhaps some Chinese banks have such capabilities that can help them manage their expansion in the United States well. We just need to find out whether this indeed is the case. In 2003, Britain's highly capable HSBC bought Household to enter the US subprime mortgage market, and later provided it did not have such capabilities.

Third, from an institution-based view, you need to understand the rules of the game, both formal and informal, governing competition in foreign markets. Failure to understand these rules can be costly. Managers at Yahoo! initially ignored the rules of the game in France, ending up with a ton of bad press as the "defender of Nazi violence," something which it could ill afford (Strategy in Action 5.3).

Finally, the savvy strategist matches entries with strategic goals. If the goal is to deter rivals in their home markets by slashing prices there (as TI did when entering Japan), then be prepared to fight a nasty price war and lose money. If the goal is to generate decent returns, then withdrawing from some tough nuts to crack may be necessary (as Wal-Mart withdrew from Germany—see Opening Case).

In conclusion, this chapter sheds considerable light on the four fundamental questions. Why firms differ in their propensity to internationalize (Question 1) boils down to the size of the firm and that of the domestic market (Figure 5.1). How firms behave (Question 2) depends on how considerations for industry competition, firm capabilities, and institutional differences influence their foreign market entry decisions (Figure 5.2). What determines the scope of the firm (Question 3)—in this case, the scope of its international involvement—fundamentally depends on how to acquire and leverage the three-pronged OLI advantages. Firms committed to owning some assets overseas through equity modes of entry and, thus, to becoming MNEs are likely to have a broader scope overseas than those unwilling to do so. Finally, entry strategies certainly have something to do with the international success and failure of firms (Question 4) since inappropriate entry strategies will torpedo overseas ventures.[69] However, appropriate entry strategies, while certainly important, are only a *beginning*. It takes a lot more to succeed overseas, as we will discuss in later chapters.

CHAPTER SUMMARY

1. *Understand the necessity to overcome the liability of foreignness*

   • When entering foreign markets, firms confront a liability of foreignness.

   • The propensity to internationalize differs among firms of different sizes and different home market sizes.

2. *Articulate a comprehensive model of foreign market entries*

   • The industry-based view suggests that industry dynamism in a host country cannot be ignored.

   • The resource-based view calls for the development of capabilities along the VRIO dimensions.

   • The institution-based view focuses on institutional constraints that foreign entrants must confront.

3. *Match the quest for location-specific advantages with strategic goals (where to enter)*

   • Where to enter depends on certain foreign countries' location-specific advantages and firms' strategic goals, such as seeking (1) natural resources, (2) market, (3) efficiency, and (4) innovation.

4. *Compare and contrast first and late mover advantages (when to enter)*

   • Each has pros and cons, and there is no conclusive evidence pointing to one direction.

5. *Follow a decision model that guides specific steps for foreign market entries (how to enter)*

   • How to enter depends on the scale of entry: Large-scale versus small-scale entries.

   • A decision model first focuses on the equity (ownership) issue.

   • The second step makes the actual selection, such as exports, contractual agreements, JVs, and WOS.

6. *Participate in three leading debates on foreign market entries*

   • The three leading debates are (1) liability versus asset of foreignness, (2) global versus regional geographic diversification, and (3) cyberspace versus conventional entries.

7. *Draw strategic implications for action*

   • Grasp the dynamism underlying the industry in a host country that you are looking into.

   • Develop overwhelming resources and capabilities to offset the liability of foreignness.

   • Understand the rules of the game—both formal and informal—governing competition in foreign markets.

   • Match efforts in market entry and geographic diversification with strategic goals.

KEY TERMS

Acquisition	Hedging	Non-equity mode
Agglomeration	Indirect export	Nontariff barrier
Build-operate-transfer (BOT) agreement	Innovation seeking	Obsolescing bargain
Co-marketing	Institutional distance	OLI advantages
Country-of-origin effect	Internalization	Ownership advantage
Cultural distance	Internalization advantage	R&D contract
Currency risk	Joint venture (JV)	Scale of entry
Direct export	Late mover advantage	Speculation
Dissemination risk	Liability of foreignness	Stage models
Efficiency seeking	Licensing/franchising agreements	Sunk cost
Equity mode	Local content requirement	Tariff barrier
Expropriation	Location-specific advantage	Trade barrier
First mover advantage	Market seeking	Turnkey project
Greenfield operation	Natural resource seeking	Wholly owned subsidiary (WOS)

CRITICAL DISCUSSION QUESTIONS

1. During the 1990s, many North American, European, and Asian MNEs set up operations in Mexico, tapping into its location-specific advantages such as (1) proximity to the world's largest economy, (2) market-opening policies associated with NAFTA membership, and (3) abundant, low-cost, and high-quality labor. None of these has changed much. Yet, by the 15th anniversary of NAFTA (2009), there is a significant movement for MNEs to curtail operations in Mexico and move to China. Why?

2. From institution- and resource-based views, identify the obstacles confronting MNEs from emerging economies interested in expanding overseas. How can such firms overcome them?

3. **ON ETHICS:** Entering foreign markets, by definition, means not investing in a firm's home country. What are the ethical dilemmas here? What are your recommendations as (1) MNE executives, (2) labor union leaders of your domestic (home country) labor forces, (3) host country officials, and (4) home country officials?

CLOSING CASE

Foreign Retailers Eye India

India has the world's highest density of retail outlets of any country. It has more than 15 million retail outlets, compared with 900,000 in the United States, whose market (by revenue) is 13 times bigger. At present, 97% of retail sales in India are made in tiny mom-and-pop shops, mostly of less than 500 square feet (46 square meters). In Indian jargon, this is known, quite accurately, as the "unorganized" retail sector. The "organized" (more modern) retail sector commands only 3% of total sales, of which 96% is in the top ten cities. The retail industry is the largest provider of jobs after agriculture, accounting for 6%–7% of jobs and 10% of GDP.

With a booming economy and a fast-growing middle class, it is not surprising that foreign retailers, such as Wal-Mart, Carrefour, Metro, and Tesco, are knocking at the door trying to expand the "organized" retail sector. However, here is one catch: The door is still closed to foreign direct investment (FDI) in the retail sector, which remains one of the last large sectors that has yet to open up to FDI. Millions of shopkeepers, supported by leftist politicians and trade unionists, are worried about the onslaught of multinationals. Citing the controversial "Wal-Mart effect" being debated in the United States and elsewhere, one Indian union leader labeled Wal-Mart "one of the ten worst corporations in the world."

In response, the reformist government that has brought India to the global spotlight since 1991 delicately tries to balance the interests of various stakeholders. FDI is still officially banned in *mass* retailing. However, a side door is now open. Foreign firms can take up to 51% equity in *single-brand* shops that sell their own products, such as Nike, Nokia, and Starbucks shops. Further, FDI in the supply chain is now permitted. Foreign firms can set up wholesale and sourcing subsidiaries that supply local mass retail partners. The first to do this was Australia's Woolworths, which in 2006 started to supply Croma stores owned by Tata Group, India's second largest conglomerate. To better compete with multinational retailers that may eventually arrive, Reliance Group, India's largest conglomerate, is now making huge waves by investing $5.5 billion to build 1,000 hypermarkets and 2,000 supermarkets to blanket the country in the next five years.

On average, Indians are still poor. Only one in 50 households has a credit card; only one in six a refrigerator. However, as in China 20 years ago, such statistics do not deter foreign entrants. Instead, these data suggest tremendous potential. Despite objections, Wal-Mart is visibly leading the foreign lobby. One of its arguments is that super-efficient retail operations will enhance efficiency throughout the entire supply chain. For example, at present, 35%–40% of fruits and vegetables in India rot while in transit. Food processing adds just 7% to the value of agricultural output, compared with 40% in China and 60% in Thailand, both of which embraced Wal-Mart. As local suppliers become more familiar with Wal-Mart's requirements, exports may naturally follow—Wal-Mart now accounts for 10% of China's exports to the United States.

Sources: Based on (1) *The Economist,* 2006, Coming to market, April 15: 69–71; (2) *The Economist,* 2006, Setting up shop, Nov 4: 73–74; (3) A. Mukherjee & N. Patel, 2005, *FDI in Retail Sector,* New Delhi: Department of Consumer Affairs.

Case Discussion Questions

1. Why is the Indian retail industry so inviting?

2. Given Wal-Mart's lack of a strong record overseas (it has various "hits and misses" when expanding overseas and does better in some countries than in others), does it have what it takes to succeed in India?

3. As an Indian government official, would you recommend the full-blown opening of the retail sector?

4. Assuming a positive answer on Question 3, what would be your recommended modes of entry if you were the CEO of Carrefour, Metro, Tesco, or Woolworths?

NOTES

Journal acronyms *AMJ*–*Academy of Management Journal;* *AMR*–*Academy of Management Review;* *APJM*–*Asia Pacific Journal of Management;* *ASQ*–*Administrative Science Quarterly;* *BW*–*Business Week;* *FEER*–*Far Eastern Economic Review;* *HBR*–*Harvard Business Review;* *JIBS*–*Journal of International Business Studies;* *JIM*–*Journal of International Management;* *JM*–*Journal of Management;* *JMS*–*Journal of Management Studies;* *JWB*–*Journal of World Business;* *MIR*–*Management International Review;* *MS*–*Management Science;* *SMJ*–*Strategic Management Journal*

1. T. Friedman, 2005, *The World Is Flat,* New York: Farrar, Straus, and Giroux; T. Levitt, 1983, The globalization of markets, *HBR,* May–June: 92–102.

2. P. Ghemawat, 2007, *Redefining Global Strategy,* Boston: Harvard Business School Press.

3. A. Cuervo-Carurra, M. Maloney, & S. Manrakhan, 2007, Causes of the difficulties in internationalization, *JIBS,* 38: 709–725; J. Mezias, 2002, Identifying liabilities of foreignness and strategies to minimize their effects, *SMJ,* 23: 229–244; S. Miller & A. Parkhe, 2002, Is there a liability of foreignness in global banking? *SMJ,* 23: 55–75; S. Zaheer, 1995, Overcoming the liability of foreignness, *AMJ,* 38: 341–363.

4. L. Nachum, 2003, Liability of foreignness in global competition, *SMJ,* 24: 1187–1208; B. Petersen & T. Pedersen, 2002, Coping with liability of foreignness, *JIM,* 8: 339–350.

5. X. Martin, A. Swaminathan, & W. Mitchell, 1998, Organizational evolution in the interorganizational environment, *ASQ,* 43: 566–602.

6. J. Hennart, 2007, The theoretical rationales for a multinationality-performance relationship, *MIR,* 47: 423–452.

7. T. Hutzschenreuter, T. Pederson, & H. Volberda, 2007, The role of path dependency and managerial intentionality, *JIBS,* 38: 1055–1068; D. Paul & P. Wooster, 2008, Strategic investments by US firms in transition economies, *JIBS,* 39: 249–266.

8. F. Knickerbocker, 1973, *Oligopolistic Reaction and Multinational Enterprise,* Boston: Harvard Business School Press.

9. T. Shervani, G. Frazier, & G. Challagalla, 2007, The moderating influence of firm market power on the transaction cost economics model, *SMJ,* 28: 635–652.

10. B. Elango & R. Sambharya, 2004, The influence of industry structure on the entry mode choice of overseas entrants in manufacturing industries, *JIM,* 10: 107–124.

11. M. W. Peng, 2001, The resource-based view and international business, *JM,* 27: 803–829. See also H. Barkema & O. Shvyrkov, 2007, Does top management team diversity promote or hamper foreign expansion?, *SMJ,* 28: 663–680; M. Hitt, L. Bierman, K. Uhlenbruck, & K. Shimizu, 2006, The influence of resources in the internationalization of professional service firms, *AMJ,* 49: 1137–1157.

12. H. Berry, 2006, Shareholder valuation of foreign investment and expansion, *SMJ,* 27: 1123–1140; J. Doukas & O. Kan, 2006, Does global diversification destroy firm value?, *JIBS,* 37: 352–371; S. Lee, M. Makhija, & Y. Paik, 2008, The value of real options investments under abnormal uncertainty, *JWB,* 43: 16–34.

13. C. Hill, P. Hwang, & C. Kim, 1990, An eclectic theory of the choice of international entry mode (p. 124), *SMJ,* 11: 117–128.

14. R. Tasker, 2002, Pepperoni power, *FEER,* November 14: 59–60.

15. T. Brewer, 1992, An issue-area approach to the analysis of MNE-government relations, *JIBS,* 23: 295–309; T. Murtha & S. Lenway, 1994, Country capabilities and the strategic state, *SMJ,* 15: 113–129.

16. W. Henisz & A. Delios, 2001, Uncertainty, imitation, and plant location, *ASQ,* 46: 443–475.

17. K. Meyer & S. Estrin, 2001, Brownfield entry in emerging markets, *JIBS,* 32: 574–584; N. Uhlenbruck & J. DeCastro, 2000, Foreign acquisitions in Central and Eastern Europe, *AMJ,* 43: 381–402.

18. R. Ramamurti, 2001, The obsolescing bargaining model? *JIBS,* 32: 23–40.

19. T. Agmon, 2003, Who gets what, *JIBS,* 34: 416–427.

20. *The Economist,* 2003, Selling to the developing world, December 13: 8.

21. D. Welch, 2004, How Honda is stalling in the US, *BW,* May 24: 62–63.

22. L. Jacque & P. Vaaler, 2001, The international control conundrum with exchange risk, *JIBS,* 32: 813–832;

D. Miller & J. Reuer, 1998, Firm strategy and economic exposure to foreign exchange rate movements, *JIBS*, 29: 493–514.

23. C. Hill, 2003, *International Business*, 4th ed. (p. 307), Chicago: Irwin McGraw-Hill.

24. C. Chan & S. Makino, 2007, Legitimacy and multi-level institutional environments, *JIBS*, 38: 621–638; M. Demirbag, K. Glaister, & E. Tatoglu, 2007, Institutional and transaction cost influence on MNEs' ownership strategies of their affiliates, *JWB*, 42: 418–434; S. Estrin & K. Meyer, 2004, *Investment Strategies in Emerging Economies*, Cheltenham, UK: Elgar; J. Laurila & M. Ropponen, 2003, Institutional conditioning of foreign expansion, *JMS*, 40: 725–751; J. Li, J. Yang, & D. Yue, 2007, Identity, community, and audience, *AMJ*, 50: 175–190.

25. R. Belderbos & L. Sleuwaegen, 2005, Competitive drivers and international plant configuration strategies, *SMJ*, 26: 577–593; J. Dunning, 1998, Location and the multinational enterprise, *JIBS*, 29: 45–66; R. Flores & R. Aguilera, 2007, Globalization and location choice, *JIBS*, 38: 1187–1210.

26. G. Bell, 2005, Clusters, networks, and firm innovativeness, *SMJ*, 26: 287–295; L. Canina, C. Enz, & J. Harrison, 2005, Agglomeration effects and strategic orientations, *AMJ*, 48: 565–581; E. Maitland, E. Rose, & S. Nicholas, 2005, How firms grow, *JIBS*, 36: 435–451; L. Nachum & C. Wymbs, 2005, Product differentiation, external economies, and MNE location choices, *JIBS*, 36: 415–434; S. Tallman, M. Jenkins, N. Henry, & S. Pinch, 2004, Knowledge, clusters, and competitive advantage, *AMR*, 29: 258–271.

27. D. Sethi, S. Guisinger, S. Phelan, & D. Berg, 2003, Trends in FDI flows, *JIBS*, 34: 315–326.

28. Economist Intelligence Unit, 2006, *CEO Briefing* (p. 9), London: EIU.

29. G. Smith, 2003, Mexico: Was NAFTA worth it (p. 72), *BW*, December 22: 66–72.

30. M. W. Peng & D. Wang, 2000, Innovation capability and foreign direct investment (p. 80), *MIR*, 40: 79–93.

31. A. Kalnins & W. Chung, 2004, Resource-seeking agglomeration, *SMJ*, 25: 689–699; J. M. Shaver & F. Flyer, 2000, Agglomeration economies, firm heterogeneity, and foreign direct investment in the United States, *SMJ*, 21: 1175–1193.

32. B. Kogut & H. Singh, 1988, The effect of national culture on the choice of entry mode, *JIBS*, 19: 411–432.

33. D. Xu & O. Shenkar, 2002, Institutional distance and the multinational enterprise (p. 608), *AMR*, 27: 608–618.

34. H. Barkema & R. Drogendijk, 2007, Internationalizing in small, incremental or larger steps? *JIBS*, 38: 1132–1148; K. Meyer & M. Gelbuda, 2006, Process perspectives in international business research in CEE, *MIR*, 46: 143–164.

35. E. Tsang & P. Yip, 2007, Economic distance and survival of foreign direct investments, *AMJ*, 50: 1156–1168.

36. M. Myers, C. Droge, & M. Cheung, 2007, The fit of home to foreign market environment, *JWB*, 42: 170–183.

37. J. Johanson & J. Vahlne, 2006, Commitment and opportunity development in the internationalization process, *MIR*, 46: 165–178; J. Steen & P. Liesch, 2007, A note on Penrosian growth, resource bundles, and the Uppsala model of internationalization, *MIR*, 47: 193–206.

38. *The Economist*, 2006, Don't mess with Russia, December 16: 11.

39. J. Evans & F. Mavondo, 2002, Psychic distance and organizational performance, *JIBS*, 33: 515–532.

40. G. Dowell & A. Swaminathan, 2006, Entry timing, exploration, and firm survival, *SMJ*, 27: 1159–1182; J. G. Frynas, K. Mellahi, & G. Pigman, 2006, First mover advantages in international business and firm-specific political resources, *SMJ*, 27: 321–345; M. Lieberman & D. Montgomery, 1988, First-mover advantages, *SMJ*, 9: 41–58.

41. M. W. Peng, S. Lee, & J. Tan, 2001, The *keiretsu* in Asia, *JIM*, 7: 253–276.

42. T. Isobe, S. Makino, & D. Montgomery, 2000, Resource commitment, entry timing, and market performance of foreign direct investments in emerging economies, *AMJ*, 43: 468–484.

43. L. Fuentelsaz, J. Gomez, & Y. Polo, 2002, Followers' entry timing, *SMJ*, 23: 245–264; J. Shamsie, C. Phelps, & J. Kuperman, 2004, Being late than never, *SMJ*, 25: 69–84.

44. V. Gaba, Y. Pan, & G. Ungson, 2002, Timing of entry in international market, *JIBS,* 33: 39–55.

45. M. W. Peng, 2000, Controlling the foreign agent, *MIR,* 40: 141–165; F. Suarez & G. Lanzolla, 2007, The role of environmental dynamics in building a first mover advantage theory, *AMR,* 32: 377–392.

46. Y. Luo & M. W. Peng, 1999, Learning to compete in a transition economy, *JIBS,* 30: 269–296. See also L. Lages, S. Jap, & D. Griffith, 2008, The role of past performance in export ventures, *JIBS,* 39: 304–325; A. Nadolska & H. Barkema, 2007, Learning to internationalize, *JIBS,* 38: 1170–1187; L. Qian & A. Delios, 2008, Internationalization and experience, *JIBS,* 39: 231–248.

47. A. Delios & W. Henisz, 2003, Political hazards, experience, and sequential entry strategies, *SMJ,* 24: 1153–1164; P. Padmansbhan & K. Cho, 1999, Decision specific experience in foreign ownership and establishment strategies, *JIBS,* 30: 25–44.

48. Y. Pan & D. Tse, 2000, The hierarchical model of market entry modes, *JIBS,* 31: 535–554.

49. J. Campa & M. Guillen, 1999, The internalization of exports, *MS,* 45: 1463–1478.

50. J. Dunning, 1993, *Multinational Enterprises and the Global Economy,* Reading, MA: Addison-Wesley. See also S. Agarwal & S. Ramaswami, 1992, Choice of foreign market entry mode, *JIBS,* 23: 1–27.

51. K. Brouthers, L. Brouthers, & S. Werner, 2003, Transaction cost-enhanced entry mode choices and firm performance, *SMJ,* 24: 1239–1248; E. Kaynak, M. Demirbag, & E. Tatoglu, 2007, Determinants of ownership-based entry mode choice of MNEs, *MIR,* 47: 505–530; S. Mani, K. Antia, & A. Rindfleisch, 2007, Entry mode and equity level, *SMJ,* 28: 857–866; H. Zhao, Y. Luo, & T. Suh, 2004, Transaction cost determinants and ownership-based entry mode choice, *JIBS,* 35: 524–544.

52. R. Salomon & J. M. Shaver, 2005, Export and domestic sales, *SMJ,* 26: 855–871.

53. M. W. Peng & A. Ilinitch, 1998, Export intermediary firms, *JIBS,* 29: 609–620.

54. M. W. Peng, Y. Zhou, & A. York, 2006, Behind make or buy decisions in export strategy, *JWB,* 41: 289–300; H. Trabold, 2002, Export intermediation: An empirical test of Peng and Ilinitch, *JIBS,* 33: 327–344.

55. G. Balabanis, 2000, Factors affecting export intermediaries' service offerings, *JIBS,* 31: 83–99; H. Lau, 2008, Export channel structure in a newly industrialized economy, *APJM,* 25 (in press); D. Skarmeas, C. Katsikeas, & B. Schlegelmilch, 2002, Drivers of commitment and its impact on performance in cross-cultural buyer-seller relationships, *JIBS,* 33: 757–783.

56. F. Wu, R. Sinkovics, S. T. Cavusgil, & A. Roath, 2007, Overcoming export manufacturers' dilemma in international expansion, *JIBS,* 38: 283–302.

57. A. Arora & A. Fosfuri, 2000, Wholly owned subsidiary versus technology licensing in the worldwide chemical industry, *JIBS,* 31: 555–572.

58. S. Chen & J. Hennart, 2002, Japanese investors' choice of joint ventures versus wholly-owned subsidiaries in the US, *JIBS,* 33: 1–18.

59. H. Barkema & F. Vermeulen, 1998, International expansion through start-up or acquisition, *AMJ,* 41: 7–26; A. Harzing, 2002, Acquisitions versus greenfield investments, *SMJ,* 23: 211–227.

60. R. Belderbos & J. Zou, 2007, On the growth of foreign affiliates, *JIBS,* 38: 1095–1112.

61. L. Brouthers, E. O'Connell, & J. Hadjimarcou, 2005, Generic product strategies for emerging market exports into Triad nation markets, *JMS,* 42: 225–245.

62. *The Economist,* 2006, BAE Systems: Changing places, October 28: 66–67.

63. J. Birkinshaw, P. Braunerhjelm, U. Holm, & S. Terjesen, 2006, Why do some multinational corporations relocate their headquarters overseas?, *SMJ,* 27: 681–700.

64. J. Dunning, J. Fujita, & N. Yakova, 2007, Some macro-data on the regionalization/globalization debate, *JIBS,* 38: 177–199; T. Osegowitsch & A. Sammartino, 2008, Reassessing (home-)regionalization, *JIBS,* 39: 184–196.

65. S. Collinson & A. Rugman, 2007, The regional character of Asian multinational enterprises, *APJM,* 24: 429–446; A. Rugman & A. Verbeke, 2004, A perspective on regional and global strategies of multinational enterprises, *JIBS,* 35: 3–18.

66. R. Grosse, 2005, Are the largest financial institutions really "global"?, *MIR,* 45: 129–144; L. Li, 2005, Is regional strategy more effective than global strategy in the US service industries?, *MIR,* 45: 37–57; C. Miller,

C. Choi, & S. Chen, 2005, Globalization rediscovered, *MIR,* 45: 121–128; G. Qian, L. Li, J. Li, & Z. Qian, 2008, Regional diversification and firm performance, *JIBS,* 39: 197–214; E. Yin & C. Choi, 2005, The globalization myth, *MIR,* 45: 103–120.

67. J. Goldsmith & T. Wu, 2006, *Who Controls the Internet? Illusions of a Borderless World,* New York: Oxford University Press.

68. P. Lasserre, 2003, *Global Strategic Management* (p. 390), New York: Palgrave.

69. D. Brock, T. Yaffe, & M. Dembovsky, 2006, International diversification and performance, *JIM,* 12: 473–489; M. Chari, S. Devaraj, & P. David, 2007, International diversification and firm performance, *JWB,* 42: 184–197; F. Contractor, V. Kumar, & S. Kundu, 2007, Nature of the relationship between international expansion and performance, *JWB,* 42: 401–417; D. Dow, 2006, Adaptation and performance in foreign markets, *JIBS,* 37: 212–226.

chapter 6

The Entrepreneurial Firm

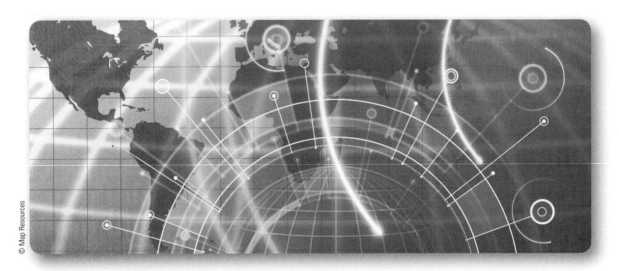

© Map Resources

KNOWLEDGE OBJECTIVES

After studying this chapter, you should be able to

1. Define entrepreneurship, entrepreneurs, and entrepreneurial firms

2. Articulate a comprehensive model of entrepreneurship

3. Identify five strategies that characterize a growing entrepreneurial firm

4. Differentiate international strategies that enter foreign markets and that stay in domestic markets

5. Participate in three leading debates concerning entrepreneurship

6. Draw strategic implications for action

Opening Case: An American Chasing the China Dream

ike Morris is an American. After graduating with an undergraduate degree in management from the University of Texas at Dallas in 1996, he joined the executive training program of a large US department store chain and then became a corporate buyer. However, he did not like life in a large corporation. After three years, he joined one of his suppliers, which was a smaller family-owned firm that manufactured small gifts and accessories. The supplier attributed its success to its early engagement with China, to which it outsourced most of its production since the 1980s. After working in the supplier's Dallas office for three years, Morris was offered the opportunity to head its China operations in 2002. Morris had never anticipated such a move, and China would be a "hardship" assignment for him, given that he did not speak Chinese. But the opportunity was irresistible, and Morris soon packed his bags and moved to Shanghai.

When Morris arrived in China in 2002, a majority of the company's products were assembled in China, but most of the components were made in Japan, Hong Kong, Taiwan, and the United States. The majority of Morris's first two years were spent on developing a local supply chain that would produce locally sourced components that met the company's quality standards. Since such a local supply chain would be developed from "scratch,"

Morris hit upon an idea: Why not set up one of these local firms by himself? He discussed this idea with trusted Chinese friends, who all supported this idea.

Morris was up-front with his employer regarding this entrepreneurial idea. When he was sent by his employer, he was asked to commit to only two years. His employer was aware that for a young, hard-charging manager like Morris, China would present numerous opportunities. The owner of his company even mentioned that after the initial two-year period, he would be willing to look into participating in opportunities that Morris might propose. Therefore, in 2004, Morris approached his employer with a proposal to open a small company that would produce components in China. This would be mutually beneficial, because Morris would remain in China (instead of returning to the United States after two years) and devote the majority of his time to his current position, while establishing an independent company on the side. This kind of relationship would be considered unconventional in many companies, but in this case, the owner of his current employer gave him the necessary blessing. As a result, the current company co-founded a new "local" supplier that provided high-quality goods at lower costs.

With the full support of Morris's current employer, he started his new company with two trustworthy Chinese partners in 2004. Morris and his current employer provided capital and marketing capability, and his Chinese partners hired the management team and built the factory. By 2007, the new company, known as a supplier offering both "US quality" and "China price," grew to over 40 employees and generated over $2 million in annual revenues. Morris and his partners were richly rewarded both financially and professionally.

By the end of 2007, Morris felt that he reached a plateau and sold his interest in the company that he co-founded in 2004. In 2008, he moved on to launch his second China venture with another friend, thus becoming a serial entrepreneur chasing the China dream.

Sources: The entrepreneur's name is disguised. Based on (1) author's interviews, (2) J. Fernandez & S. Liu, 2007, *China CEO,* Singapore: Wiley & Sons (Asia), (3) M. W. Peng, 2001, How entrepreneurs create wealth in transition economies, *Academy of Management Executive,* 15 (1): 95–108.

---

small and medium-sized enterprises (SMEs)

Firms with less than 500 employees.

entrepreneurship

The identification and exploitation of previously unexplored opportunities.

entrepreneurs

Individuals who identify and explore previously unexplored opportunities.

international entrepreneurship

A combination of innovative, proactive, and risk-seeking behavior that crosses national borders and is intended to create wealth in organizations.

How do **small and medium-sized enterprises (SMEs)** such as the two companies that Mike Morris co-founded in China grow? (SMEs are typically defined as firms with less than 500 employees.) How do they enter international markets? What are the challenges and constraints they face? This chapter deals with these and other questions. This is different from many strategy textbooks, which focus only on large firms. To the extent that every large firm started small and that some (although not all) of today's SMEs may become tomorrow's multinational enterprises (MNEs), current and would-be strategists will not gain a complete picture of the strategic landscape if they focus only on large firms. More importantly, most students will join SMEs for employment. Some readers of this book will also start up their own SMEs, thus further necessitating our attention on these numerous "Davids" instead of on the smaller number of "Goliaths."

This chapter will first define what entrepreneurship is, followed by a discussion on the nature of entrepreneurship. Next, we outline a comprehensive model of entrepreneurship informed by the three leading perspectives on strategy. Then, we introduce five major strategies and multiple ways for entrepreneurial firms to internationalize. As before, debates and extensions follow.

Entrepreneurship and Entrepreneurial Firms

Although entrepreneurship is often associated with smaller and younger firms, there is no rule banning larger and older firms from being "entrepreneurial." In fact, many large firms, which tend to be more established and bureaucratic, are often urged to become more entrepreneurial. Therefore, what exactly is entrepreneurship? Recent research suggests that firm size and age are *not* defining characteristics of entrepreneurship. Instead, **entrepreneurship** is defined as "the identification and exploitation of previously unexplored opportunities."[1] Specifically, it is concerned with "the sources of opportunities; the processes of discovery, evaluation, and exploitation of opportunities; and the set of individuals who discover, evaluate, and exploit them."[2] These individuals, thus, are **entrepreneurs,** who may be founders and owners of new businesses or managers of existing firms. Consequently, **international entrepreneurship** is defined as "a combination of innovative, proactive, and risk-seeking behavior that crosses national borders and is intended to create wealth in organizations."[3]

Although the preceding definitions suggest that SMEs are not the exclusive domain of entrepreneurship, the convention that many people often use is to associate entrepreneurship with SMEs, which, on average, may indeed be more entrepreneurial than large firms. To minimize confusion, in the remainder of this chapter, we will follow such a convention, although it is not totally accurate. That is, while we acknowledge that some managers at large firms can be very entrepreneurial,[4] we will limit the use of the term "entrepreneurs" to owners, founders, and managers of SMEs. Further, we will use the term "entrepreneurial firms" when referring to SMEs (less than 500 employees). We will label firms with more than 500 employees "large firms."

SMEs are important. Worldwide, they account for over 95% of the number of firms, create approximately 50% of total value added, and generate 60%–90% of employment (depending on the country).[5] Obviously, entrepreneurship has both rewarding and punishing aspects.[6] Many entrepreneurs will try, many SMEs will fail (for instance, approximately 60% of start-ups in the United States fail within six years).[7] Only a small number of entrepreneurs and SMEs will succeed.

A Comprehensive Model of Entrepreneurship

The "strategy tripod" consisting of the three leading perspectives on strategy—namely the industry-, resource-, and institution-based views—sheds considerable light on the entrepreneurship phenomenon. This leads to a comprehensive model illustrated in Figure 6.1.

Industry-Based Considerations

The industry-based view, exemplified by the Porter five forces framework first introduced in Chapter 2, suggests that (1) interfirm rivalry, (2) entry barriers, (3) bargaining power of suppliers, (4) bargaining power of buyers, and (5) threats of substitute products have a bearing on entrepreneurship. First, the intensity of *interfirm rivalry* has a direct impact on the probability that a new start-up will be able to make it.[8] The fewer the number of incumbent firms, the more likely they will form some sort of collusion to prevent newcomers from gaining market shares. In a worst-case scenario, a monopoly incumbent, such as Microsoft, may become so dominant that it might potentially stifle new innovation brought about by SMEs—this was the key reason why Microsoft was prosecuted by the US and EU antitrust authorities.

Entry barriers impact entrepreneurship. It is not surprising that new firm entries cluster around low entry barrier industries, such as restaurants. Conversely, capital-intensive industries hinder the chances of entrepreneurs succeeding. For example, at present no entrepreneurs in their right mind would bet their money on competing against Boeing or Airbus.

When the *bargaining power of suppliers* becomes too large, entrepreneurial solutions that can reduce such bargaining power may be sought after. For instance, Microsoft, which of course has been very entrepreneurial, is the monopoly supplier of operating systems to virtually all personal computer (PC) makers in the world, which feel uncomfortable about being compelled to purchase Microsoft products. As a result, LINUX is becoming more popular as an emerging alternative.

FIGURE 6.1   **A Comprehensive Model of Entrepreneurship**

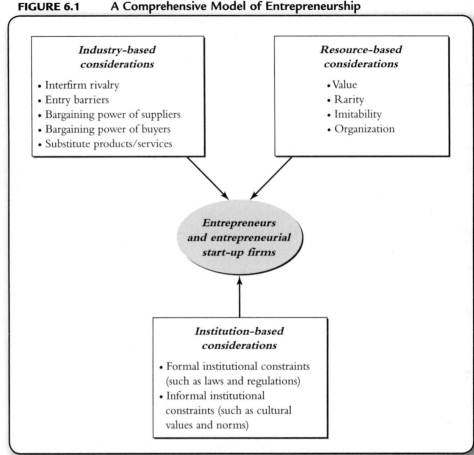

Similarly, entrepreneurs who can reduce the *bargaining power of sellers* may also find a niche for themselves. For example, a small number of national chain ("brick and mortar") bookstores used to represent the only major outlets through which hundreds of publishers could sell their books. Entrepreneurial Internet bookstores, led by Amazon, have provided more outlets for publishers, thereby reducing the bargaining power of traditional bookstores as sellers.

Substitute products/services may offer great opportunities for entrepreneurs. If entrepreneurs can bring in substitute products that can redefine the game, they can effectively chip away some of the competitive advantages held by incumbents. For example, e-mails and online payments, pioneered by entrepreneurial firms, are now substituting a large portion of faxes, express mails, and paper check printing and processing, whose incumbents are powerless to fight back.

Obviously, entrepreneurs need to carefully understand the nature of the industries they intend to join. However, one important paradox is that especially in emerging turbulent industries, the basics underlying the five forces may not be known. For example, it is often difficult to predict consumer preferences, to price innovative products, and to build capacity. However, even when the industry is conducive for entries, there is no guarantee that entrepreneurs will be successful.

Strategy in Action 6.1 - Ski in Southern Africa, Anyone?

It is hard to believe, but entrepreneurs in South Africa and neighboring Lesotho have built ski resorts on the slopes of Drakensberg mountains. These mountains are not tall by Alpine standards (3,000 meters/9,900 feet), snow is irregular, and getting in and out is difficult. Yet, Tiffindell Resort, on the South Africa side, has managed to produce a ski season every year. Between May and September (the southern hemisphere winter), over 5,000 skiers arrive. When there is not much real snow on the ground, skiers enjoy themselves on 1.5 hectares (3.7 acres) of artificial snow. This entrepreneurial venture taps into an untapped demand: Rich young customers are interested in coming to *practice* skiing in preparation for more serious winter holidays in Europe or North America. Tiffindell's rising notoriety has got itself some international competition. Afri-Ski, a rival ski resort, is opening up across the border on the Lesotho side. If Afri-Ski succeeds, Tiffindell may lose some of its novelty value. To stay

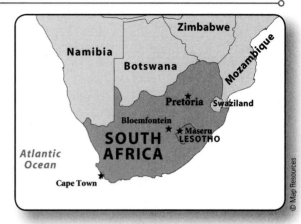

ahead of the game, Tiffindell has begun a 150 million rand ($20 million) expansion, although the venture is not reliably profitable yet.

Sources: Based on (1) *Economist*, 2003, No business like snow business, August 2: 57; (2) www.afriski.co.za; (3) www.tiffindell.co.za.

Resource-Based Considerations

The resource-based view, first introduced in Chapter 3, sheds considerable light on entrepreneurship, with a focus on its value, rarity, imitability, and organizational (VRIO) aspects (see Figure 6.1). First, entrepreneurial resources must create value.[9] For instance, networks and contacts are great potential resources for would-be entrepreneurs. However, unless they channel such networks and contacts to create economic value, such resources remain potential.

Second, resources must be *rare*. As the cliché goes, "If everybody has it, you can't make money from it." The best-performing entrepreneurs tend to have the rarest knowledge and insights about business opportunities.[10] For example, who would have thought of operating ski resorts in Africa? (See Strategy in Action 6.1.)

Third, resources must be *inimitable*. For instance, Amazon's success has prompted a number of online bookstores to directly imitate it. Amazon rapidly built the world's largest book warehouses, which ironically are "brick-and-mortar." It is Amazon's "best-in-the-breed" physical inventories—not its online presence—that are more challenging to imitate.

Fourth, entrepreneurial resources must be *organizationally* embedded. For example, although individual mercenaries have existed since the dawn of warfare, only in modern times have private military companies (PMCs) become a global industry. Entrepreneurial PMCs thrive on their organizational capabilities to provide military and security services in dangerous environments, while individuals would shy away from such conditions and even national militaries might withdraw (as in Iraq).

Institution-Based Considerations

First introduced in Chapter 4, both formal and informal institutional constraints, as rules of the game, affect entrepreneurship (see Figure 6.1). Although entrepreneurship is thriving around the globe in general, its development is unequal. Whether entrepreneurship is facilitated or retarded significantly depends on formal institutions governing how entrepreneurs start up new firms.[11] A recent World Bank study reports some striking differences in government regulations concerning start-ups such as registration, licensing, incorporation, taxation, and inspection (Figure 6.2).[12] In general, governments in developed economies impose fewer procedures (as low as two procedures and two/three days in Australia and Canada, respectively) and a lower total cost (less than 2% of per capita GNP in Denmark, New Zealand, Ireland, Sweden, United States, United Kingdom, Canada, and Finland). On the other hand, entrepreneurs confront harsher regulatory burdens in poorer countries. Brazil leads the world by requiring entrepreneurs to endure 18 procedures to obtain legal clearance to start a new firm. The Democratic Republic of Congo requires 155 days and a total cost of 487.2% per capita GNP. Overall, it is not surprising that the more entrepreneur-friendly these formal institutional requirements are, the more flourishing entrepreneurship is, and the more developed the economies will become—and vice versa.

In addition to formal institutions, informal institutions such as cultural values and norms also affect entrepreneurship.[13] Because entrepreneurs necessarily take more risks, individualistic and low uncertainty-avoidance societies tend to foster relatively more entrepreneurship, whereas collectivistic and high uncertainty-avoidance societies may result in relatively lower levels of entrepreneurship.[14] Since Chapter 4 discussed this issue at length, we will not repeat it here other than to stress its importance (see Strategy in Action 6.2 for an example). Overall, the institution-based view suggests that institutions matter. Later sections will discuss *how* they matter.

Five Entrepreneurial Strategies

This section discusses five entrepreneurial strategies: (1) growth, (2) innovation, (3) network, (4) financing/governance, and (5) harvest/exit. A sixth one, internationalization, will be highlighted in the next section. Before proceeding, it is important to note that these strategies are not mutually exclusive and that they are often pursued in combination by entrepreneurial firms.

Growth

To many individuals such as Mike Morris (see Opening Case), it is the excitement associated with a growing firm that has attracted them to become entrepreneurs.[15] Since a firm can be conceptualized as consisting of a bundle of resources (see Chapter 3), the growth of an entrepreneurial firm can be viewed as an attempt to more fully utilize currently underutilized resources.[16] What are these resources? At start-ups, they are primarily entrepreneurial vision, drive, and leadership.[17] While young firms are usually short on tangible resources (such as capital), they often have an abundant supply of intangible resources (such as entrepreneurial drive).

FIGURE 6.2   Number of Days Needed to Start Up a New Business in 36 Countries

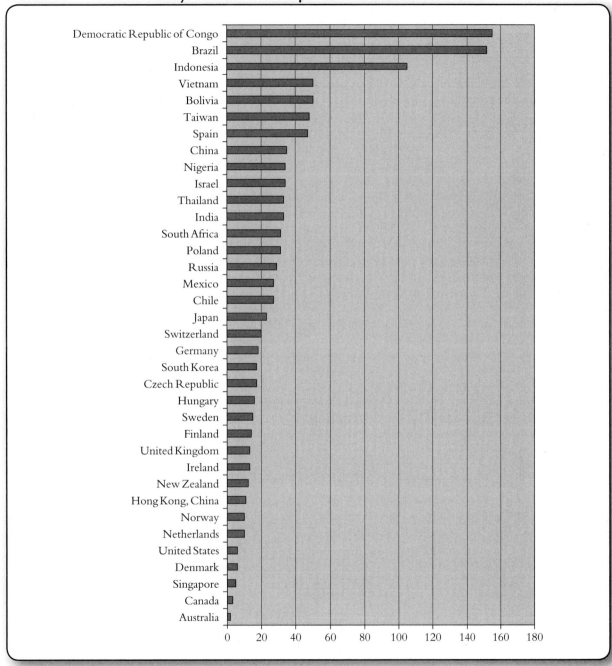

Source: Adapted from The World Bank, 2008, *Doing Business 2008*, Washington: The World Bank.

Strategy in Action 6.2 - Dealing with Counterfeiting

Ethical Challenge

Counterfeiting is an entrepreneurial strategy. A fundamental issue is while most entrepreneurs pursue legitimate business, why would many individuals and firms choose a counterfeiting strategy? Experts generally agree that the single largest determinant lies in institutional frameworks. A lack of effective formal intellectual property rights (IPR) protection seems to be a prerequisite for counterfeiting. As a new WTO member since 2001, China has significantly strengthened its IPR laws in line with the WTO TRIPS Agreement. However, what is lacking is enforcement. In America, convicted counterfeiters face fines of up to $2 million and 10 years in prison for a first offense. In China, counterfeiters will not be criminally prosecuted if their profits do not exceed approximately $10,000—few counterfeiters are dumb enough to keep records showing that they make that much money. If they are caught and are found to make less than $10,000, they can usually get away with a $1,000 fine, which is widely regarded as a (small) cost of doing business. In many cases, local governments and police have little incentive to enforce IPR laws, in fear of losing tax revenues and increasing unemployment. China is not alone in this regard. For example, in Thailand, a 2000 raid to shut down counterfeiters was blocked by 1,000 angry people organized by local officials.

To stem the tide of counterfeits, four "Es" are necessary. The first E, enforcement, even if successful, is likely to be short-lived as long as demand remains high. The other three "Es" (education, external pressures, and economic growth) require much more patient work. Education not only refers to educating IPR law enforcement officials, but also the general public about

the perils of counterfeits (fake drugs can kill, so can fake auto parts). Educational efforts hopefully will foster new norms among a new generation of entrepreneurs who will have internalized the values in favor of more ethical and legitimate businesses. External pressures have to be applied skillfully. Confronting host governments is not likely to be effective. For example, Microsoft, when encountering extensive software piracy in China, chose to collaborate with the Ministry of Electronics to develop new software instead of challenging it head-on. Microsoft figured that once the government has a stake in the sales of legitimate Microsoft products, it may have a stronger interest in cracking down on pirated software.

Finally, economic growth and home-grown brands are the most effective remedies in the long run. In the 1500s, the Netherlands (an emerging economy at that time) was busy making counterfeit Chinese porcelain. In the 1960s, Japan was the global leader for counterfeits. In the 1970s, Hong Kong grabbed this dubious distinction. In the 1980s, South Korea and Taiwan led the world. Now it is China's turn. As these countries developed their own industries, they also strengthened IPR laws. If past experience around the world is any guide, then there is hope that someday China may follow the same path.

Sources: Based on (1) *Business Week,* 2005, Fakes! February 7: 54–64; (2) D. Clark, 2006, Counterfeiting in China, *China Business Review,* January–February: 14–15; (3) *The Economist,* 2003, Imitating property is theft, May 17: 52–54; (4) C. Hill, 2007, Digital piracy: Causes, consequences, and strategic responses, *Asia Pacific Journal of Management,* 24: 9–24; (5) M. W. Peng, 2001, How entrepreneurs create wealth in transition economies, *Academy of Management Executive,* 15: 95–108.

A hallmark of entrepreneurial growth is a dynamic flexible guerrilla strategy.[18] As underdogs, entrepreneurial SMEs cannot compete against their larger and more established rivals head-on. "Going for the crumbs" (at least initially), they often engage in indirect and subtle attacks that large rivals may not immediately recognize as competitive challenges.[19] Entrepreneurial firms conserve scarce resources for crucial battles.

They often use speed and stealth to create disruption by preempting competitors, resulting in substantial first mover advantages.

Firms with an entrepreneurial growth strategy place more emphasis on action and less on analysis. While many large firms endowed with strong analytical resources often develop a refined incapacity for seizing opportunities (known as "paralysis by analysis"), many entrepreneurial firms grow by seizing certain opportunities with relatively little analysis, a classic "emergent" strategy at work.[20] For example, one study of the fastest growing firms in the United States finds that 41% had no formal business plan at all and that the other 26% had only a rudimentary, "back-of-the-envelope" plan—only 28% developed a full-blown business plan.[21] Of course, all new ventures need some analysis and planning.[22] However, there is research documenting that entrepreneurs who spent a long time in planning are no more likely to outperform individuals who seized opportunities with relatively little planning.[23]

On the other hand, it is important to caution against over-aggressiveness. Entrepreneurs, of *all* nationalities, have a tendency to be overconfident.[24] The e-commerce crash since 2000 reminds us of the perils of such overconfidence. The best entrepreneurs embrace uncertainties, yet protect themselves against excessive risk. For example, some venture capitalists, who are entrepreneurs themselves, employ well-known milestones ("rounds") of financing to stage and sequence their commitment to risky projects. Entrepreneurs failing to do so may end up suffering huge losses.

Innovation

Innovation is at the heart of an entrepreneurial mindset.[25] Israel, for example, is known for its formidable innovation capabilities at its technology companies. Well-known examples include Check Point Software (Internet and network security software) and Mirabilis (ICQ instant messaging software).[26] There is consistent evidence showing a positive relationship between a high degree of innovation and superior profitability.[27]

An innovation strategy is a specialized form of differentiation strategy (see Chapter 2).[28] It offers three advantages. First, it allows a potentially more sustainable basis for competitive advantage. Firms first to introduce new goods or services are likely to earn (quasi) "monopoly profits" until competitors emerge. If entrepreneurial firms come up with "disruptive technologies," then they may redefine the rules of competition, thus wiping out the advantages of incumbents.[29]

Second, innovation should be regarded broadly. Not only are technological breakthroughs innovations, less novel but still substantially new ways of doing business are also innovations. Most start-ups reproduce existing organizational routines, but *recombine* them to create some novel product/service offerings, such as Federal Express' (re)combination of existing air and ground assets to create a new market. For example, *Hola!,* a high-society weekly in Spain, exported its winning formula with a new focus on the British celebrities and launched *Hello!* in Britain. Edited and printed in Spain, *Hello!* has become the fastest growing British magazine.[30] While there is no technological innovation here, these are interesting cases of organizational innovation.

Finally, entrepreneurial firms are uniquely ready for innovation. Owners, managers, and employees at SMEs tend to be more innovative and risk-taking than those at large firms.[31] In fact, a key reason many SMEs are founded is because former employees of large firms are frustrated by their inability to translate innovative ideas into realities at large firms. For example, a group of programmers at IBM's German affiliate proposed to IBM that standard programming solutions could be profitably sold to clients. After their ideas were turned down, they left and founded SAP, now the number one player in the thriving enterprise resource planning (ERP) market. Innovators at large firms also have limited ability to personally profit from innovations, whose property rights usually belong to the corporation. In contrast, innovators at entrepreneurial firms are better able to reap the financial gains associated with innovations, thus fueling their motivation to charge ahead.

Network

A network strategy refers to intentionally constructing and tapping into relationships, connections, and ties that individuals and organizations have.[32] There are two kinds of networks: personal and organizational. Both are important. Prior to and during the founding phase of the entrepreneurial firm, these two networks overlap significantly. In other words, entrepreneurs' personal networks are essentially the same as the firm's organizational networks.[33] The essence of entrepreneurship can be regarded as a process to "translate" personal networks into value-adding organizational networks. Three attributes—namely, urgency, intensity, and impact—distinguish entrepreneurial networking.

First, entrepreneurial firms have a high degree of *urgency* to develop and leverage networks. Essentially, they confront a **liability of newness,** defined as the inherent disadvantage that entrepreneurial firms experience as new entrants.[34] In the absence of a track record and of tangible products (many start-ups only have an idea), start-ups do not inspire confidence and they lack legitimacy in the eyes of suppliers, customers, financiers, and other stakeholders. Therefore, start-ups urgently need to draw upon entrepreneurs' existing social networks and construct new ones to overcome the liability of newness. Convincing more legitimate and well-established individuals (as co-founders, management team members, investors, or board directors) and organizations (as alliance partners, sponsors, or customers) to lend a helping hand can boost the legitimacy of SMEs. In other words, legitimacy, an intangible but highly important resource, can be transferred. On the other hand, there is no free lunch. Entrepreneurial firms need to guard against being taken advantage of by their larger and more powerful partners.[35]

A second characteristic that distinguishes entrepreneurial networking is its *intensity*. Network relationships can be classified as strong ties and weak ties. **Strong ties** are more durable, reliable, and trustworthy relationships, whereas **weak ties** are less durable, reliable, and trustworthy.[36] Efforts to cultivate, develop, and maintain strong ties are usually more intense than weak ties. Entrepreneurs often rely on strong ties— typically 5–20 individuals—for advice, assistance, and support. Strong ties can result in trust, which grows from a long history of friendly interaction. Strong ties also lead to predictability, which refers to one party's ability to confidently predict how the other party will behave under some new circumstances. Over time, the preference for strong ties may change, and there are also benefits of weak ties (discussed later).

Finally, because of the small firm size, the contributions of entrepreneurs' personal networks tend to have a stronger *impact* on firm performance.[37] In comparison, the impact of similar networks cultivated by managers at large firms may be less pronounced because of these firms' sheer size. Moreover, being private owners, entrepreneurs can directly pocket the profits if their firms perform well, thereby motivating them to make these networks work.

liability of newness

The inherent disadvantage that entrepreneurial firms experience as new entrants.

strong ties

More durable, reliable, and trustworthy relationships cultivated over a long period of time.

weak ties

Relationships that are characterized by infrequent interaction and low intimacy.

Overall, there is strong evidence that networks, both personal and organizational, represent significant resources and opportunities, and that successful networking may lead to successful entrepreneurial performance.[38] The most advantageous positions are those well connected to a number of players who are otherwise not connected—in other words, more *centrally* located network positions are helpful. Armed with useful ties and contacts, entrepreneurs, therefore, can literally become "persons who add value by brokering the connection between others."[39]

Financing and Governance

All start-ups need to raise capital. Here is a quiz (also a joke): Of the "4F" sources of entrepreneurial financing, the first three Fs are founders, family, and friends, but what is the other F source? The answer is . . . *fools* (!). While this is a joke, it strikes a chord in the entrepreneurial world: Given the well-known failure risks of start-ups (a *majority* of them will fail), why would anybody other than fools be willing to invest in start-ups? In reality, most outside, strategic investors, who can be angels (wealthy individual investors), venture capitalists, banks, foreign entrants, and government agencies, are *not* fools. They often examine business plans, require a strong management team, and scrutinize financial reviews and analysis.[40] They also demand some assurance (such as collateral) indicating that entrepreneurs will not simply "take the money and run." Entrepreneurs need to develop relationships with these outside investors, some of which are weak ties. Turning weak-tie contacts into willing investors is always challenging.[41]

While dealing with strong-tie contacts can be quite informal (based on handshake deals or simple contracts), working with weak-tie contacts may be more formal. In the absence of a long history of interaction, weak-tie investors such as angels and venture capitalists often demand a more formal governance strategy to safeguard their investment, through a significant percentage of equity (such as 20%–40%), a corresponding number of seats on the board of directors, and a set of formal rules and policies.[42] In extreme cases, when business is not going well, venture capitalists may exercise their formal voting power and dismiss the founder CEO.[43] Entrepreneurs, therefore, have to make tradeoffs given the needs for larger-scale financing and the necessity to cede a significant portion of ownership and control rights of their "dream" firms.

Given the well-known hazards associated with start-up failures, anything that entrepreneurs can do to improve their odds would be helpful. Research indicates that the odds for survival during the crucial early years are significantly correlated with firm size—the larger, the better (Table 6.1). The upshot is that the faster start-ups can reach a certain size, the more likely they will survive the first few years in the face of the liability of newness. Since it takes a significant amount of capital (among other things) to reach a large size, entrepreneurs often make the choice of accepting more outside investment and agreeing to give up some ownership and control rights.

Internationally, the extent to which entrepreneurs draw on resources of family and friends vis-à-vis outside investors is different. In the West, only a handful of minority groups (such as Asian immigrants) can count on much financial support from family and friends, whereas in Asia, these two "Fs" (of the "4F" joke) typically contribute a great deal more.[44] This can be explained by the informal cultural norms of collectivism and the lack of formal market-supporting institutions such as venture capitalists and credit-reporting agencies in Asia.[45] Interestingly, this pattern persists after Asian immigrants arrive in the West. For example, 33% and 49% of Asian immigrant entrepreneurs

TABLE 6.1   **One- and Four-Year Survival Rates by Firm Size**

FIRM SIZE (EMPLOYEES)	CHANCES OF SURVIVING AFTER 1 YEAR	FIRM SIZE (EMPLOYEES)	CHANCES OF SURVIVING AFTER 4 YEARS
0–9	78%	0–19	50%
10–19	86%	20–49	67%
20–99	95%	50–99	67%
100–249	95%	100–499	70%
250+	100%		

Source: Adapted from J. Timmons, 1999, *New Venture Creation* (p. 33), Boston: Irwin McGraw-Hill, based on US data.

in Britain used capital from family and friends, respectively. In contrast, only 10% and 3% of native-born British entrepreneurs tapped into these two "Fs," respectively.[46]

Harvest and Exit

Entrepreneurial harvest and exit can take a number of routes, which are outlined in Table 6.2. First, selling an equity stake to an outside strategic investor (discussed earlier) can substantially increase the value of the firm and therefore offer an excellent harvest option. However, entrepreneurs must be willing to give up some ownership and control rights.

Second, selling the firm to other private owners or companies may be done with a painful discount if the business is failing, or it may carry a happy premium if the business is booming. Selling the firm is typically one of the most significant and emotionally charged events entrepreneurs confront. It is important to note that "selling out" does not necessarily mean failure. Many entrepreneurs deliberately build up businesses, in anticipation of being acquired by larger corporations and profiting handsomely.

Third, when business is not doing well, merging with another company is another alternative. The drawbacks are that the firm may lose its independence, and that some entrepreneurs may have to personally exit the firm (after receiving some compensation) to leave room for executives from another company. It is obvious that a lackluster entrepreneurial firm is not in a great position to bargain for a good deal. However, if properly structured and negotiated, a merger will allow entrepreneurs to reap the rewards for which they have worked so hard.

TABLE 6.2   **Routes of Entrepreneurial Harvest and Exit**

- Selling an equity stake
- Selling the business
- Merging with another firm
- Considering an initial public offering (IPO)
- Declaring bankruptcy

TABLE 6.3   **Advantages and Disadvantages of an Initial Public Offering (IPO)**

ADVANTAGES	DISADVANTAGES
• Improved financial condition	• Subject to the whims of financial market
• Access to more capital	• Forced to focus on the short term
• Diversification of shareholder base	• Loss of entrepreneurial control
• Ability to cash out	• New fiduciary responsibilities for shareholders
• Management and employee incentives	• Loss of privacy
• Enhanced corporate reputation	• Limits on management's freedom of action
• Greater opportunity for future acquisition	• Demands of periodic reporting

Source: Based on text in J. Kaplan, 2003, *Patterns of Entrepreneurship* (pp. 428–430), New York: Wiley.

Fourth, entrepreneurs can take their firms through an **initial public offering (IPO)**, which is the goal of many entrepreneurs. An IPO has several advantages and disadvantages (Table 6.3). Among the advantages, first and foremost is financial stability, in that the firm no longer has to constantly "beg" for money. For entrepreneurs themselves, an IPO can potentially result in financial windfalls. For the firm, stock options can be issued as incentives to motivate, attract, and retain capable employees. The IPO is also a great signal indicating that the firm has "made it." Such an enhanced reputation enables it to raise more capital to facilitate future growth such as acquisitions.

On the other hand, an IPO carries a number of disadvantages. The firm is being subject to the rational and irrational exuberance (and also pessimism) of the financial market. For example, the late 1990s saw many companies go through an IPO, whereas fewer have done so in the new millennium (thanks to the collapse of the bubble). In the IPO process, founding entrepreneurs may gradually lose their majority control. The firm, legally speaking, is no longer "theirs." Instead, founding entrepreneurs now have the new fiduciary duty to look after the interests of outside shareholders. As a result, certain constraints now restrict entrepreneurs' freedom of action. They are being scrutinized by securities authorities, shareholders, and the media, which often force firms to focus on the short term. There is also a loss of privacy, as information about personal wealth, shareholding, and compensation must often be disclosed. Some entrepreneurs, such as Ingvar Kamprad, founder of the Swedish furniture chain IKEA, and Tadao Yoshida, founder of the Japanese zippermaker YKK, have refused to go public to avoid being forced into a short-term focus by the stock market.[47]

Finally, while taking the firm through an IPO is the most triumphant way of harvest, many entrepreneurial firms that are failing do not have such a luxury. The only viable exit is often to declare bankruptcy. Each year, approximately 38,000–40,000 US businesses, most of which are start-ups, file for bankruptcy. The annual average number of bankrupt firms is approximately 14,000–15,000 in Japan, 21,000 in Germany, 47,000 in Great Britain, and 52,000 in France.[48]

Overall, a number of harvest and exit options are available to entrepreneurs. For instance, they are encouraged to think about the exit plan early in the business cycle and aim at maximizing the gains from the fruits of their labor.[49] Otherwise, they may end up having to eventually declare bankruptcy and face the consequences—definitely not something they planned on.

initial public offering (IPO)

The first round of public trading of company stock.

Internationalizing the Entrepreneurial Firm

A prevalent myth is that only large MNEs do business abroad and that SMEs mostly operate domestically. This myth, based on historical stereotypes, is being increasingly challenged, as more and more SMEs become internationalized. Further, some start-ups attempt to do business abroad from inception (see Opening Case). These are often called **"born global"** firms (or "international new ventures").[50] This section examines how entrepreneurial firms internationalize.

Transaction Costs and Entrepreneurial Opportunities

Compared with domestic transaction costs (the costs of doing business), international transaction costs are qualitatively higher.[51] On the one hand, there are numerous innocent differences in formal institutions and in informal norms (see Chapter 4). On the other hand, there may be a high level of deliberate opportunism, which is hard to detect and remedy. For example, when an unknown Saudi importer places an order from a US exporter, the US exporter may not be able to ascertain that the Saudi side will deliver payment upon receiving the goods. In comparison, most US firms are comfortable allowing domestic customers to pay within 30 or 60 days after receiving the goods. However, if foreign payment is not arriving on time (even after 30, 60, or even more days), it is difficult to assess whether firms in Saudi Arabia simply do not observe the norm of punctual payment or whether that particular importer is being deliberately opportunistic. If the latter is indeed the case, suing the Saudi importer in a Saudi court where Arabic is the official language may be so costly that it is not an option for small US exporters.

As a result, many small firms may simply say "Forget it!" when receiving an unsolicited order from abroad. Conceptually, this is an example of transaction costs being too high that many firms may choose not to pursue international opportunities. Therefore, there are always entrepreneurial opportunities that can innovatively lower some of these transaction costs, by bringing distant groups of people, firms, and countries together. Shown in Table 6.4, while entrepreneurial firms can internationalize by entering foreign markets, they can also add an international dimension without having to go abroad. Next, we discuss these strategies.

born global

Start-up companies that attempt to do business abroad from inception.

TABLE 6.4   Internationalization Strategies for Entrepreneurial Firms

Entering Foreign Markets	Staying in Domestic Markets
• Direct exports	• Indirect exports (through domestic export intermediaries)
• Franchising/licensing	• Supplier of foreign firms
• Foreign direct investment (through strategic alliances, green-field wholly owned subsidiaries, and/or foreign acquisitions)	• Franchisee/licensee of foreign brands
	• Alliance partner of foreign direct investors
	• Harvest and exit (through sell-off to, and acquisition by, foreign entrants)

International Strategies for Entering Foreign Markets

SMEs can enter foreign markets through three broad modes: (1) direct exports, (2) licensing/franchising, and (3) foreign direct investment (FDI) (see Chapter 5 for more details). First, direct exports entail the sale of products made by entrepreneurial firms in their home country to customers in other countries. This strategy is attractive because entrepreneurial firms are able to reach foreign customers directly. When domestic markets experience some downturns, sales abroad may compensate for such drops.[52] However, a major drawback is that SMEs may not have enough resources to turn overseas opportunities into profits.

A second way to enter international markets is licensing/franchising. Usually used in manufacturing industries, licensing refers to Firm A's agreement to give Firm B the rights to use A's proprietary technology (such as a patent) or trademark (such as a corporate logo) for a royalty fee paid to A by B. Franchising represents essentially the same idea, except it is typically used in service industries, such as fast food. A great advantage is that SME licensors and franchisors can expand abroad with relatively little capital of their own.[53] Foreign firms interested in becoming licensees/franchisees have to invest their own capital up front. For instance, it now costs approximately one million dollars to win a franchise from McDonald's. However, the flip side is that licensors and franchisors may suffer a loss of control over how their technology and brand names are used.

A third entry mode is FDI, which may entail strategic alliances with foreign partners, foreign acquisitions, and/or greenfield wholly owned subsidiaries. FDI has several distinct advantages. By planting some roots abroad, a firm becomes more committed to serving foreign markets. It is physically and psychologically close to foreign customers. Relative to licensing/franchising, a firm is better able to control how its proprietary technology and brand name are used. However, FDI has a major drawback, which is its cost and complexity. It requires both a nontrivial sum of capital and a significant managerial commitment. Many SMEs are unable to engage in FDI. However, there is some evidence that in the long run, FDI by SMEs may lead to higher performance, and that some SMEs can come up with sufficient resources to engage in FDI.[54]

In general, the level of complexity and required resources increases from direct exports to licensing/franchising, and finally to FDI. Traditionally, it is thought that most firms will have to go through these different "stages," and that SMEs (perhaps with few exceptions) are unable to take on FDI. These ideas—collectively known as **stage models**—posit that even for some SMEs that eventually internationalize, it entails a very slow stage-by-stage process.[55]

However, enough counter-examples of *rapidly* internationalizing entrepreneurial firms, known as the "born globals," exist to challenge stage models. Consider Logitech, now a global leader in computer peripherals.[56] It was established by entrepreneurs from Switzerland and the United States, where the firm set up dual headquarters. R&D and manufacturing were initially split between these two countries, and then quickly spread to Ireland and Taiwan through FDI. Its first commercial contract was with a Japanese company. Given the information technology advancements within the past decade, most Internet firms, because of their instant worldwide reach, have rapidly internationalized (see Closing Case).[57]

stage models

Models which suggest firms internationalize by going through predictable stages from simple steps to complex operations.

Given that most SMEs still fit the stereotype of slow (or no) internationalization and that some very entrepreneurial SMEs seem to be "born global," a key question is: What leads to rapid internationalization? The key differentiator between rapidly and slowly (or no) internationalizing SMEs seems to be the international experience of entrepreneurs.[58] If entrepreneurs, such as Mike Morris (Opening Case), have solid previous experience abroad (such as working and studying overseas and/or immigrating from certain countries), then doing business internationally is not so intimidating. Otherwise, the "fear and loathing" factor associated with the unfamiliar foreign business world may take over and entrepreneurs will simply want to avoid troubles overseas.

While many entrepreneurial firms have aggressively gone abroad, it is probably true that a majority of SMEs will be unable to do so—struggling domestically is already giving them enough headaches. However, as discussed next, some SMEs can still internationalize by staying at home.

International Strategies for Staying in Domestic Markets

Shown in Table 6.4, entrepreneurial SMEs can execute at least five strategies to internationalize without leaving their home country: (1) export indirectly, (2) become suppliers of foreign firms, (3) become licensees/franchisees of foreign brands, (4) become alliance partners of foreign direct investors, and (5) harvest and exit through sell-offs. First, whereas direct exports may be lucrative, many SMEs simply do not have the resources to handle such work. However, they still can reach overseas customers through indirect exports—exporting through domestic-based export intermediaries. Export intermediaries perform an important "middleman" function by linking sellers and buyers overseas that otherwise would not have been connected.[59] Being entrepreneurs themselves, export intermediaries facilitate the internationalization of many SMEs. Intermediaries, such as trading companies and export management companies, handle about 50% of total exports in Japan and South Korea, 38% in Thailand, and 5%–10% in the United States.[60]

A second strategy is to become suppliers of foreign firms that come to do business in one's home country. Most foreign firms, in order to save costs, are interested in looking for local suppliers. For example, one Northern Irish bakery for chilled part-bake bread secured supply contracts with an American firm, Subway, that entered Ireland in the mid-1990s. So successful was this relationship that the firm now supplies Subway franchisees throughout Europe.[61] SME suppliers thus may be able to internationalize by "piggybacking" on the larger foreign entrants.

Third, entrepreneurial firms may consider becoming licensees or franchisees of foreign brands. SMEs can learn a great deal about how to operate at world-class standards. Further, licensees and franchisees do not have to be permanently under the control of licensors and franchisors. If enough learning has been accomplished and enough capital has been accumulated, it is possible to discontinue the relationship and to reap greater entrepreneurial profits. For example, in Thailand, Minor Group, which had held the Pizza Hut franchise for 20 years, broke away from the relationship. Its new venture, The Pizza Company, is now the market leader in Thailand.[62]

A fourth strategy is to become alliance partners of foreign direct investors. Facing an onslaught of aggressive MNEs, many entrepreneurial firms may stand little chance of successfully defending their market positions. Given this, it makes great sense to follow the old adage, "If you can't beat them, join them!" While "dancing with the giants" is tricky, it seems a much better outcome than being crushed by them.

Finally, as a harvest and exit strategy, entrepreneurs may sell an equity stake or the entire firm to foreign entrants. An American couple, originally from Seattle, built a Starbucks-like coffee chain called Seattle Coffee with 60 stores in Britain. When the real Starbucks entered Britain, the couple sold the chain to Starbucks for a hefty $84 million. In light of the high failure rates of start-ups, being acquired by foreign entrants may help preserve the business in the long run.

Overall, given that international business, by definition, is a two-way business, while some entrepreneurial firms can venture abroad, others can be successfully internationalized without getting their feet wet in unfamiliar foreign waters.

Debates and Extensions

With the recent boom in entrepreneurship throughout the world, this phenomenon has continued to attract significant controversies and debates.[63] This section introduces three leading debates: (1) traits versus institutions, (2) slow internationalizers versus "born global" start-ups, and (3) anti-failure biases versus entrepreneur-friendly bankruptcy laws.

Traits versus Institutions

This is probably the oldest debate on entrepreneurship. It focuses on the question: What motivates entrepreneurs to establish new firms, while most others are simply content to work for bosses? The "traits" school of thought argues that it is personal traits that matter. Compared with non-entrepreneurs, entrepreneurs seem more likely to possess a stronger desire for achievement and are more willing to take risks and tolerate ambiguities. Overall, entrepreneurship inevitably deviates from the norm to work for others, and this deviation may be in the "blood" of entrepreneurs.[64] For example, **serial entrepreneurs** are people who start, grow, and sell several businesses throughout their career. One example is Mike Morris, an American entrepreneur chasing the China dream with multiple new ventures (see Opening Case).

Critics, however, argue that some of these traits, such as a strong achievement orientation, are not necessarily limited to entrepreneurs, but instead are characteristic of many successful individuals. Moreover, the diversity among entrepreneurs makes any attempt to develop a standard psychological or personality profile futile. Critics suggest that it is institutions—namely, the environments that set formal and informal rules of the game—that matter.[65] For example, consider the ethnic Chinese, who have exhibited a high degree of entrepreneurship throughout Southeast Asia, whereby as a minority group (usually less than 10% of the population in countries such as Indonesia and Thailand) they control 70%–80% of the wealth.[66] Yet, in mainland China, for three decades (the 1950s through the 1970s), there had been virtually no entrepreneurship, thanks to harsh communist policies. Over the last two decades, however, as government policies became relatively more entrepreneur-friendly, the institutional transitions have opened the floodgates of entrepreneurship in China.

A high-profile recent case documents how institutions constrain or enable entrepreneurship. In 2005, Baidu, a Chinese Internet start-up, listed on NASDAQ and its shares surged 354% on the same day (from $27 to $154), scoring the biggest one-day

serial entrepreneurs
People who start, grow, and sell several businesses throughout their careers.

stock surge in US capital markets since 2000. While there might be some possible "irrational exuberance" among US investors chasing "China's Google," it is evident that they did not discriminate against Baidu. The sad reality for Baidu is that, at home, it was blatantly discriminated against by the Chinese securities authorities. As a private start-up, it was not allowed to list its stock on China's stock exchanges—only state-owned firms need apply. Essentially, Baidu was pushed out of China to list in the United States, whose entrepreneur-friendly institutional frameworks, such as NASDAQ regulations, are able to facilitate more entrepreneurial success.[67] In a nutshell, it is not what is in people's "blood" that makes or breaks entrepreneurship—it is institutions that encourage or constrain entrepreneurship.

Beyond the macro societal-level institutions, more micro institutions also matter. Family background and educational attainment have been found to correlate with entrepreneurship. Children of wealthy parents, especially those who own businesses, are more likely to start their own firms. So are people who are better educated. Taken together, informal norms governing one's socioeconomic group, in terms of whether starting a new firm is legitimate or not, assert some powerful impact on the propensity to create new ventures.

Overall, this debate is an extension of the broader debate on "nature versus nurture." Most scholars now agree that entrepreneurship is the result of both nature *and* nurture.

Slow Internationalizers versus "Born Global" Start-Ups

Two components should be considered here: (1) *Can* SMEs internationalize faster than what has been suggested by traditional stage models? (2) *Should* they rapidly internationalize? The dust has largely settled on the first component: it is possible for some (but not all) SMEs to make very rapid progress in internationalization. What is currently being debated is the second component.[68]

On the one hand, advocates argue that every industry has become "global" and that entrepreneurial firms need to rapidly go after these opportunities.[69] On the other hand, stage models suggest that firms need to enter culturally and institutionally close markets first, spend enough time there to accumulate overseas experience, and then gradually move from more primitive modes such as exports to more sophisticated strategies such as FDI in distant markets. Consistent with stage models, Sweden's IKEA, for example, waited 20 years (1943–1963) before entering a neighboring country, Norway. Only more recently has it accelerated its internationalization.[70] Stage models caution that inexperienced swimmers may be drowned in unfamiliar foreign waters.

A key issue, therefore, is whether it is better for entrepreneurs to start the internationalization process soon after founding (as "born global" firms do) or to postpone until the firm has accumulated significant resources (as IKEA did). One view supports rapid internationalization.[71] Specifically, firms following the prescription of stage models, when eventually internationalizing, must overcome substantial inertia because of their domestic orientation. In contrast, firms that internationalize earlier need to overcome fewer of these barriers. Therefore, SMEs without an established domestic orientation (such as Logitech discussed earlier) may outperform their rivals that wait longer to internationalize.[72] In other words, contrary to the inherent disadvantages in internationalization associated with SMEs as suggested by stage models, there may be "inherent advantages" of being small while venturing abroad.[73]

On the other hand, some scholars argue that "the born-global view, although appealing, is a dangerous half-truth." They maintain that "You must first be successful at home, then move outward in a manner that anticipates and genuinely accommodates local differences."[74] In other words, the teachings of stage models are still relevant. Some research reports that foreign sales during the first few years of the new venture may *reduce* its chances for survival.[75] Consequently, indiscriminate advice for new ventures to "go global" may not be warranted.

Given the continuation of split findings, there are no hard and fast rules on whether entrepreneurial firms should rapidly internationalize or not. While the entrepreneurial urge to "be bold" should be encouraged, they also need to be reminded of the virtues of "not being too bold."

Anti-Failure Bias versus Entrepreneur-Friendly Bankruptcy Laws[76]

Although a majority of entrepreneurial firms fail, entrepreneurs, scholars, journalists, and government officials all share an "anti-failure" bias.[77] Everyone is interested in entrepreneurial success, and the attention to entrepreneurial failure is scant.

One of the leading debates is how to treat failed entrepreneurs who file for bankruptcy. Although we are confident that many start-ups will end up in bankruptcy, at present it is impossible to predict which ones will go under. Therefore, from an institutional standpoint, if entrepreneurship is to be encouraged, there is a need to ease the pain associated with bankruptcy by means such as allowing entrepreneurs to walk away from debt, a legal right that bankrupt American entrepreneurs appreciate. In contrast, bankrupt German entrepreneurs may remain liable for unpaid debt for up to 30 years. Further, German and Japanese managers of bankrupt firms can also be liable for criminal penalties, and some bankrupt Japanese entrepreneurs have committed suicide. Not surprisingly, many failed entrepreneurs in Germany and Japan try to avoid business exit despite escalating losses, while societal and individual resources cannot be channeled to more productive uses. Therefore, as rules of the "end game," harsh bankruptcy laws become grave *exit* barriers. They can also create significant *entry* barriers, as fewer would-be entrepreneurs may decide to launch their ventures.

At a societal level, if many would-be entrepreneurs, in fear of failure, abandon their ideas, there will not be a thriving entrepreneurial sector. Given the risks and uncertainties, it is not surprising that many entrepreneurs do not make it the first time. However, if they are given second, third, or more chances, some of them will succeed. Approximately 50% of American entrepreneurs who filed bankruptcy would resume a new venture in four years, in part due to the relatively more entrepreneur-friendly bankruptcy laws. On the other hand, a society that severely punishes failed entrepreneurs through harsh bankruptcy laws is not likely to foster widespread entrepreneurship. Failed entrepreneurs have nevertheless accumulated a great deal of experience and lessons on how to avoid their mistakes. If they drop out of the entrepreneurial game (or, in the worst case, kill themselves), their wisdom will be permanently lost (see Strategy in Action 6.3).[78]

Institutionally, there is an urgent need to remove some of our anti-failure biases and design and implement entrepreneur-friendly bankruptcy policies so that failed entrepreneurs are given more chances. At a societal level, entrepreneurial failures, while certainly painful to entrepreneurs, may be beneficial. Only through a large number of entrepreneurial experimentations—many of which will fail—can winning solutions emerge, entrepreneurship flourish, and economies develop.[79]

Strategy in Action 6.3 - Bankruptcy as Social Stigma in Japan

In Japan, where social stigma of failure is very high, bankrupt entrepreneurs often commit suicide. According to the Ministry of Health, Labor, and Welfare, the top three reasons for the cause of death for Japanese is (1) cancer, (2) heart diseases, and (3) cerebral diseases. However, among executives, the second leading cause of death is suicide. Since 2001, the number of suicides by executives and the self-employed—many are entrepreneurs—has accounted for as much as 10% of the total number of suicides committed every year. In Japan, about 30 people commit suicide per *day* for economic reasons. In one isolated rural area, so many individuals have committed suicide that the spot is now popularly known as Suicide Mountain. Interestingly, life insurance money is used to pay off the debts. In other words, some entrepreneurs strategically commit suicide to cover their debts. According to insurance companies, the largest amount of insurance premium invested by firms is often the *"kei-ei-sha hoken"* (insurance for the executives). Firms become policy holders and entrepreneurs/managers are the insured. Many entrepreneurial firms purchase such insurance not only to reduce taxes but also to hedge the risks. In other words, the death of entrepreneurs may actually help revitalize their firms when running short on cash.

Clearly, in Japan, bankruptcy is associated with extremely high levels of social stigma—and, ultimately, death. No wonder many would-be entrepreneurs are not willing to start up new businesses. Statistics show that since the 1970s, the entry rate of new firms has declined drastically and continuously, even sinking below the rate of exit from the mid-1990s. This reversal between the rate of new entry and the rate of exit has been recognized as a critical policy issue. This trend is thought to indicate a lack of entrepreneurship, which has been largely blamed for the slowdown in innovative activities and thus the "Lost Decade" (the 1990s) of Japan's economy. Since 2000, the Japanese government has implemented a series of entrepreneur-friendly policies in order to encourage new entry. However, since informal norms, values, and beliefs, such as the levels

of social stigma associated with bankruptcy, take a long period of time to evolve, whether these reforms will successfully encourage more people to become entrepreneurs remains to be seen.

Sources: This case was written by **Yasuhiro Yamakawa** (University of Texas at Dallas) under the supervision of Professor Mike W. Peng. Based on (1) Establishment and Enterprise Census, 2006, Japanese government statistics; (2) M. Gannon, 2008. *Paradoxes of Culture and Globalization.* Thousand Oaks, CA: Sage; (3) G. Hofstede, 2007, Asian management in the 21st century, *Asia Pacific Journal of Management*, 24: 411–420; (4) S.-H. Lee, M. W. Peng, & J. Barney, 2007, Bankruptcy law and entrepreneurship development: A real options perspective. *Academy of Management Review*, 32: 257–272; (5) S.-H. Lee, Y. Yamakawa, M. W. Peng, & J. Barney, 2008, How do bankruptcy laws affect entrepreneurship development? Working paper, University of Texas at Dallas; (6) Metropolitan Police Department, 2006, Suicide statistics, Tokyo; (7) D. Shepherd, 2003, Learning from business failure: Propositions of grief recovery for the self-employed, *Academy of Management Review*, 28: 318–328; (8) *Time*, 1999, The business guru's key credential: He went belly up, February 25: 46 (Asia version); (9) Y. Takahashi, 2003, Chukonen jisatsu (middle age suicide), originally cited in M. West, Dying to get out of debt: Consumer insolvency law and suicide in Japan, Working paper #03-015, University of Michigan Law School; (10) Venture Enterprise Center, 2008, Tokyo.

TABLE 6.5   **Strategic Implications for Action**

- Establish an intimate understanding of your industry to identify gaps and opportunities.
- Leverage entrepreneurial resources and capabilities.
- Push for institutions that facilitate entrepreneurship development—both formal and informal.
- When internationalizing, be bold, but not too bold.

The Savvy Entrepreneur

Entrepreneurs and their firms are quintessential engines of the "creative destruction" process underpinning global capitalism first described by Joseph Schumpeter. All three leading perspectives can shed considerable light on entrepreneurship. The industry-based view suggests that entrepreneurial firms tend to choose industries with lower entry barriers and often generate more innovative products. The resource-based view posits that it is largely intangible resources such as vision, drive, and willingness to take risk that have been fueling entrepreneurship. Finally, the institution-based view argues that the larger institutional frameworks explain a great deal about what is behind the differences in entrepreneurial and economic development around the world.

Consequently, the savvy entrepreneur can draw at least four important implications for action (Table 6.5). (1) Establish an intimate understanding of your industry to identify gaps and opportunities—alternatively, to avoid or exit from it if the threats are too strong. (2) Leverage entrepreneurial resources and capabilities, such as entrepreneurial drive, innovative capabilities, and network ties. (3) Push for more entrepreneur-friendly formal institutions, such as rules governing how to set up new firms (Figure 6.2) and how to go through bankruptcy (Strategy in Action 6.3). Entrepreneurs also need to cultivate strong informal norms granting legitimacy to entrepreneurs. Talking to high school and college students, taking on internships, and providing seed money as angels for new ventures are some of the actions that entrepreneurs can undertake. (4) When internationalizing, be bold but not too bold. Being bold does not mean being reckless. One specific insight from this chapter is that it is possible to internationalize without venturing abroad. There is a variety of international strategies that enable entrepreneurial firms to stay in domestic markets. When the entrepreneurial firm is not ready to take on higher risk abroad, this more limited involvement may be appropriate.[80]

We conclude this chapter by revisiting the four fundamental questions. Because start-ups are an embodiment of the personal characteristics of their founders, why firms differ (Question 1) and how they behave (Question 2) can be found in how entrepreneurs differ from non-entrepreneurs. What determines the scope of the firm (Question 3) boils down to how successful entrepreneurs can employ growth, innovation, network, and financing/governance strategies to expand their businesses. Finally, what determines the success and failure of firms around the globe (Question 4) depends on whether entrepreneurs can select the right industry, leverage their capabilities, and take advantage of formal and informal institutional resources—both at home and abroad.

CHAPTER SUMMARY

1. *Define entrepreneurship, entrepreneurs, and entrepreneurial firms*

    • Entrepreneurship is the identification and exploration of previously unexplored opportunities.

    • Entrepreneurs may be founders and owners of new businesses or managers of existing firms.

    • Entrepreneurial firms in this chapter are defined as SMEs that employ less than 500 people.

2. *Articulate a comprehensive model of entrepreneurship*

    • Five forces of an industry shape entrepreneurship associated with this industry.

    • Resources and capabilities largely determine entrepreneurial success and failure.

    • Institutions—both formal and informal—enable and constrain entrepreneurship around the world.

3. *Identify five strategies that characterize a growing entrepreneurial firm*

    • (1) Growth, (2) innovation, (3) network, (4) financing/governance, and (5) harvest/exit.

4. *Differentiate international strategies that enter foreign markets and that stay in domestic markets*

    • Entrepreneurial firms can internationalize by entering foreign markets, through entry modes such as (1) direct exports, (2) licensing/franchising, and (3) FDI.

    • Entrepreneurial firms can also internationalize without venturing abroad, by (1) exporting indirectly, (2) supplying foreign firms, (3) becoming licensees/ franchisees of foreign firms, (4) joining foreign entrants as alliance partners, and (5) harvesting and exiting through sell-offs to foreign entrants.

5. *Participate in three leading debates on growing and internationalizing the entrepreneurial firm*

    • (1) Traits versus institutions, (2) slow internationalizers, versus "born global" start-ups and (3) anti-failure biases versus entrepreneur-friendly bankruptcy law.

6. *Draw strategic implications for action*

    • Establish an intimate understanding of your industry to identify gaps and opportunities.

    • Leverage entrepreneurial resources and capabilities.

    • Push for institutions that facilitate entrepreneurship development—both formal and informal.

    • When internationalizing, be bold, but not too bold.

KEY TERMS

Born global	**International entrepreneurship**	**Small and medium-sized enterprise (SME)**
Entrepreneur		
	Liability of newness	**Stage model**
Entrepreneurship		**Strong ties**
Initial public offering (IPO)	**Serial entrepreneur**	**Weak ties**

CRITICAL DISCUSSION QUESTIONS

1. Why is entrepreneurship most often associated with SMEs, as opposed to larger firms?

2. Given that most entrepreneurial start-ups fail, why do entrepreneurs found so many new firms? Why are (most) governments interested in promoting more start-ups?

3. Some suggest that foreign markets are graveyards for entrepreneurial firms to over-extend themselves. Others argue that foreign markets represent the future for SMEs. If you were the owner of a small, reasonably profitable firm, would you consider expanding overseas? Why or why not?

4. ***ON ETHICS:*** Your former high school buddy invites you to join a start-up that specializes in making counterfeit products. He offers you the job of CEO and 10% of the equity of the firm. The chances of getting caught are slim. How would you respond to his proposition?

5. ***ON ETHICS:*** Everything is the same as in Question 4, except the "counterfeit" products involved are the more affordable generic drugs to combat HIV/AIDS, which would potentially help millions of patients worldwide who cannot afford the high-priced patented drugs of the Big Pharma (see Chapter 4 Opening Case). How would you respond?

CLOSING CASE

Cyworld Launches Against MySpace

In the crowded US social networking market dominated by MySpace and Facebook, Cyworld from South Korea has entered with a big splash since 2006. Cyworld is no small fry. It is the number one social network site in Internet-savvy South Korea, where 90% of the population under the age of 20 and 25% of the total population are reportedly Cyworld's registered users. The challenge is whether Cyworld can translate its home-country success overseas, especially in a culturally distant country: the United States.

Literally translated, "Cy" can mean "cyber," but it is also a play on the Korean word for relationship, so "Cyworld" can also mean "relationship world." Operated by SK Communications (a subsidiary of SK Telecom), Cyworld pioneered the concept of personal virtual space in 1999. Cyworld members cultivate on- and off-line relationships by forming buddy relationships with each other through a "minihompy" (mini-homepage or "MiniHome" in the US version), which includes a photo gallery, a message board, a guestbook, and a personal bulletin board. A user can link his/her minihompy to another user's minihompy to form a buddy relationship. These features are similar to US-based MySpace and Facebook websites.

What are the differences between Cyworld and MySpace? If MySpace is like a hip party where users vie for popularity and air time, Cyworld USA is positioned as a relaxed hangout that stresses existing relationships and hosts close to 3,000 clubs, such as "Interns Unite!" Cyworld gives social networking a twist, combining photo sharing and blogging with digital avatars who can be programmed to dance and play.

Having previously set up a local presence in China, Japan, and Taiwan, Cyworld is no stranger to doing business abroad. To prepare for its US launch in August 2006, it set up a 30-person office in San Francisco, spent approximately $10 million on 13 months of market research, and pledged to spend whatever it took to be successful in the new market. A crucial difference is that Cyworld's core audience in Korea is twenty-something college students, and the typical US member is 13 to 24, female, creative, and active in her community. To capture the hearts and minds of Cyworld's intended audience in the United States, its pre-launch odyssey was assisted by a number of US consultants and focus groups. Look-Look, a youth research agency, helped Cyworld learn about American teen culture. Native Instinct, a digital design firm, shaped the site's look and feel. The fate of the avatars (known as the "Mini-Me's") is interesting. The Japanese nixed them. American teenage focus groups, after some initial skepticism, gave them a go. But Cyworld USA made the Mini-Me's older, larger, and more ethnically diverse than their Korean counterparts.

Unfortunately, as Cyworld jumps in, a general cool-off is underway among social network users due to the avalanche of ads. Overall membership growth for the industry may have reached a plateau. In such a less hospitable environment, will Cyworld become a new social network sensation in the United States?

Sources: Based on (1) *Business Week,* 2006, The Korean upstart in MySpace's face, November 13: 72; (2) *Business Week,* 2008, Generation MySpace is getting fed up, February 18: 54–55; (3) us.cyworld.com; (4) Wikipedia, 2008, Cyworld (en.wikipedia.org).

Case Discussion Questions

1. How would you characterize the competition in this industry?

2. What are the unique resources and capabilities that Cyworld can bring to the United States?

3. What formal or informal institutions may constrain Cyworld's growth?

4. If you are a current MySpace or Facebook user, have you already visited Cyworld's site? If you have, what are the differences between MySpace/Facebook and Cyworld?

NOTES

Journal acronyms *AER–American Economic Review; AJS–American Journal of Sociology;* **AME**–*Academy of Management Executive;* **AMJ**–*Academy of Management Journal;* **AMLE**–*Academy of Management Learning and Education;* **AMR**–*Academy of Management Review;* **APJM**–*Asia Pacific Journal of Management;* **ASQ**–*Administrative Science Quarterly;* **ERD**–*Entrepreneurship and Regional Development;* **ETP**–*Entrepreneurship Theory and Practice;* **FEER**–*Far Eastern Economic Review;* **HBR**–*Harvard Business Review;* **JBV**–*Journal of Business Venturing;* **JIBS**–*Journal of International Business Studies;* **JIM**–*Journal of International Management;* **JM**–*Journal of Management;* **JMS**–*Journal of Management Studies;* **JWB**–*Journal of World Business;* **MIR**–*Management International Review;* **MS**–*Management Science;* **SMJ**–*Strategic Management Journal;* **SMR**–*MIT Sloan Management Review;* **SP**–*Sociological Perspectives*

1. M. Hitt, R. D. Ireland, S. M. Camp, & D. Sexton, 2001, Strategic entrepreneurship (p. 480), *SMJ,* 22: 479–491; J. McMullen & D. Shepherd, 2006, Entrepreneurial action and the role of uncertainty in the theory of the entrepreneur, *AMR,* 31: 132–152.

2. S. Shane & S. Venkataraman, 2000, The promise of entrepreneurship as a field of research (p. 218), *AMR,* 25: 217–226.

3. P. McDougall & B. Oviatt, 2000, International entrepreneurship (p. 903), *AMJ,* 43: 902–906.

4. J. Brikinshaw, 2000, *Entrepreneurship in the Global Firm,* London: Sage.

5. Z. Acs & C. Armington, 2006, *Entrepreneurship, Geography, and American Economic Growth,* New York:

Cambridge University Press; R. Wright & H. Etemad, 2001, SMEs and the global economy, *JIM*, 7: 151–154.

6. V. Lau, M. Shaffer, & K. Au, 2007, Entrepreneurial career success from a Chinese perspective, *JIBS*, 38: 126–146; M. Hayward, D. Shepherd, & D. Griffin, 2006, A hubris theory of entrepreneurship, *MS*, 52: 160–172; R. Lowe & A. Ziedonis, 2006, Overoptimism and the performance of entrepreneurial firms, *MS*, 52: 173–186.

7. J. Timmons, 1999, *New Venture Creation* (pp. 32–34), Boston: Irwin McGraw-Hill. See also R. Mudambi & S. Zahra, 2007, The survival of international new ventures, *JIBS*, 38: 333–352.

8. N. Huyghebaert & L. Van de Gucht, 2004, Incumbent strategic behavior in financial markets and the exit of entrepreneurial start-ups, *SMJ*, 25: 669–688.

9. R. Doern & C. Fey, 2006, E-commerce developments and strategies for value-creation, *JWB*, 41: 315–327; D. Lepak, K. Smith, & M. S. Taylor, 2007, Value creation and value capture, *AMR*, 32: 180–194.

10. L. Busenitz & J. Barney, 1997, Differences between entrepreneurs and managers in large organizations, *JBV*, 12: 9–30.

11. A. Fadahunsi & P. Rosa, 2002, Entrepreneurship and illegality, *JBV*, 17: 397–429; F. Luthans & E. Ibrayeva, 2006, Entrepreneurial self-efficacy in Central Asian transition economies, *JIBS*, 37: 92–110.

12. The World Bank, 2008, *Doing Business 2008*, Washington: The World Bank.

13. M. Minniti, W. Bygrave, & E. Autio, 2006, *Global Entrepreneurship Monitor*, Wellesley, MA: Babson College/GEM.

14. W. Baumol, 2004, Entrepreneurial cultures and countercultures, *AMLE*, 3: 316–326; A. Thomas & S. Mueller, 2000, A case for comparative entrepreneurship, *JIBS*, 31: 287–301.

15. T. Nelson, 2003, The persistence of founder influence, *SMJ*, 24: 707–724.

16. T. Eisenmann, 2006, Internet companies' growth strategies, *SMJ*, 27: 1183–1204.

17. B. Gilbert, P. McDougall, & D. Audretsch, 2006, New venture growth, *JM*, 32: 926–950.

18. K. Zhou & C. Li, 2007, How does strategic orientation matter in Chinese firms?, *APJM*, 24: 447–466.

19. M. Chen & D. Hambrick, 1995, Speed, stealth, and selective attack, *AMJ*, 38: 453–482.

20. H. Mintzberg, 1989, *Mintzberg on Management*, New York: Free Press.

21. A. Bhide, 1994, How entrepreneurs craft strategies that work (p. 152), *HBR*, March–April: 150–161.

22. F. Delmar & S. Shane, 2003, Does business planning facilitate the development of new ventures? *SMJ*, 24: 1165–1185.

23. K. Atuahene-Gima & H. Li, 2004, Strategic decision comprehensiveness and new product development outcomes in new technology ventures, *AMJ*, 47: 583–597; B. Honig & T. Karlsson, 2004, Institutional forces and the written business plan, *JM*, 30: 29–48.

24. R. McGrath & I. MacMillan, 1992, More like each other than anyone else?, *JBV*, 7: 419–429; D. Miller, 1990, *The Icarus Paradox*, New York: Harper.

25. R. Amit & C. Zott, 2001, Value creation in e-business, *SMJ*, 22: 493–520; G. Bruton, G. Dess, & J. Janney, 2007, Knowledge management in technology-focused firms in emerging economies, *APJM*, 24: 115–130; G. Lumpkin & G. Dess, 1996, Clarifying the entrepreneurial orientation construct and linking it to performance, *AMR*, 21: 135–172; M. Sarkar, R. Echambadi, R. Agarwal, & B. Sen, 2006, The effect of the innovative environment on exit of entrepreneurial firms, *SMJ*, 27: 519–539.

26. A. Saxenian, 2006, *The New Argonauts* (p. 114), Cambridge, MA: Harvard University Press.

27. H. Li & K. Atuahene-Gima, 2001, Product innovation strategy and the performance of new technology ventures in China, *AMJ*, 44: 1123–1134; P. Roberts, 1999, Product innovation, product-market competition, and persistent profitability, *SMJ*, 20: 655–670.

28. Z. Acs & D. Audretsch, 1988, Innovation in large and small firms, *AER*, 78: 678–690; S. Zahra & W. Bogner, 1999, Technology strategy and software new ventures' performance, *JBV*, 15: 135–173.

29. C. Christensen, 1997, *The Innovator's Dilemma*, Boston: Harvard Business School Press.

30. M. Guillen, 2001, *The Limits of Convergence* (p. 117), Princeton, NJ: Princeton University Press.

31. R. Agarwal, R. Echambadi, A. Franco, & M. Sarkar, 2004, Knowledge transfer through inheritance, *AMJ*, 47: 501–522; G. Qian & L. Li, 2003, Profitability of

small and medium-sized enterprises in high-technology industries, *SMJ,* 24: 881–887.

32. L. Zhou, W. Wu, & X. Luo, 2007, Internationalization and the performance of born-global SMEs, *JIBS,* 38: 673–690.

33. D. Lee & E. Tsang, 2001, The effects of entrepreneurial personality, background, and network activities on venture growth, *JMS,* 38: 583–602; H. Hoang & B. Antonic, 2003, Network-based research in entrepreneurship, *JBV,* 18: 165–187.

34. S. Human & K. Provan, 2000, Legitimacy building in the evolution of small-firm multilateral networks, *ASQ,* 45: 327–365; M. Zimmerman & G. Zeitz, 2002, Beyond survival, *AMR,* 27: 414–431.

35. D. Deeds & C. Hill, 1998, An examination of opportunistic action within research alliances, *JBV,* 14: 141–163.

36. M. Granovetter, 1973, The strength of weak ties, *AJS,* 78: 1360–1380.

37. M. W. Peng & Y. Luo, 2000, Managerial ties and firm performance in a transition economy, *AMJ,* 43: 486–501.

38. J. Baum, T. Calabrese, & B. Silverman, 2000, Don't go it alone, *SMJ,* 21: 267–294; J. Florin, M. Lubatkin, & W. Schulze, 2003, A social capital model of high-growth ventures, *AMJ,* 46: 374–384; C. Lee, K. Lee, & H. Pennings, 2001, Internal capabilities, external networks, and performance, *SMJ,* 22: 615–640; M. Sarkar, R. Echsmbadi, & J. Harrison, 2001, Alliance entrepreneurship and firm market performance, *SMJ,* 22: 701–711.

39. R. Burt, 1997, The contingent value of social capital (p. 342), *ASQ,* 42: 339–365.

40. A. Zacharakis & G. D. Meyer, 1998, A lack of insight, *JBV,* 13: 57–76.

41. A. Zacharakis, J. McMullen, & D. Shepherd, 2007, Venture capitalists' decision policies across three countries, *JIBS,* 38: 691–708.

42. W. Bygrave & J. Timmons, 1992, *Venture Capital at the Crossroads,* Boston: Harvard Business School Press.

43. A. Ranft & H. O'Neill, 2001, Board composition and high-flying founders, *AME,* 15: 126–138.

44. T. Bates, 1997, Financing small business creation, *JBV,* 12: 109–124.

45. D. Ahlstrom, G. Bruton, & K. Yeh, 2007, Venture capital in China: Past, present, and future, *APJM,* 24: 247–268; M. Wright, 2007, Venture capital in China: A view from Europe, *APJM,* 24: 269–281.

46. C. Zimmer & H. Aldrich, 1987, Resource mobilization through ethnic networks, *SP,* 30 422–455.

47. R. Larsson, K. Brousseau, M. Driver, M. Holmqvist, & V. Tarnovskaya, 2003, International growth through cooperation (p. 15), *AME,* 17 (1): 7–21.

48. S. Claessens & L. Klapper, 2002, Bankruptcy around the world, Working paper 2865, The World Bank.

49. J. Gimeno, T. Folta, A. Cooper, & C. Woo, 1997, Survival of the fittest?, *ASQ,* 42: 750–783.

50. T. Fan & P. Phan, 2007, International new ventures, *JIBS,* 38: 1113–1131; G. Knight & S. T. Cavusgil, 2004, Innovation, organizational capabilities, and the born-global firm, *JIBS,* 35: 124–141; B. Oviatt & P. McDougall, 1994, Toward a theory of international new ventures, *JIBS,* 25: 45–64.

51. A. Zacharakis, 1998, Entrepreneurial entry into foreign markets, *ETP,* spring: 23–39.

52. R. Chen & M. Martin, 2001, Foreign expansion of small firms, *JBV,* 16: 557–574.

53. A. Fosfuri, 2006, The licensing dilemma, *SMJ,* 27: 1141–1158; S. Michaels, 2000, Investments to create bargaining power, *SMJ,* 21: 497–515.

54. J. Lu & P. Beamish, 2001, The internationalization and performance of SMEs, *SMJ,* 22: 565–586; S. Zahra, R. D. Ireland, & M. Hitt, 2000, International expansion by new venture firms, *AMJ,* 43: 925–950.

55. J. Johanson & J. Vahlne, 1977, The internationalization process of the firm, *JIBS,* 4: 20–29; L. Li, D. Li, & T. Dalgic, 2004, Internationalization process of small and medium-sized enterprises, *MIR,* 44: 93–116.

56. P. McDougall, S. Shane, & B. Oviatt, 1994, Explaining the formation of international new ventures, *JBV,* 9: 469–487.

57. F. Rothaermel, S. Kotha, & H. K. Steensma, 2006, International market entry by US Internet firms, *JM,* 32: 56–82; J. Tiessen, R. Wright, & I. Turner, 2001, A model of e-commerce use by internationalizing SMEs, *JIM,* 7: 211–233.

58. S. Chetty, K. Eriksson, & J. Lindbergh, 2006, The effect of specificity of experience on a firm's perceived

importance of institutional knowledge in an ongoing business, *JIBS,* 37: 699–712; N. Coviello, 2006, The network dynamics of international new ventures, *JIBS,* 37: 713–731; Z. Fernandez & M. Nieto, 2006, Impact of ownership on the international involvement of SMEs, *JIBS,* 37: 340–351; P. Westhead, M. Wright, & D. Ucbasaran, 2001, The internationalization of new and small firms, *JBV,* 16: 333–358.

59. M. W. Peng & A. Y. Ilinitch, 1998, Export intermediary firms, *JIBS,* 29: 609–620; H. Trabold, 2002, Export intermediation: An empirical test of Peng and Ilinitch, *JIBS,* 33: 327–344.

60. M. W. Peng & A. York, 2001, Behind intermediary performance in export trade, *JIBS,* 32: 327–346; M. W. Peng, Y. Zhou, & A. York, 2006, Behind make or buy decisions in export strategy, *JWB,* 41: 289–300; S. Terjesen, C. O'Gorman, & Z. Acs, 2008, Intermediated internalization, *ERD* (in press).

61. J. Bell, R. McNaughton, & S. Young, 2001, "Born-again global" firms (p. 184), *JIM,* 7: 173–189.

62. R. Tesker, 2002, Pepperoni power, *FEER,* November 14: 59–60.

63. L. Busenitz, G. P. West, D. Shepherd, T. Nelson, G. Chandler, & A. Zacharakis, 2003, Entrepreneurship research in emergence, *JM,* 29: 285–308.

64. B. Barringer, F. Jones, & D. Neubaum, 2005, A quantitative content analysis of the characteristics of rapid-growth firms and their founders, *JBV,* 20: 663–687.

65. L. Busenitz, C. Gomez, & J. Spencer, 2000, Country institutional profiles, *AMJ,* 43: 994–1003; R. Mitchell, B. Smith, K. Seawright, & E. Morse, 2000, Cross-cultural cognitions and the venture creation decision, *AMJ,* 43: 974–993; J. Oxley & B. Yeung, 2001, E-commerce readiness, *JIBS,* 32: 705–724; H. K. Steensma, L. Marino, M. Weaver, & P. Hickson, 2000, The influence of national culture on the formation of technology alliances by entrepreneurial firms, *AMJ,* 43: 951–973.

66. H. Yeung, 2006, Change and continuity in Southeast Asian ethnic Chinese business, *APJM,* 23: 229–254.

67. Y. Yamakawa, M. W. Peng, & D. Deeds, 2008, What drives new ventures to internationalize from emerging to developed economies?, *ETP,* 32: 59–82.

68. S. Loane, J. Bell, & R. McNaughton, 2007, A cross-national study on the impact of management teams on the rapid internationalization of small firms, *JWB,* 42: 489–504; H. Sapienza, E. Autio, G. George, & S. Zahra, 2006, A capabilities perspective on the effects of early internationalization on firm survival and growth, *AMR,* 31: 914–933.

69. V. Govindarajan & A. Gupta, 2001, *The Quest for Global Dominance,* San Francisco: Jossey-Bass.

70. K. Kling & I. Goteman, 2003, IKEA CEO Anders Dahlvig on international growth, *AME,* 17: 31–45.

71. E. Autio, H. Sapienza, & J. Almeida, 2000, Effects of age at entry, knowledge intensity, and imitability in international growth, *AMJ,* 43: 909–924.

72. J. Mathews & I. Zander, 2007, The international entrepreneurial dynamics of accelerated internationalization, *JIBS,* 38: 387–403; S. Nadkarni & P. Perez, 2007, Prior conditions and early international commitment, *JIBS,* 38: 160–176.

73. P. Liesch & G. Knight, 1999, Information internationalization and hurdle rates in small and medium enterprise internationalization, *JIBS,* 30: 383–394.

74. S. Rangan & R. Adner, 2001, Profits and the Internet (pp. 49–50), *SMR,* summer: 44–53.

75. M. Lyles, T. Saxton, & K. Watson, 2004, Venture survival in a transition economy, *JM,* 30: 351–373.

76. This section draws heavily from S. Lee, M. W. Peng, & J. Barney, 2007, Bankruptcy law and entrepreneurship development, *AMR,* 32: 257–272.

77. R. McGrath, 1999, Falling forward, *AMR,* 24: 13–30.

78. D. Shepherd, 2003, Learning from business failure, *AMR,* 28: 318–328.

79. S. Lee, Y. Yamakawa, M. W. Peng, & J. Barney, 2008, How does bankruptcy law affect entrepreneurship development?, Working paper, University of Texas at Dallas. See also A. Knott & H. Posen, 2005, Is failure good?, *SMJ,* 26: 617–641.

80. M. W. Peng, C. Hill, & D. Wang, 2000, Schumpeterian dynamics versus Williamsonian considerations, *JMS,* 37: 167–184.

chapter 7

Strategic Alliances and Networks

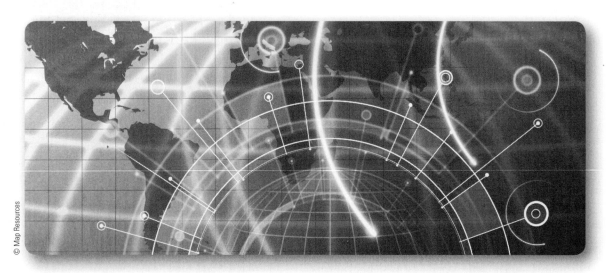

© Map Resources

KNOWLEDGE OBJECTIVES

After studying this chapter, you should be able to

1. Define strategic alliances and networks

2. Articulate a comprehensive model of strategic alliances and networks

3. Understand the decision processes behind the formation of alliances and networks

4. Gain insights into the evolution of alliances and networks

5. Identify the drivers behind the performance of alliances and networks

6. Participate in three leading debates on alliances and networks

7. Draw strategic implications for action

OPENING CASE: DANONE VERSUS WAHAHA: FROM ALLIANCE TO DIVORCE

In 1996, France's Groupe Danone SA established five joint ventures (JVs) with China's Wahaha Group, each of which Danone owned 51% and Wahaha and its employees owned the remainder. Founded in 1987, Wahaha has one of the best-known beverage brands in China. By 2006, the total number of JVs between Danone and Wahaha had grown from five to 39. A huge financial success for both Danone and Wahaha, their JVs' revenues increased from $100 million in 1996 to $2.25 billion in 2006. These JVs, which cost Danone $170 million, paid Danone a total of $307 million in dividends over the last decade. By 2006, Danone's 39 JV subsidiaries in China, jointly owned and managed by Wahaha, contributed approximately 6% of Danone's total global profits.

In addition to the JV investments with Wahaha, Danone also bought stakes in more than seven Chinese food and dairy companies, spending almost another $170 million (besides what was spent on Wahaha) over the past decade in China. In 2006, Danone became the biggest beverage maker by volume in the country, ahead of rivals such as Coca-Cola and PepsiCo. At the same time, Wahaha also pursued aggressive growth in China, some of which was beyond the scope of the JVs with Danone. By 2006, Wahaha Group controlled 70 subsidiary companies scattered throughout China. All these subsidiaries use the same brand

"Wahaha," but only 39 of them had JV relationships with Danone.

A major dispute erupted concerning Wahaha's other (non-JV) subsidiaries. In 2006, after the JVs' profits jumped 48% to $386 million, Danone wanted to buy Wahaha's *other* subsidiaries. This would enable Danone to control the "Wahaha" brand once and for all. This proposal was rejected by Wahaha's founder Zong Qinghou, who served as chairman of the 39 JVs with Danone. Zong viewed this offer as unreasonable because the book value of the non-JV subsidiaries' assets was $700 million with total profits of $130 million, while the price/earnings ratio of Danone's $500 million offer was lower than 4. Zong also asserted that the buyout would jeopardize the existence of the "Wahaha" brand, because Danone would phase it out and promote global brands such as Danone and Evian.

The heart of the dispute stemmed from the master JV agreement between Danone and Wahaha, which granted the subsidiary JVs exclusive rights to produce, distribute, and sell food and beverage products under the "Wahaha" brand. This meant that every product using the "Wahaha" brand should be approved by the board of the master JV. Danone thus claimed that the non-JV subsidiaries set up by Zong and his managers were illegally selling products using the "Wahaha" brand and

217

were making unlawful use of the JVs' distributors and suppliers. However, Zong claimed that the original JV agreement to grant exclusive rights to use the "Wahaha" brand was never approved by the Chinese trademark office and so was not in force or effect. He further stated that Danone had not made an issue when Wahaha embarked on its expansion and openly used the subsidiary JVs' assets—it seemed that Danone preferred Wahaha to shoulder the risk first. According to Zong, when Wahaha's expansion proved successful, Danone, driven by greed, wanted to reap the fruits. Finally, Zong argued that forcing Wahaha Group to grant the exclusive rights for the "Wahaha" brand to the JVs with Danone was unfair to Wahaha Group, because the French company was actively investing in other beverage companies around the country and competing with Wahaha.

The boardroom dispute spilled into the public domain when Zong publicly criticized Danone in April 2007. In response, Danone issued statements and initiated arbitrations against its Chinese partner in Stockholm, Sweden. Danone also launched a lawsuit against a company owned by Zong's daughter in the United States, alleging that it was using the Wahaha brand illegally. Outraged, Zong resigned from his board chairman position at all the JVs with Danone. Wahaha's trade union, representing about 10,000 workers of Wahaha Group, sued Danone in late 2007, demanding $1.36 million in damages. The union also froze Danone's ownership in the JVs. This made the dispute worse, and revenues of the JVs only increased 3% in 2007, 17% less than the industry's average growth.

In late 2007, both sides spent most of their energy dealing with lawsuits and arbitrations. In December 2007, pressured by the French President and the Chinese Minister of Commerce, Danone and Wahaha reached an agreement to "call off all lawsuits and arbitrations provisionally and stop all aggressive speeches against the other party." As of this writing (March 2008), no resolution was in sight—except the inevitable outcome: divorce. However, a Danone spokesman defended the JV strategy: "If we now have 30% of our sales in emerging markets and we built this in only 10 years, it's thanks to this specific [JV] strategy. We have problems with Wahaha. But we prefer to have problems with Wahaha now to not having had Wahaha at all for the last 10 years."

Sources: This case was written by **Sunny Li Sun** and **Hao Chen** (both at the University of Texas at Dallas) under the supervision of Professor Mike W. Peng. It was based on (1) *China Daily,* 2007, Chinese drinks giant brands Danone 'despicable' over lawsuit, June 8; Union files case against Danone, December 17; (2) finance.sina.com.cn/focus/2007wahaha; (3) M. W. Peng, S. L. Sun, & H. Chen, 2008, Managing divorce: How to disengage from joint ventures and strategic alliances, *Peking University Business Review,* April; (4) *Wall Street Journal,* 2007, China venture partner blames feud on Danone, June 14; Danone's China strategy is set back, June 15; Wahaha brings arbitration claim against Danone, June 18.

joint venture

A "corporate child" that is a new entity given birth and jointly owned by two or more parent companies.

Why do Danone and Wahaha establish strategic alliances? Among many forms of strategic alliances, why do they choose the **joint venture** (JV) form? Why do these financially successful JVs end up in divorce? These are some of the key questions we discuss in this chapter.

As globalization intensifies, "the least attractive way to try to win on a global basis," according to GE's former chairman and CEO Jack Welch, "is to think you can take on the world all by yourself."[1] Proliferation of strategic alliances and networks can now be seen in just about every industry and every country, resulting in an "explosion in alliances."[2] Yet, 30%–70% of all alliances and networks, such as the JVs set up by Danone and Wahaha, reportedly fail, thus necessitating our attention on their causes.

This chapter will first define strategic alliances and networks, followed by an introduction of a comprehensive model drawing upon the "strategy tripod." Then, we discuss the formation, evolution, and performance of alliances and networks, followed by debates and extensions.

Defining Strategic Alliances and Networks

Strategic alliances are voluntary agreements between firms involving exchange, sharing, or co-development of products, technologies, or services.[3] As noted in Chapter 5, the dotted area in Figure 6.3 consisting of non-equity-based contractual agreements and equity-based JVs can all be broadly considered strategic alliances. Figure 7.1 illustrates this further, visualizing alliances as a *compromise* between pure market transactions and mergers and acquisitions (M&As). **Contractual (non-equity-based) alliances** include co-marketing, research and development (R&D) contracts, turnkey projects, strategic suppliers, strategic distributors, and licensing/franchising. **Equity-based alliances** include **strategic investment** (one partner invests in another) and **cross-shareholding** (both partners invest in each other). A JV is one form of equity-based alliance. It involves the establishment of a new legally independent entity (in other words, a new firm) whose equity is provided by two (or more) partners.

Although JVs are often used as examples of alliances (see Opening Case), not *all* alliances are JVs. A JV, such as Sony Ericsson, is a "corporate child" produced by two (or more) parent firms. A non-JV, equity-based alliance can be regarded as two firms "getting married" but not having "children." For example, Renault is a strategic investor in Nissan, but both automakers still operate independently and they have *not* given birth to a new car company (which would be a JV if they did).

Strategic networks are strategic alliances formed by *multiple* firms to compete against other such groups and against traditional single firms.[4] For example, the airline industry has three multipartner alliances—Star Alliance (consisting of United Airlines, Lufthansa, Air Canada, SAS, and others), Sky Team (Delta, Air France, Korean Air, and others), and One World (American Airlines, British Airways, Cathay Pacific, Qantas, and others). These strategic networks are sometimes called **constellations.**

strategic alliances

Voluntary agreements between firms involving exchanging, sharing, or co-developing of products, technologies, or services.

contractual (non-equity-based) alliances

Alliances which are based on contracts and which do not involve the sharing of equity.

equity-based alliances

Strategic alliances which involve the use of equity.

cross-shareholding

Both partners invest in each other to become cross-shareholders.

strategic investment

One partner invests in another as a strategic investor.

FIGURE 7.1   The Variety of Strategic Alliances

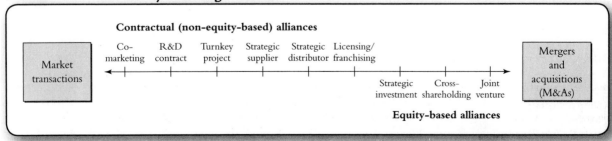

FIGURE 7.2   A Comprehensive Model of Strategic Alliances and Networks

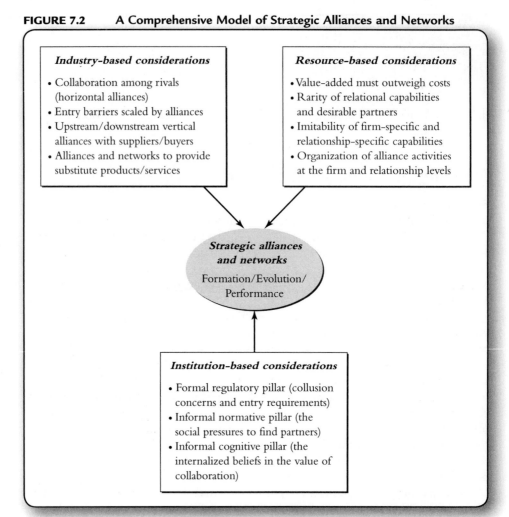

Such multilateral strategic networks are inherently more complex than single alliance relationships between two firms.[5] Overall, we will use the terms "strategic alliances" and "strategic networks" to refer to cooperative interfirm relationships.

A Comprehensive Model of Strategic Alliances and Networks

Despite the diversity of cooperative interfirm relationships, underlying each decision to engage in alliances and networks is a set of strategic considerations drawn from the "strategy tripod" discussed earlier. These considerations lead to a comprehensive model (Figure 7.2).

Industry-Based Considerations

According to the traditional industry-based view, firms are independent players interested in maximizing their own performance. In reality, most firms in any industry are embedded in a number of competitive and/or collaborative relationships, thus necessitating considerations of their alliance and network ties if we are going to realistically understand the dynamics of the five forces.[6]

First, because rivalry reduces profits, firms do not compete against each other on all occasions. Instead, many competitors collaborate by forming strategic alliances (often called **horizontal alliances**). For example, in 1983, GM and Toyota formed a JV, NUMMI, to jointly manufacture small cars in the United States. This does not suggest that these two firms are no longer competing; they still are, in most cases. What is interesting is that they decided to collaborate on a limited basis, for different purposes. GM was interested in learning how to profitably manufacture small cars, whereas Toyota was interested in learning how to operate in the United States (before operating its own wholly owned subsidiaries [WOS]). These two firms are not alone. Recently, approximately half of all strategic alliances are found to be between competitors (see Strategy in Action 7.1).[7] Sometimes, the goal is simply to tie up a competitor.

Second, while high entry barriers may deter individual firms, firms may form strategic alliances and networks to scale these walls. For instance, both Coca-Cola and Nestle were interested in entering the hot canned drinks market (such as hot coffee and tea) in Japan. However, domestic players led by Suntory built formidable entry barriers and neither Coca-Cola nor Nestle, despite their global experience, had any expertise in this particular segment largely unknown outside of Japan. Although Suntory was better than Coca-Cola at soluble coffee and tea and had a larger distribution network than Nestle, Suntory was unable to match the combined strengths of these two giants, which formed an alliance.[8] Overall, combining forces allows for lower cost and lower risk entries into new markets for partner firms.

Third, although suppliers in the five forces framework are traditionally regarded as a threat, it is not necessarily the case. First introduced in Chapter 2, it is possible to establish strategic alliances with suppliers (often called **upstream vertical alliances**), as exemplified by the Japanese *keiretsu* networks. In essence, strategic supply alliances transform the relationship from an adversarial one centered on hard bargaining to a collaborative one featuring knowledge sharing and mutual assistance. Instead of dealing with a large number of suppliers that are awarded contracts on a frequent short-term basis (such as 2.3 years, the average length of US auto supply contracts in the 1990s), strategic supply alliances rely on a smaller number of key suppliers that are awarded longer-term contracts (such as 8 years, the average length of Japanese auto supply contracts in the 1990s).[9] This helps align the interests of the focal firm with those of suppliers, which, in turn, are more willing to make specialized investments to produce better components.[10] This is not to say that bargaining power becomes irrelevant. Instead, buyer firms increase their dependence on a smaller number of strategic suppliers, whose bargaining power may, in turn, *increase*.[11] However, collaboration softens some rough edges of bargaining power by transforming a zero-sum game into a win-win proposition.

Fourth, similarly, instead of treating buyers and distributors as a possible threat, establishing strategic distribution alliances (also called **downstream vertical alliances**) may bind the focal firm and buyers and distributors together. For example, numerous hotels,

---

horizontal alliances
Strategic alliances formed by competitors.

upstream vertical alliances
Alliances with firms on the supply side (upstream).

downstream vertical alliances
Alliances with firms in distribution (downstream).

Strategy in Action 7.1 - **Russia's MiG and Sukhoi Join Hands**

During the Cold War, thousands of MiG fighter jets made by the Mikoyan Moscow Production Organization (MAPO) were synonymous with "bogeys" widely recognized and respected by military pilots in the free world. In the post-Cold War era, MAPO ran into great difficulties because the Russian government cut back its orders (no orders for new aircraft during 1992–1998) and, with the dissolution of the Warsaw Pact, Central and Eastern European air forces started to import fighters from the West. Poland, for example, ordered F-16s from the United States. MAPO thus was forced to look for new export markets. However, in new markets, MAPO found that its previously popular MiG aircraft were not as successful as those made by its traditional rival, Sukhoi Aircraft Military and Industrial Group. While Sukhoi jets had not been as famous as MiGs during the Cold War, Sukhoi scored big hits in the 1990s by securing high-profile contracts from China, India, and Vietnam, including more than 150 Su-27s as direct exports and 300 under licensed production. What was more impressive was that the Indonesian and South Korean air forces, traditionally exclusive markets for US fighters, expressed a strong interest in Sukhoi (although eventually they had to cancel because of the 1997 Asian financial crisis). In comparison, MAPO only sold 80 MiG-29s to India and Malaysia in the 1990s. As a result, MAPO found it had little choice but to cooperate with Sukhoi. To be sure, initial cooperation was limited, involving only a joint marketing strategy and a sharing of some avionics. Such cooperation, however, intensified as competition in the global arms market heated up. In 2006, both MAPO and Sukhoi, together with several other aircraft producers, were merged by the Russian government to form the new United Aircraft Building Corporation.

Sources: Based on (1) M. W. Peng, 2000, *Business Strategies in Transition Economies* (p. 96), Thousand Oaks, CA: Sage; (2) Wikipedia, 2008, (a) Mikoyan; (b) Sukhoi; (c) United Aircraft Building Corporation, en.wikipedia.org.

publishers, airlines, and car rental companies find that alliances with leading Internet distributors such as Amazon, Expedia, Priceline, and Travelocity enable them to reach more customers.

Finally, the market potential of substitute products may encourage firms to form strategic alliances and networks to materialize the commercial potential of these new products. For instance, in the drive to bring 3G wireless technology to substitute existing wireless technology to nine countries, Hutchison Whampoa, a Hong Kong–based conglomerate, has formed a number of alliances with local firms.

Resource-Based Considerations

The resource-based view, embodied in the VRIO framework, sheds considerable light on strategic alliances and networks (Figure 7.2).

VALUE

Alliances must create value.[12] The three global airline alliance networks—One World, Sky Team, and Star Alliance—create value by reducing 18%–28% of the ticket costs booked on two-stage flights compared with separate flights on the same route if these airlines were not allied.[13] Table 7.1 identifies three broad categories of value creation in terms of how advantages outweigh disadvantages. First, alliances may reduce costs, risks, and uncertainties.[14] As Google rises to preeminence, former rivals, such as eBay, Yahoo!, and Microsoft (MSN), are now exploring alliances to counter its influence while not taking on excessive risks. Second, alliances allow firms to tap into complementary assets of partners, as evidenced by the GM–Toyota JV. Third, alliances facilitate opportunities to learn from partners.[15]

Finally, an important advantage of alliances lies in their value as "real options." Conceptually, an option is the right, but not the obligation, to take some action in the future. Technically, a financial option is an investment instrument permitting its holder, having paid for a small fraction of an asset (often known as a deposit), the right to increase investment to eventually acquire it if necessary. A **real option** is an investment in real operations as opposed to financial capital.[16] A real options view has two propositions:

- In the first phase, an investor makes a relatively small, initial investment to buy an option, which leads to the right to future investment without being obligated to do so.

- The investor then holds the option until a decision point arrives in the second phase, and then decides between exercising the option or abandoning it.

For firms that are interested in eventually acquiring other companies, but that are not sure about such moves, working together in alliances thus affords an insider view to

TABLE 7.1   Strategic Alliances and Networks: Advantages and Disadvantages

ADVANTAGES	DISADVANTAGES
• Reduce costs, risks, and uncertainties	• Possibilities of choosing the wrong partners
• Gain access to complementary assets	• Costs of negotiation and coordination
• Opportunities to learn from partners	• Possibilities of partner opportunism
• Possibilities to use alliances and networks as real options	• Risks of helping nurture competitors (learning race)

real option

An option investment in real operations as opposed to financial capital.

Strategy in Action 7.2 - How to Select Partners? A Local Firm Perspective

As in human marriages, international strategic alliances involve prospective partners from two (or more) countries, each selecting partners for different purposes. Yet, much of the literature focuses on how foreign MNEs select partners in emerging economies, implicitly assuming that local firms are relatively passive and waiting to be selected. This of course is far from the truth. Some firms in emerging economies have very strong capabilities, and suitors would line up to seek relationships with them. For example, the Shanghai Automobile Industrial Corporation (SAIC) managed to have *both* Volkswagen and GM, two fierce rivals elsewhere, to be its partners in two successful JVs in China. Likewise, Baosteel, China's biggest steelmaker, has managed to attract global rivals such as Arcelor, Nippon Steel, and ThyssenKrupp that each has a JV with it. Evidently, these MNEs must swallow their pride and put up with such "polygamy" in order to access the booming Chinese economy. Similarly, the alliance portfolio of India's Tata Group reads like a "Who's Who" in the Global 500, with partners such as American Express, Bell Canada, and Hitachi.

Although many local firms do not care about the global rivalry among MNEs, local firms are often interested in using alliances to beat their own *domestic* rivals. As a result, if domestic rivals have MNE partners (let's say Heineken or DHL), local firms in retaliation often enlist the MNE competitors of their domestic rivals' MNE partners (such as Carlsberg or

FedEx). In terms of goals, while foreign MNEs are in search of partners with desirable local knowledge, production facilities, and distribution channels, local firms often use a different set of criteria. For example, Chinese, Mexican, Polish, Romanian, and Russian firms tend to focus on foreign partners' financial strengths and willingness to share expertise as their most important criteria in partner selection. While the benefits of having financially strong foreign partners are self-evident, having willing "teachers" to share knowledge—in combination with the local partners' capacity to learn—is also found to directly contribute to the performance of both the alliances and the parent firms, as found by studies in Hungary and elsewhere.

Sources: Based on (1) L. Dong & K. Glaister, 2007, National and cultural differences in international strategic alliances, *Asia Pacific Journal of Management*, 24: 191–205; (2) M. Hitt, D. Ahlstrom, T. Dacin, E. Levitas, & L. Svobodina, 2004, The institutional effects on strategic alliance partner selection in transition economies, *Organization Science*, 15: 173–185; (3) M. Kotabe, P. Aulakh, & H. Teegen, 2000, Strategic alliances in emerging Latin America, *Journal of World Business*, 35: 114–125; (4) P. Lane, J. Salk, & M. Lyles, 2001, Absorptive capacity, learning, and performance in international joint ventures, *Strategic Management Journal*, 22: 1139–1161; (5) O. Shenkar & J. Li, 1999, Knowledge search in international cooperative ventures, *Organization Science*, 10: 134–143; (6) H. K. Steensma & M. Lyles, 2000, Explaining IJV survival in a transition economy through social exchange and knowledge-based perspectives, *Strategic Management Journal*, 21: 831–851.

evaluate the capabilities of these partners. This is similar to trying on new shoes to see if they fit before buying the shoes. Since acquisitions are not only costly but also very likely to fail, alliances permit firms to *sequentially* increase their investment should they decide to pursue acquisitions. On the other hand, after working together as partners, if firms find that acquisitions are not a good idea, there is no obligation to pursue them. Overall, alliances have emerged as great instruments of real options because of their flexibility to sequentially scale *up* or scale *down* the investment.[17]

On the other hand, alliances have a number of nontrivial drawbacks. First, there is always a possibility of being stuck with the wrong partner(s). Firms are advised to choose a prospective mate with caution. Yet, the mate should also be sufficiently differentiated to provide some complementary (non–overlapping) capabilities.[18] Just like many individuals who have a hard time figuring out the true colors of their spouses before they get married, many firms find it difficult to evaluate the true intentions and capabilities of their prospective partners until it is too late.

A second disadvantage is potential partner opportunism. While opportunism is likely in any kind of economic relationship, the alliance setting may provide especially strong incentives for some (but not all) partners to be opportunistic. This is because cooperative relationships always entail some elements of trust, which may be easily abused.[19] In an alliance with Britain's Rover, Honda shared a great deal of proprietary technology beyond what was contractually called for. Honda was stunned when informed by Rover's parent firm that Rover would be sold to BMW and that Honda would be literally kicked out. Unfortunately, such an example is not an isolated incident.

Finally, alliances, especially those between rivals, can be dangerous, because they may help competitors. By opening "doors" to outsiders, alliances make it *easier* to observe and imitate firm-specific capabilities. In alliances between competitors, there is a potential **"learning race"** in which partners aim to outrun each other by learning the "tricks" from the other side as fast as possible.[20] For example, the alliance between GE and Rolls Royce to jointly develop jet engines collapsed because both firms could not resolve issues raised by their long-standing rivalry.[21]

RARITY

The second component in the VRIO framework has two dimensions: (1) capability rarity and (2) partner rarity. First, the capabilities to successfully manage interfirm relationships—often called **relational** (or **collaborative**) **capabilities**—may be rare. Managers involved in alliances require relationship skills rarely covered in the traditional business school curriculum that emphasizes competition as opposed to collaboration. To truly derive benefits from alliances, managers need to foster trust with partners, while at the same time being on guard against opportunism.[22]

As much as alliances represent a strategic and economic arrangement, they also constitute a social, psychological, and emotional phenomenon: words such as "courtship," "marriage," and "divorce" often surface. Given that the interests of partner firms do not fully overlap and are often in conflict, managers involved in alliances live a precarious existence, trying to represent the interests of their respective firms while attempting to make the complex relationship work. Given the general shortage of good relationship skills in the human population (remember: 50% of human marriages in the United States fail), it is not surprising that sound relational capabilities to successfully manage alliances are in short supply.[23]

A second aspect of rarity is **partner rarity,** defined as the difficulty to locate partners with certain desirable attributes. This stems from two sources: (1) industry structure and (2) network position. First, from an *industry structure* standpoint, in many oligopolistic industries, the number of available players as potential partners is limited. In some emerging economies whereby only a few local firms may be worthy partners, latecomers may find that potential partners have already been "cherry picked" by rivals. In the Chinese automobile industry (where WOS are not allowed), Ford, as a late mover, ended up allying with second-tier partners in China. It is hardly surprising that Ford's presence in China has been insignificant.

Second, from a *network position* perspective, firms located in the center of interfirm networks may have access to better and more opportunities (such as information, access, capital, goods, and services), and consequently may accumulate more power and influence.[24] The upshot is that firms with a high degree of **network centrality**—defined

learning race

A race in which alliance partners aim to outrun each other by learning the "tricks" from the other side as fast as possible.

relational (collaborative) capabilities

The capabilities to successfully manage interfirm relationships.

partner rarity

The difficulty to locate partners with certain desirable attributes.

network centrality

The extent to which a firm's position is pivotal with respect to others in the inter-firm network.

as the extent to which the position occupied by a firm is pivotal with respect to others in the interfirm network—are likely to be more attractive partners. Unfortunately, such firms are rare, and they are often very choosy in the kind of relationships they enter. Citigroup and Carrefour, for example, routinely turn down alliance proposals coming from all over the globe.

IMITABILITY

The issue of imitability pertains to two levels: (1) firm level and (2) alliance level. First, as noted earlier, one firm's resources and capabilities may be imitated by partners. For instance, in the late 1980s, McDonald's set up a JV with the Moscow Municipality Government that helped it enter Russia. However, during the 1990s, the Moscow mayor set up a rival fast food chain, The Bistro. The Bistro tried to eat McDonald's' lunch by replicating numerous products and practices. There was very little that McDonald's could do, because nobody sues the mayor in Moscow and hopes to win.

Another imitability issue refers to the trust and understanding among partners in successful alliances. Firms without such "chemistry" may have a hard time imitating such activities. CFM International, a JV set up by GE and Snecma to produce jet engines in France, has successfully operated for over 30 years. Rivals would have a hard time imitating such a successful relationship.

ORGANIZATION

Similarly, the organizational issues affect two levels: (1) firm level and (2) alliance/ network level. First, at the firm level, how firms are organized to benefit from alliances and networks is an important issue.[25] When the number of such relationships is small, many firms adopt a trial-and-error approach. Not surprisingly, the number of "misses" is often very high. What is problematic is that even for successful "hits," this ad hoc approach does not allow for systematic learning from these experiences. This obviously is a hazardous way of organizing for large MNEs engaging in numerous alliances and networks around the globe. In response, many firms have been developing a dedicated alliance function (parallel with traditional functions such as finance and marketing), often headed by a vice president or director with his/her own staff and resources. Such a dedicated function acts as a focal point for leveraging lessons from prior and ongoing relationships. HP, for example, has developed a 300-page decision-making manual on alliances, including 60 different tools and templates (such as alliance contracts, metrics, and checklists). It also organizes a two-day course three times a year to disseminate such learning about alliances to its managers worldwide.

At the alliance/network level, some alliance relationships are organized in a way that makes it difficult for others to replicate. There is much truth behind Tolstoy's opening statement in *Anna Karenina:* "All happy families are like one another; each unhappy family is unhappy in its own way." Given the difficulty for individuals in unhappy marriages to improve their relationship (despite an army of professional marriage counselors, social workers, friends, and family members), it is not surprising that firms in unsuccessful alliances (for whatever reason) often find it exceedingly challenging, if not impossible, to organize and manage their interfirm relationships better.

Institution-Based Considerations

Because institutions governing alliances and networks include formal and informal constraints supported by regulatory and normative/cognitive pillars, we will examine them in turn (see Figure 7.2).

FORMAL INSTITUTIONS SUPPORTED BY A REGULATORY PILLAR

Strategic alliances and networks function within formal legal and regulatory frameworks. The impact of these formal institutions can be found along two dimensions: (1) antitrust (or collusion) concerns and (2) entry mode requirements. First, many firms establish alliances with competitors. For instance, Siemens and Bosch compete in automotive components and collaborate in white goods. Cooperation between competitors is usually suspected of at least some tacit collusion by antitrust authorities (see Chapter 8). However, because integration within alliances is usually not as tight as acquisitions (which would eliminate one competitor), antitrust authorities have a higher likelihood to approve alliances as opposed to acquisitions.[26] The proposed merger between American Airlines and British Airways was blocked by both US and UK antitrust authorities. However, they have been allowed to form an alliance that has eventually grown to become the multipartner One World.

Second, formal requirements on market entry modes affect alliances and networks. In many countries, governments discourage or simply ban acquisitions to establish WOS, thereby leaving some sort of alliances with local firms to be the only entry choice for FDI. For instance, the pre-NAFTA Mexican government not only limited multinationals' entries to JVs, but also dictated the maximum ceiling of their equity position to be 49% (prior to 1994). In another example, the Fuji Xerox JV was originally proposed in 1962 as a sales company to market Xerox products in Japan, but the Japanese government refused to approve the JV unless there was some technology transfer from Xerox to Fuji.

Recently, two characteristics have arisen concerning formal government policies on entry mode requirements. First is the general trend toward more liberal policies. Many governments (such as those in Mexico and South Korea) that historically only approved JVs have now allowed WOS as an entry mode. As a result, there is now a noticeable decline of JVs and a corresponding rise of acquisitions in emerging economies.[27] A second characteristic is that despite such general movement toward more liberal policies, many governments still impose considerable requirements, especially when foreign firms acquire domestic assets. Only JVs are permitted in the strategically important Chinese automobile assembly industry and the Russian oil industry, thus eliminating acquisitions as a choice. US regulations only permit up to 25% of the equity of any US airline to be held by foreign carriers, and EU regulations limit non-EU ownership to 49% of EU-based airlines.

INFORMAL INSTITUTIONS SUPPORTED BY NORMATIVE AND COGNITIVE PILLARS

The first set of informal institutions centers on collective norms, supported by a normative pillar. A core idea of the institutional perspective is that because firms act to enhance or protect their legitimacy, copying other reputable organizations—even without knowing the direct performance benefits of doing so—may be a low-cost way to gain legitimacy. Therefore, when competitors have a variety of alliances, jumping on the alliance "bandwagon" may be perceived as a "cool" way to join the norm as opposed to ignoring industry trends.[28] In other words, informal but powerful normative pressures from the business press, investment community, and board deliberations probably drove late-mover firms such as Ford to ally with relatively obscure partners in China (discussed earlier) as opposed to having no partner and hence no presence there. For the same reason unmarried adults tend to experience some social pressure to get married, firms insisting on "going alone," especially when they experience performance problems, often confront similar pressures and criticisms from peers, analysts, investors, and the media.[29] The flipside of such a behavior is that many firms rush into interfirm relationships without adequate due diligence and then get burned.

A second set of informal institutions stresses the cognitive pillar, which centers on the internalized taken-for-granted values and beliefs that guide firm behavior. BAE Systems (formerly British Aerospace) announced in the 1990s that *all* its future aircraft development programs would involve alliances, evidently believing that an alliance strategy was the right thing to do.

Overall, both of the two core propositions that underpin the institution-based view (first introduced in Chapter 4) are applicable. The first proposition—individuals and firms rationally pursue their interests and make strategic choices within institutional constraints—is illustrated by the constraining and enabling power of the formal regulatory pillar, the informal but powerful normative pillar, and the internalized but evident cognitive pillar. The second proposition—when formal constraints fail, informal constraints may play a larger role—is also evident. This is because similar to the institutions governing human marriages, formal regulations and contracts can govern only a small (although important) portion of alliance/network behavior, and the success and failure of such relationships, to a large degree, depend on the day-in-day-out interaction between partners influenced by informal norms and cognitions.[30] This point will be expanded in more detail in the next three sections on the formation, evolution, and performance of strategic alliances and networks.

Formation

How are alliances formed? Figure 7.3 illustrates a three-stage model to address this question.[31]

Stage One: To Cooperate or Not to Cooperate?

In Stage One, a decision is made on whether to form alliances as opposed to relying on pure market transactions or acquisitions.[32] To grow by pure market transactions, the firm has to independently confront competitive challenges. This is very demanding even for resource-rich multinationals.[33] Acquisitions have some unique challenges and drawbacks (see Chapter 9). Thus, many managers conclude that alliances are the way to go.

Stage Two: Contract or Equity?

As noted in Chapter 5, the choice between contract and equity is crucial.[34] Table 7.2 identifies four driving forces. First, the key is the character of shared capabilities. The more tacit (that is, hard to describe and codify) they are, the more likely equity involvement is preferred. Although not the only source of learning, **learning by doing** is perhaps the most effective way to learn *complex* know-how. Just like individuals learning how to cook will not get the job done by reading cookbooks alone, firms learning how to produce cars will find that no amount of learning from books and reports containing codified knowledge is enough.[35] Tacit knowledge can only be acquired via learning by doing, preferably with experts as alliance partners.

learning by doing

A way of learning not by reading books but by engaging in hands-on activities.

FIGURE 7.3   Alliance Formation

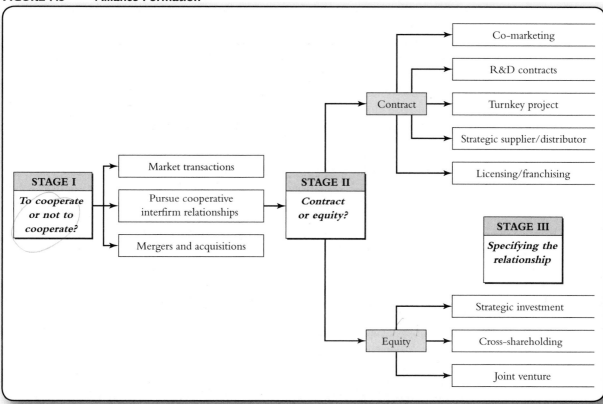

Source: Adapted from S. Tallman & O. Shenkar, 1994, A managerial decision model of international cooperative venture formation (p. 101), *Journal of International Business Studies,* 25 (1): 91–113.

A lot of tacit knowledge dealing with complex skills and know-how is embedded in specific organizational settings and is "sticky" (that is, tough to isolate from the particular firm that possesses such knowledge).[36] Hypothetically, assuming Toyota is able to codify all the tacit knowledge associated with the legendary "Toyota production system" (TPS)—something that is impossible to do in reality—and sell it, the buyer

TABLE 7.2   Equity-Based versus Non-Equity-Based Strategic Alliances and Networks

Driving Force	Equity-Based Alliances/Networks	Non-Equity-Based Alliances/Networks
Nature of shared resources (degree of tacitness and complexity)	High	Low
Importance of direct organizational monitoring and control	High	Low
Potential as real options	High (for possible upgrading to M&As)	High (for possible upgrading to equity-based relationships)
Influence of formal institutions	High (when required or encouraged by regulations)	High (when required or encouraged by regulations)

will probably find that no matter how hard it tries, it is simply unable to completely replicate TPS. This is because TPS, by definition, is firm-specific and has a high degree of "stickiness" associated with Toyota. Short of completely acquiring Toyota (an extremely costly proposition), no other firm can hope to totally master this system. Further, if many Toyota employees leave after the acquisition (a realistic scenario at most acquired firms), again, the acquirer will find that its mastery of the system is incomplete. Thus, the most realistic way to access TPS is to establish an equity-based alliance in order to learn how to "do it" side by side with Toyota, as GM did through its NUMMI JV with Toyota. In general, equity-based alliances are more likely to be formed when dealing with more complex technology and know-how (such as NUMMI) than with less complex skills that can be more efficiently transferred between two organizations (such as McDonald's franchising).

A second driving force is the importance of direct monitoring and control. Equity relationships allow firms to have at least partial direct control over joint activities on a continuing basis, whereas contractual relationships usually do not allow that.[37] In general, firms prefer equity alliances (and a higher level of equity) if they fear that their intellectual property may be expropriated.

A third driver is real options thinking. Some firms prefer to first establish contractual relationships, which can be viewed as real options (or stepping stones) for possible upgrading into equity alliances should the interactions turn out to be mutually satisfactory. Danone's interest in acquiring Wahaha's businesses may be indicative of such thinking (see Opening Case).

Finally, the choice between contract and equity also boils down to institutional constraints.[38] As noted earlier, some governments eager to help domestic firms climb the technology ladder either require or actively encourage the formation of JVs between foreign and domestic firms. The Chinese auto industry is a case in point.

Stage Three: Positioning the Relationship

Although the formation of strategic alliances has historically been assumed to be between two partners, the proliferation of interfirm relationships suggests that such thinking may need to be expanded. Given that each firm is likely to have multiple interfirm relationships, it is important to manage them as a corporate *portfolio* (or network). The combination of several individually "optimal" relationships may not create an optimal relationship portfolio for the entire firm, in light of some tricky alliances with competitors.[39] In a world of multilateral intrigues, one step down the alliance path, which may open some doors, may foreclose other opportunities. In other words, "my friend's enemy is my enemy, and my enemy's enemy is my friend." Therefore, to prevent an "alliance gridlock," carefully assessing the impact of each individual relationship *prior to its formation* on the firm's other relationships becomes increasingly important. In particular, the scope of a new relationship needs to be properly defined.

Evolution

All relationships evolve—some grow, others fail.[40] This section deals with three aspects: (1) combating opportunism, (2) evolving from strong ties to weak ties, and (3) going through a divorce.

Combating Opportunism

The threat of opportunism looms large on the horizon. Most firms want to make their relationship work, but also want to protect themselves in case the other side is opportunistic.[41] While it is difficult to completely eliminate opportunism, it is possible to minimize its threat by (1) walling off critical capabilities or (2) swapping critical capabilities through credible commitments.

First, both sides can contractually agree to wall off critical skills and technologies not meant to be shared. For example, GE and Snecma cooperated to build jet engines, yet GE was not willing to share its proprietary technology fully with Snecma. GE thus presented sealed "black box" components, the inside of which Snecma had no access to, while permitting Snecma access to final assembly. This type of relationship, in human marriage terms, is like couples whose premarital assets are protected by prenuptial agreements. As long as both sides are willing to live with these deals, these relationships can prosper.

The second approach, swapping skills and technologies, is the exact *opposite* of the first approach. Both sides not only agree not to hold critical skills and technologies back, but also make credible commitments to hold each other as a "hostage."[42] Motorola, for instance, licensed its microprocessor technology to Toshiba, which, in turn, licensed its memory chip technology to Motorola. Setting up a parallel and reciprocal relationship may increase the incentives for both partners to cooperate. For example, the agreement between France's Pernod-Ricard and America's Heublein to distribute Heublein's Smirnoff vodka in Europe was balanced by another agreement in which Heublein agreed to distribute Pernod-Ricard's Wild Turkey bourbon in the United States. In a nutshell, such mutual "hostage taking" reduces the threat of opportunism.

In human marriage terms, mutual "hostage taking" is similar to the following commitment: "Honey, I will love you forever. If I betray you, feel free to kill me. But if you dare to betray me, I'll cut your head off!" To think slightly outside the box, the precarious peace during the Cold War can be regarded as a case of mutual "hostage taking" that worked. Because both the United States and Soviet Union held each other as a "hostage," nobody dared to launch a first nuclear strike. As long as the victim of the first strike had only *one* nuclear ballistic missile submarine left (such as the American Ohio class or the Soviet Typhoon class), this single submarine would have enough retaliatory firepower to wipe the top 20 US or Soviet cities off the surface of earth, an outcome that neither of the two superpowers found acceptable (see the movie *The Hunt for Red October*). The Cold War did not turn hot in part because of such "mutually assured destruction" (MAD!)—a real military jargon.

Evolving from Strong Ties to Weak Ties

First introduced in Chapter 6, strong ties are more durable, reliable, and trustworthy relationships cultivated over a long period of time. Strong ties have two advantages.

- Strong ties are associated with the exchange of finer-grained higher-quality information.

- Strong ties serve as an informal social-control mechanism that is an alternative to formal contracts, and thus act to combat opportunism.[43] It is not surprising that many strategic alliances and networks are initially built upon strong ties among individuals and firms.

Defined as relationships characterized by infrequent interaction and low intimacy, weak ties, paradoxically, are more wide-ranging and likely to provide more opportunities. Weak ties, despite their limited ability to serve as a social-control mechanism, enjoy two advantages.

- Weak ties are less costly (requiring less time, energy, and money) to maintain.

- Weak ties excel at connecting with distant others possessing unique and novel information for strategic actions—often regarded as the *strength* of weak ties. This may be especially critical as firms search for new knowledge for cutting-edge technologies and practices.

In the same way that individuals tend to have a combination of a small number of good friends (strong ties) and a large number of acquaintances (weak ties), firms at any given point in time are likely to have a combination of strong ties and weak ties in their interfirm relationships. Both strong and weak ties "are beneficial to firms, but under different conditions—for different purposes and at different times."[44] One of the conditions influencing the types of advantages that firms require is the degree to which their strategies are designed to *exploit* current resources (such as existing connections) or *explore* new opportunities (such as future technologies).

Of particular interest to us is the distinction between "exploitation" and "exploration" noted by James March, a leading organization theorist. **Exploitation** refers to "such things as refinement, choice, production, efficiency, selection, and execution," whereas **exploration** includes "things captured by terms such as search, variation, risk taking, experimentation, play, flexibility, discovery, and innovation."[45] While both kinds of strategic activities are important and often occur simultaneously, there is a trade-off between the two because of the limited resources firms possess.[46] Thus, an *emphasis* on either set of the ties is often necessary during a particular period. In environments conducive for exploitation, strong ties may be more beneficial. Conversely, in environments suitable for exploration, weak ties may be preferred.

Many strong ties evolve to become weak ties. Examples from two contexts illustrate these dynamics. First, a new start-up often first concentrates on dense strong ties because it "seeks to exploit the current external networks and resources of the founding entrepreneur(s) to ensure its survival."[47] In the next phase, having largely exploited (and exhausted) the initial set of opportunities, the firm needs to search for new opportunities. Therefore, it shifts to exploration in order to seek new opportunities, thus calling for more weak ties with greater diversity. Amazon's changing alliance portfolio is indicative of such evolution. Initially, Amazon established strong ties with a few key publishing and distributing firms. As Amazon expanded to cover new products (toys and CDs) and new business models (auctions), it formed numerous weak ties with a variety of large suppliers, small merchants, and auction houses.

A second example is JVs formed by two partners. Over time as the initial set of opportunities are exploited and exhausted by the JV, partners, as they embark on new searches, may prefer to establish some weak-ties-based relationships with a diverse set of players. In other words, the strong ties within the JV may become too limiting. However, original partners will naturally become upset. In a human marriage, it is easy to appreciate the fury of one spouse when the other spouse is exploring other relationships (although only weak ties!). In the case of the Danone–Wahaha dispute, *both* sides were upset by the numerous relationships outside the scope of their JV relationship (see Opening Case).

exploitation

Actions captured by terms such as refinement, choice, production, efficiency, selection, and execution.

exploration

Actions captured by terms such as search, variation, risk taking, experimentation, play, flexibility, discovery, and innovation.

From Corporate Marriage to Divorce[48]

Alliances are often described as "corporate marriages" and, when terminated, "corporate divorces." Figure 7.4 portrays an alliance dissolution model. To apply the metaphor of human divorce, we focus on the two-partner alliance. The party that is the first to seek to exit is labeled the initiator, while the other party is termed the partner—for lack of a better word.

The first phase is initiation. The process begins when the initiator starts feeling uncomfortable with the alliance (for whatever reason). Wavering begins as a quiet unilateral process by the initiator, which was Daewoo in the *first* JV with General Motors (see Closing Case). After repeated demands to modify GM's behavior failed, Daewoo began to sense that the alliance was probably unsalvageable. At this point, the display of discontent became bolder. Initially, GM, the partner, might simply not "get it." The initiator's "sudden" dissatisfaction might confuse the partner. Sometimes, the partner responds by committing some grievous error, of the sort that GM seemingly made when flatly denying Daewoo's request to extend the JV's product line and market coverage. As a result, initiation tends to escalate.

The second phase is going public. The party that breaks the news first, such as Wahaha in its dispute with Danone (see Opening Case), has a first-mover advantage. By presenting a socially acceptable reason in favor of its cause, this party is able to win sympathy from key stakeholders, such as parent company executives, investors, and

FIGURE 7.4   Alliance Dissolution

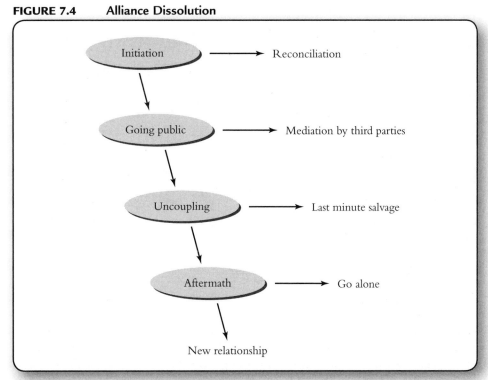

Source: Adapted from M. W. Peng & O. Shenkar, 2002, Joint venture dissolution as corporate divorce (p. 95), *Academy of Management Executive,* 16 (2): 92–105.

journalists. Not surprisingly, the initiator is likely to go public first, blaming the failure on the partner. Alternatively, the partner may preempt the move by blaming the initiator in public and establishing the righteousness of its position.

The third phase is uncoupling. Like human divorce, alliance dissolution can be friendly or hostile. In uncontested divorces, both sides attribute the separation more on, say, a change in circumstances. For example, Eli Lilly and Ranbaxy phased out their JV in India and remained friendly with each other. In contrast, contested divorces involve a party that accuses another. The worst scenario is "death by a thousand cuts," inflicted by one party at every turn (see Opening Case).

The last phase is aftermath. Like most divorced individuals, most (but not all) "divorced" firms are likely to search for new partners. Understandably, the new alliance (such as the *second* GM–Daewoo JV) is often negotiated more extensively.[49] One Italian executive reportedly signed *each* of the 2,000 pages (!) of an alliance contract.[50] However, excessive formalization may signal a lack of trust—in the same way that prenuptials may scare away some prospective human marriage partners.

Performance

Performance is a central focus for strategic alliances and networks.[51] This section discusses (1) the performance of alliances and networks and (2) the performance of parent firms.

The Performance of Strategic Alliances and Networks

There has been no consensus on what constitutes alliance performance.[52] A combination of objective measures (such as profit and market share) and subjective measures (such as managerial satisfaction) can be used (Table 7.3). Figure 7.5 shows four factors that may influence alliance performance: (1) equity, (2) learning and experience, (3) nationality, and (4) relational capabilities. However, none of them asserts an unambiguous, direct impact on performance.[53] Research has found that they may have some *correlations* with performance. First, the level of equity may be crucial. A higher level of equity is indicative of stronger commitment that is likely to result in higher performance.[54]

Second, whether firms have successfully learned from partners features prominently when assessing alliance performance.[55] Since learning is abstract in nature, experience,

TABLE 7.3   Alliance- and Network-Related Performance Measures

Alliance/Network Level	Parent Firm Level
Objective	*Objective*
• Financial performance (e.g., profitability)	• Financial performance (e.g., profitability)
• Product market performance (e.g., market share)	• Product market performance (e.g., market share)
• Stability and longevity	• Stock market reaction
Subjective	*Subjective*
• Level of top management satisfaction	• Assessment of goal attainment

FIGURE 7.5   What Is Behind Alliance Performance?

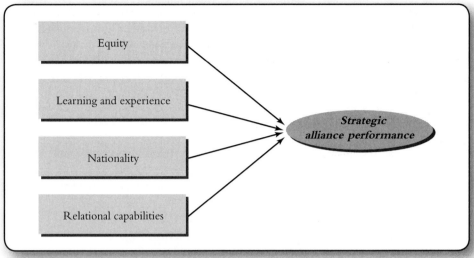

which is relatively easy to measure, is often used as a proxy.[56] While experience helps, its impact on performance is not linear. There is a limit beyond which further increase in experience may not enhance performance.[57]

Third, nationality may affect performance. For the same reason that human marriages between parties of dissimilar backgrounds are less stable than those with similar backgrounds, dissimilarities in national culture may create strains in alliances.[58] Not surprisingly, international alliances tend to have more problems than domestic ones.[59] When conflicts arise, it is often difficult to ascertain whether the other side is being opportunistic or is simply being (culturally) different.

Lastly, alliance performance may fundamentally boil down to "soft" and hard-to-measure relational capabilities. The art of relational capabilities, which is firm-specific and difficult to codify and transfer, may make or break alliances.[60] Overall, it would be naïve to think that any of these single factors such as equity, learning, nationality, and relational capabilities would guarantee success. It is their *combination* that jointly increases the odds for the success of strategic alliances.

The Performance of Parent Firms

Do parent firms benefit from strategic alliances and networks?[61] This goes back to the value-added aspect of these relationships (discussed earlier). Compared with the relative lack of consensus on alliance/network performance, there has been some convergence on the benchmarks of firm performance (such as profitability, product market share, and stock market reaction), in addition to the more subjective measure of goal attainment as perceived by management (see Table 7.3).

A number of studies report that a higher level of collaboration and shared technology is associated with better profitability and product market share for parent firms.[62] Another group of studies focuses on stock market reactions by treating each decision to enter or exit a relationship as an "event." If the event window is short enough (several days prior to and after the event), it is possible to view the "abnormal" stock returns as directly caused by that particular event. A number of such "event studies" indeed find that stock markets respond favorably to alliance activities, but only under certain circumstances, such as (1) complementarities of resources, (2) previous alliance experience, (3) ability to manage host country political risks, and (4) partner buyouts.[63] Overall, it is evident that strategic alliances and networks can create value for their parent firms, although how to make that happen remains a challenge.

Debates and Extensions

The rise of alliances and networks has generated a number of debates. Three of them are introduced here: (1) learning race versus cooperative specialization, (2) majority JVs as control mechanisms versus minority JVs as real options, and (3) alliances versus acquisitions.

Learning Race versus Cooperative Specialization[64]

An influential school of thought is the "learning race" view, contending that firms enter alliances, especially JVs, to learn and acquire partners' capabilities as quickly as possible.[65] Viewed in such a way, Eli Lilly learned enough from its JV partner Ranbaxy in India in the 1990s, and did not need Ranbaxy any more in the 2000s.[66] The JV was thus bought out to be a WOS. Likewise, Ranbaxy raced to learn from Eli Lilly's world-class technology and operations via the JV, and has now emerged to be a force to be reckoned with in the global pharmaceutical industry. Consequently, managers are advised to sharpen their firms' learning edge in order to win in such a race.

However, critics argue that the suggestion that partners should enter a JV with a racing mindset is not always justified. They question two assumptions of the learning race view, which may be unrealistic. First, the "learning race" view assumes that acquiring know-how from partners is always cost-effective. However, a major reason for entering alliances in the first place is that in-house development may be inefficient. Second, the learning race view assumes that partners are passively being exploited. In reality, other partners may be able to block access to key resources.

The second group, collectively known as the "cooperative specialization" school, posits that different firms in a relationship may want to specialize in different tasks in exchange for access to partners' contributions. This is not to suggest that learning races do not occur. To the extent these races occur, they represent more of relationship *pathologies* than the typical norms. Such pathologies can be reduced in two ways. First, it can be done through the mutual taking of hostages, such as cross-licensing (discussed earlier). Second, efforts should be made to prevent spillovers. Alliance partners have the natural economic interests to transfer knowledge to their other businesses outside the scope of collaboration (see Opening Case). One positive example is Shin Caterpillar Mitsubishi, a JV between Caterpillar and Mitsubishi. It became successful after both partners completely merged their hydraulic excavator business, thus eliminating incentives to transfer the JV know-how to their own business.

From a negative and a positive standpoint, the learning race and cooperative specialization views seem to be the two sides of the same coin. It is difficult to dismiss any one side's validity. However, overemphasizing any one side, such as the learning race view, probably is not warranted.

Majority JVs as Control Mechanisms versus Minority JVs as Real Options

A long-standing debate focuses on the appropriate level of equity in JVs. While the logic of having a higher level of equity control in majority JVs is straightforward, its actual implementation is often problematic. Asserting one party's control rights, even when justified based on a majority equity position and stronger bargaining power, may irritate the other party. This is especially likely in international JVs in emerging economies, whereby local partners often resent the dominance of Western MNEs (see Opening Case). For example, despite the obvious needs for foreign capital, technology, and management, Russian managers often refuse to acknowledge that their country, which in their view is still a superpower, is an emerging, let alone developing, country. Thus, some authors advocate a 50/50 share of management control even when the MNE has majority equity.[67]

In addition to the usual benefits associated with being a minority partner in JVs (such as low cost and less demand on managerial resources and attention), an additional benefit alluded to earlier is the ability to exercise real options. In general, the more uncertain the conditions, the higher the value of real options. In highly uncertain but potentially promising industries and countries, M&As or majority JVs may be inadvisable, because the cost of failure may be tremendous. Therefore, minority JVs are recommended *toehold* investments, seen as possible stepping stones for future scaling up—if necessary—while not exposing partners too heavily to the risks involved.[68] This may be the motive behind Danone's limited JV relationships with Wahaha, when potential in the China market was yet to be proven. However, after the uncertainties were removed, Danone was now more interested in scaling up investment by proposing to buy out Wahaha's other businesses (see Opening Case). On the other hand, real options thinking is often difficult to implement, in part because firms often find it difficult to abandon their options by killing unsuccessful relationships (what if they turn better if we try harder?).[69] As Danone found out, it is also challenging to scale up when dealing with financially successful relationships (Opening Case).

Since the real options thinking is relatively new, its applicability is still being debated.[70] While the real options logic is straightforward, its practice—when applied to acquisitions of JVs—is messy. This is because most JV contracts do not specify a previously agreed upon price for one party to acquire the other's assets. Most contracts only give the rights of first refusal to the parties, which agree to negotiate in "good faith." It is understandable that "neither party will be willing to buy the JV for more than, or sell the JV for less than its own expectation of the venture's wealth generating potential."[71] Since alliances are based on private negotiations involving no external market valuation of affected assets, how to reach an agreement on a "fair" price is tricky (see Opening Case).

Alliances versus Acquisitions

An alternative to alliances is M&As (see Chapter 9). Many firms seem to pursue M&As and alliances in isolation. While many large MNEs have an M&A function and some have set up an alliance function (discussed earlier), virtually no firm has established a combined "mergers, acquisitions, *and* alliance" function. In practice, it may be advisable to explicitly consider alliances vis-à-vis acquisitions within a single decision framework.[72] See Strategy in Action 7.3 for an example.

Strategy in Action 7.3 - Embraer's Alliances and Acquisitions

Embraer is a Brazilian manufacturer of small commercial and military aircraft. It was established in 1960 as a state-owned enterprise, but was privatized in 1994 with 60% of shares owned by private Brazilian interests (though the government retains a controlling "golden share"). It invested overseas prior to privatization (the United States in 1979, Europe in 1988) primarily to offer sales and technical support to customers in developed markets. However, after 1994—and especially in 1999—it entered into a series of strategic alliances with European groups such as EADS and Thales (France) in order to gain technology (and to reduce risk by pooling resources). Later it made acquisitions to ensure brand recognition in specialist aerospace markets. In 2004, it established a manufacturing affiliate in China (in which it owns a 51% stake), which assembles final aircraft for the Chinese and regional market. With 90% of its global sales overseas, Embraer can be regarded as one of Brazil's (indeed Latin America's) few truly global players.

Source: Excerpts from United Nations, 2006, *World Investment Report 2006: FDI from Developing and Transition Economies* (p. 159), New York and Geneva: United Nations/UN Conference on Trade and Development (UNCTAD). © United Nations, 2006.

Shown in Table 7.4, alliances, which tend to be loosely coordinated among partners, do not work well in a setting that requires a high degree of interdependence. Such a setting would call for acquisitions. Alliances work well when the ratio of soft to hard assets is relatively high (such as a heavy concentration of tacit knowledge), whereas acquisitions may be preferred when such a ratio is low. Alliances create value primarily by combining complementary resources, whereas acquisitions derive most of their value by eliminating redundant resources. Finally, consistent with real options thinking,

TABLE 7.4   Alliances versus Acquisitions

	ALLIANCES	ACQUISITIONS
Resource interdependence	Low	High
Ratio of soft to hard assets	High	Low
Source of value creation	Combining complementary resources	Eliminating redundant resources
Level of uncertainty	High	Low

Source: Based on text in J. Dyer, P. Kale, & H. Singh, 2003, Do you know when to ally or acquire? Choosing between acquisitions and alliances, Working paper, Brigham Young University.

alliances are more suitable under conditions of uncertainty, and acquisitions are more preferred when the level of uncertainty is low.

While these rules are not exactly "rocket science," "few companies are disciplined to adhere to them."[73] Consider the 50/50 JV between Coca-Cola (Coke) and Procter & Gamble (P&G) that combined their fruit drink businesses (such as Coke's Minute Maid and P&G's Sunny Delight) in 2001. The goal was to combine Coke's distribution system with P&G's R&D capabilities in consumer products. However, the stock market sent a mixed signal in response, pushing P&G's stock 2% *higher* and Coke's 6% *lower* on the day of the announcement. For three reasons, Coke probably could have done better by simply acquiring P&G's fruit drink business. First, a higher degree of integration would be necessary to derive the proposed synergies. Second, because Coke's distribution assets were relatively easy-to-value hard assets, while P&G's R&D capabilities were hard-to-value soft assets, the risk was higher for Coke. Finally, little uncertainty existed regarding the popularity of fruit drinks and so investors found it difficult to understand why Coke would share 50% of this fast-growing business with P&G, a laggard in the industry. Not surprisingly, the JV was quickly terminated within six months.

On the other hand, many M&As (such as DaimlerChrysler) would have probably been better off had the firms pursued alliances, at least initially. Overall, acquisitions may be overused as a first step to access resources in another firm, whereas alliances, guided by a real options logic, can provide a great deal of flexibility to scale up or scale down investments.

The Savvy Strategist

While traditionally firm strategy is, by definition, about how a single firm strategizes, the recent rise of alliances and networks has significantly expanded the strategic horizon by highlighting *interfirm* strategy. This new "alliance revolution" has introduced a new perspective to the strategy field. Instead of concentrating on competition only, a new generation of strategists needs to be savvy at *both* competition and cooperation—in other words, "co-opetition."[74]

The savvy strategist thus draws three important implications for action (Table 7.5). First, improving relational (collaborative) capabilities is crucial for the success of strategic alliances and networks. Given that excellent relational skills are rare among the population in general (think of the high divorce rates) and that the business school curriculum often emphasizes competition at the expense of collaboration, you need to work extra hard to be good at collaboration. The do's and don'ts outlined in Table 7.6 will provide a useful start.

TABLE 7.5   Strategic Implications for Action

- Improve relational (collaborative) capabilities crucial for the success of strategic alliances and networks.
- Understand and master the rules of the game governing alliances and networks around the world.
- Carefully weigh the pros and cons of alliances vis-à-vis those of acquisitions.

TABLE 7.6　　**Improving the Odds for Alliance Success**

AREA	DO'S AND DON'TS
Contract versus "chemistry"	No contract can cover all elements of the relationship. Relying on a detailed contract does not guarantee a successful relationship. It may indicate a lack of trust.
Warning signs	Identify symptoms of frequent criticism, defensiveness (always blaming others for problems), and stonewalling (withdrawal during a fight).
Invest in the relationship	Like married individuals working hard to invigorate their ties, alliances require continuous nurturing. Once a party starts to waver, it is difficult to turn back the dissolution process.
Conflict resolution mechanisms	"Good" married couples also fight. Their secret weapon is to find mechanisms to avoid unwarranted escalation of conflicts. Managers need to handle conflicts—inevitable in any alliance—in a credible, responsible, and controlled fashion.

Source: Based on text in M. W. Peng & O. Shenkar, 2002, Joint venture dissolution as corporate divorce (pp. 101–102), *Academy of Management Executive*, 16 (2): 92–105.

Second, you need to understand the rules of the game governing alliances and networks—both formal and informal—around the world. Formal rules dictating alliances to be the preferred mode of entry and banning WOS would make it necessary to embark on an alliance strategy, as Eli Lilly did when entering India in the 1990s. Over time, such rules have been relaxed and WOS allowed, thus enabling some reconsideration of Eli Lilly's JV strategy. Informal norms and values are also important. In the absence of a legal mandate for alliances, the norms for entering emerging economies used to be in favor of alliances (see Opening Case). However, the recent trend has moved toward phasing out alliances and establishing stronger controls over subsidiaries in emerging economies.[75]

Third, you need to carefully weigh the pros and cons associated with alliances and acquisitions. Diving into alliances (or acquisitions) without considering the other option may be counterproductive, as Coca-Cola found out after it established a JV with P&G on fruit drinks. Considering alliances vis-à-vis acquisitions within an *integrated* decision framework may be necessary.

Overall, this chapter sheds considerable light on the four fundamental questions in strategy. The answers to Questions 1 (Why firms differ?) and 2 (How firms behave?) boil down to how different industry-, resource-, and institution-based considerations drive alliance and network actions. What determines the scope of the firm (Question 3)—or more specifically, the scope of the alliance in this context—can be found in the strategic goals behind these relationships. Some alliances may have a wide scope in anticipation of an eventual merger (such as the Renault–Nissan alliance), while other alliances may have a limited scope, keeping the partners fiercely competitive in other aspects (such as the GM–Toyota JV). Finally, the international success and failure of strategic alliances and networks (Question 4) is fundamentally determined by how firms develop, possess, and leverage "soft" relational capabilities when managing their interfirm relationships, in addition to "hard" assets such as technology and capital. In conclusion, there is no doubt that strategic alliances and networks are difficult to manage. But managing is hardly ever simple, whether managing external relationships or internal units.

Chapter Summary

1. *Define strategic alliances and networks*

   - Strategic alliances are voluntary agreements between firms involving the exchange, sharing, or co-development of products, technologies, or services.

   - Strategic networks are strategic alliances formed by multiple firms.

2. *Articulate a comprehensive model of strategic alliances and networks*

   - Industry-, resource-, and institution-based considerations form the backbone of a comprehensive model of strategic alliances and networks.

3. *Understand the decision processes behind the formation of alliances and networks*

   - Principal phases of alliance and network formation include (1) deciding whether to cooperate or not, (2) determining whether to pursue contractual or equity modes, and (3) positioning the particular relationship.

4. *Gain insights into the evolution of alliances and networks*

   - Three aspects of evolution highlighted are (1) combating opportunism, (2) evolving from strong ties to weak ties, and (3) turning from corporate marriages to divorces.

5. *Identify the drivers behind the performance of alliances and networks*

   - At the alliance/network level, (1) equity, (2) learning and experience, (3) nationality, and (4) rational capabilities are found to affect alliance and network performance.

6. *Participate in three leading debates on alliances and networks*

   - Three leading debates highlighted are (1) learning race versus cooperative specialization, (2) majority JVs as control mechanisms versus minority JVs as real options, and (3) alliances versus acquisitions.

7. *Draw strategic implications of action*

   - Improve relational (collaborative) capabilities.

   - Understand and master the rules of the game governing alliances and networks around the world.

   - Carefully weigh the pros and cons of alliances vis-à-vis those of acquisitions.

Key Terms

Constellation	Downstream vertical alliance	Exploration
Contractual (non-equity-based) alliance	Equity-based alliance	Horizontal alliance
Cross-shareholding	Exploitation	Joint venture

Learning by doing	Real option	Strategic investment
Learning race	Relational (collaborative) capability	Strategic network
Network centrality		Upstream vertical alliance
	Strategic alliance	
Partner rarity		

CRITICAL DISCUSSION QUESTIONS

1. Some argue that at a 30%–70% failure rate (depending on different studies), strategic alliances and networks have a strikingly high failure rate and that firms need to scale down their alliance and network activities. Others suggest that this failure rate is not particularly higher than the failure rate of new entrepreneurial start-ups, internal corporate ventures, new products launched by single companies, and M&As. Therefore, such a failure rate is not of grave concern. How would you join this debate?

2. **ON ETHICS:** Firms often do not reveal (and try to hide) their true intentions during courtship and negotiation stages prior to forming strategic alliances and networks. What are the ethical dilemmas here?

3. **ON ETHICS:** Some argue that engaging in a "learning race" is unethical. Others believe that a "learning race" is part and parcel of alliance relationships, especially those with competitors. What do you think?

CLOSING CASE

General Motors and Daewoo: Married, Divorced, and Married Again

In 1984, General Motors (GM) and Daewoo formed a 50/50 joint venture (JV) named the "Daewoo Motor Company," each contributing $100 million equity. The JV would produce the Pontiac LeMans, based on GM's popular Opel Kadett model developed by GM's wholly owned German subsidiary Opel. Commentators hailed the alliance as a brilliant outcome of a corporate "marriage" of German technology and Korean labor (whose cost was low at that time). As a win-win combination, GM would tackle the small car market in North America and eventually expand into Asia, whereas Daewoo would gain access to superior technology.

Unfortunately, the alliance was problematic. By the late 1980s, Korean workers at the JV launched a series of bitter strikes to demand better pay. Ultimately, the JV had to more than double their wages, wiping out the low-cost advantage. Equally problematic was the poor quality of the LeMans. Electrical systems and brakes often failed. US sales plummeted to 37,000 vehicles in 1991, down 86% from the 1988 high.

However, Daewoo argued that the poor sales were not primarily due to quality problems, but due to GM's poor marketing efforts that had not treated the LeMans as one of GM's own models. Further, Daewoo was deeply frustrated by GM's determination to block its efforts to export cars to Eastern Europe, which Daewoo saw as its ideal market. GM's reasoning was that Eastern Europe was Opel's territory.

Gradually, Daewoo secretly developed independent car models, while GM initially was unaware of these activities. Once Daewoo launched competing car models, the troubles associated with this JV, long rumored by the media, became strikingly evident.

The picture of an "ideal couple" with a "perfect kid" (the JV) was now replaced by the image of a dysfunctional family where everybody was pointing fingers at each other.

In 1992, GM and Daewoo divorced, with Daewoo buying out GM's equity for $170 million. While GM exited the problematic JV, it was left without a manufacturing base in Korea. Daewoo, on the other hand, embarked upon one of the most ambitious marches into emerging economies, building a dozen auto plants in Indonesia, Iran, Poland, Ukraine, Uzbekistan, and Vietnam. In the process, Daewoo borrowed an astounding $20 billion, leading to its collapse during the 1997 Asian economic crisis.

In an interesting turn of events, GM and Daewoo joined hands again. Despite its bankruptcy, Daewoo attempted to avoid GM and strongly preferred a takeover by Ford. But Ford took a pass. Then, GM entered the negotiation, eventually forming a new JV, called "GM Daewoo Auto and Technology Company," with Daewoo's Korean creditors in 2001. The terms of this marriage were quite different from the previous one. Instead of a 50/50 split, GM was now in the driver's seat, commanding a 67% stake (with a bargain-basement price of $400 million)—in essence, a GM acquisition in disguise.

This time, GM has fully integrated GM Daewoo into its global strategy, because GM now has uncontested control. GM Daewoo makes cars in South Korea and Vietnam and exports them to over 140 countries. One of the most decisive moves is to phase out the Daewoo brand tarnished by quality problems and financial turbulence, except in South Korea and Vietnam. GM has labeled a vast majority of cars built by GM Daewoo as Chevrolet, a brand that GM usually pitches as more American than the Stars and Stripes. In the United States, Latin America, and Eastern Europe, the GM Daewoo–built Chevrolet Aveo has become one of the best-selling compact cars, beating the Toyota Echo and the Hyundai Excel. In addition to finished cars, GM Daewoo also makes kits to be assembled by local factories in China, Colombia, India, Thailand, and Venezuela. In three years, GM Daewoo's worldwide sales of cars and kits reached one million, up from 400,000 when GM took over. That makes GM Daewoo one of the best-performing units of the troubled Detroit automaker.

Sources: Based on (1) *Business Week*, 2004, Daewoo: GM's hot new engine, November 29: 52–53; (2) *Business Week*, 2005, Made in Korea, assembled in China, August 1: 48; (3) M. W. Peng & O. Shenkar, 2002. Joint venture dissolution as corporate divorce, *Academy of Management Executive*, 16: 92–105; (4) Wikipedia, 2008, GM Daewoo, en.wikipedia.org.

Case Discussion Questions

1. Are the conditions in the automobile industry facilitating or constraining an alliance strategy?

2. In the first JV, did GM and Daewoo have the necessary relational capabilities to make the JV work?

3. In the second JV, have the partners improved their relational capabilities?

4. How does this case inform the debate on alliances versus acquisitions?

NOTES

Journal acronyms *AME*–*Academy of Management Executive;* *AMJ*–*Academy of Management Journal;* *AMR*–*Academy of Management Review;* *APJM*–*Asia Pacific Journal of Management;* *BW*–*Business Week;* *CMR*–*California Management Review;* *HBR*–*Harvard Business Review;* *IBR*–*International Business Review;* *JFE*–*Journal of Financial Economics;* *JIBS*–*Journal of International Business Studies;* *JIM*–*Journal of International Management;* *JM*–*Journal of Management;* *JMS*–*Journal of Management Studies;* *JWB*–*Journal of World Business;* *MIR*–*Management International Review;* *MS*–*Management Science;* *OSc*–*Organization Science;* *SMJ*–*Strategic Management Journal*

1. Cited in J. Reuer, 2004, Introduction (p. 2), in J. Reuer (ed.), *Strategic Alliances,* New York: Oxford University Press.

2. F. Contractor & P. Lorange (eds.), 2002, *Cooperative Strategies and Alliances,* Amsterdam: Elsevier.

3. R. Gulati, 1998, Alliances and networks (p. 293), *SMJ,* 19: 293–317.

4. T. Das & B. Teng, 2002, Alliance constellations, *AMR*, 27: 445–456; B. Gomes-Casseres, 1996, *The Alliance Revolution*, Cambridge, MA: Harvard University Press.

5. C. Dhanaraj & A. Parkhe, 2003, Orchestrating innovation networks, *AMR*, 31: 659–669; S. Lazzarini, 2007, The impact of membership in competing alliance constellations, *SMJ*, 28: 345–367; M. Zeng & X. Chen, 2003, Achieving cooperation in multiparty alliances, *AMR*, 28: 587–605.

6. R. Gulati, N. Nohria, & A. Zaheer, 2000, Strategic networks, *SMJ*, 21: 203–215.

7. D. Gnyawali & R. Madhavan, 2001, Cooperative networks and competitive dynamics (p. 431), *AMR*, 26: 431–445.

8. J. Dyer & H. Singh, 1998, The relational view (p. 667), *AMR*, 23: 660–679.

9. J. Dyer, 1997, Effective interfirm collaboration, *SMJ*, 18: 543–556.

10. M. Subramani & N. Venkatraman, 2003, Safeguarding investments in asymmetric relationships, *AMJ*, 46: 46–62.

11. D. Harrison, 2004, Is a long-term business relationship an implied contract?, *JMS*, 41: 107–125.

12. J. Dyer & N. Hatch, 2006, Relation-specific capabilities and barriers to knowledge transfers, *SMJ*, 27: 701–719; A. Madhok & S. Tallman, 1998, Resources, transactions, and rents, *OSc*, 9: 326–339; N. Park, J. Mezias, & J. Song, 2004, A resource-based view of strategic alliances and firm value in the electronic marketplace, *JM*, 30: 7–27.

13. *The Economist*, 2003, Open skies and flights of fancy (p. 67), October 4: 65–67.

14. R. R. Sampson, 2007, R&D alliances and firm performance, *AMJ*, 50: 364–386.

15. B. Bourdeau, J. Cronin, & C. Voorhees, 2007, Modeling service alliances, *SMJ*, 28: 609–622; A. Tiwana & M. Keil, 2007, Does peripheral knowledge complement control?, *SMJ*, 28: 623–634.

16. B. Kogut, 1991, JVs and the option to expand and acquire, *MS*, 37: 19–33; T. Tong & J. Reuer, 2007, Real options in multinational corporations, *JIBS*, 38: 215–230.

17. T. Folta & K. Miller, 2002, Real options in equity partnerships, *SMJ*, 23: 77–88; M. Santoro & J. McGill,

2005, The effect of uncertainty and asset co-specialization on governance in biotechnology alliances, *SMJ*, 26: 1261–1269.

18. F. Rothaermel & W. Boeker, 2008, Old technology meets new technology, *SMJ*, 29: 47–77.

19. S. Currall & A. Inkpen, 2002, A multilevel approach to trust in JVs, *JIBS*, 33: 479–495.

20. G. Hamel, 1991, Competition for competence and inter-partner learning within strategic alliances, *SMJ*, 12: 83–103; J. Hennart, T. Roehl, & D. Zietlow, 1999, "Trojan horse" or "workhorse"? *SMJ*, 20: 15–29.

21. J. Lampel & J. Shamsie, 2000, Probing the unobtrusive link (p. 590), *SMJ*, 21: 593–602.

22. L. Mesquita, 2007, Starting over when the bickering never ends, *AMR*, 32: 72–91.

23. G. Lorenzoni & A. Lipparini, 1999, The leveraging of interfirm relationships, *SMJ*, 20: 317–338.

24. T. Pollock, J. Porac, & J. Wade, 2004, Constructing deal networks, *AMR*, 29: 50–72.

25. D. Gerwin, 2004, Coordinating new product development in strategic alliances, *AMR*, 29: 241–257.

26. Federal Trade Commission, 2000, *Antitrust Guidelines for Collaborations among Competitors*, Washington: FTC.

27. M. W. Peng, 2006, Making M&As fly in China, *HBR*, March: 26–27. See also M. Desai, C. F. Foley, & J. Hines, 2004, The costs of shared ownership, *JFE*, 73: 323–374; P. Kale & J. Anand, 2006, The decline of emerging economy JVs, *CMR*, 48: 62–76; S. Rossi & P. Volpin, 2004, Cross-country determinants of M&As, *JFE*, 74: 277–304; H. K. Steensma, L. Tihanyi, M. Lyles, & C. Dhanaraj, 2005, The evolving value of foreign partnerships in transitioning economies, *AMJ*, 48: 213–235.

28. M. T. Dacin, C. Oliver, & J. Roy, 2007, The legitimacy of strategic alliances, *SMJ*, 28: 169–187.

29. M. Guillen, 2002, Structural inertia, imitation, and foreign expansion, *AMJ*, 45: 509–525; J. Lu, 2002, Intra- and inter-organizational imitative behavior, *JIBS*, 33: 19–38.

30. F. Jeffries & R. Reed, 2000, Trust and adaptation in relational contracting, *AMR*, 25: 873–882; Y. Luo, 2002, Contract, cooperation, and performance in international joint ventures, *SMJ*, 23: 903–919; L. Poppo & T. Zenger, 2002, Do formal contracts and relational governance function as substitutes or

complements?, *SMJ*, 23: 707–725; P. Saparito, C. Chen, & H. Sapienza, 2004, The role of relational trust in bank-small firm relationships, *AMJ*, 47: 400–410.

31. This section draws heavily from S. Tallman & O. Shenkar, 1994, A managerial decision model of international cooperative venture formation, *JIBS*, 25: 91–113.

32. J. Hagedoorn & G. Duysters, 2002, External sources of innovative capabilities, *JMS*, 39: 167–188.

33. S. Park, R. Chen, & S. Gallagher, 2002, Firm resources as moderators of the relationship between market growth and strategic alliances in semiconductor start-ups, *AMJ*, 45: 527–545.

34. Y. Wang & S. Nicholas, 2007, The formation and evolution of non-equity alliances in China, *APJM*, 24: 131–150.

35. M. Colombo, 2003, Alliance form, *SMJ*, 24: 1209–1229; P. Kale & H. Singh, 2007, Building firm capabilities through learning, *SMJ*, 28: 981–1000.

36. R. Jensen & G. Szulanski, 2004, Stickiness and the adaptation of organizational practices in cross-border knowledge transfers, *JIBS*, 35: 508–523; B. Simonin, 2004, An empirical investigation of the process of knowledge transfer in international strategic alliances, *JIBS*, 35: 407–427.

37. Y. Pan & X. Li, 2000, JV formation of very large multinational firms, *JIBS*, 31: 179–189.

38. J. Hagedoorn, D. Cloodt, & H. van Kranenburg, 2005, Intellectual property rights and the governance of international R&D partnerships, *JIBS*, 36: 175–186.

39. W. Hoffmann, 2007, Strategies for managing a portfolio of alliances, *SMJ*, 28: 827–856; D. Lavie, C. Lechner, & H. Singh, 2007, The performance implications of timing of entry and involvement in multipartner alliances, *AMJ*, 50: 578–604; J. Reuer & R. Ragozzino, 2006, Agency hazards and alliance portfolios, *SMJ*, 27: 27–43; B. Silverman & J. Baum, 2002, Alliance-based competitive dynamics, *AMJ*, 45: 791–806.

40. S. Makino, C. Chan, T. Isobe, & P. Beamish, 2007, Intended and unintended termination of international joint ventures, *SMJ*, 28: 1113–1132; J. Robins, S. Tallman, & K. Fladmoe-Lindquist, 2002, Autonomy and dependence of international cooperative ventures, *SMJ*, 23: 881–901.

41. S. White & S. Lui, 2005, Distinguishing costs of cooperation and control in alliances, *SMJ*, 26: 913–932.

42. Y. Zhang & N. Rajagopalan, 2002, Inter-partner credible threat in IJVs, *JIBS*, 33: 457–478.

43. P. Adler & S. Kwan, 2002, Social capital, *AMR*, 27: 17–40; B. Koka & J. Prescott, 2002, Strategic alliances as social capital, *SMJ*, 23: 795–816.

44. T. Rowley, D. Behrens, & D. Krackhardt, 2000, Redundant governance structures (p. 383), *SMJ*, 21: 369–386.

45. J. March, 1991, Exploration and exploitation in organizational learning (p. 71), *OSc*, 2: 71–87.

46. F. Rothaermel & D. Deeds, 2004, Exploration and exploitation alliances in biotechnology, *SMJ*, 25: 201–221.

47. J. Hite & W. Hesterly, 2001, The evolution of firm networks (p. 282), *SMJ*, 22: 275–286; R. Madhavan, B. Koka, & J. Prescott, 1998, Networks in transition, *SMJ*, 19: 439–459.

48. This section draws heavily from M. W. Peng & O. Shenkar, 2002, JV dissolution as corporate divorce, *AME*, 16: 92–105.

49. J. Reuer & A. Arino, 2007, Strategic alliance contracts, *SMJ*, 28: 313–330.

50. A. Arino & J. Reuer, 2004, Designing and renegotiating strategic alliance contracts (p. 44), *AME*, 18: 37–48.

51. J. Child & Y. Yan, 2003, Predicting the performance of IJVs, *JMS*, 40: 284–320; A. Goerzen, 2007, Alliance networks and firm performance, *SMJ*, 28: 487–509; D. Jolly, 2005, The exogamic nature of Sino-foreign JVs, *APJM*, 22: 285–306.

52. A. Arino, 2003, Measures of strategic alliance performance, *JIBS*, 34: 66–79; A. Goerzen & P. Beamish, 2005, The effect of alliance network diversity on MNE performance, *SMJ*, 26: 333–354; J. Lu & D. Xu, 2006, Growth and survival of IJVs, *JM*, 32: 426–448; P. Meschi, 2005, Stock market valuation of JV sell-offs, *JIBS*, 36: 688–700; A. Mohr, 2006, A multiple constituency approach to IJV performance measurement, *JWB*, 41: 247–260; A. Shipilov, 2006, Network strategy and performance of Canadian investment banks, *AMJ*, 49: 590–604; A. Yan & M. Zeng, 1999, IJV instability, *JIBS*, 30: 397–414.

53. A. Gaur & J. Lu, 2007, Ownership strategies and survival of foreign subsidiaries, *JM,* 33: 84–110; A. Madhok, 2006, How much does ownership really matter? *JIBS,* 37: 4–11.

54. J. Barden, H. K. Steensma, & M. Lyles, 2005, The influence of parent control structure on parent conflict in Vietnamese IJVs, *JIBS,* 36: 156–174; C. Dhanaraj & P. Beamish, 2004, Effect of equity ownership on the survival of IJVs, *SMJ,* 25: 295–305; W. Newburry, Y. Zeira, & O. Yeheskel, 2003, Autonomy and effectiveness of equity IJVs in China, *IBR,* 12: 395–419.

55. R. Aguilera, 2007, Translating theoretical logics across borders, *JIBS,* 38: 38–46; P. Lane, J. Salk, & M. Lyles, 2001, Absorptive capacity, learning, and performance in IJVs, *SMJ,* 22: 1139–1161; M. Lyles & J. Salk, 1996, Knowledge acquisition from foreign parents in IJVs, *JIBS,* 27: 877–903; K. Meyer, 2007, Contextualizing organizational learning, *JIBS,* 38: 27–37; E. Tsang, 2002, Acquiring knowledge by foreign partners from IJVs in a transition economy, *SMJ,* 23: 835–854.

56. R. Sampson, 2005, Experience effects and collaborative returns in R&D alliances, *SMJ,* 26: 1009–1031.

57. Y. Luo & M. W. Peng, 1999, Learning to compete in a transition economy, *JIBS,* 30: 269–296.

58. J. Kaufmann & H. O'Neill, 2007, Do culturally distant partners choose different types of JVs?, *JWB,* 42: 435–448; V. Pothukuchi, F. Damanpour, J. Choi, C. Chen, & S. Park, 2002, National and organizational culture differences and IJV performance, *JIBS,* 33: 243–265; D. Sirmon & P. Lane, 2004, A model of cultural differences and international alliance performance, *JIBS,* 35: 306–319.

59. D. Hambrick, J. Li, K. Xin, & A. Tsui, 2001, Compositional gaps and downward spirals in IJV management groups, *SMJ,* 22: 1033–1053.

60. K. Brouthers & G. Mamossy, 2006, Post-formation processes in Eastern and Western European JVs, *JMS,* 43: 203–229; R. Krishnan, X. Martin, & N. Noorderhaven, 2006, When does trust matter to alliance performance? *AMJ,* 49: 894–917.

61. D. Lavie, 2007, Alliance portfolios and firm performance, *SMJ,* 28: 1187–1212.

62. A. Afuah, 2000, How much do your co-opetitors' capabilities matter in the face of technological change?, *SMJ,* 21: 387–404; J. Baum, T. Calabrese, & B. Silverman, 2000, Don't go it alone, *SMJ,* 21: 267–294.

63. B. Anand & T. Khanna, 2000, Do firms learn to create value?, *SMJ,* 21: 295–316; H. Merchant & D. Schendel, 2000, How do international joint ventures create shareholder value?, *SMJ,* 21: 723–737.

64. This section draws heavily from M. Zeng & J. Hennart, 2002, From learning races to cooperative specialization, in F. Contractor & P. Lorange (eds.), *Cooperative Strategies and Alliances* (189–210), Amsterdam: Elsevier.

65. Hamel, 1991, Competition for competence. See also P. Dussauge, B. Garrette, & W. Mitchell, 2000, Learning from competing partners, *SMJ,* 21: 99–126.

66. N. Celly & C. Dhanaraj, 2004, Eli Lilly in India, Ivey case study 9B04M016, University of Western Ontario.

67. C. Choi & P. Beamish, 2004, Split management control and international joint venture performance, *JIBS,* 35: 201–215; H. K. Steensma & M. Lyles, 2000, Explaining IJV survival in a transition economy, *SMJ,* 21: 831–851.

68. T. Tong, J. Reuer, & M. W. Peng, 2008, International joint ventures and the value of growth options, *AMJ* (in press).

69. R. Adner & D. Levinthal, 2004, What is *not* a real option, *AMR,* 29: 74–85.

70. R. McGrath, W. Ferrier, & A. Mendelow, 2004, Real options as engines of choice and heterogeneity, *AMR,* 29: 86–101; J. Reuer & M. Leiblein, 2000, Downside risk implications of multinationality and international joint ventures, *AMJ,* 43: 203–214.

71. T. Chi, 2000, Option to acquire or divest a joint venture, *SMJ* (p. 671), 21: 665–687.

72. P. Kale, J. Dyer, & H. Singh, 2002, Alliance capability, stock market response, and long-term alliance success, *SMJ,* 23: 747–767; D. Yiu & S. Makino, 2002, A choice between JV and WOS, *OSc,* 13: 667–683.

73. J. Dyer, P. Kale, & H. Singh, 2004, When to ally and when to acquire, *HBR* (p. 113), July–August: 109–115.

74. A. Brandenburger & B. Nablebuff, 1996, *Co-opetition,* New York: Doubleday.

75. J. Xia, J. Tan, & D. Tan, 2008, Mimetic entry and bandwagon effect, *SMJ,* 29: 195–217.

chapter 8

Global Competitive Dynamics

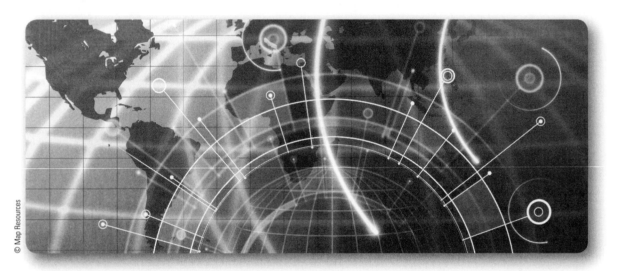

© Map Resources

KNOWLEDGE OBJECTIVES

After studying this chapter, you should be able to

1. Articulate the "strategy as action" perspective

2. Understand the industry conditions conducive for cooperation and collusion

3. Explain how resources and capabilities influence competitive dynamics

4. Outline how antitrust and antidumping laws affect domestic and international competition

5. Identify the drivers for attacks, counterattacks, and signaling

6. Discuss how local firms fight multinational enterprises (MNEs)

7. Participate in two leading debates concerning competitive dynamics

8. Draw strategic implications for action

Opening Case: Unilever Fights Procter & Gamble

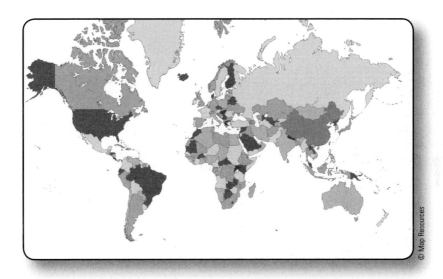

© Map Resources

With twin headquarters in the United Kingdom and the Netherlands, Unilever competes in three major geographical areas: Europe, the Americas, and Asia-Pacific-Africa (APA). Unilever contests in three product markets: foods (such as Knorr soups), personal care (such as Calvin Klein cosmetics), and fabric care (such as Omo detergent). Combining geographic and product dimensions, Unilever thus has presence in nine (3×3) specific markets. Its main global rival in these nine markets is the US-based Procter & Gamble (P&G), whose leading brands include Folgers coffee (foods), Pampers diapers (personal care), and Tide detergent (fabric care).

A fundamental question for Unilever is: how to channel resources that can provide the best opportunities to outcompete P&G in this global "war"?

Table 8.1 helps answer this question. Because both Unilever and P&G dominate their home markets, room for further growth in Europe is limited and chances in the Americas are not great. Thus, growing the APA markets becomes imperative. Of the three product markets, Unilever can thrust into APA foods where P&G is still weak. For example, Hindustan Lever (HLL), Unilever's Indian subsidiary, acquired a number of local firms, boosting its market share in ice cream from zero in the 1990s to 75% in the mid-2000s.

In APA fabric care, because P&G's strengths are strong, Unilever has to assemble massive forces to launch price wars. In China where P&G is very strong, Unilever dropped the price of its Omo detergents by 40% in 1999. Because P&G was distracted elsewhere, it took two years to match

TABLE 8.1   Unilever versus P&G

	ATTRACTIVENESS TO UNILEVER	P&G's CLOUT
Europe foods	High	Low
Europe personal care	High	Moderate
Europe fabric care	High	Low
Americas foods	Low	High
Americas personal care	Low	High
Americas fabric care	Low	High
Asia-Pacific-Africa foods	High	Low
Asia-Pacific-Africa personal care	High	High
Asia-Pacific-Africa fabric care	High	High

Unilever's prices, thus ceding its leading position as a foreign branded detergent in China to Unilever. India is a major APA fabric care market where Unilever is stronger, as HLL dominates the detergents market with a 40% share. The challenge there is how to defend its stronghold, where P&G has been launching a series of price attacks. In 2004, P&G slashed prices for Ariel and Tide detergents by 25%–50%, forcing HLL to respond similarly. By 2008, P&G clearly gained fabric care market share in India, and HLL's growth slowed down.

Overall, while winning or losing these "campaigns" does not guarantee that Unilever and P&G will win or lose the global "war," systematic thinking focusing on one market at a time definitely is helpful. In other words, strategists at Unilever and P&G plotting the battles need to simultaneously think global and act local.

Sources: Based on (1) Author's interviews, 2003–2007; (2) Bloomberg, 2008, Unilever growth to sputter as P&G takes market share in India (www.bloomberg.com); (3) I. MacMillan, A. van Putten, & R. McGrath, 2003, Global gamesmanship, *Harvard Business Review,* May: 62–71.

competitive dynamics

Actions and responses undertaken by competing firms.

competitor analysis

The process of anticipating rivals' actions in order to both revise a firm's plan and prepare to deal with rivals' responses.

In the long rivalry between Unilever and P&G, why did they take certain actions but not others? Once one side initiates an action, how does the other respond? These are some of the key questions in this chapter, which focuses on such **competitive dynamics**—actions and responses undertaken by competing firms.[1] Since one firm's actions are rarely unnoticed by rivals, the initiating firm would naturally like to predict rivals' responses *before* making its own move.[2] This process is called **competitor analysis,** advocated a long time ago by the ancient Chinese strategist Sun Tzu's teaching to not only know "yourself" but also "your opponents."

Recall that Chapter 1 introduced the "strategy as plan" and "strategy as action" schools. This chapter elaborates on the "strategy as action" school. As military officers have long known, a good plan never lasts longer than the first contact with the enemy because the enemy does not act according to our plan (!). Thus, strategy's defining feature is action, not planning. This chapter first highlights the "strategy as action" perspective, followed by a comprehensive model. Then, attack, counterattack, and signaling are outlined, with one interesting extension on how local firms fight multinational enterprises (MNEs) in emerging economies. Debates and extensions follow.

FIGURE 8.1   **Strategy as Action**

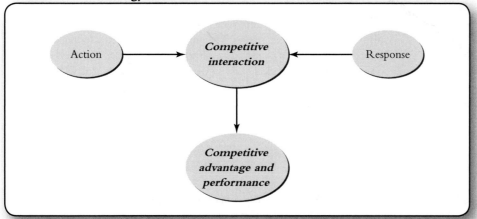

Source: From *Strategy for Action, Industry Rivalry and Coordination*, 1st edition by C.M. Grimm and K.G. Smith, p. 62. Copyright © 1997. Reprinted with permission of South-Western, a division of Cengage Learning: www. cengagerights.com. Fax 800 730-2215.

Strategy as Action

The heart of this chapter is the "strategy as action" perspective (Figure 8.1). It suggests that the essence of strategy is interaction—actions and reactions that lead to competitive advantage. Firms, like militaries, often compete aggressively. Note the military tone of terms such as "attacks," "counterattacks," and "price wars."[3] In other words, it often seems that "business is war."

So, business is war—or is it? It is obvious that military principles cannot be completely applied, because the marketplace, after all, is not a battlefield whose motto is "Kill or be killed." If fighting to the death destroys the "pie," there will be nothing left. In business, it is possible to compete and win without having to kill the opposition. In a nutshell, business is simultaneously war *and* peace (see Strategy in Action 8.1). Alternatively, most competitive dynamics concepts can also be explained in terms of sports analogies. Sports fans know terms such as "offense" and "defense" very well.

While militaries fight over territories, waters, and air spaces, firms compete in markets along product and geographic dimensions (see Opening Case). **Multimarket competition** occurs when firms engage the same rivals in multiple markets.[4] Because a multimarket competitor can respond to an attack not only in the attacked market but also in other markets in which both firms meet, its challenger has to think twice before launching an attack. In other words, while firms "act local," they have to "think global." Because firms recognize their rivals' ability to retaliate in multiple markets, such multimarket competition may result in *reduction* of competitive intensity among rivals, an outcome known as **mutual forbearance,** which we will discuss in more detail next.

Overall, the "strategy tripod" sheds considerable light on competitive dynamics, leading to a comprehensive model (Figure 8.2). The next three sections discuss the three "legs" for the tripod.

multimarket competition

Firms engage the same rivals in multiple markets.

mutual forbearance

Multimarket firms respect their rivals' spheres of influence in certain markets and their rivals reciprocate, leading to tacit collusion.

Strategy in Action 8.1 - Cisco versus Huawei: War and Peace

Founded in 1986, Cisco is a worldwide leader in networking for the Internet. Numerous rivals challenged Cisco, but none was threatening enough—until the rise of Huawei. Founded in 1987, Huawei distinguished itself as an aggressive company that led the telecommunications equipment market in China. It is remarkable that Huawei, despite being a non-state-owned company, was able to not only beat all state-owned rivals but also a series of multinationals in China. In 1999, Huawei launched an overseas drive. Starting with $50 million sales (4% of overall sales) in international markets in 1999, Huawei's sales outside of China reached $11 billion (65% of overall sales) in 2006. What is Huawei's secret weapon? Relative to offerings from competitors such as Cisco, Lucent, Nokia, and Siemens, Huawei's products offer comparable performance at a 30% lower price. This is music to the ears of telecom operators. As a result, Huawei not only penetrated many emerging economies, but also achieved significant breakthroughs in developed markets such as Japan and Western Europe. As of 2007, Huawei served 31 of the world's top 50 telecom operators, including Vodafone, Telefonica, KPN, FT/Orange, and Italia Telecom. Yet, North America remained the toughest nut to crack.

In 2002, Huawei turned its guns on North America—Cisco's stronghold. In Supercomm 2002 (a trade show) in Atlanta, Huawei's debut in North America, two guests visited the Huawei booth and asked detailed questions for 20 minutes. Only after the two guests left did one of Huawei's executives recognize that one of the guests was John Chambers, Cisco's CEO. Chambers thus personally experienced the aggressive arrival of his archrival from China. Thanks to Huawei, Cisco's sales in China peaked in 2001 at $1 billion and then never reached anything above $600 million. Correspondingly Cisco's share in the Chinese router market dropped from 80% to 50%. In North America, facing suspicious buyers, Huawei offered "blind" performance tests on Huawei and Cisco machines whose logos were removed. Buyers often found that the only difference was price.

Cisco's response was both audacious and unexpected. On January 22, 2003, Cisco filed a lawsuit in Texas, alleging that Huawei unlawfully copied and misappropriated Cisco's software and documentation. Cisco's actions totally caught Huawei off guard—the first time it was sued by a foreign rival. Even the day of the attack was deliberately chosen. It was right before Spring Festival, the main annual holiday in China. Thus, none of the Huawei top executives was able to spend a day with their family in the next few weeks. The media noted that this lawsuit squarely put Huawei "on the map" as Cisco's acknowledged enemy number one.

Huawei's response was also interesting. Huawei noted that as a firm that consistently invested at least 10% of its sales on R&D, it had always respected intellectual property rights (IPR). In addition to hiring top American lawyers, Huawei also announced a joint venture with Cisco's rival 3Com several days before the court hearing in March 2003. Consequently, 3Com's CEO, Bruce Claflin, provided testimonial supporting Huawei. By using an American CEO to fight off another American firm, Huawei thus skillfully eroded the "us versus them" feeling permeating this case at a time when "China bashing" was in the air.

While both Cisco and Huawei fought in court, negotiations between them, often involving American and Chinese officials, also intensified. In July 2004, Cisco dropped the case. While the details of the settlement were confidential, *both* Cisco and Huawei declared victory. Huawei agreed to change the software and documentation in question, thus partially meeting Cisco's goals. More importantly, Cisco delayed Huawai's North America offensive by one and a half years. Huawei not only refuted most of Cisco's accusations, but also showcased its technological muscle under intense media spotlight for which it did not have to spend a penny. In part thanks to this high-profile case, Huawei's international sales *doubled*—from approximately $1 billion in 2003 to $2 billion in 2004. Clearly, Huawei rapidly became a force to be reckoned with. In

Strategy in Action 8.1 - (continued)

December 2005, Chambers visited Huawei and for the first time met its CEO Ren Zhengfei. The former plaintiff and defendant shook hands and had friendly discussions like pals, as if nothing had happened between them.

Sources: I thank Sunny Li Sun (University of Texas at Dallas) for his assistance. Based on (1) cisco.com; (2) *Cisco Systems, Inc. et al. v. Huawei Technologies, Co., Ltd. et al., Civil Action No. 2:03-CV-027,* Marshall, TX: US District Court for the Eastern District of Texas; (3) huawei.com; (4) J. Wu & Y. Ji (2006), *Huawei's World,* Beijing: China CITIC Press.

Industry-based Considerations

Collusion and Prisoners' Dilemma

Industry-based considerations are fundamentally concerned with the very first of the Porter five forces, rivalry among competitors in an industry (see Chapter 2). Issues associated with entry barriers and substitutes, the other two of the five forces, also figure prominently. Because Chapter 2 has already discussed rivalry at length, we will not repeat it here. What we highlight here is that most firms in an industry, if given a choice, would probably prefer a reduced level of competition. "People of the same trade seldom meet together, even for merriment and diversion," wrote Adam Smith in *The Wealth of Nations* (1776), "but their conversation often ends in a conspiracy against the public." In modern jargon, this means that competing firms in an industry may have an incentive to engage in **collusion,** defined as collective attempts to reduce competition.

Collusion can be tacit or explicit. Firms engage in tacit collusion when they *indirectly* coordinate actions by signaling their intention to reduce output and maintain pricing above competitive levels. Explicit collusion exists when firms *directly* negotiate output and pricing and divide markets. Explicit collusion leads to a **cartel**—an output- and price-fixing entity involving multiple competitors. A cartel is also known as a trust, whose members have to trust each other in honoring agreements. Since the Sherman Act of 1890, cartels have often been labeled "anticompetitive" and outlawed by **antitrust laws** in many countries.

In addition to antitrust laws, collusion is often crushed by the weight of its own incentive problems. Chief among these problems is prisoners' dilemma, which underpins **game theory.** The term "prisoners' dilemma" derives from a simple game in which two prisoners suspected of a major joint crime (such as burglary) are separately interrogated and told that if either one confesses, the confessor will get a one-year sentence while the other will go to jail for ten years. Since the police do not have strong incriminating evidence for the more serious burglary charges, if neither confesses, both will be convicted of a lesser charge (such as trespassing) each for two years. If both confess, both will go to jail for ten years. At a first glance, the solution to this problem seems clear enough. The maximum *joint* payoff would be for neither of them to confess. However, even if both parties agree not to confess before they are arrested, there are still tremendous incentives to confess.

collusion

Collective attempts between competing firms to reduce competition.

cartel

An entity that engages in output- and price-fixing, involving multiple competitors. Also known as a trust.

antitrust laws

Laws that attempt to curtail anticompetitive business practices such as cartels and trusts.

game theory

A theory which focuses on competitive and cooperative interaction (such as in a prisoners' dilemma situation).

FIGURE 8.2   A Comprehensive Model of Global Competitive Dynamics

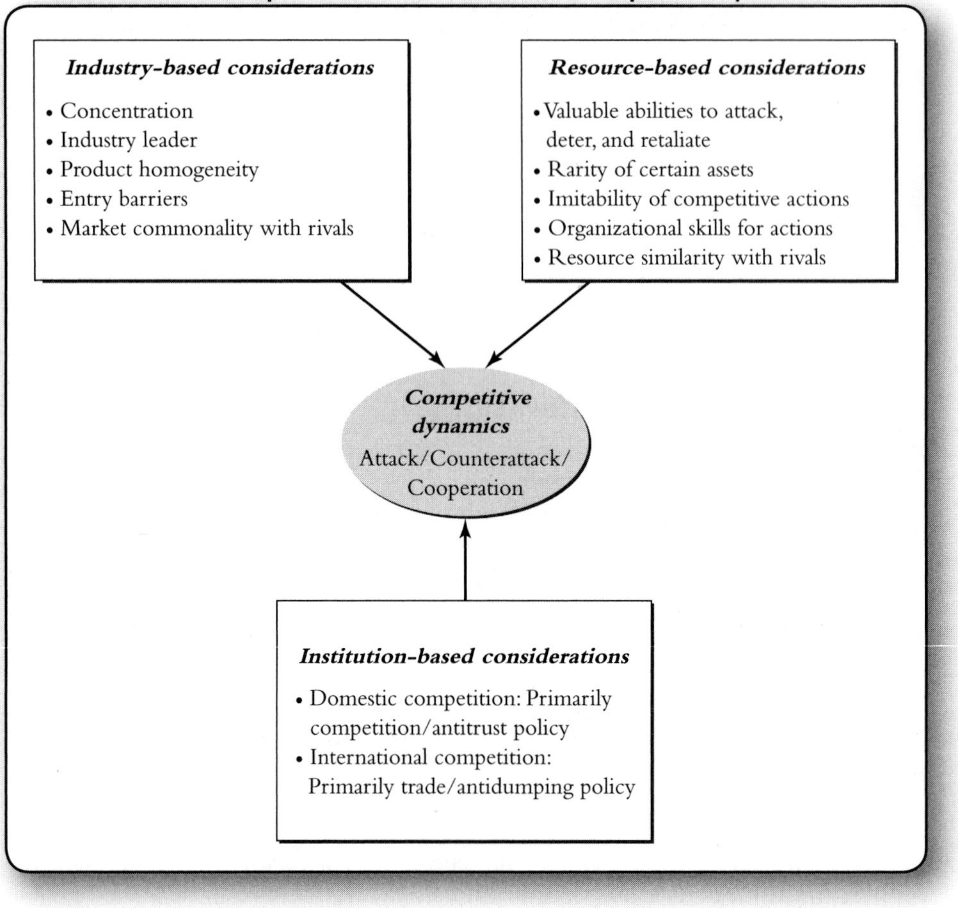

Translated to an airline setting, Figure 8.3 illustrates the payoff structure for both airlines A and B in a given market, let's say, between Sydney, Australia, and Auckland, New Zealand. Assuming a total of 200 passengers, Cell 1 represents the most ideal outcome for both airlines to maintain the price at $500 and each gets 100 passengers and makes $50,000—the "industry" revenue reaches $100,000. However, in Cell 2, if B maintains its price at $500 while A drops it to $300, B is likely to lose all customers. Assuming perfectly transparent pricing information on the Internet, who would want to pay $500 when you can get a ticket for $300? Thus, A may make $60,000 on 200 passengers and B gets nobody. In Cell 3, the situation is reversed. In both Cells 2 and 3, although the industry *decreases* revenue by 40%, the price dropper *increases* its revenue by 20%. Thus, both A and B have strong incentives to reduce price and hope the other side becomes a "sucker." However, neither likes to be a "sucker." Thus, both A and B may want to chop prices, as in Cell 4, whereby each still gets 100 passengers. But both firms as well as the industry end up with a 40% reduction of revenue. A key insight of game theory is that even if A and B have a prior agreement to fix the price at $500, both still have strong incentives to cheat, thus pulling the industry to Cell 4 whereby both are clearly worse off.

FIGURE 8.3 **A Prisoners' Dilemma for Airlines and Payoff Structure (assuming a total of 200 passengers)**

	Airline A	
	Action 1 A keeps price at $500	Action 2 A drops price to $300
Airline B Action 1 B keeps price at $500	(Cell 1) A: $50,000 B: $50,000	(Cell 2) A: $60,000 B: 0
Action 2 B drops price to $300	(Cell 3) A: 0 B: $60,000	(Cell 4) A: $30,000 B: $30,000

Industry Characteristics and Collusion vis-à-vis Competition

Given the benefits of collusion and incentives to cheat, what industries are conducive for collusion vis-à-vis competition? Five factors emerge (Table 8.2). The first relevant factor is the number of firms or—more technically—the **concentration ratio,** defined as the percentage of total industry sales accounted for by the top four, eight, or twenty firms. In general, the higher the concentration, the easier it is to organize collusion. In a high-concentration, two-firm interaction (Figure 8.3), when the situation deteriorates to Cell 2, B may choose *not* to respond with "tit-for-tat" because it would land in the undesirable Cell 4. Instead, B may choose to retaliate by dropping prices in other markets. This sends a relatively clear signal urging A to go back to Cell 1 in the

TABLE 8.2 **Industry Characteristics and Possibility of Collusion vis-à-vis Competition**

COLLUSION POSSIBLE	COLLUSION DIFFICULT (COMPETITION LIKELY)
• Few firms (high concentration)	• Many firms (low concentration)
• Existence of an industry price leader	• No industry price leader
• Homogeneous products	• Heterogeneous products
• High entry barriers	• Low entry barriers

• High market commonality
  (mutual forbearance)
	• Lack of market commonality
	  (no mutual forbearance)

concentration ratio

The percentage of total industry sales accounted for by the top four, eight, or twenty firms.

Sydney–Auckland market. Now imagine there are 10 airlines in the Sydney–Auckland market (a low concentration situation) and six launch some price cutting. The situation becomes much more complicated. Even when the four remaining airlines prefer *not* to join such a campaign in this particular market, their low price retaliations elsewhere, intended to signal to the six price droppers to come to their "senses," send an ambiguous signal. This is because the six price droppers may (mis)interpret the retaliatory actions in their other markets not as a response to their price reductions in the Sydney–Auckland market, but rather, as an "invasion" of their other markets. Therefore, instead of increasing prices in the Sydney–Auckland market, they may also drop prices in other markets. Given the high likelihood that the six airlines that drop prices may not "get it," the four remaining airlines may well decide to simply slash their prices in the Sydney–Auckland market, thus pushing the entire industry into a downward spiral (Cell 4 in Figure 8.3). This happens in many industries with numerous rivals, where price competition is the norm.

Second, the existence of a **price leader**—a firm that has a dominant market share and sets "acceptable" prices and margins in the industry—helps maintain order and stability needed for tacit collusion. The price leader can signal to the entire industry with its own pricing behavior, when it is appropriate to raise or reduce prices, without jeopardizing the overall industry structure. The price leader also possesses the **capacity to punish,** defined as sufficient resources to deter and combat defection. To combat cheating, the most frequently used punishment entails undercutting the defector by flooding the market with deep discounts, thus making the defection fruitless. Such punishment is very costly because it will bring significant financial losses in the short run. However, if small-scale cheating is not dealt with, defection may become endemic, and the price leader will have the most to lose if collusion collapses. Thus, the price leader needs to have both the willingness and capabilities to carry out punishments and bear the costs. On the other hand, an industry without an acknowledged price leader is likely to be more chaotic. Prior to the 1980s, GM played the price leader role, announcing in advance the percentage of price increases, and expecting Ford and Chrysler to follow (which they often did). Should the latter two step "out of bounds," GM would punish them. However, more recently, when Asian and European challengers refuse to follow GM's lead, GM is no longer willing and able to play this role. Thus, the industry has become much more competitive.

Third, an industry with homogeneous products, in which rivals are forced to compete on price (rather than differentiation), is likely to lead to collusion.[5] Because price competition is often "cut throat," firms may have stronger incentives to collude. Since 1990, many firms in commodity industries around the globe, such as shipping and vitamins, have been convicted for price fixing.

Fourth, an industry with high entry barriers for new entrants (such as shipbuilding) is more likely to facilitate collusion than an industry with low entry barriers (such as restaurants). New entrants are likely to ignore the existing industry "order," to introduce less homogeneous products with newer technologies (in other words, "disruptive technologies"), and to violate industry norms cultivated through social relationships.[6] As "mavericks," new entrants "can be thought of as loose cannons in otherwise placid and calm industries."[7]

Finally, **market commonality,** defined as the degree of overlap between two competitors' markets, also has a significant bearing on the intensity of rivalry.[8] Multimarket

price leader

A firm that has a dominant market share and sets "acceptable" prices and margins in the industry.

capacity to punish

Having sufficient resources to deter and combat defection.

market commonality

The degree that two competitors' markets overlap.

firms may respect rivals' spheres of influence in certain markets and their rivals may reciprocate, leading to tacit collusion. To make that happen, firms need to establish multimarket contact, by following each other to enter new markets. Thus, when Carlsberg enters a new country, Heineken will not be far behind.

Mutual forbearance, due to a high degree of market commonality, primarily stems from two factors: (1) deterrence and (2) familiarity. Deterrence is important because a high degree of market commonality suggests that if a firm attacks in one market, its rivals have the ability to engage in **cross-market retaliation,** leading to a costly all-out war nobody can afford. Familiarity is the extent to which tacit collusion is enhanced by a firm's awareness of the actions, intentions, and capabilities of rivals. Repeated interactions lead to such familiarity, resulting in more mutual respect.

Overall, the industry-based perspective has generated a voluminous body of insights on competitive dynamics. Recall from Chapter 2 that the predecessor of this perspective is industrial organization (IO) economics, whose goal is to facilitate competition through regulation. IO economics has been influential in competition/antitrust policy. For example, concentration ratios used to be mechanically applied by US antitrust authorities. For many years (until 1982), if an industry's top-four firm concentration ratio exceeded 20%, it would *automatically* trigger an antitrust investigation. However, since the 1980s, such a mechanical approach has been abandoned, in part because "cartels have formed in markets that bear few of the suggested structural criteria and have floundered in some of the supposedly ideal markets."[9] Evidently, industry-based considerations, while certainly insightful, are unable to tell the complete story, thus calling for contributions from resource- and institution-based perspectives to shed light on competitive dynamics, as outlined in the next two sections.

Resource-based Considerations

A number of resource-based imperatives, informed by the VRIO framework first outlined in Chapter 4, drive decisions and actions associated with competitive dynamics (see Figure 8.2).

Value

Firm resources must create value when engaging rivals. For example, the ability to attack in multiple markets—of the sort Gillette (now part of P&G) possessed when launching its Sensor razors in 23 countries *simultaneously*—throws rivals off balance, thus adding value. Likewise, the ability to rapidly respond to challenges also adds value.[10] Another example is a dominant position in key markets (such as flights in and out of Dallas/Fort Worth for American Airlines). Such a strong sphere of influence poses credible threats to rivals, which understand that the firm will defend its core markets vigorously.

One way to add value is patenting. While patents are obviously valuable, firms are expanding their scale and scope of patenting, resulting in a "patent race."[11] Microsoft now files approximately 3,000 patents a year, up from a mere five in 1990. Intel sits on 10,000 patents. Only about 5% of patents end up having any economic value. So why do firms spend so much money on the "patent race" (on average, half a million dollars in R&D for one patent)? The answer is primarily defensive and competitive. The

cross-market retaliation

Retaliation in other markets when one market is attacked by rivals.

Strategy in Action 8.2 - Publish or Perish in Patent Race

The patent system is often characterized as a "winner take all" system. The winner, specifically the patenting firm, will have its intellectual property protected for the duration of the patent. Ceding a patent to a competitor often spells substantial economic losses for the losing firm, which has to pay its competitor for using the patent. In some cases, firms losing the patent race may perish by dropping out of the market.

However, firms losing a patent race do not necessarily have to perish. Under the "first to invent" rule used by the US Patent and Trademark Office (USPTO), some losing firms will be unable to obtain a patent because rivals invented such technology earlier. Nevertheless, losing firms can still prevent rivals from winning the race. The losing firms' weapon of choice is *preemptive* publication of scientific results. A hallmark of any patent system is the nonobviousness test—to qualify for a patent, an invention cannot be obvious to a person skilled in the field. Because any publication immediately becomes part of the prior art, the strategy of preemptive publishing allows a firm unable to win the patent race to render an otherwise nonobvious invention obvious and, thus, unpatentable. In other words, preemptive publications raise the bar for patentability.

Further, preemptive publications neither have to be "peer reviewed" nor have to be "in print." Publications in a firm's own journal—or even on its own website—may suffice as long as they appear *before* the date of invention and are accessible by the public.

Overall, winners do not "take all" in patent races. Firms losing patent races can publish their way out. When successfully implemented, a strategy of preemptive publishing can not only block winning firms from obtaining a patent, but also make new information available to all at no extra cost—a clear benefit to the society.

Sources: Based on (1) S. Merrill et al., 2004, *A Patent System for the 21st Century*, Washington: National Research Council; (2) G. Parchomovsky, 2000, Publish or perish, *Michigan Law Review*, 98: 926–952.

proliferation of patents makes it very easy for one firm to unwittingly infringe on rivals' parents. When being challenged, a firm without a defensive portfolio of patents is at a severe disadvantage: It has to pay its rivals for using their patents. On the other hand, a firm with strong patents can challenge rivals for their infringements, thus making it easier to reach some understanding—or mutual forbearance. Patents, thus, become a valuable weapon in fighting off rivals. Primarily for this reason, Huawei now files about 2,500 patents a year (Strategy in Action 8.1).

On the other hand, for follower firms unable to win the patent race, one way to attack patenting firms is to challenge the value of the patents. Strategy in Action 8.2 illustrates how follower firms can disrupt patenting firms' strategies through scientific publishing.

Rarity

Either by nature or nurture (or both), certain assets are very rare, thus generating significant advantage in competitive dynamics. Singapore Airlines, in addition to claiming one of the best locations connecting Europe and Asia Pacific as its home base, has often been rated as the world's best airline. This combination of both geographic advantage and man-made reputation advantage is rare, thus allowing Singapore Airlines to always charge higher prices and equip itself with newer and better equipment. It is the first airline in the world to fly the all new A380.

Imitability

Most rivals watch each other and probably have a fairly comprehensive (although not necessarily accurate) picture of how their rivals compete. However, the next hurdle lies in how to imitate successful rivals. It is well known that fast-moving rivals tend to perform better.[12] Even when armed with this knowledge, slow-moving firms will find it difficult to imitate rivals' actions. Many major airlines have sought to imitate discount carriers such as Southwest but have failed repeatedly.

Organization

Some firms are better organized for competitive actions, such as stealth attacks and answering challenges "tit-for-tat."[13] An intense "warrior-like" culture not only requires top management commitment, but also employee involvement down to the "soldiers in the trenches." It is such a self-styled "wolf" culture that has propelled Huawei to become Cisco's leading challenger (Strategy in Action 8.1). It is difficult for slow-moving firms to suddenly wake up to become more aggressive.[14]

On the other hand, more centrally coordinated firms may be better mutual forbearers than firms whose units are loosely controlled. For an MNE competing with rivals across many countries, a mutual forbearance strategy requires some units, out of respect for rivals' sphere of influence, to sacrifice their maximum market gains by withholding some efforts. Of course, such coordination helps other units with dominant market positions to maximize performance, thus helping the MNE as a whole. Successfully carrying out such mutual forbearance calls for organizational reward systems and structures (such as those concerning bonuses and promotions) that encourage cooperation between units (see Chapter 10). Conversely, if a firm has competitive reward systems and structures (for example, bonuses linked to unit performance), unit managers may be unwilling to give up market gains for the greater benefits of other units and the whole firm, thus undermining mutual forbearance.[15]

Resource Similarity

Resource similarity is defined as "the extent to which a given competitor possesses strategic endowment comparable, in terms of both type and amount, to those of the focal firm."[16] Firms with a high degree of resource similarity are likely to have similar competitive actions. For instance, American Airlines and Japan Airlines may have a higher degree of resource similarity than the degree of resource similarity between American Airlines and Travelocity.

If we put together resource similarity and market commonality (discussed earlier), we can yield a framework of competitor analysis for any pair of rivals (Figure 8.4). In Cell 4, because two firms have a high degree of resource similarity but a low degree of market commonality (little mutual forbearance), the intensity of rivalry is likely to be the highest. Conversely, in Cell 1, since both firms have little resource similarity but a high degree of market commonality, the intensity of their rivalry may be the lowest. Cells 2 and 3 present an intermediate level of competition.

For example, prior to the 1996 entry of Fox (a US-based subsidiary of Rupert Murdoch's News Corporation), the US television news market was in Cell 2. The intensity of rivalry was the second *lowest* because the Big Three networks (ABC, CBS, and NBC) had high market commonality (all focusing on the United States) and high

resource similarity

The extent to which a given competitor possesses strategic endowments comparable to those of the focal firm.

FIGURE 8.4   A Framework for Competitor Analysis between a Pair of Rivals

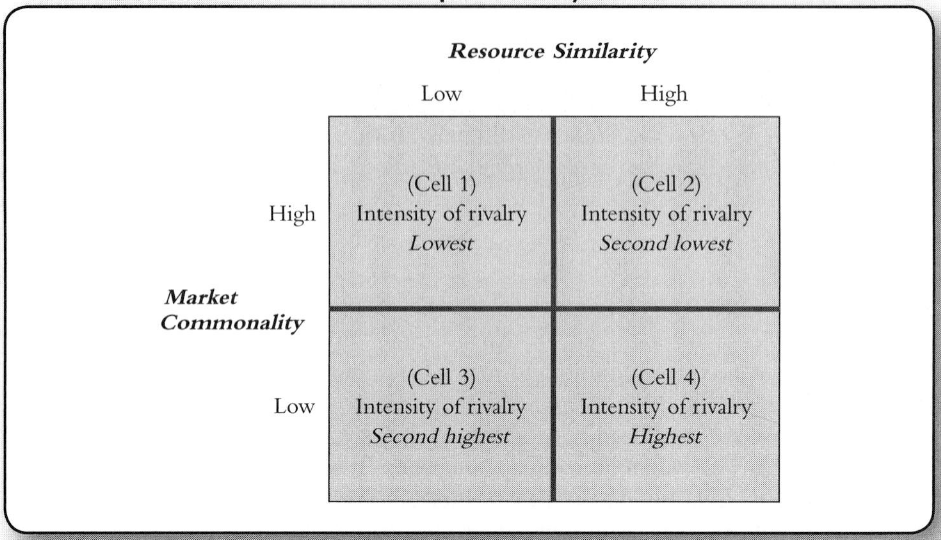

Sources: Adapted from (1) M. Chen, 1996, Competitor analysis and interfirm rivalry: Toward a theoretical integration (p. 108), *Academy of Management Review,* 21: 100–134 and (2) J. Gimeno & C. Y. Woo, 1996, Hypercompetition in a multimarket environment: The role of strategic similarity and multimarket contact in competitive de-escalation (p. 338), *Organization Science,* 7: 322–341.

resource similarity (TV programming). However, Fox's entry has transformed the game.[17] In addition to its Australian roots, News Corporation is a global player with presence in Asia, Canada, and Europe. In other words, while Fox shares high resource similarity with the Big Three, it has low market similarity with the Big Three, which have very little non-US presence. The upshot? The industry is now in Cell 4 with the *highest* intensity of rivalry. That is why Fox can beat up the Big Three, with little fear of its non-US markets being retaliated against. Fox is now the most watched news channel in the United States, reaching 96% of US households. The Big Three thus pay a heavy price for their US-centric mentality. Overall, conscientious mapping along the dimensions outlined in Figure 8.4 can help managers sharpen their analytical focus, allocate resources in proportion to the degree of threat each rival presents, and avoid nasty surprises.

Fighting Low-Cost Rivals[18]

A leading challenge for incumbents is how to deal with low-cost rivals. By the early 1990s, Costco, Dell, Southwest Airlines, and Wal-Mart showed their low-cost teeth. Now, low-cost rivals pop up around the world, such as Ireland's Ryanair in airlines and India's Ranbaxy and Israel's Teva in generic drugs. For incumbents, ignoring them will be dangerous, but do incumbents have the necessary capabilities to fight low-cost rivals? Figure 8.5 suggests a framework for responding to low-cost rivals.

This framework suggests that incumbents need to resist the urge to initiate price wars in an effort to drive out low-cost rivals. From an institution-based view, predatory pricing may be illegal in many countries (see next section). From a resource-based

FIGURE 8.5   How to Fight a Low-Cost Rival

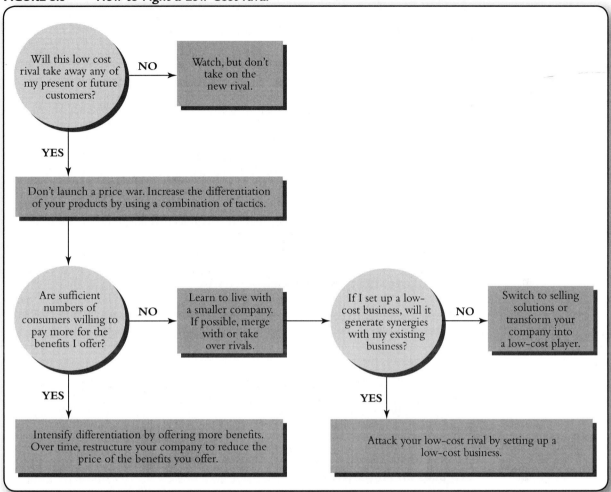

Source: Adapted from N. Kumar, 2006, Strategies to fight low-cost rivals, *Harvard Business Review* (p. 107), December: 104–112.

view, in a race to the bottom, incumbents *usually* lose, because low-cost rivals have much better capabilities in the low-cost game. K-Mart not only failed to beat Wal-Mart on price, but also dragged itself into bankruptcy. Similarly, United Airlines dueled Southwest, and British Airways (BA) took on Ryanair. In the end, Southwest has soared but United has crash landed into bankruptcy (repeatedly). Ryanair has operating margins three times those of BA (23% versus 7%) and is now worth more than BA in capitalization.

One advice for incumbents is to enhance differentiation and convince customers to pay for such benefits (see Chapter 2). Apple designs cool gadgets. Target charges a small premium above Wal-Mart prices, as opposed to trying to beat Wal-Mart prices.

However, when differentiation fails and incumbents are forced to go downmarket, they need to take a hard look at the O aspect from a VRIO standpoint: Do they have the necessary organizational capabilities to effectively compete against low-cost rivals? Incumbents tend to have the delusion that based on their experience, they can easily replicate low-cost operations. In the 1990s, most major airlines launched no-frills operations, such as BA's Go, Continental Lite, Delta Express, KLM's Buzz, SAS's Snowflake, and United's Shuttle. Since then, *all* these operations have been shut down or sold off, indicative of both a lack of organizational capabilities and a lack of ability to learn "new tricks."

Eventually, while incumbents may (hopefully successfully) transform themselves to become low-cost players, they may also switch to selling solutions. For example, IBM switched from selling hardware, whose markets are eroded by low-cost rivals, to selling high-end solutions. IBM now sells whatever combination of hardware, software, and services that customers prefer, whether that means selling IBM products or rivals' offerings. The leading piano maker Steinway now focuses on the "experience," and sells a large number of pianos made by its low-cost rival, Pearl River from China, which has formidable manufacturing firepower but limited branding capabilities.

Institution-based Considerations

In a nutshell, the institution-based view advises managers to be well versed in the "rules of the game" governing domestic and international competition. Surprisingly, the existing global (or mainstream) strategy textbooks have relatively little (or sometimes no) coverage on the institutions governing competitive dynamics. This is unfortunate because a lack of understanding of these institutions may land otherwise successful firms (such as Microsoft) in deep trouble. In a nutshell, the institution-based view argues that free markets are not necessarily free. This section focuses on formal institutions governing domestic and international competition.

Formal Institutions Governing Domestic Competition: A Focus on Antitrust

competition policy

Policy governing the rules of the game in competition, which determine the institutional mix of competition and cooperation that gives rise to the market system.

antitrust policy

Competition policy designed to combat monopolies, cartels, and trusts.

Formal institutions governing domestic competition are broadly guided by **competition policy,** which "determines the institutional mix of competition and cooperation that gives rise to the market system."[19] Of particular relevance to us is **antitrust policy** designed to combat monopolies and cartels.[20] Competition/antitrust policy seeks to balance efficiency and fairness. While efficiency is relatively easy to understand, it is often hard to agree on what is fairness (see Strategy in Action 8.3 on Google). In the United States, fairness means equal opportunities for incumbents and new entrants. It is "unfair" for incumbents to raise entry barriers to shut out new entrants. However, in Japan, fairness means the *opposite*—that is, incumbents that have invested in and nurtured an industry for a long time deserve to be protected from the intrusion brought by new entrants. What Americans approvingly describe as "market dynamism" is negatively labeled by Japanese as "market turbulence;" the Japanese ideal is "orderly competition" (in other words, incumbent dominance—see Integrative Case on the Japanese bookselling industry). Overall, the American antitrust policy is *proconsumer*, whereas the Japanese approach is *proincumbent*. It is difficult to argue who is right or wrong here, but we need to be aware of such crucial differences.

Strategy in Action 8.3 - Who's Afraid of Google?

Ethical Challenge

Rarely if ever has a company risen so fast in so many ways as Google, the world's most popular search engine. This is true by just about any measure: the growth in its market value and revenues; the number of people clicking in search of news, the nearest pizza parlor, or a satellite image of their neighbor's garden; the volume of its advertisers; or the number of its lawyers and lobbyists.

Such an ascent is enough to evoke concerns—both paranoid and justified. The list of constituencies that hate or fear Google grows by the week. Television networks, book publishers, and newspaper owners feel Google has grown by using their content without paying for it. Telecom firms such as AT&T and Verizon are miffed that Google prospers, in their eyes, by free-riding on the bandwidth they provide—especially when it is about to bid against them in a forthcoming auction for radio spectrum. Many small firms hate Google because they relied on exploiting its search formulas to win prime positions in its rankings, but dropped to the Internet's equivalent of Hades after Google tweaked these algorithms.

And now come the politicians. Libertarians dislike Google's deal with China's censors. Conservatives moan about its uncensored videos. But the big new fear has to do with the privacy of its users. Google's business model assumes that people will entrust it with ever more information about their lives, to be stored in the company's "cloud" of remote computers. These data begin with the logs of a user's searches (in effect, a record of his interests) and his responses to advertisements. Often they extend to the user's e-mail, calendar, contacts, documents, spreadsheets, photos, and videos. They could soon include even the user's medical records and precise location (determined from his or her mobile phone).

More JP Morgan than Bill Gates

Google is often compared to Microsoft (another enemy, incidentally), but its evolution is actually closer to that of the banking industry. Just as financial institutions grew to become depositories of people's money, and thus guardians of private information about their finances, Google is now turning into a custodian of a far wider and more intimate range of information about individuals. Yes, this applies also to all rivals such as Yahoo! and Microsoft. But Google, through the sheer speed with which it accumulates this treasure of information, will be the one to test the limits of what society can tolerate.

It does not help that Google is often seen as arrogant. Granted, this complaint often comes from sour-grapes rivals. But many others are put off by Google's cocksure assertion of its own holiness, as if it merited unquestioning trust. This after all is the firm that chose "Don't be evil" as its corporate motto and that explicitly intones that its goal is "not to make money," as its boss, Eric Schmidt, puts it, but to "change the world." Its ownership structure is set up to protect that vision.

Ironically, there is something rather cloudlike about the multiple complaints surrounding Google. The issues are best parted into two cumuli: a set of "public" arguments about how to regulate Google; and a set of "private" ones for Google's managers, to deal with the strategy the firm needs to get through the coming storm. On both counts, Google—contrary to its own propaganda—is much better judged as just like any other "evil" money-grabbing company.

Grab the Money

This view has arisen because, from the public point of view, the main contribution of all companies to society comes from making profits, not giving things away. Google is a good example of this. Its "goodness" stems less from all that guff about corporate altruism than from Adam Smith's invisible hand. It provides a service that others find very useful—namely, helping people find information (at no charge) and letting advertisers promote their wares to those people in a finely targeted way.

(continued)

Given this, the onus of proof is with Google's would-be prosecutors to prove it is doing something wrong. On antitrust, the price that Google charges its advertisers is set by auction, so its monopolistic clout is limited; and it has yet to use its dominance in one market to muscle into others the way Microsoft did. The same presumption of innocence goes for copyright and privacy. Google's book-search product, for instance, arguably helps rather than hurts publishers and authors by rescuing books from obscurity and encourages readers to buy copyrighted works. And, despite Big Brotherish talk about knowing what choices people will be making tomorrow, Google has not betrayed the trust of its users over their privacy. If anything, it has been better than its rivals in standing up to prying governments in both America and China.

That said, conflicts of interest will become inevitable—especially with privacy. Google in effect controls a dial that, as it sells ever more services to you, could move in two directions. Set to one side, Google could voluntarily destroy very quickly any user data it collects. That would assume privacy, but it would limit Google's profits from selling to advertisers information about what you are doing, and make those services less useful. If the dial is set to the other side and Google hangs on to the information, the services will be more useful, but some dreadful intrusions into privacy would occur.

The answer, as with banks in the past, must lie somewhere in the middle; and the right point for the dial is likely to change, as circumstances change. That will be the main public interest in Google. But, as the bankers (and Bill Gates) can attest, public scrutiny also creates a private challenge for Google's managers: Just how should they present their case?

One obvious strategy is to allay concerns over Google's trustworthiness by becoming more transparent and opening up more of its processes and plans to scrutiny. But it also needs a deeper change of heart. Pretending that, just because your founders are nice young men and you give away lots of services, society has no right to question your motives no longer seems sensible. Google is a capitalistic tool—and a useful one. Better, surely, to face the coming storm on that foundation, than on a trite slogan that could be your undoing.

Source: The Economist, 2007, Who's afraid of Google? September 1: 9. © The Economist Newspaper Group.

collusive price setting

Monopolists or collusion parties setting prices at a level higher than the competitive level.

predatory pricing

(1) Setting prices below costs in the short run to destroy rivals and (2) intending to raise prices to cover losses in the long run after eliminating rivals.

As examples, Table 8.3 illustrates the three major US antitrust laws and five landmark cases. Competition/antitrust policy focuses on (1) collusive price setting and (2) predatory pricing. **Collusive price setting** refers to price setting by monopolists or collusion parties at a level higher than competitive level. The largest case prosecuted on collusive pricing is the global vitamin cartel of the 1990s, artificially jacking up prices by 30%–40%.[21]

Another area of concern is **predatory pricing,** defined as (1) setting prices below cost *and* (2) intending to raise prices to cover its losses in the long run after eliminating rivals ("an attempt to monopolize"). This is an area of significant contention. First, it is not clear what exactly "cost" is. Second, even when firms are found to be selling below cost, US courts have ruled that if rivals are too numerous to eliminate, one firm cannot recoup its losses due to low prices by jacking up prices. Then its pricing cannot be labeled "predatory." This seems to be the case in most industries. Thus, the two legal tests have made it extremely difficult to win a predation case in the United States.[22]

TABLE 8.3 Major Antitrust Laws and Landmark Cases in the United States

MAJOR ANTITRUST LAWS	LANDMARK CASES
Sherman Act of 1890	**Standard Oil (1911)**
• It is illegal to monopolize or attempt to monopolize an industry.	• Had a US market share exceeding 85%.
• "Every person who shall monopolize, or attempt to monopolize, or combine or conspire with any person or persons, to monopolize any part of the trade or commerce among the several states, or with foreign nations, shall be deemed guilty of a misdemeanor."	• Found guilty of monopolization.
	• Dissolved into several smaller firms.
	Aluminum Company of America (ALCOA) (1945)
• Explicit collusion is clearly illegal.	• Had 90% of the US aluminum ingot market.
• Tacit collusion is in a gray area, although the spirit of the law is against it.	• Found guilty of monopolization.
	• Ordered to subsidize rivals' entry and sold plants.
Clayton Act of 1914	**IBM (1969–1982)**
• Created the Federal Trade Commission (FTC) to regulate the behavior of business firms.	• Had 70% US computer market share.
• Empowered the FTC to prevent firms from engaging in harmful business practices.	• Sued by DOJ for monopolization, unfair product bundling, and predatory pricing.
	• Case dropped by the Reagan Administration.
Hart-Scott-Rodino (HSR) Act of 1976	**AT&T (1974–1982)**
• Empowered the Department of Justice (DOJ) to require firms to submit internal documents.	• A legal "natural monopoly" since the 1900s.
	• Still sued by DOJ for monopolization, in particular its efforts to block new entrants.
• Empowered state attorneys general (AGs) to initiate triple-damage suits.	• Reached a settlement with the Reagan Administration resulting in a breakup.
	Microsoft (1990–2001)
	• MS-DOS and Windows had an 85% market share.
	• Sued by DOJ, FTC, and 22 state AGs for monopolization and illegal product bundling.
	• Settled in 1994, ordered to split into two in 2000, judgment to split the firm reversed on appeal in 2001, settled again in 2001.
	• Found guilty by the EU in 2004 (lost appeal in 2007).

A third area of concern is **extraterritoriality,** namely, the reach of one country's laws to other countries. US courts have taken it upon themselves to *unilaterally* punish non-US cartels (some of which may be legal elsewhere), such as the diamond cartel led by De Beers (see Integrative Case "Is a Diamond Forever?"). It is not surprising that such US actions often irritate foreign governments and firms. More recently, the EU evidently has taken a page from the US antitrust playbook.

extraterritoriality
The reach of one country's laws to other countries.

It threatened to veto the merger between Boeing and McDonnell Douglas and successfully torpedoed the proposed merger between GE and Honeywell. In 2004, Microsoft, which cleared antitrust hurdles with the US authorities in 2002, was subject to antitrust penalties imposed by the EU. In 2007, Microsoft lost its appeal in an EU court. Without a doubt, in the age of globalization, extraterritorial applications of domestic competition/antitrust laws create tension among governments and firms. The EU's recent ruling against Microsoft was criticized as a "new form of protectionism" by the American side.[23]

Since the Reagan era, US antitrust enforcement has become more permissive. It is not an accident that strategic alliances among competitors have proliferated since the 1980s (see Chapter 7). However, despite improved clarity and permissiveness, the legal standards for interfirm cooperation are still ambiguous. In the absence of international harmonization of antitrust policy, it is crucial that firms be aware of these ambiguities when planning their actions, especially when operating under the jurisdiction of multiple governments.

Formal Institutions Governing International Competition: a Focus on Antidumping

In the same spirit of predatory pricing, **dumping** is defined as (1) an exporter selling below cost abroad and (2) planning to raise prices after eliminating local rivals. While domestic predation is usually labeled "anticompetitive," cross-border dumping is often emotionally accused to be "unfair." Antidumping laws are laws that punish foreign firms accused of dumping.

Consider the following two scenarios. First, a steel producer in *Indiana* enters a new market, Texas. In Texas, it offers prices lower than those in Indiana, resulting in a 10% market share in Texas. Texas firms have two choices. The first one is to initiate a lawsuit against the Indiana firm for "predatory pricing." However, it is difficult to prove (1) that the Indiana firm is selling below cost *and* (2) that its pricing is an "attempt to monopolize." Under US antitrust laws, a predation case like this will have no chance of succeeding. In other words, domestic competition/antitrust laws offer no hope for protection. Thus, Texas firms are most likely to opt for their second option—to retaliate in kind by offering lower prices to customers in Indiana, leading to lower prices in both Texas and Indiana.

Now in the second scenario, the "invading" firm is not from Indiana but *India*. Holding everything else constant, Texas steel firms can argue that the Indian firm is dumping. Under US **antidumping laws,** Texas steel producers "would almost certainly obtain legal relief on the very same facts that would not support an antitrust *claim*, let alone antitrust relief."[24] Note that imposing antidumping duties on Indian steel imports reduces the incentive for Texas firms to counterattack by entering India, resulting in *higher* prices in both Texas and India, where consumers are hurt. These two scenarios are not merely hypothetical; they are highly realistic. An OECD study in Australia, Canada, the EU, and the US reports that 90% of the practices found to be unfair dumping in these countries would never have been questioned under their own antitrust laws if used by a domestic firm in making a domestic sale.[25] In a nutshell, foreign firms are discriminated against by the formal rules of the game.

dumping

An exporter selling below cost abroad and planning to raise prices after eliminating local rivals.

antidumping laws

Laws that punish foreign companies that engage in dumping in a domestic market.

Discrimination is also evident in the actual investigation of antidumping. A case is usually filed by a domestic firm with the relevant government authorities—in the United States, they are the International Trade Administration (a unit of the Department of Commerce) and International Trade Commission (an independent government agency). Then, these government agencies send lengthy questionnaires to accused foreign firms, requesting comprehensive, proprietary data on their cost and pricing, in English, using US generally accepted accounting principles (GAAP), within 30–45 days. Many foreign defendants fail to provide such data on time. The investigation can have four outcomes:

- If no data are forthcoming from abroad, the accusing firm can easily win.

- If foreign firms do provide data, the accusing firm can still argue that these unfair foreigners have lied—"There is no way their costs can be so low!" In the case of Louisiana versus Chinese crawfish growers, the authenticity of the $9 per *week* salary made by Chinese workers was a major point of contention.

- Even if the low cost data are verified, US (and EU) antidumping laws allow the complainant to argue that these data are not "fair." In the case of China, the argument goes, its cost data reflect huge distortions due to government intervention because China is still a "nonmarket" economy—the wage may be low, but workers may be provided with low-cost housing and benefits subsidized by the government. The crawfish case thus boiled down to how much it would cost to raise hypothetical crawfish in a market economy (in this particular case, Spain was mysteriously chosen). Because Spanish costs were about the same as Louisiana costs, the Chinese were found guilty of dumping in America by selling below *Spanish* costs. Thus, 110%–123% import duties were levied on Chinese crawfish.

- The fourth possible outcome is that the defendant wins the case. But this happens to only 5% of the antidumping cases in the United States.[26]

Simply filing an antidumping petition (regardless of the outcome), one study finds, may result in a 1% increase of the stock price for US listed firms (an average of $46 million increase in market value).[27] Evidently, Wall Street knows that Uncle Sam is "on your side." It is thus not surprising that antidumping cases have now proliferated throughout the world. Although the EU and the US have initiated the largest number of cases, on per dollar of imports, Argentina and South Africa have 20 times more cases than the US, India, seven times, and Brazil, five times.[28]

While some argue that the differences between domestic and international business are only a matter of degree, in the case of antidumping, we see some fundamentally different treatments of domestic and international firms. It is ironic that the rising tide of globalization in the last two decades has been accompanied by the rising proliferation of antidumping cases, which are allowed under the WTO. The message to firms interested in doing business abroad is clear: Their degree of freedom in overseas pricing is significantly less than that in domestic pricing.

In summary, the institution-based view suggests that institutional conditions such as the availability of antidumping protection are not just the "background." They directly determine what weapons a firm has in its arsenal to wage competitive battles. Next, we outline two main action items.

Attack and Counterattack

In the form of price cuts, advertising campaigns, market entries, and new product introductions, an **attack** can be defined as an initial set of actions to gain a competitive advantage, and a **counterattack** is consequently defined as a set of actions in response to an attack. This section focuses on: (1) What are the main kinds of attacks? (2) What kinds of attacks are more likely to be successful?

Three Main Types of Attack[29]

The three main types of attack are (1) thrust, (2) feint, and (3) gambit. Shown in Figure 8.6, **thrust** is the classic frontal attack with brute force.[30] A case in point is the "browser war." In 1996, Netscape had 90% of the browser market, and Microsoft (Explorer) had less than 5%. After Microsoft's frontal attack, Netscape's market share fell to 14%, whereas Microsoft's rose to 86% in 1998.[31]

A **feint,** in basketball, is one player's effort to fool his/her defender, pretending he/ she would go one way but instead charging ahead another way. Shown in Figure 8.7, in competitive dynamics, a feint is a firm's attack on a focal arena important to a competitor but one that is not the attacker's true target area.[32] The feint is followed by the attacker's commitment of resources to its actual target area. Consider the "Marlboro war" between Philip Morris and R. J. Reynolds (RJR). In the early 1990s, both firms' traditional focal market, the United States, experienced a 15% decline over the previous decade. Both were interested in Central and Eastern Europe (CEE), which grew rapidly. Philip Morris executed a feint in the United States by dropping 20% off the price on its flagship brand, Marlboro, on one *day* (April 2, 1993, which became known as the "Marlboro Friday"). Confronting this ferocious and sudden move, RJR diverted

attack

An initial set of actions to gain competitive advantage.

counterattack

A set of actions in response to attacks.

thrust

The classic frontal attack with brute force.

feint

A firm's attack on a focal arena important to a competitor, but not the attacker's true target area.

FIGURE 8.6   Thrust

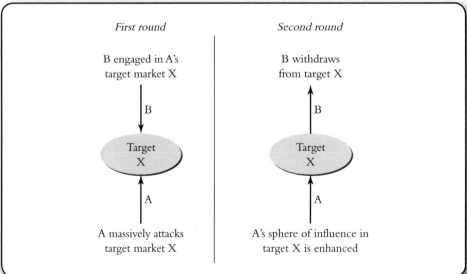

Source: Adapted from R. G. McGrath, M. Chen, & I. C. MacMillan, 1998, "Multimarket maneuvering in uncertain spheres of influence: Resource diversion strategies" (p. 729), from *Academy of Management Review,* 23: 724–740. © 1998. Reprinted by permission of Academy of Management Review via Copyright Clearance Center.

FIGURE 8.7   Feint

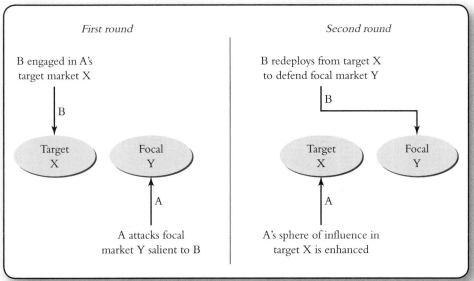

First round

B engaged in A's
target market X

B

Target
X

Focal
Y

A

A attacks focal
market Y salient to B

Second round

B redeploys from target X
to defend focal market Y

B

Target
X

Focal
Y

A

A's sphere of influence in
target X is enhanced

Source: Adapted from R. G. McGrath, M. Chen, & I. C. MacMillan, 1998, "Multimarket maneuvering in uncertain spheres of influence: Resource diversion strategies" (p. 729), from *Academy of Management Review*, 23: 724–740.

substantial resources earmarked for CEE to defend its US market. Philip Morris was thus able to rapidly establish its dominant sphere of influence in CEE.[33]

A **gambit,** in chess, is a move that sacrifices a low-value piece in order to capture a high-value piece. The competitive equivalent is to withdraw from a low-value market to attract rivals to divert resources into it in order to capture a high-value market (Figure 8.8). For example, Gillette and Bic competed in both razors and lighters. Gillette was stronger in razors and Bic was stronger in lighters. Gillette in 1984 withdrew *entirely* from lighters and devoted its attention to razors. Bic accepted the gambit and diverted razor resources to lighters. The gambit can be regarded as an exchange of the spheres of influence between Gillette and Bic, each with a stronger position in one market.

Awareness, Motivation, and Capability

Obviously, unopposed attacks are more likely to be successful. Thus, attackers need to understand the three drivers for counterattacks: (1) awareness, (2) motivation, and (3) capabilities.[34]

- If an attack is so subtle that rivals are not *aware* of it, then the attacker's objectives are likely to be attained. One interesting idea is the "blue ocean strategy" that avoids attacking core markets defended by rivals.[35] A thrust on rivals' core markets is very likely to result in a bloody price war—in other words, a "red ocean." In the 1990s, Netscape drew tremendous publicity by labeling Microsoft the "Death Star" (of the movie *Star Wars* fame) and predicting that the Internet would make Windows obsolete. Such a challenge helped make Netscape Microsoft's number-one enemy, leading to the demise of Netscape (or its drowning in the "red ocean").[36]

gambit

A firm's withdrawal from a low-value market to attract rival firms to divert resources into the low-value market so that the original withdrawing firm can capture a high-value market.

FIGURE 8.8　　　**Gambit**

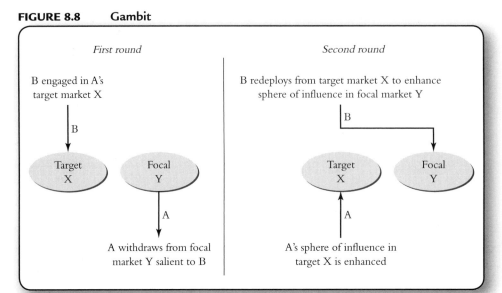

Source: Adapted from R. G. McGrath, M. Chen, & I. C. MacMillan, 1998, Multimarket maneuvering in uncertain spheres of influence: Resource diversion strategies (p. 733), *Academy of Management Review,* 23: 724–740.

- *Motivation* is also crucial. If the attacked market is of marginal value, managers may decide not to counterattack. Consider how China's Haier entered the US white goods market. Although Haier dominates its home country with a broad range of products, it chose to enter the US market in a most non-threatening segment: mini-bars for hotels and dorms. Does anyone remember the brand of the mini-bar in the last hotel room where you stayed? Evidently, not only did you fail to pay attention to that brand, but incumbents such as GE and Whirlpool also dismissed this segment as peripheral and low margin. In other words, they were not motivated to counterattack. Thanks in part to the incumbents' lack of motivation to counterattack, Haier now commands a 50% US market share in compact refrigerators, and has built a factory in South Carolina to go after more lucrative product lines.

- Even if an attack is identified and a firm is motivated to respond, it requires strong *capabilities* to carry out counterattacks—as discussed in our earlier section on resources.

Cooperation and Signaling

Some firms choose to compete, and others choose to cooperate. How to signal one's intention to cooperate in order to *reduce* competitive intensity? Short of illegally talking directly to rivals, firms have to resort to signaling—that is, "While you can't talk to your competitors on pricing, you can always *wink* at them." We outline four means of such winking:

- A non-aggression (also known as "fat cat") strategy refers to active investment in non-threatening ways so as not to provoke attacks on a firm's core markets. For example, IKEA actively invests in the wooden self-assembly segment of the furniture market. At the same time, it has announced that it has no intention to enter the traditional factory-assembled furniture segment, thus discouraging traditional furniture firms to enter IKEA's core market.

- While a non-aggression strategy reduces competition by *not* entering new markets, a second strategy, market entry, may also have the same effect. Firms may enter new markets, not really to challenge incumbents but to seek mutual forbearance by establishing multimarket contact. Thus, MNEs often chase each other, entering one country after another.[37] Airlines that meet in many routes are often less aggressive than airlines that meet in one or a few routes.[38]

- Firms can send an open signal for a truce. As GM faced grave financial difficulties in 2005, Toyota's chairman told the media at press conferences *twice* that Toyota would "help GM" by raising Toyota prices in the United States. As far as signaling goes, Toyota's signal could not have been more unambiguous, short of talking directly to GM, which would be illegal. Toyota, of course, was self-interested. Should GM indeed declare bankruptcy, Toyota would attract all the "machine-gun fire" from protectionist backlash. Nevertheless, US antitrust authorities reportedly took note of Toyota's remarks—essentially an open message to GM for price fixing.[39]

- Sometimes firms can send a signal to rivals by enlisting the help of governments. Because direct negotiations with rivals on what consists of "fair" pricing are often illegal, holding such discussions is legal under the auspices of government investigations. Thus, filing an antidumping petition or suing a rival does not necessarily indicate a totally hostile intent; sometimes, it signals to the other side: "We don't like what you are doing; it's time to talk." Cisco dropped its case against Huawei after both firms negotiated a solution, mediated by both Chinese and US governments (see Strategy in Action 8.1).

Reduced to its core, cooperation among competitors fundamentally boils down to a repeated game in which players accommodate each other to avoid conflict. Thomas Schelling, a leading theorist on conflict resolution and a Nobel laureate, argues that conflict is essentially a way of bargaining and that maintenance of cooperation is a protracted series of successful bargains.[40] Sometimes such bargaining is explicit. However, explicit bargaining can easily become explicit collusion and is no longer allowed legally. As a result, "bargaining" often takes place through signals and actions, which in theory speak louder than words. However, conflicting objectives, imperfect information processing, and deliberate actions to mislead (such as feints noted earlier) often result in misunderstandings, which tend to lead to an escalation of competition and consequently a collapse of cooperation. Because of significant incentive problems (noted earlier), collusion is often difficult to sustain. For example, the average duration of cartels recently convicted by US and EU authorities lasted only six years.[41]

Overall, because of the sensitive nature of interfirm cooperation designed to reduce competition, we do not know a lot about them. However, to the extent that business is both war and peace, strategists need to pay as much attention to making peace with rivals as fighting wars against them.

Local Firms versus Multinational Enterprises

While managers, students, and journalists are often fascinated by MNE rivals such as Coke/Pepsi, SAP/Oracle, and Sony/Samsung, much less is known about how local firms cope when confronting the MNE onslaught. Local firms can adopt four strategic postures outlined in Figure 8.9.[42]

In Cell 3, in some industries, the pressures to globalize are relatively low and local firms' strengths lie in a deep understanding of local markets. Therefore, a **defender** strategy, by leveraging local assets in areas which MNEs are weak, is often called for. For example, in Israel, facing an onslaught from MNE cosmetics firms, a number of local firms turned to focus on products suited to the Middle Eastern climate and managed to defend their turf. Ahava has been particularly successful, in part because of its highly unique components extracted from the Dead Sea that MNEs cannot find elsewhere.[43] In essence, we can view such a defender strategy as a *gambit*, through which local firms cede some markets (such as mainstream cosmetics) to MNEs while building strongholds in other markets.

In Cell 4, in some industries where pressures for globalization are relatively low, local firms may possess some skills and assets that are transferable overseas, thus leading to an **extender** strategy. This strategy centers on leveraging home-grown competencies abroad. For instance, Asian Paints controls 40% of the house paint market in India. Asian Paints developed strong capabilities tailored to the unique environment in India, characterized by thousands of small retailers serving numerous low-income consumers who only want small quantities of paint that can be diluted to save money. Such capabilities are not only a winning formula in India, but also in much of the

defender

A strategy that leverages local assets in areas which MNEs are weak

extender

A strategy that centers on leveraging home-grown competencies abroad by expanding into similar markets.

FIGURE 8.9   How Local Firms in Emerging Economies Respond to Multinationals

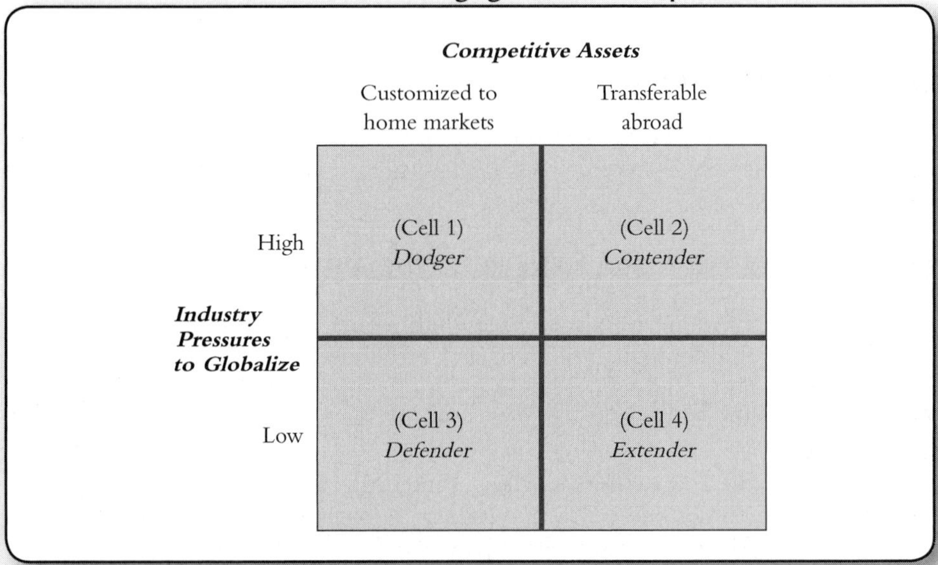

Source: Adapted from N. Dawar & T. Frost, 1999, Competing with giants: Survival strategies for local companies in emerging markets (p. 122), *Harvard Business Review*, March–April: 119–129.

developing world. In contrast, MNEs, whose business model typically centers on affluent customers in developed economies, have had a hard time coming up with profitable low-end products. Overall, Asian Paints' strategy can be viewed as a *thrust* charging into new markets.

Cell 1 depicts a most difficult situation for local firms that compete in industries with high pressures for globalization. Thus, a **dodger** strategy is necessary. This is largely centered on cooperating through joint ventures (JVs) with MNEs, as well as sell-offs to MNEs. In the Chinese automobile industry, *all* major local automakers have entered JVs with MNEs. In the Czech Republic, Skoda was sold by the government to Volkswagen. The essence of this strategy is that to the extent that local firms are unable to successfully compete head-on against MNEs, cooperation becomes necessary. In other words, if you can't beat them, join them!

Finally, in Cell 2, some local firms, through a **contender** strategy, engage in rapid learning and then expand overseas. A number of Chinese mobile phone makers such as TCL and Bird have rapidly caught up with global heavyweights such as Motorola and Nokia. By 2003, local firms, from a 5% market share five years ago, commanded more than 50% market share in China. Engaging in a "learning race," TCL and Bird have now embarked on an overseas *thrust*. Leading video game companies in China are attempting to do the same (see Closing Case).

In China, after the initial dominance, MNEs are not always "kings of the hill." In numerous industries (such as sportswear and home appliance), many MNEs have been "dethroned." While weak local players are washed out, some of the leading local players (such as Huawei in Strategy in Action 8.1), having won the game in the highly competitive domestic environment, now challenge MNEs overseas. In the process, they become a new breed of MNEs themselves.[44] As a group, foreign MNEs in China are not as profitable as local firms (except state-owned ones).[45] The upshot? Local firms are not necessarily "sitting ducks" when facing the onslaught of MNEs in emerging economies.

Debates and Extensions

Numerous debates revolve around this sensitive area. We outline two of the most significant ones: (1) strategy versus IO economics and antitrust policy, and (2) competition versus antidumping.

Strategy versus IO Economics and Antitrust Policy

This debate is between strategy and IO economics and its public policy brainchild, competition/antitrust policy. Antitrust officials tend to be trained in economics and law but not in business. Thus, individuals with little sense of how real strategic decisions are made end up making and enforcing rules governing competition. Antitrust officials have some deep-seated suspicion of especially large companies that, if not "tamed," may allegedly leverage and abuse their competitive advantage. Such disconnect naturally breeds mutual suspicion and frustration between strategists and antitrust officials.

While this debate goes on in many parts of the world, it is in the United States that it has become most heavily contested. Because the United States has the world's oldest and most developed antitrust frameworks (dating back to the 1890 Sherman Act), the

dodger

A strategy that centers on cooperating through joint ventures with MNEs and/or sell-offs to MNEs.

contender

A strategy that centers on rapid learning and then expanding overseas.

US debate is also the most watched in the world. Therefore, our discussion here primarily draws on US materials. This does not mean that we are adopting a US-centric perspective here (which is a tendency that this book endeavors to *combat*); we just use the crucial US debate as a *case study* that may have global implications elsewhere.

In this debate, strategists have made four arguments. First, antitrust laws, influenced by IO economics, were created in response to the old realities of mostly domestic competition—the year 1890 for the Sherman Act is not a typo for 1990 (!). However, the largely global competition today indicates that a dominant firm in one country (think of Boeing) does not automatically translate into a dangerous monopoly. The existence of foreign rivals (such as Airbus) forces the large domestic incumbent to be more competitive. The "strategy as action" perspective suggests that *all* advantages are temporary and that they may disappear when rivals launch new (and often surprise) attacks. Richard D'Aveni, who coined the term "hypercompetition," argues that, "Applying traditional US antitrust enforcement in an environment of hypercompetition is like driving a Model T on an expressway. The law moves too slowly to keep up with the traffic."[46]

Second, the very actions accused to be "anticompetitive" may actually be highly "competitive" or "hypercompetitive." The hypercompetitive Microsoft was charged for its "anticompetitive" behavior by US (and EU) authorities. Its alleged crime? Not *voluntarily* helping its competitors (!).

Third, US antitrust laws create strategic confusion. Because intent to destroy rivals is a smoking gun of antitrust cases, managers are forced to use milder language. Don't say, or write in an e-mail, "We want to beat competitors!"—otherwise, managers may end up in court. In contrast, foreign firms often use war-like language: Komatsu is famous for its slogan "Encircling Caterpillar!" and Honda for "Annihilate, crush, and destroy Yamaha!" The inability to talk straight creates confusion among lower level managers and employees. Unfortunately, a confused firm is not likely to be aggressive.

Finally, US antitrust laws may be unfair, because these laws discriminate *against* US firms. If GM and Ford were to propose to jointly manufacture cars, antitrust officials would have turned them down, citing an (obvious!) intent to collude. Ironically, GM was allowed to make cars with Toyota, starting in 1983. Now after 25 years, Ford is no longer the second largest automaker in America—you guessed it, Toyota is now the second largest automaker in the United States. The upshot? American antitrust laws have helped Toyota but hurt Ford. This does not seem very fair, to say the least.

Given the importance of such a debate, it is unfortunate that *none* of the other strategy textbooks discusses it. They may be doing the field a disservice by not confronting this debate head-on. The outcome of this debate may to a large degree shape future competition in the world.

Competition versus Antidumping

Two arguments exist against the practice of imposing antidumping restrictions on foreign firms. First, because dumping centers on selling "below cost," it is often difficult (if not impossible) to prove the case given the ambiguity concerning "cost." The second argument is that if foreign firms are indeed selling below cost, so what? This is simply a (hyper)competitive action. When entering a new market, virtually all firms lose money on Day 1 (and often in Year 1). Until some point when the firm breaks even, it will lose money because it sells below cost. Domestically, cases abound of such dumping, which are perfectly legal. For example, we all receive numerous coupons in the mail offering free or cheap goods. Coupon items are frequently sold (or given away) below cost. Do consumers complain about such good deals? Probably not. "If the foreigners are kind enough (or dumb enough) to sell their goods to our country below cost, why should we complain?"[47]

A classic response is: What if, through "unfair" dumping, foreign rivals drive out local firms and then jack up prices? Given the competitive nature of most industries, it is often difficult (if not impossible) to eliminate all rivals and then recoup losses by charging higher monopoly prices. The fear of foreign monopoly is often exaggerated by special interest groups who benefit at the expense of consumers in the entire country. Joseph Stiglitz, a Nobel laureate in economics and then chief economist of the World Bank, wrote that antidumping duties "are simply naked protectionism" and one country's "fair trade laws" are often known elsewhere as "unfair trade laws."[48]

One solution is to phase out antidumping laws and use the same standards against domestic predatory pricing. Such a waiver of antidumping charges has been in place between Australia and New Zealand, between Canada and the US, and within the EU. Thus, a Canadian firm, essentially treated as a US firm, can be accused of predatory pricing but cannot be accused of dumping in the United States. Since antidumping is about "us versus them," such harmonization represents essentially an expanded notion of "us." However, domestically, as noted earlier, a predation case is very difficult to make. In such a way, competition can be fostered, aggressiveness rewarded, and "dumping" legalized.

The Savvy Strategist

If capitalism, according to Joseph Schumpeter, is about "creative destruction," then the "strategy as action" perspective highlights how such power of creative destruction is unleashed in the marketplace. Consequently, three implications for action emerge for the savvy strategist (Table 8.4). First, you need to thoroughly understand the nature of your industry that may facilitate competition or cooperation. Consider music, software, and film industries, where digital piracy is accelerating thanks to broadband Internet connections and peer-to-peer networks. Table 8.5 advises incumbents (copyright holders) to view pirates as competitors and new entrants. Thus, lower cost and enhanced differentiation, derived from the industry-based view, may prove effective in fighting digital piracy.

TABLE 8.4   Strategic Implications for Action

- Thoroughly understand the nature of your industry that may facilitate competition or cooperation.
- Strengthen resources and capabilities that more effectively compete and/or cooperate.
- Understand the rules of the game governing domestic and international competition around the world.

TABLE 8.5   Strategic Responses to Digital Piracy

- Not only compete but also cooperate with pirates by adopting a permissive stance, especially when there are strong network effects and the copyright holder is competing with rivals to get its offering established as a standard.

- Provide free samples, instead of having pirates serve the demand for samples whose quality may be questionable.

- Exercise cost leadership by lowering the price of the legal good in order to deter entry by pirates.

- Enhance differentiation by offering something extra to consumers who pay full price for the legal good.

- Change the incentives of buyers of pirate products (such as music companies' support for Apple's iTune services).

- Influence the norms associated with digital piracy, by legally challenging and punishing major offenders.

Source: Based on text in C. Hill, 2007, Digital piracy: Causes, consequences, and strategic responses, *Asia Pacific Journal of Management*, 24 (1): 9–25.

Second, you and your firm need to strengthen capabilities that more effectively compete and/or cooperate. In attacks and counterattacks, subtlety, frequency, complexity, and unpredictability are helpful. In cooperation, market similarity and mutual forbearance may be better. As Sun Tzu advised, you not only need to "know yourself," but also "know your opponents" by developing skills and instincts in competitor analysis and thinking like your opponents (see Figure 8.4).

Third, you need to understand the rules of the game governing competition around the world. Domestically, aggressive language such as "Let's beat competitors" may not be allowed in countries such as the United States. Remember, an e-mail, like a diamond, is "forever," and "deleted" e-mails are still stored on the server that can be uncovered. However, carefully crafted ambitions such as Wal-Mart's "We want to be number one in grocery business" are legal, because such wording (at least on paper) shows no illegal intention to destroy rivals. Too bad 31 US supermarket chains declared bankruptcy since Wal-Mart charged into groceries in the 1990s—just a tragic coincidence (!).[49]

The necessity to understand the rules of the game is crucial when venturing abroad. What is legal domestically may be illegal elsewhere. Imagine the shock that Chinese managers may generate when they venture abroad and approach rivals in the United States to discuss pricing—legal in China. They would be prosecuted in the United States. Another crucial area is antidumping. Many Chinese managers are surprised that their low-cost strategy is labeled "illegal" dumping in the very countries that often brag about "free market" competition. In reality, "free markets" are not free. However, managers well-versed in the rules of the game may launch subtle attacks without incurring the wrath of antidumping officials. Imports commanding less than 3% market share less than 3% in a 12-month period are regarded by US antidumping laws as "negligible imports" not worthy of investigation.[50] Thus, foreign firms not crossing such a "red line" would be safe.

In terms of the four fundamental questions, why firms differ (Question 1) and how firms behave (Question 2) boil down to how the "strategy tripod" influences competitive dynamics. What determines the scope of the firm around the globe. (Question 3) is driven, in part, by an interest in establishing mutual forbearance with multimarket rivals—in other words, "the best defense is a good offense." Finally, what determines the success and failure of firms around the globe (Question 4), to a large extent, depends on how firms carry out their competitive and cooperative actions. Overall, given that business is simultaneously war *and* peace, a winning formula, as in war and chess, is "Look ahead, reason back."

CHAPTER SUMMARY

1. *Articulate the "strategy as action" perspective*

    • Underpinning the "strategy as action" perspective, competitive dynamics refers to actions and responses undertaken by competing firms.

2. *Understand the industry conditions conducive for cooperation and collusion*

    • Such industries tend to have (1) a small number of rivals, (2) a price leader, (3) homogenous products, (4) high entry barriers, and (5) high market commonality (mutual forbearance).

3. *Explain how resources and capabilities influence competitive dynamics*

    • Resource similarity and market commonality can yield a powerful framework for competitor analysis.

4. Outline how antitrust and antidumping laws affect domestic and international competition

    • Domestically, antitrust laws focus on collusion and predatory pricing.

    • Internationally, antidumping laws discriminate against foreign firms and protect domestic firms.

5. *Identify the drivers for attacks, counterattacks, and signaling*

    • The three main types of attacks are (1) thrust, (2) feint, and (3) gambit. Counterattacks are driven by (1) awareness, (2) motivation, and (3) capability.

    • Without talking directly to competitors, firms can signal to rivals through various means.

6. *Discuss how local firms fight MNEs*

    • When confronting MNEs, local firms can choose a variety of strategic choices: (1) defender, (2) extender, (3) dodger, and (4) contender. They may not be as weak as many people believe.

7. *Participate in two leading debates concerning competitive dynamics*

    • The two leading debates are (1) strategy versus IO economics and antitrust policy, and (2) competition versus antidumping.

8. *Draw strategic implications for action*

- Thoroughly understand the nature of your industry that may facilitate competition or cooperation.

- Strengthen resources and capabilities that more effectively compete and/or cooperate.

- Understand the rules of the game governing domestic and international competition around the world.

KEY TERMS

Antidumping laws	Concentration ratio	Game theory
Antitrust laws	Contender	Market commonality
Antitrust policy	Counterattack	Market retaliation
Attack	cross-market retaliation	Multimarket competition
Capacity to punish	Defender	Mutual forbearance
Cartel	Dodger	Predatory pricing
Collusion	Dumping	Price leader
Collusive price setting	Extender	Resource similarity
Competition policy	Extraterritoriality	Thrust
Competitive dynamics	Feint	
Competitor analysis	Gambit	

CRITICAL DISCUSSION QUESTIONS

1. **ON ETHICS:** As CEO of a US firm, you feel the price war in your industry is killing profits for all firms. However, you have been warned by corporate lawyers not to openly discuss pricing with rivals, whom you know personally (you went to school with them). How would you signal your intentions?

2. **ON ETHICS:** As a CEO, you are concerned that your firm and your industry in the United States are being devastated by foreign imports. Trade lawyers suggest that you file an antidumping case against leading foreign rivals and assure you a win. Would you file an antidumping case or not? Why?

3. **ON ETHICS:** As part of a feint attack, your firm (firm A) announces that in the next year, it intends to enter country X where the competitor (firm B) is very strong. Your firm's real intention is to march into country Y where B is very weak. There is actually *no* plan to enter X. However, in the process of trying to "fool" B, customers, suppliers, investors, and the media are also being intentionally misled. What are the ethical dilemmas here? Do the pros of this action outweigh its cons?

CLOSING CASE

Fighting the Online Video Game Wars in China

The video game industry has two main segments. The first is personal computer (PC)- and console-based games, such as Nintendo's Wii, Sony's Playstation and PSP handhelds, and Microsoft's Xbox. The second is a relatively new line of online video games, where players (known as "gamers") compete in virtual worlds populated with thousands of players in large games known as massively multiplayer online games (MMOGs).

With an army of close to 40 million gamers, China is emerging as a major battleground for video game wars, commanding $1 billion in revenue in the country in 2007, a figure that could double by 2010. As you read this case, China is on course to surpass South Korea to be the top market in Asia. In the next decade, China is likely to be the world's largest online video game market.

In the 1990s, the Chinese video game industry was growing slowly and not profitably. Rampant piracy and low income levels made it unattractive to Nintendo, Sony, and Microsoft. Further, the business model adopted in developed economies, based on sales of consoles and game cartridges to make a profit, made very slow progress in China. This was because the average Chinese found it prohibitively expensive to buy consoles or PCs. High-speed Internet connection, although quickly becoming more available, was expensive and thus rare in Chinese households.

In 2001, an innovative new business model pioneered by domestic firms significantly lowered the cost of playing games. This model centered on buying pre-paid cards for a small fee to use a PC at an Internet café. Games were hosted on secure company servers and accessed from Internet cafés. "Killing two birds with one stone," this new model solved two major problems: the high cost to play and piracy. Since gamers only paid a few cents per hour, games now became affordable to numerous groups, ranging from school kids to retirees living on fixed incomes. Piracy was also largely eliminated because game content was maintained on secure company servers.

The impact of this innovation was immediate and profound. Instead of saving a lot of money to buy

expensive equipment, anyone could go to an Internet café to have a good time now. This has steered the market toward MMOGs and away from consoles. China's explosive growth has not escaped the attention of major international game companies such as Nintendo, Sony, and Microsoft. However, the China market does not play to these firms' traditional strengths in console games, thus forcing them to adapt and acquire new capabilities in MMOGs.

Foreign firms eyeing China will find the market dominated by three strong domestic players: (1) Shanda, (2) NetEase, and (3) The9, Ltd. Shanda was a leader in the pre-paid card movement and, as a result, was successfully listed on NASDAQ (as SNDA) in 2004. However, facing rising competition, Shanda in 2005 started to give away games for free and to charge for in-game items and upgrades. NetEase is the current market leader, strong on content built on Chinese mythology. Its top-selling game *Westward Journey* enjoyed 1.3 million *concurrent* users during its peak play time. The company generating the hottest buzz is The9, Ltd., which obtained a license for *World of Warcraft* (*WoW*) from the Irvine, California-based Blizzard Entertainment. *WoW* is the most successful online video game in history, generating close to $1 billion a year in worldwide income. In China, *WoW* smashed opening-day sale records for the industry and now boasts more than 3.5 million subscribers (including an estimated 100,000 "gold farmers," gamers who are employed *full*-time to play *WoW* in order to acquire virtual currency to be sold to other players for real money). In its first year, 2006, *WoW* raked in 99% of The9's $126 million revenue, which enabled The9 to fund new game development activities.

For foreign firms salivating for the spoils of China's video game wars, the fundamental question is: How to play the games when industry rules are fast changing and unpredictable? Sony and Microsoft are cultivating the console market. Microsoft operates an incubation center in Chengdu to help third-party developers create Xbox-compatible content. Sony is also working with local game developers. The Walt Disney Internet Group is partnering with Shanda to develop new games that include Disney characters. Blizzard has acquired a game development studio in Shanghai to incorporate China flavor into its next-generation games.

Not to be left alone, the Chinese government has intervened in two ways. First, upset with game addiction and other health concerns (one gamer died in 2007 after playing three consecutive *days* in an Internet café), the government has now demanded that game companies include "fatigue controls" that will halt the game after several hours. Second, the Ministry of Culture announced that it would ban games "threatening state security, damaging the nation's glory, disturbing social order, and infringing on others' legitimate rights." Starting in 2004, the Ministry every year published a list of recommended games that were deemed "healthy" and "intelligent." Not surprisingly, all 35 games on these lists, as of 2008, were domestic games.

Finally, Chinese firms are not likely to sit around to see their home market invaded. Building on domestic success, they may become major game exporters to Asia and the rest of the world. Chinese firm Kingsoft's *Perfect World* has already entered Japan and South Korea. In 2008, China's CDC Games launched in North America a *manga*-style MMOG, *Lunia*, which is very popular in China and Japan.

Sources: Based on (1) BBC, 2007, China censors online video games, June 1, newsvote.bbc.co.uk; (2) J. Dibbell, 2007, The life of the Chinese gold farmer, *The New York Times*, June 17, www.nytimes.com; (3) R. Ewing, 2007, China's online video game wars, *China Business Review*, July–August: 45–49; (4) Money Central, 2008, CDC Games launches popular manga-style online video game in North America, February 22, news.moneycentral.msn.com; (5) Xinhua, 2008, Chinese authority lists 10 "suitable" e-games for teenagers, February 9, www.xinhuanet.com.

Case Discussion Questions

1. Drawing on industry-based considerations, explain why China's video game industry has experienced such explosive growth.

2. What differentiates winning firms from losing and also-run firms in this industry?

3. Do foreign game companies, such as Nintendo, Sony, Microsoft, and Blizzard, have what it takes to win in China?

4. Using Figure 8.9, explain in which cell(s) leading domestic Chinese video game companies are located. Further, predict the outcome of the video game wars waged between Chinese and foreign game companies.

Notes

Journal acronyms *AME–Academy of Management Executive; AMJ–Academy of Management Journal; AMR–Academy of Management Review; APJM–Asia Pacific Journal of Management; BW–Business Week; CJE–Canadian Journal of Economics; HBR – Harvard Business Review; IE–International Economy; JEP–Journal of Economic Perspectives; JIBS–Journal of International Business Studies; JIM–Journal of International Management; JM–Journal of Management; JMS–Journal of Management Studies; JWB–Journal of World Business; LRP–Long Range Planning; MS–Management Science; OSc–Organization Science; SMJ–Strategic Management Journal*

1. D. Ketchen, C. Snow, & V. Hoover, 2004, Research on competitive dynamics, *JM*, 30: 779–804.

2. L. Capron & O. Chatain, 2008, Competitors' resource-oriented strategies, *AMR*, 33: 97–121.

3. V. Rindova, M. Becerra, & I. Contardo, 2004, Enacting competitive wars, *AMR*, 29: 670–686.

4. J. Gimeno & C. Woo, 1999, Multimarket contact, economies of scope, and firm performance, *AMJ*, 43: 239–259.

5. C. Campbell, G. Ray, & W. Muhanna, 2005, Search and collusion in electronic markets, *MS*, 51: 497–507; M. Semadeni, 2006, Minding your distance, *SMJ*, 27: 169–187.

6. M. Benner, 2007, The incumbent discount, *AMR*, 32: 703–720; C. Christensen, 1997, *The Innovator's Dilemma*, Boston: Harvard Business School Press; C. Hill & F. Rothaermel, 2003, The performance of incumbent firms in the face of radical technological innovation, *AMR*, 28: 257–274.

7. J. Barney, 2002, *Gaining and Sustaining Competitive Advantage* (p. 359), Upper Saddle River, NJ: Prentice Hall. See also J. Stephen, J. Murmann, W. Boeker, & J. Goodstein, 2003, Bringing managers into theories of multimarket competition, *OSc*, 14: 403–421.

8. M. Chen, 1996, Competitor analysis and interfirm rivalry (p. 106), *AMR*, 21: 100–134.

9. D. Spar, 1994, *The Cooperative Edge: The Internal Politics of International Cartels* (p. 5), Ithaca, NY: Cornell UP.

10. J. R. Baum & S. Wally, 2003, Strategic decision speed and firm performance, *SMJ*, 24: 1107–1129.

11. This paragraph draws heavily from *The Economist*, 2005, A market for ideas, October 22: 1–18.

12. W. Ferrier, K. Smith, & C. Grimm, 1999, The role of competitive action in market share erosion and industry dethronement, *AMJ*, 42: 372–388.

13. D. Basdeo, K. Smith, C. Grimm, V. Rindova, & P. Derfus, 2006, The impact of market actions on firm reputation, *SMJ*, 27: 1205–1219; G. Vroom & J. Gimeno, 2007, Ownership form, managerial incentives, and the intensity of rivalry, *AMJ*, 50: 901–922.

14. C. Pegels, Y. Song, & B. Yang, 2000, Management heterogeneity, competitive interaction groups, and firm performance, *SMJ*, 21: 911–923.

15. B. Golden & H. Ma, 2003, Mutual forbearance, *AMR*, 28: 479–493; A. Kalnins, 2004, Divisional multimarket contact within and between multiunit organizations, *AMJ*, 47: 117–128.

16. Chen, 1996, Competitor analysis and interfirm rivalry (p. 107). See also W. Desarbo, R. Grewal, & J. Wind, 2006, Who competes with whom?, *SMJ*, 27: 101–129; L. Fuentelsaz & J. Gomez, 2006, Multipoint competition, strategic similarity, and entry into geographic markets, *SMJ*, 27: 477–499.

17. H. Ma, 1998, Mutual forbearance in international business (p. 140), *JIM*, 4: 129–147.

18. N. Kumar, 2006, Strategies to fight low-cost rivals, *HBR*, December: 104–112.

19. E. Graham & D. Richardson, 1997, Issue overview (p. 5), in E. Graham & D. Richardson (eds.), *Global Competition Policy*, 3–46, Washington: Institute for International Economics.

20. J. Clougherty, 2005, Antitrust holdup source, cross-national institutional variation, and corporate political strategy implications for domestic mergers in a global context, *SMJ*, 26: 769–790.

21. M. W. Peng, 2009, *Global Business* (p. 306), Cincinnati: South-Western Cengage Learning.

22. E. Fox, 1997, US and EU competition law (pp. 351–352), in E. Graham & D. Richardson (eds.), *Global Competition Policy*, 339–354, Washington: Institute for International Economics.

23. *The Economist*, 2007, A matter of sovereignty, September 22: 75–76.

24. R. Lipstein, 1997, Using antitrust principles to reform antidumping law (p. 408, original italics), in E. Graham & D. Richardson (eds.), *Global Competition Policy*, 405–438, Washington: Institute for International Economics.

25. OECD, 1996, *Trade and Competition: Frictions after the Uruguay Round* (p. 18), Paris: OECD.

26. T. Prusa, 2001, On the spread and impact of antidumping (p. 598), *CJE*, 34: 591–611.

27. S. Marsh, 1998, Creating barriers for foreign competitors, *SMJ*, 19: 25–37.

28. M. Finger, F. Ng, & S. Wangchuk, 2001, Antidumping as safeguard policy (p. 6), Working paper, World Bank.

29. This section draws heavily from R. McGrath, M. Chen, & I. MacMillan, 1998, Multimarket maneuvering in uncertain spheres of influence, *AMR*, 23: 724–740.

30. M. Chen & I. MacMillan, 1992, Nonresponse and delayed response to competitive moves, *AMJ*, 35: 359–370.

31. D. Yoffie & M. Kwak, 2001, *Judo Strategy* (p. 193), Boston: Harvard Business School Press.

32. G. Stalk, 2006, Curveball: Strategies to fool the competition, *HBR*, September: 115–122.

33. I. MacMillan, A. van Putten, & R. McGrath, 2003, Global gamesmanship, *HBR*, May: 62–71.

34. M. Chen, K. Su, & W. Tsai, 2007, Competitive tension, *AMJ*, 50: 101–118; T. Yu & A. Cannella, 2007, Rivalry between multinational enterprises, *AMJ*, 50: 665–686.

35. W. C. Kim & R. Mauborgne, 2005, *Blue Ocean Strategy*, Boston: Harvard Business School Press.

36. M. Cusumano & D. Yoffie, 1998, *Competing on Internet Time*, New York: Free Press.

37. F. Knickerbocker, 1973, *Oligopolistic Reaction and Multinational Enterprise*, Boston: Harvard Business School Press. See also G. McNamara & P. Vaaler, 2000, The influence of competitive positioning and rivalry in emerging market risk assessment, *JIBS*, 31: 337–347; K. Ito & E. Rose, 2002, Foreign direct investment location strategies in the tire industry, *JIBS*, 33: 593–602; L. Thomas & K. Weigelt, 2000, Product location choice and firm capabilities, *SMJ*, 21: 897–909.

38. J. Baum & H. Korn, 1996, Competitive dynamics of interfirm rivalry, *AMJ*, 39: 255–291.

39. *USA Today*, 2005, Price remarks by Toyota chief could be illegal, June 10: 5B.

40. T. Schelling, 1980, *The Strategy of Conflict*, Cambridge, MA: Harvard University Press.

41. S. Evenett, M. Levenstein, & V. Suslow, 2001, International cartel enforcement (p. 1226), *IE*, 24: 1221–1245.

42. This section draws heavily from N. Dawar & T. Frost, 1999, Competing with giants, *HBR*, March–April: 119–129.

43. D. Lavie & A. Fiegenbaum, 2000, Strategic reaction of domestic firms to foreign MNC dominance, *LRP*, 33: 651–672.

44. J. Mathews, 2006, Dragon multinationals, *APJM*, 23: 5–27.

45. D. Xu, Y. Pan, C. Wu, & B. Yim, 2006, Performance of domestic and foreign-invested enterprises in China, *JWB*, 41: 261–274.

46. D'Aveni, 1994, *Hypercompetition* (p. 358); J. Kerstetter, 2004, Trustbusters are on the wrong trail, *BW*, June 21: 48.

47. R. Griffin & M. Pustay, 2003, *International Business*, 3rd ed. (p. 241), Upper Saddle River, NJ: Prentice Hall.

48. J. Stiglitz, 2002, *Globalization and Its Discontent* (pp. 172–173), New York: Norton.

49. C. Fishman, 2006, *The Wal-Mart Effect*, New York: Penguin.

50. M. Czinkota & M. Kotabe, 1997, A marketing perspective of the US International Trade Commission's antidumping actions (p. 183), *JWB*, 32: 169–187.

Competition in the Chinese Automobile Industry[1]

Qingjiu (Tom) Tao
Lehigh University

How do various foreign and domestic automakers compete in the fastest growing automobile market in the world?

For automakers seeking relief from a global price war caused by overcapacity and recession, China is the only game in town. With just ten vehicles per 1,000 residents in China as of 2006 (as opposed to 940 in the United States and 584 in Western Europe), there seems to be plenty of growth opportunities. Not surprisingly, nearly every major auto company has jumped into China, quickly turning the country into a new battleground for dominance in this global industry. In addition, China has become a major auto parts supplier. Of the world's top 100 auto parts suppliers, 70% have a presence in China.

China vaulted past Japan in 2006 to become the world's number-two vehicle market (after the United States). In 2006, car sales in China were up 37%, and sales of all vehicles including trucks and buses (7.2 million in total) were up 25%. Reports of record sales, new production, and new venture formations were plenty. After China's accession to the World Trade Organization (WTO) in 2001, the industry has been advancing by leaps and bounds. At the global level, China has moved to the third position in production behind the United States and Japan, and is slated to produce 8.5 to 9 million vehicles in 2007. Around 50% of the world's activity in terms of capacity expansion is seen in China (see Exhibit 1).

Because the Chinese government does not approve wholly owned subsidiaries for foreign carmakers (even after the WTO accession), foreign firms interested in final-assembly operations have to set up joint ventures (JVs) or licensing deals with domestic players. By the mid-1990s, most major global auto firms had managed to enter the country through these means (Exhibit 2).

Among the European companies, Volkswagen (VW), one of the first entrants (see the following), has dominated the passenger car market. In addition, Fiat-Iveco and Citroen are expanding.

Japanese and Korean automakers are relatively late entrants. In 2003, Toyota finally committed $1.3 billion to a 50/50 JV. Guangzhou Honda, Honda's JV, quadrupled its capacity by 2004. Formed in 2003, Nissan's new JV with Dongfeng, which is the same partner for the Citroen JV, is positioned to allow Nissan to make a full-fledged entry. Meanwhile, Korean auto players are also keen to participate in the China race, with Hyundai and Kia having commenced JV production recently.

American auto companies have also made significant inroads into China. General Motors (GM) has an important JV in Shanghai, whose cumulative investment by 2006 would be $5 billion. Although Ford does not have a high-profile JV as GM, it nevertheless established crucial strategic linkages with several of China's second-tier automakers. DaimlerChrysler's Beijing Jeep venture, established since the early 1980s, has continued to maintain its presence.

The Evolution of Foreign Direct Investment (FDI) in the Automobile Industry

In the late 1970s, when Chinese leaders started to transform the planned economy to a market economy, they realized that China's roads were largely populated by inefficient, unattractive, and often unreliable vehicles that needed to be replaced. However, importing large quantities of vehicles would be a major drain on

---

[1] This case was written by Qingjiu (Tom) Tao (Lehigh University). © Qingjiu (Tom) Tao. Reprinted with permission.

EXHIBIT 1   Automobile Production Volume and Growth Rate in China (1996–2006)

YEAR	1996	1997	1998	1999	2000	2001	2002	2003	2004	2005	2006
VOLUME (IN MILLIONS)	1.475	1.585	1.629	1.832	2.068	2.347	3.251	4.443	5.070	5.718	7.280
GROWTH RATE	1.5%	7.5%	2.8%	12.5%	12.9%	13.2%	38.5%	37.7%	14.1%	12.8%	27.3%

Source: Yearbook of China's Automobile Industry (1996–2006).

EXHIBIT 2   Timing and Initial Investment of Major Car Producers

	FORMATION	INITIAL INVESTMENT (IN MILLIONS OF US$)	FOREIGN EQUITY	CHINESE PARTNER	FOREIGN PARTNER
Beijing Jeep	1983	223.93	42.4%	Beijing Auto Works	Chrysler
Shanghai Volkswagen	1985	263.41	50%	SAIC	Volkswagen
Guangzhou Peugeot	1985	131.4	22%	Guangzhou Auto Group	Peugeot
FAW VW	1990	901.84	40%	First Auto Works	Volkswagen
Wuhan Shenlong Citroen	1992	505.22	30%	Second Auto Works	Citroen
Shanghai GM	1997	604.94	50%	SAIC	GM
Guangzhou Honda	1998	887.22	50%	Guangzhou Auto Group	Honda
Changan Ford	2001	100.00	50%	Changan Auto motors	Ford
Beijing Hyundai	2002	338.55	50%	Beijing Auto Group	Hyundai
Tianjin Toyota	2003	1300.00	50%	First Auto Works	Toyota

the limited hard currency reserves. China thus saw the need to modernize its automobile industry. Attracting FDI through JVs with foreign companies seemed to be ideal. However, unlike the new China at the dawn of the 21st century, which attracted automakers of every stripe, China in the late 1970s and early 1980s was not regarded as attractive by many global automakers. In the early 1980s, Toyota, for example, refused to establish JVs with Chinese firms even when invited by the Chinese authorities (Toyota chose to invest in a more

promising market, the United States, in the 1980s). In the first wave, three JVs were established during 1983–1984 by VW, American Motors,[2] and Peugeot, in Shanghai, Beijing, and Guangzhou, respectively. These three JVs thus started the two decades of FDI in China's automobile industry.

FDI activities occurred in two distinct phases in China's automobile industry. The first phase was from the early 1980s to the early 1990s, as exemplified by the three early JVs mentioned previously. The second phase

---

[2] American Motors was later acquired by Chrysler, which, in turn, was acquired by Daimler to form DaimlerChrysler. More recently (in 2007), DaimlerChrysler divested the Chrysler part. Between 1983 and 2005, the JV in China maintained its name as "Beijing Jeep Corporation" while experiencing ownership changes. In 2005, its name was changed to "Beijing Benz-DaimlerChrysler Automotive Co., Ltd." At the time of this writing (late 2007), it is not clear how the JV's name may change further to reflect the divestiture of Chrysler.

EXHIBIT 3   Evolution of Relative Market Share among Major Auto Manufacturers in China

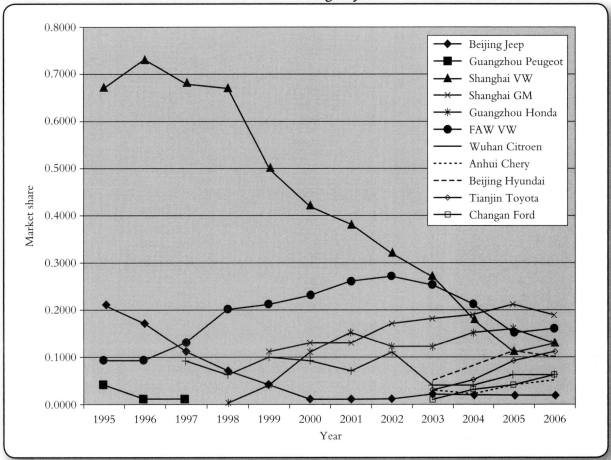

was from the mid-1990s to the present. Because of the reluctance of foreign car companies, only approximately 20 JVs were established by the end of 1989. FDI flows into this industry started to accelerate sharply from 1992. The accumulated number of foreign-invested enterprises was 120 in 1993, a number that skyrocketed to 604 in 1998, with the cumulated investment reaching $20.9 billion.

The boom of the auto market, especially during the early 1990s, brought significant profits to early entrants such as Shanghai VW and Beijing Jeep. The bright prospect attracted more multinationals to invest. This new wave of investment then resulted in an overcapacity. Combined with the changing customer base from primarily selling fleets to government agencies, state-owned enterprises, and taxi companies to selling individual cars to private buyers, the auto market has turned into a truly competitive arena. The WTO entry in 2001 has further intensified the competition as government regulations weaken. Given the government mandate for JV entries and the limited number of worthy local firms as partners, multinationals have to fight their way in to secure the last few available local partners. By the end of 2002, almost all major Chinese motor vehicle assemblers set up JVs with foreign firms. For the numerous foreign automakers that entered China, the road to the Great Wall has been a bumpy and crowded one. Some firms lead, some struggle, and some have had to drop out. The leading players are profiled in Exhibit 3.

Volkswagen

After long and difficult negotiations that began in 1978, VW in 1984 entered a 50/50 JV with the Shanghai Automotive Industrial Corporation (SAIC) to produce the Santana model using completely knocked down (CKD) kits. The Santana went on to distinguish itself as China's first mass-produced modern passenger car. As a result, VW managed to establish a solid market position. Four years later, VW built on its first-mover advantage and secured a second opening in the China market when the central authorities decided to establish two additional passenger car JVs. After competing successfully against GM, Ford, Nissan, Renault, Peugeot, and Citroen, VW was selected to set up a second JV with the First Auto Works (FAW) in Changchun in northeast China in 1988 for CKD assembly of the Audi 100 and the construction of a state-of-the-art auto plant to produce the VW Jetta in 1990.

Entering the China market in the early 1980s, VW took a proactive approach in spite of great potential risks. The German multinational not only committed enormous financial resources but also practiced a rather bold approach in its dealings in China. This involved a great deal of high-level political interaction with China's central and local government authorities for which the German government frequently lent its official support. Moreover, VW was willing to avail the Chinese partners of a broad array of technical and financial resources from its worldwide operations. For example, in 1990 VW allowed FAW a 60% stake in its JV while furnishing most of the manufacturing technology and equipment for its new FAW-Volkswagen Jetta plant in Changchun. Moreover, VW has endeavored to raise the quality of locally produced components and parts. Undoubtedly, for the remainder of the 1980s and most of the 1990s, VW enjoyed significant first-mover advantages. With a market share (Shanghai VW and FAW VW combined) of more than 70% for passenger cars over a decade, VW, together with its Chinese partners, benefited considerably from the scarcity of high-quality passenger cars and the persistence of a seller's market.

However, by the late 1990s, the market became a more competitive buyer's market. As the leading incumbent, VW has been facing vigorous challenges brought by its global rivals, which by the late 1990s had made serious commitments to compete in China. Consequently, VW's passenger car market share in China dropped from over 70% in 1999 to 39% in 2004. In 2005, GM took the number-one position in China from FAW VW. How to defend VW's market position thus is of paramount importance.

General Motors

In 1995, GM and SAIC, which was also VW's partner, signed a 50/50, $1.57 billion JV agreement—GM's first JV in China—to construct a greenfield plant in Shanghai. The new plant was designed to produce 100,000 sedans per year, and it was decided to produce two Buick models modified for China. The plant was equipped with the latest automotive machinery and robotics and was furnished with process technology transferred from GM's worldwide operations. Initially, GM Shanghai attracted a barrage of criticisms about the huge size of its investment and the significant commitments to transfer technology and design capabilities to China. These criticisms notwithstanding, GM management reiterated on numerous occasions that China was expected to become the biggest automotive market in the world within two decades and that China represented the single most important emerging market for GM.

Since launching Buick in China in 1998, GM literally started from scratch. Unlike its burdens at home, GM is not saddled with billions in pensions and health care costs. Its costs are competitive with rivals, its reputation does not suffer, and it does not need to shell out $4,000 per vehicle in incentives to lure new buyers—even moribund brands such as Buick are held in high esteem in China. Consequently, profits are attractive: The $437 million profits GM made in 2003 in China, selling just 386,000 cars, compares favorably with $811 million profits it made in North America on sales of 5.6 million autos. In 2004, GM had about 10,000 employees in China and operated six JVs and two wholly owned foreign enterprises (which were allowed to be set up more recently in non-final assembly operations). Boasting a combined manufacturing capacity of 530,000 vehicles sold under the Buick, Chevrolet, and Wuling nameplates, GM offers the widest portfolio of products among JV manufacturers in China. Seeing China sales rise 32% to nearly 880,000 vehicles, GM recently announced plans to build hybrids in China.

Peugeot

Together with VW and American Motors (the original partner for the Beijing Jeep JV), Peugeot was one of the first three entrants in the Chinese automobile industry. It started to search for JV partners in 1980 and in 1985 set up a JV, Guangzhou Peugeot, in south China. The JV mainly produced the Peugeot 504 and 505, both out-of-date models of the 1970s. While many domestic users complained about the high fuel consumption, difficult maintenance, and expensive parts, the French car manufacturer netted huge short-term profits at approximately $480 million by selling a large amount of CKD kits and parts. Among its numerous problems, the JV also reportedly repatriated most of its profits and made relatively few changes to its 1970s-era products, whereas VW in Shanghai reinvested profits and refined its production, introducing a new "Santana 2000" model in the mid-1990s. Around 1991, Guangzhou Peugeot accounted for a nearly 16% share of the domestic passenger car market. But it began to go into the red in 1994, with its losses amounting to $349 million by 1997, forcing Peugeot to retreat from China. It sold its interest in the JV to Honda in 1998 (see later in this case).

While the sour memories of the disappointing performance of its previous JV were still there, Peugeot (now part of PSA Peugeot Citroen) decided to return to the battlefield in 2003. This time, the Paris-based carmaker seemed loaded with ambitious expectations to grab a slice of the country's increasingly appealing auto market sparked by the post-WTO boom. One of its latest moves is an agreement in 2003 under which PSA Peugeot Citroen would further its partnership with Hubei-based Dongfeng Motor, one of China's top three automakers that originally signed up as a JV partner with Citroen, to produce Peugeot vehicles in China. According to the new deal, a Peugeot production platform would be installed at the Wuhan plant of the JV, Dongfeng Citroen. Starting from 2004, the

new facility has turned out car models tailored for domestic consumers, including the Peugeot 307, one of the most popular models in Europe since 2003.

Honda

Peugeot's 1998 pullout created a vacuum for foreign manufacturers that missed the first wave of FDI into this industry. These late entrants included Daimler-Benz, GM, Opel (a German subsidiary of GM), and Hyundai. Against these rivals, Honda entered and won the fierce bidding war for the takeover of an existing auto plant in Guangzhou of the now defunct Guangzhou Peugeot JV. The partner selection process followed a familiar pattern: Beijing was pitting several bidders against each other to extract a maximum of capital, technology, and manufacturing capabilities, as well as the motor vehicle types deemed appropriate for China. Honda pledged to invest $887 million and committed the American version of the Honda Accord, whose production started in 1999. Two years later, Guangzhou Honda added the popular Odyssey minivan to its product mix. In less than two years, Honda had turned around the loss-making Peugeot facility into one of China's most profitable passenger car JVs.

It is important to note that well before its JV with the Guangzhou Auto Group, Honda had captured a significant market share with exports of the popular Honda Accord and a most effective network of dealerships and service and repair facilities all over China. These measures helped Honda not only attain an excellent reputation and brand recognition, but also strengthened Honda's bargaining power with Chinese negotiators.

Emerging Domestic Players

The original thinking behind the Open Door policy of China's auto market forming JVs with multinationals was to access capital and technology and develop Chinese domestic partners into self-sustaining independent players. However, this market-for-technology strategy failed to achieve its original goal. Cooperation with foreign car companies did bring in capital and technology, but also led to an overdependence on foreign technology and an inadequate capacity (or even incentive) for independent innovations. By forming JVs with all the major domestic manufacturers and controlling brands, designs, and key technologies, multinational companies effectively eliminated domestic competition for most of the last two decades. Only in the last few years have Chinese manufacturers started to design, produce, and market independent brands. In 2006, domestic companies controlled some 27% of the domestic market (mostly in entry- to mid-level segments). They have become masters at controlling costs and keeping prices down, with a typical Chinese auto worker earning $1.95 an hour compared to his German counterpart who makes $49.50 an hour.

Ironically, the breakthrough came from newly established manufacturers without foreign partners. Government-owned Chery (Qirui) Automobile, which started with $25 million using secondhand Ford production equipment, produced only 2,000 vehicles six year ago.[3] In 2006, it sold 305,236 cars, a surge of 118% over 2005, with plans to double that again by 2008. Privately owned Geely Group obtained its license only six years ago and began with crudely built copycat hatchbacks powered by Toyota-designed engines. With an initial output of 5,000 cars in 2001, Geely today produces 180,000 a year, with various models of sedans and sports cars, including those equipped with self-engineered six-cylinder engines.

Beyond the domestic market, Chery now exports cars to 29 countries. In 2006, the company produced 305,000 cars and exported 50,000. Chery cars are expected to hit the European market later in 2007. It signed a deal with DaimlerChrysler to produce Dodge brand vehicles for the US and Western Europe markets in the near future. Geely Group plans to buy a stake in the UK taxi-maker Manganese Bronze Holdings and start producing London's black taxis in Shanghai. It also aims to sell its affordable small vehicles in the US within several years.

In an effort to get closer to overseas markets, the Chinese players are starting to open overseas factories, too. Chery has assembly operations in Russia, Indonesia, Iran, and Egypt. The company now is planning to extend its reach in South America by opening an assembly plant to produce its Tigo brand sport-utility vehicle in Uruguay. Brilliance produces vehicles in three overseas factories in North Korea, Egypt, and Vietnam, and Geely has a factory in Russia.

The Road Ahead

Looking ahead, the tariff and non-tariff barriers will gradually be removed in post-WTO China. Increasing vehicle imports after trade liberalization will put pressure on the existing JVs that assemble cars in China and force them to improve their global competitiveness. Otherwise, locally produced vehicles, even by JVs with multinational automakers, with no advantage in regards to models, prices, sales networks, component supplies, and client services, will have a hard time surviving.

Despite China's low per capita income overall, a large wealthy entrepreneurial class has risen with significant purchasing power thanks to two decades of economic development. The average price of passenger cars sold in China in 2008 is about $20,000, whereas the average car price in countries such as Brazil, India, and Indonesia is $6,000–$8,000. China, for example, is BMW's biggest market for the most expensive imported 7-Series sedan, outstripping even the United States—even though Chinese buyers pay double what Americans pay and often in cash.

However, vehicle imports will not exceed 8% of the market in the foreseeable future. China's automobile industry, which has almost exclusively focused on the domestic market, still has much room for future development and will maintain an annual growth rate of 20% for the next few years. In

---

[3] In May 2005, GM sued Chery in a Chinese court for counterfeiting the design of a vehicle developed by GM's South Korean subsidiary Daewoo. While this case created some media sensation, in November 2005, the parties, encouraged by the Chinese government, reached "an undisclosed settlement." The settlement terms were not revealed. It was not known whether Chery had to pay for its alleged infringement or whether it was barred from using the purportedly infringing design (http://iplaw.blogs.com/content/2005/11/gm_piracy_case_.html).

the long run, as domestic growth inevitably slows, market competition and industry consolidation will become fiercer. The entry barrier will be higher and resource development will become more crucial to the sustainability of competitive advantage. In order to survive and maintain healthy and stable growth, China's JV and indigenous automobile companies, having established a solid presence domestically, must be able to offer their own products in a competitive manner in the global market.

No doubt, the road to success in China's automobile industry is fraught with potholes. As latecomers, Hyundai, Toyota, Honda, and Nissan had fewer options in the hunt for appropriate JV partners and market positioning than did first-mover VW in the 1980s. All through the early 1990s, foreign auto companies were solicited to enter China and encountered little domestic competition or challenge. This situation has changed significantly. Today, the industry is crowded with the world's top players vying for a share of this dynamic market. Success in China may also significantly help contribute to the corporate bottom line for multinationals that often struggle elsewhere. For example, China, having surpassed the United States, is now Volkswagen's largest market outside of Germany. One-quarter of Volkswagen's corporate profits now come from China.

Two competing scenarios now confront executives contemplating a move into China or expansion within China: (1) At the current rate of rapid foreign and domestic investment, the Chinese industry will rapidly develop overcapacity. Given the inevitable cooling of the economy's overall growth, a bloodbath propelled by self-inflicted wounds, such as massive incentives, looms on the horizon. (2) Given the low penetration of cars among the vast Chinese population whose income is steadily on the rise, such a rising tide will be able to lift all boats—or wheels—for a long while to come.

Sources: Based on (1) W. Arnold, 2003, The Japanese automobile industry in China, JPRI Working Paper No. 95; (2) *The Economist*, 2003, Cars in China: The great leap forward, February 1: 53–54; (3) G. Edmondson, 2004, Volkswagen slips into reverse, *BusinessWeek*, August 9: 40; (4) H. Huang, 1999, Policy reforms and foreign direct investment: The case of the Chinese automotive industry, *Fourin*, 9 (1): 3–66; (5) M. W. Peng, 2000, Controlling the foreign agent: How governments deal with multinationals in a transition economy, *Management International Review*, 40 (2): 141–166; (6) Q. Tao, 2004, The Road to Success: A Resource-Base View of Joint Venture Evolution in China's Auto Industry, Ph.D. dissertation, University of Pittsburgh; (7) D. Welch, 2004: GM: Gunning it in China, *BusinessWeek*, June 21: 112–115; (8) G. Zeng & W. Peng, 2003, China's automobile industry boom, *Business Briefing: Global Automobile Manufacturing & Technology 2003*, 20–22. (9) E. Thun, 2006. *Changing lanes in China.* (10) D. Roberts, 2007, China's auto industry takes on the world, *BusinessWeek*, March 28.

Case Discussion Questions

1. Why do all multinational automakers choose to use FDI to enter this industry? What are the drawbacks of using other entry modes such as exporting and licensing?

2. Some early entrants (such as Volkswagen) succeeded, while some early entrants (such as Peugeot) failed. Similarly, some late entrants (such as Honda) did well and some late entrants (such as Ford) continue to struggle. From a resource-based standpoint, what role does entry timing play in determining performance?

3. From an institution-based view, explain the initial reluctance of most multinational automakers to enter China in the 1980s. What happened that made them change their minds more recently?

4. You are a board member at one of the major multinational companies and have just heard two presentations at a board meeting outlining two contrasting scenarios regarding the outlook of the Chinese automobile industry in the last paragraph of the case. Would you vote "Yes" or "No" for a $2 billion proposal to fund a major FDI project in China?

Unilever's "Fair & Lovely" Whitening Cream[1]

Aneel Karnani
University of Michigan

Unilever is aggressively marketing "Fair & Lovely,"—a skin whitening cream in many countries in Asia and Africa—and in particular, India. It is doing well financially. However, it is not necessarily doing good, and its actions may have negative implications on the public welfare.

The idea that companies can do well by doing good has caught the attention of executives, academics, and public officials. The annual report of virtually every large company claims that its mission is to serve some larger social purpose besides making profits. The theme of the Academy of Management conference in 2006 asserts that "there is more to corporate success than the financial bottom line," and goes on to argue that companies can accomplish some positive social goals without suffering financially. Leading international institutions, such as the United Nations (UN), also accept this logic and seek to create partnerships between the private sector, governments, and civil society. For example, the UN Global Compact promotes good corporate citizenship by asking companies to assume responsibilities in the areas of human rights, labor standards, environment, and anti-corruption.

The popular "bottom of the pyramid" (BOP) proposition argues that large private firms can make significant profits by selling to the poor, and in the process help eradicate poverty (Prahalad, 2004). The World Resources Institute, a leading think tank, has based its "development through enterprise" program on the notion of "eradicating poverty through profit: making business work for the poor." C. K. Prahalad further argues that "it is absolutely possible to do well while doing good" (*Time*, 2005).

According to the "doing well by doing good" (DWDG) proposition, firms have a corporate social responsibility to achieve some larger social goals, and can do so without a financial sacrifice. This appealing proposition that you can have your cake and eat it too has convinced many people.

But, is the DWDG proposition empirically valid? To help answer this question, this paper examines in depth the case of "Fair & Lovely," a skin whitening cream marketed by Unilever in many countries in Asia and Africa, and, in particular, India by Hindustan Lever Limited (HLL), the Indian subsidiary of Unilever. I chose this particular case study because Fair & Lovely is mentioned as a positive example of doing good by Hammond and Prahalad (2004), two of the most visible proponents of the BOP proposition. Both Unilever and HLL are frequently mentioned in the BOP literature as examples of companies doing good (for example, Prahalad, 2004; Balu, 2001; Hart, 2005). HLL explicitly states on its website that its corporate social responsibility is rooted in its Corporate Purpose—the belief that "to succeed requires the highest standards of corporate behaviour towards our employees, consumers and the societies and world in which we live." Niall Fitzgerald (2003), then Chairman of Unilever, said in a speech that "CSR is inherent in everything we do." The choice of this case study is also appropriate because both Unilever and HLL are doing well; Unilever is one of the most successful multinational firms in the fast-moving consumer goods business, while HLL is the dominant firm in its markets in India.

---

[1] This case was written by Aneel Karnani (University of Michigan) and originally published as "Doing Well by Doing Good—Case Study: "'Fair and Lovely' Whitening Cream" in *Strategic Management Journal,* 28 (2007): 1351–1357. © 2007 John Wiley & Sons, Ltd. Reprinted with permission. Case discussion questions are added by Mike W. Peng.

This paper shows that Fair & Lovely is indeed doing well; it is one of the more profitable and faster growing brands in Unilever and HLL's portfolios. It is, however, not doing good, and I demonstrate Fair & Lovely's negative impact on the public welfare. One counterfactual example does not invalidate the DWDG proposition, nor its subset, the BOP proposition. However, the empirical support for these propositions is largely anecdotal (for example, Prahalad, 2004). It is, therefore, reasonable to use the case study approach to discuss the validity and limitations of these propositions. Moreover, the choice of the case—one that *a priori* would be expected to support the DWDG proposition—strengthens the counter argument. I conclude with thoughts on alternative mechanisms to reconcile the divergence between private profits and public welfare.

Doing Well

Fair & Lovely, the largest selling skin whitening cream in the world, is clearly doing well. First launched in India in 1975, Fair & Lovely held a commanding 50%–70% share of the skin whitening market in India in 2006, a market that is valued at over $200 million and growing at 10%–15% per annum (Marketing Practice, 2006). Fair & Lovely was the second-fastest growing brand in HLL's portfolio of 63 brands, with a growth rate of 21.5% per year (HLL, 2002). Its two closest rival competitors, both produced by local Indian firms, CavinKare's brand Fairever and Godrej's FairGlow, have a combined market share of only 16%. Claiming to possess a customer base of 27 million Indian customers who use its product regularly, Fair & Lovely has successfully launched new product formulations, from lotions to gels and soaps. Fair & Lovely is marketed by Unilever in 40 countries in Asia, Africa, and the Middle East, with India being the largest single market. Fair & Lovely is certainly doing well financially.

Created by HLL's research laboratories, Fair & Lovely claims to offer dramatic whitening results in just six weeks. A package sold in Egypt displays one face six times, in an ever-whitening progression, and includes "before" and "after" photos of a woman who presumably used the product. On its website the company calls its product "the miracle worker," which is "proven to deliver one to three shades of change" (Leistokow, 2003). HLL claims that its special patented formulation safely and gently controls the dispersion of melanin in the skin without the use of harmful chemicals frequently found in other skin lightening products. (Higher concentrations of melanin lead to darker skin.)

Doing Good

Not surprisingly, HLL claims Fair & Lovely is doing good by fulfilling a social need. They argue that 90 percent of Indian women want to use whiteners because it is "aspirational . . . . A fair skin is like education, regarded as a social and economic step up" (Luce and Merchant, 2003). More importantly, independent researchers have applauded Fair & Lovely for doing good. Hammond and Prahalad (2004) cite the comments of a young female street sweeper who expressed pride in using a fashion product that will prevent the hot sun from taking as great a toll on her skin as it did on her parents'. According to Hammond and Prahalad, she now "has a choice and feels empowered because of an affordable consumer product formulated for her needs." Further, they assert that by providing a choice to the poor, HLL is allowing the poor to exercise a basic right that improves the quality of their lives. HLL is making the poor better off by providing "real value in dignity and choice." It seems to be doing well by doing good.

Not Doing Good

Since Fair & Lovely is not categorized as a pharmaceutical product, Unilever has not been required to prove efficacy. However, many dermatologists *do* dispute its efficacy and claim that fairness creams cannot be effective without the use of skin bleaching agents such as hydroquinone, steroids, mercury salts, and other harmful chemicals, which Fair & Lovely does not contain (Islam et al., 2006). "Whitening creams sell like hot cakes, although there is no documented benefit," says Preya Kullavanijaya (2000), director of the Institute of Dermatology, Thailand. Dr. R. K. Pandhi, head of the Department of Dermatology at All India Institute of Medical Sciences in Delhi, says that he "has never come across a medical study that substantiated such claims [of whitening]. No externally applied cream can change your skin color" (Sinha, 2000). Professor A. B. M. Faroque, Chair of the Department of Pharmaceutical Technology, the University of Dhaka, Bangladesh, also questions the efficacy of fairness products, and Fair & Lovely in particular (Islam et al., 2006).

Faroque adds that, ironically, despite the obsession with fair skin, dark skin is actually healthier and less vulnerable to skin diseases than lighter skin. Dark skin contains more melanin, which protects it from the sun and hence, reduces the incidences of skin disease. Whitening creams pose a special risk in developing countries where dermatologists and general medical practitioners are typically not the first to be consulted on the treatment of skin diseases (Kullavanijaya, 2000). Patients often seek the advice of beauticians, family, friends, and pharmacists before going to a licensed medical professional. This risk is aggravated by the fact that potent topical medicines are widely available without a prescription.

Controversial Advertisements

One TV commercial aired in India (often referred to as the Air Hostess advertisement) "showed a young, dark-skinned girl's father lamenting he had no son to provide for him, as his daughter's salary was not high enough—the suggestion being that she could not get a better job or get married because of her dark skin. The girl then uses the cream [Fair & Lovely], becomes fairer, and gets a better-paid job as an air hostess—and makes her father happy" (BBC News, 2003). In a Fair & Lovely advertisement aired in Malaysia, a train attendant fails to catch the attention of her love interest, a businessman who buys a ticket from her every day, until she appears one day with fairer skin as a result of using Fair & Lovely (Prystay, 2002).

Unilever has followed a similar advertising strategy for Fair & Lovely in all the countries where it is sold. Advertising is a major element of its marketing mix, although the exact amount spent on advertising is a proprietary secret. It is reported that Unilever spent $7 million on advertising Fair & Lovely in Bangladesh, a much smaller market than India (Islam et al., 2006). In India, it was among the most advertised brands during the World Cup in 2002 (Chandran, 2003).

Fair & Lovely's heavily aired television commercials typically contain the message of a depressed woman with few prospects that gains a brighter future by either attaining a boyfriend/husband or a job after becoming markedly fairer, which is emphasized in the advertisements with a silhouette of her face lined up dark to light. It is interesting to note that in the print and TV advertisements, as the woman becomes "whiter" she also becomes noticeably happier! (Some recent Fair & Lovely TV ads can be seen on the website YouTube.) Such commercials have attracted much public criticism, especially from women's groups, in many countries, from India to Malaysia to Egypt.

Brinda Karat, General Secretary of the All India Democratic Women's Congress (AIDWC), calls the Fair & Lovely advertising campaign "highly racist" (BBC News, 2003). The Air Hostess "advertisement is demeaning to women and it should be off the air." Karat calls the advertisement "discriminatory on the basis of the color of skin," and "an affront to a woman's dignity" (Leistikow, 2003).

The AIDWC campaign culminated in the Indian government banning two Fair & Lovely advertisements, including the notorious Air Hostess advertisement, in 2003. Ravi Shankar Prasad, India's Information and Broadcasting Minister, said "I will not allow repellent advertisements such as this to be aired" (Luce and Merchant, 2003). "Fair & Lovely cannot be supported because the advertising is demeaning to women and the women's movement," the minister said (Doctor and Narayanswamy, 2003). The ban solely applied to two specific commercials in India. However, Fair & Lovely continues to run other advertisements with similar messages in India with little apparent change.

"We want stricter controls over these kinds of ads," says Senator Jaya Partiban, President of the national women's wing of the Malaysian Indian Congress (Prystay, 2002). "Those [Unilever] ads are incredible," says Malaysian social activist Cynthia Gabriel. "Whitening creams are capitalizing on a market that's quite racist and biased toward people who are lighter" (Prystay, 2002). Unilever insists it never meant to convey a message that could be interpreted to have racial undertones.

Unilever's Response

Unilever has countered the criticism it has received for its Fair & Lovely advertisements by saying that complexion is one of the Asian standards of beauty and that it is a dimension of personal grooming: "A well-groomed person usually has an advantage in life" (Islam et al., 2006). Arun Adhikari, executive director for personal products at HLL, suggests that the company has not done anything wrong, ". . . historically Fair & Lovely's thoroughly researched advertising depicted a 'before and after' effect. The current commercials show a negative and positive situation. We are not glorifying the negative but we show how the product can lead to a transformation, with romance and a husband the pay-off" (Luce and Merchant, 2003).

HLL went a step further in defending its advertising strategy. After the Indian government banned two Fair & Lovely commercials in 2003, the company was unrepentant and argued that its Fair & Lovely commercials were about "choice and economic empowerment for women" (Luce and Merchant, 2003). Hammond and Prahalad (2004) clearly buy this argument, and use exactly the same words when they say that the poor sweeper woman who uses Fair & Lovely "has a choice and feels empowered."[2]

As discussed earlier, various women's movements obviously do not buy this argument. They say it is not empowerment. At best, it is a mirage, and at worst, it serves to entrench a woman's disempowerment. The way to truly empower a woman is to make her less poor, financially more independent, and better educated. Social and cultural changes also must occur that eliminate the prejudices that are the cause of such deprivations. If the woman was truly empowered, say the women's groups, she would likely refuse to buy a skin whitener in the first place.

Target Market

The target market for Fair & Lovely is predominantly young women aged 18–35 (Srisha, 2001). Disturbingly, "there is repeated evidence that schoolgirls in the 12–14 years category widely use fairness creams" (Ninan, 2003). The poor also are a significant target market for Fair & Lovely. HLL marketed the product in "affordable" small size pouches to facilitate purchase by the poor. As mentioned, Hammond and Prahalad (2004) cite Fair & Lovely as an example of a product targeted at the poor or those at the "bottom of the pyramid." Sam Balsara, president of the Advertising Agencies Association of India, said, "Fair & Lovely did not become a problem today. It's been making inroads into poor people's budgets for a long time. I remember being told back in 1994 by mothers in a Hyderabad slum that all their daughters regularly used Fair & Lovely" (Ninan, 2003).

Constraints on Free Markets

Fair & Lovely is clearly doing well; it is a profitable and high-growth brand for Unilever in many countries, especially in India. The company is not breaking any laws; millions of women voluntarily buy the product and seem to be loyal customers. However, it is unlikely Unilever is fulfilling some "positive social goal" and might even be working to the detriment of a larger social objective. This paper does not mean to demonize Unilever, but there is no reason to canonize it either.

Should women have the right to buy Fair & Lovely? Absolutely, yes. None of the women's groups wants to ban the product. Should Unilever have the right to make profits by selling these products? Yes, it is a free market. Unilever, after all, did not create the sexist and racist prejudices that, at least, partially feed the demand for this product. Unfortunately, it is likely that the company has helped sustain these prejudices, however unwittingly—and that is the critical point here.

In a classic free market argument, HLL says, "the protests of women's activist groups bear no relationship to the popularity of Fair & Lovely, the best selling brand [in India's skin whitener market]" (Luce and Merchant, 2003). There is an evident contradiction between this argument and HLL's explicit espousal of corporate social responsibility. An even bigger problem might be that the market for Fair & Lovely is subject to market failure, and the free market ideology cannot be applied wholesale.

---

[2] C. K. Prahalad is a member of the board of directors of HLL.

One reason for possible market failure is the lack of information, especially about the efficacy of the Fair & Lovely product. A second reason is the vulnerability of the consumers, who are victims of racist and sexist prejudices; the poor are further disadvantaged by being ill informed, not well-educated, and perhaps even illiterate. This concern becomes greater when it affects children, who also are using the product.

Even if there is no market failure, countries might choose to constrain free markets for a larger social purpose. Many developing countries in Asia, Africa, and the Middle East suffer from deep and pervasive sexist and racist prejudices. To help reduce these prejudices, it might be sensible to constrain advertisements that perpetuate these prejudices. For example, it is more difficult to launch and sustain a movement to empower women in the pervasive presence of sexist advertisements. These advertisements drown out the efforts and voices of women's organizations that are working to promote equality and social justice for women in their countries.

When the profit-maximizing behavior of firms results in negative consequences to the public welfare, constraints must be imposed on the behavior of said firms. Constraints can be achieved via four mechanisms: corporate social responsibility, self-regulation by industry, activism by civil society, and government regulation. The firm could constrain its own behavior because it exercises corporate social responsibility, even though this may involve some financial penalty. A second possibility is for firms in an industry (or industries) to self-regulate their conduct, perhaps to reduce free-rider problems and to preempt government regulation. The third possibility is for civil society to pressure companies to act in the public interest. Finally, the government could regulate firm conduct to improve the public welfare.

These four mechanisms are, of course, not mutually exclusive; they can reinforce each other. For example, civil activism might lead to government regulation, as in the case of Fair & Lovely. Or, the threat of government regulation might make self-regulation more effective. The four mechanisms, broadly defined, do exhaust the possibilities in practice. Whistle blowing by employees and media exposure can be considered as forms of civil activism and might reinforce another mechanism.

The preceding discussion supports the position that profit-maximizing behavior by Fair & Lovely is not in the public interest. In the following, I examine four possible ways to constrain Unilever's behavior, and show that none of these approaches is particularly effective in the case of Fair & Lovely.

Corporate Social Responsibility

As stated earlier, HLL explicitly states on its website that its corporate social responsibility is rooted in its Corporate Purpose—the belief that "to succeed requires the highest standards of corporate behavior towards our employees, consumers, and the societies and world in which we live." However, it seems that Unilever (and HLL) are not living up to these professed "highest standards," at least, in the case of Fair & Lovely. But, to be fair to Unilever, it is far from alone in this hypocritical behavior. Crook (2005) in a survey on corporate social responsibility (CSR) concludes that for most large public companies, "CSR is little more than a cosmetic treatment."

It is possible that HLL top management genuinely believes its own rhetoric that Fair & Lovely "empowers" women. There is a wide gap between this belief and the position of civil activists that Fair & Lovely advertising is demeaning to women. One possible cause of this gap might be the fact that the top management (as mentioned in the annual report) and board of directors of HLL is exclusively male. Maybe HLL needs to more actively listen to its customers and civil society.

Self-regulation

The ideal solution to socially objectionable advertising is self-regulation by advertisers, advertising agencies, and the media. It is "ideal" in the sense that it involves the least amount of intervention into free markets. Industry in most countries, including India, attempts to implement self-regulation of advertising.

The Advertising Standards Council of India (ASCI), a self-regulatory body, was formed in 1985 by advertisers and advertising agencies. It acts as an intermediary between the advertising industry and the Indian government in order to prevent undue government intervention and censorship of advertisements. The organization claims an 80% compliance record, which they believe shows that self-regulation is working. The evidence, however, does not support such a conclusion. The ASCI does not screen all advertisements run in India. Rather, it only reviews commercials that have received complaints and has only recently begun developing more comprehensive guidelines and standards after pressuring from the Indian government.

"[O]ut of the top 250 advertisers not even 100 are members of the ASCI," says Gualbert Pereira, secretary general of ASCI (Doctor and Narayanswamy, 2003). If an advertiser is not a member of the ASCI, there is little the organization can do to police the behavior of the advertiser. Some members drop out allegedly because of unfavorable rulings on their ads. Moreover, compliance by its members is voluntary and there is no legal penalty for noncompliance.

ASCI operates with very limited resources. The annual membership fees range from $55 to $1100. The ASCI financial statements for the year 2001–2002 showed less than $200,000 in fees collected. ASCI operates out of "ramshackle" offices with a staff of five people (Doctor and Narayanswamy, 2003). By contrast, the Advertising Standards Association in the UK employs 150 people in a five-story building and expects members to contribute a fraction of their advertising budget.

Advertisers often take advantage of the time it takes ASCI to render its verdicts to run the full course of their advertising campaigns. Overall, ASCI's "diktats are honored more in name than in spirit . . . It is clearly a case of good intentions but very little action to back them up" (Doctor and Narayanswamy, 2003).

Civil Society Activism

Another source of constraints on free markets to increase public welfare and achieve some positive social goals is activism by civil society (organizations such as consumer movements, NGOs, and charitable foundations). Activism by civil society has succeeded even when there are no governmental regulations. Witness, for example, the recent pressure on McDonald's to introduce healthier menu options.

The Indian government banned two Fair & Lovely advertisements after a year-long campaign led by the All India Democratic Women's Congress. Even after this arduous battle, it was a hollow victory. There has been no significant change in the marketing of Fair & Lovely.

Government Regulation

When the pursuit of private profits by firms leads to a reduction in public welfare, the ultimate solution, of course, is government regulation. Advocates of the free market correctly see this solution as a last resort. Just as there are examples of market failure, examples abound of government failure. Regulation often ends up making the situation worse and reducing public welfare. For example, the overzealous regulation of advertising might end up stifling creativity and free speech, which hurts legitimate and economically desirable businesses.

In the case of Fair & Lovely, governments in India and other countries have done virtually nothing to constrain the behavior of Unilever. The Indian Association of Dermatologists, Venereologists, and Leprologists (IADVL) says that the current situation is unacceptable, and condemns the lack of a law to regulate the sale of skin whitening products. "Actually, these are drugs," says Anil Gangoo, president of IADVL, "that are sold as cosmetics, to avoid legal control." His association has tried to draw the government's attention to this issue many times. The authorities promise to look into it, but never act. "The cosmetics lobbies are very powerful," explains Gangoo (Dussault, 2006).

Conclusion

"Doing well by doing good" is a seductive proposition that has understandably captured the attention and imagination of many executives, academics, and public officials. Problems arise when there is a divergence between private profits and public welfare. In such cases, there is a need to constrain markets, which is particularly difficult in developing countries. Governments in developing countries often lack the political will, resources, and competence to successfully restrain powerful firms. Corruption makes the situation even worse. These countries also often lack the institutional maturity and public support needed for effective action by civil society and for self-regulation by the industry. As these countries develop economically, politically, and socially, such shortcomings will be remedied. Meanwhile, CSR is their best hope.

References

R. Balu, 2001, Strategic innovation: Hindustan Lever, Ltd., *Fast Company*, 47: 120.

BBC News, 2003, India debates "racist" skin cream ads, *BBC News*, July 24, http://news.bbc.co.uk/2/hi/south_asia/3089495.stm [March 30, 2007].

R. Chandran, 2003, All for self-control, *Business Line*, April 24, http://www.thehindubusinessline.com/catalyst/2003/04/24/stories/2003042400020100.htm [March 30, 2007].

C. Crook, 2005, The good company, *The Economist*, January 20.

V. Doctor & H. Narayanswamy, 2003, Ban for the buck, *The Economic Times*, April 2.

A. M. Dussault, 2006, Light headed, *The Hindu*, February 24.

N. Fitzgerald, 2003, CSR: Rebuilding trust in business, http://www.unilever.com/Images/A%20Perspective%20on%20Corporate%20Social%20Responsibility%20in%20the%2021st%20Century_tcm13-5520.pdf [March 30, 2007].

A. Hammond & C. K. Prahalad, 2004, Selling to the poor, *Foreign Policy*, May–June.

S. L. Hart, 2005, Capitalism at the Crossroads, Philadelphia, PA: Wharton School Publishing.

HLL, 2002, Analysts meeting: Results, http://www.hll.com/investor/Quarterly%20Results/2002/Q1ResultsPresentation02.pdf [March 30, 2007].

K. S. Islam, H. S. Ahmed, E. Karim, & A. M. Amin, 2006, Fair factor, *Star Weekend Magazine*, May 12.

N. Leistikow, 2003, Indian women criticize "Fair & Lovely" ideal, *Women's eNews*, April 28, http://www.womensenews.org/article.cfm/dyn/aid/1308/context/archive [March 30, 2007].

E. Luce & K. Merchant, 2003, India orders ban on advert saying fairer equals better for women, *Financial Times*, March 20.

Marketing Practice, 2006, http://marketingpractice.blogspot.com/2006_02_01_archive.html [March 30, 2007].

S. Ninan, 2003, Seeing red with this pitch, *The Hindu*, March 16.

C. K. Prahalad, 2004, *Fortune at the Bottom of the Pyramid: Eradicating Poverty through Profits*, Philadelphia, PA: Wharton School Publishing.

C. Prystay, 2002, Critics say ads for skin whiteners capitalize on Malaysian prejudice, *The Wall Street Journal*, April 30.

S. Sinha, 2000, Fair & growing, *India Today,* December 4.

D. Srisha, 2001, Fairness wars, Case study, ICFAI Center for Management Research, Hyderabad, India.

The Economic Times, 2003, Ban for the buck, April 2; *Time*, 2005, Selling to the poor, April 17.

Case Discussion Questions

1. The author argues that Unilever's "Fair & Lovely" is doing well but not doing good. Do you agree?

2. Milton Friedman argued that "the business of business is business." How can this argument help Unilever defend its case if you were a Unilever executive?

3. If you were an Indian government official or social activist, what would be your proposed solution?

Pearl River's International Strategy[1]

Yuan Lu
Chinese University of Hong Kong

The CEO of China's (and the world's) largest pianomaker seeks advice on how to enter international markets.

In March 2000, Tong Zhicheng, CEO of China's Pearl River Piano Group (PRPG) Corporation, received a group of professors from business schools in Hong Kong and the United States. He enthusiastically showed them around the company's product presentation hall and workshops. "Do you think American customers would like my products?" he asked an American professor. "Yeah, why not?" the professor replied, "They are good pianos with low prices. However, the American piano market has matured; therefore, it is not easy to survive there."

So, how to enter the American market? This was the major strategic challenge confronting Tong for some time. Over the preceding few years, the company had begun exporting to Asian and European markets, but Tong believed it was the right time to think about the US market.

Company Background

PRPG started as a state-owned enterprise (SOE). The group corporation was developed from a piano factory established in 1956 in the southern city of Guangzhou. When it was founded, the factory had less than 100 employees and produced only 13 pianos a year (one of which was exported to Hong Kong). As most production procedures involved manual skills, the factory's capacity was limited, less than 1,000 units a year. The factory branded its products "Pearl River Piano" since it was located next to the Pearl River. Throughout the 1960s and the 1970s, Pearl River pianos were not well known in China since the better-known brands were the Star

Sea made by the Beijing Piano Factory and the Ni Er (named after a famous musician) made by the Shanghai Piano Factory.

A strategic turnaround occurred in the early 1980s after the Chinese government decided to embark on economic reforms. One of China's early reform programs was to delegate decision autonomy to enterprise levels. In the mid-1980s, the factory was granted autonomy for imports and exports, which encouraged it to search for partners and markets abroad. It became the first piano builder in China to import foreign technologies and expatriate experts. In 1987, the factory was expanded to become Pearl River Piano Industrial Corporation, and in 1996, after merging with a few smaller musical instrument companies, it formed Pearl River Piano Group Corporation.

Pianos originated in Europe, where the first stringed instrument was the harp in ancient times. The modern piano took a long time to develop. For instance, the keyed monochords were developed approximately in the 12th century. In 1709, Bartolomeo Cristofori, an Italian harpsichord maker, made an instrument that was later regarded as the first piano. He called it the *gravicembalo col piano e forte*, or "harpsichord that plays soft and loud." In the late 18th century, pianomaking flourished in Vienna. The piano at that time had a wood frame, two strings per note, and leather-covered hammers. Mozart, for example, composed his concertos and sonatas on such a piano. The 18th and 19th centuries were the most exciting time for piano builders because the Industrial Revolution brought innovations to piano production, such as high-quality steel for making strings.

[1] This case was written by Yuan Lu (Chinese University of Hong Kong). It is intended to be used for class discussions rather than to illustrate either effective or ineffective handling of an administrative situation. The author would like to thank Mr. Tong Zhicheng for his kindness of offering opportunities of interviews and visits to the company. © Yuan Lu. Reprinted with permission.

In terms of basic technology, today's piano is almost the same as that of the late 19th century.

A piano is made up of more than 8,000 components, requiring more than 200 labor hours to produce and employing more than 300 production procedures. Normally, piano builders introduced production assembly lines in order to improve efficiency, but it was commonly believed that a high-quality piano could only be made by craftsmen using their skills and experiences to make and tune each product.

1992 to 1999: Tong's Strategy

Tong joined the piano factory when he was 16 and started his career as a piano builder by first working as a junior craftsman. He recalled his career development as the following:

> "PRPG was a small-scale company at that time [when I joined it], so I was able to try a variety of jobs. I worked as a repairman, and then I became the head of the repair department. Afterwards, I was promoted to be the head of three other departments: overseas sales, domestic sales, and supplies. After that, I was sent to Macau [a former Portuguese colony south of Guangzhou that was returned to Chinese sovereignty in 1999] and set up a new factory. In 1991, I was sent back to the headquarters and in 1992, I was appointed CEO."[2]

After Tong assumed the CEO position, he introduced two strategic pillars: innovation and quality. Innovation included the importation of new technology in production and quality measurement and product innovation by developing a wide range of pianos to meet the upper-, medium-, and low-end markets. PRPG invested approximately $60 million to upgrade production lines. The company established an expert team consisting of more than 40 technicians and computerized product design, tuning, and product quality analysis. It further developed more than 70 different styles and eight families of pianos.

The second strategic pillar was to enhance quality. The company introduced Total Quality of Management in 1988. In 1996, it introduced ISO 9000 and was certified in 1998. The company also established a joint venture with Yamaha in 1995. The joint venture licensed Yamaha technology to make key components (such as framework) and then became a key supplier to Yamaha in China. Through this partnership, PRPG learned how to make a world-class, high-quality product.

As CEO, Tong did not like to stay in his office but maintained his tradition of walking around in production lines and chatting with workers. He once said to visitors, "Every piano is my son." He told employees:

> "By striving to compete with other manufacturers that have a much longer history of building pianos, Pearl River has put its employees and management on notice that we will accept nothing short of perfection."[3]

Tong realized that innovation and quality improvement were perhaps not enough to make his products competitive with Western-built pianos. Since a piano was traditionally a European musical instrument, it was imperative that a Chinese piano builder, such as PRPG, identify a distinctive position in the marketplace in order to win the competition.

Chinese Pianos with Western Cultural Properties

Piano builders can be categorized as those targeting upper-, medium-, and low-end markets. A company targeting the upper market typically developed competitive advantages based on a long history of reputation, sophisticated procedures, luxury materials, beautiful styles and painting, and high-quality piano performance. Usually, European pianos targeted the upper market. Customers in this market segment included professionals for world-class concerts, upper-class households, and collectors. However, although European piano makers enjoyed their long history of developing pianos, the United States became an important piano building base as well as a large market. For example, Steinway pianos were usually regarded as the best in the world. The company, which is now based

---

[2] Hang Lung Center for Organizational Research Newsletter. Fall 2000. Globalization ambition and management philosophy: An interview with Mr. Tong Zhicheng, CEO of Pearl River Piano Group.

[3] Pearl River Piano Group homepage: http://www.pearlriverpiano.com/eprp/aboutus.html#Origins.

in the United States, was created in 1853 by German immigrant Henry Engelhard Steinway. For 150 years, Steinway has been dedicated to the ideal of making the finest pianos in the world. Due to sophisticated production procedures, as well as characteristics of the small market niche, companies in this market segment usually had a small production volume. For instance, Steinway only produced about 2,000 pianos a year. To compete with this strategy, handcraft skills, history, reputation, and preferences of well-known piano players became the key factors to success.

Many piano builders, particularly late entrants from Asia to this industry, targeted the medium- and low-end markets. The strategy adopted by these companies focused on efficiency, which was achieved through large-scale production. For example, Yamaha was the largest piano builder in the world. Its production capability could reach over 150,000 sets a year. Companies positioning themselves to target the medium- and low-end markets competed primarily on price.

PRPG adopted the second strategy and focused on the mass customer market as its dominant niche. However, Tong's ambition was to produce the best pianos in the world like Steinway. He clearly knew that it was difficult to replicate Steinway's success. His strategic ambition therefore was to propel Pearl River Piano to become an upper-class brand while improving both its product quality and reputation. Tong believed that he could make the best product, next only to Steinway. To achieve this goal, he had to make his pianos better than the products of most overseas piano builders, particularly those produced by Asian competitors.

How to do that? Tong believed that the piano is a distinctive piece of work that integrates both technology and culture, and that he must make his pianos sound like European products and project an image of "European culture." He said that although PRPG might need a few years to catch up to the world-class piano builders by importing technologies and expert knowledge for quality enhancement, it would take a much longer time to understand and master the piano culture.

To make employees and managers understand not only technology but also the Western culture associated with pianos, Tong invited seven foreign expatriates from Germany and the United States as consultants and advisors who came every six months to work with PRPG technicians and workers. Moreover, Tong stressed the necessity to maintain manual work in key production procedures, although the company installed two computerized laboratories to test products. "Do you know the difference between products made by machine and made by hand?" Tong once said to his employees. "A piano made by machine sounds like a machine. A piano made by hands sounds like a human being. The best piano should be made by heart not by machine." To make handcrafted pianos, Tong trained 100 highly skilled technicians who tested and adjusted every product manually. He also encouraged managers to learn to play piano, and he himself was an excellent pianist.

Building Sales Networks and Brand

Tong had rich experience in sales and marketing both domestically and internationally. PRPG was the first piano builder in China to establish a nationwide distribution network. Tong created strategic alliances with distributors, musical schools, and colleges, and numerous famous pianists who were invited to be advisors to promote Pearl River pianos. By 2000, PRPG had more than 130 strategic alliances throughout the country, in addition to 208 sales units.

Tong's ambition was to make Pearl River Piano a world-class brand. In fact, when he began to introduce innovation and quality strategies, he noted the importance of brand. Since 1996, he consciously promoted Pearl River Piano as a national brand. His strategy was to make his brand known in domestic and international markets by allying famous pianists. Tong sponsored various types of piano concerts and competitions, such as the Chinese Works Piano Competition 2000 in Hong Kong. Tong also established close personal relationships with many world-renowned piano players (such as Lazar Erman) and recommended that they play Pearl River pianos in their concerts.

The Internationalization Challenge

By the end of 2000, PRPG was the largest piano builder in China, the second largest in the world (next to Yamaha), with an annual production capacity of over 100,000 pianos. The company had more than 4,000 employees with a total asset value of approximately $130 million. While it also diversified into other musical instruments, its center of gravity was definitely piano, with more than 50% of the piano market in China. However, Tong did not seem satisfied with this progress. Although there was room to grow in China, competition became tougher than a few years ago. Hundreds of private companies began entering the market and competed through their low-quality and low-price products.

Tong thus turned his eyes on international markets, specifically the US market. When asked "What would PRPG's prospects be without globalization?" he answered:

> "The company could still survive [by staying in China] under some constraints. However, it is impossible for an entrepreneur to stay at the same position permanently. In fact, an entrepreneur is an aggressor in the business world. . . . We are still developing. We have made some progress, but not yet a great success. . . . PRPG has laid the foundations for globalization, but we cannot claim that our global outreach is well established yet. I guess it will take another three years to build a more solid foundation."[4]

When compared with other Chinese piano builders, PRPG had gained some experience in exporting. Tong believed that although the piano market in the United States was mature, his products could carve out a market niche. Because of the expensive labor costs in the United States and the necessity to rely on manual skills when building pianos, Pearl River pianos could take advantage of cheap labor costs in China combined with high product quality to eventually win American customers.

The company actually started making efforts to enter the US market a few years ago. While relying upon traditional direct exports, Tong also tried to seek a US piano builder as a partner to penetrate the market but this attempt did not succeed. He realized that most Americans still viewed Chinese products as cheap and low quality. In addition, it was difficult to get a strategic alliance partner because an American piano builder would perceive him as a competitor instead of a partner. To build a strategic alliance with an American company, PRPG might also have to introduce the American partner to the Chinese market, as an exchange for its entry to the US market. This would add a new rival in China's increasingly crowded domestic market. Therefore, Tong needed to calculate carefully what he could offer to the partner and what he wanted from the partnership.

Searching for various alternatives to enter the US market did not stop Tong's pace. In 1999, he set up a sales subsidiary in the United States as the platform upon which to further expand. However, he believed that although direct exports might be effective in the short run, the company should do something else in the long term. He viewed the company's mission to enter the US market as a crucial stage toward building the Pearl River Piano brand name internationally. "What should I do next?" he frequently asked his managers and consultants. And it was on that morning back in March of 2000 that he asked the same question to the Hong Kong and American professors who visited him.

Case Discussion Questions

1. Drawing on industry-, resource-, and institution-based views, explain how PRPG, from its humble roots, managed to become China's largest and the world's second largest piano producer.

2. Why did Tong believe that PRPG must engage in significant internationalization (instead of the current direct export strategy) at this point?

3. If you were one of the professors who visited Tong in March of 2000, how would you have briefed him about the pros and cons of various foreign market entry options?

4. Again, if you were one of those professors, what method would you have suggested as a way to tackle the US market?

---

[4] See Hang Lung Center for Organizational Research Newsletter. Fall 2000. Globalization ambition and management philosophy: An interview with Mr. Tong Zhicheng, CEO of Pearl River Piano Group.

Is a Diamond (Cartel) Forever?[1]

Mike W. Peng
University of Texas at Dallas

South Africa's De Beers successfully managed the global diamond cartel throughout the 20th century. However, it is encountering major challenges in the 21st century.

The longest running and probably the most successful cartel in the modern world is the international diamond cartel headed by De Beers of South Africa. The cartel system underpinning the $64 billion a year industry is, according to *The Economist*, "curious and anomalous—no other market exists, nor would anything similar be tolerated in a serious industry." While De Beers successfully managed this cartel throughout the 20th century, it is now confronting major challenges in the 21st century. How did the cartel start? What are its driving forces? What are its current challenges? This case addresses these questions.

The Cartel

Although historically diamonds were rare, the discovery of South African diamond mines by the end of the 19th century brought an avalanche of stones to the global market. A key reason diamond prices were so expensive was because of the deeply ingrained perception of scarcity. Consequently, if there was an oversupply, prices could plummet. Cecil Rhodes, an English tycoon who founded the De Beers Mines in South Africa in 1875, sought to solve this problem by focusing on two areas. First, Rhodes realized that supply from South Africa, the only significant producer in the world at that time, should be limited. Second, because producers (diggers) had little control over the quality and quantity of their output, they preferred to deal with an indiscriminate buyer willing to purchase both spectacular and mediocre

stones. Since most output would be mediocre stones, producers preferred to remove any uncertainty and to be able to sell *all* of their output. On the other hand, buyers (merchants) needed to secure a steady supply of stones (both high and low ends) in order to generate sufficient volume to polish and then retail. Rhodes's solution was to create an ongoing agreement between a single producer and a single buyer in which supply was kept low and prices high.

Putting his idea in action, Rhodes bought out all the major South African mines in the 1890s and formed a diamond merchants' association in the country, called the "Diamond Syndicate," to which he would sell his output. In such "single-channel marketing," all members of the syndicate pledged to buy diamonds from Rhodes and sell them in specific quantities and prices. With such an explicit scheme

[1] This case was written by Mike W. Peng (University of Texas at Dallas) and supported by a National Science Foundation CAREER grant (SES 0552089) for educational purposes. This case was entirely based on media publications. The views expressed are those of the author and not those of the NSF. The author thanks Erin Pleggenkuhle-Miles for her excellent research assistance. © Mike W. Peng. Reprinted with permission.

of quantity- and price-fixing, the diamond cartel was born. After Rhodes's death in 1902, the De Beers's empire was strengthened by Ernest Oppenheimer, a German diamond merchant who had founded his own company, Anglo-American, in South Africa. Through cross-shareholdings, members of the Oppenheimer family still control both De Beers's and Anglo-American to this day.

Industry Attributes

Most cartels collapse due to organizational and incentive problems. The longevity of the De Beers cartel, now running for more than 100 years, thus is an amazing case study of how to effectively run a cartel. At least three industry attributes contribute to the cartel's longevity. First, the industry has an extraordinarily high concentration. In Rhodes's day, De Beers not only controlled all of South African (and hence virtually worldwide) production, but also controlled all sales through its wholly owned subsidiary, Central Selling Organization (CSO), in London.

Second, De Beers is the undisputed price leader. Sales of rough diamonds (called "sights") are managed by the CSO to an exclusive group of "cherry picked" merchants (known as "sightholders") from cities such as Antwerp, Johannesburg, Mumbai, New York, and Tel Aviv. Sightholders would inform the CSO of their preferences for quantity and quality. The CSO then matched them with inventory. During each sight, the CSO offered each sightholder a preselected parcel. The buyer either took it or left it—no bargaining was permitted. Buyers usually took the parcel. If buyers did not like the system, they would not be invited again. This tactic allowed De Beers to control, down to the carat, exactly what and how many stones entered the market and at what price. To maintain the exclusivity of the sightholders, their number was reduced from approximately 350 in the 1970s to less than 100 sightholders in the 2000s.

Third, the friendly social relationships among participants of the cartel—for the most part—facilitate its long-term viability. "It's a personal business, face to face," said De Beers's current chairman Nicky Oppenheimer (Ernest's grandson), "In uranium, everybody brings their lawyers. In diamonds, there are no lawyers sitting around. It's a handshake business."

Firm Capabilities

At least three firm-specific attributes are also behind the longevity of De Beer's cartel. First, De Beers has a very clear strategy: Expand demand, limit supply, and maximize long-term profit. In the postwar decades, thanks to De Beers advertising (which amounted to $180 million in 2003, in addition to $270 million spent by its clients), diamond engagement rings have become almost compulsory in North America, Western Europe, and Japan. Increasingly anniversary rings are made of diamonds as well. The purpose of the recent "diamonds are forever" campaign is simply to prevent the emergence of a market for secondhand diamonds, which would significantly increased supply. Consequently, De Beers historically has been able to take advantage of very inelastic demand to set prices, largely constrained only by the number of engagements, and to a lesser extent major anniversaries, in any given year.

Second, De Beers exhibits a high level of flexibility to adapt to new challenges. By the 1950s, South Africa was no longer the leading producer. Today, only 12% of the worldwide production is from South Africa, while Botswana and Russia outperform South Africa in rough diamond production by a wide margin (Exhibit 1). Out of necessity, De Beers had to reach out to other producers. It offered its capital and expertise to African producers in Botswana, Angola, and Namibia. As a result, De Beers still controls approximately 40% of the worldwide production—it is still the biggest diamond miner but no longer that dominant. If producers declined offers for joint production, De Beers would urge them to sell to De Beers. Appreciating the benefits of cooperation and the hazards of oversupply, many producers agreed. Even during the heyday of the former Soviet Union, which for political reasons did not acknowledge any business dealings with the then Apartheid-era South Africa, the Soviet government entered secret agreements with De Beers to participate in such collusion. The producers typically agreed to sell rough diamonds *only* to De Beers, which dictated prices. De Beers promised to purchase *all* of the output, rain or shine (prices might fluctuate due to changing demand), resulting in its huge stockpiles of diamonds. In exchange, the producers reaped the traditional benefits of a cartel: stable prices, guaranteed purchases, and little competition.

EXHIBIT 1   Rough Diamond Production by Value

COUNTRY	ROUGH DIAMOND PRODUCTION
Botswana	26.0%
Russia	17.8%
South Africa	11.8%
Canada	11.4%
Angola	8.1%
Democratic Republic of Congo	8.0%
Australia	4.5%
Namibia	5.7%
Others	6.7%
Total Value	$12.7 billion

Source: Based on figure in *The Economist,* 2007, Changing facets (p. 76), February 24: 75–76.

At present, De Beers still controls approximately 50% of the rough diamond sales worldwide (Exhibit 2).

Perhaps most strikingly, De Beers possesses both the unique will and capability to enforce cartel arrangements. As in all cartels, the incentives to cheat are tremendous: Both producers and buyers are interested in cutting De Beers out of the process. As a price leader with a significant capacity to punish, De Beers's reactions are typically swift and powerful. In 1981, President Mobutu Seko of Zaire (now known as the Democratic Republic of Congo) announced that his country, the world's leading producer of industrial diamonds, had broken away from De Beers by directly marketing its diamonds. Although only 3% of De Beers's sales were lost, its "world order" would be at stake if such actions went unpunished. Consequently, De Beers drew on its stockpiles to flood the market, driving the price of Zairian industrial diamonds from $3 per carat to $1.80 and wiping out any financial gains the Zairians had hoped to grab. While incurring disproportional losses, De Beers had made its point. In 1983, Zaire crawled back on its knees and De Beers agreed, but only at terms much less favorable than those offered before.

In another example, many sightholders in Tel Aviv, a major diamond cutting and trading center, began to hoard diamonds purchased from the CSO in the late 1970s, hoping to combat Israel's rampant inflation. The disappearance of a substantial amount of diamonds from global circulation tightened supply, leading to skyrocketing prices and encouraging merchants elsewhere to also hoard and profit. While De Beers actually benefited from such higher prices in the short run, it realized that in the long run such an uncontrolled speculative bubble would burst. In response, in 1978, De Beers purged one third of CSO sightholders and

EXHIBIT 2   De Beers Diamond Production and Sales

PERCENTAGE OF WORLD TOTAL	1990	2007
De Beers production of rough diamonds	45%	40%
De Beers sales of rough diamonds	80%	50%

Source: Based on text in *The Economist,* 2007, Changing facets (p. 75), February 24: 75–76.

kicked out the most aggressive Israeli speculators and some non-Israeli merchants who had done business with the Israelis. Cut off from their CSO supplies, speculative merchants were forced to draw down their stockpiles, thus restoring prices to normal levels and leading to a "soft landing" from the speculative fever.

Institutional Constraints and Maneuvers

De Beers is also a skillful player in understanding and manipulating the rules of the game. In South Africa, half of the stock market is composed of the stocks of De Beers, Anglo-American, and their vast empire of related firms in the conglomerate. They control the pillar of South Africa's economy, namely, strategic minerals. For obvious reasons, the South African government—both during and after Apartheid—is on friendly terms with De Beers, whose cartel has no fear of being prosecuted. Likewise, De Beers maintains friendly relationships with most governments of diamond-producing countries. Its secret deals with the former Soviet government were indicative of its superb persuasive power, driving home the point that economics was more important than ideology (even during the heyday of the Cold War).

While De Beers historically has entered a number of joint production arrangements with host country governments in Botswana, Angola, and the Democratic Republic of Congo, it would ship all its rough diamond output mined from Africa to London, where the diamonds would be sorted and then sold (by the CSO noted earlier). However, the rules of the game are now changing. African governments are increasingly interested in cutting and polishing diamonds mined from their countries, which would add about 50% to the value of rough diamonds. This process is known as "beneficiation"—locating diamond processing activities in countries where the stones are extracted. "I am not going to say that beneficiation is something everyone in the [De Beers] business desires," acknowledged Gareth Penny, De Beers's managing director in a 2007 interview, "but in the end, diamond resources are national resources. . . Beneficiation is not about altruism but about good business; it creates much closer relationships with our partners."

In 2004, when the licenses for De Beers's two most profitable mines in Botswana came up for renewal, the Botswana government negotiated a beneficiation agreement with De Beers. In case De Beers disagreed, Botswana threatened to impose an export levy on rough diamond exports. In the end, De Beers agreed to sort in Botswana *all* the diamonds from its numerous sources around the world in a new $83 million facility entirely funded by De Beers. Botswana further demanded that De Beers's sightholders also cut the diamonds in Botswana. Since Botswana is the current leader, producing 26% of rough diamonds in the world, De Beers and its sightholders had little choice but to agree. These operations in Botswana will commence in 2009. Not surprisingly, governments in Angola and the Democratic Republic of Congo are also salivating for a piece of the action beyond mere diamond mining.

Finally, De Beers faces one major institutional headache: The US government argued that De Beers and its cartel are in clear violation of US antitrust laws, and unsuccessfully tried to prosecute it in 1945, 1974, and 1994. De Beers managed to stay beyond the extraterritorial reach of US laws until recently, since it had no legal presence and no (direct) sales in the US. All its diamonds are sold in London, and then sightholders can export them to the US, which is legal. Technically, the imported diamonds are no longer De Beers's—they belong to independent sightholders. However, with 50% of the retail diamond buyers in the United States, these legal actions have prevented De Beers executives from being able to visit their buyers and retailers in the United States for fear of being arrested. Clearly, a solution is necessary.

Current Challenges

Overall, the De Beers group, which is now widely diversified despite its center of gravity in diamonds, has been highly successful. In over 100 years of history, it only lost money in 1915, 1932, and 2007. At present, De Beers employs approximately 23,000 people in more than 25 countries, including 20 mines currently in production in Africa and joint ventures and partnerships in Canada, Russia, and Australia. In 2007, De Beers posted an annual loss of $521 million despite strong sales of $6.84 billion due to a nearly $1 billion impairment charge on its Canadian operations. Although 2007 was a difficult year given the general weakness of the global economy, higher fuel costs, and cost overruns at its new Canadian mines, rough diamond prices rose an average of 7.5% in the second half of 2007, which encouraged De Beers to continue to invest heavily in exploration for new diamonds.

Looking ahead, De Beers' three main challenges lie in (1) adapting to the changing industry structure, (2) dealing with pressures for corporate social responsibility, and (3) overcoming formal institutional barriers preventing it from directly operating in its largest market, the United States.

First, in terms of industry structure, De Beers is no longer a monopolist. It is a leading player in an oligopoly that increasingly has to accommodate new players. Today, the cartel is less of a cartel than what it used to be. The rise of the then Soviet and now Russian mines in Siberia, which now produce 18% of the global output, poses sufficient market power to threaten De Beers's standing. The leading Russian producer, Alrossa, has collaborated with Lev Leviev Group, a leading Israeli diamond merchant headed by a Russian-speaking Uzbeki-born Israeli citizen. They have reduced sales of rough diamonds to De Beers, polished more diamonds in Russia, and marketed them directly. Outraged, De Beers, which invited Lev Leviev to become a sightholder in 1987, removed its privileges of a sightholder in 1995. But the tide is difficult for De Beers to turn back. However, on the bright side, with the increasingly difficult-to-control cartel, De Beers no longer needs to focus exclusively on defending the cartel and the industry at large. Instead, it has more freedom to make decisions to maximize its own profits, such as buying fewer stones at uneconomical prices.

Second, De Beers has been facing mounting pressures for corporate social responsibility (CSR) on at least three fronts. The first was the $1.2 billion worth of "conflict diamonds" that floated to the global market as a result of the civil war in Angola and Sierra Leone in the 1990s. In its traditional role of a buyer of the last resort, De Beers felt compelled to purchase the new supply; otherwise, it risked losing its tight grip on global supply. However, with "blood on its hands," De Beers encountered a public relations disaster, especially after the UN imposed sanctions on "conflict diamonds." Eventually, under tremendous pressure of consumer boycotts and activist campaigns, De Beers in 2000 initiated a "Kimberly Process" which, together with almost 70 governments and all the big industry players, committed the industry to a strict certification process for the legitimate origin of diamonds. The "Kimberly Process" has been in effect since 2003 and has reduced the number of conflict diamonds to 0.2% of global production. In 2006–2007, the Hollywood movie *Blood Diamond* again renewed public interest in conflict diamonds, yet De Beers reported that the movie did not dent diamond sales.

A second CSR area is the HIV/AIDS disaster, reportedly affecting 25% of the adult population in southern Africa. In 2003, De Beers became the first mining company to extend health insurance free of charge to HIV-positive employees and their spouses and partners in South Africa, Botswana, and Namibia. This insurance coverage would remain in effect for employees after retirement or retrenchment.

A third CSR area is environmental protection. Diamond mining, if not properly managed, can easily cause environmental problems. De Beers thus has to pay careful attention to the environment footprint of its operations. All its major operations have been ISO14001 certified.

Finally, facing rising competition, De Beers has sought to flex its muscle by developing a De Beers brand of diamonds and other luxury goods. In 2000, it formed a joint venture with a leading luxury goods firm, LVMH, and opened a De Beers LV store in London and three stores-within-stores in Tokyo. However, its plan to open a flagship store in New York was frustrated because of the US government ban on its business due to its alleged antitrust violations. Nicky Oppenheimer, De Beers's current chairman, openly wrote in his "chairman's statement" in the *2003 Annual Report* that De Beers's core strategy was "to bend all our efforts to increasing worldwide demand for our product and ensure that diamond jewelry would henceforth outperform the rest of the luxury goods market"—in other words, increase demand, limit supply, and jack up price, exactly the "criminal" acts as charged by the US government. Essentially acknowledging "guilty as charged," Oppenheimer's 1999 speech to alumni of the Harvard Business School contained the following statements:

- "We set out, as a matter of policy, to break the commandments of Mr. Sherman [principal lawmaker for the Sherman Act of 1890]. We make no pretence that we are not seeking to manage the diamond market, to control supply, to manage prices, and to act collusively with our partners in the business."

- "This form of single channel marketing has exercised an extraordinary beneficial influence upon the whole of the diamond industry and particularly to many of the economies of Africa."

- "It is no accident that diamond prices have been more stable when compared with other commodities. The positive trend in rough diamond prices is due to De Beers's marketing efforts. And this is an effort which is in the interest of both the producer and the consumer, a strange and illogical coming together of opposites."

- "I believe that the attitude of the [US] Justice Department is at odds with American foreign policy, which seeks to support the reconstruction and development of Africa. . . . It is always hard to argue that you are the exception to the rule, but in the case of De Beers and the ultimate luxury—diamonds—I believe a review of US antitrust laws should form part of a new framework for engagement with Africa. Indeed, it would be in line with the spirit of the African Growth and Opportunity Act."

Is the Cartel Forever?

Before the first edition of *Global Strategic Management* went to press, in July 2004, De Beers agreed to pay a $10 million fine to the US government, thus ending a 60-year-long impasse—it was first charged by the US government in 1945 and this recently settled case was initiated in 1994. Before the second edition went to press, in January 2008, media reported that De Beers agreed to settle the charges with a total payment of $295 million in the United States. The following is the entire excerpt from www.debeersgroup.com under "Ethics: Resolution of Actions in the United States" (accessed February 14, 2008):

In July 2004, De Beers entered a plea agreement with the US Department of Justice to resolve criminal charges against the company for an alleged conspiracy to fix the price of industrial diamonds. On the basis of payment of a US$10 million fine, the United States agreed it would not bring further criminal charges against De Beers, related companies, or any current or former directors, officers, employees, and agents for any act related to those price-fixing allegations as set out in the indictment. This marked the first important step in resolving US litigation issues outstanding against the company.

In November 2005, De Beers announced that an agreement had been reached, and a preliminary approval order issued, to settle the majority of civil class action suits filed against the company in the United States. Since then, in March 2006, the three remaining civil class action suits were added to the November settlement agreement, resulting in an overriding global settlement agreement totaling US$295 million, which has received preliminary court approval.

This settlement does not involve any admission of liability on the part of De Beers but will bring an end to all outstanding class actions. This represents an important step to improving our reputation in the largest diamond consumer market in the world and stands as clear evidence of our commitment to competition law compliance. De Beers continues to cooperate with the Court of the District of New Jersey to seek resolution of this litigation.

As part of the class action settlement, De Beers agreed to offer injunctive relief, which includes a general commitment to comply with antitrust laws of the United States, and specific prohibited conduct with third-party producers and sightholders. Injunctive relief is a typical component of class action settlements in the United States. The injunctive relief further demonstrates our clear commitment to operating in accordance with competition laws around the world.

The $295 million De Beers agreed to pay would be divided roughly in half between diamond merchants and consumers. Anyone who bought retail diamonds in the United States between 1994 and 2006 could potentially get a refund, regardless of whether these diamonds came from De Beers or not, because diamonds prices were allegedly fixed and controlled by De Beers. The exact amount each consumer would get depends on the number of eligible buyers who claimed a refund. At a maximum of 32% of a purchase price, a consumer could get up to $640 back on a $2,000 ring. However, here is a catch: if everyone claimed a refund, only $2 would come back on a $2,000 ring. The upshot? "Definitely don't show this story to your friends," said a *Chicago Tribune* article published on January 21, 2008.[2]

As captured by the title of the *Chicago Tribune* article, "Diamond refunds are a consumer's best friend," consumers who unexpectedly receive refunds will naturally be happy. De Beers's executives are also pleased because they can now travel to the United States without fear of arrest and the firm can now operate a flagship De Beers jewelry shop on Fifth Avenue in New York. However, a question looming large on the horizon for De Beers executives and antitrust officials is: Has the longest-running cartel really come to an end? This truly is a billion dollar question.

Sources: Based on (1) J. Burns & D. Spa, 2000, *Forever: De Beers and U.S. Antitrust Law,* Harvard Business School case study 9-700-082; (2) *Chicago Tribune,* 2008, Diamond refunds are a consumer's best friend, January 21 (www.chicagotribune.com); (3) A. Cockburn, 2002, Diamonds: The real story, *National Geographic,* March: 2–35; (4) *The Economist,* 2004, Rumors are forever, February 28: 62; (5) *The Economist,* 2004, The cartel isn't forever, July 17: 60–62; (6) *The Economist,* 2005, Rough and tumble, October 29: 66; (7) *The Economist,* 2007, Changing facets, February 24: 75–76; (8) *Financial Times,* 2007, De Beers cedes diamond grip to African states, November 29 (www.ft.com); (9) *Financial Times,* 2008, De Beers hit by $1bn charge, February 8 (www.ft.com); (10) *Forbes,* 2003, The billionaire who cracked De Beers, September 15: 108–115; (11) Reuters, 2008, De Beers sees "challenging" 2008 for diamond sector, February 11 (www.reuters.com); (12) D. Spa, 1994, *The Cooperative Edge: The Internal Politics of International Cartels,* Ithaca, NY: Cornell University Press; (13) www.debeersgroup.com; (14) www.diamondclassaction.com.

Case Discussion Questions:

1. Most cartels fail within a short period of time due to organizational and incentive problems. Why is the diamond cartel so long lasting (spanning the entire 20th century and still going, despite some recent loss of power)?

2. Drawing on industry-, resource-, and institution-based views, explain why De Beers has been phenomenally successful.

3. Given the multidimensional current challenges, what are opportunities for De Beers? What are threats? What kinds of strengths and weaknesses does De Beers have when dealing with these challenges?

4. Discuss the future of the rivalry between De Beers and Leviev, especially in the new arena of retail competition with branded jewelry. What does the future hold for both firms?

---

[2] If you are reading this case after May 19, 2008, forget about the refund, which ends after this date. See www.diamondclassaction.com.

chapter 9

Diversification and Acquisitions

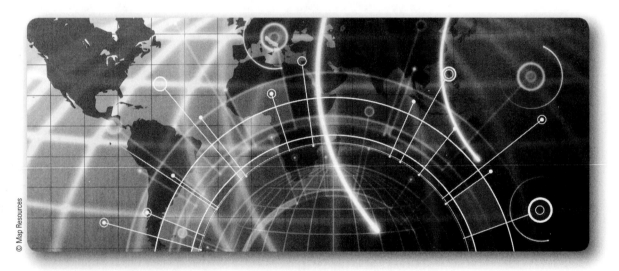

© Map Resources

KNOWLEDGE OBJECTIVES

After studying this chapter, you should be able to

1. Define product diversification and geographic diversification

2. Articulate a comprehensive model of diversification

3. Gain insights into the motives and performance of acquisitions

4. Enhance your understanding of restructuring

5. Participate in two leading debates on diversification, acquisitions, and restructuring

6. Draw strategic implications for action

OPENING CASE: RENAULT-NISSAN

As part of the recent restructuring in the global automobile industry, in 1999, Renault injected $5 billion to acquire 37% of Nissan's equity. Acquiring Nissan enabled Renault to broaden its geographic scope by expanding to Asia, where it had been weak. At that time, Nissan, despite its historical glory, had a faded brand, awesome debt loads, and an uncertain future.

Although the deal was called an "alliance" as a euphemism, there was no doubt Renault was in charge. An executive from Renault, Carlos Ghosn, a Brazilian-born Frenchman of Lebanese ancestry, was first named Nissan's chief operating officer (COO) in 2000 and then its chief executive officer (CEO) in 2001. At that time, a total of 43 of the 46 Nissan models sold in Japan were unprofitable. Nicknamed "Le Cost Cutter," Ghosn ruled that no new model would be developed unless it made money. Since 2000, Ghosn shut down five plants in Japan, reduced the work force by 21,000 (14% of the total—all in Japan), and shifted more production of new models to the United States. Nissan returned to profitability in 2001. In 2005, Ghosn was appointed CEO of Renault, while still serving as CEO of Nissan.

By most measures, the combined Renault–Nissan group has shown enviable performance. Moving from selling less than five million vehicles in 1999 to more than six million in 2007, the group surged to become the world's third largest automobile group (in volume), behind General Motors and Toyota. Since 1999, Renault's share price grew 151%, while the CAC 40 group listed in France grew only 25%. During the same period, Nissan's share price jumped 197%, while the Nikkei index crawled up by only 6%.

What is behind the success of the combined Renault–Nissan group? In the words of Ghosn himself, writing in the *Harvard Business Review,* the key was to balance the needs for radical strategic changes and the respect for Nissan's identity and the self-esteem of its employees:

> "Those two goals—making changes and safeguarding identity—can easily come into conflict; pursuing them both entails a difficult and sometimes precarious balancing act. This was particularly true in this case. I was, after all, an outsider—non-Nissan, non-Japanese . . . I knew that if I tried to dictate changes from above, the effort would backfire, undermining morale and productivity. But if I was too passive, the company would simply continue its downward spiral."

On the one hand, Ghosn and his team ditched the time-honored seniority system in Nissan and installed a performance-based promotion system. Not surprisingly, they received a lot of flak for undermining the Japanese "culture." Yet, over time, a new culture focusing on performance emerged, which would have been unthinkable in the old Nissan. On the other hand, they created nine cross-functional teams involving 500 Nissan managers. The teams were not only responsible for coming up with recommendations that became the input for the corporate-wide revival plan, but were also the watchdogs for their implementation.

Another key was relentless efforts in integration. Not only did Renault and Nissan actively cooperate in joint engineering, production, and distribution around the world, in 2002 they also set up a 50/50 jointly owned company, Renault–Nissan bv, registered in a third country, The Netherlands ("bv" refers to a closed limited liability company known as *besloten vennootschap* under Dutch law).

Renault–Nissan bv hosts a group-wide Alliance Board and manages two joint companies: Renault–Nissan Purchasing Organization (RNPO) and Renault–Nissan Information Services (RNIS). Of note is RNPO, founded in 2001 to optimize purchasing performance across the combined group. By 2008, RNPO was covering 83% of all Renault and Nissan purchases, leveraging the significant purchasing power of the combined group.

Sources: Based on (1) C. Ghosn, 2002, Saving the business without losing the company, *Harvard Business Review,* 80 (1): 37–45; (2) *International Herald Tribune,* 2008, Nissan-Renault alliance still going strong, February 28, www.iht.com; (3) Renault, 2007, *Renault Nissan Alliance Facts and Figures 2006,* Paris: Renault; (4) Wikipedia, 2008, The Renault Nissan alliance, en.wikipedia.org.

---

corporate-level strategy (also known as **corporate strategy**)

Strategy about how a firm creates value through the configuration and coordination of its multimarket activities.

business-level strategy

Strategy which builds competitive advantage in a discrete and identifiable market.

diversification

Adding new businesses to the firm that are distinct from its existing operations.

product diversification

Entries into new product markets and/or business activities that are related to a firm's existing markets and/or activities.

Why did Renault choose to broaden its *geographic* scope by acquiring Nissan in Japan? Why didn't it, for example, broaden its *product* scope by acquiring firms in other industries? What can firms do to improve their odds for successfully diversifying, acquiring, and restructuring? These are some of the strategic questions we will address in this chapter.

Starting from this chapter, Part III (Chapters 9, 10, 11, and 12) focuses on **corporate-level strategy** (or, in short, **corporate strategy**), which is how a firm creates value through the configuration and coordination of its multimarket activities. In comparison, Part II (Chapters 5, 6, 7, and 8) has dealt with **business-level strategy,** defined as ways to build competitive advantage in an identifiable market. While business-level strategy is very important, for larger, multimarket firms, corporate-level strategy is equally or perhaps more important.[1] In other words, an understanding of corporate-level strategy helps us see the "forest," whereas business-level strategy focuses on "trees."

In this chapter, we focus on a key aspect of corporate strategy, **diversification,** which is adding new businesses to the firm that are distinct from its existing operations. Diversification is probably the single most researched, discussed, and debated topic in strategy. It can be accomplished along two dimensions. The first is **product diversification**—through entries into different industries. The second is **geographic diversification**—through entries into different countries. Although market entries can entail strategic alliances and green-field investments (see Chapter 5), our focus here is on mergers and acquisitions (M&As) and restructuring.

We will first introduce product diversification and geographic diversification. Then, we will develop a comprehensive model, drawing on the "strategy tripod." Acquisitions and restructuring are examined next, followed by debates and extensions.

Product Diversification

Most firms start as small businesses focusing on a single product or service with little diversification—known as a **single business strategy.** Over time, a product diversification strategy, with two broad categories (related and unrelated), may be embarked upon.

Product-Related Diversification

Product-related diversification refers to entries into new product markets and/or activities that are related to a firm's existing markets and/or activities. The emphasis is on **operational synergy** (also known as **scale economies** or **economies of scale**), defined as increases in competitiveness beyond what can be achieved by engaging in two product markets and/or activities separately. In other words, firms benefit from declining unit costs by leveraging product relatedness—that is, $2 + 2 = 5$. The sources of operational synergy can be (1) technologies (such as common platforms), (2) marketing (such as common brands), and (3) manufacturing (such as common logistics).[2] For instance, Renault and Nissan, through RNPO, pooled their purchasing together to derive lower cost and better synergy for their related operations around the world (see Opening Case).

Product-Unrelated Diversification

Product-unrelated diversification refers to entries into industries that have no obvious product-related connections to the firm's current lines of business.[3] For example, General Electric (GE) competes in appliances, lighting fixtures, aircraft engines, broadcasting, and financial services. Product-unrelated diversifiers (such as GE) are called **conglomerates,** and their strategy is known as **conglomeration.** Instead of operational synergy, conglomerates focus on **financial synergy** (also known as **scope economies** or **economies of scope**)—namely, increases in competitiveness for each individual unit financially controlled by the corporate headquarters beyond what can be achieved by each unit competing independently as standalone firms.

The mechanism to obtain financial synergy is different from that for obtaining operational synergy. The key role of corporate headquarters is to identify and fund profitable investment opportunities. In other words, a conglomerate serves as an **internal capital market** that channels financial resources to high-potential high-growth areas.[4] Given there are active external capital markets that try to do the same, a key issue is whether units affiliated with conglomerates in various industries (such as GE's aircraft engine division) outperform their standalone independent competitors in respective industries (such as Snecma). Stated differently, at issue is whether corporate headquarters can do a *better* job in identifying and taking advantage of profitable opportunities than external capital markets. If conglomerate units beat standalone rivals (which is something most GE units consistently do), then there is a **diversification premium** (or conglomerate advantage)—in other words, product-unrelated diversification adds value.[5] Otherwise, there can be a **diversification discount** (or conglomerate disadvantage), when conglomerate units are better off by competing as standalone entities (see Closing Case). Shown in Strategy in Action 9.1, the sum of the value of the units affiliated with Beatrice, when sold individually, was *larger* than the value of the conglomerate as a whole, a clear indication that in this case, conglomeration destroyed value.

---

geographic diversification

Entries into new geographic markets.

single business strategy

A strategy which focuses on a single product or service with little diversification.

product-related diversification

Entries into new product markets and/or business activities that are related to a firm's existing markets and/or activities.

operational synergy

Synergy derived by having joint shared activities, personnel, and technologies.

scale economies (economies of scale)

Reductions in per unit costs by increasing the scale of production.

product-unrelated diversification

Entries into industries that have no obvious product-related connections to the firm's current lines of business.

conglomerates

Product-unrelated diversifiers.

conglomeration

A strategy of product-unrelated diversification.

Strategy in Action 9.1 - **Beatrice: The Rise and Fall of a US Conglomerate**

Ethical Challenge

Founded in rural Nebraska in a town called Beatrice, the firm began as a small dairy producer in 1891. In the next several decades, Beatrice became a leading dairy firm through acquisitions. But in 1956, the Federal Trade Commission (FTC) charged Beatrice for possessing "excessive" market power, forcing it to divest plants and preventing it from acquiring other dairy firms.

The FTC action inadvertently forced Beatrice to embark on product-unrelated diversification. By 1975, only 21% of its earnings were in dairy. Industries in which Beatrice established a presence included bakeries, beverages, chemicals, cold storage, confectionery, garden, graphic arts, home, and printing. All targets were private family-run businesses, whose owners (now division managers) were largely left alone provided that financial results were satisfactory. Corporate headquarters did *not* try to integrate the new units, and the word "synergy" was *never* used in annual reports during 1952–1976. Sales grew from $235 million in 1952 to $5.6 billion in 1976. The return to shareholders averaged more than 14% per year and the capital market reacted favorably. By 1976, as a far-flung conglomerate (Figure 9.3), Beatrice operated in 27 countries.

Since 1976, with two new CEOs (one during 1976–1979 and another during 1979–1985), Beatrice moved toward more centralization, by organizing the firm into six groups in search of "synergies." It unleashed an expensive corporate-wide "We're Beatrice" marketing campaign. Headquarters staff increased from 161 in 1976 to 750 in 1985. The second CEO also had a tendency to get involved in operational details. In addition, the acquisition strategy also changed toward making high-profile, expensive acquisitions of publicly traded firms such as Tropicana (1978) and Esmark (1984). Unfortunately, the capital market started to heavily discount Beatrice's stock. During 1976–1985, every acquisition was met with a *reduction* in market value, and a total of $2 billion in market value was destroyed. In 1985, the CEO was forced to resign. Later that year, Beatrice was taken over by a management team advised by a leading private equity firm, Kohlberg, Kravis, and Robert (KKR), in the then-largest leveraged buyout (LBO) in history with $1 billion in premium to shareholders. Starting in 1986, Beatrice started to sell off divisions such as Avis and Tropicana. In 1990, the remaining Beatrice sold itself to ConAgra for $1.3 billion. In all, proceeds from asset sales reached $11.1 billion, which was 19% *more* than Beatrice's equity at the time of the LBO ($9.3 billion).

The story of Beatrice (1891–1990) is a fascinating history of the evolution of corporate diversification in the United States in the 20th century. Beatrice experienced over 400 acquisitions and 90 divestitures. The pre-1976 Beatrice created value by acquisitions, the 1976–1985 Beatrice destroyed value by acquisitions, and the post-1986 Beatrice created value by divestitures. One interesting speculation, from an ethical standpoint, is whether managers making these decisions *knowingly* or *unknowingly* made mistakes.

Sources: Based on (1) G. Baker, 1992, Beatrice: A study in the creation and destruction of value, *Journal of Finance,* 47: 1081–1119; (2) T. Stuart & D. Collis, 1991, *Beatrice Companies— 1985,* Harvard Business School case study.

Product Diversification and Firm Performance

The relationship between product diversification and firm performance has received significant attention. Hundreds of studies, mostly conducted in the West, suggest that, on average (although not always), performance may increase as firms shift from single business strategies to product-related diversification, but performance may decrease as

FIGURE 9.1   Product Diversification and Firm Performance

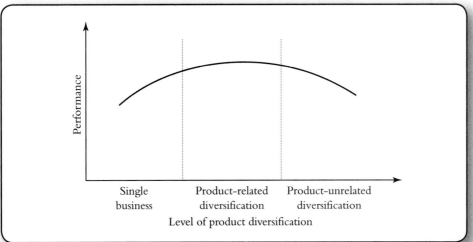

Source: From *Competing for Advantage*, 1st edition by R.E. Hoskisson, M.A. Hitt and R.D. Ireland, p. 228. Copyright © 2004. Reprinted with permission of South-Western, a division of Cengage Learning: www. cengagerights.com. Fax 800 730-2215

firms change from product-related to -unrelated diversification—in other words, the linkage seems to be an inverted U shape (Figure 9.1).[6] Essentially "putting all your eggs in one basket," a single business strategy can be potentially risky and vulnerable. "Putting your eggs in different baskets," product-unrelated diversification may reduce risk, but its successful execution requires strong organizational capabilities that many firms lack (discussed later). Consequently, product-related diversification, essentially "putting your eggs in *similar* baskets," has emerged as a balanced way to both reduce risk and leverage synergy since the 1970s.[7]

However, important caveats exist. Not all product-related diversifiers outperform unrelated diversifiers. In an age of "core competence," the continuous existence and prosperity of the likes of GE, Siemens, and Virgin Group suggest that for a small group of highly capable firms, conglomeration may still add value in developed economies. Moreover, in emerging economies, a conglomeration strategy seems to be persisting, with some units (such as those affiliated with South Korea's Samsung Group, India's Tata Group, and Turkey's Koc Group) outperforming standalone competitors.[8] The reason many conglomerates fail is not because this strategy is inherently unsound, but because firms fail to implement it. Conglomeration calls for corporate managers to impose a strict financial discipline on constituent units and hold unit managers accountable—of the sort GE's former chairman and CEO, Jack Welch, famously imposed on all divisions, "Either become the world's top one or two in your industry, or expect your unit to be sold." However, most corporate managers are not so "ruthless," and they may tolerate poor performance of some units, which can be subsidized by better units. By robbing the better units to aid the poor ones, corporate managers in essence practice "socialism." Over time, better units may lose their incentive to do well, as a result, and eventually *corporate* performance suffers.

financial synergy

The increase in competitiveness for each individual unit that is financially controlled by the corporate headquarters beyond what can be achieved by each unit competing independently as standalone firms.

scope economies (economies of scope)

Reduction in per unit costs and increases in competitiveness by enlarging the scope of the firm.

internal capital market

A term used to describe the internal management mechanisms of a product-unrelated diversified firm (conglomerate) which operate as a capital market inside the firm.

diversification premium

Increased levels of performance because of association with a product-diversified firm (also known as conglomerate advantage).

diversification discount

Reduced levels of performance because of association with a product-diversified firm (also known as conglomerate discount).

FIGURE 9.2   Geographic Diversification and Firm Performance: An S Curve

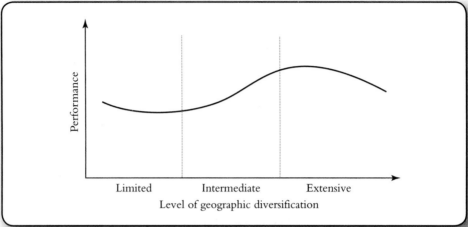

Sources: Adapted from F. Contractor, S. K. Kundu, & C.-C. Hsu, 2003, "A three stage theory of international expansion: The link between multinationality and performance in the service sector" (p. 7), *Journal of International Business Studies,* 34: 5–18.

Geographic Diversification

Although geographic diversification can be done within one country (expanding from one city or state to another), in this chapter we focus on **international diversification,** namely, the number and diversity of countries in which a firm competes (see also Chapter 5).

Limited versus Extensive International Scope

Two broad categories of geographic diversification can be identified. The first is limited international scope, such as US firms focusing on NAFTA markets and Spanish firms concentrating on Latin America. The emphasis is on geographically and culturally adjacent countries in order to reduce the liability of foreignness (see Chapters 4 and 6 for details). The second category is extensive international scope, maintaining a substantial presence beyond geographically and culturally neighboring countries. For example, the largest market for Honda is North America, accounting for 54% of its sales (twice as large as 27% of its sales in its home region, Asia). While neighboring countries are not necessarily "easy" markets, success in distant countries obviously calls for a stronger set of advantages to compensate for the liability of foreignness there.

Geographic Diversification and Firm Performance

international diversification

The number and diversity of countries in which a firm competes.

In this age of globalization, we frequently hear the calls for greater geographic diversification: All firms need to go "global," non-international firms need to start venturing abroad, and firms with a little international presence should widen their geographic scope. The ramifications for firms failing to heed such calls presumably are grave. However, the evidence is *not* fully supportive of this popular view. As captured by the S curve in Figure 9.2, two findings emerge.[9] First, at a low level of internationalization, there is a U-shaped relationship between geographic scope and firm performance, which suggests an initially negative effect of international expansion on performance before the positive returns are realized. This stems from the well-known hazard of liability of foreignness (see Chapter 5). Second, at moderate to high levels of internationalization, there is an inverted U shape, implying a positive relationship between geographic scope and firm performance—but only to a certain extent, beyond which further expansion is again detrimental. In other words, the conventional wisdom—"the more global, the better"—is actually misleading.

Not all firms have been sufficiently involved overseas to experience the ups and downs captured by the S curve in Figure 9.2. Many studies report a U-shaped relationship, because they only sample firms in the early to intermediate stages of internationalization.[10] Small inexperienced firms are often vulnerable during the initial phase of overseas expansion. On the other hand, many other studies document an inverted U shape, because their samples are biased for larger firms with moderate to high levels of diversification.[11] Many large multinational enterprises (MNEs) have a "flag planting" mentality, bragging about in how many countries they have a presence. However, their performance, beyond a certain limit, often suffers, thus necessitating some withdrawals. Wal-Mart, for example, had to withdraw from Germany and South Korea recently.

Given this complexity, it is hardly surprising there is a great debate about geographic diversification.[12] Shown in Figure 9.2, there indeed is an intermediate range within which firm performance increases with geographic scope, leading some studies that sample firms in this range to conclude that "there is value in internationalization itself because geographic scope is found to be related to higher firm profitability."[13] However, other studies, which sample firms with a high level of geographic scope, caution that "multinational diversification is apparently less valuable in practice than in theory."[14] Consequently, the recent consensus emerging out of the debate is to not only acknowledge the validity of both perspectives, but also to specify conditions under which each perspective (geographic diversification *helps* or *hurts* firm performance) is likely to hold.[15]

Combining Product and Geographic Diversification

Although most studies focus on a single dimension of diversification (product or geographic) that is already very complex, in practice, most firms (except single-business firms with no interest to internationalize) have to entertain both dimensions of diversification *simultaneously*.[16] Figure 9.3 illustrates the four possible combinations. Firms in Cell 3 are **anchored replicators,** because they focus on product-related diversification and a limited geographic scope. They seek to replicate a set of activities in related industries in a small number of countries anchored by the home country. Cardinal Health, a leading US pharmaceutical distributor, pursues such a strategy.

Firms in Cell 1 can be called **multinational replicators** because they engage in product-related diversification on one hand and far-flung multinational expansion on the other. Most automakers, such as Renault and Nissan in the Opening Case, have pursued this combination.

Firms in Cell 2 can be labeled as **far-flung conglomerates** because they pursue both product-unrelated diversification and extensive geographic diversification. MNEs such as Bombardier, GE, Mitsui, Samsung, Siemens, and Vivendi Universal serve as cases in point.

anchored replicators

Companies that seek to replicate a set of activities in related industries in a small number of countries anchored by the home country.

multinational replicators

Firms which engage in product-related diversification on one hand and far-flung multinational expansion on the other hand.

far-flung conglomerates

Conglomerate firms which pursue both extensive product-unrelated diversification and extensive geographic diversification.

FIGURE 9.3   Combining Product and Geographic Diversification

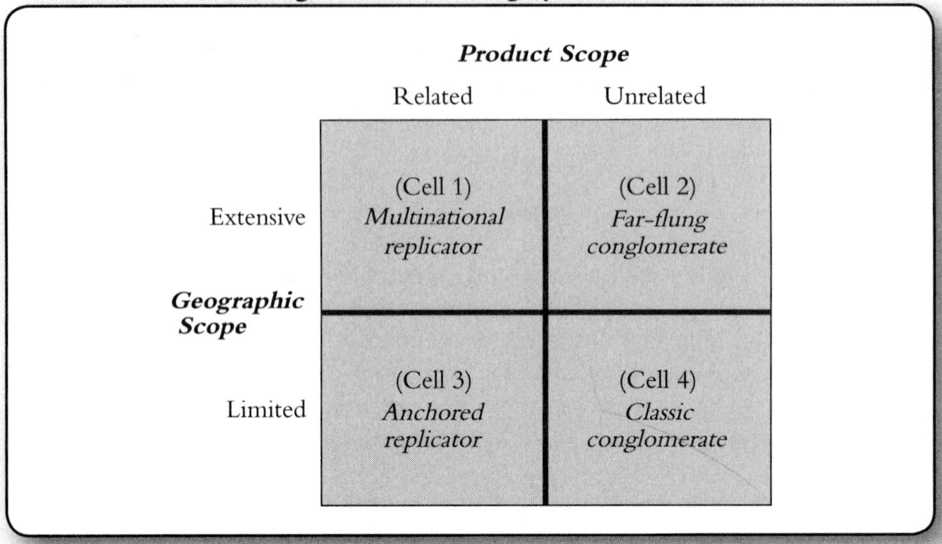

Finally, in Cell 4 we find **classic conglomerates,** which engage in product-unrelated diversification within a small set of countries centered on the home country. Current examples include India's Tata Group, Turkey's Koc Group, and China's Hope Group.

Overall, migrating from one cell to another, although difficult, is possible. For instance, most of the current multinational replicators (Cell 1) can trace their roots as anchored replicators (Cell 3). One interesting migratory pattern in the last two decades is that many classic conglomerates, such as Finland's Nokia and South Korea's Samsung, that formerly dominated multiple unrelated industries in their home countries, have reduced their product scope but significantly expanded their geographic scope—in other words, migrating from Cell 4 to Cell 1.[17] In broad strategic terms, this means that the costs for doing business abroad have declined and that the costs for managing conglomeration have risen. In other words:

Costs in Cell 4 (managing conglomeration while mostly staying at home) > Costs in Cell 1 (doing business abroad while mostly staying at home) but maintaining product relatedness in diversification)

Further, asserting that firms in a particular cell will outperform those in other cells is naïve if not foolhardy. In *every* cell, we can find both highly successful and highly unsuccessful firms. Next, we explore why this is the case.

A Comprehensive Model of Diversification

classic conglomerate

Companies that engage in product-unrelated diversification within a small set of countries centered on the home country.

Why do firms diversify? The "strategy tripod" suggests a comprehensive model of diversification (Figure 9.4) to answer this complex and important question.

Industry-Based Considerations

A straightforward motivation for diversification is the growth opportunities in an industry. If an industry has substantial growth opportunities (such as biotechnology),

FIGURE 9.4   A Comprehensive Model of Diversification

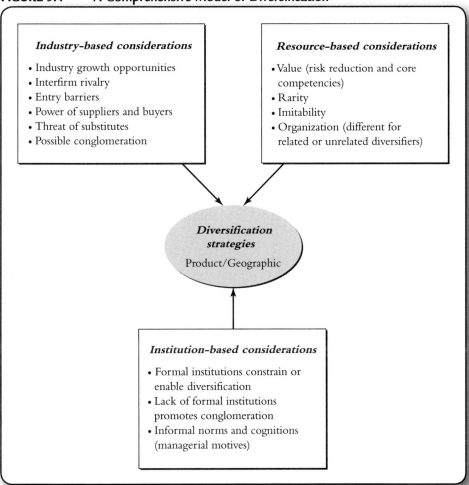

most incumbents have an incentive to engage in product-related and/or international diversification. However, if it is a "sunset" industry (think of typewriters), many incumbents may exit and pursue opportunities elsewhere.[18]

In addition to growth opportunities, the structural attractiveness of an industry, captured by the five forces framework, also has a significant bearing on diversification. Recall that the first force, interfirm rivalry, is primarily manifested through two competitive strategies: cost leadership and differentiation. Pursuing each of them may motivate firms to diversify. A cost leadership strategy may encourage firms to seek opportunities for product-related diversification. For example, PepsiCo, a cost leader, recently diversified into sports drinks. When demand for carbonated beverages, such as Mountain Dew, flattened out (at least in the United States), PepsiCo's considerable distribution capabilities could find some synergy by adding the newly acquired Gatorade products. A differentiation strategy can also lead to product-related diversification. Most of us saw the one-and-only (differentiated) Disney movie *Lion King*. Little did

Strategy in Action 9.2 - Indian Companies on a Buying Binge

One striking indicator of Indian companies' coming of age is the bidding war for Britain's Jaguar and Land Rover car businesses in 2007–2008. *Both* firms shortlisted by Jaguar and Land Rover's owner, Ford Motor Company, were Indian: Tata Motors and Mahindra & Mahindra. Of the two, Tata Motors, a part of Tata Group, won the bidding war and bought Jaguar and Land Rover in March 2008. Britain's leading magazine, *The Economist*, noted the irony: "The future of these two grand old badges will be shaped not in Coventry, cradle of the British motor industry, but in Pune, home of Tata Motors."

The ambition and confidence exhibited by Tata Motors and Mahindra & Mahindra are not uncommon among leading Indian companies these days. In the past few years, thanks to rapid domestic growth, their average profit margins are approximately 10%—more than twice the global average. With spare cash, Indian companies have been marauding acquisitively. While India's IT trio—Wipro, Infosys, and Tata Consulting Services (TCS)—have acquired a series of Western businesses, non-IT companies have also intensified their foreign acquisitions. Tata Group, for example, recently bought Britain's Tetley Tea, Singapore's NatSteel, and South Korea's Daewoo Trucks. The group claimed that it looks beyond sheer size in search of a strategic fit when making acquisitions. Since Indian acquisitions are so recent, no major foreign acquisition has failed so far.

However, given that globally, approximately 70% of acquisitions end up in failure, how successful the inexperienced Indian acquirers will be in managing their acquired businesses remains to be seen.

Sources: Based on (1) *Economic Times*, 2008, Tatas seek long-term pact with Ford, March 15, economictimes.indiatimes.com; (2) *The Economist*, 2007, Marauding maharajahs, March 31: 71–72; (3) *The Economist*, 2008, The challengers, January 12: 62–64.

we know that Disney unleashed a total of 150 (!) related products based on *Lion King* (such as children's books and toys) and made $3 billion.

Second, entry barriers do not always deter new entrants. For entrants determined to march into the focal industry or country, high entry barriers often result in acquisitions, as opposed to green-field entries. Shown in Strategy in Action 9.2, for India's new breed of MNEs, acquiring incumbents to gain immediate market access is an efficient way to overcome entry barriers.

The bargaining power of suppliers and buyers may prompt firms to broaden their scope, by acquiring suppliers upstream and/or buyers downstream. For example, Sony, diversifying downstream, has now become a leading player in movies and music.

The threat of substitutes also has a bearing on diversification. Kodak and Fuji have been threatened by Canon, Samsung, and HP, which diversified into digital cameras—a substitute for photographic films. None of these electronics firms had been regarded as a rival by Kodak and Fuji until recently.

In summary, the industry-based view, by definition, has largely focused on product-related diversification with an industry focus (often in combination with geographic diversification). Next, we introduce resource- and institution-based considerations to enrich this discussion.

Resource-Based Considerations

Shown in Figure 9.4, the resource-based view—outlined by the VRIO framework—has a set of complementary considerations underpinning diversification strategies.

VALUE

Does diversification create value? The answer is "Yes," but only under certain conditions.[19] Compared with non-diversified single-business firms, diversified firms are able to spread risk. Even for overdiversified firms that have to restructure, no one is returning to a single business with no diversification. The most optimal point tends to be some moderate level of diversification.

Beyond risk reduction, diversification can create value by leveraging certain core competencies, resources, and capabilities. Honda, for instance, is renowned for its product-related diversification by leveraging its core competence in internal combustion engines. It not only competes in automobiles and motorcycles, but also in boat engines and lawnmowers.

RARITY

For diversification to add value, firms must have unique skills to execute such a strategy. In 2004, an executive team at China's Lenovo planned to acquire IBM's PC division—a significant move in geographic diversification. The team confronted Lenovo's suspicious board that raised a crucial question: if a venerable American technology company had failed to profit from the PC business, did Lenovo have what it takes to do better when managing such a complex global business? The answer was actually "No." The board gave its blessing to the plan only after the acquisition team agreed to not only acquire the business, but also to recruit top American executives.

IMITABILITY

While many firms undertake acquisitions, a much smaller number of them have mastered the art of post-acquisition integration.[20] Consequently, firms that excel in integration possess *hard-to-imitate* capabilities. At Northrop, integrating acquired businesses has progressed to a "science." Each must conform to a carefully orchestrated plan listing nearly 400 items, from how to issue press releases to which accounting software to use. Unlike its bigger defense rivals such as Boeing and Raytheon, Northrop thus far has not stumbled with any of the acquisitions.

ORGANIZATION

Fundamentally, whether diversification adds value boils down to how firms are organized to take advantage of the benefits while minimizing the costs. Since Chapter 10 will be devoted to organizational issues in geographic diversification, here we focus on

TABLE 9.1   **Product-Related versus Product-Unrelated Diversification**

	PRODUCT-RELATED DIVERSIFICATION	PRODUCT-UNRELATED DIVERSIFICATION
Synergy	Operational synergy	Financial synergy
Economies	Economies of scale	Economies of scope
Control emphasis	Strategic (behavior) control	Financial (output) control
Organizational structure	Centralization	Decentralization
Organizational culture	Cooperative	Competitive
Information processing	Intensive rich communication	Less intensive communication

product diversification. Given the recent popularity of product-related diversification, many people believe that product-unrelated diversification is an inherently value-destroying strategy. However, this is not true. With proper organization, product-unrelated diversification can add value.

Shown in Table 9.1, product-related diversifiers need to foster a centralized organizational structure with a cooperative culture.[21] The key is to explore operational linkages among various units, and some units may need to be pulled back to coordinate with other units. For example, to maximize corporate profits, Disney's animation division producing the movie *Lion King* had to wait before launching the movie until its merchandise divisions were ready to hawk related merchandise. If animation managers' bonuses were linked to the annual box-office receipts of the movie, they would obviously be eager to release the movie. But if bonuses were linked with overall corporate profits, then animation managers would be happy to assist and coordinate with their merchandise colleagues and would not mind waiting for a while. Consequently, corporate headquarters should not evaluate division performance solely based on strict financial targets (such as sales). The principal control mechanism is **strategic control** (or **behavior control**), based on largely subjective criteria to monitor and evaluate units' contributions with rich communication between corporate and divisional managers.

However, the best way to organize conglomerates is exactly the *opposite*. The emphasis is on **financial control** (or **output control**), based on largely objective criteria (such as return on investment) to monitor and evaluate units' performance. Because most corporate managers have experience in only one industry (or a few industries) and none realistically can be an expert in the wide variety of unrelated industries represented in a conglomerate, corporate headquarters is forced to focus on financial control, which does not require a lot of rich industry-specific knowledge. Otherwise, corporate managers will experience a tremendous **information overload** (too much information to process). Consequently, the appropriate organizational structure is decentralization with substantial divisional autonomy—in other words, structurally separate units.[22] To keep divisional managers focused on financial performance, their compensation should be directly linked with quantifiable unit performance. Thus, the relationship among various divisions is competitive, each trying to attract a larger share of corporate investments. Such competition within an internal capital market is similar to standalone firms competing for more funds from the external capital market. The Virgin Group, for example, considers itself as "a branded venture-capital firm" whose portfolio includes airlines, railways, beverages, and music stores. The corporate headquarters supplies a common brand (Virgin) and leaves divisional managers "alone" as long as they deliver sound performance.

strategic control (or behavior control)

Controlling subsidiary/unit operations based on whether they engage in desirable strategic behavior (such as cooperation).

financial control (or output control)

Controlling subsidiary/unit operations strictly based on whether they meet financial/output criteria.

information overload

Too much information to process.

Overall, the key to adding value through either product-related or -unrelated diversification is the appropriate match between diversification strategy and organizational structure and control.[23] Conglomerates often fail when corporate managers impose a more centralized structure undermining lower-level autonomy (see Strategy in Action 9.1).

Institution-Based Considerations

Given that it is a combination of formal and informal institutions that drives firm strategies such as diversification, we examine each set of institutions in turn.

FORMAL INSTITUTIONS

Formal institutions affect diversification strategies. The rise of conglomerates in the 1950s and 1960s in developed economies was inadvertently promoted by formal constraints designed to curtail product-related diversification. In the United States, the post-1950 antitrust authorities viewed product-related diversification (especially mergers), designed to enhance firms' market power within an industry, as "anticompetitive" and challenged them (Strategy in Action 9.1). Thus, firms seeking growth (such as Beatrice) were forced to look beyond their industry, triggering a great wave of conglomeration. By the 1980s, the US government changed its mind and no longer critically scrutinized related mergers within the same industry. It is not a coincidence that the movement to dismantle conglomerates and focus on core competencies has taken off since the 1980s.

Similarly, the popularity of conglomeration in emerging economies is often underpinned by their governments' protectionist policies. Conglomerates (often called **business groups** in emerging economies) can leverage connections with governments by obtaining licenses, arranging financing (often from state-owned or -controlled banks), and securing technology. As long as protectionist policies prevent significant foreign entries, conglomerates can dominate domestic economies. However, when governments start to dismantle protectionist policies, competitive pressures from foreign multinationals (as well as domestic non-diversified rivals) may intensify. These changes may force conglomerates to improve performance by reducing their scope (see Closing Case).[24]

Likewise, the significant rise of geographic diversification undertaken by numerous firms can be attributed, at least in part, to the gradual opening of many economies initiated by formal market-supporting and -opening policy changes. (Strategy in Action 9.3 discusses M&As in China.)

INFORMAL INSTITUTIONS

Informal institutions can be found along normative and cognitive dimensions. Normatively, managers often seek to behave in ways that will not cause them to be noticed as different and consequently singled out for criticism by shareholders, board directors, and the media. Therefore, when the norm is to engage in conglomeration, more and more managers may simply follow such a norm. Poorly performing firms are especially under such normative pressures. While early movers in conglomeration (such as GE) may indeed have special skills and insights to make such a complex strategy work, many late movers probably do not have these capabilities and simply jump on the "bandwagon" when facing poor performance.[25] Over time, this explains—at least partially—the massive disappointment with conglomeration in developed economies.

business groups

A term to describe a conglomerate, which is often used in emerging economies.

Strategy in Action 9.3 - Making M&As Fly in China

The first wave of foreign direct investment (FDI) in China, in the 1980s, mostly took the form of joint ventures (JVs). A second wave followed in the 1990s in the form of wholly foreign-owned enterprises (WFOEs). Now a third wave of FDI—cross-board mergers and acquisitions (M&As)—is gaining strength.

Consider the forces driving this third wave. China has a massive appetite for FDI; it is one of the world's largest FDI recipients. Yet, M&As account for only 10% to 15% of FDI flowing into China, compared with approximately 70% of FDI outside of China that takes the form of M&As. One reason for this disparity is that, until China joined the World Trade Organization in 2001, national regulations often encouraged (or required) foreign entrants to form JVs or set up WFOEs, while explicitly discouraging M&As. But China has since gradually loosened the regulations that govern foreign takeovers of Chinese assets, especially state-owned enterprises (SOEs), and has made explicit moves to attract foreign M&As. In many industries, including financial services and manufacturing, constraints on M&As are just now being lifted. At the same time, Chinese firms are increasingly engaging in cross-border M&As of their own. To the extent that the Chinese government supports the outbound M&As, it must in most cases clear the path for inbound M&As, according to international norms of reciprocity.

Given the environment, how should foreign companies proceed? In many ways, strategies for M&As in China overlap with those for M&As elsewhere. But recent research has uncovered some idiosyncrasies that are specific to acquisitions in China. First, Chinese SOEs are rife with organizational slack. Government agencies have restructured some SOEs to reduce underutilized resources and to make the SOEs more attractive M&A targets for foreign firms. While slack usually indicates inefficiency, in certain firms, some slack—such as unabsorbed cash flow in the form of depreciation funds, reserve funds, and retained earnings—may indicate the potential for increased performance, actually enhancing targets' attractiveness.

Second, it is well known that many Chinese SOEs maintain three sets of books: one set that exaggerates performance, so they can brag to administrative superiors; one that underreports performance, for tax purposes; and one that is fairly accurate, for managers themselves. Acquisition targets are likely to show foreign negotiators the bragging books initially. As a result, foreign firms need to be aggressive in conducting due diligence to uncover an accurate picture of targets' assets and resources. This is particularly relevant when investigating slack.

Finally, most Western firms launching JVs and WFOEs in China have believed that ethnic Chinese managers—those from overseas Chinese economies, such as Hong Kong and Taiwan, who are well versed in the local language—were the best choice for running their operations in China. Meanwhile, they have presumed that Western managers would be less effective because of language and cultural barriers. But evidence from recent research suggests the *opposite*: Using surveys, interviews, and other tools, researchers find that ethnic Chinese managers hired by Western companies to run these businesses are, on average, *less* effective than their non-Chinese counterparts, as measured by the length of their tenures and attainment of performance goals. How could this be?

Strategy in Action 9.3 - (continued)

One reason appears to be that ethnic Chinese managers often struggle with an ambiguous managerial identity: Western corporate headquarters views them as "us," while local Chinese employees also expect them to be "us." When these managers favor headquarters on issues where headquarters and locals conflict—such as whether Western employees and locals should receive equal compensation or whether chopsticks or forks should be used at company banquets—local employees may regard them as traitors of sorts. That corrodes employees' trust, ultimately undermining ethnic Chinese managers' performance. On the other hand, employees give Western managers the benefit of the doubt. They expect these managers to behave differently, to commit cultural errors, and to show allegiance to the parent firm. This tolerance by local employees of Western managers'

differences can enhance these managers' confidence and performance.

Of course, not every non-Chinese manager outperforms every ethnic Chinese manager. It is clear, however, that managerial effectiveness in China does not depend on one's ability to use chopsticks. This point is crucial as more M&As flow into China and more acquiring companies staff their target firms' management.

Source: Adapted from M. W. Peng, 2006, Making M&As fly in China, *Harvard Business Review*, March: 26–27. For underlying research, see (1) Z. Lin, M. W. Peng, H. Yang, & S. Sun, 2008, What drives M&As in China and America? Networks, learning, and institutions, Working paper, University of Texas at Dallas; (2) M. W. Peng, 2005, From China strategy to global strategy, *Asia Pacific Journal of Management*, 22: 123–141; (3) J. Tan & M. W. Peng, 2003, Organizational slack and firm performance during economic transitions, *Strategic Management Journal*, 24: 1249–1263.

Another informal driver for conglomeration is the cognitive dimension—namely, the internalized beliefs that guide managerial behavior.[26] Managers may have motives to advance their personal interests that are not necessarily aligned with the interests of the firm and its shareholders. These are called managerial motives for diversification, such as (1) reduction of managers' employment risk and (2) pursuit of power, prestige, and income. Because single-business firms are vulnerable to economy-wide ups and downs (such as recessions), managers' jobs and careers may be at risk. Thus, managers may have an interest to diversify their firms in order to reduce their own employment risk. In addition, since power, prestige, and income are typically associated with a larger firm size, some managers may have self-interested incentives to overdiversify their firms, resulting in value destruction. Such excessive diversification is known as empire building (see Chapter 11).[27]

In summary, the institution-based view suggests that formal and informal institutional conditions directly shape diversification strategy.[28] Taken together, the industry-, resource-, and institution-based views collectively explain how the scope of the firm evolves around the world.

The Evolution of the Scope of the Firm[29]

At its core, diversification is essentially driven by economic benefits and bureaucratic costs. **Economic benefits** are the various forms of synergy (operational or financial) discussed earlier. **Bureaucratic costs** are the additional costs associated with a larger, more diversified organization, such as more headcounts and more complicated information systems. Overall, it is the difference between the benefits and costs that leads to certain

economic benefits

Benefits brought by the various forms of synergy in the context of diversification.

bureaucratic costs

The additional costs associated with a larger, more diversified organization, such as more employees and more expensive information systems.

FIGURE 9.5   What Determines the Scope of the Firm?

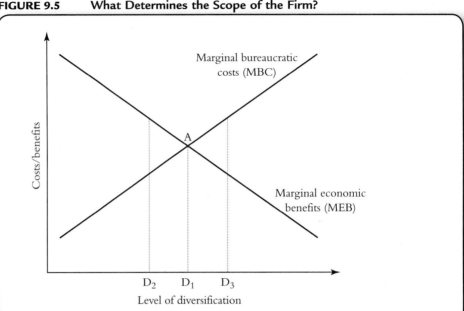

Source: Adapted from G. Jones & C. Hill, 1988, "Transaction cost analysis of strategy-structure choices" (p. 166), JOURNAL, 9: 159-172. Reprinted by permission of John Wiley & Sons Limited.

marginal economic benefits (MEB)

The economic benefits of the last unit of growth (such as the last acquisition).

marginal bureaucratic costs (MBC)

The bureaucratic costs of the last unit of organizational expansion (such as the last subsidiary established).

diversification strategies. Since the economic benefits of the last unit of growth (such as the last acquisition) can be defined as **marginal economic benefits** (MEB) and the additional bureaucratic costs incurred as **marginal bureaucratic costs** (MBC), the scope of the firm is thus determined by a comparison between MEB and MBC.[30] Shown in Figure 9.5, the optimal scope is at point A, where the appropriate level of diversification should be D_1. If the level of diversification is D_2, some economic benefits can be gained by moving up to D_1. Conversely, if a firm overdiversifies to D_3, reducing the scope to D_1 becomes necessary. Thus, how the scope of the firm evolves over time can be analyzed by focusing on MEB and MBC.

In the United States (Figure 9.6), between the 1950s and 1970s, if we hold MBC constant (an assumption relaxed later), the MEB curve shifted upward, resulting in an expanded scope of the firm on average (moving from D_1 to D_2). This is because of (1) growth opportunities within the same industry through product-related diversification, especially for large firms, were blocked by formal institutions such as antitrust policies, (2) the emergence of organizational capabilities to derive financial synergy from conglomeration, and (3) the diffusion of these actions through imitation, leading to an informal but visible norm among managers that such product-unrelated growth was legitimate. During that time, external capital markets, which were less sophisticated, were supportive, believing that conglomerates had an advantage in allocating capital (see Strategy in Action 9.1).

However, by the early 1980s, significant transitions occurred along industry, resource, and institutional dimensions. First, M&As within the same industry were no longer critically scrutinized by the government, making it unnecessary to focus on

FIGURE 9.6 **The Evolution of the Scope of the Firm in the United States: 1950–1970 and 1970–1990**

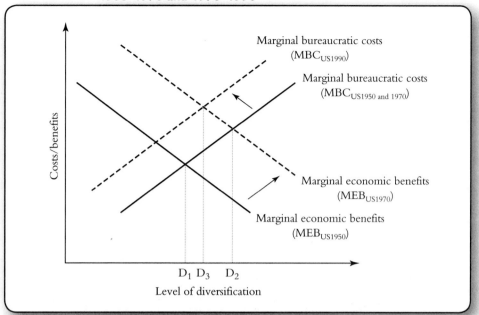

Source: M. W. Peng, S.-H. Lee, & D. Wang, 2005, What determines the scope of the firm over time? A focus on institutional relatedness (p. 627), from *Academy of Management Review*. © 2005. Reprinted by permission of Academy of Management Review via Copyright Clearance Center.

unrelated diversification in different industries. Second, a resource-based analysis suggests that given the VRIO hurdles, it would be extremely challenging—though not impossible—to derive competitive advantage from conglomeration (discussed earlier). In other words, with an expanded scope of the firm, MBC also increased, often outpacing the increase in MEB (Figure 9.6). Many firms (such as Beatrice) overdiversified and destroyed value. Consequently, a dramatic reversal in US investor sentiment occurred toward conglomeration: Positive in the 1960s, neutral in the 1970s, and negative in the 1980s (Strategy in Action 9.1). Parallel to these developments, external capital markets became better developed, with more analysts and more transparent and real-time reporting, all of which allowed for more efficient channeling of financial resources to high-potential firms. As a result, the conglomerate advantage serving as an internal capital market became less attractive. Finally, informal norms and cognitions changed, as managers increasingly became more disciplined and focused on shareholder value maximization and believed that reducing the scope of the firm was the "right" thing to do. All these combined to push the appropriate scope of the firm from D_2 to D_3 in Figure 9.6 by the 1990s.

Globally, an interesting extension is to understand the puzzle as to why conglomeration, which has been recently discredited in developed economies, is not only in vogue but also in some (but not all) cases adds value in emerging economies. Figure 9.7 shows how conglomerates in emerging economies may add value at a higher level of diversification, whereby firms in developed economies are not able to. This analysis relies on two crucial and reasonable assumptions. The first is that at a given level of

FIGURE 9.7   **The Optimal Scope of the Firm: Developed versus Emerging Economies at the Same Time**

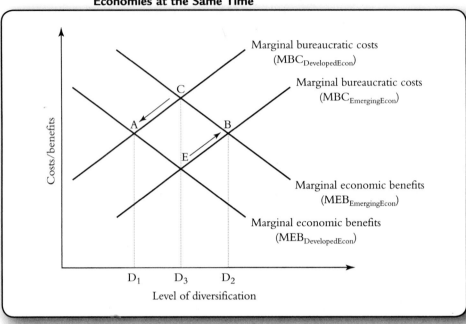

Source: M. W. Peng, S.-H. Lee, & D. Wang, 2005, What determines the scope of the firm over time? A focus on institutional relatedness (p. 628), from *Academy of Management Review.* © 2005. Reprinted by permission of Academy of Management Review via Copyright Clearance Center.

diversification, $MEB_{EmergingEcon} > MEB_{DevelopedEcon}$. This is primarily because under-developed external capital markets in emerging economies make conglomerates as internal capital markets more attractive.

A second assumption is that at a given level of diversification, $MEB_{EmergingEcon} < MBC_{DevelopedEcon}$. In emerging economies, because of the weaknesses of formal institutions, informal constraints rise to play a *larger* role in regulating economic exchanges (see Chapter 4). Most conglomerates in these countries are family firms, whose managers rely more on informal personal (and often family) relationships to get things done. Relative to firms in developed economies, firms in emerging economies typically feature a lower level of bureaucratization, formalization, and professionalization, which may result in lower bureaucratic costs.

Consequently, for any scope between D_1 and D_2 (such as D_3) in Figure 9.7, firms in developed economies at point C need to be downscoped toward point A (D_1), whereas there is still room to gain for firms in emerging economies at point E, which can move up to point B (D_2). However, bear in mind that conglomerates in emerging economies confront the same problem that plagues those in developed economies: The wider the scope, the harder it is for corporate headquarters to coordinate, control, and invest properly in different units. It seems evident that for conglomerates in emerging economies, there is also a point beyond which further diversification may backfire. As shown in the Closing Case on South Korean conglomerates, the conglomerate advantage is especially likely to be eroded when external capital markets in emerging economies become better developed.

Overall, industry dynamics, resource repertoires, and institutional conditions are not static, nor are diversification strategies. The next two sections describe two primary means for expanding and contracting the scope of the firm—through acquisitions and restructuring, respectively.

Acquisitions

Setting the Terms Straight

Although the term **mergers and acquisitions (M&As)** is often used, in reality, acquisitions dominate the scene. An **acquisition** is transfer of the control of assets, operations, and management from one firm (target) to another (acquirer), the former becoming a unit of the latter. A **merger** is the combination of assets, operations, and management of two firms to establish a new legal entity. Only approximately 3% of cross-border M&As are mergers. Even many so-called "mergers of equals" turn out to be one firm taking over another (such as DaimlerChrysler). A recent *World Investment Report* published by the United Nations opines that "The number of 'real' mergers is so low that, for practical purposes, 'M&As' basically mean 'acquisitions.'"[31] Consequently, we will use the two terms, "M&As" and "acquisitions," interchangeably.

Specifically, we focus on cross-border (international) M&As, whose various types are illustrated by Figure 9.8. Cross-border activities represent approximately 30% of all M&As, and M&As represent the largest proportion (about 70%) of FDI flows.

There are three primary categories of M&As: (1) horizontal, (2) vertical, and (3) conglomerate. **Horizontal M&As** refer to deals involving competing firms in the same industry (such as BP/Amoco).[32] Approximately 70% of the cross-border M&As are horizontal. **Vertical M&As,** another form of product-related diversification, are deals that allow the focal firms to acquire suppliers (upstream) and/or buyers (downstream) (such as Sony/Columbia Pictures). About 10% of cross-border M&As are vertical ones. **Conglomerate M&As** are transactions involving firms in product-unrelated industries (such as Vivendi/Universal). Roughly 20% of cross-border M&As are conglomerate deals.

The terms of M&As can be friendly or hostile. In **friendly M&As,** the board and management of a target firm agree to the transaction. **Hostile M&As** (also known as **hostile takeovers**) are undertaken against the wishes of the target firm's board and management, who reject M&A offers. In the United States, hostile M&As are more frequent, reaching 14% of all deals in the 1980s (although the number went down to 4% in the 1990s). Internationally, hostile M&As are very rare, accounting for less than 0.2% of all deals and less than 5% of total value.

Motives for Mergers and Acquisitions

What drives M&As? Table 9.2 shows three drivers: (1) synergistic, (2) hubris, and (3) managerial motives, which can be illustrated by the three leading perspectives.[33] In terms of synergistic motives, the most frequently mentioned industry-based rationale is to enhance and consolidate market power.[34] For example, after a series of M&As in three years (such as Renault/Nissan), the top ten automakers increased their global market share from 69% in 1996 to 80% in 1999.[35]

mergers and acquisitions (M&As)

Firms either merging with or acquiring other firms.

acquisition

The transfer of control of assets, operations, and management from one firm (target) to another (acquirer); the former becoming a unit of the latter.

merger

The combination of assets, operations, and management of two firms to establish a new legal entity.

horizontal M&As

Merger and acquisition deals involving competing firms in the same industry.

vertical M&As

Merger and acquisition deals involving suppliers (upstream) and/or buyers (downstream).

conglomerate M&As

M&As deals involving firms in product-unrelated industries.

FIGURE 9.8   Cross-border M&As

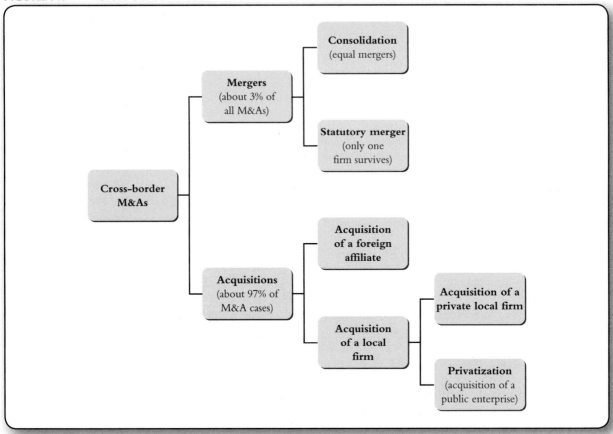

Source: Adapted from United Nations, 2000, World Investment Report 2000 (p. 100), New York: UN

friendly M&As

Mergers and acquisitions in which the board and management of a target firm agree to the transaction (although they may initially resist).

hostile M&As (also known as hostile takeovers)

Mergers and acquisitions undertaken against the wishes of the target firm's board and management, who reject M&A offers.

From a resource-based view, the most important synergistic rationale is to leverage superior resources.[36] Lufthansa recently acquired Air Dolomiti, an award-winning regional airline in northern Italy. While many small airlines drop out, Lufthansa's willingness to leverage its superior resources helps ensure Air Dolomiti's presence in the skies. Finally, another motive is to gain access to complementary resources, as evidenced by Lenovo's interest in IBM's worldwide client base.

In terms of synergistic motives, from an institution-based view, acquisitions are often a response to formal institutional constraints and transitions in search of synergy.[37] It is not a coincidence that the number of cross-border M&As has skyrocketed in the last two decades. This is the same period during which trade and investment barriers have gone down and FDI has risen.[38]

While all the synergistic motives, in theory, add value, hubris and managerial motives reduce value. **Hubris** refers to managers' overconfidence in their capabilities.[39] Managers of acquiring firms make two very strong statements.[40] The first is that "We can manage *your* assets better than you [target firm managers] can!" The second statement is even bolder, because acquirers of publicly listed firms always have to pay an

TABLE 9.2   **Motives Behind Mergers and Acquisitions**

	INDUSTRY-BASED ISSUES	RESOURCE-BASED ISSUES	INSTITUTION-BASED ISSUES
Synergistic Motives	• Enhance and consolidate market power • Overcome entry barriers • Reduce risk • Scope economies	• Leverage superior managerial capabilities • Access to complementary resources • Learning and developing new skills	• Respond to formal institutional constraints and transitions • Take advantage of market openings and globalization
Hubris Motives		• Managers' overconfidence in their capabilities	• Herd behavior—following norms and chasing fads of M&As
Managerial Motives			• Self-interested actions such as empire-building guided by informal norms and cognitions

acquisition premium (an above-the-market price to acquire another firm).[41] This is essentially saying: "We are smarter than the market!" To the extent that the capital market is (relatively) efficient and that the market price of target firms reflects their intrinsic value, there is simply no hope to profit from such acquisitions. Even when we assume the capital market to be inefficient, it is still apparent that when the premium is too high, acquiring firms must have overpaid.[42] This is especially true when multiple firms bid for the same target, the winning acquirer may suffer from the "winner's curse" from auctions—that is, the winner has overpaid. From an institution-based view, many managers join the acquisition "bandwagon," after some first-mover firms start doing deals in an industry. The fact that M&As come in "waves" speaks volumes about such a herd behavior. Eager to catch up, many late movers in such "waves" may rush in, prompted by a "Wow! Get it!" mentality. Not surprisingly, many deals go bust.

While the hubris motives suggest that managers may *unknowingly* overpay for targets, managerial motives posit that for self-interested reasons, some managers may have *knowingly* overpaid the acquisition premium for target firms. Driven by such norms and cognitions, some managers may have deliberately overdiversified their firms through M&As (see Chapter 11 for details).

Overall, synergistic motives add value, and hubris and managerial motives destroy value. They may *simultaneously* coexist. Next, we discuss how they impact performance.

Performance of Mergers and Acquisitions

Despite the popularity of M&As, their performance record is rather sobering. As many as 70% of M&As reportedly fail. On average, acquiring firms' performance does not improve after acquisitions and is often negatively affected.[43] Target firms, after being acquired, often perform worse than when they were independent standalone firms.[44] The only identifiable group of winners is shareholders of target firms, who may experience, on average, a 24% increase in their stock value during the period of the transaction (thanks to the acquisition premium).[45] Shareholders of acquiring firms experience a 4% loss of their stock value during the same period. The combined wealth of shareholders of both acquiring and target firms is marginally positive, less than 2%.[46] While

hubris

Managers' overconfidence in their capabilities.

acquisition premium

The difference between the acquisition price and the market value of target firms.

TABLE 9.3   **Symptoms of Merger and Acquisition Failures**

	PROBLEMS FOR ALL M&As	PARTICULAR PROBLEMS FOR CROSS-BORDER M&As
Pre-acquisition: ***Overpayment for targets***	• Managers overestimate their ability to create value • Inadequate pre-acquisition screening • Poor strategic fit	• Lack of familiarity with foreign cultures, institutions, and business systems • Inadequate number of worthy targets • Nationalistic concerns against foreign takeovers (political and media levels)
Post-acquisition: ***Failure in integration***	• Poor organizational fit • Failure to address multiple stakeholder groups' concerns	• Clashes of organizational cultures compounded by clashes of national cultures • Nationalistic concerns against foreign takeovers (firm and employee levels)

these findings are mostly from three decades of M&A data in the United States (where half of the global M&As take place and most of the M&A research is done), they probably also apply to cross-border acquisitions.

Why do many acquisitions fail? Problems can be identified in both pre- and post-acquisition phases (Table 9.3). During the pre-acquisition phase, because of executive hubris and/or managerial motives, acquiring firms may overpay targets—in other words, they fall into a "synergy trap."[47] For example, in 1998, when Chrysler was profitable, Daimler-Benz paid $40 billion, a 40% premium over its market value, to acquire it. Given that Chrysler's expected performance was already built into its existing share price, at a *zero* premium, Daimler-Benz's willingness to pay for such a high premium was indicative of (1) strong managerial capabilities to derive synergy, (2) high levels of hubris, (3) significant managerial self-interests, or (4) all of the above. As it turned out, by the time Chrysler was sold in 2007, it fetched only $7.4 billion, destroying four-fifths of the value.

Another primary pre-acquisition problem is inadequate screening and failure to achieve **strategic fit,** which is the effective match of complementary strategic capabilities. For example, the $35 billion acquisition (claimed as a "merger") of Sweden's Astra by Britain's Zeneca—both in the pharmaceutical industry—in 1999 might lack strategic fit. While the combined firm had greater scale economies, both had a large number of soon-to-expire patents that would no longer serve as entry barriers to deter generic drug manufacturers.[48]

Internationally, because of greater institutional and cultural distances, these pre-acquisition problems can be even worse.[49] In addition, in oligopolistic industries (such as automobiles and pharmaceuticals) where the number of worthy targets may be small, once rivals start to "cherry pick" targets, other firms may feel a greater urgency to "rush in," failing to adequately consider crucial strategic fit issues. In addition, nationalistic concerns against foreign acquisitions may erupt. When Dubai Ports World (DP World) from the United Arab Emirates tried to acquire US ports in 2006, nationalistic sentiments torpedoed the deal.[50]

During the post-acquisition phase, numerous integration problems may pop up. Even when the acquiring firms have paid attention to strategic fit, it is important to also consider **organizational fit,** which is the similarity in cultures, systems, and structures. One study reports that a striking 80% of acquiring firms do *not* analyze organizational fit with targets.[51] For instance, on paper, Daimler-Benz and Chrysler had a good strategic fit both in terms of complementary product lines and geographic scope. But there

strategic fit

The complementarity of partner firms' "hard" skills and resources, such as technology, capital, and distribution channels.

organizational fit

The complementarity of partner firms' "soft" organizational traits, such as goals, experiences, and behaviors, that facilitate cooperation.

seemed to be inadequate organizational fit. American managers resented the dominance of German managers, who promised that the deal would be a "merger of equals." German top executives disliked being paid two-thirds less than their Chrysler colleagues. These cultural clashes led to a mass exodus of American managers leaving Chrysler—a common phenomenon in acquired firms.[52]

Another issue is the failure to address multiple stakeholders' concerns during integration, which involves job losses, restructured responsibilities, diminished power, and much else that is stressful (see Opening Case). Shown in Figure 9.9, substantial concerns arise among a variety of stakeholders, such as investors and customers, as well as employees at all levels. Most companies focus on task issues (such as standardizing financial reporting) first, and pay inadequate attention to people issues, resulting in low morale and high turnover, especially among its best talents.[53]

In cross-border M&As, integration difficulties may be much worse, because clashes of organizational cultures are compounded by clashes of national cultures.[54] When Four Seasons acquired a hotel in Paris, the simple "American" request that employees smile at customers was resisted by French employees and laughed at by the local media as "la culture Mickey Mouse."[55]

Overall, although acquisitions are often the largest capital expenditures most firms ever make, they are frequently the worst planned and executed activities of all. Unfortunately, when merging firms try to sort out the mess, competitors are likely to launch aggressive attacks to take advantage of the chaos (see Chapter 8). When DaimlerChrysler struggled with postmerger chaos, BMW overtook Mercedes-Benz to become the world's number-one luxury carmaker. Adding all of the above, it is hardly surprising that most M&As fail.

FIGURE 9.9   Concerns of Different Stakeholders During M&As

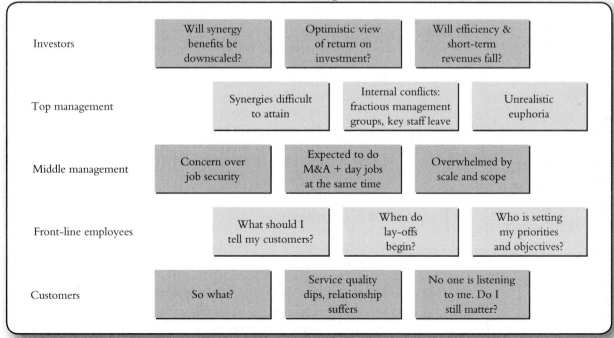

Restructuring

Setting the Terms Straight

Although the term **"restructuring"** normally refers to adjustments to firm size and scope through either diversification (expansion or entry), divestiture (contraction or exit), or both,[56] its most common definition is *reduction* of firm size and scope—we will adopt this more frequently used definition here. There is a historical reason behind this one-sided use of the word "restructuring." By the 1980s and 1990s when this word surfaced in our vocabulary, many firms suffered from overdiversification and became interested in reducing size and scope. Using this definition, there are two primary ways of restructuring: (1) **downsizing** (reducing the number of employees through lay-offs, early retirements, and outsourcing),[57] and (2) **downscoping** (reducing the scope of the firm through divestitures and spin-offs).[58] Another side of downscoping is **refocusing,** namely, narrowing the scope of the firm to focus on a few areas.

Motives for Restructuring

We can draw on industry-, resource-, and institution-based views to understand the motives for restructuring.[59] From an industry-based view, restructuring is often triggered by a rising level of competition within an industry (such as telecommunications).[60] Given that a primary motivation for M&As is to eliminate redundant assets, industries experiencing a high level of M&As (such as automobiles in Opening Case) not surprisingly often unleash major restructuring efforts.[61]

The resource-based view suggests that while restructuring may bring some benefits, significant costs also arise (such as organizational chaos, anxiety, and low morale). When most rivals restructure, these activities may not generate sustainable value, are not rare, and cause organizational problems. In short, it is "not possible for firms to 'save' or 'shrink' their way to prosperity."[62]

From an institution-based perspective, by the 1980s and 1990s, firms in developed economies increasingly felt pressure from capital markets to restructure.[63] Managers increasingly accepted restructuring to be a part of legitimate business undertaking.[64] However, strong institutional pressures *against* restructuring also exist. In the United States, restructuring, job loss, and outsourcing have been controversial issues in every presidential election since the 1990s. In Germany, all "redundancies" must, by law, be negotiated by workers' councils (unions), whose members understandably are not keen to vote themselves out of jobs. In Central and Eastern Europe where some restructuring is often urgently needed, many managers are reluctant to do so.[65] In Asia, even after the rude awakening of the 1997 financial crisis, restructuring has still been "sporadic and glacially slow."[66] Overall, corporate restructuring is not widely embraced around the world.[67]

Debates and Extensions

The two leading debates discussed here will be (1) product relatedness versus other forms of relatedness and (2) acquisitions versus alliances.

Product Relatedness versus Other Forms of Relatedness

What exactly is relatedness? While the idea of product relatedness is seemingly straightforward, it has attracted at least three significant points of contention. First, how to

restructuring

(1) Adjusting firm size and scope through either diversification (expansion or entry), divestiture (contraction or exit), or both. (2) Reducing firm size and scope.

downsizing

Reducing the number of employees through lay-offs, early retirements, and outsourcing.

downscoping

Reducing the scope of the firm through divestitures and spin-offs.

refocusing

Narrowing the scope of the firm to focus on a few areas.

actually measure product relatedness remains debatable.[68] Starbucks now sells music CDs in its coffee shops. Are coffee and music related? The answer would be both "yes" and "no," depending on how you measure relatedness. Amazon not only sells books, but also hawks apparel, furniture, movies, power tools, TVs, and dozens of other product categories. Are these products related? From a production standpoint, they certainly are not. But from a distribution/shopping standpoint, a compelling case can be made that these products are related—think of the numerous products Wal-Mart carries.

Second, beyond measurement issues, an important school of thought, known as the **"dominant logic"** school, argues that it is not only the visible product linkages that can count as "product relatedness." Rather, it is a set of common underlying dominant logic that connects various businesses in a diversified firm.[69] Consider Britain's easyGroup, which operates easyJet (airline), easyCinema, and easyInternetcafé, among others. Underneath its conglomerate skin, a dominant logic is to actively manage supply and demand. Early and/or non-peak-hour customers get cheap deals (such as 20 cents a movie), and late and/or peak-hour customers pay a lot more. Charges at the Internet cafés rise as the seats fill up. While many firms (such as airlines) practice such "yield management," none has been so aggressive as the easyGroup. Thus, instead of treating the easyGroup as an "unrelated conglomerate," perhaps we may label it a "related yield management firm."

Finally, from an institution-based view, some "product unrelated" conglomerates may be linked by **institutional relatedness,** defined as "a firm's informal linkages with dominant institutions in the environment which confer resources and legitimacy."[70] For example, sound informal relationships with government agencies, in countries (usually emerging economies) where such agencies control crucial resources such as licensing, financing, and labor pools, would encourage firms to leverage such relationships by entering multiple industries. In emerging economies, solid connections with banks—a crucial financial institution—may help raise financing to enter multiple industries, whereas standalone entrepreneurial start-ups without such connections often have a hard time securing financing.[71] This idea helps explain why in developed economies, e-commerce is dominated by new start-ups (such as Amazon and eBay), whereas in emerging economies it is dominated by new units of old-line conglomerates (such as Hong Kong's Wharf and Singapore's Sembcorp). It seems that despite the Western advice to downscope, some conglomerates in emerging economies have recently *expanded* their scope by entering new industries such as e-commerce. In other words, a firm, which is classified as a "product unrelated" conglomerate, may actually enjoy a great deal of institutional relatedness.

Acquisitions versus Alliances

Despite the proliferation of acquisitions, their lackluster performance has led to a debate regarding whether they have been overused. Strategic alliances are an alternative to acquisitions (see Chapter 7). However, many firms seem to have plunged straight into "merger mania." Even when many firms pursue both M&As and alliances, they are often undertaken in isolation.[72] While many large MNEs have an M&A function and some have set up an alliance function, virtually no firm has established a combined "mergers, acquisitions, *and* alliance" function. In practice, it may be advisable to explicitly compare and contrast acquisitions vis-à-vis alliances.[73]

Compared with acquisitions, strategic alliances, despite their own problems, cost less and allow for opportunities to learn from working with each other before engaging in full-blown acquisitions.[74] Many poor acquisitions (such as DaimlerChrysler) would

dominant logic

A common underlying theme that connects various businesses in a diversified firm.

institutional relatedness

A firm's informal linkages with dominant institutions in the environment that confer resources and legitimacy.

TABLE 9.4   Strategic Implications for Action

- Understand the nature of your industry that may call for diversification, acquisitions, and restructuring.
- Develop capabilities that facilitate successful acquisitions and restructuring.
- Master the rules of the game governing acquisitions and restructuring around the world.

probably have been better off had firms pursued alliances first. At present, it is inconclusive whether alliances are actually better than acquisitions. Nevertheless, it seems imperative that firms seriously and thoroughly investigate alliances as an alternative to acquisitions (see Chapter 7 for details).

The Savvy Strategist

Guided by the three leading perspectives that lead to the "strategy tripod," the savvy strategist draws three important implications for action (Table 9.4). First, understand the nature of your industry that may call for diversification, acquisitions, and restructuring. In some "sunset" industries, diversification out of them is a must. In new hot-growth industries and countries, new entrants often feel compelled to acquire in order to ensure a timely presence (see Strategy in Action 9.2 and 9.3).

Second, you and your firm need to develop capabilities that facilitate successful acquisitions and restructuring by following the suggestions outlined in Table 9.5. These would include do not overpay for targets and focus on both strategic and organizational fit.[75] At GE, acquisition management is a full-time job, involving 230 full-time employees. Some firms deploy ad hoc teams when needed. During the HP–Compaq merger, the integration team numbered more than 1,500.[76] While approaches vary, no firm can afford to take acquisitions, especially the integration phase, lightly.

Finally, you need to master the rules of the game—both formal and informal—governing acquisitions around the world. In 2004, when Lenovo acquired IBM's PC division, it faced US government scrutiny. IBM had a better understanding of the necessity for the new Lenovo to maintain an "American" image, by persuading Lenovo to give up the idea of having dual headquarters in China and the United States and set up its world headquarters in the United States. This highly symbolic action

TABLE 9.5   Improving the Odds for Acquisition Success

AREA	DO'S AND DON'TS
Pre-acquisition	• Do not overpay for targets and avoid a bidding war when premiums are too high. • Engage in thorough due diligence concerning both strategic fit and organizational fit.
Post-acquisition	• Address the concerns of multiple stakeholders and try to keep the best talents. • Be prepared to deal with roadblocks thrown out by people whose jobs and power may be jeopardized.

made it easier to win approval from the US government. In contrast, in 2001, GE and Honeywell proposed to merge and cleared US antitrust scrutiny. Yet, they failed to anticipate the power of the EU antitrust authorities to torpedo the deal.[77] These two otherwise highly capable firms should have done more "homework"—known in the jargon as due diligence—on the institutional side.

In terms of the four most fundamental questions, this chapter directly answers Question 3: What determines the scope of the firm? Industry conditions, resource repertoire, and institutional frameworks shape corporate scope. In addition, why firms differ (Question 1) and how firms behave (Question 2) boil down to why and how they choose different diversification strategies. Finally, what determines the success and failure of firms around the globe? The answer lies in whether they can successfully overcome the challenges associated with diversification, acquisitions, and restructuring.

CHAPTER SUMMARY

1. *Define product diversification and geographic diversification*

   - Product-related diversification focuses on operational synergy and scale economies.

   - Product-unrelated diversification (conglomeration) stresses financial synergy and scope economies.

   - Geographically diversified firms can have a limited or extensive international scope.

   - Most firms pursue product and geographic diversification simultaneously.

2. *Articulate a comprehensive model of diversification*

   - The "strategy tripod" suggests industry-, resource-, and institution-based factors for diversification.

3. *Gain insights into the motives and performance of acquisitions*

   - Most M&As are acquisitions.

   - M&As are driven by (1) synergistic, (2) hubris, and/or (3) managerial motivations.

4. *Enhance your understanding of restructuring*

   - Restructuring involves downsizing, downscoping, and refocusing.

5. *Participate in two leading debates on diversification, acquisitions, and restructuring*

   - (1) Product relatedness versus other forms of relatedness and (2) acquisitions versus alliances.

6. *Draw strategic implications for action*

   - Understand the nature of your industry that may call for diversification, acquisitions, and restructuring.

   - Develop capabilities that facilitate successful acquisitions and restructuring.

   - Master the rules of the game governing acquisitions and restructuring around the world.

KEY TERMS

Acquisition	Economic benefit	Merger and acquisition (M&A)
Acquisition premium	Far-flung conglomerate	
Anchored replicator	Financial control (output control)	Multinational replicator
Bureaucratic cost		Operational synergy
Business group	Financial synergy	Organizational fit
Business-level strategy	Friendly M&A	Product diversification
Classic conglomerate	Geographic diversification	Product-related diversification
Conglomerate	Horizontal M&A	Product-unrelated diversification
Conglomerate M&A	Hostile M&A (hostile takeover)	Refocusing
Conglomeration	Hubris	Restructuring
Corporate-level strategy (corporate strategy)	Information overload	Scale economies (economies of scale)
	Institutional relatedness	
Diversification	Internal capital market	Scope economies (economies of scope)
Diversification discount		Single business strategy
Diversification premium	International diversification	Strategic control (behavior control)
Dominant logic	Marginal bureaucratic cost	
Downscoping	Marginal economic benefit	Strategic fit
Downsizing	Merger	Vertical M&A

CRITICAL DISCUSSION QUESTIONS

1. Some argue that shareholders can diversify their stockholdings and that there is no need for corporate diversification to reduce risk. The upshot is that any excess earnings (known as "free cash flows"), instead of being used to acquire other firms, should be returned to shareholders as dividends and that firms should pursue more focused strategies. Do you agree or disagree with this statement? Why?

2. Unrelated product diversification (conglomeration) is widely discredited in developed economies. However, in some cases it still seems to add value in emerging economies. Is this interest in conglomeration likely to hold or decrease in emerging economies over time? Why?

3. **ON ETHICS:** As a CEO, you are trying to decide whether to acquire a foreign firm. The size of your firm will double after this acquisition and it will become the largest in your industry. On one hand, you are excited about the opportunities

to be a leading captain of industry and the associated power, prestige, and income (you expect your income to double next year). On the other hand, you have just read this chapter and are troubled by the fact that 70% of M&As reportedly fail. How would you proceed?

CLOSING CASE

From Diversification Premium to Diversification Discount in South Korea

Large conglomerates (business groups), such as Samsung, Hyundai, LG, and Daewoo, are called *chaebol*s in South Korea (hereafter Korea). They dominate the economy, contributing approximately 40% of Korea's GDP as of 1996. In 1996, Samsung had 80 subsidiaries, Hyundai 57, LG 49, and Daewoo 30—scattered in different industries such as automobiles, chemicals, construction, electronics, financial services, insurance, semiconductors, shipbuilding, and steel. Why and how did *chaebol*s, all from humble roots in focused industries, grow to become such sprawling conglomerates? The chairman of LG shared an intriguing story:

"My father and I started a cosmetic cream factory in the late 1940s. At that time, no company could supply us with plastic caps of adequate quality for cream jars, so we had to start a plastic business. Plastic caps alone were not sufficient to run the plastic molding plant, so we added combs, toothbrushes, and soap boxes. This plastics business also led us to manufacture electric fan blades and telephone cases, which in turn led us to manufacture electrical and electronic products and telecommunications equipment. The plastics business also took us into oil refining, which needed a tanker shipping company. The oil refining company alone was paying an insurance premium amounting to more than half the total revenue of the then-largest insurance company in Korea. Thus, an insurance company was started."

What the story does not reveal is the visible hand of the Korean government, which channeled financial resources to fund *chaebol*s' growth. In the meantime, the government protected domestic markets from foreign competition. However, the cozy protected environment did not last forever. Because Korea's eagerness to join the OECD prior to its accession in 1996 resulted in external pressures to open the economy, the government gradually removed import restrictions. In addition, capital markets became more open and vibrant. At the same time, labor costs rose sharply. Internationally, *chaebol* products were often stuck in the middle between high-end Japanese offerings and low-end Chinese merchandise.

Confronting such rising environmental turbulence by the 1990s, *chaebol*s increased their scope. The average number of affiliates of the top 30 *chaebol*s grew from 17 per group in 1987 to 22 in 1996, a 30% increase. In the process, they took on a high level of debt, based on extensive cross-guarantees among group member firms. Banks were happy to provide loans, believing that *chaebol*s were "too big to fail." The debt/equity ratio ended up being, on average,

FIGURE 9.10   **A 10% Diversification Premium in 1984–1987 Turned into a 5% Discount in 1994–1996**

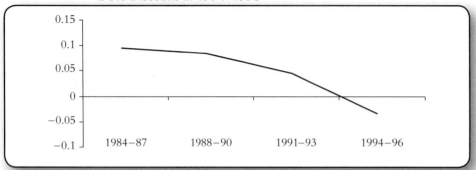

Source: Adapted from K. B. Lee, M. W. Peng, & K. Lee, 2008, From diversification premium to diversification discount during institutional transitions (p. 63), *Journal of World Business,* 43: 47–65. A value above the horizontal line indicates a diversification premium, and a value below the horizontal line indicates a diversification discount.

617% for the top 30 *chaebols*. In some extreme cases, New Core's debt/equity ratio was 1,225%, Halla's was 2,066%, and Jinro's was 3,765%.

Unfortunately, by the time the Asian economic crisis of 1997 struck, *chaebols* took an enormous beating. Their excessive borrowing and reckless growth were sharply criticized. Of the 30 top *chaebols* in 1996, close to half of them, including New Core, Halla, and Jinro, have gone through bankruptcy proceedings or bank-sponsored restructuring programs. Daewoo, ranked number four in 1996, has literally been broken up. All surviving *chaebols* have sold businesses and substantially reduced their scope.

In retrospect, signs of *chaebols'* troubles had been like writings on the wall before the crisis. There was indeed a time *chaebols* carried a diversification *premium,* with affiliates outcompeting comparable independent firms (about 10% higher sales during 1984–1987). However, rising environmental turbulence coupled with growing firm size proved to be a lethal combination. By 1994–1996, there was a diversification *discount,* with *chaebol* member firms selling at 5% less than comparable independent firms (Figure 9.10). Finally, the better developed external capital markets further eroded the *chaebols'* advantage to operate an internal capital market.

With hindsight, it is amazing to see *chaebols* being applauded as the champions of Korean economic development and a worthy organizational model for other developing economies to emulate prior to 1997. Since 1997, *chaebols* were often painted with a

negative brush and blamed for the country's economic crisis. Both positions seem extreme. *Chaebols* probably were neither "paragons" nor "parasites." Their roles changed. *Chaebols* as conglomerates did add value during earlier days. But past some point of inflection (probably the early 1990s as shown in Figure 9.10), their drawbacks started to outweigh their benefits.

Sources: Based on (1) S. J. Chang, 2006, Business groups in East Asia: Post-crisis restructuring and new growth, *Asia Pacific Journal of Management,* 23: 407–417; (2) H. Kim, R. Hoskisson, L. Tihanyi, & J. Hong, 2004, The evolution and restructuring of diversified business groups in emerging markets: The lessons from *chaebols* in Korea, *Asia Pacific Journal of Management,* 21: 25–48; (3) K. B. Lee, M. W. Peng, & K. Lee, 2008, From diversification premium to diversification discount during institutional transitions, *Journal of World Business,* 43: 47–65; (4) M. W. Peng & A. Delios, 2006, What determines the scope of the firm over time and around the world? *Asia Pacific Journal of Management,* 23: 385–405.

Case Discussion Questions

1. Drawing on industry-, resource-, and institution-based views, explain why conglomeration (product-unrelated diversification) became a dominant corporate strategy in postwar Korea.

2. What turned *chaebols'* diversification premium into a diversification discount?

3. Some argue that *chaebols* as an organizational species will die. How does the future look for *chaebols* in Korea, and for conglomerates in emerging economies in general?

NOTES

Journal acronyms *AME–Academy of Management Executive;* **AMJ***–Academy of Management Journal;* **AMR***–Academy of Management Review;* **APJM***–Asia Pacific Journal of Management;* **ASQ***–Administrative Science Quarterly;* **CMR***–California Management Review;* **EJ***–Economic Journal;* **HBR***–Harvard Business Review;* **JB***–Journal of Business;* **JEP***–Journal of Economic Perspectives;* **JFE***–Journal of Financial Economics;* **JIBS***–Journal of International Business Studies;* **JM***–Journal of Management;* **JMS***–Journal of Management Studies;* **JWB***–Journal of World Business;* **LRP***–Long Range Planning;* **MIR***–Management International Review;* **OSc***–Organization Science;* **SMJ***–Strategic Management Journal.*

1. R. Adner & C. Helfat, 2003, Corporate effects and dynamic managerial capabilities, *SMJ,* 24: 1011–1025; E. Bowman & C. Helfat, 2001, Does corporate strategy matter?, *SMJ,* 22: 1–23.

2. C. St. John & J. Harrison, 1999, Manufacturing-based relatedness, synergy, and coordination, *SMJ,* 20: 129–145; I. Stern & A. Henderson, 2004, Within-business diversification in technology-intensive industries, *SMJ,* 25: 487–505.

3. D. Miller, M. Fern, & L. Cardinal, 2007, The use of knowledge for technological innovation within diversified firms, *AMJ,* 50: 308–326.

4. J. Liebeskind, 2000, Internal capital markets, *OSc,* 11: 58–76; J. Shackman, 2007, Corporate diversification, vertical integration, and internal capital markets, *MIR,* 47: 479–504.

5. K. B. Lee, M. W. Peng, & K. Lee, 2008, From diversification premium to diversification discount during institutional transitions, *JWB,* 43: 47–65.

6. L. Palich, L. Cardinal, and C. C. Miller, 2000, Curvilinearity in the diversification-performance linkage, *SMJ,* 21: 155–174.

7. R. Rumelt, 1974, *Strategy, Structure, and Economic Performance,* Boston: Harvard Business School Press.

8. M. W. Peng & A. Delios, 2006, What determines the scope of the firm over time and around the world?, *APJM,* 24: 385–405. See also A. Chacar & G. Vissa, 2005, Are emerging economies less efficient?, *SMJ,* 26: 933–946; A. Chakrabarti, K. Singh, & I. Mahmood, 2007, Diversification and performance, *SMJ,* 28: 101–120; B. Kedia, D. Mukherjee, & S. Lahiri, 2006, Indian business groups, *APJM,* 23: 559–577; T. Khanna & J. Rivkin, 2001, Estimating the performance effects of

business groups in emerging markets, *SMJ,* 22: 45–74; M. Li, K. Ramaswamy, & B. Petitt, 2006, Business groups and market failures, *APJM,* 24: 439–452; Y. Lu & J. Yao, 2006, Impact of state ownership and control mechanisms on the performance of group affiliated companies in China, *APJM,* 23: 485–504; X. Ma, X. Yao, & Y. Xi, 2006, Business group affiliation and firm performance in a transition economy, *APJM,* 23: 467–484.

9. F. Contractor, S. Kundu, & C. Hsu, 2003, A three-stage theory of international expansion, *JIBS,* 34: 5–18; J. Lu & P. Beamish, 2004, International diversification and firm performance, *AMJ,* 47: 598–609.

10. N. Capar & M. Kotabe, 2003, The relationship between international diversification and performance in service firms, *JIBS,* 34: 345–355; G. Qian, 1997, Assessing product-market diversification of US firms, *MIR,* 37: 127–149.

11. L. Gomes & K. Ramaswamy, 1999, An empirical examination of the form of the relationship between multinationality and performance, *JIBS,* 30: 173–188.

12. M. Chari, S. Devaraj, & P. David, 2007, International diversification and firm performance, *JWB,* 42: 184–197; J. Doukas & L. Lang, 2003, Foreign direct investment, diversification, and firm performance, *JIBS,* 34: 153–172; Y. Fang, M. Wade, A. Delios, & P. Beamish, 2007, International diversification, subsidiary performance, and the mobility of knowledge resources, *SMJ,* 28: 1053–1064; M. Hitt, L. Tihanyi, T. Miller, & B. Connelly, 2006, International diversification, *JM,* 32: 831–867; M. Kotabe, S. Srinivasan, & P. Aulakh, 2002, Multinationality and firm performance, *JIBS,* 33: 79–97.

13. A. Delios & P. Beamish, 1999, Geographic scope, product diversification, and the corporate performance of Japanese firms (p. 724), *SMJ,* 20: 711–727.

14. J. M. Geringer, S. Tallman, & D. Olsen, 2000, Product and international diversification among Japanese multinational firms (p. 76), *SMJ,* 21: 51–80.

15. A. Goerzen & P. Beamish, 2003, Geographic scope and multinational enterprise performance, *SMJ,* 24: 1289–1306.

16. A. Goerzen & S. Makino, 2007, Multinational corporation internationalization in the service sector, *JIBS,* 38: 1149–1169; M. Hitt, R. Hoskisson, & H. Kim, 1997, International diversification, *AMJ,* 40: 767–798;

L. Nachum, 2004, Geographic and industrial diversification of developing country firms, *JMS*, 41: 273–294; S. Tallman & J. Li, 1996, Effects of international diversity and product diversity on the performance of multinational firms, *AMJ*, 39: 179–196; M. Wiersema & H. Bowen, 2008, Corporate diversification, *SMJ*, 29: 115–132.

17. K. Meyer, 2006, Global focusing, *JMS*, 43: 1109–1144.

18. C. Park, 2003, Prior performance characteristics of related and unrelated acquirers, *SMJ*, 24: 471–480; K. Ramaswamy, 1997, The performance impact of strategic similarity in horizontal mergers, *AMJ*, 40: 697–715.

19. J. Bercovitz & W. Mitchell, 2007, When is more better?, *SMJ*, 28: 61–79; L. Capron & J. Shen, 2007, Acquisitions of private vs. public firms, *SMJ*, 28: 891–911; S. Karim, 2006, Modularity in organizational structure, *SMJ*, 27: 799–823; J. Macher & C. Boerner, 2006, Experience and scale and scope economies, *SMJ*, 27: 845–865; K. Uhlenbruck, M. Hitt, & M. Semadeni, 2006, Market value effects of acquisitions involving Internet firms, *SMJ*, 27: 899–913.

20. J. Haleblian, J. Kim, & N. Rajagopalan, 2006, The influence of acquisition experience and performance on acquisition behavior, *AMJ*, 49: 357–370.

21. N. Argyres, 1996, Capabilities, technological diversification, and divisionalization, *SMJ*, 17: 395–410.

22. C. O'Reilly & M. Tushman, 2004, The ambidextrous organization, *HBR*, April: 74–81.

23. C. Hill, M. Hitt, & R. Hoskisson, 1992, Cooperative versus competitive structures in related and unrelated diversified firms, *OSc*, 3: 501–521.

24. M. Guillen, 2000, Business groups in emerging economies, *AMJ*, 43: 362–380; T. Khanna & K. Palepu, 2000, The future of business groups in emerging markets, *AMJ*, 43: 268–285; R. Hoskisson, A. Cannella, L. Tihanyi, & R. Faraci, 2004, Asset restructuring and business group affiliation in French civil law countries, *SMJ*, 25: 525–539.

25. K. Carow, R. Heron, & T. Saxton, 2004, Do early birds get the returns?, *SMJ*, 25: 563–585.

26. C. Marquis & M. Lounsbury, 2007, Vive la resistance, *AMJ*, 50: 799–820; P. Thornton, 2001, Personal versus market logics of control, *OSc*, 12: 294–311.

27. P. Wright, M. Kroll, & D. Elenkov, 2002, Acquisition returns, increase in firm size, and CEO compensation, *AMJ*, 45: 599–608; P. Wright, M. Kroll, A. Lado, &

B. Van Ness, 2002, The structure of ownership and corporate acquisition strategies, *SMJ*, 23: 41–54.

28. B. Kogut, G. Walker, & J. Anand, 2002, Agency and institutions, *OSc*, 13: 162–178; M. Mayer & R. Whittington, 2003, Diversification in context, *SMJ*, 24: 773–781; W. Wan & R. Hoskisson, 2003, Home country environments, corporation diversification strategies, and firm performance, *AMJ*, 46: 27–45.

29. This section draws heavily from M. W. Peng, S. Lee, & D. Wang, 2005, What determines the scope of the firm over time? A focus on institutional relatedness, *AMR*, 30: 622–633.

30. G. Jones & C. Hill, 1988, Transaction cost analysis of strategy-structure choice, *SMJ*, 9: 159–172.

31. United Nations, 2000, *World Investment Report 2000* (p. 99), New York: United Nations.

32. M. Lubatkin, W. Schulze, A. Mainkar, & R. Cotterill, 2001, Ecological investigation of firm effects on horizontal mergers, *SMJ*, 22: 335–358.

33. K. Brouthers, P. van Hastenburg, & J. van den Ven, 1998, If most mergers fail why are they so popular?, *LRP*, 31: 347–353; A. Seth, K. Song, & R. Pettit, 2000, Synergy, managerialism, or hubris?, *JIBS*, 31: 387–405.

34. R. Krishnan, S. Joshi, & H. Krishnan, 2004, The influence of mergers on firms' product-mix strategies, *SMJ*, 25: 587–611.

35. *World Investment Report 2000* (p. 128).

36. J. Anand & A. Delios, 2002, Absolute and relative resources as determinants of international acquisitions, *SMJ*, 23: 119–134; P. Puranam & K. Srikanth, 2007, What they know vs. what they do, *SMJ*, 28: 805–825; T. Saxton & M. Dollinger, 2004, Target reputation and appropriability, *JM*, 30: 123–147.

37. W. Schneper & M. Guillen, 2004, Stakeholder rights and corporate governance, *ASQ*, 49: 263–295.

38. J. Doh, 2000, Entrepreneurial privatization strategies, *AMR*, 25: 551–571; K. Meyer & S. Estrin, 2007, *Acquisition Strategies in European Emerging Markets*, London: Palgrave; K. Uhlenbruck & J. DeCastro, 2000, Foreign acquisitions in Central and Eastern Europe, *AMJ*, 43: 381–402.

39. R. Roll, 1986, The hubris hypothesis of corporate takeovers, *JB*, 59: 197–216.

40. P. Buckley & P. Ghauri, 2002, *International Mergers and Acquisitions* (p. 2), London: Thomson.

41. T. Laamanen, 2007, On the role of acquisition premium in acquisition research, *SMJ*, 28: 1359–1369.

42. S. Moeller, F. Schlingemann, & R. Stulz, 2004, Firm size and the gains from acquisitions, *JFE*, 73: 201–228.

43. D. King, D. Dalton, C. Daily, & J. Covin, 2004, Meta-analyses of post-acquisition performance, *SMJ*, 25: 187–200.

44. R. Kapoor & K. Lim, 2007, The impact of acquisitions on the productivity of inventors at semiconductor firms, *AMJ*, 50: 1133–1155.

45. D. Datta, G. Pinches, & V. Narayanan, 1992, Factors influencing wealth creation from M&As, *SMJ*, 13: 67–84.

46. G. Andrade, M. Mitchell, & E. Stafford, 2001, New evidence and perspectives on mergers, *JEP*, 15: 103–120.

47. M. Sirower, 1997, *The Synergy Trap*, New York: Free Press. See also M. Hayward & D. Hambrick, 1997, Explaining the premiums paid for large acquisitions, *ASQ*, 42: 103–127.

48. M. Hitt, J. Harrison, & R. D. Ireland, 2001, *Mergers and Acquisitions* (p. 89), New York: Oxford University Press.

49. I. Bjorkman, G. Stahl, & E. Vaara, 2007, Cultural differences and capability transfer in cross-border acquisitions, *JIBS*, 38: 658–672.

50. C. Gopinath, 2009, DP World, in M. W. Peng, *Global Business* (pp. 111–115), Cincinnati: South-Western Cengage Learning.

51. T. Grubb & R. Lamb, 2000, *Capitalize on Merger Chaos* (p. 14), New York: Free Press.

52. A. Buchholtz, B. Ribbens, & I. Houle, 2003, The role of human capital in postacquisition CEO departure, *AMJ*, 46: 506–514; R. Davis & A. Nair, 2003, A note on top management turnover in international acquisitions, *MIR*, 43: 171–183; J. Krug & W. H. Hegarty, 2001, Predicting who stays and leaves after an acquisition, *SMJ*, 22: 185–196.

53. J. Birkinshaw, H. Bresman, & L. Hakanson, 2000, Managing the post-acquisition integration process, *JMS*, 37: 395–425; C. Homburg & M. Bucerius, 2006, Is speed of integration really a success factor of M&As?, *SMJ*, 27: 347–367; E. Vaara, 2003, Post-acquisition integration as sensemaking, *JMS*, 40: 859–894.

54. J. Child, D. Faulkner, & R. Pitkethly, 2001, *The Management of International Acquisitions*, Oxford, UK: Oxford University Press; K. Meyer & E. Lieb-Doczy, 2003, Post-acquisition restructuring as evolutionary process, *JMS*, 40: 459–482; K. Uhlenbruck, 2004, Developing acquired foreign subsidiaries, *JIBS*, 35: 109–123.

55. R. Hallowell, D. Bowen, & C. Knoop, 2002, Four Seasons goes to Paris (p. 19), *AME*, 16: 7–24.

56. D. Bergh, R. Johnson, & R. DeWitt, 2008, Restructuring through spin-off or sell-off, *SMJ*, 29: 133–148.

57. A. Budros, 1999, A conceptual framework for analyzing why organizations downsize, *OSc*, 10: 69–82; M. Hayward & K. Shimizu, 2006, De-commitment to losing strategic action, *SMJ*, 27: 541–557.

58. R. Hoskisson & M. Hitt, 1994, *Downscoping*, New York: Oxford University Press.

59. G. Bruton, D. Ahlstrom, & J. Wan, 2003, Turnaround in East Asian firms, *SMJ*, 24: 519–540.

60. D. Hatfield, J. Liebeskind, & T. Opler, 1996, The effects of corporate restructuring on aggregate industry specialization, *SMJ*, 17: 55–72.

61. L. Capron, W. Mitchell, & A. Swaminathan, 2001, Asset divestiture following horizontal acquisitions, *SMJ*, 22: 817–844.

62. W. Cascio, 2002, Strategies for responsible restructuring (p. 81), *AME*, 16: 80–91.

63. E. Zuckerman, 2000, Focusing the corporate product, *ASQ*, 45: 591–619.

64. K. Shimizu, 2007, Prospect theory, behavioral theory, and the threat-rigidity hypothesis, *AMJ*, 50: 1495–1514.

65. I. Filatotchev, T. Buck, & V. Zhukov, 2000, Downsizing in privatized firms in Russia, Ukraine, and Belarus, *AMJ*, 43: 286–304.

66. M. Carney, 2004, The institutions of industrial restructuring in Southeast Asia (p. 174), *APJM*, 21: 171–188.

67. M. Makhija, 2004, The value of restructuring in emerging economies, *SMJ*, 25: 243–267.

68. A. Pehrsson, 2006, Business relatedness and performance, *SMJ*, 27: 265–282; J. Robins & M. Wiersema, 2003, The measurement of corporate portfolio strategy, *SMJ*, 2003: 39–59.

69. C. K. Prahalad & R. Bettis, 1986, The dominant logic, *SMJ*, 7: 485–501. See also A. Ilinitch & C. Zeithaml, 1995, Operationalizing and testing Galbraith's center

of gravity theory, *SMJ,* 16: 401–410; D. Ng, 2007, A modern resource-based approach to unrelated diversification, *JMS,* 44: 1481–1502.

70. Peng, Lee, & Wang, 2005, What determines the scope of the firm over time? (p. 623).

71. N. Le, S. Venkatesh, & T. Nguyen, 2006, Getting bank financing, *APJM,* 23: 209–227.

72. X. Yin & M. Shanley, 2008, Industry determinants of the "merger versus alliance" decision, *AMR* (in press).

73. D. Yiu & S. Makino, 2002, The choice between joint venture and wholly owned subsidiary, *OSc,* 13: 667–683.

74. P. Porrini, 2004, Can a previous alliance between an acquirer and a target affect acquisition performance? *JM,* 30: 545–562.

75. L. Capron & N. Pistre, 2002, When do acquirers earn abnormal returns?, *SMJ,* 23: 781–795; R. Larsson & S. Finkelstein, 1999, Integrating strategic, organizational, and human resource perspectives on M&As, *OSc,* 10: 1–26; J. Reuer, O. Shenkar, & R. Ragozzino, 2004, Mitigating risk in international M&As, *JIBS,* 35: 19–32; F. Vermeulen & H. Barkema, 2001, Learning through acquisitions, *AMJ,* 44: 457–477.

76. R. Burgelman & W. McKinney, 2006, Managing the strategic dynamics of acquisition integration, *CMR,* 48: 6–27.

77. N. Aktas, E. Bodt, & R. Roll, 2007, Is European M&A regulation protectionist?, *EJ,* 117: 1096–1121.

chapter 10

Multinational Strategies, Structures, and Learning

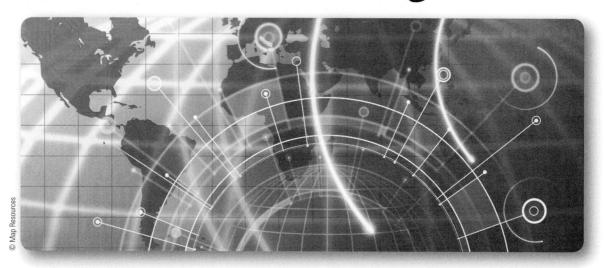

© Map Resources

KNOWLEDGE OBJECTIVES

After studying this chapter, you should be able to

1. Understand the four basic configurations of multinational strategies and structures

2. Articulate a comprehensive model of multinational strategy, structure, and learning

3. Outline the challenges associated with learning, innovation, and knowledge management

4. Participate in two leading debates on multinational strategy, structure, and learning

5. Draw strategic implications for action

OPENING CASE: TOYOTA AS (ALMOST) NUMBER ONE

Over the past three decades, during which every automaker has been allegedly "learning from Toyota," Toyota has widened the performance gap between itself and the rest of the pack. From humble roots, it has risen to (almost) become the number one automaker by volume in the world. The year 2007 marked the 70th anniversary of its founding and the 50th anniversary of its first exports to the United States. In 2007, Toyota sold 9.4 million vehicles globally, only about 3,000 fewer than General Motors (GM). In other words, Toyota almost dethroned GM, which has occupied the top spot since 1931. The media speculated that Toyota might have deliberately shied away from being number one to both avoid potential protectionist backlash in the United States and also to keep its own employees from becoming too arrogant. Currently, Toyota is the most profitable automaker, while GM and Ford have been suffering huge losses. Market capitalization says it all: Toyota is now worth more than the American Big Three combined and more than Honda and Nissan put together.

Toyota has evolved from being an exporter that made all its econobox cars in Japan to a far-flung enterprise that now makes a full range of vehicles in Argentina, Australia, Brazil, Britain, Canada, China, the Czech Republic, France, India, Indonesia, Malaysia, Mexico, Pakistan, the Philippines, Poland, Russia, South Africa, Thailand, Turkey, the United States, and Vietnam. Its rise is neither quick nor inevitable. In the crucial US market, in 1970, Toyota had only a 2% sliver, whereas GM commanded 40%. Its market share moved up to 3% in 1980, 8% in 1990, and 9% in 2000. Its US market share entered double digits for the first time only in 2006, when it rose to 13% and GM's declined to 26%. In 2007, Toyota's US market share grew to 16% and GM's fell to 24%. Recently, Toyota's growth has been accelerating. In 1995, it had 26 factories. In 2007, it had 63. In the past six years, Toyota added significant new capacity to make three million cars—the only other automaker to boost production that fast was Ford Motor Company, under the original Henry Ford in the early 1900s.

As Toyota blossoms around the world, a leading challenge is how to keep Toyota "Toyota." Recently, a series of un-Toyota-like quality problems have shown "cracks" in its armor. In 2007, America's influential *Consumer Reports* magazine pushed three vehicles from its recommended list (the Camry V6 sedan, the Lexus GS, and the Tundra pickup truck) and opined that it would "no longer recommend any new or re-designed Toyota models without reliability data on a specific design." In other words, Toyota models are no longer automatically assumed to be reliable. Toyota executives are concerned because Toyota's legendary quality reputation, which took decades to establish, could erode quickly. After being ranked 28th out of 36 vehicle brands by J.D. Power in a customer satisfaction survey in 2007, Toyota unleashed a program labeled "EM^2" (everything matters *exponentially*) to take a hard look into its operations.

To cope with its growing pains, Toyota has recently taken three crucial steps. First, it formally codified and disseminated the Toyota Way. For decades, Toyota had preached its principles, without writing them down, through socialization. However, the tacit and intangible nature of these principles made it very challenging for non-Japanese employees to grasp. In 2001, Toyota formally documented the "Toyota Way"—its core values centered on "continuous improvement" and "respect for people." According to Toyota's president Katsuaki Watanabe, it would serve as "a bible for overseas executives."

Second, Toyota beefed up training. Since rapid growth has led to 45% of its production being outside Japan, it has become harder to keep things the Toyota Way. Training centers have recently been set up not only in Japan, but also in Britain, India, Thailand, and the United States. At the factory level, Toyota has spent many years developing a cadre of 2,000 coordinators who act as teachers (*sensei*) for overseas operations. However, there are not enough of them. In response, Toyota has been retaining Japanese managers who are over 60 years old if they wish to continue to work. While some of them prefer not to work overseas, they nevertheless free up younger Japanese managers who can then be sent overseas.

Finally, Toyota has realized that a one-way diffusion of knowledge from headquarters and Japanese plants to the rest of the world may not be enough. As a result, it is facilitating more learning and knowledge transfer among overseas subsidiaries, especially from more established subsidiaries such as Toyota Canada and Toyota Kentucky that have a history of close to 20 years. It has sent employees from these subsidiaries to serve as coordinators overseas, the first time using non-Japanese *sensei* to train other non-Japanese employees.

Sources: Based on (1) *Business Week,* 2007, Toyota's all-out drive to stay Toyota, December 3: 54–56; (2) *Business Week,* 2007, Why Toyota is afraid of being number one, March 5: 42–50; (3) *The Economist,* 2007, A wobble on the road to the top, November 10: 85–87; (4) K. Watanabe, 2007, Lessons from Toyota's long drive, *Harvard Business Review,* July–August: 74–83; (5) Yahoo! Finance, 2008, Toyota falls short of GM in global sales, January 23, biz.yahoo.com.

How can multinational enterprises (MNEs) such as Toyota strategically manage growth around the world? How can they learn country tastes, global trends, and market transitions that may call for structural changes? How can they improve the odds for better innovation? These are some of the key questions we address in this chapter. Importantly, this is the topic that traditional "global strategy" textbooks emphasize. Because this book broadens the scope of "global strategy" to be "strategy around the globe" (see Chapter 1), we have already covered a wider set of topics, including strategy issues confronting smaller entrepreneurial firms (Chapter 6). This chapter covers very important material that underlines the success and failure of larger MNEs.

We start by discussing the crucial relationship between four strategies and four structures. Next, a comprehensive model drawing from the "strategy tripod" sheds light on these issues. Then, we discuss worldwide learning, innovation, and knowledge management. Debates and extensions follow.

Multinational Strategies and Structures

This section first introduces an (integration-responsiveness framework) centered on the pressures for cost reductions and local responsiveness. We then outline the four strategic choices and the four corresponding organizational structures that MNEs typically adopt.

Pressures for Cost Reductions and Local Responsiveness

MNEs primarily confront two sets of pressures: those for cost reductions and local responsiveness. The framework that deals with these two sets of pressures is called the **integration-responsiveness framework,** because (cost pressures often call for global integration and because local responsiveness urges MNEs to adapt locally)" In both domestic and international competition, pressures for cost reductions are almost universal. What is unique in international competition is the pressure for **local responsiveness,** which is reflected in different consumer preferences and host country demands. Consumer preferences vary tremendously around the world. For example, beef-based hamburgers brought by McDonald's obviously would find no customers in India, a land where cows are sacred. Host country (demands and expectations) add to the pressures for local responsiveness. Throughout Europe, Canadian firm Bombardier manufactures an "Austrian version" of railcars in Austria, a "Belgian version" in Belgium, and so on. Bomdardier believes that such local responsiveness, although not required, is essential for making sales to railway operators in Europe, which tend to be state-owned.

Taken together, while (being locally responsive) certainly makes local customers and governments happy, these actions unfortunately increase cost. Given the universal interest in lowering cost, a natural tendency is to downplay (or ignore) the different needs and wants of various local markets and to market a "global" version of products and services—ranging from the "world car" to the "global song." The intellectual underpinning of the movement to "globalize" offerings can be traced to a 1983 article published by Theodore Levitt, with a self-explanatory title: "The Globalization of Markets."[2] Levitt argued that there is a worldwide convergence of consumer tastes. As evidence, Levitt pointed out that Coke Classic, Levi Strauss jeans, and Sony TV were successful on a worldwide basis. He predicted that such convergence would characterize most product markets in the future.

Levitt's article has often been used as the intellectual underpinning propelling many MNEs to globally integrate their products, while minimizing local adaptation. Ford experimented with "world car" designs. MTV pushed ahead with the belief that viewers would flock to "global" (essentially American) programming. Unfortunately, most of these experiments have not been successful. Ford has found wide-ranging differences among consumer tastes around the globe (see Strategy in Action 10.1), and MTV has eventually realized that there is no "global song." In a nutshell, one size does not fit all.[3] Next, we discuss how MNEs can (pay attention to both dimensions of cost reductions *and* local responsiveness.)

Four Strategic Choices

Based on the integration-responsiveness framework, Figure 10.1 plots the four strategic choices for MNEs: (1) home replication, (2) localization, (3) global standardization, and (4) transnational.[4] Each strategy has a set of pros and cons outlined in Table 10.1.

integration-responsiveness framework

A framework of MNE management on how to simultaneously deal with two sets of pressures for global integration and local responsiveness.

local responsiveness

The necessity to be responsive to different customer preferences around the world.

Strategy in Action 10.1 - The Ups and Downs at Ford

Ford Motor Company was always more international than its two Detroit rivals, General Motors (GM) and Chrysler. In the 1960s, Ford of Europe was set up to consolidate operations in Britain and Germany. This structure was ahead of its time and was imitated by rivals. While the top brass at GM all featured American guys, Ford's top management ranks have featured executives from Argentina, Australia, Britain, and Germany.

In 1993, the rise of Alex Trotman, a Scot who had worked for Ford since 1955, as Ford's chairman and CEO personified Ford's international character. In the 1960s, while working for Ford of Europe, Trotman wrote a proposal on global consolidation that, while not implemented, would prove prophetic. It advocated many of the tenets that would later be incorporated into Ford's global restructuring of the mid-1990s—under Trotman's leadership. Known as Ford 2000, the restructuring transformed Ford from several regional groups (Asia Pacific, Europe, North America, and South America) into one presumably seamless global organization with factories and sales companies reporting instantly across oceans spanned by broadband links. Ford 2000 drained power from the regions back to Dearborn (a Detroit suburb where Ford is headquartered). However, the end result, exemplified by a "world car," the Ford Mondeo, proved disappointing. The Mondeo was a hit in Europe where drivers preferred more engine performance, but it flopped as the Ford Contour and Mercury Mystique in America where rider comfort was more preferred. Powerful regional managers and country heads naturally resented the loss of power. It simply did not make any sense for a factory manager in Cologne, Germany, to report to a global chief of manufacturing 3,000 miles away in Dearborn. However, few dared to declare the emperor naked.

In 1999, Trotman passed the baton to the next CEO, Jacques Nasser, a Lebanese-born executive who grew up in Australia. Recognizing the problems associated with Ford 2000, Nasser quickly reversed large parts of Ford 2000. Europe and South America regained regional power. Nasser went on a shopping spree, acquiring Volvo Cars from Volvo and Range Rover from BMW and consolidating Mazda in the Ford portfolio. Unfortunately, Nasser's tenure was full of upheaval not only associated with Ford 2000 and the serial acquisitions, but also with the faulty Bridgestone/Firestone tires that caused numerous Ford Explorer sport utility vehicles (SUVs) to accidentally roll over. Such upheaval caused Ford to take its eye off the ball. At the same time, Asian and European rivals turned up the heat on Ford by challenging it even in its stronghold markets for large SUVs and light trucks, where Ford had made most of its profits in the 1990s. As an executive, Nasser was widely viewed as too abrasive, alienating employees, suppliers, and eventually the Ford family that still controlled 40% equity. By 2001, Nasser was forced to resign by chairman Bill Ford (the original Henry Ford's great grandson).

From 2001–2006, Bill Ford acted as both chairman and CEO, but failed to turn the company around. Instead, the automaker continued its downward spiral and its US market share reached a historical low of 16%. In 2006, Bill Ford hired Alan Mullaly as the new CEO. Mullaly used to head Boeing's fabled commercial plane division. All eyes are now on Mullaly to see how Boeing's best pilot can pull Ford out of a hard landing.

Sources: Based on (1) *Business Week,* 2006, Ford's new top gun, September 18: 30–34; (2) *The Economist,* 2005, A hard lesson in globalization, April 30: 63; (3) Wikipedia, 2008, Ford Motor Company, en.wikipedia.org.

Home replication strategy, often known as "international" (or "export") strategy, emphasizes the international replication of home country–based competencies, such as (production scales, distribution efficiencies, and brand power.) In manufacturing, this is usually manifested in an export strategy. In services, this is often done through licensing

FIGURE 10.1 **Multinational Strategies and Structures: The Integration-Responsive Framework**

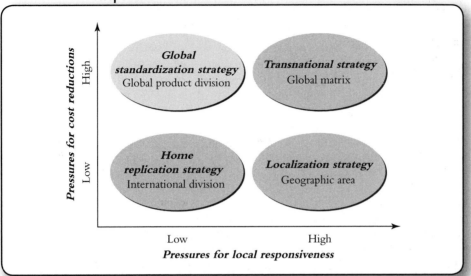

Note: In some other textbooks, "home replication" may be referred to as "international" or "export" strategy, "localization" as "multidomestic" strategy, and "global standardization" as "global" strategy. Some of these labels are confusing, because one can argue that all four strategies here are "international" or "global," thus resulting in some confusion if we label one of these strategies as "international" and another as "global." The present set of labels is more descriptive and less confusing.

and franchising. This strategy is relatively easy to implement and usually the first one adopted when firms venture abroad.

On the disadvantage side, this strategy suffers from a lack of local responsiveness because it focuses on the home country. This makes sense when the majority of a firm's customers are domestic. However, when the firm aspires to broaden its international scope to reach more foreign customers, failing to be mindful of foreign customers' needs and wants may result in their alienation. For instance, Wal-Mart, when entering Brazil, set up

home replication strategy

A strategy which emphasizes the international replication of home country–based competencies such as production scales, distribution efficiencies, and brand power.

TABLE 10.1 **Four Strategic Choices for Multinational Enterprises**

	ADVANTAGES	DISADVANTAGES
Home replication	• Leverages home country-based advantages • Relatively easy to implement	• Lack of local responsiveness • May result in foreign customer alienation
Localization	• Maximizes local responsiveness	• High costs due to duplication of efforts in multiple countries • Too much local autonomy
Global standardization	• Leverages low-cost advantages	• Lack of local responsiveness • Too much centralized control
Transnational	• Cost efficient while being locally responsive • Engages in global learning and diffusion of innovations	• Organizationally complex • Difficult to implement

localization (multidomestic) strategy

An MNE strategy which focuses on a number of foreign countries/ regions, each of which is regarded as a standalone local (domestic) market worthy of significant attention and adaptation.

global standardization strategy

An MNE (global) strategy that relies on the development and distribution of standardized products worldwide to reap the maximum benefits from low-cost advantages.

centers of excellence

MNE subsidiaries explicitly recognized as a source of important capabilities, with the intention that these capabilities be leveraged by and/or disseminated to other subsidiaries.

worldwide mandate

The charter to be responsible for one MNE function throughout the world.

transnational strategy

An MNE strategy which endeavors to be cost efficient, locally responsive, and learning driven simultaneously.

an exact copy of its stores in the United States, with a large number of *American* footballs. Unfortunately, in Brazil, the land of soccer that won five World Cups, nobody (except a few homesick American expatriates in their spare time) plays American football.

Localization (multidomestic) strategy is an extension of the home replication strategy. Localization strategy focuses on a number of foreign countries/regions, each of which is regarded as a standalone "local" market worthy of significant attention and adaptation. While sacrificing global efficiencies, this strategy is effective when there are clear differences among national and regional markets and low pressures for cost reductions. MTV started with a home replication strategy (literally broadcasting American programming) when first venturing overseas. It has now switched to localization. For Western Europe alone, MTV now has eight channels, each in a different language.

In terms of disadvantages, the localization strategy must shoulder high costs due to the duplication of efforts in multiple countries. The costs of producing such a variety of programming at MTV are obviously greater than the costs of producing one set of programming. As a result, this strategy is only appropriate in industries where the pressures for cost reductions are not significant. Another drawback is potentially too much local autonomy. Each subsidiary regards its country to be so unique it is difficult to introduce corporate-wide changes. For example, Unilever had 17 country subsidiaries in Europe in the 1980s and it took as long as four *years* to "persuade" all 17 subsidiaries to introduce a single new detergent across Europe.

As the opposite of the localization strategy, **global standardization strategy** is sometimes simply referred to as "global strategy." Its hallmark is the development and distribution of standardized products worldwide in order to reap the maximum benefits from low-cost advantages. While both the home replication and global standardization strategies minimize local responsiveness, a crucial difference is that an MNE pursuing a global standardization strategy is not limited to basing its major operations at home. In a number of countries, the MNE may designate "**centers of excellence**," defined as subsidiaries explicitly recognized as a source of important capabilities, with the intention that these capabilities be leveraged by and/or disseminated to other subsidiaries.[5] For example, Merck Frosst Canada, the Canadian subsidiary of Merck, is a center of excellence in R&D. Centers of excellence are often given a **worldwide** (or **global**) **mandate**—namely, the charter to be responsible for one MNE function throughout the world. HP's Singapore subsidiary, for instance, has a worldwide mandate to develop, produce, and market all of HP's handheld products.

In terms of disadvantages, a global standardization strategy obviously sacrifices local responsiveness. This strategy makes great sense in industries where pressures for cost reductions are paramount and pressures for local responsiveness are relatively minor. However, as noted earlier, in numerous industries, ranging from automobiles to consumer products, a "one-size-fits-all" strategy may be inappropriate. Consequently, arguments such as "all industries are becoming global" and "all firms need to pursue a global (standardization) strategy" are potentially misleading.

Transnational strategy aims to capture "the best of the two worlds" by endeavoring to be both cost efficient and locally responsive.[6] In addition to cost efficiency and local responsiveness, a third hallmark of this strategy is global learning and diffusion of innovations. Traditionally, the diffusion of innovations in MNEs is a one-way flow, from the home country to various host countries—the label "home replication" says it all (!). Underpinning such a one-way flow is the assumption that the home country is the best location for generating innovations, an assumption that is increasingly challenged by critics, who make two points. First, given that innovations are inherently risky and uncertain, there is no guarantee that the home country will always generate the highest-quality innovations.[7] Second, for many large MNEs, their subsidiaries have acquired a variety of innovation capabilities, some of which may have the potential for wider applications elsewhere.[8] For instance, GM has ownership stakes in Daewoo, Opel, Saab, Subaru, and Suzuki, as well as the Shanghai GM joint venture with China's SAIC. Historically, GM employed a localization strategy and each subsidiary decided what cars to produce by themselves. Consequently, some of these subsidiaries developed locally formidable but globally underutilized innovation capabilities. It makes sense for GM to tap into some of these local capabilities (such as Daewoo's prowess in small cars) for wider applications (see Chapter 7 Closing Case).

Taking these two points together, MNEs that engage in a transnational strategy promote global learning and diffusion of innovations in multiple ways. Innovations not only flow from the home country to host countries (which is the traditional flow), but also flow from host countries to the home country and flow among subsidiaries in multiple host countries (see Opening Case).[9]

On the disadvantage side, a transnational strategy is organizationally complex and difficult to implement. The large amount of knowledge sharing and coordination may slow down decision speed. Simultaneously trying to achieve cost efficiencies, local responsiveness, and global learning places contradictory demands on MNEs (to be discussed in the next section).

Overall, it is important to note that given the various pros and cons, there is no optimal strategy. The new trend in favor of a transnational strategy needs to be qualified with an understanding of its significant organizational challenges. This point leads to our next topic.

Four Organizational Structures

Also shown in Figure 10.1 are four organizational structures, which are appropriate for the four strategic choices outlined earlier: (1) international division structure, (2) geographic area structure, (3) global product division structure, and (4) global matrix structure.

International division is typically set up when firms initially expand abroad, often engaging in a home replication strategy. For example, Figure 10.2 shows Cardinal Health's

international division

A structure typically set up when firms initially expand abroad, often engaging in a home replication strategy.

FIGURE 10.2   International Division Structure at Cardinal Health

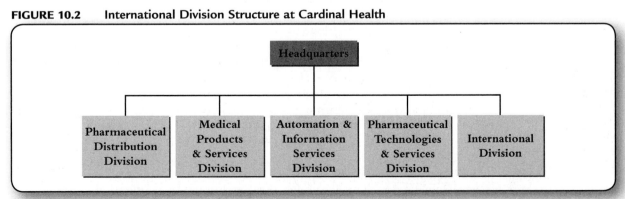

Sources: Based on author's interview and www.cardinal.com. Headquartered in Dublin, Ohio (a suburb of Columbus), Cardinal Health is a *Fortune* 20 company.

FIGURE 10.3   Geographic Area Structure at Avon Products

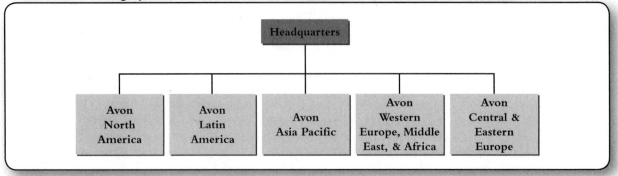

Source: Adapted from avoncompany.com. Headquartered in New York, Avon Products, Inc., is the company behind numerous "Avon ladies" around the world.

geographic area structure

An organizational structure which organizes the MNE according to different countries and regions, and is the most appropriate structure for a multidomestic strategy.

country (regional) manager

The business leader in charge of a specific country (or region) for an MNE.

global product division

An organizational structure which assigns global responsibilities to each product division.

global matrix

An organizational structure often used to alleviate the disadvantages associated with both geographic area and global product division structures, especially for MNEs adopting a transnational strategy.

new addition of an international division, in addition to its four product divisions that focus on the US health care markets. Although this structure is intuitively appealing, it often leads to two problems. First, foreign subsidiary managers, whose input is channeled through the international division, are not given sufficient voice relative to the heads of domestic divisions.[10] Second, by design, the international division serves as a "silo" whose activities are not coordinated with the rest of the firm that focuses on domestic activities. Consequently, many firms phase out this structure after their initial stage of overseas expansion.

Geographic area structure organizes the MNE according to different geographic areas (countries and regions). It is the most appropriate structure for a localization strategy. Figure 10.3 illustrates Avon's structure. A geographic area can be a country or a region, led by a **country** (or **regional**) **manager.** Each area is largely standalone. In contrast to the limited voice of subsidiary managers in the international division structure, country and regional managers carry a great deal of weight in a geographic area structure. Paradoxically, *both* the strengths and weaknesses of this structure lie in its local responsiveness. While being locally responsive can be a virtue, it also encourages the fragmentation of the MNE into highly autonomous hard-to-control "fiefdoms."[11]

Global product division structure, which is the opposite of the geographic area structure, supports the global standardization strategy. Figure 10.4 shows such an example from EADS, whose most famous unit is Airbus. This structure treats each product division as a standalone entity with full worldwide—as opposed to domestic or regional—responsibilities. This structure greatly facilitates attention to pressures for cost efficiencies, because it allows for consolidation on a worldwide (or at least regional) basis and reduces inefficient duplication in multiple countries. Recently, because of the popularity of the global standardization strategy (noted earlier), the global product division structure is on the rise. Ford has phased out the geographic area structure in favor of the global product division structure, although its drawback is that local responsiveness suffers (see Strategy in Action 10.1).

Global matrix alleviates the disadvantages associated with both geographic area and global product division structures, especially for MNEs adopting a transnational strategy. Shown in Figure 10.5, its hallmark is the sharing and coordination of responsibilities between product divisions and geographic areas in order to be both cost efficient

FIGURE 10.4   **Global Product Division Structure at European Aeronautic Defense and Space Company (EADS)**

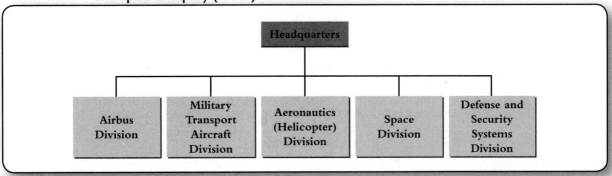

Source: Adapted from www.eads.com. Headquartered in Munich, Germany and Paris, France, EADS is the largest commercial aircraft maker and the largest defense contractor in Europe.

and locally responsive. In this hypothetical example, the country manager in charge of Japan—in short, the Japan manager—reports to Product Division 1 and Asia Division, both of which have equal power.

While this structure in theory supports the goals of the transnational strategy, in practice, it is often difficult to deliver. The reason is simple: While managers (such as the Japan manager) usually find there is enough headache dealing with one boss, they do not appreciate having to deal with two bosses, who are often in conflict (!). For example, Product Division 1 may decide that Japan is too tough a nut to crack and that there are more promising markets elsewhere, thus ordering the Japan manager to *curtail* her investment and channel resources elsewhere. This makes sense because Product

FIGURE 10.5   **A Hypothetical Global Matrix Structure**

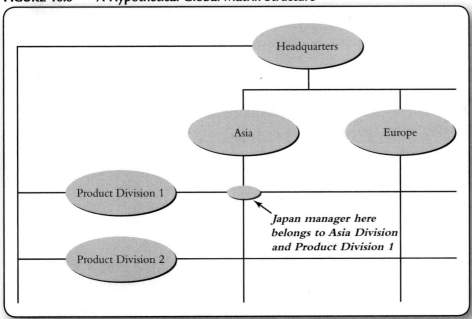

Division 1 cares about its global market position and is not wedded to any particular country. However, Asia Division, which is evaluated by how well it does in Asia, may beg to differ. It argues that to be a leading player in Asia, it cannot afford to be a laggard in Japan. Therefore, Asia Division demands that the Japan manager *increase* her investment in the country. Facing these conflicting demands, the Japan manager, who prefers to be "politically correct," does not want to make any move before consulting corporate headquarters. Eventually, headquarters may provide a resolution. However, in the process, crucial time may be lost and important windows of opportunity for competitive actions may be missed.

Taken together, the matrix structure, despite its merits on paper, may add layers of management, slow down decision speed, and increase cost while not showing performance improvement. There is no conclusive evidence for the superiority of this structure.[12] Having experimented with the matrix structure, many MNEs, such as the highly visible Swiss-Swedish conglomerate ABB, have now moved back to the simpler and easier-to-manage global product structure. Even when matrix is still in place, global product divisions are often given more power than geographic area divisions. The following quote from the then-CEO of an early adopter of the matrix structure, Dow Chemical, is sobering:

> We were an organization that was matrixed and depended on teamwork, but there was no one in charge. When things went well, we didn't know whom to reward; and when things went poorly, we didn't know whom to blame. So we created a global product division structure, and cut out layers of management. There used to be 11 layers of management between me and the lowest level employees, now there are five.[13]

Overall, the positioning of the four structures in Figure 10.1 is not random. They evolve from the relatively simple international division through either geographic area or global product division structures and may finally reach the more complex global matrix stage. It is important to note that not every MNE experiences all these structural stages and the evolution is not necessarily one direction (consider, for example, ABB's withdrawal from the matrix structure).

The Reciprocal Relationship Between Multinational Strategy and Structure

In one word, the relationship between strategy and structure is *reciprocal*. Three ideas stand out:

- Strategy usually drives structure.[14] The fit between strategy and structure, as exemplified by the *pairs* in each of the four cells in Figure 10.1, is crucial.[15] A misfit, such as combining a global standardization strategy with a geographic area structure, may have grave consequences.

- The relationship is not one-way. As much as strategy drives structure, structure also drives strategy. The unworkable matrix structure has called into question the wisdom of the transnational strategy.

- Strategies are not static, nor are structures. It is often necessary to change strategy, structure, or both.[16] In Europe, many MNEs traditionally pursued a localization strategy supported by the geographic area structure (such as the 17 European subsidiaries for Unilever). However, significant integration within the European Union has made such a formerly value-adding strategy/structure match obsolete. Consequently, many MNEs have now moved toward a pan-European strategy (a mini-version of the global standardization strategy) with a region-wide structure. Unilever, for instance, created a Lever Europe group to consolidate the 17 subsidiaries.

A Comprehensive Model of Multinational Strategy, Structure, and Learning

Having outlined the basic strategy/structure configurations, let us introduce a comprehensive model that, as before, draws on the "strategy tripod" (see Figure 10.6).

Industry-Based Considerations

Why are MNEs structured differently? Why do they emphasize different forms of learning and innovation? For example, industrial-products firms (such as semiconductors) tend to adopt global product divisions, and consumer-goods companies (such as cosmetics) often rely on geographic area divisions. Industrial-products firms typically emphasize technological innovations, whereas consumer-goods companies place premiums on learning consumer trends and generating repackaged and recombined products as marketing innovations (such as Heinz's marketing of *green* ketchup that appeals to children). A short answer is that the different nature of their industries provides a clue. Industrial-products firms value technological and engineering knowledge that is not location-specific (such as how to most efficiently make semiconductor chips). Consumer-goods industries, on the other hand, require deep knowledge about consumer tastes that is location-specific (such as what kinds of potato chips consumers in Hungary or Honduras would prefer).[17]

In addition, the five forces framework again sheds considerable light on the issue at hand. Within a given industry, as competitors increasingly match each other in cost efficiencies and local responsiveness, their rivalry naturally focuses on learning and innovation.[18] This is especially the case in oligopolistic industries (such as automobiles and cosmetics), whose number of competitors has shrunk recently because of mergers and acquisitions (see Chapter 9).

Entry barriers also shape MNE strategy, structure, and learning. Why do many MNEs phase out the multidomestic strategy and geographic area division structure by consolidating production in a small number of world-scale facilities? One underlying motivation is that smaller suboptimal-scale production facilities, scattered in a variety of countries, are not effective deterrents against potential entrants. Massive, world-scale facilities in strategic locations can serve as more formidable deterrents. For example, Honda built a world-scale factory for the Accord in Ohio.

The bargaining power of suppliers and buyers also has a bearing. When buyer firms move internationally, they increasingly demand integrated offerings from their suppliers—that is, the ability to buy the same supplies at the same price and quality in

FIGURE 10.6   A Comprehensive Model of Multinational Strategy, Structure, and Learning

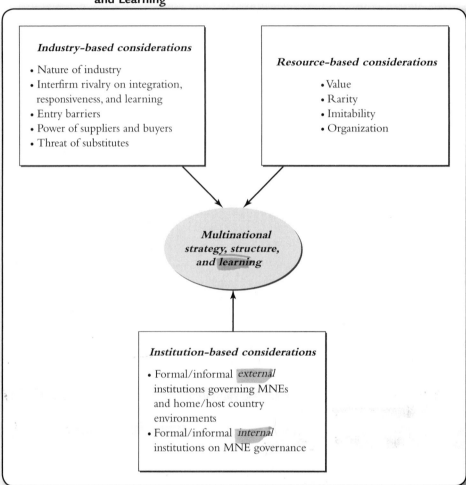

every country in which they operate. Components suppliers are thus often forced—or at least encouraged (!)—to internationalize. Otherwise, suppliers run the risk of losing a substantial chunk of business. Not surprisingly, as Toyota invested in China recently, *all* of its top 30 suppliers set up factories in adjacent areas at their own expenses.

The threat of substitute products has a direct bearing on learning and innovation. R&D often generates innovative substitutes. 3M's Post-It notes, for example, can partially substitute for glue and tape. Personal computers have made typewriters obsolete.

Resource-Based Considerations

Shown in Figure 10.6, the resource-based view, exemplified by the VRIO framework, adds a number of insights.[19] First, the question of value needs to be confronted. As noted earlier, when making structural changes, whether the new structure (such as matrix) adds concrete value is crucial. Another example is the value of innovation.[20]

A vast majority of innovations fail to reach market, and most new products that do reach market end up being financial failures. There is a crucial difference between an innovator and a *profitable* innovator. The latter not only has plenty of good ideas, but also lots of complementary assets (such as appropriate organizational structures and marketing muscles) to add value to innovation (see Chapter 3).[21] Philips, for example, is a great innovator, having invented rotary shavers, videocassettes, and compact discs (CDs). However, its ability to profit from these innovations lags behind that of Samsung, Sony, and Matsushita, which have much stronger complementary assets.

A second question is rarity. Certain strategies or structures may be in vogue at one point in time. When rivals all move toward a global standardization strategy, this strategy cannot become a source of differentiation. To improve global coordination, many MNEs spend millions of dollars on enterprise resource planning (ERP) packages provided by SAP and Oracle. However, such packages are designed for broad-appeal implementation, thus providing no firm-specific advantage for the adopting firm.

Even when capabilities are valuable and rare, they must be hard to imitate. Formal structures are easier to observe and imitate than informal ones. This is one of the reasons why the informal flexible matrix is in vogue now. The informal flexible matrix "is less a structural classification than a broad organizational concept or philosophy, manifested in organizational capability and management mentality."[22] It is a lot harder to imitate an intangible mentality than to imitate a tangible structure.

The last hurdle is organization, namely, how MNEs are organized, both formally and informally, around the world. As discussed earlier, if MNEs are able to derive the organizational benefits of the matrix without being burdened by a formal matrix structure (that is, building an informal flexible invisible matrix), they are likely to outperform rivals.

Institution-Based Considerations

MNEs face two sets of the "rules of the game": Formal and informal institutions governing (1) *external* relationships and (2) *internal* relationships. Each is discussed in turn.

FORMAL AND INFORMAL *EXTERNAL* INSTITUTIONS.

Externally, MNEs are subject to the formal institutional frameworks erected by various home- and host-country governments.[23] For instance, home-country governments may for political reasons discourage or ban MNEs from structuring certain operations in "sensitive" countries. After the Cold War was over, US defense firms such as Boeing and Lockheed Martin were eager to set up R&D subsidiaries in Russia, whose rocket scientists were some of the best (and certainly cheapest!) in the world. These firms have been warned by the US government not to perform any mission-critical R&D there.

Host-country governments, on the other hand, often attract, encourage, or coerce MNEs into undertaking activities that they may otherwise abdicate. Basic manufacturing generates low-paying jobs, does not provide sufficient technology spillovers (foreign technology being diffused domestically), and carries little prestige. Advanced manufacturing, R&D, and regional headquarters, on the other hand, generate higher-paying and better jobs, provide more technology spillovers, and lead to better prestige.[24] Thus, host-country governments (such as those in China, Hungary, and Singapore) often use a combination of "carrots" (such as tax incentives and infrastructure upgrades) and "sticks" (like threats to block market access) to attract MNE investments in higher value–added areas.

In addition to formal institutions, MNEs also confront a series of informal institutions governing their relationships with *home* countries.[25] In the United States, despite heated media debates, few laws today ban US-based MNEs from aggressively setting up overseas subsidiaries. However, managers contemplating such moves must take into account the informal, but vocal, backlash against such activities, which often result in domestic job losses (see Closing Case).

Numerous elements of informal institutions must also be handled when dealing with *host* countries. For instance, Airbus spends 40% of its procurement budget with US suppliers in more than 40 states. While there is no formal requirement for Airbus to "farm out" supply contracts in the United States, its sourcing decisions are guided by the informal norm of reciprocity: If one country's suppliers are involved with Airbus, airlines based in that country are more likely to buy Airbus aircraft.

FORMAL AND INFORMAL *INTERNAL* INSTITUTIONS

How MNEs are governed internally is determined by various formal and informal "rules of the game." Formally, the organizational charts in Figures 10.2–10.5 specify reporting relationships.[26] Most MNEs have systems of evaluation, reward, and punishment in place based on these formal rules.

What the formal organizational charts do not reveal are the informal "rules of the game." The nationality of the head of foreign subsidiaries is such an example.[27] Given the lack of formal regulations, MNEs essentially have three choices when appointing a head of a subsidiary:

- A home-country national (such as an American for a subsidiary of a US-headquartered MNE in India)

- A host-country national (such as an Indian for the same subsidiary)

- A third-country national (such as an Australian for the preceding subsidiary)

MNEs from different countries have different norms when making these appointments. Most Japanese MNEs seem to follow an informal rule: Heads of foreign subsidiaries, at least initially, need to be Japanese nationals.[28] In comparison, European MNEs are more likely to appoint host- and third-country nationals to lead subsidiaries. As a group, US MNEs' practices seem to be between Japanese and European practices. These staffing approaches may reflect strategic differences.[29] Home-country nationals, especially those long-time employees of the same MNE at home, are more likely to have developed a better understanding of the informal workings of the firm and to be better socialized into its dominant norms and values (see Opening Case). Consequently, the Japanese propensity to appoint home-country nationals is conducive for their preferred global standardization strategy that values globally coordinated actions. Conversely, the European comfort in appointing host- and third-country nationals is indicative of European MNEs' (traditional) preference for a localization strategy.

Beyond the nationality of subsidiary heads, the nationality of top executives at the highest level (such as chairman and CEO) seems to follow another informal rule: They are (almost always) home-country nationals. To the extent that top executives are ambassadors of the firm and that the MNE's country of origin is a source of differentiation (a German MNE is often perceived to be different from an Italian MNE), home-country nationals would seem to be the most natural candidates for top positions.

However, in the eyes of stakeholders such as employees and governments around the world, a top echelon consisting of largely one nationality does not bode well for an MNE aspiring to "globalize" everything it does. Some critics even argue that this "glass ceiling" reflects "corporate imperialism."[30] Consequently, such leading MNEs as Citigroup, Coca-Cola, GSK, Nissan, PepsiCo, and Sony have appointed foreign-born executives to top posts. Such foreign-born bosses bring substantial diversity to the organization, which may be a plus. However, such diversity puts an enormous burden on these non-native executives to clearly articulate the values and exhibit behaviors expected of senior managers of an MNE associated with a particular country.[31] Proctor & Gamble (P&G), for example, appointed Durk Jager, a native of the Netherlands, to be its chairman and CEO in 1999. Unfortunately, Jager's numerous change initiatives almost brought the venerable company to a grinding halt and he was quickly fired in 2000. Since then, the old rule is back: P&G has been led by an American executive.[32]

Overall, while formal internal rules on how the MNE is governed may reflect conscientious strategic choices, informal internal rules are often taken for granted and deeply embedded in administrative heritages, thus making them difficult to change.

Worldwide Learning, Innovation, and Knowledge Management

Knowledge Management

Underpinning the recent emphasis on worldwide learning and innovation is the emerging interest in knowledge management. **Knowledge management** can be defined as the structures, processes, and systems that actively develop, leverage, and transfer knowledge. Some scholars argue that knowledge management is *the* defining feature of MNEs.[33]

Many managers regard knowledge management as simply information management. Taken to an extreme, "such a perspective can result in a profoundly mistaken belief that the installation of sophisticated information technology (IT) infrastructure is the be-all and end-all of knowledge management."[34] Knowledge management not only depends on IT but also more broadly on informal social relationships within the MNE. This is because there are two categories of knowledge: (1) explicit knowledge and (2) tacit knowledge. **Explicit knowledge** is codifiable (that is, can be written down and transferred with little loss in its richness). Virtually all the knowledge captured, stored, and transmitted by IT is explicit. **Tacit knowledge** is noncodifiable and its acquisition and transfer require hands-on practice.[35] For instance, mastering a driving manual (containing a ton of explicit knowledge) without any road practice does not make you a good driver. Tacit knowledge is evidently more important and harder to transfer and learn—it can be acquired only through learning by doing (driving in this case). Consequently, from a resource-based view, explicit knowledge captured by IT may be strategically *less* important. What counts is the hard-to-codify and -transfer tacit knowledge.

Knowledge Management in Four Types of MNEs

Differences in knowledge management among the four types of MNEs in Figure 10.1 fundamentally stem from the interdependence (1) between the headquarters and foreign subsidiaries and (2) among various subsidiaries (Table 10.2).[36] In MNEs pursuing a home replication strategy, such interdependence is moderate and the role of subsidiaries is largely to adapt and leverage parent company competencies. Thus, knowledge on

knowledge management

The structures, processes, and systems that actively develop, leverage, and transfer knowledge.

explicit knowledge

Knowledge that is codifiable (that is, it can be written down and transferred without losing much of its richness).

tacit knowledge

Knowledge that is not codifiable (that is, hard to be written down and transmitted without losing much of its richness).

TABLE 10.2   **Knowledge Management in Four Types of Multinational Enterprises**

STRATEGY	HOME REPLICATION	LOCALIZATION	GLOBAL STANDARDIZATION	TRANSNATIONAL
Interdependence	Moderate	Low	Moderate	High
Role of foreign subsidiaries	Adapting and leveraging parent company competencies	Sensing and exploiting local opportunities	Implementing parent company initiatives	Differentiated contributions by subsidiaries to integrate worldwide operations
Development and diffusion of knowledge	Knowledge developed at the center and transferred to subsidiaries	Knowledge developed and retained within each subsidiary	Knowledge mostly developed and retained at the center and key locations	Knowledge developed jointly and shared worldwide
Flow of knowledge	Extensive flow of knowledge and people from headquarters to subsidiaries	Limited flow of knowledge and people in both directions (to and from the center)	Extensive flow of knowledge and people from center and key locations to subsidiaries	Extensive flow of knowledge and people in multiple directions

Sources: Adapted from (1) C. Bartlett & S. Ghoshal, 1989, *Managing Across Borders: The Transnational Solution* (p. 65), Boston: Harvard Business School Press; (2) T. Kostova & K. Roth, 2003, Social capital in multinational corporations and a micro-macro model of its formation (p. 299), *Academy of Management Review,* 28 (2): 297–317.

new products and technologies is mostly developed at the center and flown to subsidiaries, representing the traditional "one-way" flow. Starbucks, for instance, insists on replicating its US coffee shop concept around the world, down to the elusive "atmosphere."

In MNEs adopting a localization strategy, the interdependence is low. Knowledge management centers on developing knowledge that can best tackle local markets. Ford of Europe used to develop cars for Europe, with limited flow of knowledge from and toward headquarters (see Strategy in Action 10.1).

In MNEs pursuing a global standardization strategy, the interdependence is increased. Knowledge is developed and retained at the center and a few "centers of excellence." Consequently, there is an extensive flow of knowledge and people from headquarters and these centers to other subsidiaries. For example, Yokogawa Hewlett-Packard, HP's subsidiary in Japan, won a coveted Japanese Deming Award for quality. The subsidiary was then charged with transferring such knowledge to the rest of HP, which resulted in a ten-fold improvement in *corporate*-wide quality in ten years.[37]

A hallmark of transnational MNEs is a high degree of interdependence and extensive bidirectional flows of knowledge.[38] For example, extending a popular ice cream developed in Argentina based on a locally popular caramelized milk dessert, Häagen-Dazs introduced this flavor, Dulce De Leche, throughout the United States and Europe. Within one year, it became the second most popular Häagen-Dazs ice cream (next only to vanilla).[39] Particularly fundamental to transnational MNEs are knowledge flows among dispersed subsidiaries, each not only developing locally relevant knowledge but also aspiring to contribute globally beneficial knowledge that enhances *corporate*-wide competitiveness of the MNE as a whole (see Siemens' ShareNet in Strategy in Action 10.2).

Strategy in Action 10.2 - Siemens' ShareNet

How can Siemens tap into and rejuvenate its 475,000 employees' comprehensive knowledge and expertise that is geographically dispersed in 190 countries? Since 1998, Siemens has developed a knowledge management (KM) system, ShareNet, that endeavors to put its employees' combined knowledge to work.

The ShareNet initiative went through four steps. Step one was concept definition. ShareNet was envisioned to not only handle explicit knowledge, but also tacit knowledge. To overcome the drawbacks of traditional repository-based KM systems, the new system had to integrate interactive components such as a forum for urgent requests and a platform for sharing rich knowledge. The ShareNet team wanted to avoid the usual Siemens practice of rolling out initiatives from Munich, Germany, to the rest of the MNE—such a practice often backfired.

The second step was the global rollout for 39 countries in 1999. Siemens addressed the bias of both global integration and local responsiveness by adopting a "glocal" approach. While strategic direction was maintained in Munich, ShareNet managers were appointed to local subsidiaries. Importantly, these ShareNet managers were not expats from the headquarters, but rather people from the subsidiaries assigned to become the nucleus in their regions. To jump start the system, ShareNet managers held local workshops, and encouraged participants to post an unsolved problem as an urgent request that would be sent to all users worldwide. Without exception, by the end of the day, the posting would get at least one reply, and inevitably, the person who had posted it would be "stunned." Not surprisingly, every workshop was followed by an increase in urgent requests from that country.

To be sure, resistance was extensive. In Germany, attitude toward the English-only ShareNet was negative initially. Some employees thought that a Germany-based firm should use German. Although the English proficiency of German employees was relatively high, many employees still dared not post a question in a forum where thousands of people could see their grammatical or spelling errors. Over time, such resistance was gradually overcome as users personally saw the benefit from using the system.

The third step was generating momentum. Many people said: "I don't have time for this." Others put it more bluntly: "Why do I have to share?" In 2000, Siemens provided incentives for local country managers, and rewarded a country's overall participation. For a successful sale resulting from ShareNet collaboration, a bonus was given to both the country that had contributed the knowledge and the country that used it. Individuals were rewarded with various prizes, such as mobile phones, books, and even trips to visit knowledge exchange partners.

The fourth step was sustaining performance. By 2002, ShareNet had 19,000 users in more than 80 countries, supported by 53 ShareNet managers in different countries. Yet, not everything was rosy. The post-"9/11" downturn forced corporate-wide layoffs. After restructuring, the ShareNet team was trimmed to less than ten members worldwide. To demonstrate the value added, the ShareNet team documented €5 million in direct profits that had been generated by the KM system. On balance, ShareNet was considered a huge success.

Sources: Based on (1) *The Economist,* 2007, Home and abroad, February 10: 7–8; (2) www.siemens.com; (3) T. Stewart & L. O'Brien, 2005, Transforming an industrial giant, *Harvard Business Review,* February: 115–122; (4) S. Voelpel, M. Dous, & T. Davenport, 2005, Five steps to creating a global knowledge-sharing system, *Academy of Management Executive,* 19: 9–23.

Globalizing Research and Development (R&D)

R&D represents a crucial arena for knowledge management. Relative to production and marketing, only more recently has R&D emerged as an important function to be internationalized—often known as innovation-seeking investment (see Chapter 5).[40]

The intensification of competition for innovation drives the globalization of R&D. Such R&D provides a vehicle to access a foreign country's local talents and expertise.[41] Recall earlier discussions in Chapter 5 on the importance of *agglomeration* of high-caliber innovative firms within a country. For foreign firms, a most effective way to access such a cluster is to be there through FDI—as Shiseido did in France by setting up a perfume lab there.

From a resource-based standpoint, a fundamental basis for competitive advantage is innovation-based firm heterogeneity (being different).[42] Decentralized R&D performed by different locations and teams around the world virtually guarantees that there will be persistent heterogeneity in the solutions generated.[43] GSK for example, has aggressively spun off R&D units, because it realizes that adding more researchers in centralized R&D units does not necessarily enhance global learning and innovation.

Overall, the scale and scope of R&D by MNE units in host countries have grown significantly. On a worldwide basis, 16% of business R&D is now conducted by MNEs in host countries. Of course, this percentage varies, between 72% in Ireland and 2% in South Korea. The percentage for Hungary, China, and the United States is 63%, 24%, and 14%, respectively.[44] Given such a significant presence, it is not surprising that host-country governments increasingly value such "foreign" R&D.

Problems and Solutions in Knowledge Management[45]

Institutionally, how MNEs employ the formal and informal "rules of the game" has a significant bearing behind the success or failure of knowledge management. Shown in Table 10.3, a number of informal "rules" can become problems in knowledge management. In knowledge acquisition, many MNEs prefer to invent everything internally. However, for large firms, R&D actually offers *diminishing* returns.[46] Consequently, a new model, "open innovation," is emerging.[47] It relies on more collaborative research, among various internal units, external firms, and university labs. Evidence shows firms that skillfully share research outperform those that fail to do so.[48]

In knowledge retention, the usual problems of employee turnover are compounded when such employees are key R&D personnel, whose departure will lead to knowledge leakage.[49] In knowledge outflow, there is the "How does it help me?" syndrome. Specifically, managers of the source subsidiary may view the outbound sharing of knowledge as a diversion of scarce time and resources (see Strategy in Action 10.2).

TABLE 10.3   Problems in Knowledge Management

ELEMENTS OF KNOWLEDGE MANAGEMENT	COMMON PROBLEMS
Knowledge acquisition	Failure to share and integrate external knowledge
Knowledge retention	Employee turnover and knowledge leakage
Knowledge outflow	"How does it help me?" syndrome and "knowledge is power" mentality
Knowledge transmission	Inappropriate channels
Knowledge inflow	"Not invented here" syndrome and absorptive capacity

Source: Adapted from A. Gupta & V. Govindarajan, 2004, *Global Strategy and Organization* (p. 109), New York: Wiley.

Further, some managers may believe that "knowledge is power"—monopolizing certain knowledge may be viewed as the currency to acquire and retain power within the MNE.[50]

Even when certain subsidiaries are willing to share knowledge, inappropriate transmission channels may still torpedo effective sharing.[51] It is tempting to establish **global virtual teams,** which do not meet face-to-face, to transfer knowledge. Unfortunately, such teams often have to confront tremendous communication and relationship barriers.[52] Videoconferences can hardly show body language and Skype often breaks down. Thus, face-to-face meetings are often still necessary. Finally, recipient subsidiaries may block successful knowledge inflows due to two problems. First, the "not invented here" syndrome creates a resistance to ideas from other units. Second, recipients may have limited **absorptive capacity**—the "ability to recognize the value of new information, assimilate it, and apply it."[53]

As solutions to combat these problems, corporate headquarters can manipulate the formal "rules of the game," such as (1) tying bonuses to measurable knowledge outflows and inflows, (2) using high-powered corporate- or business-unit-based incentives (as opposed to individual- and single-subsidiary-based incentives), and (3) investing in codifying tacit knowledge (such as the codification of the Toyota Way illustrated in the Opening Case). Siemens used some of these measures when promoting its ShareNet (see Strategy in Action 10.2). However, these formal policies fundamentally boil down to the very challenging (if not impossible) task of how to accurately measure inflows and outflows of tacit knowledge. The nature of tacit knowledge simply resists such formal bureaucratic practices. Consequently, MNEs often have to rely on a great deal of informal integrating mechanisms, such as (1) facilitating management and R&D personnel networks among various subsidiaries through joint teamwork, training, and conferences and (2) promoting strong organizational (that is, MNE-specific) cultures and shared values and norms for cooperation among subsidiaries.[54]

Instead of using traditional formal command-and-control structures that are often ineffective, knowledge management is best facilitated by informal **social capital,** which refers to the informal benefits individuals and organizations derive from their social structures and networks.[55] Because of the existence of social capital, individuals are more likely to go out of their way to help friends and acquaintances. Consequently, managers of the China subsidiary are more likely to help managers of the Chile subsidiary with needed knowledge if they know each other and have some social relationship. Otherwise, managers of the China subsidiary may not be as enthusiastic to provide such help if the call for help comes from managers of the Cameroon subsidiary, with whom there is no social relationship. Overall, the micro informal interpersonal relationships among managers of various units may greatly facilitate macro inter-subsidiary cooperation among various units—in short, a **micro-macro link.**[56]

Debates and Extensions

The question of how to manage complex MNEs has led to numerous debates, some of which have been discussed earlier (such as the debate on the matrix structure). Here we outline two of the leading debates not previously discussed: (1) corporate controls versus subsidiary initiatives and (2) customer-focused dimensions versus integration, responsiveness, and learning.

---

global virtual teams

Teams whose members are physically dispersed in multiple locations in the world. They cooperate on a virtual basis.

absorptive capacity

The ability to absorb new knowledge by recognizing the value of new information, assimilating it, and applying it.

social capital

The informal benefits individuals and organizations derive from their social structures and networks.

micro-macro link

Micro, informal interpersonal relationships among managers of various units may greatly facilitate macro, interorganizational cooperation among various units.

Corporate Controls versus Subsidiary Initiatives

One of the leading debates on how to manage large firms is centralization versus decentralization. Within an MNE, the debate boils down to central controls versus subsidiary initiatives. A starting point is that subsidiaries are not necessarily at the receiving end of commands from headquarters. When headquarters promote certain practices (such as quality circles), some subsidiaries will be in full compliance, others may pay lip service to them, and still others may simply refuse to adopt them, citing local differences.[57]

In addition to reacting to headquarters' demands differently, some subsidiaries may actively pursue their own *subsidiary*-level strategies and agendas.[58] These activities are known as **subsidiary initiatives,** defined as the proactive and deliberate pursuit of new opportunities by a subsidiary to expand its scope of responsibility (see Strategy in Action 10.3). Many authors argue that such initiatives may inject a much needed spirit of entrepreneurship throughout the larger bureaucratic MNE.

However, from the perspective of corporate headquarters, it is hard to distinguish between good-faith subsidiary initiative and opportunistic "empire building."[59] A lot is at stake when determining which subsidiaries would become "centers of excellence" with worldwide mandates.[60] Subsidiaries that fail to attain this status may see their roles marginalized and, in the worst case, their facilities closed. Subsidiary managers are often host-country nationals (such as Canadian managers at Honeywell Canada in Strategy in Action 10.3), who would naturally prefer to strengthen their subsidiary. However, these tendencies, although very natural and legitimate, are not necessarily consistent with the MNE's *corporate*-wide goals. These tendencies, if not checked and controlled, can surely lead to chaos.

Customer-Focused Dimensions versus Integration, Responsiveness, and Learning[61]

As discussed earlier, juggling the three dimensions of integration, responsiveness, and learning has often made the global matrix structure so complex it is unworkable. However, instead of simplifying, many MNEs have added new dimensions. Often, new customer-focused dimensions of structure are placed on top of an existing structure, resulting in a four- or five-dimension matrix.

Of the two primary customer-focused dimensions, the first is a **global account structure** to supply customers (often other MNEs) in a coordinated and consistent way across various countries. Most original equipment manufacturers (OEMs)—namely, contract manufacturers that produce goods *not* carrying their own brands (such as the makers of Nike shoes and Microsoft Xbox)—use this structure. Singapore's Flextronics, the world's largest electronics OEM, has dedicated global accounts for Dell, Palm, and Sony Ericsson. The second customer-focused dimension is the oft-used **solutions-based structure.** For instance, as a "customer solution" provider, IBM will sell whatever combination of hardware, software, and services that customers prefer, whether that means selling IBM products or rivals' offerings.

The typical starting point is to put in place temporary solutions rather than create new layers or units. However, this ad hoc approach can quickly get out of control, resulting in subsidiary managers' additional duties of reporting to three or four "informal bosses" (acting as global account managers) on top of their "day jobs." Eventually, new formal structures may be called for, resulting in more bureaucracy.

subsidiary initiative

The proactive and deliberate pursuit of new business opportunities by an MNE's subsidiary to expand its scope of responsibility.

global account structure

A customer-focused structure that supplies customers (often other MNEs) in a coordinated and consistent way across various countries.

solutions-based structure

An MNE organization structure which caters to the needs of providing solutions for customers' problems.

𝒮𝓉𝓇𝒶𝓉𝑒𝑔𝓎 𝒾𝓃 𝒜𝒸𝓉𝒾𝑜𝓃 10.3 - A Subsidiary Initiative at Honeywell Canada

Ethical Challenge

Honeywell Limited is a wholly owned Canadian subsidiary—hereafter "Honeywell Canada"—of the Minneapolis-based Honeywell, Inc. Until the mid-1980s, Honeywell Canada was a traditional branch plant that mainly produced for the Canadian market, in volumes approximately one-tenth of those of the main manufacturing operations in Minneapolis. By the late 1980s, the winds of change unleashed by the US-Canadian Free Trade Agreement (later to become NAFTA in the 1990s) threatened the very survival of Honeywell Canada, whose relatively inefficient (suboptimal scale) operations could face closure when the high tariffs came down and Made-in-USA products could enter Canada duty-free. Canadian managers in the subsidiary entrepreneurially proposed to the headquarters that their plant be given the mandate in certain product lines to produce for all of North America. In exchange, they agreed to shut down some inefficient lines. Although some US managers were understandably negative, the head of the homes division was open-minded. Negotiations followed and the Canadian proposal was eventually adopted. Consequently, Honeywell Canada was designated as a Honeywell "Center of Excellence" for valves and actuators. At present, Honeywell Canada is Canada's leading controls company.

While this is a successful case of subsidiary initiative, a potential ethical problem is that, from a corporate

headquarters' standpoint, it is often difficult to ascertain whether the subsidiary is making good-faith efforts acting in the best interest of the MNE or the subsidiary managers are primarily promoting their own self-interests, in the areas of power, prestige, and their own jobs. How corporate headquarters can differentiate good-faith efforts from more opportunistic maneuvers remains a challenge.

Sources: Based on (1) J. Birkinshaw, 2000, *Entrepreneurship in the Global Firm* (p. 26), London: Sage; (2) www.honeywell.ca; (3) www.honeywell.com.

So what is the solution when confronting the value-added potential of customer-focused dimensions and their associated complexity and cost? One solution is to *simplify*. For instance, ABB, when facing grave performance problems, transformed its sprawling "Byzantine" matrix structure to a mere two global product divisions: power technology and automation.

The Savvy Strategist

MNEs are the ultimate large, complex, and geographically dispersed business organizations. To manage effectively, four clear implications emerge for the savvy strategist (Table 10.4). First, understand the nature and evolution of your industry in order to

TABLE 10.4   Strategic Implications for Action

- Understand the evolution of your industry to come up with the right strategy-structure configurations.
- Develop learning and innovation capabilities to leverage multinational presence as an asset— "think global, act local."
- Master the external rules of the game governing MNEs and home/host country environments.
- Be prepared to change the internal rules of the game governing MNE management.

come up with the right strategy-structure configurations. When the Japanese automobile industry was primarily exporting, Toyota naturally adopted a home replication strategy supported by an international division. However, as the industry evolved to become more geographically dispersed in terms of production and innovation, Toyota's strategy and structure had to adapt and progress in order to keep up (see Opening Case).

Second, managers need to actively develop learning and innovation capabilities to leverage multinational presence. A winning formula is "*think global, act local.*" Failing to do so may be costly. From 1999–2000, many Ford Explorer SUVs accidentally rolled over and killed many people in the United States. Most of these accidents were caused by faulty tires made by Japan's Bridgestone and its US subsidiary Firestone. Before the number of US accidents skyrocketed, an alarming number of accidents had already taken place in warmer weather countries such as Brazil and Saudi Arabia and local managers dutifully reported them to headquarters in Japan and the United States. Unfortunately, these reports were dismissed by higher-ups as "driver error" or "road conditions." Bridgestone (and Firestone) thus failed to leverage its multinational presence as an asset—it should have learned from these reports and proactively probed into the potential for similar accidents in cooler weather countries (tires depreciate faster in warmer weather). In the end, many more lives were lost.

Third, mastering the external rules of the game governing MNEs and home/host country environments becomes a must. In 2000, Philips took advantage of home country rules concerning antidumping (see Chapter 8) by suing Chinese firms for dumping in the EU. However, after Philips upset the Chinese government, its sales in China, its second largest market after the United States, immediately dropped by 10% (from $5.5 billion in 2000 to $5 billion in 2001). Trying to repair the damage, in 2003 Philips' board held its first meeting outside of Amsterdam in Beijing and visited Chinese officials. It also moved its Asia headquarters from Hong Kong to Shanghai and set up R&D units in Xian.

Finally, managers need to understand and be prepared to change the internal rules of the game governing MNE management. Different strategies and structures call for different internal rules of the game. Some facilitate and others constrain MNE actions. It is impossible for a home replication firm to entertain having a foreigner as its CEO. Yet, as an MNE becomes more global in its operations, its managerial outlook needs to be broadened as well. While not every MNE needs to appoint a foreign-born executive as its head, the foreign-born bosses at Coca-Cola, Nissan, PepsiCo, and Sony represent one of the strongest signals about these firms' global outlook.

CHAPTER SUMMARY

1. *Understand the four basic configurations of multinational strategies and structures*

   - Governing multinational strategy and structure is an integration-responsiveness framework.

   - There are four strategy/structure pairs: (1) home replication strategy/international division structure, (2) localization strategy/geographic area structure, (3) global standardization strategy/global product division structure, and (4) transnational strategy/global matrix structure.

2. *Articulate a comprehensive model of multinational strategy, structure, and learning*

   - Industry-based considerations drive a number of decisions affecting strategy, structure, and learning.

   - Management of MNE strategy, structure, and learning needs to take VRIO into account.

   - MNEs are governed by external and internal rules of the game around the world.

3. *Outline the challenges associated with learning, innovation, and knowledge management*

   - Knowledge management primarily focuses on tacit knowledge.

   - Globalization of R&D calls for capabilities to combat a number of problems associated with knowledge creation, retention, outflow, transmission, and inflow.

4. *Participate in two leading debates on multinational strategy, structure, learning, and innovation*

   - (1) Corporate controls versus subsidiary initiatives and (2) customer-focused dimensions versus integration, responsiveness, and learning.

5. *Draw strategic implications for action*

   - Understand the evolution of your industry to come up with the right strategy-structure configurations.

   - Develop learning and innovation capabilities around the world—"think global, act local."

   - Master the external rules of the game from home/host country environments.

   - Be prepared to change the internal rules of the game governing MNEs.

KEY TERMS

Absorptive capacity	**Explicit knowledge**	**Global product division**
Center of excellence	**Global account structure**	**Global standardization strategy**
Country (regional) manager	**Global matrix**	

Global virtual team	Local responsiveness	Subsidiary initiative
Home replication strategy	Localization (multi-domestic) strategy	Tacit knowledge
Integration-responsiveness framework	Micro–macro link	Transnational strategy
International division	Social capital	Worldwide (global) mandate
Knowledge management	Solutions-based structure	

CRITICAL DISCUSSION QUESTIONS

1. In this age of globalization, some gurus argue that all industries are becoming global and that all firms need to adopt a global standardization strategy. Do you agree? Why or why not?

2. **ON ETHICS:** You are the head of the best-performing subsidiary in an MNE. Because bonus is tied to subsidiary performance, your bonus is the highest among managers of all subsidiaries. Now headquarters is organizing managers from other subsidiaries to visit and learn from your subsidiary. You worry that if your subsidiary is no longer the star unit when other subsidiaries' performance catches up, your bonus will go down. What are you going to do?

3. **ON ETHICS:** You are a corporate R&D manager at Boeing and are thinking about transferring some R&D work to China, India, and Russia, where the work performed by a $70,000 US engineer reportedly can be done by an engineer in one of these countries for less than $7,000. However, US engineers at Boeing have staged protests against such moves. US politicians are similarly vocal concerning job losses and national security hazards. What are you going to do?

CLOSING CASE

Ethical Challenge

Moving Headquarters Overseas

While a majority of MNEs have been moving money, technology, and jobs around the world, a small but increasing number of them have also moved their headquarters (HQ) overseas. In general, there are two levels of HQ: *business unit* HQ and *corporate* HQ. At the business unit level, examples are numerous. In 2004, Nokia moved its corporate finance HQ from Helsinki, Finland, to New York. In 2006, IBM's global procurement office moved from New York to Shenzhen, China. Examples for corporate HQ relocations are fewer, but they tend to be of a higher

profile. In 1981, Tetra Pak, a packaging company that pioneered the soft package for beverages, moved its corporate HQ from Sweden to Switzerland. In the early 1990s, HSBC moved its corporate HQ from Hong Kong to London. Similarly, Anglo American, Old Mutual, and SAB (later to become SABMiller after acquiring Miller Beer) moved from South Africa to London. In 2004, News Corporation moved its corporate HQ from Melbourne, Australia, to New York. In 2005, China's Lenovo set up its corporate HQ in North Carolina, home of IBM's former PC division that Lenovo acquired. The question is: Why?

If you have moved from one house to another in the same city, you can easily appreciate the logistical challenges (and nightmares!) associated with relocating HQ overseas. A simple answer is that the benefits of such moves must significantly outweigh their drawbacks. At the business unit level, the answer is straightforward: the "center of gravity" of the activities of a business unit may pull its HQ toward a host country. See the following letter to suppliers from IBM's chief procurement officer informing them of the move to China:

IBM Global Procurement is taking a major step toward developing a more geographically distributed executive structure . . . By anchoring the organization in this location, we will be better positioned to continue developing the skills and talents of our internal organization in the region . . . Clearly, this places us closer to the core of the technology supply chain which is important, not only for IBM's own internal needs, but increasingly for the needs of external clients whose supply chains we are managing via our Procurement Services offering. As IBM's business offerings continue to grow, we must develop a deeper supply chain in the region to provide services and human resource skills to clients both within Asia and around the world.

At least four strategic rationales lie at the corporate level. First, a leading symbolic value is an unambiguous statement to various stakeholders that the firm is a global—rather than domestic or local—player. News Corporation's corporate HQ relocation to New York is indicative of its global status, as opposed to being a relatively parochial firm from "down under." Lenovo's coming of age as a global player is no doubt underpinned by the establishment of its worldwide HQ in the United States.

Second, there may be significant efficiency gains. If the new corporate HQ is in a major financial center such as New York or London, the MNE can have more efficient, more direct, and more frequent communication with institutional shareholders, financial analysts, and investment banks. The MNE also

increases its visibility in a financial market. This can result in greater liquidity for the stock, a broader shareholder base, and greater market capitalization. Three leading (former) South African firms, Anglo American, Old Mutual, and SABMiller, have now joined the ranks of the FTSE 100—the top 100 UK-listed firms by capitalization.

Third, firms may benefit from their visible commitment to the laws and regulations of the new host country. By making such a commitment, firms benefit from the higher-quality legal and regulatory regime they now operate under. These benefits are especially crucial for firms from emerging economies where local rules are not world-class. A lack of confidence about South Africa's political stability drove Anglo American, Old Mutual, and SABMiller to London. By coming to London, HSBC likewise endeavored to deviate from its Hong Kong roots at a time before the 1997 handover when the future of Hong Kong was uncertain.

Finally, by moving (or threatening to move) HQ locations, firms enhance their bargaining power vis-à-vis that of their (original) home country governments. For example, Tetra Pak's move of its corporate HQ to Switzerland was driven primarily by the owners' tax disputes with the Swedish government. The message is clear: If the home country government treats us harshly, we will pack our bags.

The last point, of course, is where the ethical and social responsibility controversies erupt. Relatively small Western economies, such as Sweden, the Netherlands, and Canada, run the risk of losing a number of their leading firms once they "make it." Although the absolute number of jobs lost is not great, these are high-quality (and high-paying) jobs that every government would prefer to see. More alarmingly, if a sufficient number of HQs move overseas, this could lead to serious ramifications, such as other high-quality service providers (like lawyers, bankers, and accountants) following them. In response, proposals are floating to offer tax incentives for these "foot-loose" MNEs to keep HQ at home. However, critics question why these wealthy MNEs (and executives often known as "fat cats") need to be subsidized (or bribed), while many other sectors and individuals are struggling.

Sources: Based on (1) J. Birkinshaw, P. Braunerhjelm, U. Holm, & S. Terjesen, 2006, Why do some multinational corporations relocate their headquarters overseas?, *Strategic Management Journal*, 27: 681–700; (2) IBM, 2006, IBM Procurement headquarters moves to Shenzhen, China, May 22, www-03.ibm.com; (3) Wikipedia, 2008, (a) Lenovo Group and (b) SABMiller, en.wikipedia.org.

Case Discussion Questions

1. What are the drawbacks and benefits associated with moving business unit HQ and corporate HQ to another country?

2. If you were a CEO or a business unit head, under what conditions would you consider moving your HQ?

3. If you were a government official in the MNE's home country, what could you do to discourage such moves of multinational HQs out of the country?

NOTES

Journal acronyms *AME–Academy of Management Executive;* ***AMJ**–Academy of Management Journal;* ***AMR**–Academy of Management Review;* ***APJM**–Asia Pacific Journal of Management;* ***ASQ**–Administrative Science Quarterly;* ***BW**–Business Week;* ***HBR**–Harvard Business Review;* ***IBR**–International Business Review;* ***JIBS**–Journal of International Business Studies;* ***JIM**–Journal of International Management;* ***JM**–Journal of Management;* ***JMS**–Journal of Management Studies;* ***JWB**–Journal of World Business;* ***MIR**–Management International Review;* ***OSc**–Organization Science;* ***SMJ**–Strategic Management Journal*

1. J. Birkinshaw, S. Ghoshal, C. Markides, J. Stopford, & G. Yip (eds.), 2003, *The Future of the Multinational Company*, London: Wiley; C. K. Prahalad & Y. Doz, 1987, *The Multinational Mission*, New York: Free Press; J. Stopford & L. Wells, 1972, *Managing the Multinational Enterprise*, New York: Basic Books.

2. T. Levitt, 1983, The globalization of markets, *HBR*, May–June: 92–102.

3. A. Rugman, 2001, *The End of Globalization*, New York: AMACOM.

4. A. Harzing, 2000, An empirical analysis and extension of the Bartlett and Ghoshal typology of MNCs, *JIBS*, 31: 101–120.

5. T. Frost, J. Birkinshaw, & P. Ensign, 2002, Centers of excellence in MNCs (p. 997), *SMJ*, 23: 997–1018; G. Reger, 2004, Coordinating globally dispersed research centers of excellence, *JIM*, 10: 51–76.

6. C. Bartlett & S. Ghoshal, 1989, *Managing Across Borders*, Boston: Harvard Business School Press.

7. B. Ambos & B. Schlegelmilch, 2007, Innovation and control in the multinational firm, *SMJ*, 28: 473–486;

N. Anand, H. Gardner, & T. Orris, 2007, Knowledge-based innovation, *AMJ*, 50: 406–428; H. Berry, 2006, Leaders, laggards, and the pursuit of foreign knowledge, *SMJ*, 27: 151–168; J. Cantwell, J. Dunning, & O. Janne, 2004, Towards a technology-seeking explanation of US direct investment in the United Kingdom, *JIM*, 10: 5–20; W. Chen & K. Miller, 2007, Situational and institutional determinants of firm's R&D search intensity, *SMJ*, 28: 369–381.

8. J. Birkinshaw & N. Hood, 1998, Multinational subsidiary evolution, *AMR*, 23: 773–796; J. Manea & R. Pearce, 2006, MNEs' strategies in Central and Eastern Europe, *MIR*, 46: 235–255.

9. J. Cantwell & R. Mudambi, 2005, MNE competence-creating subsidiary mandates, *SMJ*, 26: 1109–1128; K. Ruckman, 2005, Technology sourcing through acquisitions, *JIBS*, 36: 89–103.

10. B. Lamont, V. Sambamurthy, K. Ellis, & P. Simmonds, 2000, The influence of organizational structure on the information received by corporate strategies of MNEs, *MIR*, 40: 231–252; Y. Ling, S. Floyd, & D. Baldrige, 2005, Toward a model of issue-selling by subsidiary managers in MNCs, *JIBS*, 36: 637–654.

11. U. Andersson, M. Forsgren, & U. Holm. 2007, Balancing subsidiary influence in the federative MNC, *JIBS*, 38: 802–818; R. Edwards, A. Ahmad, & S. Ross, 2002, Subsidiary autonomy, *JIBS*, 33: 183–191; S. Johnston & B. Menguc, 2007, Subsidiary size and the level of subsidiary autonomy in MNCs, *JIBS*, 38: 787–801; S. Miller & L. Eden, 2006, Local density and foreign subsidiary performance, *AMJ*, 49: 341–355.

12. T. Devinney, D. Midgley, & S. Venaik, 2000, The optimal performance of the global firm, *OSc*, 11: 674–695.

13. R. Hodgetts, 1999, Dow Chemical CEO William Stavropoulos on structure (p. 30), *AME*, 13: 29–35.

14. A. Chandler, 1962, *Strategy and Structure*, Cambridge, MA: MIT Press.

15. J. Wolf & W. Egelhoff, 2002, A reexamination and extension of international strategy-structure theory, *SMJ*, 23: 181–189.

16. G. Benito, B. Grogaard, & R. Narula, 2003, Environmental influences on MNE subsidiary roles, *JIBS*, 34: 443–456; T. Malnight, 2001, Emerging structural patterns within MNCs, *AMJ*, 44: 1187–1210; T. Murtha, S. Lenway, & R. Bagozzi, 1998, Global mind-sets and cognitive shift in a complex MNC, *SMJ*, 19: 97–114; S. Venaik, D. Midgley, & T. Devinney, 2005, Dual paths to performance, *JIBS*, 36: 655–675; R. Whitley, G. Morgan, W. Kelley, & D. Sharpe, 2003, The changing Japanese multinational, *JMS*, 40: 643–672.

17. T. Chi, P. Nystrom, & P. Kircher, 2004, Knowledge-based resources as determinants of MNC structure, *JIM,* 10: 219–38.

18. K. Atuahene-Gima, 2003, The effects of centrifugal and centripetal forces on product development speed and quality, *AMJ*, 46: 359–373; E. Morgan & F. Fai, 2007, Innovation, competition, and change in IB, *MIR*, 47: 631–638.

19. P. Cloninger, 2004, The effect of service intangibility on revenue from foreign markets, *JIM*, 10: 125–146; A. Delios & P. Beamish, 2001, Survival and profitability, *AMJ*, 44: 1028–1039; E. Danneels, 2002, The dynamics of product innovation and firm competencies, *SMJ*, 23: 1095–1122.

20. K. Ojah & L. Monplaisir, 2003, Investors' valuation of global product R&D, *JIBS*, 34: 457–472.

21. Y. Su, E. Tsang, & M. W. Peng, 2008, How do internal capabilities and external partnerships affect innovativeness? Working paper, University of Texas at Dallas.

22. Bartlett & Ghoshal, 1989, *Managing Across Borders* (p. 209).

23. A. Hillman & W. Wan, 2005, The determinants of MNE subsidiaries' political strategies, *JIBS*, 36: 322–340.

24. Y. Akbar & J. McBride, 2004, MNE strategy, FDI, and economic development, *JWB*, 39: 89–105; T. Buck, X. Liu, Y. Wei, & X. Liu, 2007, The trade development path and export spillovers in China, *MIR*, 47: 683–706; K. Meyer, 2004, Perspectives on MNEs in emerging economies, *JIBS*, 35: 259–276.

25. J. Laurila & M. Ropponen, 2003, Institutional conditioning of foreign expansion, *JMS*, 40: 725–751; T. Kostova & S. Zaheer, 1999, Organizational legitimacy under conditions of complexity, *AMR*, 24: 64–81; R. Ramamurti, 2004, Developing countries and MNEs, *JIBS*, 35: 277–283.

26. W. Sine, H. Mitsuhashi, & D. Kirsch, 2006, Revisiting Burns and Stalker, *AMJ*, 49: 121–132.

27. N. Nooderhaven & A. Harzing, 2003, The "country-of-origin effect" in MNCs, *MIR*, 43: 47–66.

28. P. Beamish & A. Inkpen, 1998, Japanese firms and the decline of the Japanese expatriate, *JWB*, 33: 35–50; R. Belderbos & M. Heijltjes, 2005, The determinants of expatriate staffing by Japanese multinationals in Asia, *JIBS*, 36: 341–354.

29. Y. Paik & J. Sohn, 2004, Expatriate managers and MNCs' ability to control international subsidiaries, *JWB*, 39: 61–71.

30. C. K. Prahalad & K. Lieberthal, 1998, The end of corporate imperialism, *HBR*, 76 (4): 68–79.

31. L. Palich & L. Gomez-Mejia, 1999, A theory of global strategy and firm efficiency, *JM*, 25: 587–606; L. Yaconi, 2001, Cross-cultural role expectations in nine European country-units of an MNE, *JMS*, 38: 1187–1215.

32. *BW*, 2003, P&G: New and improved, July 7: 52–63.

33. N. Anand, H. Gardner, & T. Morris, 2007, Knowledge-based innovation, *AMJ*, 50: 406–428; N. Foss & T. Pedersen, 2005, Organizing knowledge processes in the MNC, *JIBS*, 35: 340–349; M. Haas & M. Hansen, 2007, Different knowledge, different benefits, *SMJ*, 28: 1133–1153; B. Kogut & U. Zander, 1993, Knowledge of the firm and the evolutionary theory of the MNC, *JIBS*, 24: 625–645; G. Szulanski & R. Jensen, 2006, Presumptive adaptation and the effectiveness of knowledge transfer, *SMJ*, 27: 937–957; S. Tallman & A. Phene, 2007, Leveraging knowledge across geographic boundaries, *OSc*, 18: 252–260.

34. A. Gupta & V. Govindarajan, 2004, *Global Strategy and Organization* (p. 104), New York: Wiley.

35. G. Bruton, G. Dess, & J. Janney, 2007, Knowledge management in technology-focused firms in emerging economies, *APJM*, 24: 115–130; R. Coff, D. Coff, & R. Eastvold, 2006, The knowledge-leveraging paradox,

AMR, 31: 452–465; T. Felin & W. Hesterly, 2007, The knowledge-based view, *AMR*, 32: 195–218; X. Martin & R. Salomon, 2003, Knowledge transfer capacity and its implications for the theory of the MNE, *JIBS*, 34: 356–373; U. Schultze & C. Stabell, 2004, Knowing what you don't know?, *JMS*, 41: 549–573.

36. N. Adler & N. Hashai, 2007, Knowledge flows and the modeling of the MNE, *JIBS*, 38; 639–657; K. Hewett, M. Roth, & K. Roth, 2003, Conditions influencing headquarters and foreign subsidiary roles in marketing activities and their effects on performance, *JIBS*, 34: 567–585; M. Kotabe, D. Dunlap-Hinkler, R. Parente, & H. Mishra, 2007, Determinants of cross-national knowledge transfer and its effect on firm innovation, *JIBS*, 38: 259–282; Y. Luo & H. Zhao, 2004, Corporate link and competitive strategy in MNEs, *JIM*, 10: 77–105; D. Minbaeva, 2007, Knowledge transfer in MNCs, *MIR*, 47: 567–593; R. Nag, K. Corley, & D. Gioia, 2007, The intersection of organizational identity, knowledge, and practice, *AMJ*, 50: 821–847; C. Williams, 2007, Transfer in context, *SMJ*, 28: 867–889.

37. M. Porter, H. Takeuchi, & M. Sakakibara, 2000, *Can Japan Compete?* (p. 80), Cambridge, MA: Perseus.

38. T. Frost & C. Zhou, 2005, R&D co-practice and "reverse" knowledge integration in MNCs, *JIBS*, 36: 676–687; Y. Luo & M. W. Peng, 1999, Learning to compete in a transition economy, *JIBS*, 30: 269–296; S. Mu, D. Gnyawali, & D. Hatfield, 2007, Foreign subsidiaries' learning from local environments, *MIR*, 47: 79–102.

39. Y. Doz, J. Santos, & P. Williamson, 2001, *From Global to Metanational*, Boston: Harvard Business School Press.

40. K. Asakawa & A. Som, 2008, Internationalizing R&D in China and India, *APJM*, 25 (in press); R. Belderbos, 2003, Entry mode, organizational learning, and R&D in foreign affiliates, *SMJ*, 24: 235–255; P. Criscuolo & R. Narula, 2007, Using multi-hub structures for international R&D, *MIR*, 47: 639–660; W. Kuemmerle, 1999, The drivers of FDI into R&D, *JIBS*, 30: 1–24; M. Zedtwitz, O. Gassman, & R. Boutellier, 2004, Organizing global R&D, *JIM*, 10: 21–49.

41. M. W. Peng & D. Wang, 2000, Innovation capability and foreign direct investment, *MIR*, 40: 79–83; J. Penner-Hahn & J. M. Shaver, 2005, Does international R&D increase patent output?, *SMJ*, 26: 121–140.

42. G. Vegt, E. Vliert, & X. Huang, 2005, Location-level links between diversity and innovative climate depend on national power distance, *AMJ*, 48: 1171–1182; G. Verona, 1999, A resource-based view of product development, *AMR*, 24: 132–142.

43. F. Sanna-Randaccio & R. Veugelers, 2007, Multinational knowledge spillovers with decentralized R&D, *JIBS*, 38: 47–63.

44. UNCTAD, 2005, *World Investment Report 2005* (p. 136), New York and Geneva: United Nations/ UNCTAD.

45. This section draws heavily from Gupta & Govindarajan, 2004, *Global Strategy and Organization*.

46. H. Greve, 2003, A behavioral theory of R&D expenditures and innovations, *AMJ*, 46: 685–702.

47. U. Andersson, M. Forsgren, & U. Holm, 2002, The strategic impact of external networks, *SMJ*, 23: 979–996; D. Gerwin & J. Ferris, 2004, Organizing new product development projects in strategic alliances, *OSc*, 15: 22–37; A. Lam, 2003, Organizational learning in multinationals, *JMS*, 40: 673–703; W. McCutchen, P. Swamidas, & B. Teng, 2004, R&D risk-taking in strategic alliances, *MIR*, 44: 53–67; M. Mol, P. Pauwels, P. Matthyssens, & L. Quintens, 2004, A technological contingency perspective on the depth and scope of international outsourcing, *JIM*, 10: 287–305; R. Narula & G. Duysters, 2004, Globalization and trends in international R&D alliances, *JIM*, 10: 199–218; W. Sheremata, 2004, Competing through innovation in network markets, *AMR*, 29: 359–377.

48. J. Spencer, 2003, Firms' knowledge-sharing strategies in the global innovation system, *SMJ*, 24: 217–233; K. Laursen & A. Salter, 2006. Open for innovation, *SMJ*, 27: 131–150; M. Yamin & J. Otto, 2004, Patterns of knowledge flows and MNE innovative performance, *JIM*, 10: 239–258.

49. Q. Yang & C. Jiang, 2007, Location advantages and subsidiaries' R&D activities, *APJM*, 24: 341–358.

50. I. Bjorkman, W. Barner-Rasmussen, & L. Li, 2004, Managing knowledge transfer in MNCs, *JIBS*, 35: 443–455; R. Mudambi & P. Navarra, 2004, Is knowledge power?, *JIBS*, 35: 385–406.

51. G. Szulanski & R. Jensen, 2006, Presumptive adaptation and the effectiveness of knowledge transfer, *SMJ*, 27: 937–957.

52. S. Chevrier, 2003, Cross-cultural management in multinational project groups, *JWB*, 38: 141–149; K. Goodall & J. Roberts, 2003, Only connect, *JWB*, 38: 150–160; K. Lagerstrom & M. Andersson, 2003, Creating and sharing knowledge within a transnational team, *JWB*, 38: 84–95; R. Lunnan & T. Barth, 2003, Managing the exploration vs. exploitation dilemma in transnational "bridging teams," *JWB*, 38: 110–126; M. Maznevski & K. Chudoba, 2000, Building space over time, *OSc*, 11: 473–492; A. Mendez, 2003, The coordination of globalized R&D activities through project teams organization, *JWB*, 38: 96–109; D. Schweiger, T. Atamer, & R. Calori, 2003, Transnational project teams and networks, *JWB*, 38: 127–140; M. Zellmer-Bruhn & C. Gibson, 2006, Multinational organization context, *AMJ*, 49: 501–518.

53. W. Cohen & D. Levinthal, 1990, Absorptive capacity, *ASQ*, 35: 128–152; J. Hong, R. Snell, & M. Easterby-Smith, 2006, Cross-cultural influences on organizational learning in MNCs, *JIM*, 12: 408–429; J. Jansen, F. Bosch, & H. Volberda, 2005, Managing potential and realized absorptive capacity, *AMJ*, 48: 999–1015; P. Lane, B. Koka, & S. Pathak, 2006, The reification of absorptive capacity, *AMR*, 31: 833–863; D. Minbaeva, T. Pedersen, I. Bjorkman, C. Fey, & H. Park, 2003, MNC knowledge transfer, subsidiary absorptive capacity, and HRM, *JIBS*, 34: 586–599; G. Todorova & B. Durisin, 2007, Absorptive capacity, *AMR*, 32: 774–786; S. Zahra & G. George, 2002, Absorptive capacity, *AMR*, 27: 185–203.

54. H. Kim, J. Park, & J. Prescott, 2003, The global integration of business functions, *JIBS*, 34: 327–344; I. Manev & W. Stevenson, 2001, Nationality, cultural distance, and expatriate status, *JIBS*, 32: 285–304; S. O'Donnell, 2000, Managing foreign subsidiaries, *SMJ*, 21: 525–548; M. Subramaniam & N. Venkatraman, 2001, Determinants of transnational new product development capability, *SMJ*, 22: 359–378; E. Tsang, 2002, Acquiring knowledge by foreign partners from international joint ventures in a transition economy, *SMJ*, 23: 835–854.

55. A. Inkpen & E. Tsang, 2005, Social capital, networks, and knowledge transfer, *AMR*, 30: 146–165; T. Kostova & K. Roth, 2003, Social capital in MNCs and a micro-macro model of its formation, *AMR*, 28: 297–317; M. Subramanian & M. Youndt, 2005, The influence of intellectual capital on the types of innovation capabilities, *AMJ*, 48: 450–463.

56. M. W. Peng & Y. Luo, 2000, Managerial ties and firm performance in a transition economy, *AMJ*, 43: 486–501.

57. T. Kostova & K. Roth, 2002, Adoption of an organizational practice by subsidiaries of multinational corporations, *AMJ*, 45: 215–233.

58. B. Allred & K. S. Swan, 2004, Contextual influences on international subsidiaries' product technology strategy, *JIM*, 10: 259–286; M. Geppert, K. Williams, & D. Matten, 2003, The social construction of contextual rationalities in MNCs, *JMS*, 40: 617–641; J. Medcof, 2001, Resource-based strategy and managerial power in networks of internationally dispersed technology units, *SMJ*, 22: 999–1012; K. Moore, 2001, A strategy for subsidiaries, *MIR*, 41: 275–290.

59. D. Vora, T. Kostova, & K. Roth, 2007, Roles of subsidiary managers in MNCs, *MIR*, 47: 595–620.

60. S. Feinberg, 2000, Do world product mandates really matter?, *JIBS*, 31: 155–167.

61. This section draws heavily from J. Birkinshaw & S. Terjesen, 2003, The customer-focused multinational, in Birkinshaw et al. (eds.), *The Future of the Multinational Company* (115–127).

chapter 11

Corporate Governance

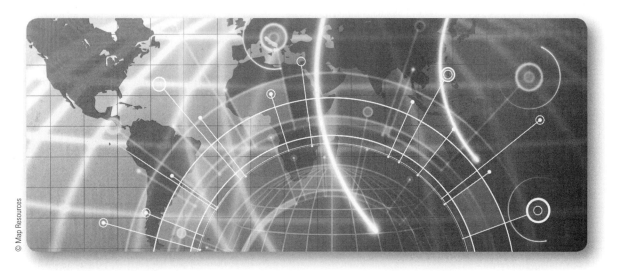

© Map Resources

KNOWLEDGE OBJECTIVES

After studying this chapter, you should be able to

1. Differentiate various ownership patterns around the world

2. Articulate the role of managers in both principal–agent and principal–principal conflicts

3. Explain the role of the board of directors

4. Identify voice- and exit-based governance mechanisms and their combination as a package

5. Acquire a global perspective on how governance mechanisms vary around the world

6. Elaborate on a comprehensive model of corporate governance

7. Participate in two leading debates on corporate governance

8. Draw strategic implications for action

OPENING CASE: THE PRIVATE EQUITY CHALLENGE

Private equity is the hottest new buzzword in corporate governance around the world. Private equity firms often take an underperforming publicly listed firm off the stock exchange, add some heavy dose of debt, throw in sweet "carrots" to incumbent managers, and trim all the "fat" (typically through layoffs). Private equity firms get paid by (1) the fees and (2) the profits reaped when they take the private firms public again through a new initial public offering (IPO).

Private equity first emerged in the 1980s, with a stream of deals peaked by Kohlberg Kravis Robert's (KKR) $25 billion takeover of RJR Nabisco in 1988—then the highest price paid for a public firm. While KKR disciplined deadwood managers who destroyed shareholder value, it received a ton of bad press, cemented in a best-selling book *Barbarians at the Gate* that portrayed KKR as a greedy and barbarous raider.

After the RJR Nabisco deal, the private equity industry stagnated during the 1990s. However, in the 2000s, private equity has scaled new heights, growing from 0.25% of world GDP in 2000 to 1.5% in 2007. In 1991, just 57 private equity firms existed. In 2007, close to 700 were in the chase. Private equity deals now represent about 25% of all mergers and acquisitions (M&As) in the world (and about 35% in the United States). Since 2005, Europe has had more actions (measured by deal values) than the United States. In 2007, Cerberus Capital Management,

a private equity firm, purchased Chrysler from DaimlerChrysler for $7.4 billion. APAX Partners, another private equity shop, spent $7.75 billion to buy Thomson Learning (the publisher of this book, now Cengage Learning) from The Thomson Corporation listed in New York (NYSE: TOC) and Toronto (TSX: TOC)—the publisher of *this book*.

Private equity has always been controversial. Proponents argue that private equity is a response to the corporate governance deficiency of the public firm. Private equity excels in four ways:

- Private owners, unlike dispersed individual shareholders, care deeply about the return on investment. Private equity firms always send experts to sit on the board and are hands-on in managing.

- A high level of debt imposes strong financial discipline to minimize waste.

- Private equity turns managers from agents to principals with substantial equity, thus providing a powerful incentive to them. Private equity firms pay managers more generously, but also punish failure more heavily. Managers' compensation at companies under private ownership, according to a leading expert, Michael Jensen, is *20 times* more sensitive to performance than at companies listed publicly. On average, private equity makes the *same* managers, managing the *same* assets, perform much more effectively.

- Finally, privacy is fabulous. For managers, no more short-term burden to "meet the numbers" for Wall Street, no more heavy-duty paperwork from regulators (an especially crushing load thanks to the Sarbanes-Oxley Act since 2002), and better yet, no more disclosure in excruciating detail of how much they are paid (an inevitable invitation to be labeled "fat cats"). Top managers under private ownership are indeed *fatter* cats. It is not surprising that more managers prefer a quieter but far more lucrative life.

All of the above, according to critics, are exactly what is wrong with private equity. In addition to "barbarians," private equity has also been labeled "asset strippers" and "locusts." As high executive compensation at public firms has already become a huge controversy, private equity has further increased the income inequality between the high financiers and top managers as one group and the rest of us as another group. Private equity has rapidly proliferated around the world. Some of the fuss reflects the shock in countries suddenly facing the full rigor of Anglo-American private equity. In Germany, some politicians in 2005 labeled foreign private equity groups as "locusts who feast on German firms for profit before spitting them out." In South Korea, Lone Star Funds of Dallas was initially hailed in 2003 as a brave outsider willing to save troubled Korean firms. However, in 2006, when Lone Star tried to cash out by selling its 51% equity of Korea Exchange Bank, unions took to the street to protest and prosecutors issued a warrant to arrest its co-founder for alleged financial manipulation.

To be sure, private equity results in job cuts, but the same would happen if targets were acquired by public firms. Private buyers do not intentionally set out to destroy their prize. Their record as corporate citizens is no more barbaric than that of public firms. In a record-breaking $45 billion buyout in 2007, Texas Pacific and KKR jointly took over a Texas utility TXU (NYSE: TXU). Private owners paid shareholders a 25% premium, gave retail customers a 10% price cut, and forced TXU to jettison plans to build eight dirty coal-fired power plants—hailed by environmentalists as a major victory.

Sources: Based on (1) *Business Week,* 2006, Public score for private equity, December 4: 48; (2) *The Economist,* 2006, In the shadows of debt, September 23: 79–81; (3) *The Economist,* 2006, The benefits of privacy, March 18: 65; (4) *The Economist,* 2007, Barbarians in dock, March 3: 12; (5) *The Economist,* 2007, Better pay for all, January 20: 18–19; (6) *The Economist,* 2007, The trouble with private equity, July 7: 11; (7) *The Economist,* 2007, The uneasy crown, February 10: 74–76; (8) M. Jensen, 1989, Eclipse of the public corporation, *Harvard Business Review,* September: 61–74; (9) A. von Nordenflycht, 2007, Is public ownership bad for professional service firms? *Academy of Management Journal,* 50: 429–445.

corporate governance

The relationship among various participants in determining the direction and performance of corporations.

Why has private equity emerged as a major alternative form of governance compared with the publicly listed corporation? What are the differences between the two? What is the most optimal way to govern corporations so that investors will reap returns? These are some of the key questions addressed in this chapter, which focuses on how to govern the corporation around the world. **Corporate governance** is "the relationship among various participants in determining the direction and performance of corporations."[1] The primary participants are (1) owners, (2) managers, and (3) boards of directors—collectively known as the "tripod" underpinning corporate governance (Figure 11.1).

FIGURE 11.1   The Tripod of Corporate Governance

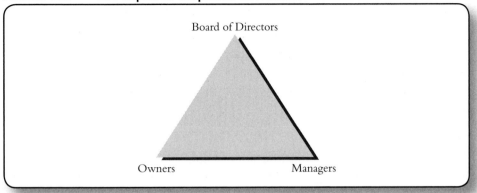

We start by discussing each of the three legs of the "tripod." Next, we introduce internal and external governance mechanisms from a global perspective. Then, a comprehensive model drawn from the "strategy tripod" is outlined. As before, debates and extensions follow.

Owners

Owners provide capital, bear risks, and own the firm. Three broad patterns exist: (1) concentrated versus diffused ownership, (2) family ownership, and (3) state ownership.

Concentrated versus Diffused Ownership

Founders usually start up firms and completely own and control them. This is referred to as **concentrated ownership and control.** However, at some point, if the firm aspires to grow and needs more capital, the owners' desire to keep the firm in family hands will have to accommodate the arrival of other shareholders. Approximately 80% of listed US firms and 90% of listed UK firms are now characterized by **diffused ownership,** with numerous small shareholders but none with a dominant level of control.[2] In such firms, there is a **separation of ownership and control,** in that ownership is dispersed among many small shareholders and control is largely concentrated in the hands of salaried professional managers who own little (or no) equity.

If majority or dominant owners (such as founders) do not personally run the firm, they are naturally interested in keeping a close eye on how the firm is run. However, dispersed owners, each with a small stake, have neither incentives nor resources to do so. Most small shareholders do not bother to show up at annual shareholder meetings. They prefer to free ride and hope that other shareholders will properly monitor and discipline managers. If small shareholders are not happy, they will simply sell the stock and invest elsewhere. However, if all shareholders behave in this manner, then no shareholder would care and managers would end up acquiring significant *de facto* control power.

The rise of institutional investors, such as professionally managed mutual funds and pension pools, has significantly changed this picture.[3] Institutional investors have both incentives and resources to closely monitor and control managerial actions. The increased

concentrated ownership and control

Ownership and control rights concentrated in the hands of owners.

diffused ownership

An ownership pattern involving numerous small shareholders, none of which has a dominant level of control.

separation of ownership and control

The dispersal of ownership among many small shareholders, and control of the firm is largely concentrated in the hands of salaried, professional managers who own little (or no equity).

size of institutional holdings limits the ability of institutional investors to dump the stock, because when one's stake is large enough, selling out depresses the share price and harms the seller.

While the image of widely held corporations is a reasonably accurate description of most modern large US and UK firms, it is *not* the case in other parts of the world. Outside the Anglo-American world, there is relatively little separation of ownership and control. Most large firms are typically owned and controlled by families or the state.[4] Next, we turn our attention to such firms.

Family Ownership

The vast majority of large firms throughout continental Europe, Asia, Latin America, and Africa feature concentrated family ownership and control.[5] On the positive side, family ownership and control may provide better incentives for the firm to focus on long-term performance. It may also minimize the conflicts between owners and professional managers typically encountered in widely owned firms.[6] However, on the negative side, family ownership and control may lead to the selection of less qualified managers (who happen to be the sons, daughters, and relatives of founders), the destruction of value because of family conflicts, and the expropriation of minority shareholders (discussed later).[7] At present, there is no conclusive evidence on the positive or negative role of family ownership and control on the performance of large firms.[8]

State Ownership

Other than families, the state is another major owner of firms in many parts of the world. Since the 1980s, one country after another—ranging from Britain to Brazil to Belarus—realizes that their **state-owned enterprises (SOEs)** often perform poorly. SOEs suffer from an incentive problem. Although in theory all citizens (including employees) are owners, in practice, they have neither the rights to enjoy dividends generated from SOEs (as shareholders would), nor the rights to transfer or sell "their" property. SOEs are *de facto* owned and controlled by government agencies far removed from ordinary citizens and employees. Thus, there is little motivation for SOE managers and employees to improve performance, which they can hardly benefit from personally. In a most cynical fashion, SOE employees in the former Soviet Union summed it up well: "They pretend to pay us and we pretend to work." As a result, a wave of privatization has hit the world since the 1980s.[9] The SOE share has declined from more than 10% of global GDP in 1979 to 5% today.[10]

Managers

Managers, especially executives on the **top management team (TMT)** led by the **chief executive officer (CEO),** represent another crucial leg of the corporate governance "tripod."

Principal–Agent Conflicts

The relationship between shareholders and professional managers is a relationship between principals and agents—in short, an **agency relationship. Principals** are persons (such as owners) delegating authority, and **agents** are persons (such as managers) to

---

state-owned enterprises (SOE)

A firm owned and controlled by the state (government).

top management team (TMT)

The team consisting of the highest level of executives of a firm led by the CEO.

chief executive officer (CEO)

The top executive in charge of the strategy and operations of a firm.

agency relationship

The relationship between principals and agents.

principals

Persons (such as owners) who delegate authority.

agents

Persons (such as managers) to whom authority is delegated.

whom authority is delegated. **Agency theory** suggests a simple yet profound proposition: To the extent that the interests of principals and agents do not completely overlap, there will *inherently* be **principal–agent conflicts.** These conflicts result in **agency costs,** including (1) the principals' costs of monitoring and controlling the agents and (2) the agents' costs of bonding (signaling that they are trustworthy).[11] In a corporate setting, when shareholders (principals) are interested in maximizing the long-term value of their stock, managers (agents) may be more interested in maximizing their own power, income, and perks.

Manifestations of agency problems include excessive executive compensation, on-the-job consumption (such as corporate jets), low-risk short-term investments (such as maximizing current earnings while cutting long-term R&D), and empire building (such as value-destroying acquisitions). Consider executive compensation. In 1980, the average US CEO earned approximately 40 times what the average blue-collar worker earned. Today, the ratio is 400 times.[12] Despite some performance improvement, it seems difficult to argue that the average firm CEO improved performance 10 times faster than her workers since 1980, and thus deserved a pay package worth the salary of 400 workers today.[13] In other words, one can "smell" some agency costs.

Directly measuring agency costs, however, is difficult. In one of the most innovative (and hair-raising) attempts to directly measure agency costs, one study finds that some sudden CEO *deaths* (plane crashes or heart attacks) are accompanied by an increase in share prices of their firms.[14] These CEOs reduced agency costs that shareholders had to shoulder by dropping dead (!). Conversely, we could imagine how much value these CEOs destroyed when they had been alive. The capital market, sadly (and some may even say cruelly), was pleased with such human tragedies.

The primary reason agency problems persist is because of **information asymmetries** between principals and agents—that is, agents such as managers almost always know more about the property they manage than principals do. While it is possible to reduce information asymmetries through governance mechanisms, it is not realistic to completely eliminate agency problems.

Principal–Principal Conflicts

Since concentrated ownership and control by families is the norm in many parts of the world, different kinds of conflicts are at play. One of the leading indicators of concentrated family ownership and control is the appointment of family members as board chairman, CEO, and other TMT members. In East Asia, approximately 57% of the corporations have board chairmen and CEOs from the controlling families.[15] In continental Europe, the number is 68%.[16] The families are able to do so, because they are controlling (although not necessarily majority) shareholders. For example, in 2003, the 30-year-old James Murdoch became CEO of British Sky Broadcasting (BSkyB), Europe's biggest satellite broadcaster, in the face of loud minority shareholder resistance. The reason? James' father is Rupert Murdoch who controlled 35% of BSkyB and chaired the board.

The BSkyB case is a classic example of the conflicts in family-owned and -controlled firms. Instead of between principals (shareholders) and agents (professional managers), the primary conflicts are between two classes of principals: controlling shareholders and minority shareholders—in other words, **principal–principal conflicts**[17] (Figure 11.2 and Table 11.1). Family managers such as Rupert and James Murdoch, who represent (or are)

agency theory

The theory about principal-agent relationships (or agency relationships in short). It focuses on principal-agent conflicts.

principal-agent conflicts

Conflicts of interests between principals (such as shareholders) and agents (such as professional managers).

agency costs

The costs associated with principal-agent relationships. They are the sum of (1) principals' costs of monitoring and controlling agents, (2) agents' costs of bonding, and (3) the residual loss because the interests of the principals and the agents do not align.

information asymmetries

Asymmetric distribution of information between two sides. For example, in principal-agent relationships, agents almost always know more about the property they manage than principals do.

principal-principal conflicts

Conflicts of interests between two classes of principals: controlling shareholders and minority shareholders.

FIGURE 11.2   Principal–Agent Conflicts and Principal–Principal Conflicts

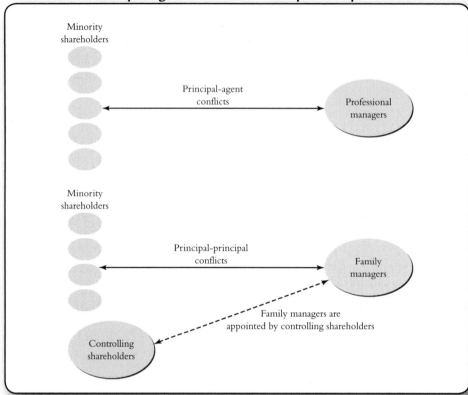

Source: Adapted from M. Young, M. W. Peng, D. Ahlstrom, G. Bruton, & Y. Jiang, 2008, Corporate governance in emerging economies: A review of the principal-principal perspective (p. 200), *Journal of Management Studies*, 45: 196–220.

TABLE 11.1   Principal–Agent versus Principal–Principal Conflicts

	PRINCIPAL–AGENT CONFLICTS	PRINCIPAL–PRINCIPAL CONFLICTS
Ownership pattern	Dispersed—shareholders holding 5% of equity are regarded as "blockholders."	Dominant—often greater than 50% of equity is controlled by the largest shareholders.
Manifestations	Strategies that benefit entrenched managers at the expense of shareholders (such as shirking, excessive compensation, and empire building).	Strategies that benefit controlling shareholders at the expense of minority shareholders (such as minority shareholder expropriation and cronyism).
Institutional protection of minority shareholders	Formal constraints (such as courts) are more protective of shareholder rights. Informal norms adhere to shareholder wealth maximization.	Formal institutional protection is often lacking. Informal norms are typically in favor of controlling shareholders.
Market for corporate control	Active, at least in principle as the "governance mechanism of last resort."	Inactive even in principle. Concentrated ownership thwarts notions of takeover.

Source: Adapted from M. Young, M. W. Peng, D. Ahlstrom, G. Bruton, & Y. Jiang, 2008, Corporate governance in emerging economies: A review of the principal-principal perspective (p. 202), *Journal of Management Studies*, 45: 196–220.

controlling shareholders, may advance family interests at the expense of minority shareholders. Controlling shareholders' dominant position as *both* principals and agents (managers) may allow them to override traditional governance mechanisms designed to curtail principal–agent conflicts. For example, the board of directors will hardly be effective when the CEO being evaluated is the son of the board chairman.

The result of concentrated ownership by families is that family managers may have the potential to engage in **expropriation** of minority shareholders, defined as activities that enrich controlling shareholders at the expense of minority shareholders. For example, managers from the controlling family may simply divert resources from the firm for personal or family use. This activity is vividly nicknamed "**tunneling**"—digging a tunnel to sneak resources out.[18] While such "tunneling" (often known as "corporate theft") is illegal, expropriation can be legally done through **related transactions,** whereby controlling owners sell firm assets to another firm they own at below-market prices or spin off the most profitable part of a public firm and merge it with another private firm of theirs.

Overall, while corporate governance practice and research traditionally focuses on how to control professional managers because of the separation of ownership and control in US and UK firms, how to govern family managers in firms with concentrated ownership and control is of equal or probably higher importance around the world.

Board of Directors

As an intermediary between owners and managers, the board of directors oversees and ratifies strategic decisions and evaluates, rewards, and if necessary penalizes top managers.

Key Features of the Board

These include (1) composition, (2) leadership structure, and (3) interlocks.

BOARD COMPOSITION

Otherwise known as the insider/outsider mix, board composition has recently attracted significant attention. **Inside directors** are top executives of the firm. The trend around the world is to introduce more **outside directors,** defined as non-management members of the board. Outside directors are presumably more independent and can better safeguard shareholder interests.[19] In the post-Enron era, many US firms have added outside directors.

Although there is a widely held belief in favor of a higher proportion of outside directors, academic research has *failed* to empirically establish a link between the outsider/insider ratio and firm performance (see Strategy in Action 11.1).[20] Even "stellar" firms with a majority of outside directors on the board (on average 74% of outside directors at Enron, Global Crossing, and Tyco before their scandals erupted) can still be plagued by governance problems.[21] It is possible that some of these outside directors are *affiliated* directors who may have family, business, and/or professional relationships with the firm or firm management. In other words, such affiliated outside directors are not necessarily "independent." For example, outside directors on Japanese boards often come from banks, other member firms of the same *keiretsu*, and their parent firms.[22]

LEADERSHIP STRUCTURE

Whether the board is led by a separate chairman or by the CEO who doubles as a chairman—a situation known as **CEO duality**—is also important. From an agency theory standpoint, if the board is to supervise agents such as the CEO, it seems

---

expropriation
Activities that enrich controlling shareholders at the expense of minority shareholders

tunneling
Activities of managers from the controlling family of a corporation to divert resources from the firm for personal or family use.

related transactions
Controlling owners sell firm assets to another firm they own at below-market prices or spin off the most profitable part of a public firm and merge it with another of their private firms.

inside directors
Directors serving on corporate boards who are also full-time managers of these companies.

outside directors
Non-management members of the board.

CEO duality
When the board is led by the CEO, who doubles as a chairman.

Strategy in Action 11.1 - Outside Directors in Chinese Corporations

Corporate governance reforms in China primarily aim to curtail principal–agent conflicts in state-owned enterprises (SOEs). Although in theory all citizens are owners, in practice they have neither the rights to enjoy dividends generated from SOEs (as real shareholders would), nor the rights to transfer or sell "their" property. Further, they have zero influence in corporate governance. Not surprisingly, in traditional SOEs, principal–agent problems are rampant. Many managers abuse state assets, run SOEs into the ground, and are undisciplined.

During the reform era, the government, in an effort to tighten governance, has listed a large number of traditional SOEs on the Shanghai and Shenzhen Stock Exchanges. Such listed firms are still owned and controlled by the state acting as a majority shareholder, but they also include other investors, such as institutional, individual, and foreign investors. Influenced by agency theory, Chinese policymakers, academics, and journalists widely believe that introducing outside (presumably independent) directors will curb principal–agent problems and enhance these firms' financial performance. Consequently, as of 2002, listed companies in China are legally required to appoint outside directors to their boards. Do outside directors *really* have a positive influence on financial performance?

The answer from my recent research is: Not really! From a resource-based view, even though a few outside directors may make a difference, if every firm has them, outside directors are no longer rare and are unable to help differentiate one firm from another. From an institution-based view, many outside directors are appointed for "window dressing" purposes. Many outside directors fail to show up at board meetings (and if they did show up, they evidently took a nap during the meetings). Finally, how independent some of these outside directors are remains questionable. Some may have family and/or professional relationships with inside managers.

My recent research from Russia also reports a similar lack of impact of outside directors on firm performance. In conclusion, policy prescription inspired by agency theory, such as the necessity to appoint outside directors, needs to be embraced with caution in emerging economies.

Sources: Based on (1) M. W. Peng, 2004, Outside directors and firm performance during institutional transitions, *Strategic Management Journal*, 25: 453–471; (2) M. W. Peng, T. Buck, & I. Filatotchev, 2003, Do outside directors and new managers help improve firm performance? An exploratory study in Russian privatization, *Journal of World Business*, 38: 348–360; (3) M. W. Peng, S. Zhang, & X. Li, 2007, CEO duality and firm performance during China's institutional transitions, *Management and Organization Review*, 3: 205–225; (4) M. Young, M. W. Peng, D. Ahlstrom, G. Bruton, & Y. Jiang, 2008, Corporate governance in emerging economies: A review of the principal-principal perspective, *Journal of Management Studies*, 45: 196–220.

imperative that the board be chaired by a separate individual. Otherwise, how can the CEO be evaluated by the body that he/she chairs? However, a corporation led by two top leaders (a board chairman and a CEO) may lack a unity of command and experience top-level conflicts. Not surprisingly, there is significant divergence across countries. For instance, while a majority of the large UK firms separate the two top jobs, most large US firms combine them. A practical difficulty often cited by US boards is that it is very hard to recruit a capable CEO without the board chairman title.

Around the world, both practices exist. Academic research is inconclusive on whether CEO duality (or non-duality) is more effective.[23] Today, however, pressures have arisen around the world for firms to split the two jobs to at least show that they are serious about controlling the CEO.

BOARD INTERLOCKS

Who the directors are and where they come from are also important. Directors tend to be economic and social elites who share a sense of camaraderie and reciprocity. When one person affiliated with one firm sits on the board of another firm, an **interlocking directorate** has been created. Firms often establish relationships through such board appointments. For instance, outside directors from financial institutions often facilitate financing. Outside directors experienced in acquisitions may help the focal firms engage in these practices.[24]

In the United States, Frank Carlucci, a former Secretary of Defense and chairman of the Carlyle Group (a leading private equity firm) himself, served on 20 boards (!) at one time. In Hong Kong, the most heavily connected director, David Li, chairman of the Bank of East Asia, sat on nine boards.[25] Critics argue that such directors are unlikely to effectively monitor management. In fact, one of the boards David Li served on was Enron's. In the post-Enron environment, such practices are increasingly rare.

The Role of Boards of Directors

In a nutshell, boards of directors perform (1) control, (2) service, and (3) resource acquisition functions. Boards' effectiveness in serving the control function stems from their independence, deterrence, and norms, as discussed next:

- The ability to effectively control managers boils down to how independent directors are. Outside directors who are personally friendly and loyal to the CEO are unlikely to challenge managerial decisions. Exactly for this reason, CEOs often nominate family members, personal friends, and other independent but passive directors.[26]

- There is a lack of deterrence on the part of directors should they fail to protect shareholder interests. Courts usually will not second-guess board decisions in the absence of bad faith or insider dealing. Directors are often protected from the consequences of bad decisions.

- When challenging management, directors have few norms to draw on. Directors who "stick their necks out" by confronting the CEO in meetings tend to be frozen out of board deliberations.[27] When they raise a point, nobody picks it up.

In addition to control, another important function of the board is service—primarily advising the CEO.[28] Finally, another crucial board function is resource acquisition for the focal firm, often through interlocking directorates.[29]

Overall, until recently, many boards of directors simply "rubber stamp" (approve without scrutiny) managerial actions. Prior to the 1997 economic crisis, many South Korean boards did not bother to hold meetings and so board decisions were literally "rubber stamped"—not even by directors themselves, but by corporate secretaries who stamped the seals of all the directors, which were kept in the corporate office. However, change is in the air throughout the world. In South Korea, board meetings are now regularly held and seals are personally stamped by the directors themselves.

Directing Strategically

If boards are to function effectively, being a director is one of the most demanding jobs, calling for an active "nose in but hands off" approach. Given the comprehensive functions of control, service, and resource acquisition and the limited time and resources

interlocking directorate

A situation whereby two or more firms share one director affiliated with one firm who serves on multiple boards.

TABLE 11.2   Outside Directors versus Inside Directors

	PROS	CONS
Outside directors	• Presumably more independent from management (especially the CEO). • More capable of monitoring and controlling managers. • Good at financial control.	• Independence may be illusionary. • "Affiliated" outside directors may have family or professional relationships with the firm or management. • Not good at strategic control.
Inside directors	• Have first-hand knowledge about the firm. • Good at strategic control.	• Non-CEO inside directors (executives) may not be able to control and challenge the CEO.

directors have, directors must strategically prioritize. How directors strategically prioritize differs significantly around the world. In US and UK firms, the traditional focus, which stems from their separation of ownership and control, is on the boards' control function. While the service function is still important, the resource acquisition role, although important in practice, tends to be criticized by policymakers, activists, and the media, who often regard activities such as interlocking directorates as "collusive." Consequently, recent US regulations, especially the Sarbanes-Oxley (SOX) Act of 2002, emphasize the control function to almost the exclusion of the resource acquisition function. Some scholars have voiced concerns that such a lack of balance may lead to unhealthy board functioning in the future.

Since outside directors are not likely to have enough first-hand knowledge about the firm, they are thus forced to focus on financial performance targets and numbers—known as financial control (see Table 11.2). Financial control may encourage CEOs to focus on the short term, at the expense of long-term shareholder interests (such as maximizing current earnings by reducing R&D). Therefore, inside directors, who are executives, can bring first-hand knowledge to board deliberations, allowing for a more sophisticated understanding of some managerial actions (such as investing in the future while not maximizing current earnings). A board informed by such inside views is able to exercise strategic control, basing its judgment beyond a mere examination of financial numbers. It seems that a healthy board requires both kinds of control, thus calling for a balanced composition of insiders and outsiders.

In the rest of the world, many boards are established and modeled after Anglo-American boards. However, the similarities between them are often more in form than in substance. In practice, a great deal of emphasis is placed on resource acquisition—through interlocking directorates and cross-shareholdings. The service role is less pronounced, and the control function is often hardly detectable.[30] Overall, while boards in theory should perform the three roles of control, service, and resource acquisition, in practice the relative emphasis differs significantly across countries.

Governance Mechanisms as a Package

Governance mechanisms can be classified as internal and external ones—otherwise known as voice-based and exit-based mechanisms, respectively. **Voice-based mechanisms** refer to shareholders' willingness to work with managers, usually through the board, by

voice-based mechanisms

Corporate governance mechanisms which focus on shareholders' willingness to work with managers, usually through the board of directors, by "voicing" their concerns.

"voicing" their concerns. **Exit-based mechanisms** indicate that shareholders no longer have patience and are willing to "exit" by selling their shares. This section outlines these mechanisms.

Internal (Voice-Based) Governance Mechanisms

The two internal governance mechanisms typically employed by boards can be characterized as (1) "carrots" and (2) "sticks." In order to better motivate managers, increasing executive compensation as "carrots" is often a must. Stock options that help align the interests of managers and shareholders have become increasingly popular.[31] The underlying idea is pay for performance, which seeks to link executive compensation with firm performance.[32] While in principle this idea is sound, in practice it has a number of drawbacks. If accounting-based measures (such as return on sales) are used, managers are often able to manipulate numbers to make them look better. If market-based measures (such as stock prices) are adopted, stock prices obviously are subject to too many forces beyond managers' control. Consequently, the pay-for-performance link in executive compensation is usually not very strong.[33]

   In general, boards are likely to use "carrots" before considering "sticks." However, when facing continued performance failures, boards may have to dismiss the CEO.[34] Approximately 40% of all CEO changes in recent years are sackings for underachievement.[35] In brief, boards seem to be more "trigger-happy" recently. Because top managers must shoulder substantial firm-specific employment risk (a fired CEO is extremely unlikely to run another publicly traded company), they naturally demand more generous compensation—a premium on the order of 30% or more—before taking on new CEO jobs. This in part explains the rapidly rising levels of executive compensation.

External (Exit-Based) Governance Mechanisms

There are three external governance mechanisms: (1) market for product competition, (2) market for corporate control, and (3) market for private equity. Product market competition is a powerful force compelling managers to maximize profits and, in turn, shareholder value. However, from a corporate governance perspective, product market competition *complements* the market for corporate control and the market for private equity, each of which is outlined next.

THE MARKET FOR CORPORATE CONTROL. This is the main external governance mechanism, otherwise known as the takeover market or the mergers and acquisitions (M&A) market (see Chapter 9). It is essentially an arena where different management teams contest for the control rights of corporate assets. As an external governance mechanism, the market for corporate control serves as a disciplining mechanism of last resort when internal governance mechanisms fail. The underlying logic is spelled out by agency theory, which suggests that when managers engage in self-interested actions and internal governance mechanisms fail, firm stock will be undervalued by investors. Under these circumstances, other management teams, which recognize an opportunity to reorganize or redeploy the firm's assets and hence to create new value, bid for the rights to manage the firm. The market for corporate control was relatively inactive prior to the 1980s. However, since the 1980s, a large wave of M&As and restructuring has emerged (see Chapter 9).

exit-based mechanisms

Corporate governance mechanisms which focus on exit, indicating that shareholders no longer have patience and are willing to "exit" by selling their shares.

How effective is the market for corporate control? Three findings emerge:[36]

- On average, shareholders of target firms earn sizable acquisition premiums.

- Shareholders of acquiring firms experience slight but insignificant losses.

- A substantially higher level of top management turnover occurs following M&As.

In summary, while internal mechanisms aim at "fine-tuning," the market for corporate control enables the "wholesale" removal of entrenched managers. As a radical approach, the market for corporate control has its own limitations. It is very costly to wage such financial battles, because acquirers must pay an acquisition premium. In addition, a large number of M&As seem to be driven by acquirers' sheer hubris or empire building,[37] and the long-term profitability of post-merger firms is not particularly impressive (see Chapter 9).

Nevertheless, the net impact, at least in the short run, seems to be positive, because the threat of takeovers does limit managers' divergence from shareholder wealth maximization. In Japan, an increasingly credible threat of takeovers has been rising. For example, Minolta was recently taken over by HOYA. As a result, more and more Japanese managers are now paying attention to their firms' stock prices. Of course, the number of M&A cases in Japan is still small, but a rising threat itself is already having some effect on managerial behavior.[38]

THE MARKET FOR PRIVATE EQUITY. Instead of being taken over, a large number of publicly listed firms have gone private by tapping into **private equity**—equity capital invested in private (non-public) companies (see Opening Case). Private equity is primarily (but not always) invested through **leveraged buyouts (LBOs).** In an LBO, private investors, often in partnership with incumbent managers, issue bonds and use the cash raised to buy the firm's stock—in essence replacing shareholders with bondholders and transforming the firm from a public to a private entity. As another external governance mechanism, private equity utilizes the bond market, as opposed to the stock market, to discipline managers. LBO-based private equity transactions are associated with three major changes in corporate governance:

- LBOs change the incentives of managers by providing them with substantial equity stakes.

- The high amount of debt imposes strong financial discipline.

- LBO sponsors closely monitor the firms they have invested in.

private equity

equity capital invested in private (non-public) companies.

leveraged buyout (LBO)

A means by which private investors, often in partnership with incumbent managers, issuebonds and use the cash raised to buy the firm's stock.

Overall, evidence suggests that LBOs improve efficiency, at least in the short run.[39] However, the picture is less clear regarding the long run, because earlier studies find that LBOs may have forced managers to reduce investments in long-term R&D.[40] However, more recent research reports (1) that private equity-backed firms have more focused patents that generate better economic returns, and (2) that such firms do not suffer from a reduction of R&D in the long run.[41] Around the world, private equity has grown by leaps and bounds in recent years, from 0.25% of world GDP in 2000 to 1.5% in 2007, now representing approximately 25% of all M&A activities (see Opening Case for more details).

Internal Mechanisms + External Mechanisms = Governance Package

Taken together, the internal and external mechanisms can be considered a "package."[42] Michael Jensen, a leading agency theorist, argues that in the United States, failures of internal governance mechanisms in the 1970s activated the market for corporate control in the 1980s.[43] Managers initially resisted. However, over time, many firms that are not takeover targets or that have successfully defended themselves against such attempts end up restructuring and downsizing—doing exactly what "raiders" would have done had these firms been taken over. In other words, the strengthened external mechanisms force firms to improve their internal mechanisms.

Overall, since the 1980s, American managers have become much more focused on stock prices, resulting in a new term, "**shareholder capitalism**," which has been spreading around the world.[44] In Europe, executive stock options become popular and M&As more frequent.[45] In Russia, after the 1998 collapse, there are now some traces of modern corporate governance.[46]

A Global Perspective

Illustrated in Figure 11.3, different corporate ownership and control patterns around the world lead to a different mix of internal and external mechanisms. The most familiar type is Cell 4, exemplified by most large US and UK firms. While external governance mechanisms (M&As and private equity) are active, internal mechanisms are relatively weak due to the separation of ownership and control that gives managers significant *de facto* control power.

FIGURE 11.3   A Global Perspective on Internal and External Governance Mechanisms

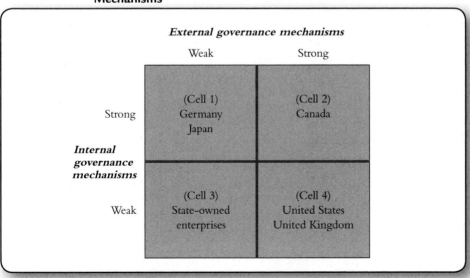

Source: Cells 1, 2, and 4 are adapted from E. R. Gedajlovic & D. M. Shapiro, 1998, Management and ownership effects: Evidence from five countries (p. 539), *Strategic Management Journal,* 19: 533–553. The label of Cell 3 is suggested by the present author.

shareholder capitalism

A view of capitalism which suggests that the most fundamental purpose for firms to exist is to serve the economic interests of shareholders (also known as capitalists).

TABLE 11.3   Two Primary Families of Corporate Governance Systems

CORPORATIONS IN THE UNITED STATES AND UNITED KINGDOM	CORPORATIONS IN CONTINENTAL EUROPE AND JAPAN
Anglo-American corporate governance models	German-Japanese corporate governance models
Market-oriented high-tension systems	Bank-oriented network-based systems
Rely mostly on exit-based external mechanisms	Rely mostly on voice-based internal mechanisms
Shareholder capitalism	Stakeholder capitalism

The opposite can be found in Cell 1, namely, firms in continental Europe and Japan where the market for corporate control is relatively inactive (although there is more activity recently). Consequently, the primary governance mechanisms remain concentrated ownership and control.

Overall, the Anglo-American and continental European-Japanese (otherwise known as German-Japanese) systems represent the two primary corporate governance families in the world, with a variety of labels (see Table 11.3). Given that both the United States and United Kingdom as a group and continental Europe and Japan as another group are highly developed successful economies, it is difficult and probably not meaningful to argue whether the Anglo-American or German-Japanese system is better.[47] Evidently, each has different strengths and weaknesses.

Some other systems do not easily fit into such a dichotomous world. Placed in Cell 2, Canada has *both* a relatively active market for corporate control and a large number of firms with concentrated ownership and control—over 380 of the 400 largest Canadian firms are controlled by a single shareholder.[48] Canadian managers thus face powerful internal and external constraints.

Finally, SOEs (of all nationalities) are in an unfortunate position of both weak external and internal governance mechanisms (Cell 3). Pre-reform SOEs in the former Soviet bloc and China serve as a case in point. Externally, the market for corporate control did not exist. Internally, managers were supervised by officials who acted as *de facto* "owners" with little control (Strategy in Action 11.1).

Overall, firms around the world are governed by a combination of internal and external mechanisms. For firms in Cells 1, 2, and 4, there is some partial substitution between internal and external mechanisms (for example, weak boards may be partially substituted by a strong market for corporate control). However, it is not viable to be stuck in Cell 3 with both weak internal and external mechanisms in the long run, thus triggering the move to privatize SOEs, as outlined next.

Strengthening Governance Mechanisms through Privatization

From a corporate governance standpoint, the global wave of privatization of SOEs is a movement to migrate out of the unfortunate Cell 3 in Figure 11.3.[49] An important question, of course, is: Which direction to go? SOEs in developed economies, upon privatization, would naturally migrate from Cell 3 to the respective cells for the private-firm counterparts in their own countries (such as Cell 1 for German firms and Cell 4 for UK firms).

What is fascinating is the privatization directions for SOEs in countries such as Poland and Russia, which historically do not belong to any of the other three cells.

When Central and Eastern European (CEE) countries started to privatize their SOEs in the early 1990s, the Anglo-American governance model featuring dispersed shareholders and a strong market for corporate control was often recommended by foreign advisors, who were often American and British nationals. However, most policymakers and practitioners in CEE argued that in the absence of functioning capital markets, it would not be realistic to move from Cell 3 to Cell 4 directly. Instead, a two-phase model of privatization was typically adopted, first through buyouts by employees (to secure their support) and then via the introduction of outside investors and new managers (to facilitate restructuring). Overall, privatization in CEE often moved SOEs first from Cell 3 to Cell 1 and then attempted to move toward Cell 4.

Two decades of privatization in CEE (and other parts of the world) suggest three lessons:[50]

- Privatization to insiders helps improve the performance of *small* firms, because such ownership and control is an efficient way to better motivate managers and employees.

- In *large* corporations, similar privatization to insiders, without external governance pressures, is hardly conducive for needed restructuring. Throughout CEE, managers are deeply entrenched because of their high ownership positions.[51]

- Outside ownership and control, preferably by blockholders, funds, foreigners, and/or banks, are more likely to facilitate restructuring.[52] Such outside ownership and control do not happen frequently, because incumbent managers do not necessarily welcome such outside "intrusion." However, when outside investors such as institutional investors do come in, they may actively assert their power.[53]

Overall, there is evidence that privatization may work because improved governance and better motivation, while far from perfect, tend to lead to better firm performance.[54] Given that it takes a combination of well-developed internal and external mechanisms as a package to properly govern the firm, it is not surprising that the privatization journey is far from being completed.

A Comprehensive Model of Corporate Governance

As before, the "strategy tripod" drawn from the three leading perspectives leads to a comprehensive model (Figure 11.4). This section discusses these three views in turn.

Industry-Based Considerations

The nature of industry sometimes questions certain widely accepted conventional wisdom regarding (1) outside directors, (2) insider ownership, and (3) CEO duality.[55] Having more outside directors on the board is often regarded as a performance-enhancing practice. However, such thinking ignores industry differences. In industries characterized by a rapid pace of innovation requiring significant R&D investments (such as IT), outside directors are found to have a *negative* impact on firm performance.[56] This is because of the necessity for directors to have intimate knowledge and solid experience, and because of the necessity for firms to embark on more complex and novel strategies in such industries, which require more strategic control. In contrast, outside directors tend to focus on financial control, which may be inappropriate in these industries.

FIGURE 11.4   A Comprehensive Model of Corporate Governance

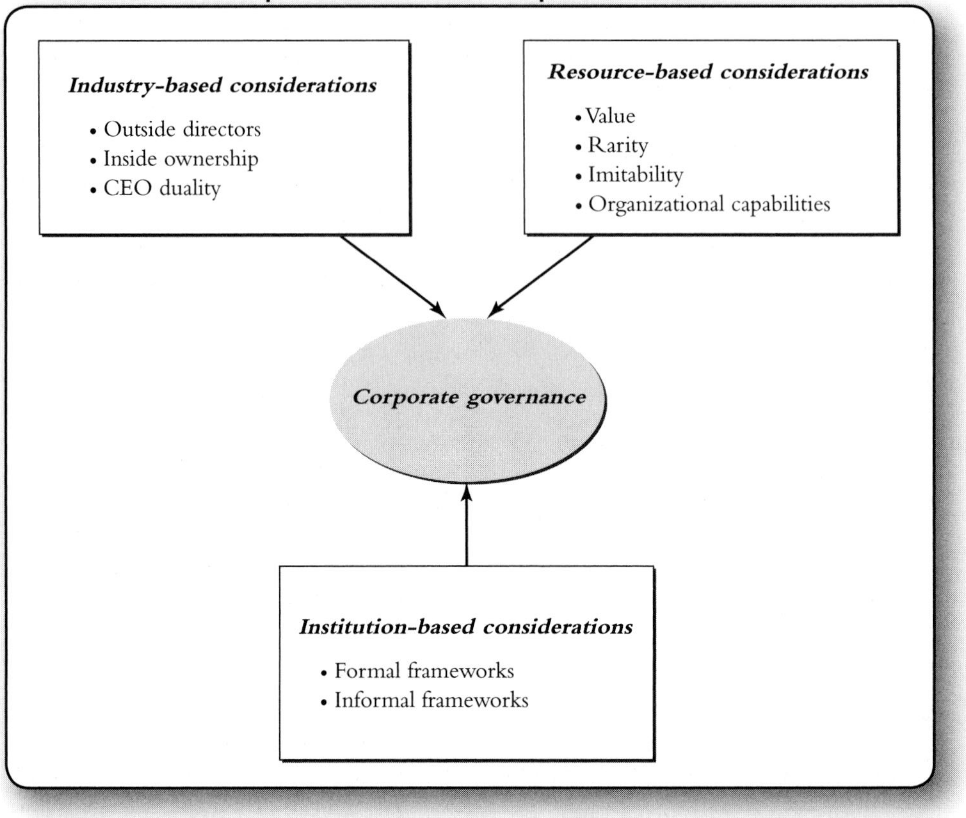

Another example is the widely noted link between inside management ownership and firm performance. Research finds that for firms in low-growth stable industries, there is *no* such relationship.[57] Only in relatively high-growth turbulent industries has this relationship been found. While increased insider ownership is designed to encourage managers to take more risks, opportunities to profitably take such risks probably may be more likely in high-growth turbulent industries.[58]

A third example is the often criticized practice of CEO duality. In industries experiencing great turbulence, the presence of a single leader may allow a faster and more unified response to changing events.[59] These benefits may outweigh the potential agency costs brought by such duality.

Overall, governance practices need to create a fit with the nature of the industry in which firms are competing. This cautions against universal prescriptions of certain "best" practices.

Resource-Based Considerations

managerial human capital

The skills and abilities acquired by top managers.

From a corporate governance standpoint, some of the most *v*aluable, *r*are, and hard-to-*i*mitate firm-specific resources (the first three in the VRIO framework) are the skills and abilities of top managers and directors—often regarded as **managerial human capital**.[60] Some of these capabilities are highly unique, such as international experiences.

Executives without such first-hand experience are often handicapped when they try to expand overseas. In addition, the social networks of these executives, often through board interlocks, are highly unique and likely to add value.[61] Also, top managerial talents are hard-to-imitate—unless they are hired away by rival firms.

In another example, the ability to successfully list on a high-profile exchange such as New York Stock Exchange (NYSE) and London Stock Exchange (LSE) is valuable, rare, and hard-to-imitate. In 1997, the valuations of foreign firms listed in New York were 17% higher than their domestic counterparts in the same country that were either unable or unwilling to list abroad.[62] Now, despite hurdles such as SOX, the select few that are able to list in New York are rewarded more handsomely: Their valuations are now 37% higher than comparable groups of domestic firms in the same country.[63] London-listed foreign firms do not enjoy such high valuations. This is classic resource-based logic at work: Precisely because it is much more challenging to list in New York in the SOX era, the small number of foreign firms that are able to do this are truly exceptional, not only in product market capabilities but also in governance effectiveness (see Strategy in Action 11.2). Thus, they deserve much higher valuations.

The last crucial component in the VRIO framework is O: organizational. It is within an organizational setting (in TMTs and boards) that managers and directors function.[64] Overall, the few people at the top of an organization can make a world of difference. Governance mechanisms need to properly motivate and discipline them to make sure they make a positive impact.

Institution-Based Considerations

FORMAL INSTITUTIONAL FRAMEWORKS. There is a fundamental difference between the separation of ownership and control in (most) Anglo-American firms and the concentration of ownership and control in the rest of the world. Why is there such a difference? While explanations abound, a leading reason is an institutional one. In brief, better formal legal protection of shareholder rights, especially those held by *minority* shareholders, in the United States and United Kingdom encourages founding families to dilute their equity to attract minority shareholders and delegate day-to-day management to professional managers. Given reasonable investor protection, founding families themselves (such as the Rockefellers) may, over time, feel comfortable becoming minority shareholders of the firms they founded. On the other hand, when formal legal and regulatory institutions are dysfunctional, founding families *must* run their firms directly. In the absence of investor protection, bestowing management rights to outside professional managers may invite abuse and theft.[65]

Strong evidence exists that the weaker the formal legal and regulatory institutions protecting shareholders, the more concentrated ownership and control rights become— in other words, there is some substitution between the two. Common-law countries (the United States, United Kingdom, and former British colonies) generally have the strongest legal protection of investors and the lowest concentration of corporate ownership.[66] Within common-law countries, such ownership concentration is higher for firms in emerging economies (such as Hong Kong, India, Israel, and South Africa) than developed economies (such as Australia, Canada, Ireland, and New Zealand). In short, concentrated ownership and control is an answer to potentially rampant principal–agent conflicts in the absence of sufficient legal protection of shareholder rights.

Strategy in Action 11.2 - Sarbanes-Oxley and New York

Ethical Challenge

Not too long ago, listing in New York—either at the New York Stock Exchange (NYSE) for large firms or NASDAQ for small firms—was widely viewed as a rite of passage for ambitious non-US firms. Such listings not only offered direct access to the world's largest capital market, but also an invaluable global cachet. In 2000, nine of the top ten initial public offerings (IPOs) came to New York. New York's rivals, London and Hong Kong, did not seem to matter much: In 2000, NYSE and NASDAQ commanded 60% of worldwide IPO proceeds, while London took away only 8% and Hong Kong received 5%. New York's dominance seemed untouchable.

However, winds change. In 2006, New York was beaten by *both* London (London Stock Exchange [LSE] for large firms and the new Alternative Investment Market [AIM] for small firms) and Hong Kong. Many non-US firms are shying away from New York, which grabbed an embarrassingly low 17% of the worldwide IPO proceeds in 2006. In comparison, London took away 21% and Hong Kong 18%. Of the top 25 global IPOs in 2006, only one took place in New York. London is positioning itself as a natural home for firms from Europe, Russia, and Israel. Hong Kong benefits from the gush of Chinese listings. There is more at stake than simple bragging rights on who is bigger. If US exchanges fail to attract new overseas listings, they will lose out on the trading that follows—the lifeblood of capital markets. Wall Street's decline could also translate into lost American jobs and reduced economic growth, especially in New York. In 2006, New York's mayor Michael Bloomberg published a high-profile article with an alarming title: "To save New York, learn from London."

So, what happened? Most of the finger pointing is directed to the Sarbanes-Oxley (SOX) Act of 2002. Enacted in the wake of the Enron scandal, SOX meant to enhance the protection of shareholders, a noble goal. However, in the rush to do something,

lawmakers failed to account for compliance costs, which have skyrocketed. Regarded by executives as the corporate equivalent of a root canal, SOX compliance costs come with a tab of $2 million to $8 million per firm in the first year alone—billions of dollars across all US-listed firms. This burden is disproportionately heavy for smaller listed firms. Former Ohio congressman Michael Oxley, who cosponsored SOX, admitted in a 2007 interview that the compliance costs "proved to be much more expensive than anticipated." However, listed US firms have no choice but to be in compliance.

SOX has driven away many US firms that do have a choice. About 50 smaller US firms that might have listed on NASDAQ went to list instead on London's AIM, and hundreds of others are considering the same move. Many non-US firms are saying to New York: "No, thanks!" Listing in New York (or any foreign location) is never free. It always boils down to a cost-benefit analysis. The benefits are typically the lower cost of capital and higher

Strategy in Action 11.2 - (continued)

company valuation. The costs are typically reporting and compliance requirements and costs related to enforcement by securities authorities and lawsuits by shareholders. SOX has dramatically increased these costs, and has emboldened American shareholders to sue foreign firms. This is not a theoretical possibility. Within *days* of listing in New York in 2003, China Life, an insurer, was sued by shareholders for its alleged failure to disclose old liabilities. Since then, China's big banks all chose to list first in friendlier Hong Kong.

However, defenders of SOX argue that New York, with or without SOX, has always demanded the highest level of corporate governance. There is a reason that, on average, only one in ten public firms from outside the United States would list in New York: The other nine may not be good enough. In other words, if shady Russian firms go to London, so be it! As an example, consider PartyGaming, an online gambling company headquartered in Gibraltar and listed on LSE since 2005. Until 2006, 90% of its revenues had come from US residents, although online gambling was illegal in the United States. PartyGaming's prospectus for LSE did disclose this risk, noting that it "takes comfort in an apparent unwillingness or inability" of US authorities to enforce the law. A firm with such a dubious business model obviously would not have qualified for a New York listing if it had applied. In October 2006, US authorities swiftly moved to ban money transfers

to gambling sites such as PartyGaming. Its stock dropped 60% in 24 hours. SOX defenders suggest that firms such as PartyGaming are exactly the kind of shady outfits that SOX is designed to weed out from listing in New York—London may win the listings war, but London investors can get burned.

Although SOX has some defenders, its popularity is low among practitioners. Your author has personally experienced this at a recent corporate governance conference at the University of Texas at Dallas in November 2007, where Oxley was the keynote speaker. Before Oxley was brought into the room, the session chair half-jokingly said to everybody: "Get your slingshots out!" When Oxley was brought to the podium, I naturally applauded. However, I quickly stopped after only one *second*, because I realized that in a room packed with over 200 people, I was the *only* one clapping (!).

Sources: Based on (1) *BusinessWeek*, 2006, London's freewheeling exchange, November 27: 40; (2) *BusinessWeek*, 2007, Michael Oxley's next act, April 9: 104; (3) C. Doidge, A. Karolyi, & R. Stulz, 2004, Why are foreign firms listed in the US worth more? *Journal of Financial Economics*, 71: 205–238; (4) *The Economist*, 2006, Down on the street, November 25: 69–71; (5) *The Economist*, 2006, What's wrong with Wall Street, November 25: 11; (6) The Honorable Michael Oxley, 2007, The status of corporate governance in the first decade of the 21st century, keynote speech, "Balancing Stakeholder Interests" Conference, Institute for Excellence in Corporate Governance, University of Texas at Dallas, November 1, www.utdallas.edu/news/archive/2007/11-01-001.html.

However, what is good for controlling shareholders is not necessarily good for minority shareholders and for an economy. As noted earlier, the minimization of principal–agent conflicts through concentration of ownership and control, unfortunately, introduces more principal–principal conflicts. Consequently, many potential minority shareholders may refuse to invest. "How to avoid being expropriated as a minority shareholder?" one popular saying in Asia suggests, "Don't be one!" If minority shareholders are informed enough to be aware of these possibilities and still decide to invest, they are likely to discount the shares floated by family owners, resulting in lower corporate valuations, fewer publicly traded firms, inactive and smaller capital markets, and, in turn, lower levels of economic development in general.

Given that almost every country desires vibrant capital markets and economic development, it seems puzzling that Anglo-American-style investor protection is not universally embraced. It is important to note that at its core, corporate governance ultimately is a choice about *political* governance. For largely historical reasons, most countries have made hard-to-reverse political choices. For example, the German practice of "codetermination" (employees control 50% of the votes on supervisory boards) is an outcome of political decisions made by postwar German governments.[67] If German firms had US/UK-style dispersed ownership and still allowed employees to control 50% of the votes on supervisory boards, these firms would end up becoming *employee*-dominated firms. Thus, concentrated ownership and control becomes a natural response.

Changing political choices, although not impossible, will encounter significant resistance, especially from incumbents (such as German labor unions or Asian families) who benefit from the present system.[68] In the nine countries of East Asia (excluding China), the top-15 families, on average, control approximately 53% of the listed assets and 39% of the GDP. Some of the leading business families not only have great connections with the government, sometimes they *are* the government. For example, two recent prime ministers of Italy and Thailand—Silvio Berlusconi and Thaksin Shinawatra, respectively—came from leading business families in these countries.

Only when extraordinary events erupt would some politicians muster sufficient political will to initiate major corporate governance reforms. The spectacular corporate scandals in the United States (such as Enron) are an example of such extraordinary events prompting more serious political reforms in the form of SOX and other regulatory changes (see Strategy in Action 11.2).

INFORMAL INSTITUTIONAL FRAMEWORKS. An interesting question is: In the last two decades around the world, why and how have informal norms and values concerning corporate governance changed to such a great extent? In the United States and United Kingdom, the idea of shareholder capitalism has graduated from minority view to orthodoxy. In the rest of the world, this idea is rapidly spreading. At least three sources of these changes can be identified: (1) the rise of capitalism, (2) the impact of globalization, and (3) the global diffusion of "best practices."

First, recent changes in corporate governance around the world are part of the greater political, economic, and social movement embracing capitalism.[69] The triumph of capitalism naturally boils down to the triumph of *capitalists* (otherwise known as shareholders). However, "free markets" are not necessarily free. Even some of the most developed countries have experienced significant governance failures, calling for a sharper focus on shareholder value.

Second, at least three aspects of recent globalization have a bearing on corporate governance.

- Thanks to more trade and investment, firms with different governance norms increasingly come into contact and expose their differences. Being aware of alternatives, shareholders as well as managers and policymakers are no longer easily persuaded that "our way" is the most natural and most efficient way of corporate governance.[70]

TABLE 11.4   Selected Corporate Governance (CG) Codes Around the World Since the 1990s

DEVELOPED ECONOMIES	EMERGING ECONOMIES
Cadbury Report (United Kingdom, 1992)	King Report (South Africa, 1994)
Dey Report (Canada, 1994)	Confederation of Indian Industry Code of CG (India, 1998)
Bosch Report (Australia, 1995)	Korean Stock Exchange Code of Best Practice (Korea, 1999)
CG Forum of Japan Code (Japan, 1998)	Mexican Code of CG (Mexico, 1999)
German Panel on CG Code (Germany, 2000)	Code of CG for Listed Companies (China, 2001)
Sarbanes-Oxley Act (United States, 2002)	Code of Corporate Conduct (Russia, 2002)

- **Foreign portfolio investment (FPI)**—foreigners purchasing stocks and bonds—has scaled new heights. These investors naturally demand better shareholder protection before committing their funds.

- The global thirst for capital has prompted many firms to pay attention to corporate governance. Many foreign firms, for example, have listed their stock in New York and London. In exchange for such privileges, they have to be in compliance with US and UK listing requirements (Strategy in Action 11.2).

Third, the changing norms and values are also directly promoted by the global diffusion of codes of "best practices." Led by Britain's Cadbury Report in 1992, the global proliferation of such codes is striking (Table 11.4). A lot of these codes are advisory and not legally binding. However, there are strong pressures for firms to "voluntarily" adopt these codes. In Russia, although adopting the 2002 Code of Corporate Conduct is in theory voluntary, firms that opt not to adopt have to publicly explain why, essentially naming and shaming themselves.

In addition, the Organization for Economic Cooperation and Development (OECD) has spearheaded efforts to globally diffuse "best practices." In 1999, it published the *OECD Principles of Corporate Governance,* suggesting that the overriding objective of the corporation should be to optimize shareholder returns over time.[71] The *Principles* are non-binding even for the 30 OECD member countries. Nevertheless, the global norms seem to be moving toward the *Principles.* For example, China and Taiwan (neither are OECD members) have recently taken a page from the *Principles* and allowed for class action lawsuits brought by shareholders.

Slowly but surely, change is in the air in almost every country. Although some companies and countries may adopt such changes for "window dressing" purposes, over time, some of the new shapes and forms of corporate governance may indeed change deeply held cognitive beliefs.

Debates and Extensions

Recent changes in corporate governance are often driven by significant debates, some of which have already been discussed. This section discusses two other major debates: (1) opportunistic agents versus managerial stewards and (2) global convergence versus divergence.

foreign portfolio investment (FPI)

Foreigners' purchase of stocks and bonds in one country. They do not directly manage operations.

Opportunistic Agents versus Managerial Stewards

Agency theory assumes managers to be agents who may engage in self-serving opportunistic activities if left to their own devices. However, critics contend that most managers are likely to be honest and trustworthy. Managerial mistakes may be due to a lack of competence, information, or luck, and not necessarily due to self-serving motives. Thus, it may not be fair to characterize all managers as opportunistic agents. Although very influential, agency theory has been criticized as an "anti-management theory of management."[72] A "pro-management" theory, **stewardship theory,** has emerged recently. It suggests that most managers can be viewed as owners' stewards.[73] Safeguarding shareholders' interests and advancing organizational goals, as opposed to one's own self-serving agenda, will maximize (most) managers' own utility functions.

Stewardship theorists agree that agency theory is useful when describing a certain portion of managers and under certain circumstances (such as under siege during take-over battles).[74] However, if all principals view all managers as self-serving agents with control mechanisms to put managers on a "tight leash," some managers, who initially view themselves as stewards, may be so frustrated that they end up engaging in the very self-serving behavior agency theory seeks to minimize. In other words, as a self-fulfilling prophecy, agency theory may *induce* agency problems.[75]

Global Convergence versus Divergence

Another leading debate is whether corporate governance is converging or diverging globally. Convergence advocates argue that globalization unleashes a "survival-of-the-fittest" process by which firms will be forced to adopt globally best (essentially Anglo-American) practices.[76] Global investors are willing to pay a premium for stock in firms with Anglo-American-style governance, prompting other firms to follow. Most of the recent governance codes (Table 11.4) largely draw from core Anglo-American concepts. The OECD has been promoting these Anglo-American principles as the "gold" standard. As a result, shareholder activism, an unheard of phenomenon in many parts of the world, is now becoming more visible (see Closing Case).

One interesting phenomenon often cited by convergence advocates is **cross-listing,** namely, listing shares on foreign stock exchanges (see Strategy in Action 11.2). Such cross-listing is primarily driven by the desire to tap into larger pools of capital. Foreign firms thus must comply with US and UK securities laws and adopt Anglo-American corporate governance norms. There is evidence, for instance, that Japanese firms listed in New York and London, compared with those listed at home, are more concerned about shareholder value.[77] A US or UK listing can be viewed as a signal of the firm's commitment to strengthen shareholder value, resulting in higher valuations.

Critics contend that governance practices will continue to diverge throughout the world.[78] For example, promoting more concentrated ownership and control is often recommended as a solution to combat principal–agent conflicts in US and UK firms. However, making the same recommendation to reform firms in continental Europe, Asia, and Latin America may be counterproductive or even disastrous. The main problem there is that controlling shareholders typically already have too much ownership

stewardship theory

A theory which suggests that managers should be regarded as stewards of owners' interests.

cross-listing

Firms list their shares on foreign stock exchanges.

and control.[79] Finally, some US and UK practices differ significantly. In addition to the split on CEO duality (the UK against, the US for) discussed earlier, none of the US anti-takeover defenses (such as "poison pills") is legal in the UK.

In the case of cross-listed firms, divergence advocates make two points. First, compared to US firms, these foreign firms have significantly larger boards, more inside directors, lower institutional ownership, and more concentrated ownership.[80] In other words, cross-listed foreign firms do not necessarily adopt US governance norms and practices before or after listing. Second, despite the popular belief that US and UK securities laws would apply to cross-listed foreign firms, in practice, these laws have rarely been effectively enforced against foreign firms' "tunneling."[81]

At present, complete divergence is probably unrealistic, especially for large firms in search of capital from global investors. Complete convergence also seems unlikely. What is more likely is "cross vergence"—balancing the expectations of global investors and those of local stakeholders.[82]

The Savvy Strategist

In the corporate governance arena, the savvy strategist capitalizes on three strategic implications for action (Table 11.5). First, understand the nature of principal–agent and principal–principal conflicts to create better governance mechanisms. For example, the rise of private equity is a direct response to principal–agent conflicts typically found in publicly listed firms. Amazingly, private equity typically makes the *same* managers, managing the *same* assets, perform much more effectively. In terms of mechanisms to alleviate principal–principal conflicts, one practice is to introduce a second controlling (dominant) shareholder that may monitor and constrain the action of the first controlling shareholder.

Second, savvy strategists need to develop firm-specific capabilities to differentiate on governance dimensions. In Japan, Sony stands out. In 1970, it became the first Japanese firm to list in New York, London, and Amsterdam. In the 1990s, it reduced the number of directors from 39 to a more manageable 10. In 2002, its board became dominated by outsiders.[83] From 15% in 1990, Sony's foreign equity ownership increased to 45% in 2000. In contrast, the ratio for all listed Japanese firms only increased from 4% in 1990 to 13% in 2000. Sony thus reaps significant benefits from more foreign investment and therefore a lower cost of capital.

Third, savvy strategists need to understand the rules, anticipate changes, and be aware of differences, especially when doing business abroad. Consider the two examples in

TABLE 11.5   Strategic Implications for Action

- Understand the nature of principal-agent and principal-principal conflicts to create better governance mechanisms.
- Develop firm-specific capabilities to differentiate a firm on corporate governance dimensions.
- Master the rules affecting corporate governance, anticipate changes, and be aware of differences.

Strategy in Action 11.3 - Infosys

In India, a leading IT firm Infosys has emerged as an exemplar in corporate governance. It leads the pack, by being the first Indian firm to follow US generally accepted accounting principles (GAAP), the first to offer stock options to all employees, and one of the first to introduce outside directors. Since its listings in Bombay in 1993 (BSE: 500209) and NASDAQ in 1999 (as INFY), it has gone far beyond disclosure requirements mandated by both Indian and US standards. On NASDAQ, Infosys *voluntarily* behaves like a US domestic issuer, rather than subjecting itself to the less stringent standards of a foreign issuer. In interviews, Infosys executives dismiss the idea that its governance practices are fueled by its interest in attracting capital, of which it has plenty. Instead, the primary reason cited is to gain credibility with Western customers in the rough-and-tumble software product market. In other words, excellent governance practices make Infosys stand out in the product market.

Sources: Based on (1) T. Khanna & K. Palepu, 2004, Globalization and convergence in corporate governance, *Journal of International Business Studies*, 35: 484–507; (2) www.infosys.com; (3) Wikipedia, 2008, Infosys, en.wikipedia.org.

Strategy in Action 11.2. While PartyGaming, until 2006, had an excellent understanding of the rules (the nonenforcement of the US ban on online gambling), it had failed to anticipate the swift regulatory changes that brought down its business almost overnight (the enforcement to ban money transfers to gambling sites since October 2006). In retrospect, PartyGaming made at least one wise decision—not trying to list in New York, whereby its disclosure that 90% of its revenues came from illegal online gambling by US residents would have failed to pass regulatory screening. In contrast, China Life made a huge mistake by coming to New York and failing to understand American investor sentiments. It thought it could have it both ways: tapping into the vast US investor pool and hiding some liabilities without full disclosure (evidently a common practice at home). Unfortunately, some American shareholders dragged China Life to court in New York within *days* of its listing.

Overall, a better understanding of corporate governance can help us answer the four fundamental questions in strategy. First, why do firms differ? Firms differ in corporate governance because of the different nature of industries, different abilities to motivate and discipline managers, and different institutional frameworks. Second, how do firms behave? Given that most corporations throughout the world have similar basic components of corporate governance (owners, managers, and boards), the primary sources of differences stem from how these components relate to and interact with each other to set the direction of the corporate ship. Third, what determines the scope of the firm? From a corporate governance standpoint, a wide scope may be indicative of managers' empire building and risk reduction. Finally, what determines the success and failure of firms around the globe? Although research is still inconclusive, there is reason to believe—in the aggregate and in the long run—that better governed firms will be rewarded with a lower cost of capital and consequently better firm performance (see Strategy in Action 11.3).[84] In other words, as firms increasingly match each other on products, services, and technologies, corporate governance may become one of the last frontiers of competitive differentiation, thus urging firms to "race to the top."

CHAPTER SUMMARY

1. *Differentiate various ownership patterns (concentrated/diffused, family, and state ownership)*

   - Owners represent the first leg in the "tripod" for corporate governance.

   - In the United States and United Kingdom, firms with separation of ownership and control dominate. Elsewhere, firms with concentrated ownership and control in the hands of families or governments are predominant.

2. *Articulate the role of managers in both principal–agent and principal–principal conflicts*

   - In firms with separation of ownership and control, the primary conflicts are principal–agent conflicts.

   - In firms with concentrated ownership, principal–principal conflicts prevail.

3. *Explain the role of the board of directors*

   - The board of directors performs (1) control, (2) service, and (3) resource acquisition functions.

   - Around the world, boards differ in composition, leadership structure, and interlocks.

4. *Identify voice- and exit-based governance mechanisms and their combination as a package*

   - Internal voice-based mechanisms and external exit-based mechanisms combine as a package to determine corporate governance effectiveness. The market for corporate control and the market for private equity are two primary means of external mechanisms.

5. *Acquire a global perspective on how governance mechanisms vary around the world*

   - Different combinations of internal and external governance mechanisms lead to four main groups.

   - Privatization around the world represents efforts to enhance governance effectiveness.

6. *Elaborate on a comprehensive model of corporate governance*

   - Industry-, institution-, and resource-based views shed considerable light on governance issues.

7. *Participate in two leading debates on corporate governance*

   - (1) Opportunistic agents versus managerial stewards and (2) global convergence versus divergence.

8. *Draw strategic implications for action*

   - Understand the nature of principal–agent and principal–principal conflicts.

   - Develop firm-specific capabilities to differentiate on corporate governance dimensions.

   - Master the rules affecting corporate governance, anticipate changes, and be aware of differences.

KEY TERMS

Agency cost	Expropriation	Private equity
Agency relationship	Foreign portfolio investment (FPI)	Related transaction
Agency theory	Information asymmetry	Separation of ownership and control
Agent	Inside director	Shareholder capitalism
Chief executive officer (CEO)	Interlocking directorate	State-owned enterprise (SOE)
CEO duality	Leveraged buyout (LBO)	Stewardship theory
Concentrated ownership and control	Managerial human capital	Top management team (TMT)
Corporate governance	Outside director	Tunneling
Cross-listing	Principal	Voice-based mechanism
Diffused ownership	Principal–agent conflict	
Exit-based mechanism	Principal–principal conflict	

CRITICAL DISCUSSION QUESTIONS

1. Some argue that the Anglo-American-style separation of ownership and control is an inevitable outcome in corporate governance. Others contend that this is one variant (among several) on how large firms can be effectively governed and that it is not necessarily the most efficient form. What do you think?

2. Recent corporate governance reforms in various countries urge (and often require) firms to add more outside directors to their boards and separate the jobs of board chairman and CEO. Yet, academic research has not been able to conclusively support the merits of both practices. Why?

3. *ON ETHICS:* As a chairman/CEO, you are choosing two candidates for one outside independent director position on your board. One is another CEO, a long-time friend whose board you have served for many years. The other is a known shareholder activist whose tag line is "No need to make fat cats fatter." Placing him on the board will earn you kudos among analysts and journalists for inviting a leading critic to scrutinize your work. However, he may try to prove his theory that CEOs are overpaid—in other words, your own compensation could be on the line. Whom would you choose?

CLOSING CASE

David Webb: A Shareholder Activist in Hong Kong

Although Hong Kong may have a reputation to house one of the world's most sophisticated financial markets, minority shareholders have a tradition of being abused by controlling shareholders. Although Hong Kong regulations were largely cut and pasted from British statutes, the nature of Hong Kong's listed firms means that the laws leave gaping loopholes that are exploited by controlling shareholders. Since most listed British firms do not have controlling shareholders, the board is apt to fairly reflect the interests of all shareholders. However, in Hong Kong, 32 of the 33 "blue chips" in the Hang Seng Index, except HSBC, have controlling shareholders—a single person or group of persons, typically from a family, who control the board.

Crusading against such an Establishment, David Webb, who was one of the 50 "Stars of Asia" featured by *BusinessWeek*, is a unique character in the emerging shareholder activism movement in Hong Kong. Webb, a native of England and an Oxford University graduate, moved to Hong Kong in 1991. He worked in investment banking and corporate finance until 1998 when he retired to become a full-time investor. His www.webb-site.com now boasts 9,000 subscribers. He is an outspoken critic at many shareholder meetings and an advocate for minority shareholders. He says that over 90% of listed companies have a shareholder who owns more than 20% and has *de facto* control. He believes where either a family or a government controls most listed companies, minority shareholders tend to be abused. "He has been an important voice in promoting good corporate governance," said David O'Rear, chief economist for the Hong Kong General Chamber of Commerce.

As it stands now, the families that control most Hong Kong companies simply appoint directors and railroad their elections through at shareholder meetings. After buying 10 shares in each of the 33 companies that make up the Hang Seng Index, Webb has been regularly attending shareholder meetings and demanding formal votes on *all* proposals. That does not win him many friends among the tycoon set accustomed to doing cozy deals without outside scrutiny. Webb recognizes that the primary problems in corporate governance in Hong Kong—and also across Asia—arise from the concentrated ownership and control of companies.

Webb has been using his website to help increase awareness of the problem. In 2006, he recommended minority shareholders of Henderson Investment Ltd. to vote against the buyout offer from its parent company, Henderson Land Development Co., because the controlling shareholders did not offer a fair price in such a related transaction. He was pleased to see that minority shareholders vetoed the buyout plan. In the "Hall of Shame" on his website, he lists the companies under investigation by the Hong Kong authorities and writes analyses exposing instances where shareholders seem to be cheated or overlooked.

One of Webb's key targets is often the government of the Hong Kong Special Administrative Region, itself a major investor in the local market, even though the government has also turned to him for advice. Webb has been invited to serve on a number of corporate governance reform committees. In 2007, he was reappointed to Takeovers Panel and Takeovers Appeal Committee in the Hong Kong Securities and Futures Commission. Webb opined: "There is a reform process here, but it is incredibly slow. I take the position that it's better to lobby from the inside rather than the outside . . . You can't rock the boat if you are swimming around outside it."

Sources: This case was written by Professor **Yi Jiang** (California State University, East Bay). It is based on (1) G. Wehrfritz, 2005, Safe haven? The slippery slope, *Newsweek International Edition,* May 2 (online); (2) V. England, 2005, Spotlight: A crusader in Hong Kong, *International Herald Tribune,* August 20 (online); (3) H. Wan, 2006, Henderson Investment slumps on rejected buyout offer, *Bloomberg,* January 23 (online); (4) SFC Appoints Takeovers Panel and Takeovers Appeal Committee Members, www.sfc.hk, March 30, 2007; (5) M. Young, M. W. Peng, D. Ahlstrom, G. Bruton, & Y. Jiang, 2008, Corporate governance in emerging economies: A review of the principal-principal perspective, *Journal of Management Studies,* 45: 196-220; (6) www.webb-site.com.

Case Discussion Questions

1. What is the primary type of conflict in corporate governance in Hong Kong? Why do transplanted British laws and regulations seem ineffective?

2. What are Webb's motivations? Why aren't there many minority shareholders in Hong Kong who actively participate in corporate governance like Webb?

3. How effective are Webb's "in your face" challenges of the current practices? Will these challenges change the prevailing norms, values, and regulations on corporate governance in Hong Kong?

4. If you were Webb, what would be your recommendations to reform corporate governance in Hong Kong, Asia, and emerging economies more broadly?

NOTES

Journal acronyms *AER*–*American Economic Review;* *AME*–*Academy of Management Executive;* *AMJ*–*Academy of Management Journal;* *AMR*–*Academy of Management Review;* *APJM*–*Asia Pacific Journal of Management;* *ASQ*–*Administrative Science Quarterly;* *BW*–*BusinessWeek;* *JAE*–*Journal of Accounting and Economics;* *JEL*–*Journal of Economic Literature;* *JEP*–*Journal of Economic Perspectives;* *JF*–*Journal of Finance;* *JFE*–*Journal of Financial Economics;* *JIBS*–*Journal of International Business Studies;* *JM*–*Journal of Management;* *JMS*–*Journal of Management Studies;* *JPE*–*Journal of Political Economy;* *JWB*–*Journal of World Business;* *MIR*–*Management International Review;* *MOR*–*Management and Organization Review;* *OSc*–*Organization Science;* *RES*–*Review of Economics and Statistics;* *SMJ*–*Strategic Management Journal*

1. R. Monks & N. Minow, 2001, *Corporate Governance* (p. 1), Oxford, UK: Blackwell. See also M. Benz & B. Frey, 2007. Corporate governance, *AMR,* 32: 92–104.

2. R. Stulz, 2005, The limits of financial globalization (p. 1618), *JF,* 60: 1595–1638.

3. K. Schnatterly, K. Shaw, & W. Jennings, 2008, Information advantages of large institutional owners, *SMJ,* 29: 219–227; L. Tihanyi, R. Johnson, R. Hoskisson, & M. Hitt, 2003, Institutional ownership differences and international diversification, *AMJ,* 46: 195–211.

4. R. La Porta, F. Lopez-de-Silanes, & A. Shleifer, 1999, Corporate ownership around the world, *JF,* 54: 471–517.

5. M. Carney & E. Gedajlovic, 2002, The coupling of ownership and control and the allocation of financial resources, *JMS,* 39: 123–146; S. Thomson & T. Pederson, 2000, Ownership structure and economic performance in the largest European companies, *SMJ,* 21: 689–705.

6. R. Anderson & D. Reeb, 2003, Founding-family ownership and firm performance, *JF,* 58: 1301–1328.

7. S. Chang, 2003, Ownership structure, expropriation, and performance of group-affiliated companies in Korea, *AMJ,* 46: 238–254; W. Schulze, M. Lubatkin, R. Dino, & A. Buchholtz, 2001, Agency relationships in family firms, *OSc,* 12: 99–116.

8. M. W. Peng & Y. Jiang, 2008, Family ownership and control of large corporations: The good, the bad, the irrelevant—and why, Working paper, University of Texas at Dallas.

9. M. W. Peng, T. Buck, & I. Filatotchev, 2003, Do outside directors and new managers help improve firm performance? An exploratory study in Russian privatization, *JWB,* 38: 348–360.

10. W. Megginson & J. Netter, 2001, From state to market, *JEL,* 39: 321–389.

11. M. Jensen & W. Meckling, 1976, Theory of the firm, *JFE,* 3: 305–360.

12. *BW,* 2002, How to fix corporate governance, May 6: 69–78.

13. J. Combs & M. Skill, 2003, Managerialist and human capital explanations for key executive pay premiums, *AMJ,* 46: 63–77.

14. W. Johnson, R. Magee, N. Nagarajan, & H. Newman, 1985, An analysis of the stock price reaction to sudden executive deaths, *JAE,* 7: 151–174.

15. S. Claessens, S. Djankov, & L. Lang, 2000, The separation of ownership and control in East Asian corporations, *JFE,* 58: 81–112.

16. M. Faccio & L. Lang, 2002, The ultimate ownership of Western European corporations, *JFE,* 65: 365–395.

17. M. Young, M. W. Peng, D. Ahlstrom, G. Bruton, & Y. Jiang, 2008, Corporate governance in emerging economies: A review of the principal-principal perspective, *JMS,* 45: 196–220.

18. S. Johnson, R. La Porta, F. Lopez-de-Silanes, & A. Shleifer, 2000, Tunneling, *AER,* 90: 22–27.

19. A. Ellstrand, L. Tihanyi, & J. Johnson, 2002, Board structure and international political risk, *AMJ,* 45: 769–777; S. T. Certo, 2003, Influencing initial public offering investors with prestige, *AMR,* 28: 432–446.

20. D. Dalton, C. Daily, A. Ellstrands, & J. Johnson, 1998, Meta-analytic reviews of board composition, leadership structure, and financial performance, *SMJ,* 19: 269–290; Y. Kor, 2006, Direct and interaction effects of top management team and board compositions on R&D investment strategy, *SMJ,* 27: 1081–1099; M. Kroll, B. Walters, & S. Le, 2007, The impact of board composition and top management team ownership structure on post-IPO performance in young entrepreneurial firms, *AMJ,* 50: 1198–1216.

21. S. Finkelstein & A. Mooney, 2003, Not the usual suspects, *AME,* 17: 101–113.

22. E. Gedajlovic & D. Shapiro, 2002, Ownership structure and firm profitability in Japan, *AMJ,* 45: 565–575.

23. B. R. Baliga, R. C. Moyer, & R. Rao, 1996, CEO duality and firm performance, *SMJ,* 17: 41–53; M. W. Peng, S. Zhang, & X. Li, 2007, CEO duality and firm performance during China's institutional transitions, *MOR,* 3: 205–225.

24. R. Gulati & J. Westphal, 1999, Cooperative or controlling? *ASQ,* 44: 473–506.

25. K. Au, M. W. Peng, & D. Wang, 2000, Interlocking directorates, firm strategies, and performance in Hong Kong (p. 32), *APJM,* 17: 29–47.

26. T. Pollock, H. Fischer, & J. Wade, 2002, The role of power and politics in the repricing of executive options, *AMJ,* 45: 1172–1183; J. Westphal & I. Stern, 2007, Flattery will get you everywhere, *AMJ,* 50: 267–288.

27. J. Westphal & P. Khanna, 2004, Keeping directors in line, *ASQ,* 48: 361–399.

28. N. Athanassiou & D. Nigh, 1999, The impact of US company internationalization on top management team advice networks, *SMJ,* 20: 93–92; M. Carpenter & J. Westphal, 2001, The strategic context of external network ties, *AMJ,* 44: 639–660; J. Westphal & J. Fredrickson, 2001, Who directs strategic change?, *SMJ,* 22: 1113–1137.

29. M. W. Peng, 2004, Outside directors and firm performance during institutional transitions, *SMJ,* 25: 453–471.

30. M. Young, D. Ahlstrom, G. Bruton, & E. Chan, 2001, The resource dependence, service, and control functions of boards of directors in Hong Kong and Taiwanese firms, *APJM,* 18: 223–244.

31. C. Devers, R. Wiseman, & R. M. Holmes, 2007, The effects of endowment and loss aversion in managerial stock option valuation, *AMJ,* 50: 191–208; T. Eisenmann, 2002, The effects of CEO equity ownership and firm diversification on risk taking, *SMJ,* 23: 513–534; M. Goranova, T. Alessandri, P. Brandes, & R. Dharwadkar, 2007, Managerial ownership and corporate diversification, *SMJ,* 28: 211–225; J. McGuire & E. Matta, 2003, CEO stock options, *AMJ,* 46: 255–265; J. O'Conner, R. Priem, J. Coombs, & K. M. Gilley, 2006, Do CEO stock options prevent or promote fraudulent financial reporting?, *AMJ,* 49: 483–500; W. G. Sanders & A. Tuschke, 2007, The adoption of institutionally contested organizational practices, *AMJ,* 50: 33–56.

32. A. Bruce, T. Buck, & B. Main, 2005, Top executive remuneration, *JMS,* 42: 1493–1506; C. Cadsby, F. Song, & F. Tapon, 2007, Sorting and incentive effects of pay for performance, *AMJ,* 50: 387–405; T. Cho & W. Shen, 2007, Changes in executive compensation following an environmental shift, *SMJ,* 28: 747–754; P. Fiss, 2006, Social influence effects and managerial compensation evidence from Germany, *SMJ,* 27: 1013–1031; L. Gomez-Mejia, R. Wiseman, & B. Dykes, 2005, Agency problems in diverse contexts, *JMS,* 42: 1507–1517; M. Larraza-Kintana, R. Wiseman, L. Gomez-Mejia, & T. Welbourne, 2007, Disentangling compensation and employment

risks using the behavioral agency model, *SMJ*, 28: 1001–1019; M. Makri, P. Lane, & L. Gomez-Mejia, 2006, CEO incentives, innovation, and performance in technology-intensive firms, *SMJ*, 27: 1057–1080; P. Wright, M. Kroll, J. Krug, & M. Pettus, 2007, Influences of top management team incentives on firm risk taking, *SMJ*, 28: 81–89.

33. L. Bebchuk & J. Fried, 2004, *Pay without Performance*, Cambridge, MA: Harvard University Press; J. Wade, J. Porac, T. Pollock, & S. Graffin, 2006, The burden of celebrity, *AMJ*, 49: 643–660.

34. W. Shen & T. Cho, 2005, Exploring involuntary executive turnover through a managerial discretion framework, *AMR*, 30: 843–854; Y. Zhang & N. Rajagopalan, 2004, When the known devil is better than an unknown god, *AMJ*, 47: 483–500.

35. *The Economist*, 2003, Coming and going, October 25: 12–14.

36. G. Jarrell, J. Brickley, & J. Netter, 1988, The market for corporate control, *JEP*, 2: 49–68; J. Krug & W. Hegarty, 1997, Postacquisition turnover among US top management teams, *SMJ*, 18: 667–675.

37. N. Hiller & D. Hambrick, 2007, Conceptualizing executive hubris, *SMJ*, 26: 297–319.

38. T. Yoshikawa & J. McGuire, 2008, Change and continuity in Japanese corporate governance, *APJM*, 25: 5–24.

39. P. Phan & C. Hill, 1995, Organizational restructuring and economic performance in leveraged buyouts, *AMJ*, 38: 704–739.

40. W. Long & D. Ravenscraft, 1993, LBOs, debt, and R&D intensity, *SMJ*, 14: 119–136.

41. J. Lerner, P. Stromberg, & M. Sorensen, 2008, Private equity and long-run investment, in J. Lerner & A. Gurung (eds.), *The Global Economic Impact of Private Equity Report 2008* (pp. 27–42), Geneva, Switzerland: World Economic Forum.

42. K. Rediker & A. Seth, 1995, Boards of directors and substitution effects of governance mechanisms, *SMJ*, 16: 85–99.

43. M. Jensen, 1993, The modern industrial revolution, exit, and failure of internal control systems, *JF*, 48: 831–880.

44. P. Fiss & E. Zajac, 2004, The diffusion of ideas over contested terrain, *ASQ*, 49: 501–534; W. Schneper &

M. Guillen, 2004, Stakeholder rights and corporate governance, *ASQ*, 49: 263–295.

45. A. Tuschke & W. G. Sanders, 2003, Antecedents and consequences of corporate governance reform, *SMJ*, 24: 631–649.

46. T. Buck, 2003, Modern Russian corporate governance, *JWB*, 38: 299–313; D. McCarthy & S. Puffer, 2008, Interpreting the ethicality of corporate governance decisions in Russia, *AMR*, 33: 11–31.

47. A. Shleifer & R. Vishny, 1997, A survey of corporate governance (p. 774), *JF*, 52: 737–783.

48. E. Gedajlovic & D. Shapiro, 1998, Management and ownership effects (p. 536), *SMJ*, 19: 533–553.

49. A. Cuervo, 2000, Explaining the variation in the performance effects of privatization, *AMR*, 25: 581–591.

50. K. Meyer & M. W. Peng, 2005, Probing theoretically into Central and Eastern Europe, *JIBS*, 36: 600–621; R. Ramamurti, 2000, A multilevel model of privatization in emerging economies, *AMR*, 25: 525–551.

51. I. Filatotchev, T. Buck, & V. Zhukov, 2000, Downsizing privatized firms in Russia, Ukraine and Belarus, *AMJ*, 43: 286–304.

52. K. Uhlenbruck & J. DeCastro, 2000, Foreign acquisitions in Central and Eastern Europe, *AMJ*, 43: 381–402.

53. B. Belev, 2003, Institutional investors in Bulgarian corporate governance reform, *JWB*, 38: 361–374.

54. P. Mar & M. Young, 2001, Corporate governance in transition economies, *JWB*, 36: 280–302.

55. A. Henderson, D. Miller, & D. Hambrick, 2006, How quickly do CEOs become obsolete?, *SMJ*, 27: 447–460.

56. E. Zajac & J. Westphal, 1994, The costs and benefits of managerial incentives and monitoring in large US corporations, *SMJ*, 15: 121–142.

57. M. Li & R. Simerly, 1998, The moderating effect of environmental dynamism on the ownership-performance relationship, *SMJ*, 19: 169–179.

58. M. Carpenter, T. Pollock, & M. Leary, 2003, Testing a model of reasoned risk-taking, *SMJ*, 24: 803–820.

59. B. Boyd, 1995, CEO duality and firm performance, *SMJ*, 16: 301–312; W. Judge, I. Naoumova, & N. Koutzevol, 2003, Corporate governance and firm performance in Russia, *JWB*, 38: 385–396.

60. R. Castanias & C. Helfat, 2001, The managerial rents model, *JM,* 27: 661–678.

61. C. Collins & K. Clark, 2003, Strategic human resource practices, top management team social networks, and firm performance, *AMJ,* 46: 740–751; M. Geletkanycz, B. Boyd, & S. Finkelstein, 2001, The strategic value of CEO external directorate networks, *SMJ,* 22: 889–898.

62. C. Doidge, A. Karolyi, & R. Stulz, 2004, Why are foreign firms listed in the US worth more?, *JFE,* 71: 205–238.

63. *The Economist,* 2007, Down on the street (p. 70), November 25: 69–71.

64. Z. Simsek, 2007, CEO tenure and organizational performance, *SMJ,* 28: 653–662.

65. M. Burkart, F. Panunzi, & A. Shleifer, 2003, Family firms, *JF,* 58: 2167–2201.

66. R. La Porta, F. Lopez-de-Silanes, A. Shleifer, & R. Vishny, 1998, Law and finance, *JPE,* 106: 1113–1155.

67. T. Buck & A. Shahrim, 2005, The translation of corporate governance changes across national cultures, *JIBS,* 36: 42–61.

68. R. Rajan & L. Zingales, 2003, The great reversals, *JFE,* 69: 5–50.

69. G. Drori, Y. Jang, & J. Meyer, 2006, Sources of rationalized governance, *ASQ,* 51: 205–229.

70. P. David, T. Yoshikawa, M. Chari, & A. Rasheed, 2006, Strategic investments in Japanese corporations, *SMJ,* 27: 591–600; L. Oxelheim & T. Randoy, 2005, The Anglo-American financial influence on CEO compensation in non-Anglo-American firms, *JIBS,* 36: 470–483.

71. OECD, 1999, *OECD Principles of Corporate Governance,* Paris: OECD.

72. L. Donaldson, 1995, *American Anti-management Theories of Management,* Cambridge, UK: Cambridge University Press.

73. J. Davis, F. D. Schoorman, & L. Donaldson, 1997, Toward a stewardship theory of management, *AMR,* 22: 20–47; P. Lee & H. O'Neill, 2003, Ownership structure and R&D investments of US and Japanese firms, *AMJ,* 46: 212–225.

74. P. Lane, A. Cannella, & M. Lubatkin, 1998, Agency problems as antecedents to unrelated mergers and diversification, *SMJ,* 19: 555–578.

75. S. Ghoshal & P. Moran, 1996, Bad for practice, *AMR,* 21: 31–47.

76. P. Witt, 2004, The competition of international corporate governance systems, *MIR,* 44: 309–333.

77. T. Yoshikawa & E. Gedajlovic, 2002, The impact of global capital market exposure and stable ownership on investor relations practices and performance of Japanese firms, *APJM,* 19: 525–540.

78. R. Aguilera & G. Jackson, 2003, The cross-national diversity of corporate governance, *AMR,* 28: 447–465.

79. G. Bruton, D. Ahlstrom, & J. Wan, 2003, Turnaround in East Asian firms, *SMJ,* 24: 519–540.

80. G. Davis & C. Marquis, 2003, The globalization of stock markets and convergence in corporate governance, in R. Swedberg (eds.), *Economic Sociology of Capitalist Institutions,* Cambridge, UK: Cambridge University Press.

81. J. Siegel, 2003, Can foreign firms bond themselves effectively by renting US securities laws?, *JFE,* 75: 319–359.

82. C. Crossland & D. Hambrick, 2007, How national systems differ in their constraints on corporate executives, *SMJ,* 28: 767–789; T. Khanna, J. Kogan, & K. Palepu, 2006, Globalization and similarities in corporate governance, *RES,* 88: 69–90; C. Kwok & S. Tadesse, 2006, National culture and financial systems, *JIBS,* 37: 227–247.

83. T. Yoshikawa, L. Tsui-Auch, & J. McGuire, 2008, Corporate governance reform as institutional innovation, *OSc* (in press).

84. R. Coff, 1999, When competitive advantage doesn't lead to performance, *OSc,* 10: 119–133; O. Gottschalg & M. Zollo, 2007, Interest alignment and competitive advantage, *AMR,* 32: 418–437.

chapter 12

Corporate Social Responsibility

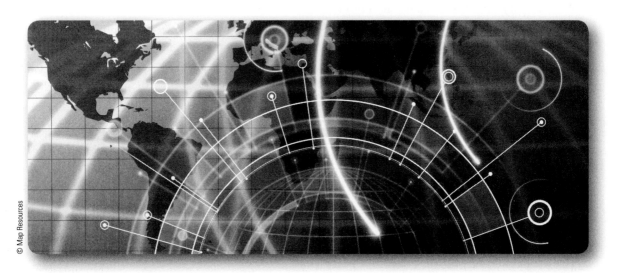

© Map Resources

KNOWLEDGE OBJECTIVES

After studying this chapter, you should be able to

1. Articulate what a stakeholder view of a firm is

2. Develop a comprehensive model of corporate social responsibility

3. Participate in three leading debates concerning corporate social responsibility

4. Draw strategic implications for action

Opening Case: Plan A at Marks & Spencer

Founded in 1884, Marks & Spencer (M&S) is a leading UK retailer. In 2007, it had 70,000 employees, 570 stores in the United Kingdom and 240 stores in 34 other countries, serving approximately 16 million customers. It had 2,000 suppliers, over 20,000 farms, and 250,000 workers who helped produce products carried by M&S. In 2007, M&S launched an ambitious, corporate-wide Plan A—a five-year plan that addressed some of the biggest social and environmental challenges with 100 concrete commitments that it aspired to achieve by 2012. Every store had a dedicated Plan A champion. Plan A was divided into five areas, each with approximately 20 goals slated for achievement by 2012. These areas, with leading examples, were:

- Climate change: becoming carbon neutral for all its UK and Irish operations

- Waste reduction: sending no waste to landfill

- Sustainable raw materials: tripling sales of organic food

- Fair partnership with suppliers: introducing random checking of suppliers to ensure that M&S's Global Sourcing Principles are being adhered to at all times

- A healthy lifestyle for customers and employees: introducing more nutritionally balanced food, with more informative labeling, no artificial coloring, and a reduced amount of salt

In Plan A's first year (2007), M&S reduced energy-related CO_2 emissions from its stores and offices by 55,000 tons, opened three pilot "eco-stores," and completed a carbon footprint assessment for its food business. Among its numerous actions, one example was an effort to reduce plastic shopping bags, which were always given away to shoppers free of charge. M&S argued that from an environmental standpoint, plastic bags are not "free" because they are not biodegradable and will be stuck in landfills essentially forever. Starting in April 2007, its 50 stores in Southwest England and Northern Ireland gave customers a free cloth Bag for Life. After four weeks, these trial stores started charging 10 pence (US$0.20) for each Bag for Life (which would be replaced free of charge when worn out), and 5 pence (US$0.10) for each plastic food carrier bag. The effect was immediate: in trial stores, the customers' use of food carrier bags dropped by over 70% and M&S also sold eight times more Bags for Life than it did in 2006. Throughout all its stores, M&S cashiers simply asked shoppers: "Do you need a carrier?" Overall, between April and December 2007, M&S reduced its use of plastic bags by 11% across all its stores—a total of 37 million *fewer* bags given out. All profits from the sale of bags in 2007, over £80,000 (US$160,000), went to an environmental charity, Groundwork, to support environmental regeneration projects. Based on these successful trials, M&S rolled out its program to charge for shopping bags in all its UK and Irish stores in May 2008.

Although clearly motivated by considerations for corporate social responsibility (CSR), M&S has been careful not to label this program a "CSR" plan. The committee in charge of Plan A is called a "How We Do Business" (HWDB) Committee. Where does the term "Plan A" come from? According to Plan A's website:

We're doing this because it's what you want us to do. It's also the right thing to do. We're calling it Plan A because we believe it's now the only way to do business. There is no Plan B.

After only its first year, Plan A already earned a number of kudos from various CSR groups. M&S led the global retail sector in the Dow Jones Sustainability Index. It was awarded the World Environment Center Gold Medal for Sustainable Business. In the UK, it received recognition from Greenpeace (top retailer for using wood from sustainable sources), from Compassion in World Farming (top retailer for high food animal welfare standards), and from the National Consumer Council (for operating market-leading green supermarkets). Yet, not all was rosy. In autumn 2007, some nongovernmental organizations (NGOs) challenged M&S, demanding that it be more aspirational in its commitments to improve labor standards. In response, M&S increased the number of labor experts from 7 to 23 on the visitation teams for labor standards compliance and promised to do more.

Sources: Based on (1) *The Economist,* 2008, Just good business, January 19: 3–6; (2) M&A, 2007, *Plan A News,* plana. marksandspencer.com; (3) M&S, 2008, *Plan A: Year 1 Review,* January 15, plana.marksandspencer.com.

---

corporate social responsibility (CSR)

The social responsibility of corporations. It pertains to consideration of, and response to, issues beyond the narrow economic, technical, and legal requirements of the firm to accomplish social benefits along with the traditional economic gains that the firm seeks.

stakeholder

Any group or individual who can affect or is affected by the achievement of the organization's objectives.

Although Marks and Spencer (M&S) aspires to be one of the most socially responsible firms, the Opening Case raises three crucial questions: (1) Why does it label its main committee in charge of Plan A as a How We Do Business (HWDB) committee? (2) In light of the challenges launched against M&S by some NGOs, can a firm ever be socially responsible enough? (3) When a firm pursues a social mission, is it setting itself up to be a target? Obviously, these questions have no easy answers. This chapter helps you answer these and other questions concerning **corporate social responsibility** (CSR)—"consideration of, and response to, issues beyond the narrow economic, technical, and legal requirements of the firm to accomplish social benefits along with the traditional economic gains which the firm seeks."[1] Although historically issues concerning CSR have been on the "backburner" of strategy discussions, these issues are increasingly brought to the forefront of corporate agendas.[2] While this chapter is positioned as the last in this book, by no means do we suggest that CSR is the least important topic. Instead, we believe that this chapter is one of the best ways to *integrate* all three leading perspectives on strategy, namely, industry-, resource-, and institution-based views.[3] The comprehensive nature of CSR is evident in our Opening Case on M&S.

At the heart of CSR is the concept of **stakeholder,** which is "any group or individual who can affect or is affected by the achievement of the organization's objectives."[4] Shown in Figure 12.1, while shareholders certainly are an important group of stakeholders, other stakeholders include managers, non-managerial employees (hereafter "employees"), suppliers, customers, communities, governments, and social and environmental groups.

FIGURE 12.1   A Stakeholder View of the Firm

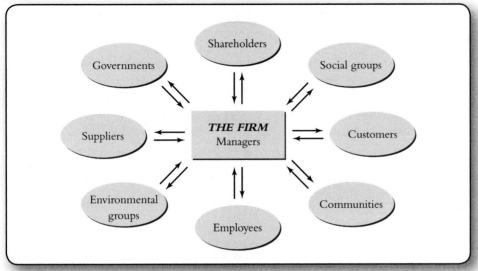

Source: Adapted from T. Donaldson & L. Preston, 1995, The stakeholder theory of the corporation: Concepts, evidence, and implications (p. 69), *Academy of Management Review,* 20: 65–91.

Since Chapter 11 has already dealt with shareholders at length, this chapter focuses on *non-shareholder stakeholders,* which we term "stakeholders" here for compositional simplicity. A leading debate on CSR is whether managers' efforts to promote the interests of these stakeholders are at odds with their fiduciary duty (required by law) to safeguard shareholder interests.[5] To the extent that firms are *not* social agencies and that their primary function is to serve as economic enterprises, it is certainly true that firms should not (and are unable to) take on all the social problems of the world. Yet on the other hand, failing to heed to certain CSR imperatives may be self-defeating in the long run. Therefore, the key is how to strategize with CSR.

The remainder of this chapter introduces a stakeholder view of the firm, and then discusses a comprehensive model of CSR drawn from the "strategy tripod." Debates and extensions then follow.

A Stakeholder View of the Firm

A Big Picture Perspective

A stakeholder view of the firm, with a quest for global sustainability, represents a "big picture." A key goal for CSR is **global sustainability,** which is defined as the ability "to meet the needs of the present without compromising the ability of future generations to meet their needs."[6] It not only refers to a sustainable social and natural environment, but also sustainable capitalism.[7] Globally, at least three sets of drivers are related to the urgency of sustainability in the 21st century:[8]

- Rising levels of population, poverty, and inequity associated with globalization call for new solutions. The repeated protests staged around the world since the Seattle protests in 1999 (see Chapter 1) are but tips of an iceberg of antiglobalization sentiments.

global sustainability

The ability to meet the needs of the present without compromising the ability of future generations to meet their needs.

Strategy in Action 12.1 - Is Icelandic Glacial Really "Carbon Neutral"?

Ethical Challenge

Icelandic Glacial is a new entrant in the thriving bottled water industry that hawks its products with "green" images of snow-capped mountains and crystal-clear water. Coming from pollution-free Iceland, Icelandic Glacial is being distributed in the United States by Anheuser-Busch, which bought a 20% stake in Icelandic Glacial in 2006. Boldly, Icelandic Glacial has claimed that it is entirely "carbon neutral," having eliminated any contribution to global warming. Although Icelandic buys "carbon offsets" to alleviate the environmental effects of ocean shipping, *BusinessWeek* reported that Icelandic has conveniently ignored the pollution generated by trucking its bottles around the country. In general, making, filling, and shipping billions of bottles by the bottled water industry generates 8.4 million tons of carbon dioxide emissions in the United States alone, equivalent to 2.2 million cars on the road. Further, bottled water is sold in plastic bottles, which will eventually make their way to landfills. These are not biodegradable and will remain there as permanent

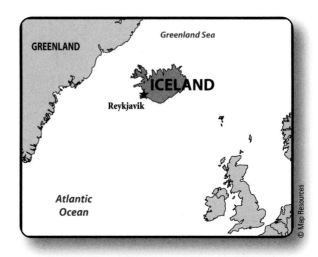

trash forever. So is Icelandic Glacial—or any bottled water you enjoy—really "green"?

Sources: Based on (1) *BusinessWeek,* 2007, How green is that water? August 13: 68; (2) www.icelandicglacial.com.

- Compared with the relatively eroded power of national governments in the wake of globalization, nongovernmental organizations (NGOs) and other civil society stakeholders have increasingly assumed the role of monitor and in some cases enforcer of social and environmental standards.[9]

- Industrialization has created irreversible effects on the environment.[10] Global warming, pollution, soil erosion, and deforestation have become problems demanding solutions (see Strategy in Action 12.1).[11]

Drivers underpinning global sustainability are complex and multidimensional. For multinational enterprises (MNEs) with operations spanning the globe, their CSR areas, shown in Table 12.1, seem mind-boggling. This bewilderingly complex "big picture" forces managers to *prioritize*.[12] To be able to do that, primary and secondary stakeholders must be identified.[13]

primary stakeholder groups

Constituents on which the firm relies for its continuous survival and prosperity.

Primary and Secondary Stakeholder Groups

Primary stakeholder groups are constituents the firm relies on for its continuous survival and prosperity.[14] Shareholders, managers, employees, suppliers, customers—together with governments and communities whose laws and regulations must be obeyed and

TABLE 12.1   Corporate Social Responsibilities for Multinational Enterprises (MNEs) Recommended by International Organizations

MNEs and Host Governments

- Should not interfere in the internal political affairs of the host country (OECD, UN)

- Should consult governmental authorities and national employers' and workers' organizations to ensure that their investments conform to the economic and social development policies of the host country (ICC, ILO, OECD, UN)

- Should reinvest some profits in the host country (ICC)

MNEs and Laws, Regulations, and Politics

- Should respect the right of every country to exercise control over its natural resources (UN)

- Should refrain from improper or illegal involvement in local politics (OECD)

- Should not pay bribes or render improper benefits to public servants (OECD, UN)

MNEs and Technology Transfer

- Should develop and adapt technologies to the needs of host countries (ICC, ILO, OECD)

- Should provide reasonable terms and conditions when granting licenses for industrial property rights (ICC, OECD)

MNEs and Environmental Protection

- Should respect the host country laws and regulations concerning environmental protection (OECD, UN)

- Should supply to host governments information concerning the environmental impact of MNE activities (ICC, UN)

MNEs and Consumer Protection

- Should preserve the safety and health of consumers by disclosing appropriate information, labeling correctly, and advertising accurately (UN)

MNEs and Employment Practices

- Should cooperate with host governments to create jobs in certain locations (ICC)

- Should give advance notice of plant closures and mitigate the adverse effects (ICC, OECD)

- Should respect the rights for employees to engage in collective bargaining (ILO, OECD)

MNEs and Human Rights

- Should respect human rights and fundamental freedoms in host countries (UN)

Sources: Based on (1) ICC: The International Chamber of Commerce Guidelines for International Investment (www.iccwbo.org); (2) ILO: The International Labor Office Tripartite Declarations of Principles Concerning Multinational Enterprises and Social Policy (www.ilo.org); (3) OECD: The Organization for Economic Cooperation and Development Guidelines for Multinational Enterprises (www.oecd.org); (4) UN: The United Nations Code of Conduct on Transnational Corporations (www.un.org).

to whom taxes and other obligations may be due—are typically considered primary stakeholders.

Secondary stakeholder groups are defined as "those who influence or affect, or are influenced or affected by, the corporation, but they are not engaged in transactions with the corporation and are not essential for its survival."[15] Environmental groups (such as Greenpeace) often take it upon themselves to promote pollution reduction technologies. Fair labor practice groups (such as Fair Labor Association) frequently challenge firms that allegedly fail to provide decent labor conditions for employees. While the firm does not depend on secondary stakeholder groups for its survival, such groups may have the potential to cause significant embarrassment and damage to a firm—think of Nike in the 1990s.

A key proposition of the stakeholder view of the firm is that instead of only pursuing the economic bottom line, such as profits and shareholder returns, firms should pursue a more balanced set, called the **triple bottom line,** consisting of *economic, social,* and *environmental* performance, by simultaneously satisfying the demands of all stakeholder groups.[16] To the extent that some competing demands obviously exist, it seems evident that the CSR proposition represents a dilemma. In fact, it has provoked a fundamental debate, which is introduced next.

secondary stakeholder groups

Stakeholders who influence or affect, or are influenced or affected by, the corporation, but they are not engaged in transactions with the corporation and are not essential for its survival.

triple bottom line

A performance yardstick consisting of economic, social, and environmental performance.

A Fundamental Debate

The CSR debate centers on the nature of the firm in society. Why does the firm exist? Most people would intuitively answer: "To make money." Milton Friedman, a former University of Chicago economist and Nobel laureate who passed away in 2006, had eloquently argued: "The business of business is business."[17] The idea that the firm is an economic enterprise seems uncontroversial. At issue is whether the firm is *only* an economic enterprise.

One side of the debate argues that "the social responsibility of business is to increase its profits," which is the title of Friedman's influential article mentioned earlier that was published in 1970. This free market school of thought draws upon Adam Smith's idea that pursuit of economic self-interest (within legal and ethical bounds) leads to efficient markets. Free market advocates believe that the first and foremost stakeholder group is shareholders, whose interests managers have a fiduciary duty to look after. To the extent that the hallmark of our economic system remains capitalism, the providers of capital—namely, capitalists or shareholders—deserve a commanding height in managerial attention. In fact, since the 1980s, a term that explicitly places shareholders as the single most important stakeholder group, namely, *shareholder capitalism*, has become increasingly influential around the world (see Chapter 11).

Free market advocates argue that if firms attempt to attain social goals, such as providing employment and social welfare, managers will lose their focus on profit maximization (and its derivative, shareholder value maximization).[18] Consequently, firms may lose their character as capitalistic enterprises and become *socialist* organizations. This perception of socialist organization is not a pure argumentative point, but an accurate characterization of numerous state-owned enterprises (SOEs) throughout the pre-reform Soviet Union, Central and Eastern Europe, and China, as well as other developing countries in Africa, Asia, and Latin America. Privatization, in essence, is to remove the social function of these firms and restore their economic focus through private ownership (see Chapter 11). Overall, the free market school is increasingly influential around the world. It has also provided much of the intellectual underpinning for globalization spearheaded by MNEs.

It is against such a formidable and influential school of thought that the CSR movement has emerged. CSR advocates argue that a free market system that takes the pursuit of self-interest and profit as its guiding light—although in theory constrained by rules, contracts, and property rights—may in practice fail to constrain itself, thus often breeding greed, excesses, and abuses.[19] Firms and managers, if left to their own devices, may choose self-interest over public interest. While not denying that shareholders are important stakeholders, CSR advocates argue that all stakeholders have an *equal* right to bargain for a "fair deal."[20] Given stakeholders' often conflicting demands, the very purpose of the firm, instead of being a profit-maximizing entity, is argued to serve as a vehicle for coordinating their interests. Of course, a very thorny issue in the debate is whether all stakeholders indeed have an equal right and how to manage their (sometimes inevitable) conflicts.[21]

Starting in the 1970s as a peripheral voice in an ocean of free market believers, the CSR school of thought has slowly but surely made progress in becoming a more central part of strategy discussions. It has two driving forces. First, even as free markets march around the world, the gap between the haves and have-nots has *widened*. Although many emerging economies have been growing by leaps and bounds, the per capita income gap between developed economies and much of the developing world has widened. While 2% of the world's children living in America enjoy 50% of the world's toys, one-quarter of the children in Bangladesh and Nigeria are in their countries' work force.[22] Even within developed economies such as the United States, the income gap between the upper and lower echelons of society has widened. In 1980, the average American CEO was paid 40 times more than the average worker. The ratio is now above 400. Although American society accepts a greater income inequality than many others do, aggregate data of such widening inequality, which both inform and numb, often serve as a stimulus for reforming the "leaner and meaner" capitalism. However, the response from free market advocates is that to the extent there is competition, there will always be *both* winners and losers. What CSR critics describe as "greed" is often translated as "incentive" in the vocabulary of free market advocates.

A second reason behind the rise of the CSR movement seems to be waves of disasters and scandals. For example, in 1984, a toxic accident at Union Carbide's Bhopal, India, plant killed over 3,000 people and injured another 300,000. In 1989, the oil tanker *Exxon Valdez* spilled a tanker-load of oil in the pristine waters of Alaska. In 2001–2002, corporate scandals of Enron, WorldCom, Royal Ahold, and Parmalat rocked the world. Not surprisingly, new disasters and scandals often propel CSR to the forefront of public policy and management discussions.

Overall, managers as a stakeholder group are unique in that they are the only group that is positioned at the center of all these relationships.[23] It is important to understand how they make decisions concerning CSR, as illustrated next.

A Comprehensive Model of Corporate Social Responsibility

While some people view that CSR is not an integral part of strategy, a comprehensive model of CSR drawn from the "strategy tripod" (Figure 12.2) shows that the three traditional perspectives on strategy can shed considerable light on CSR with relatively little adaptation and extension. This section articulates why this is the case.

Industry-Based Considerations

The industry-based view, exemplified by the five forces framework, can be extended to help understand the emerging competition on CSR.

RIVALRY AMONG COMPETITORS. The more concentrated an industry is, the more likely competitors will recognize their mutual interdependence based on old ways of doing business that are not up to the higher CSR standards (see Chapter 8). Under such circumstances, it is easier for incumbents to resist CSR pressures. For example, when facing mounting pressures to reduce car emission levels, the Big Three carmakers in the United States—together with their allies in the oil industry—lobbied politicians, challenged the science of global climatic change, and pointed to the high costs of reducing emissions.[24] This strategy seemed to have worked initially, when in 2001 the Bush administration pulled out of the Kyoto Protocol, a treaty committed to lower emission levels, which the United States signed in 1997. A corollary, however, is that when the number of rivals increases, it becomes more difficult to sustain a united front against CSR pressures.

FIGURE 12.2   A Comprehensive Model of Corporate Social Responsibility

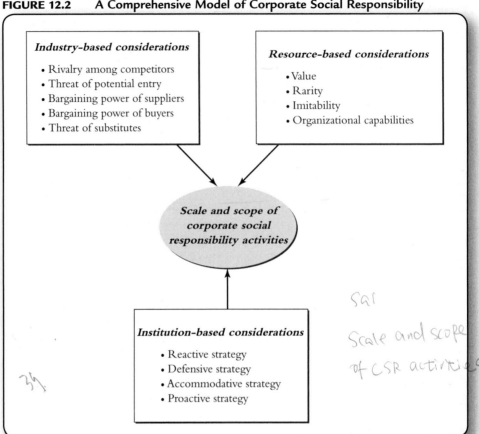

THREAT OF POTENTIAL ENTRY. How can incumbents raise entry barriers to deter potential entrants? Some evidence exists that experience accumulated from being first movers in pollution control technologies can create entry barriers that favor incumbents.[25] The two major types of pollution control technologies have their differences. The first is more proactive, *pollution prevention*. Like defects, pollution typically reveals flaws in product design or production. Pollution prevention technologies reduce or eliminate pollutants by using cleaner alternatives, often resulting in more superior products (such as fuel cells for cars). The second pollution control area is more reactive, "end-of-pipe" *pollution reduction*, often added as a final step to capture pollutants prior to their discharge.[26] Their effectiveness is not equal. The technologies likely to give incumbents the most effective entry barrier are in the area of proactive pollution prevention.[27] For instance, at Dow Chemical, the return on pollution prevention projects in its Waste Reduction Always Pays (WRAP) program averaged better than 60% in the 1990s. Chevron's Save Money and Reduce Toxics (SMART) and 3M's Pollution Prevention Pays (3P) programs are similar examples that not only deliver direct, triple-bottom-line benefits, but also heighten entry barriers for potential entrants.[28]

BARGAINING POWER OF SUPPLIERS. If socially and environmentally conscious suppliers provide unique, differentiated products with few or no substitutes, their bargaining power is likely to be substantial. For example, Coca-Cola is the sole provider of Coke syrup to its bottlers around the world, most of which are independently owned by franchisees. Coca-Cola is thus able to assert its bargaining power by requiring that all its bottlers certify that their social and environmental practices are responsible. Coca-Cola also encourages its bottlers to support social programs, such as financing start-up kiosks in South Africa and Vietnam, donating free drinks to earthquake victims in China, and promoting reading among school children in 42 countries, including the United States.

BARGAINING POWER OF BUYERS. By leveraging their bargaining power, individual and corporate buyers interested in CSR may extract substantial concessions from the focal firm. An example of the power of individual consumers is the controversy regarding Shell's 1995 decision to sink an oil platform in the North Sea. It led to strong protests organized by Greenpeace in Germany, which caused an 11% drop in Shell gas station sales in one month. Such pressures forced Shell to reverse its decision and dismantle the oil platform on shore at great cost.[29]

An example of how corporate buyers extract concessions is the recent efforts made by Nike, which acted in response to criticisms for its failure to eradicate "sweatshops" throughout its supply chain. Although Nike does not own its supplier factories, Nike is able to enact a worldwide monitoring program for all supplier factories, using both internal and third-party auditors. For "clean" contractors that have never engaged in "sweatshop" practices, this simply adds a ton of work such as documentation and hosting of auditors, as well as extra costs. For "sweatshop" operators, this requires some fundamental and costly change to the way they do business. Not surprisingly both groups initially resisted Nike's efforts. Nevertheless, Nike has been able to "just do it," by throwing its weight around.

Finally, buyers can increase bargaining power when they are in great difficulties. Dying HIV/AIDS patients in Africa, Asia, and Latin America, backed by their governments and CSR groups, often demand that pharmaceutical firms headquartered in rich, developed economies (1) donate free drugs, (2) lower drug prices, and (3) release patents to allow for local manufacturing of cheaper generic versions of the same drugs. While pharmaceutical firms have been resisting these attempts, they may eventually be forced to give in (see Chapter 4 Opening Case).

THREAT OF SUBSTITUTES. If substitutes are superior to existing products and costs are reasonable, they may attract more customers. For example, wind power, which is much more environmentally friendly than fossil-fuel sources of power, such as oil and coal, and safer than nuclear power, may have great potential. In this regard, the establishment of a Wind Energy group at General Electric (GE) seems to be a proactive step in exploring this substitute technology. It is true that at present, wind power requires heavy government subsidies in order to become commercially viable. However, its future is likely to be promising, given the increasing depletion of fossil fuel, the sky-rocketing oil prices, and the growing awareness of the risks associated with conventional technologies (such as the risk of terrorism at nuclear power plants).[30] Overall, the possible threat of substitutes requires firms to vigilantly scan the larger environment, instead of narrowly focusing on the focal industry.

TURNING THREATS TO OPPORTUNITIES. Taken together, the five forces framework suggests two lessons. First, it reinforces the important point that not all industries are equal in terms of their exposure to CSR challenges. Energy- and materials-intensive industries (such as chemicals) are more vulnerable to environmental scrutiny. Labor-intensive industries (such as apparel) are more likely to be challenged on fair labor practice grounds. However, despite varying degrees of exposure, no industry may be completely immune from CSR. Table 12.2 shows the widening list of industries challenged by environmentalists, one of the core CSR groups, over the last four decades.

Given the increasingly inescapable responsibility to be good corporate citizens, the second lesson is that industries and firms may want to selectively but proactively turn some of these threats into opportunities.[31] For example, instead of treating NGOs as threats, Home Depot, Lowe's, and Unilever have their sourcing policies certified by NGOs. Dow Chemical has established community advisory panels in most of its locations worldwide. Many managers traditionally treat CSR as a nuisance, involving heavy regulation, added costs, and unwelcome liability. Such an attitude may underestimate strategic business opportunities associated with CSR. The most proactive managers and the companies they lead are far-sighted enough to embrace CSR challenges through selective but preemptive investments and sustained engagement—in essence, making their CSR activities a source of *differentiation*, as opposed to an additional item of cost (see Opening Case).

Resource-Based Considerations

CSR-related resources can include (1) *tangible* technologies and processes and (2) *intangible* skills and attitudes.[32] The VRIO framework can shed considerable light on CSR.

VALUE. Do a firm's CSR-related resources and capabilities add value? For many large firms, especially MNEs, their arsenal of financial, technological, and human resources can be applied toward a variety of CSR causes. For example, firms can choose to appease antinuclear groups by refusing to purchase energy from nuclear power plants, or to respond to human rights groups by not doing business in (or with) countries accused of human rights violations. These activities are known as **social issue participation** that is not directly related to the management of primary stakeholders. Research suggests that these activities may actually *reduce* shareholder value.[33] Overall, although social issue participation may create some remote social and environmental value, to the extent that one of the legs of the tripod of triple bottom line is economic, these abilities do not qualify as value-adding firm capabilities.

In contrast, expertise, techniques, and processes associated with the direct management of primary stakeholder groups are likely to add value.[34] For example, US companies excelling in diversity programs may gain a leg up when dealing with two primary stakeholder groups: employees and customers. Between 2000 and 2020, the number of Hispanic, African, Asian, and Native Americans will reportedly grow by 42 million, whereas Caucasians will rise by a mere 10 million.[35] Many companies compete on diversity via internships, scholarships, and aggressive recruiting of minority candidates. Firms most sought after by minority employees and customers must have possessed some very valuable capabilities in the competition for the hearts and minds (and wallets) of the future.[36]

social issue participation

Firms' participation in social causes not directly related to managing primary stakeholders.

TABLE 12.2   Industries Challenged by Environmentalists

1960s	1970s	1980s	1990s
Coal mining and pollution	Aerosols	Aerosols	Aerosols
Detergents	Airports	Agriculture	Agriculture
Mining	Asbestos	Airports	Air-conditioning
Pesticides	Automobiles (*see Closing Case*)	Animal testing	Airlines and airports
Water (dams)	Biotechnology	Automobiles (*see Closing Case*)	Animal testing
	Chemicals	Biotechnology	Armaments
	Coal mining and pollution	Chemicals	Automobiles (*see Closing Case*)
	Deep sea fishing	Coal mining and pollution	Banking
	Detergents	Computers	Biotechnology
	Heavy trucks	Deep sea fishing	Catering
	Metals	Detergents	Chemicals
	Nuclear power	Fertilizers	Coal mining and pollution
	Oil tankers	Forestry	Computers
	Packaging	Incineration	Detergents
	Passenger jets	Insurance	Dry cleaning
	Pesticides	Landfill	Electrical equipment
	Pulp mills	Nuclear power	Electricity supply
	Tobacco	Oil tankers	Fashion
	Toxic waste	Onshore oil and gas	Fertilizers
	Transport	Packaging	Fish farming (*see Strategy in Action 12.2*)
	Water	Paints	Fishing
	Whaling	Pesticides	Forestry
		Plastics	Incineration
		Pulp and paper	Insurance
		Refrigeration	Landfill
		Supermarkets	Meat processing
		Tobacco	Mining
		Toxic waste	Motorways
		Tropical hardwoods	Nuclear power
		Tuna fishing	Office supplies
		Water	Oil tankers
		Whaling	Onshore oil and gas
			Packaging
			Paints
			Pesticides
			Plastics
			Property
			Pulp and paper
			Refrigeration
			Shipping
			Supermarkets
			Textiles
			Tires
			Tobacco
			Tourism
			Toxic waste
			Transport
			Tropical hardwoods
			Water

Source: Adapted from J. Elkington, 1994, Towards the sustainable corporation: Win-win-win business strategies for sustainable development (p. 95), *California Management Review,* winter: 90–100.

RARITY. If competitors also possess certain valuable resources, then the focal firm is not likely to gain a significant advantage by having them. For example, both Home Depot and Lowe's have their suppliers in Brazil, Indonesia, and Malaysia certify—via external verification by NGOs such as the Forest Stewardship Council—that their sources are from renewable forests. These complex processes require strong management capabilities, such as negotiating with local suppliers, coordinating with NGOs, and disseminating such information to stakeholders. Since both competitors possess capabilities to manage these processes, they become valuable but common (not rare) resources.

IMITABILITY. Although valuable and rare resources may provide some competitive advantage, such advantage will only be temporary if competitors are able to imitate.[37] Only resources that are not only valuable and rare but also hard-to-imitate can help firms entertain some sustainable competitive advantage. For example, pollution *prevention* technologies may provide firms with a significant advantage, whereas pollution *reduction* technologies may offer no such advantage. This is because the relatively simple "end-of-pipe" pollution reduction technologies can be more easily imitated. On the other hand, pollution prevention technologies are more complex and are more integrated with the entire chain of production. Rivals often have a harder time imitating such complex capabilities.

In addition, at some firms, CSR-related capabilities are deeply embedded in very idiosyncratic managerial and employee skills, attitudes, and interpretations.[38] The socially complex way of channeling these people's energy and conviction toward CSR cannot be easily imitated. For example, the enthusiasm and energy that M&S devotes to CSR are very difficult to imitate (see Opening Case). Although M&S may not please every NGO, it is difficult to argue that M&S's Plan A is "faking."

ORGANIZATION. Is the firm organized to exploit the full potential of CSR?[39] Numerous components within a firm may be relevant, such as formal management control systems and informal relationships between managers and employees. These components are often called complementary assets (see Chapter 3), because, by themselves, complementary assets are difficult to generate advantage. However, these complementary assets, when combined with valuable, rare, and hard-to-imitate capabilities, may enable a firm to fully utilize its CSR potential.

For example, assume Firm A is able to overcome the three hurdles mentioned earlier (V, R, and I) by achieving a comprehensive understanding of some competitors' "best practices" in pollution prevention. Although Firm A has every intention of implementing such "best practices," chances are they may not work unless Firm A also possesses a number of complementary assets. This is because process-focused best practices of pollution prevention are not in isolation and are often difficult to separate from a firm's other activities. These best practices require a number of complementary assets, such as a continuous emphasis on process innovation and an uncompromising quest to reduce costs. These complementary assets are not developed as part of new environmental strategies; rather, they are grown from more general business strategies (such as differentiation).[40] If such complementary assets are already in place, they are available to be leveraged in the new pursuit of best CSR practices. Otherwise, single-minded imitation is not likely to be effective.[41]

THE CSR-ECONOMIC PERFORMANCE PUZZLE. The resource-based view helps solve a major puzzle in the CSR debate since the 1970s. The puzzle—and a source of frustration to CSR advocates—is why there is no conclusive evidence of a direct, positive link between CSR and *economic* performance, such as profits and shareholder returns.[42] Although some studies indeed report a *positive* relationship,[43] others find a *negative* relationship[44] or *no* relationship.[45] While there can be a number of explanations for this intriguing mess, a resource-based explanation suggests that because of capability constraints discussed earlier, many firms are not cut out for a CSR-intensive (differentiation) strategy. Since all studies have some sampling bias (no study is "perfect"), studies oversampling firms not ready for a high level of CSR activities are likely to report a negative relationship between CSR and economic performance, and studies oversampling firms ready for CSR may find a positive relationship. Also, studies with more balanced (more random) samples may fail to find any statistically significant relationship. In summary, since each firm is different (a basic assumption of the resource-based view), not every firm's economic performance is likely to benefit from CSR.

Institution-Based Considerations

The institution-based view sheds considerable light on the gradual diffusion of the CSR movement and the strategic responses of firms.[46] At the most fundamental level, regulatory pressures underpin *formal* institutions, whereas normative and cognitive pressures support *informal* institutions. The strategic response framework consisting of (1) reactive, (2) defensive, (3) accommodative, and (4) proactive strategies, first introduced in Chapter 4 (see Table 4.7), can be extended to explore how firms make CSR decisions, as illustrated in Table 12.3.

TABLE 12.3   The US Chemical Industry Responds to Environmental Pressures

PHASE	STRATEGIC RESPONSE	REPRESENTATIVE STATEMENTS FROM THE INDUSTRY'S TRADE JOURNAL, *CHEMICAL WEEK*
1962–1970	Reactive	Denied the severity of environmental problems and argued that these problems could be solved independently through the industry's technological prowess.
1971–1982	Defensive	"Congress seems determined to add one more regulation to the already 27 health and safety regulations we must answer to. This will make the EPA [Environmental Protection Agency] a chemical czar. No agency in a democracy should have that authority" (1975).
1983–1988	Accommodative	"The EPA has been criticized for going too slow . . . Still, we think that it is doing a good job" (1982). "Critics expect an overnight fix. The EPA deserves credit for its pace and accomplishments" (1982).
1989–present	Proactive	"Green line equals bottom line—The Clean Air Act (CAA) equals efficiency. Everything you hear about the 'costs' of complying with the CAA is probably wrong . . . Wiser competitors will rush to exploit the Green Revolution" (1990).

Source: Adapted from A. Hoffman, 1999, Institutional evolution and change: Environmentalism and the US chemical industry, *Academy of Management Journal,* 42: 351–371 for the phases and statements. Hoffman's last phase ended in 1993; its extension to the present is done by the present author.

Reactive strategy is indicated by relatively little or no support by top management to CSR causes.[47] Firms do not feel compelled to act in the absence of disasters and outcries. Even when problems arise, denial is usually the first line of defense. Put another way, the need to accept some CSR is neither internalized through cognitive beliefs, nor does it result in any norms in practice. That leaves only formal regulatory pressures to compel firms to be in compliance. For example, in America, food and drug safety standards that we take for granted today were fought by food and drug companies in the early half of the 20th century. The very basic idea that food and drugs should be tested before they could be sold to customers and patients was bitterly contested. Thousands of people ended up dying because of unsafe foods and drugs. As a result, the Food and Drug Administration (FDA) was progressively granted more powers. This era is not necessarily over since today many dietary-supplement makers, whose products are beyond the FDA's reach, continue to sell untested "supplements" and deny responsibility.[48]

Defensive strategy focuses on regulatory compliance. There may be some piece-meal involvement by top management, but the attitude is generally one of viewing CSR as an added cost or nuisance. Firms admit responsibility, but often fight it. After the establishment of the Environmental Protection Agency (EPA) in 1970, the US chemical industry resisted the intrusion of the EPA (Table 12.3). The regulatory requirements were at significant odds with the norms and cognitive beliefs held by industry members at that time.

How do various institutional pressures change firms' behavior? In the absence of informal normative and cognitive beliefs, formal regulatory pressures are the only feasible way to push firms ahead. A key insight of the institution-based view is that individuals and organizations make *rational* choices given the right kind of incentives. For example, one efficient way to control pollution is to make polluters pay some "green" taxes. These can range from gasoline retail taxes to landfill charges on waste disposal. However, how demanding these regulatory pressures should be remains controversial. One side of the debate argues that tough environmental regulation may lead to higher costs and reduced competitiveness, especially when competing with foreign rivals not subject to such demanding regulations. In other words, there is no "free environmental lunch."[49]

However, CSR advocates, endorsed by former vice president Al Gore and strategy guru Michael Porter, argue that stringent environmental regulation may force firms to innovate, however reluctantly, thus benefiting the competitiveness of an industry and a country.[50] The recent battle over corporate average fuel economy (CAFE) in the United States is a case in point (see Closing Case).

Accommodative strategy is characterized by some support from top managers, who may increasingly view CSR as a worthwhile endeavor. Since formal regulations may be in place and informal social and environmental pressures on the rise, the CSR concern may be shared by a number of firms, thus leading to the emergence of some new industry norms. Further, some new managers passionate about, or sympathetic toward, CSR causes may have joined the organization, whereas some traditional managers may change their outlook, leading to increasingly strong cognitive beliefs that CSR is the right thing to do. In other words, from both normative and cognitive standpoints, it becomes legitimate—a matter of social obligation—to accept responsibility and do all that is required.[51] In the US chemical industry, such a transformation probably took place in the early 1980s (see Table 12.3).

reactive strategy

A strategy that is passive about corporate social responsibility. Firms do not act in the absence of disasters and outcries. When problems arise, denial is usually the first line of defense.

defensive strategy

A strategy that is defensive in nature. Firms admit responsibility, but often fight it.

accommodative strategy

A strategy that tries to accommodate corporate social responsibility considerations into decision making.

One tangible action firms often take to indicate their willingness to accept CSR is to adopt **codes of conduct** (sometimes called **codes of ethics**). Firms under the most intense CSR criticisms, such as those in the sportswear industry, often actively engage in these activities. Interestingly (but not surprisingly), the content of these codes varies by individual firm, industry, and country.[52] US codes of conduct tend to pay less attention to immediate production concerns and more attention to secondary stakeholder issues, such as welfare of the community and environmental protection. European codes concentrate more on production activities, such as quality management and limiting the environmental footprint of activities. Hong Kong codes tend to focus narrowly on corruption prevention but pay less attention to broader CSR issues.

There is an intense debate regarding the diffusion of codes of conduct. First, some argue that firms may not necessarily be sincere. This *negative* view suggests that given the rising interest in CSR, firms may be compelled to appear to be sensitive to CSR by "window dressing."[53] Many firms may chase fads by following what others are doing, while not having truly internalized the need to genuinely address CSR concerns. Second, an *instrumental* view suggests that CSR activities simply represent a useful instrument to make good profits. According to Toyota's critics in the debate on tougher fuel efficiency standards in the United States, firms such as Toyota are not necessarily becoming more "ethical" (see Closing Case). Finally, a *positive* view believes that (at least some) firms may be self-motivated to "do it right" regardless of social pressures. Codes of conduct tangibly express values that organizational members view as central and enduring.[54]

The institution-based view suggests that all three perspectives are probably valid. This is to be expected given how institutional pressures work to instill value. Regardless of actual motive, the fact that firms are embarking on some tangible CSR journey is encouraging, and indicative of the rising *legitimacy* of CSR on the management agenda.[55] Even for firms adopting codes of conduct only for "window dressing" purposes, publicizing a set of CSR criteria against which they can be judged opens doors for more scrutiny by concerned stakeholders (see Closing Case). These pressures are likely to encourage these firms' internal transformation to become better and more self-motivated corporate citizens. For example, it probably is fair to say that Nike is a more responsible corporate citizen today than what it was in 1990.

From a CSR perspective, the best firms employ a **proactive strategy** with CSR by constantly anticipating responsibility and endeavoring to do more than is required. Top management not only supports and champions CSR activities, but also views CSR as a source of differentiation.[56] For example, in 1990, BMW anticipated its emerging responsibility associated with the German government's proposed "take-back" policy. It not only designed easier-to-disassemble cars, but also signed up the few high-quality dismantler firms as part of an exclusive recycling infrastructure. Further, BMW actively participated in public discussions and succeeded in establishing the BMW approach as the German national standard for automobile disassembly. Other car companies were thus required to follow BMW's lead. However, they were left to fight over smaller, lower-quality dismantlers or develop an in-house dismantling infrastructure from scratch, both of which cost more, whereas BMW scored points on the triple bottom line.

Proactive firms often engage in three areas of activities. First, like BMW, they actively participate in regional, national, and international policy discussions. To the

codes of conduct (codes of ethics)

A set of written policies and standards for corporate conduct and ethics.

proactive strategy

A strategy that focuses on proactive engagement in corporate social responsibility.

extent that policy discussions today may become regulations in the future, it seems better to get involved early and (hopefully) steer the course toward a favorable direction. Otherwise, relatively passive firms are likely to see regulations to which they have little input being imposed on them.[57] In short, "if you're not at the table, you're on the menu."[58]

Second, proactive firms often build alliances with stakeholder groups.[59] Many firms collaborate with NGOs. Because of the historical tension and distrust, these "sleeping-with-the-enemy" alliances are not easy to handle. The key lies in identifying relatively short-term manageable projects of mutual interest. For instance, UPS collaborated with the Alliance for Environmental Innovation to help packaging material suppliers reduce almost 50% of their air pollution and 12% of their energy use.[60]

Third, proactive firms often engage in *voluntary* activities that go beyond what is required by regulations.[61] While there are numerous examples of industry-specific self-regulation,[62] an area of intense global interest is the pursuit of the International Standards Organization (ISO) 14001 certification of environment management system (EMS). Headquartered in Switzerland, ISO is an influential NGO consisting of national standards bodies of 111 countries. Launched in 1996, the ISO 14001 EMS has become the gold standard for CSR-conscious firms.[63] Although not required by law, many MNEs, such as Ford, IBM, and Skanska, have adopted ISO 14001 standards in all their facilities worldwide. Firms such as GM, Siemens, and Toyota have demanded that all of their top-tier suppliers be ISO 14001–certified.

From an institutional perspective, these areas of proactive activities are indicative of the normative and cognitive beliefs held by many managers on the importance of doing the right thing. While there is probably a certain element of "window dressing" and a quest for better profits, it is obvious that these efforts provide some tangible social and environmental benefits.

MAKING STRATEGIC CHOICES. The typology of (1) reactive, (2) defensive, (3) accommodative, and (4) proactive strategies is an interesting menu provided for different firms to choose. At present, the number of proactive firms is still a minority. While many firms are compelled to do something, a lot of CSR activities probably are still "window dressing." Only sustained pressures along regulatory, normative, and cognitive dimensions may push and pull more firms to do more.[64] Research by M&S after Plan A's first year (see Opening Case) has yielded interesting data on the distribution of its consumers and employees along these four dimensions (Table 12.4). Since CSR strategies cannot be embarked upon in a vacuum, a firm's particular strategy needs to have some alignment with the CSR propensity of its consumers, employees, and other

TABLE 12.4   Distribution of Marks & Spencer's Consumers and Employees

CONCEPTUAL CATEGORY	M&S'S LABEL	PERCENTAGE OF CONSUMERS	PERCENTAGE OF EMPLOYEES
Reactive	"Not my problem"	24%	1%
Defensive	"What's the point"	38%	21%
Accommodative	"If it's easy"	27%	54%
Proactive	"Green crusaders"	11%	24%

Source: Based on text in Marks & Spencer, 2008, *Plan A: Year 1 Review* (p. 16), January 15, plana.marksandspencer.com.

stakeholders. In other words, it is not realistic to implement a proactive strategy when the firm has numerous reactive employees and consumers.

Debates and Extensions

Without exaggeration, the entire subject of CSR is about debates (see Strategy in Action 12.2 for an example). Some may even debate whether CSR belongs in a global strategy text. *None* of the other global strategy (or mainstream "strategic management") textbooks has a full chapter devoted to CSR in addition to another full chapter on ethics, cultures, and institutions (see Chapter 4). It is not far-fetched to suggest that there is a big debate between this chapter (focusing on stakeholder capitalism) and Chapter 11 (focusing on shareholder capitalism). Here, we discuss three recent, previously unexplored debates particularly relevant for international operations: (1) domestic versus overseas social responsibility, (2) race to the bottom ("pollution haven") versus race to the top, and (3) active versus inactive CSR engagement overseas.

Domestic versus Overseas Social Responsibility

Given that corporate resources are limited, resources devoted to overseas CSR, unfortunately, often mean fewer resources devoted to domestic CSR.[65] Consider two *primary* stakeholder groups: domestic employees and communities. Expanding overseas, especially toward emerging economies, may not only increase corporate profits and shareholder returns, but also provide employment to host countries and develop these economies at the "base of the pyramid," all of which have noble CSR dimensions (see Chapter 1 Closing Case). However, this is often done at the expense of domestic employees and communities. One can vividly appreciate the devastation of job losses on such employees and communities, by watching the 1998 movie *The Full Monty*, which took place in Sheffield, England, the former steel capital of Europe and the world. Laid-off steel mill workers eventually took up an "alternative" line of work (male strip dancing). To prevent such a possible fate, in 2004, DaimlerChrysler's German unions had to scrap a 3% pay raise and endure an 11% increase in work hours (from 35 to 39 hours) with no extra pay in exchange for promises that 6,000 jobs would be kept in Germany for eight years—otherwise, their jobs would go to the Czech Republic, Poland, and South Africa. However, such labor deals will probably only slow down, not stop, the outgoing tide of jobs from developed economies. The wage differentials are just too great. "When we find a certain product can be made with a 50% decrease in salary costs in another country," argued a German executive, "we cannot avoid that if we want to stay competitive."[66]

To the extent that few (or no) laid-off German employees would move to the neighboring Czech Republic and Poland to seek work (and forget about moving to China, India, or South Africa), most of them end up being social welfare recipients in Germany. Thus, one may argue that MNEs shirk their CSR by increasing the social burdens of their home countries. Executives making these decisions are often criticized by the media, unions, and politicians. However, from a corporate governance perspective, especially the "shareholder capitalism" variant, MNEs are doing nothing wrong by maximizing shareholder returns (see Chapter 11).

Strategy in Action 12.2 - Salmon, Salmon, Everywhere

Ethical Challenge

There has been an explosion in the global supply of salmon recently, but this rise in numbers is not due to an increase in the wild salmon catch, which has been in steady decline for decades. Instead, as wild Atlantic salmon disappear (wild Pacific salmon are still relatively safe), salmon farming (aquaculture) has increased.

Starting in Norway as a cottage industry in the late 1960s, salmon farming quickly spread to Britain, Canada, Iceland, and Ireland in the 1970s; the United States in the 1980s; and Chile in the 1990s. Farm-raised salmon live in sea cages. They are fed pellets to speed growth (twice as fast as in the wild), pigments to mimic the pink wild salmon flesh, and pesticides to kill the lice that go hand-in-hand with an industrial feedlot. Atlantic salmon farming (still dominated by Norwegian firms; followed by Chilean companies) has exploded into a $2 billion-a-year global business that produces 700,000 tons of fish annually. In comparison, the wild salmon catch in the Atlantic (only allowed by Britain and Ireland) is only 3,000 tons a year. In essence, it is Atlantic salmon farming companies that have transformed salmon from a rare and expensive seasonal delicacy to a common chicken of the sea to be enjoyed by everyone year-round. In addition, Atlantic salmon farming has taken commercial fishing pressure off wild salmon stocks and provided employment to depressed maritime regions. For example, in economically depressed western Scotland, salmon aquaculture employs approximately 6,400 workers.

But, here is the catch: Farm-raised salmon have (1) fouled the nearby sea, (2) spread diseases and sea lice, and (3) led to a large number of escaped fish. Each of these problems has become a growing controversy. First, heavy concentration of fish in a tiny area—up to 800,000 in one floating cage—leads to food and fecal waste that promotes toxic algae blooms, which, in turn, have led to closure of shellfishing in nearby waters. Second, sea lice outbreaks at fish farms in Ireland, Norway, Scotland, and the United States have had a devastating effect on wild salmon and other fish. The third problem lies in escaped salmon. In Scotland, approximately 300,000 farmed fish escape every year. Research has found that escaped salmon interbreed

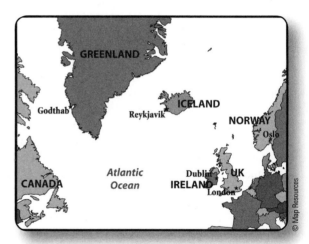

with wild salmon. In Norwegian rivers that are salmon spawning grounds, 10%–35% of the "wild" fish are found to be escaped salmon.

Wild salmon are an amazing species, genetically programmed to be able to find their spawning grounds in rivers after years of wandering in the sea. Although at present, only one egg out of every 4,000 is likely to complete such an epic journey, salmon has been a magic fish in the legends of Iceland, Ireland, Norway, and Scotland. These legends are threatened by the escaped farm-raised salmon and the hybrid they produce with wild salmon, because genetically homogenous salmon, descended from aquaculture fish, are ill suited to find these rivers and could also leave the species less able to cope with threats such as disease and climate change. In short, the biodiversity of the wild salmon stocks, already at dangerously low levels, is threatened by fish farming. Defenders of fish farming, however, argue that *all* farming alters, and sometimes damages, the environment. If modern agriculture featuring pesticides and fertilizers were invented today, it probably would be banned. They argue that there is no reason the aquaculture industry needs to be held to higher standards.

Sources: Based on (1) *BusinessWeek,* 2006, Fished out, September 4: 56–64; (2) *The Economist,* 2003, The promise of a blue revolution, August 9: 19–21; (3) F. Montaigne, 2003, Everybody loves Atlantic Salmon: Here's the catch, *National Geographic,* 204 (1): 100–123.

The heart of this debate boils down to a fundamental point that frustrates CSR advocates: In a capitalist society, it is shareholders (otherwise known as *capitalists*) who matter at the end of the day. According to Jack Welch, GE's former chairman and CEO:

> Unions, politicians, activists—companies face a Babel of interests. But there's only one owner. A company is for its shareholders. They own it. They control it. That's the way it is, and the way it should be.[67]

When firms have enough resources, it would be nice to take care of domestic employees and communities. However, when confronted with relentless pressures for cost cutting and restructuring, managers have to prioritize.[68] Paradoxically, in this age of globalization, while the CSR movement is on the rise, the great migration of jobs away from developed economies is also accelerating. While people and countries at the base of the global pyramid welcome such migration, domestic employees and communities in developed economies, as well as unions and politicians, frankly hate it. Not surprisingly, this politically explosive debate is likely to heat up in the years to come.

Active versus Inactive CSR Engagement Overseas

Active CSR engagement is now increasingly expected of MNEs. MNEs that fail to do so are often criticized by NGOs. In the 1990s, Shell was harshly criticized for "not lifting a finger" when the Nigerian government brutally cracked down on rebels in the Ogoni region in which Shell operated. However, such well-intentioned calls for greater CSR engagement are in direct conflict with a long-standing principle governing the relationship between MNEs and host countries: non-intervention in local affairs (see the *first* bullet point in Table 12.1).

The non-intervention principle originated from concerns that MNEs might engage in political activities against the national interests of the host country. Chile in the 1970s serves as a case in point. After the democratically elected socialist President Salvador Allende had threatened to expropriate the assets of ITT (a US-based MNE) and other MNEs, ITT, allegedly in connection with the Central Intelligence Agency (CIA), promoted a coup that killed President Allende. Consequently, the idea that MNEs should not interfere in the domestic political affairs of the host country has been enshrined in a number of codes of MNE conduct (see Table 12.1).

However, CSR advocates have been emboldened by some MNEs' actions during the apartheid era in South Africa, when local laws required racial segregation of the workforce. While many MNEs withdrew, those that remained were encouraged by the Sullivan Principles to challenge the apartheid system, undermining the government's base of power. BP, for example, desegregated its employees. Emboldened by the successful removal of the apartheid regime in South Africa in 1994, CSR advocates have unleashed a new campaign, stressing the necessity for MNEs to engage in actions that often constitute political activity, in particular in the human rights area. Shell, after its widely criticized (lack of) action in Nigeria, has explicitly endorsed the United Nations Declaration on Human Rights and supported the exercise of such rights "within the legitimate role of business" since 1996.

But, what exactly is the "legitimate role" of CSR initiatives in host countries? In almost every country, there are local laws and norms that some foreign MNEs may find objectionable. In Estonia, ethnic Russians are being discriminated against. In many Arab countries, women do not have the same legal rights as men. In the United States, a number of groups (ranging from Native Americans to homosexuals) claim to be discriminated against. At the heart of this debate is whether foreign MNEs should spearhead efforts to remove some of these discriminatory practices or should remain politically neutral by conforming to current host country laws and norms. This obviously is a nontrivial challenge.

Race to the Bottom ("Pollution Haven") versus Race to the Top

In global business, a controversial "pollution haven" debate has arisen. One side argues that because of heavier environmental regulation in developed economies, MNEs may have an incentive to shift pollution-intensive production to developing countries, whose environmental standards may be lower. To attract investment, developing countries may enter a "race to the bottom" by lowering (or at least not tightening) environmental standards, and some may become "pollution havens."[69]

The other side argues that globalization does not necessarily have negative effects on the environment in developing countries to the extent suggested by the "pollution haven" hypothesis. This is largely due to many MNEs' *voluntary* adherence to environmental standards higher than those required by host countries.[70] One study finds that US capital markets significantly reward these practices, thus refuting the perspective that being green constitutes a liability that depresses market value.[71] In general, most MNEs reportedly outperform local firms in environmental management.[72] The underlying motivations behind MNEs' voluntary "green practices" can be attributed to (1) worldwide CSR pressures in general, (2) CSR demands made by customers in developed economies, and (3) requirements of MNE headquarters for worldwide compliance of higher CSR standards (such as ISO 14001). Although it is difficult to suggest that the "race to the bottom" does not exist, MNEs as a group do not necessarily add to the environmental burden in developing countries. Some MNEs, such as Dow, may facilitate the diffusion of better environmental technologies to these countries.

The Savvy Strategist

Concerning CSR, the industry-, resource-, and institution-based views suggest three clear implications for action (Table 12.5). First, given the increasingly inescapable responsibility to be good corporate citizens, managers may want to integrate CSR

TABLE 12.5   Strategic Implications for Action

- Integrate CSR as part of the core activities and processes of the firm.
- Pick your CSR battles carefully—don't blindly imitate other firms' CSR activities.
- Understand the rules of the game, anticipate changes, and seek to shape and influence such changes.

as part of the core activities of the firm—instead of "faking it" and making cosmetic changes. M&S provides a case in point (Opening Case). Many managers traditionally treat CSR as a nuisance, involving regulation, added costs, and liability. Such an attitude may underestimate potential business opportunities associated with CSR.

Second, savvy managers need to pick CSR battles carefully. The resource-based view suggests an important lesson, which is captured by Sun Tzu's timeless teaching: "Know yourself, know your opponents." While your opponents may engage in high-profile CSR activities that allow them to earn bragging rights while contributing to their triple bottom line, blindly imitating these practices, while not knowing enough about "yourself" (you as a manager and the firm/unit you lead), may lead to some disappointment. Instead of always chasing the newest best practices, firms are advised to select CSR practices that fit with their *existing* resources, capabilities, and especially complementary assets.[73]

Third, savvy strategists need to understand the formal and informal rules of the game, anticipate changes, and seek to shape such changes. In the case of carbon offsetting, although the US government has refused to ratify the Kyoto Protocol, many far-sighted US managers realize that as more countries around the world join Kyoto, competitors based in these countries may gain a strong "green" advantage.[74] Therefore, many US firms voluntarily participate in CSR activities not (yet) mandated by US law, in anticipation of more stringent environmental requirements down the road.

For current and would-be strategists, this chapter has clearly shown that from a CSR perspective, we can revisit the four fundamental questions. First, why do firms differ in CSR activities? Firm differences can be found in (1) industry structures, (2) resource repertoire, and (3) formal and informal institutional pressures. Second, how do firms behave in the CSR arena? Some are reactive and defensive, others are accommodative, and still others are proactive. Third, what determines a firm's CSR scope? While industry structures, resource bases, and formal institutional pressures are likely to ensure some minimal involvement, firms with a broad range of CSR engagements are likely to be characterized by a large percentage of managers and employees who intrinsically feel the need to "do it right" (see Table 12.4). In other words, it fundamentally boils down to differences in informal normative and cognitive beliefs held by managers and employees. Finally, what determines the success and failure of firms around the world? No doubt, CSR will increasingly become an important part of the answer. The best performing firms are likely to be those that can integrate CSR activities into the core economic functions of the firm while addressing social and environmental concerns.[75]

The globally ambiguous and different CSR standards, norms, and expectations make many managers uncomfortable. As a result, many managers continue to relegate CSR to the "backburner." However, this does not seem to be the right attitude for current and would-be strategists who are studying this book—that is, *you*. It is important to note that we live in a dangerous period of global capitalism. In the *post-Seattle, post-9/11,* and *post-Enron* world (see Chapter 1), managers, as a unique group of stakeholders, have an important and challenging responsibility to safeguard and advance capitalism. From a CSR standpoint, this means building more humane, more inclusive, and fairer firms that not only generate wealth and develop economies, but also respond to changing societal expectations concerning the social and environmental role of the firm around the world.[76]

CHAPTER SUMMARY

1. *Articulate what a stakeholder view of the firm is*

   - A stakeholder view of the firm urges companies to pursue a more balanced triple bottom line, consisting of economic, social, and environmental performance.

   - Despite the fierce defense of the free market school, especially its shareholder capitalism variant, the CSR movement has now become a more central part of strategy discussions.

2. *Develop a comprehensive model of corporate social responsibility*

   - The industry-based view argues that the nature of different industries drives different CSR strategies.

   - The resource-based view posits that not all CSR satisfies the VRIO requirements.

   - The institution-based view suggests that when confronting CSR pressures, firms may employ (1) reactive, (2) defensive, (3) accommodative, and (4) proactive strategies.

3. *Participate in three leading debates concerning corporate social responsibility*

   - (1) Domestic versus overseas social responsibility, (2) active versus inactive CSR engagement overseas, and (3) race to the bottom versus race to the top.

4. *Draw strategic implications for action*

   - Integrate CSR as part of the core activities and processes of the firm.

   - Pick your CSR battles carefully—don't blindly imitate other firms' CSR activities.

   - Understand the rules of the game, anticipate changes, and seek to influence such changes.

KEY TERMS

Accommodative strategy	Global sustainability	Secondary stakeholder groups
Code of conduct (code of ethics)	Primary stakeholder groups	Social issue participation
Corporate social responsibility (CSR)	Proactive strategy	Stakeholder
Defensive strategy	Reactive strategy	Triple bottom line

CRITICAL DISCUSSION QUESTIONS

1. In a landmark *Dodge v. Ford* case in 1919, Michigan State Supreme Court determined whether Henry Ford could withhold dividends from the Dodge brothers (and other shareholders of the Ford Motor Company) to engage in what today

would be called CSR activities. With a resounding "No," the court opined that "A business organization is organized and carried on primarily for the profits of the stockholders." If the court in your country were to decide on this case this year (or in 2019), what do you think would be the likely outcome?

2. **ON ETHICS:** Some argue that investing in emerging economies greatly facilitates economic development at the base of the global economic pyramid. Others contend that moving jobs to low-cost countries not only abandons CSR for domestic employees and communities in developed economies, but also exploits the poor in these countries and destroys the environment. If you were (1) the CEO of an MNE headquartered in a developed economy, (2) the leader of a labor union in the home country of the MNE mentioned here that is losing a lot of jobs, or (3) the leader of an environmental NGO in the low-cost country in which the MNE invests, how would you participate in this debate?

3. **ON ETHICS:** Hypothetically, your MNE is the largest foreign investor in (1) Vietnam where religious leaders are being persecuted or (2) Estonia where ethnic Russian citizens are being discriminated against by law. As the country manager there, you are being pressured by NGOs of all stripes to help the oppressed groups in these countries. But you also understand that the host government could be upset if your firm is found to engage in local political activities deemed inappropriate. These activities, which you personally find distasteful, are not directly related to your operations. How would you proceed?

CLOSING CASE

Ethical Challenge

Which Side Is Toyota On?

Toyota has carefully crafted its "green" image, substantiated by its Prius hybrid model. Yet, in late 2007, Toyota suddenly became a target for environmental groups, its usual allies. A new coalition of environmental groups simply named itself Truth About Toyota and dedicated itself to naming and shaming Toyota's alleged hypocrisy. The following are a sample of news titles from other sources collected and disseminated by www.truthabouttoyota.com: (1) Stuck in some green mud, (2) Toyota: Moving backward, and (3) Toyota's betrayal.

What happened? In the eyes of environmentalists, Toyota betrayed them by joining the "bad boys"—General Motors (GM), Ford, and Chrysler—to lobby against efforts in the US Congress to aggressively increase fuel economy standards, known as the corporate average fuel economy (CAFE) regulations.

Supporters for tougher CAFE regulations wanted to pass legislation that would mandate an average 35 miles per gallon for *both* cars and light trucks by 2020—up from 27.5 miles per gallon for cars and 22.2 for light trucks (including minivans and sports utility vehicles [SUVs]) in 2007. Toyota and its allies supported an alternative, less progressive proposal that would set the CAFE levels at 35 miles per gallon for cars and 32 for light trucks by 2022. Toyota's decision to support the less aggressive increase of fuel efficiency was most likely driven by its recent introduction of fuel-thirsty trucks, especially its giant Tundra pickup. According to www.truthabouttoyota.com, Toyota's fleetwide pollution is higher today than it was 20 years ago.

In response to Toyota's alleged "betrayal," outraged Prius owners in several US cities staged protests against Toyota. In a public letter to Toyota, nine US environmental leaders wrote on October 11, 2007:

> Toyota Motor Corporation's efforts to lobby Congress to weaken, delay, or eliminate the bipartisan Senate measure stands in marked contrast to its public statements and its marketing to consumers. Furthermore, it appears that Toyota is applying a double standard when the company simultaneously complied with strict Japanese fuel economy standards yet lobbies members of the US House and Senate against more modest improvements here in the United States . . . As the world's leading automaker and a leader in advanced vehicle technology, Toyota should be setting the industry standard, not stooping to the lowest common denominator.

In Toyota's defense, a *Wall Street Journal* article opined: "The profitless Prius wouldn't exist if not for the non-hybrids that keep Toyota in business . . . [Toyota's position] would let automakers continue to make big vehicles that happen to be the ones Americans, with their dollars, show they actually want."

In the end, Toyota and its allies lost. On December 6, 2007, the Energy Independence and Security Act was passed, calling for a 35-miles-per-gallon CAFE level for *both* cars and light trucks by 2020. On January 13, 2008, Toyota's president Katsuaki Watanabe gave a speech at a Detroit auto show:

> In ten years, we have sold 1.25 million hybrids globally and nearly 750,000 in North America in less than eight years. Last year, we sold more than a quarter-million hybrids in the US alone . . . Last month, the US Congress agreed on an energy bill calling for a 35-mpg CAFE by 2020. Toyota strongly supports this long-overdue legislation.

However, as always, we will not wait until the deadline to comply. I have issued a challenge to our engineers to meet the new standard well in advance of 2020. I believe it can be done, it should be done, and that Toyota is capable of doing it.

The political storm did not seem to affect Toyota's sales of hybrid models—at least initially. In January 2008, of a total of 22,392 hybrid units sold in the United States (a 27% increase over January 2007), 18,652 units (83% of the hybrid market) went to Toyota. Of these, 11,379 Prius units were sold, commanding a 37% increase over January 2007. In addition, 12% of the Camry sedans (3,750 units) and 17% of the Highlander SUVs (2,143 units) sold in January 2008 were hybrid vehicles.

Sources: Based on (1) Green Car Congress, 2008, Reported US sales of hybrids up 27.3% in January 2008, February 7, www.greencarcongress. com; (2) H. Jenkins, 2007, Cheap shot at Toyota, *Wall Street Journal*, October 24, online.wsj.com; (3) S. Nadel et al., 2007, Letter to Shigeru Hayakawa, Chairman and CEO, Toyota Motor North America, October 11, www.truthabouttoyota.com; (4) Toyota, 2008, Remarks by Katsuaki Watanabe at Toyota International Media Reception, 2008 NAIAS Detroit, January 13, pressroom.toyota.com; (5) Wikipedia, 2008, Corporate average fuel economy, en.wikipedia.org; (6) www. truthabouttoyota.com.

Case Discussion Questions

1. If you were a Toyota executive, would you have decided to lobby against tougher CAFE standards?

2. If you were a Prius owner, would you have joined the protests against Toyota's "betrayal"?

3. If you were a Tundra owner, what would be your view on this debate?

4. If you were shopping for a hybrid, would Toyota's president's remarks influence your decision (either positively or negatively)? Do these remarks matter?

NOTES

Journal acronyms *AME–Academy of Management Executive;* ***AMJ**–Academy of Management Journal;* ***AMP**–Academy of Management Perspectives;* ***AMR**–Academy of Management Review;* ***APJM**–Asia Pacific Journal of Management;* ***ASQ**–Administrative Science Quarterly;* ***BEQ**–Business Ethics Quarterly;* ***BW**–BusinessWeek;* ***CMR**–California Management Review;* ***HBR**–Harvard Business Review;* ***JBE**–Journal of Business Ethics;* ***JIBS**–Journal of International Business Studies;* ***JIM**–Journal of International Management;* ***JM**–Journal of Management;* ***JMS**–Journal of Management Studies;* ***JWB**–Journal of World Business;* ***MS**–Management Science;* ***NYTM**–The New York Times*

Magazine; **OSc**–*Organization Science;* **OSt**–*Organization Studies;* **SMJ**–*Strategic Management Journal.*

1. K. Davis, 1973, The case for and against business assumption of social responsibilities (p. 312), *AMJ,* 16: 312–322. See also R. Aguilera, R. Rupp, C. Williams, & J. Ganapathi, 2007, Putting the S back in CSR, *AMR,* 32: 836–863; D. Etzion, 2007, Research on organizations and the natural environment, 1992–present, *JM,* 33: 637–664; C. Marquis, M. Glynn, & G. Davis, 2007, Community isomorphism and corporate social action, *AMR,* 32: 925–945; A. McWilliams, D. Siegel, & P. Wright, 2006, Corporate social responsibility, *JMS,* 43: 1–18; K. Starkey & A. Crane, 2003, Toward green narrative, *AMR,* 28: 220–237.

2. P. Godfrey, 2005, The relationship between corporate philanthropy and shareholder wealth, *AMR,* 30: 777–798; T. Jones, W. Felps, & G. Bigley, 2007, Ethical theory and stakeholder-related decisions, *AMR,* 32: 137–155; J. Post, L. Preston, & S. Sachs, 2002, *Redefining the Corporation,* Stanford, CA: Stanford University Press.

3. Y. He, Z. Tian, & Y. Chen, 2007, Performance implications of nonmarket strategy in China, *APJM,* 24: 151–169; K. O'Shaughnessy, E. Gedajlovic, & P. Reinmoeller, 2007, The influence of firm, industry, and network on the corporate social performance of Japanese firms, *APJM,* 24: 283–304.

4. E. Freeman, 1984, *Strategic Management: A Stakeholder Approach* (p. 46), Boston: Pitman; T. Rowley & M. Moldoveanu, 2003, When will stakeholder groups act?, *AMR,* 28: 204–219.

5. P. David, M. Bloom, & A. Hillman, 2007, Investor activism, managerial responsiveness, and corporate social performance, *SMJ,* 28: 91–100.

6. World Commission on Environment and Development, 1987, *Our Common Future* (p. 8), Oxford: Oxford University Press.

7. S. Hart, 2005, *Capitalism at the Crossroads,* Philadelphia: Wharton School Publishing; R. Rajan & L. Zingales, 2003, *Saving Capitalism from the Capitalists,* New York: Crown.

8. S. Hart & M. Milstein, 2003, Creating sustainable value, *AME,* 17: 56–67.

9. J. Doh & T. Guay, 2006, CSR, public policy, and NGO activism in Europe and the United States, *JMS,* 43: 47–73.

10. P. Romilly, 2007, Business and climate change risk, *JIBS,* 38: 474–480.

11. C. Seelos & J. Mair, 2007, Profitable business models and market creation in the context of deep poverty, *AMP,* November: 49–63; A. Scherer & G. Palazzo, 2007, Toward a political conception of corporate responsibility, *AMR,* 32: 1096–1120.

12. J. Coombs & K. M. Gilley, 2005, Stakeholder management as a predictor of CEO compensation, *SMJ,* 26: 827–840; B. Husted & D. Allen, 2006, CSR in the MNE, *JIBS,* 37: 838–849; G. Kassinis & N. Vafeas, 2006, Stakeholder pressures and environmental performance, *AMJ,* 49: 145–159; S. Sharma & I. Henriques, 2005, Stakeholder influences on sustainability practices in the Canadian forest products industry, *SMJ,* 26: 159–180.

13. C. Eesley & M. Lenox, 2006, Firm responses to secondary stakeholder action, *SMJ,* 27: 765–781; R. Mitchell, B. Agle, & D. Wood, 1997, Toward a theory of stakeholder identification and salience, *AMR,* 22: 853–886.

14. T. Kochan & S. Rubinstein, 2000, Toward a stakeholder theory of the firm, *OSc,* 11: 367–386; R. Wolfe & D. Putler, 2002, How tight are the ties that bind stakeholder groups?, *OSc,* 13: 64–80.

15. M. Clarkson, 1995, A stakeholder framework for analyzing and evaluating corporate social performance (p. 107), *AMR,* 20: 92–117.

16. T. Donaldson & L. Preston, 1995, The stakeholder theory of the corporation, *AMR,* 20: 65–91; J. Elkington, 1997, *Cannibals with Forks: The Triple Bottom Line of 21ˢᵗ Century Business,* New York: Wiley.

17. M. Friedman, 1970, The social responsibility of business is to increase its profits, *NYTM,* September 13: 32–33.

18. M. Jensen, 2002, Value maximization, stakeholder theory, and the corporate objective function, *BEQ,* 12: 235–256.

19. C. Nielsen, 2005, Competition within the US national security regime, *JIM,* 11: 497–517.

20. R. Buchholz, 2004, The natural environment, *AME,* 18: 130–133; O. Ferrell, 2004, Business ethics and customer stakeholders, *AME,* 18: 126–129.

21. J. Mahoney, 2008, Towards a stakeholder theory of strategic management, Working paper, University of Illinois.

22. J. Margolis & J. Walsh, 2003, Misery loves companies, *ASQ,* 48: 268–305.

23. K. Basu & G. Palazzo, 2008, Corporate social responsibility, *AMR,* 33: 122–136.

24. D. Levy & D. Egan, 2003, A neo-Gramscian approach to corporate political strategy, *JMS,* 40: 803–829.

25. T. Dean & R. Brown, 1995, Pollution regulation as a barrier to new firm entry, *AMJ,* 38: 288–303.

26. J. A. Aragon-Correa, 1998, Strategic proactivity and firm approach to the natural environment, *AMJ,* 41: 556–567; M. Russo & P. Fouts, 1997, A resource-based perspective on corporate environmental performance and profitability, *AMJ,* 40: 534–559.

27. R. Klassen & D. C. Whyback, 1999, The impact of environmental technologies on manufacturing performance, *AMJ,* 42: 599–615.

28. S. Hart, 1995, A natural-resource-based view (p. 993), *AMR,* 20: 986–1014.

29. P. Christmann & G. Taylor, 2002, Globalization and the environment (p. 123), *AME,* 16 (3): 121–135.

30. M. Russo, 2003, The emergence of sustainable industries, *SMJ,* 24: 317–331.

31. S. Sharma, 2000, Managerial interpretations and organizational context as predictors of corporate choice of environmental strategy, *AMJ,* 43: 681–697.

32. R. Chan, 2005, Does the natural-resource-based view of the firm apply in an emerging economy?, *JMS,* 42: 625–675; J. A. Aragon-Correa & S. Sharma, 2003, A contingent resource-based view of proactive corporate environmental strategy, *AMR,* 28: 71–88; A. Marcus & M. Anderson, 2006, A general dynamic capability, *JMS,* 43: 19–46.

33. A. Hillman & G. Keim, 2001, Shareholder value, stakeholder management, and social issues, *SMJ,* 22: 125–139; M. Meznar, D. Nigh, & C. Kwok, 1998, Announcements of withdrawal from South Africa revisited, *AMJ,* 41: 715–730.

34. W. Judge & T. Douglas, 1998, Performance implications of incorporating natural environmental issues into the strategic planning process, *JMS,* 35: 241–262.

35. *BW,* 2003, Diversity is about to get more elusive, not less, July 7: 30–31.

36. D. Turban & D. Greening, 1996, Corporate social performance and organizational attractiveness to prospective employees, *AMJ,* 40: 658–672.

37. S. Sharma & H. Vredenburg, 1998, Proactive corporate environmental strategy and the development of competitively valuable organizational capabilities, *SMJ,* 19: 729–754.

38. L. Andersson & T. Bateman, 2000, Individual environmental initiative, *AMJ,* 43: 548–570; M. Cordano & I. Frieze, 2000, Pollution reduction preferences of US environmental managers, *AMJ,* 43: 627–641; C. Egri & S. Herman, 2000, Leadership in the North American environmental sector, *AMJ,* 43: 571–604; C. Ramus & U. Steger, 2000, The roles of supervisory support behaviors and environmental policy in employee "ecoinitiatives" at leading-edge European companies, *AMJ,* 43: 605–626.

39. N. Darnall & D. Edwards, 2006, Predicting the cost of environmental management system adoption, *SMJ,* 27: 301–320; M. Russo & N. Harrison, 2005, Organizational design and environmental performance, *AMJ,* 48: 582–593.

40. M. Delmas, M. Russo, & M. Montes-Sancho, 2007, Deregulation and environmental differentiation in the electric utility industry, *SMJ,* 28: 189–209.

41. P. Christmann, 2000, Effects of best practices of environmental management on cost advantage, *AMJ,* 43: 663–680.

42. M. Barnett & R. Salomon, 2006, Beyond dichotomy, *SMJ,* 27: 1101–1122; J. Harrison & R. E. Freeman, 1999, Stakeholders, social responsibility, and performance, *AMJ,* 42: 479–487; A. Lockett, J. Moon, & W. Visser, 2006, CSR in management research, *JMS,* 43: 115–136; A. Mackey, T. Mackey, & J. Barney, 2007, CSR and firm performance, *AMR,* 32: 817–835; M. Orlitzky, F. Schmidt, & S. Rynes, 2003, Corporate social and financial performance, *OSt,* 24: 403–441; D. Schuler & M. Cording, 2006, A corporate social performance-corporate financial performance behavioral model for consumers, *AMR,* 31: 540–558; V. Strike, J. Gao, & P. Bansal, 2006, Being good while being bad, *JIBS,* 37: 850–862.

43. S. Berman, A. Wicks, S. Kotha, & T. Jones, 1999, Does stakeholder orientation matter?, *AMJ,* 42: 488–506; S. Waddock & S. Graves, 1997, The corporate social performance-financial performance link, *SMJ,* 18: 303–319.

44. D. Vogel, 2005, The low value of virtue, *HBR,* June: 26.

45. B. Agle, R. Mitchell, & J. Sonnenfeld, 1999, What matters to CEOs?, *AMJ,* 42: 507–525.

46. J. Campbell, 2007, Why would corporations behave in socially responsible ways?, *AMR,* 32: 946–967; P. Christmann, 2004, Multinational companies and the natural environment, *AMJ,* 47: 747–760; D. Waldman

et al., 2006, Cultural and leadership predictions of CSR values of top management, *JIBS,* 37: 823–837.

47. I. Henriques & P. Sadorsky, 1999, The relationship between environmental commitment and managerial perceptions of stakeholder importance, *AMJ,* 42: 87–99.

48. P. Hilts, 2003, *Protecting America's Health,* New York: Knopf.

49. L. Amine, 2003, An integrated micro- and macrolevel discussion of global green issues, *JIM,* 9: 373–393.

50. A. Gore, 1992, *Earth in the Balance,* New York: Harper Row; M. Porter & M. Kramer, 2006, Strategy and society, *HBR,* December: 78–92.

51. S. Banerjee, 2001, Managerial perceptions of corporate environmentalism, *JMS,* 38: 489–513; D. Matten & A. Crane, 2005, Corporate citizenship, *AMR,* 30: 166–179.

52. A. Kolk & R. Vam Tulder, 2004, Ethics in international business, *JWB,* 39: 49–60; G. Weaver, 2001, Ethics programs in global businesses, *JBE,* 30: 3–15.

53. P. Bansal & I. Clelland, 2004, Talking trash, *AMJ,* 47: 93–103.

54. C. Robertson & W. Crittenden, 2003, Mapping moral philosophies, *SMJ,* 24: 385–392; J. van Oosterhout, P. Heugens, & M. Kaptein, 2006, The internal morality of contracting, *AMR,* 31: 521–539.

55. O. Boiral, 2007, Corporate greening through ISO 14001, *OSc,* 18: 127–146; J. Howard-Grenville & A. Hoffman, 2003, The importance of cultural framing to the success of social initiatives in business, *AME,* 17: 70–84.

56. O. Branzei, T. Ursacki-Bryant, I. Vertinsky, & W. Zhang, 2004, The formation of green strategies in Chinese firms, *SMJ,* 25: 1075–1095.

57. D. Schuler, K. Rehbein, & R. Cramer, 2002, Pursuing strategic advantage through political means, *AMJ,* 45: 659–672.

58. *The Economist,* 2007, Everybody's green now (p. 6), June 2: 6.

59. B. Arya & J. Salk, 2006, Cross-sector alliance learning and effectiveness of voluntary codes of CSR, *BEQ,* 16: 211–234; C. Hardy, T. Lawrence, & D. Grant, 2005, Discourse and collaboration, *AMR,* 30: 58–77; J. Selsky & B. Parker, 2005, Cross-sector partnerships to address social issues, *JM,* 31: 849–873.

60. D. Rondinelli & T. London, 2003, How corporations and environmental groups cooperate, *AME,* 17: 61–76.

61. P. Bansal & K. Roth, 2000, Why companies go green, *AMJ,* 43: 717–737.

62. A. King & M. Lenox, 2000, Industry self-regulation without sanctions, *AMJ,* 43: 698–716.

63. R. Jiang & P. Bansal, 2003, Seeing the need for ISO 14001, *JMS,* 40: 1047–1067; A. King, M. Lenox, & A. Terlaak, 2005, The strategic use of decentralized institutions, *AMJ,* 48: 1091–1106.

64. A. Carroll, 2004, Managing ethically with global stakeholders, *AME,* 18 (2): 114–120.

65. J. Logsdon & D. Wood, 2002, Business citizenship, *BEQ,* 12: 155–188; D. Rousseau & R. Batt, 2007, Global competition's perfect storm, *AMP,* 21: 16–23; J. Snider, R. Paul, & D. Martin, 2003, CSR in the 21st century, *JBE,* 48: 175–188.

66. *BW,* 2004, European workers' losing battle (p. 41), August 9: 41.

67. J. Welch & S. Welch, 2006, Whose company is it anyway?, *BW,* October 9: 122.

68. A. Sundaram & A. Inkpen, 2004, The corporate objective revisited, *OSc,* 15: 350–363.

69. H. J. Leonard, 1988, *Pollution and the Struggle for a World Product,* Cambridge: Cambridge University Press.

70. P. Christmann & G. Taylor, 2006, Firm self-regulation through international certifiable standards, *JIBS,* 37: 863–878; A. Rugman & A. Verbeke, 1998, Corporate strategy and international environmental policy, *JIBS,* 29: 819–833.

71. G. Dowell, S. Hart, & B. Yeung, 2000, Do corporate global environmental standards create or destroy market value?, *MS,* 46: 1059–1074.

72. J. Child & T. Tsai, 2005, The dynamic between MNC strategy and institutional constraints in emerging economies, *JMS,* 42: 95–126.

73. A. McWilliams & D. Siegel, 2001, Corporate social responsibility, *AMR,* 26: 117–127.

74. J. Lash & F. Wellington, 2007, Competitive advantage on a warming planet, *HBR,* March: 95–102.

75. B. Husted & J. Salazar, 2006, Taking Friedman seriously, *JMS,* 43: 75–91.

76. N. Gardberg & C. Fombrun, 2006, Corporate citizenship, *AMR,* 31: 329–346; A. Peredo & J. Chrisman, 2006, Toward a theory of community-based enterprise, *AMR,* 31: 309–328.

Sunflower Company[1]

Aldas Pranas Kriauciunas
Purdue University

An entrepreneurial Lithuanian company endeavors to survive and prosper by adapting to changing market conditions in a transition economy.

Business survival in a transition economy encompasses many challenges. Founded in the then newly independent country of Lithuania, Sunflower has not only survived, but has grown for over 15 years under difficult conditions. Through planning and luck, it has met challenges head-on, but one of its greatest challenges—international expansion—is still ahead. To understand the firm, its history is presented in five periods: start of the firm (1992 to 1994); expansion of the firm (1995 to 1998); crisis period (1999 to 2000); recovery (2001 to 2004); and EU membership (2005 to present).

Start (1992 to 1994)

Sunflower was founded in 1992 in Vilnius, the capital of Lithuania. Lithuania is located on the eastern coast of the Baltic Sea and is somewhat smaller than the US state of Indiana. The country has a population of 3.5 million and had one of the fastest growing economies in Europe from 2001 onward. Lithuania's economy is based on a broad industrial base (chemicals, metal processing, construction materials, food processing, and light industry), as well as solid transportation and service sectors. See Exhibit 1 for additional information.

The Sunflower Company was started with $30,000 initial capital. As indicated in Exhibit 2, the firm started with three employees: the director (founder), an accountant, and a sales agent. In the early 1990s, many opportunities existed in the new economy. It was easy to register a new company, demand for new products was high, and competition was still low. However, annual inflation exceeded 500%, the country did not have its own currency, and organized crime robbed firms or required protection money to leave firms alone.

In the early 1990s, it was very difficult to get a loan from a bank. Domestic banks were primarily interested in large companies and had little interest in new or start-up companies. The country had no foreign banks and the laws forbade companies from borrowing money from private individuals. To get around these restrictions, many companies had two sets of books. One set was presented to tax authorities, while another set reflected the actual financial situation of

---

[1] This case was written by Aldas Pranas Kriauciunas (Purdue University). It is based on interviews with the founder of Sunflower Company. The name of the company has been changed to ensure confidentiality. © Aldas Pranas Kriauciunas. Reprinted with permission.

EXHIBIT 1   Lithuania: Macro-Economic Data

YEAR	GDP CHANGE	INFLATION	CUMULATIVE FDI (€)	AVERAGE MONTHLY WAGE (US$)	UNEMPLOYMENT RATE	INTEREST RATE
1992	-15.0%	1150%	---	$18	3.0%	88%
1993	-10.0%	180%	---	$50	4.0%	30%
1994	-5.0%	40%	0.42 billion	$100	5.0%	24%
1995	3.8%	12%	0.55 billion	$150	5.5%	24%
1996	4.5%	7%	0.8 billion	$175	6.8%	16%
1997	7.0%	3%	1.2 billion	$225	7.5%	12%
1998	5.0%	0%	1.9 billion	$300	8.5%	13%
1999	-4.0%	0%	2.4 billion	$285	10.1%	13%
2000	3.0%	1%	2.7 billion	$270	11.5%	11%
2001	7.9%	0.6%	3.1 billion	$273	12.5%	8%
2002	6.8%	-1.0%	3.8 billion	$348 ($288[a])	11.3%	6%
2003	9.0%	-1.3%	4.0 billion	$441 ($304[a])	10.3%	5%
2004	7.0%	2.9%	4.7 billion	$402	8.7%	5.7%
2005	7.5%	3.0%	7.0 billion	$452	6.9%	4.7%
2006	7.5%	4.5%	8.4 billion	$641	4.7%	5.4%
2007	8.0%	8.1%	10.0 billion[b]	$855	4.3%	8.6%

[a] On February 2, 2002, Lithuania changed its exchange rate system to peg its currency to the euro, rather than the US dollar. Average monthly wages for 2002 and 2003 are reported based on the floating exchange rate. Figures in parentheses are dollar amounts based on the previous fixed exchange rate.

[b] Figure is through the third quarter of 2007.

the company, including loans from individuals. However, by 1994 banks started giving short-term loans to new firms.

One challenge for the firm was deciding what work to focus on. As Exhibit 3 shows, the firm sold metal and many other products in its first years. It even tried selling sandwiches and snacks during the visit of Pope John Paul II to Lithuania in 1993. Each product was introduced with the intent of meeting some niche demand. Since there were almost no management books or journals written in Lithuanian, small companies relied on a hit-or-miss approach in deciding what to sell.

Expansion (1995 to 1998)

As the firm grew, the set of problems and opportunities changed. Finding qualified employees continued to be a problem. This problem became even more acute from 1997 to 1998 when the prime minister significantly raised salaries for government workers. Since these government workers made up one-third of all employed people in the country, this put upward pressure on all wages. The increasing number of foreign companies in Lithuania also paid premium wages. Therefore, it became harder for small companies to hire good employees. To keep turnover low, Sunflower

EXHIBIT 2   Annual Company Data

YEAR	# OF EMPLOYEES	REVENUE (US$)	PRE-TAX PROFITS (US$)
1992	3	$15,000	N/A
1993	10	$150,000	-$7,000
1994	11	$185,000	$10,000
1995	17	$366,000	$20,000
1996	12	$455,000	$14,000
1997	23	$1,375,000	$149,000
1998	28	$1,576,250	$30,000
1999	36	$1,375,000	$18,000
2000	48	$1,650,000	$12,000
2001	45	$2,100,000	$23,000
2002	54	$2,700,000	$24,000
2003	52	$3,500,000	$22,000
2004	69	$3,700,000	-$70,000
2005	58	$3,228,000	$183,000
2006	26	$4,110,000	$129,000
2007	32 (+1 in Latvia)	$6,010,000	$166,000
2008	35 (+3 in Latvia)	$7,850,000	$214,000

All information based on December 31 of the calendar year.
2008 figures are based on March 2008 projections.

made sure salaries were paid on time, lent money to employees for personal needs, and let employees use company vehicles over the weekend. This increased employee loyalty to the firm. During this period, working with banks became easier. In late 1994, the company received its first loan—for six months at an annual rate of 40%. Western suppliers noticed the success of the company and began to sell equipment through a credit line. In this stage of growth, the product lines of the company changed significantly. The firm shifted its attention to two new areas: tire repair and store display systems.

Development of the Tire Repair Division

In 1994, competition in the current product lines increased, while simultaneously the demand for new products also increased. At that time, only two companies in Lithuania were selling tire repair equipment. Both demand and competition were growing, which provided an opportunity for Sunflower to enter into this new market. The director's education background was in transportation, so he was interested in expanding into this area. He saw that the number of cars was growing in Lithuania, indicating an increased demand for tire and car repair services. Additionally, he looked

EXHIBIT 3   **Product Lines by Year**

Product	92	93	94	95	96	97	98	99	00	01	02	03	04	05	06	07	08
Washing machines	+	+															
Tea	+	+	+														
Ferrous metals	+	+	+														
Soup		+	+														
Spices		+	+														
Matches		+	+														
Chocolate cream		+	+														
Shoes		+	+														
Coffee		+	+														
Detergent		+	+														
Candy		+	+														
Cookies		+	+														
Bras		+	+														
Calculators			+														
Lightbulbs			+	+													
Store display systems			+	+	+	+	+	+	+	+	+	+	+	+			
Service station equipment			+	+	+	+	+	+	+	+	+	+	+	+	+	+	+
Tire repair materials			+	+	+	+	+	+	+	+	+	+	+	+	+	+	+
Tires				+	+	+	+	+	+								
Car windshields				+	+												
Service station tools								+	+	+	+	+	+	+	+	+	+
Auto diagnostic equipment								+	+	+	+	+	+	+	+	+	+
Kitchen cabinets									+	+	+	+	+	+			
Office furniture											+	+	+	+			
Hotel furniture											+	+	+	+			

at trends in Poland, which was approximately three years ahead of Lithuania in regards to the tire repair market. In Poland, car repair shops were already buying new equipment.

To receive training, the firm's technicians traveled to Poland to visit tire repair equipment vendors. These vendors became Sunflower's initial partners and were very helpful as the company entered the tire repair market in Lithuania. The Polish partners provided training on the products and market analysis. In late 1995, Sunflower began to bypass the Polish middlemen and buy directly from Western suppliers. Buying direct helped reduce the purchase costs of the equipment.

The competition in this market increased annually. The company decided to deal with competition by specializing in a key segment. Sunflower chose tire repair as the area of specialty and was able to provide everything associated with that line of work: equipment, materials, and consultations. Entry was achieved in three stages: (1) establishing a network of sales agents throughout the country; (2) starting an advertising campaign; and (3) helping companies prepare business plans so they could get financing to buy the firm's equipment. At one time, the company had a 50% market share of its niche market, largely by attracting clients that no one had targeted before.

Development of the Store Display Division

In the mid-1990s, there was an increase in the number of small stores in Lithuania as well as the remodeling of existing stores. These stores needed new shelves, display cases, layout design, and related products. Since one of Sunflower's employees was an architect, this seemed like an area of high potential for the company. To learn about designing in-store displays, the company's staff took trips to Poland to learn about the market and materials used and began to import store display cases and shelving materials.

The market for store displays, cases, and shelves can be split into two parts: food stores and non-food stores. Sunflower targeted both parts of the market, but did not do well in either segment. Food stores needed refrigeration systems, but the company did not have sufficient technical experience for that line of work. Attention to the food stores took time and energy away from focusing on the non-food stores where the company could have done well. Additionally,

two changes occurred in the market in a short period of time. The first change was that the competition moved from Polish suppliers to Italian suppliers for higher-quality materials. The second change was that competitors began to produce display cases and shelves from raw materials rather than purchasing completed units. These two changes allowed the competition to increase quality and cut prices. The sales in this area for Sunflower fell in 1998 and 1999.

Crisis (1999 to 2000)

In August 1998, Russia devalued its currency, the ruble. The effect hit Lithuania in late 1999 and the economy contracted. Although retail sales fell 15%, capital investments fell 50%. This significantly affected Sunflower since both its product lines were investment-type goods and fewer retail stores and tire repair shops were opening up.

Tire Repair Equipment

It became more difficult for companies to finance purchases and investments. Banks reduced lending, making it difficult for smaller companies to get loans. One solution initiated by Sunflower's director was to broker agreements between Lithuanian service stations and foreign companies such as Shell, Mobil, and BP. The agreement provided exclusive distributorships for motor oil through Lithuanian service stations. The foreign company also financed tire repair materials and equipment, which Sunflower would supply. The second solution was for Sunflower to become involved in the leasing process. Since Lithuanian collateral laws were not fully developed, many leasing companies sprung up. Sunflower learned how to prepare documents for leasing companies, so that leasing companies only had to process the paperwork. In this way, the leasing company financed the equipment, Sunflower kept sales going, and the service stations received the equipment they needed.

Store Display

Sunflower was being pushed out of the store display market. The management decided to enter store furniture production and predicted that the Russian crisis would end in the fall of 1999. The strategy was to start up production when the market would be in the recovery stage and market entry would be easier. However, the economic crisis grew worse and production began during the worst phase of the recession. The company director was ready to initiate layoffs. However, a large unexpected contract with a new store in Uzbekistan (Central Asia) to install all its shelving and display cases allowed the division to keep working even when local demand was low.

Kitchen Cabinet Production

Production of store displays began in November 1999 and kitchen furniture production began in December 1999. The kitchen cabinet market had a lot of competition. To compete, Sunflower purchased multitask equipment with short set-up times. This allowed them to undertake special orders at half the price of the competition. Additionally, the competition was laying off production workers and managers due to the impact of the Russian economic crisis. Sunflower hired these employees and quickly built a strong production division. Through these steps, in March 2000, Sunflower won one of the top awards in Lithuania's largest annual furniture exhibition for its kitchen furniture, even though the competition was much larger with annual revenues of $15 million to $20 million, employing from 500 to 800 workers.

Recovery (2001 to 2004)

As Lithuania's economy began to recover, the company prepared to take advantage of predicted demand increase. The firm standardized production processes to improve quality and delivery times, established ties with strategic partners and suppliers, increased the length of loans to three years, and invested $150,000 to purchase and renovate much larger production facilities.

The tire repair market faced a different set of challenges. The number of small, independent service stations was falling and the importance of large, domestic service station chains was increasing. The surviving independent chains were forming their own networks to give themselves better bargaining power, but they only made up 15% percent of the market. Foreign companies were trying to lock-in local companies

in long-term contracts and also establishing contracts with service stations in smaller cities.

On May 1, 2004, Lithuania became a member of the European Union. Overnight, the country became part of a market with over 350 million inhabitants. Sunflower's revenues had increased 20% percent over the past year due to increased foreign interest in furniture. Exports westward were rising but the quality, price, and delivery requirements were stricter than what the company had faced previously. The company had already paid fines due to late delivery. Foreign companies expanding in Lithuania were placing orders for Sunflower's furniture and store display systems. However, the orders were based on low labor costs, which were likely to increase in the future. Being part of the EU meant the firm could focus even more than before, but it was not clear what to focus on. The director was considering how to adjust the firm's strategy, handle the continued growth of the company, and take advantage of increased demand.

EU Membership (2005 to Present)

From the start of EU membership, Sunflower tried to balance both product lines. However, the firm found it could not compete with low-cost Chinese labor for furniture manufacturing. In the director's view, the Chinese factories were very strong in high-volume manufacturing. Also, the labor costs in Lithuania were increasing too quickly for the company to be competitive. Due to these reasons, the director sold the furniture manufacturing lines to another company in mid-2005. He also arranged for the employees to be transferred, and the building was rented out to the company purchasing the equipment. This turned out to be a good decision since the company that took over the furniture operations has not been able to invest in new technology, and labor costs have increased even more quickly than expected.

The tire repair market has continued to grow. Although consolidation has occurred, Sunflower has done well as a supplier rather than as a competitor. The company continues to provide a package of materials, equipment, training, repair, and leasing assistance. Foreign companies have not moved into this market, as it is rather small and the pay rates for services (as opposed to manual labor) are rather low.

The sale of the furniture business allowed the company to improve its tire repair support business. In 2005, Sunflower provided all its agents with hand-held billing/printer devices that allowed for real-time inventory ordering and tracking, along with printing bills and receipts for customers. In early 2007, the company installed GPS tracking devices on all technician automobiles throughout the country. This allowed the supervisor to track each vehicle and ensure that the billing for repairs matched the time the technician spent on-site. The director indicated that performance improved quickly, since the technicians could not lie to the supervisor about where they were located.

In 2007, the company decided to enter the Latvian market. This was the first international expansion for the company. They had considered entering Belarus in 1998, but the Russian crisis made conditions unfavorable. The Latvian market is favorable since the tire repair market is underdeveloped, especially with respect to suppliers. Also, since Latvia is an EU member, the new Sunflower employees in Latvia report directly to the manager in Vilnius, Lithuania. There is no overhead and the employees initially work from home. The employees there sell the same items as in Lithuania. They also have the same handheld devices and their cars, too, are equipped with the GPS tracking devices. By the end of 2008, the director expects that just under 10% of Sunflower's revenue will come from Latvia. Future geographic expansion targets are Estonia or Poland.

Looking ahead, the director sees four challenges for the company:

1. *Splitting the company up and/or selling a part of the company*. The firm could be split in four ways: sales network (in Lithuania and Latvia), equipment specialists, repair technicians, and real estate (the rented-out factory). Although the first three work well together, there is no requirement that Sunflower own all those pieces.

2. *Retaining people*. Currently, 67% of costs are people-related, for items such as salary, training, and communications. The director has initiated a program through which employees are vested after five years. However, it will become even more difficult to keep employees given EU-wide employment opportunities that are now available to Lithuanians.

3. *Applying information technology*. Currently, one supervisor can track about 15 employees. Over time, the director believes this number can increase to 30. Over the past several years, the amount of overhead had not increased even as the number of salespeople and specialists increased. Sunflower needs to find a balance between effective technology and effective management.

4. *Managing country and regional economic factors*. Although large economic crises such as that in the 1990s are not expected, regional or cyclical slowdowns are possible. The director believes that with good employees, the firm can adjust to any economic situation. Hence, the priority on retaining employees.

Case Discussion Questions

1. Why has Sunflower been successful even though it has frequently changed its product lines and strategy? Would this approach work in established markets?

2. How has Lithuania's economic development and EU membership created both opportunities and challenges?

3. How should Sunflower address its four main challenges?

3i Group and Little Sheep[1]

Lily Fang
INSEAD

Roger Leeds
Johns Hopkins University, School of Advanced International Studies

How and why an unlikely yet productive relationship was forged between a large, well-established global private equity firm and a rapidly growing Chinese restaurant chain.

> Many people grow a company like raising a pig. The pig gets fat; you kill it and make money. I grow my company like raising a son. The average life span of a restaurant is less than three years in China. I want Little Sheep to last a century.
>
> —Zhang Gang, Founder, Little Sheep Catering Chain Co.

> Helping a great business to realize its potential takes a lot more than just capital. It is ultimately about the people, thus your relationship with the management team and the sort of support you can provide, such as introductions to key industry expertise and relevant operational best practice, is very important.
>
> —Anna Cheung, 3i Partner, China

3i Group Plc

3i Group plc is one of the oldest private equity firms in the world, with a track record dating back to 1945 when the British government and a consortium of banks founded two organizations—the Industrial and Commercial Finance Corporation (ICFC) and the Finance Corporation for Industry (FCI)—to bridge the financing gap afflicting small and medium-sized enterprises (SMEs) in the aftermath of World War II.[2] In 1975, these two corporations merged, and in 1983 the combined entity was renamed 3i—"investors in industry." In 1994, 3i was listed on the London Stock Exchange, becoming the first large private equity fund to go public and have access to permanent capital. 3i invests in a wide variety of businesses through its five lines: buyouts, growth capital, venture capital, infrastructure, and quoted private equity (see Exhibit 1).[3]

Expanding its geographic footprint beyond the UK and Europe, 3i today has offices in 14 countries across Europe, Asia, and the United States, and has made investments in more than 30 countries. The firm opened its first Asia office in Singapore in 1997, followed by a second office in Hong Kong four years later, and offices in Shanghai, Mumbai, and Beijing subsequently. During fiscal year 2006, 16% of the group's new investments were in Asia. Alongside the geographic shift, 3i's investment strategy has also evolved, with an

---

[1] This case was written by Lily Fang (INSEAD) and Roger Leeds (SAIS, Johns Hopkins University). It was originally published in 2008 as "3i Group plc and Little Sheep" by the World Economic Forum USA, Inc., as part of *Globalization of Alternative Investments Working Papers, Volume 1 The Global Economic Impact of Private Equity Report 2008*. Edited by Josh Lerner and Anuradha Gurung. (www.weforum.org/pdf/cgi/Full_Report.pdf). © 2008 World Economic Forum, Lily Fang, and Roger Leeds. Reprinted with permission.

[2] The perceived funding gap—the "Macmillan gap"—was scrutinized back in 1929 in a report by a committee under the chairmanship of Lord Macmillan. The founding of ICFC, predecessor of 3i, was closely linked to one suggestion in the Macmillan Report.

[3] 3i's growth capital and venture capital investments are made from its balance sheet, while the group invests in buyouts through its €5 billion Eurofund V. During 2007, both the infrastructure and quoted private equity business lines raised new funds that are listed on the London Stock Exchange.

EXHIBIT 1   Summary Information on 3i's Business Lines

		Growth Capital	Venture Capital	Infrastructure	Quoted Public Equity	Total
	Buyouts					
3i's own capital	1,281	1,460	741	469	20	3,971
Third-party funds	2,129	227	15	385	0	2,756
Total	3,410	1,687	756	854	20	6,727

Figures (in millions £)

Source: 3i Annual Report 2007.

emphasis on making fewer, larger, and more sector-focused investments. In Asia, the group's average investment size has been about $40–$50 million, and sectors in focus included consumer-related goods and services, health care and energy.

These changes in investment strategy were consistent with a decision to become more actively involved in its portfolio companies, returning to the firm's original *modus operandi* as an "investor in industry." To better serve its portfolio companies, 3i developed two unique programs: People Program and Business Development Practice. *People Program* is a highly sophisticated approach to cultivating relationships internationally with seasoned executives and industry experts whom 3i regularly calls upon to assist the deal team at various stages of the investment process, from due diligence to post-investment operational support. While many private equity groups rely upon industry experts, 3i's *People Program* is unique in its scale and 20-year history of building an enviable Rolodex. Chris Rowlands, 3i's managing director for Asia, explained: "At 3i, this is not a nice-to-have, or an afterthought. This is at the heart of our investment model."

The second distinctive 3i program, the *Business Development Practice*, is a dedicated resource to help 3i's portfolio companies expand their operations internationally. Initially this grew out of a demand from European firms wanting to gain entry to Asia, but the team is increasingly working with Asian firms seeking to tap into the European and US markets,

and Rowlands believes it "is not only a service for our portfolio companies, but we believe it directly increases our investment value as well."

Inner Mongolia Little Sheep Catering Chain Co., Ltd.

Entrepreneurial Beginnings

In 1999, an entrepreneur called Zhang Gang founded Little Sheep Catering Chain Co. in Inner Mongolia, one of the most remote and underdeveloped corners of the world. One of the five autonomous regions in China, Inner Mongolia's economy was primarily agrarian and until the 1990s had ranked among the country's poorest regions. But this began to change dramatically with the economic reform programs initiated by Deng Xiaoping in the 1980s. The combination of a reform-minded regional government and rich natural resources provided strong impetus for Inner Mongolia's economic growth. By 2006, Inner Mongolia had been transformed into one of the wealthiest regions in terms of GDP per capita.[4]

Although with no formal business education, Zhang (ethnic Han Chinese) was an opportunistic and intuitive businessman long before he founded Little Sheep. A short stint as a factory worker in Baotou Steel Factory at an early age led Zhang to conclude that a career as a worker in a state-owned factory would be "very repressive." He then ventured into

---

[4] In 2006, Inner Mongolia's GDP per capita ranked number 10 among Chinese regions, behind only nine wealthy coastal provinces (GDP per capita ranking data from wikipedia.com, November 2007).

clothes retailing while still a teenager and, by the early 1990s, had accumulated enough capital to enter the cell phone business, eventually rising to become the sole distributor of cell phone equipment in Inner Mongolia.

Zhang initially thought about entering the food business as a hobby. He focused on a popular dish in Northern China called "hot pot"—a pot of boiling soup that sits atop a small, table-top stove to which diners add thinly sliced meat and vegetables. Traditionally, the cooked food is then dipped in flavored sauces. Zhang wanted to improve the soup base so there would be no need to dip the cooked food in sauces—he wanted to create a healthier and more naturally flavored hot pot. After many trials and tastings, he finally settled on a unique recipe containing over 60 spices and herbs. Only then did he begin thinking about it as a business. "It made sense—I always wanted to have a basic business, selling something simple that people wanted," he recalled.

Zhang named his venture Little Sheep because locally raised lamb is a staple in the Mongolian diet, and thinly sliced lamb would be the specialty in his new restaurant. He opened the first Little Sheep restaurant in Baotou, a large city in Inner Mongolia on August 8, 1999, and it was an instant success. By the second day, long lines of customers queued up outside the restaurant, an unprecedented phenomenon in a city where people were unaccustomed to waiting in line for supper. Based on this early success, Zhang managed to open two additional restaurants in Baotou within two months, with an equally enthusiastic customer response.

The Trademark Battle

As Zhang witnessed the surprising popularity of Little Sheep, his business intuition immediately set in. Once word spread about the phenomenal early success of the restaurants, he knew others would try to replicate his business model and even use the Little Sheep name, undermining the brand value. As early as October 1999, just as he was opening his second and third restaurants, Zhang submitted his first application to the National Trademark Office, the official government agency in charge of intellectual property matters. This proved to be the start of a battle that would drag on for nearly seven years, until Little Sheep was finally awarded trademark protection in June 2006. Ironically, it took Little Sheep longer to be granted trademark protection in China than in several overseas markets. Reflecting on this drawn-out experience with the government authorities, Zhang lamented that this was his "single biggest headache" during the entire history of the firm. Not only would this have an unexpected impact on Little Sheep's growth strategy, it also would sow the seeds in Zhang's mind to bring Little Sheep to the public market.

Rapid Growth and Strategic Re-orientation

The extraordinary success of the first three restaurants spurred Zhang to expand with lightning speed throughout the country. By the end of 2002, just over three years after opening the doors to his first restaurant in Baotou, the company had established a nationwide chain of more than 500 restaurants. Ironically, the lack of trademark protection was as much a driver of rapid expansion as the founder's ambition and entrepreneurial talent. "I didn't have the luxury to wait. I had to move fast to grab market. Otherwise, anyone could start a Little Sheep and we had no legal recourse to fight back," Zhang explained.

But this success came at a high cost, and by the end of 2002 the company was suffering from serious growing pains. While the rapid expansion had been primarily driven by an aggressive franchise strategy, the company's thin management ranks resulted in very weak oversight of the franchisees. The problems were aggravated when media reports began to appear claiming substandard quality and service in certain Little Sheep franchise stores, inevitably damaging the brand.

At the end of 2002, Zhang faced a critical decision: Should the company curtail growth and scale back the franchises until his management team could be strengthened, even though this would result in the immediate loss of substantial franchise fees? If so, he would risk alienating a growing roster of franchise applicants who were waiting to capitalize on the brand and open Little Sheep restaurants. Resisting the temptation to maximize short-term profits, Zhang decided to temporarily halt the awarding of new franchises in the following year. In addition, he initiated efforts to more closely monitor the performance of the existing franchises, and designated one of his long-time lieutenants, Zhang Zhan Hai, to be in charge of the task.

EXHIBIT 2   **Major Events in Little Sheep's Corporate History**

Date	Event
Aug-99	First Little Sheep restaurant opened
Oct-99	Second and third Little Sheep restaurants opened, making it a chain
May-01	Little Sheep set up subsidiary company in Shanghai
Jan-02	Little Sheep set up subsidiary company in Beijing
Jan-02	Little Sheep set up subsidiary company in Shenzhen
Aug-02	Little Sheep passed ISO9001 certification and China national "Green Food" certification
Jan-03	Little Sheep set up R&D and production facility for seasonings
Jan-04	Little Sheep set up subsidiary company in Hong Kong
May-04	Little Sheep opened its first restaurant in Hong Kong
Nov-04	Little Sheep became the only restaurant business to enter the "China Top 500 Businesses" list, ranking #451
Nov-04	Little Sheep obtained the "Prestigious Brand" designation in China
May-05	Little Sheep entered the "Inner Mongolia Top 50 Private Businesses" list, ranking #2
Aug-05	Little Sheep's brand was evaluated at 5.5 billion RMB, and entered "China Top 500 Most Valuable Brands" list, ranking #95
Aug-05	Little Sheep entered "China Top 500 Service Businesses" list, ranking #160 (#1 among food companies)
Sep-05	Little Sheep obtained the "China Top 100 Food Businesses" title for the third time, ranking #2
Oct-05	Little Sheep opened its first overseas direct-ownership restaurant in Toronto, Canada
Dec-05	Little Sheep entered the "China Top 500 Quality" list and "China Food and Beverages Top 10 Quality" list
May-06	Little Sheep was named one of "Inner Mongolia's Most Respected 50 Businesses"
Jun-06	Little Sheep's trademark was formally awarded

Source: Compiled from company documents.

3i's Investment in Little Sheep

Management's Goal

Gradually, Zhang's decision to scale back the expansion began to pay off. In 2004, the company strengthened its management ranks significantly by hiring as senior vice president of finance, industry veteran Lu Wen Bing, former vice president of Meng Niu (Mongolian Cow), a well-known Inner Mongolia–based dairy company. Lu brought much needed financial discipline and internal control to the company, and by 2005

Little Sheep's performance had clearly rebounded as the company collected a number of prestigious regional and national business awards, including the Little Sheep brand being ranked 95th by the World Brand Lab among "The 500 Most Valuable Chinese Brands." According to Ministry of Commerce statistics, the company had the second largest market share among China's restaurant chains, behind only the fast-food giant KFC. (See Exhibit 2 for a major-events timeline in Little Sheep's corporate history up to the 3i investment, and Exhibit 3 for the company's

EXHIBIT 3   **Little Sheep's Footprint in China (as of the end of 2005)**

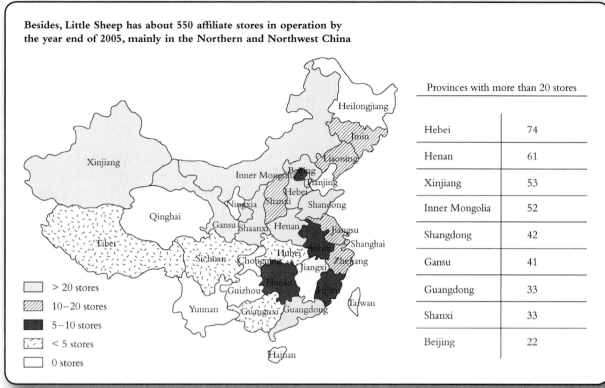

Besides, Little Sheep has about 550 affiliate stores in operation by the year end of 2005, mainly in the Northern and Northwest China

Provinces with more than 20 stores	
Hebei	74
Henan	61
Xinjiang	53
Inner Mongolia	52
Shangdong	42
Gansu	41
Guangdong	33
Shanxi	33
Beijing	22

Legend:
- > 20 stores
- 10–20 stores
- 5–10 stores
- < 5 stores
- 0 stores

Sources: Company documents.

footprint in China at the end of 2005, just before the 3i investment.)

Notwithstanding this renewed success, Zhang recognized that sustaining the company's growth would require not only financial resources but, more importantly, additional industry expertise. Like many Chinese entrepreneurs, Zhang came to believe that the ultimate validation for Little Sheep's success would be a public listing, preferably on an overseas exchange.[5] This would give the company a diversified source of capital, as well as brand recognition, and subject it to market discipline. His preference for an overseas listing was rooted in his concern about the lax listing standards on the domestic Chinese exchanges; he preferred instead an international listing. But to prepare

for an initial public offering (IPO), he believed that the company needed to attract not only additional capital, but also a partner with the capability to provide much-needed industry knowledge and expertise. "What we lacked were high-level professionals from the food and beverage industry who could help take Little Sheep to the next, higher level . . . . We needed a partner that could help us prepare for an IPO outside China," explained Zhang.

Origin of the Deal

Little Sheep's extraordinary growth and brand name recognition attracted many willing investors, including such prestigious investment banks as Morgan Stanley

---

[5] At the time, the Chinese A-share market was also closed for new public listing.

EXHIBIT 4   Growth Statistics for the Chinese Restaurant Industry

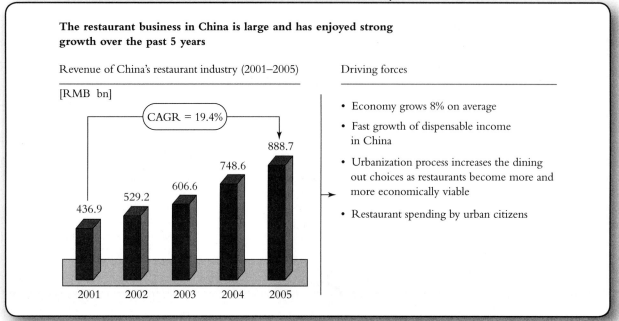

The restaurant business in China is large and has enjoyed strong growth over the past 5 years

Revenue of China's restaurant industry (2001–2005)

[RMB bn]

CAGR = 19.4%

888.7
748.6
606.6
529.2
436.9

2001   2002   2003   2004   2005

Driving forces

- Economy grows 8% on average
- Fast growth of dispensable income in China
- Urbanization process increases the dining out choices as restaurants become more and more economically viable
- Restaurant spending by urban citizens

Source: Company documents.

and Goldman Sachs. At 3i, Little Sheep was spotted by an associate director, Daizong Wang, a Wharton MBA who had recently joined the group after a four-year stint with Goldman Sachs in Hong Kong. As 3i's investment strategy in Asia was becoming more sector-focused, Wang was assigned to study the food and beverage sector, which had been growing at a rate twice as fast as China's GDP for over 15 years. As the Chinese economy began to shift towards more consumption-led growth, Wang believed that consumer-related sectors such as restaurants would offer a tremendous upside (see Exhibit 4).

Wang also noticed that even though the sector was experiencing rapid growth, prior to 2005 there had been no private equity investments due to the lack of scale in typical restaurant businesses. Unfazed, he began to analyze the market share rankings of restaurant chains in China to screen for investment targets. Little Sheep ranked second, occupying 6.2%

of the entire restaurant and catering market, behind KFC.[6] Intrigued by Little Sheep's ability to achieve scale unlike most other restaurants, Wang realized that simplicity was the key to Little Sheep's business model: "The Chinese restaurant business is fragmented because it is difficult to standardize. In most restaurants, the largest cost component is the chef, but it is difficult to achieve consistency. Little Sheep is different because customers cook their own food in the hot pot, which eliminates the need for a chef. This do-it-yourself style of dining and the ease of standardization made this business capable of scale." In fact, these characteristics made hot-pot restaurants a significant subsector of the total restaurant industry, accounting for more than 20% of all consumer spending on restaurants, with Little Sheep the clear market leader with one-third of total hot-pot revenue (see Exhibit 5). Based on this analysis, Daizong Wang concluded, "From the very beginning, I wanted to invest in this business."

---

[6] According to *Euromonitor,* Little Sheep has a higher, 9.9% market share among China's full-service restaurant chains, excluding fast food.

EXHIBIT 5   Hot Pot Restaurant as a Subsector of the Dining Industry

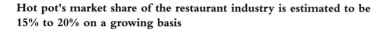

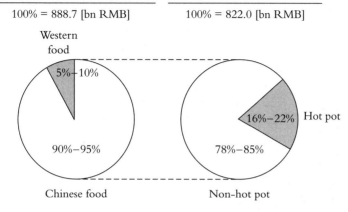

Hot pot's market share of the restaurant industry is estimated to be 15% to 20% on a growing basis

Total restaurant industry in 2005	Chinese food volume in 2005	Comments
100% = 888.7 [bn RMB]	100% = 822.0 [bn RMB]	

Western food

5%–10%

90%–95%

Chinese food

16%–22% Hot pot

78%–85%

Non-hot pot

Comments

- Calculation based on data from China Restaurants in Chain Statistics Yearbook

- Hot pot market share shows an upward trend
  - 14.7% in 2003
  - 21.2% in 2004

- A sample telephone survey conducted by Roland Berger staff showed on average hot pot dining represents 15%–20% of overall restaurant spending

Source: Company documents.

His next step, in August 2005, was to cold call Little Sheep's senior vice president of finance, Lu Wen Bing. After making his pitch to Lu, whom Wang found "surprisingly open minded [about private equity]," he was invited to a formal meeting in Baotou, Little Sheep's headquarters. Reflecting on the initial exchange, Wang said: "At a time when few in China understood the difference between private equity and investment banking, Lu was very sophisticated and ahead of the curve." It turned out that earlier in his career, Lu had worked on the senior management team of Meng Niu when it received a widely publicized investment from Morgan Stanley and CDH, a well-known Chinese private equity fund. Based on this previous experience, he was *predisposed* to working with a private equity investor.

Winning the Mandate

After the initial meeting in August, 3i engaged in a four-month competition with other private equity suitors, including Goldman Sachs and Morgan Stanley, before finally being awarded the Little Sheep mandate. During this period, Anna Cheung, a 3i partner based in Hong Kong, was assigned as the senior member on the team working with Wang to secure the mandate. The investment team flew to Baotou frequently, getting to know Little Sheep's senior management team, and explaining 3i's investment philosophy. At the same time, they spoke with a number of research analysts covering the Hong Kong and Chinese restaurant sector to learn more about the sector, and shared their findings with Little Sheep senior management. The team also tapped into 3i's network of industry experts (via 3i's *People Program*) and identified Nish Kankiwala, former president of Burger King International, as a suitable advisor for Little Sheep. As the top executive at one of the world's largest fast-food restaurant chains, Kankiwala would bring a wealth of sorely needed knowledge about the franchise business. At the request of the 3i team, Kankiwala flew to Beijing and spent a number of days meeting with Little Sheep's entire senior management team, learning the ups and downs of the company's performance, and discussing the relevance of his own experience to Little Sheep's future strategy. This was the first time that Little Sheep management had direct access to a world-class expert with a deep understanding of their business and they were impressed by 3i's commitment and ready access to this caliber of expertise.

But the specter of Goldman Sachs continued to lurk in the background. Wang heard that his former Goldman colleagues were visiting Little Sheep in Baotou in late 2005, so he immediately flew to Baotou and was "prepared to sit there until we signed the term sheet." His persistence paid off and four months after Wang's August cold call, 3i signed a term sheet with Little Sheep, agreeing to a $25 million equity investment for a minority stake in the company. (Prax Capital, a private equity fund focused on Chinese investments, invested $5 million as a co-investor.) The transaction closed six months later in June 2006, and 3i's real value-add to the company began to take shape.

Post-investment Value Creation

Forming a Strategic Blueprint

During the six-month period between the signing of the mandate in late 2005 and the final closing in June 2006, 3i worked closely with Little Sheep management to clarify a number of strategic questions the company needed to address. An agreement was reached to engage Roland Berger, a strategic consulting company, to provide fact-based analysis as a basis for resolving some of the most pressing issues.

Based on extensive data collection and analysis, the consultants made a number of specific recommendations, such as optimal store size and location in different submarkets,[7] and how the company should overhaul its existing franchises (as described in the next section). These findings and recommendations became the basis of a blueprint that outlined a step-by-step effort to professionalize and improve the company's operations. When the analysis and recommendations were presented to the Little Sheep board, the response was highly favorable.

Mapping Strategy to Operations: The 180-Day Plan

Aided by the strategic insights gained from Roland Berger's report, 3i's Wang drafted a "180-day plan," a detailed work plan of tasks that the company needed to address in the ensuing six months, including specific financial, legal, operational, and HR issues (see Exhibit 6). After discussing the plan with management and obtaining their full commitment to executing it, its progress was then continuously tracked and updated. 3i partner Anna Cheung explained: "The 180-day plan helped to provide structure and a time frame that gave all parties involved a goal to work towards."

This detailed level of post-investment involvement is standard for all 3i investments, and it confirmed for Little Sheep management that 3i was willing and able to provide the nonfinancial benefits they had been seeking from their private equity investor.

Strengthening the Management Team and the Board

Both 3i and Little Sheep understood clearly that a critical task for the company prior to a public listing was strengthening the management team and board structure. Little Sheep's management team had a high level of integrity and drive, but lacked depth: the entire top management team consisted of founder and CEO, Zhang; a senior vice president of finance; and three regional vice presidents (see Exhibit 7). Even more significantly, as Wang remarked, "the company lacked systems such as centralized operation management, new-store development, and marketing teams, which were crucial for the company to continue to grow in a coordinated manner." Through the years, the company had been carried forward almost entirely by a small team of managers united and motivated by the founder's sheer personal strength and charm. "The founder, Mr Zhang, is an inspirational person," remarked Cheung. As one of Zhang's lieutenants would confirm, he was "the heart and soul" of the business. But there was a pressing need to recruit additional professional managers, install management information systems, and revamp the structure and responsibilities of the board.

In this regard, 3i was instrumental in helping Little Sheep gradually put a strong team and a governance system in place. Once 3i made the investment, Cheung and Wang both joined the board as non-executive

---

[7] For example, based on profitability analysis, the consultants found that the optimal store size for tier-1, tier-2, and tier-3 cities are 1,200 m^2, 600 m^2, and 300 m^2, respectively, and that the reason for most underperforming stores (profitability < 5% of sales) was due to a wrong store location.

EXHIBIT 6   An Excerpt from the "180-Day Plan"

#	ISSUES	TIMING	ACTION/OUTPUT
I.	**Legal**		
. . .			
g.	Lease agreement	Within 6 months.	- Renew lease agreements that have expired or are to expire soon by 31 July 2006. - Revise certain lease agreements (identified in legal due diligence) by 31 July 2006. - . . .
. . .			-
i.	Other permits and certificates	Within 12 months.	- Obtain necessary certificates or evidence for compliance with fire safety, environmental protection, and sewage fees within 12 months.
II.	**Financial**		
a.	Internal system	Within 3 months – report and recommendations; within 12 months – adoption of recommendations.	- . . . - Engage a leading accountant to examine systems, processes, controls, and information capture to ensure robust, speedy, and accurate information flow. - Report outlining adequacy of existing systems and recommendations for improvements to be presented at first Board meeting post-completion. Satisfactory system should be in place in 12 months. - . . .
. . .			
III.	**Business and Operations**		
. . .			
c.	New site selection	By 31 September 2006.	- Standardize and formalize the location assessment process. - Set up a dedicated team responsible for new site selection for the whole group. - Establish a set of criteria and parameters, such as those in Roland Berger's report. - . . .
. . .			
e.	Store-level operational improvement	Assign responsibilities and agree on an action plan within 3 months.	- Refine the operations manual. - Step up staff trainings and communications. - Enhance internal audit and increase the frequency of store checks. - Implement the KPI benchmark at city/provincial, regional, and national levels.
. . .			-

Source: Company documents.

EXHIBIT 7   Little Sheep's Management Team before 3i's Investment

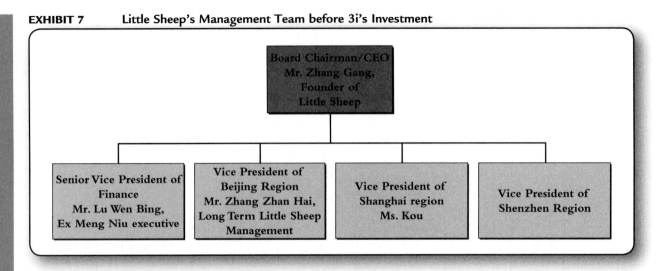

directors. 3i also recruited two additional independent directors with strong industry experience: Nish Kankiwala, the former president of Burger King International, who played a part in the deal initiation process; and Yuka Yeung, CEO of the KFC franchise in Hong Kong. Both individuals had extensive experience in the food industry and were exactly the type of high-level industry people Little Sheep had been looking for.

Instead of viewing these new directors as outsiders, however, Little Sheep's top management enthusiastically welcomed them as partners capable of adding considerable value to the company. When 3i proposed four board meetings per year, Little Sheep came back and asked for more. "Little Sheep is the only company I have worked with that has asked for more board meetings . . . . Zhang is an extraordinary entrepreneur, but he was very humble and eager to learn. This is one of the most impressive things about the company," Cheung commented.

The newly constituted board immediately began to focus on adding depth to the management team. Up to this point, Zhang had served as both the board chairman and the CEO and had tended to delegate much of routine management to members of his senior management team. One of the first 3i recommendations was to recruit a full-time CEO dedicated to overseeing day-to-day management of the business. "We practically insisted on it," recalled Wang.

In addition, based on 3i's recommendation, the board agreed to create new positions for a COO and a CFO, but emblematic of China's thin supply of professional managers, it would take more than a year to recruit the right candidates. (See Exhibit 8 for Little Sheep's organization chart as of October 2007.)

Creating a Standards Committee

Until these three new senior executives could be recruited, an interim management solution was needed. 3i proposed—and the board agreed—to create a Standards Committee consisting of Little Sheep's existing management team, plus Wang. The committee's purpose was to serve as interim CEO, focusing especially on enhancing the communication and coordination among the three regional operations until a proper headquarters could be set up. From June to September 2006, the committee met biweekly to discuss detailed operational matters and make decisions to be carried out by the three regional VPs. Gradually, as internal communication improved and key headquarters functions were established, the Standards Committee evolved to become a series of monthly meetings focused more on long-term strategic issues, such as new-store developments, marketing, and budgeting. Finally, in November 2007, with the establishment of Little Sheep's new national operation headquarters in Shanghai, the committee was formally dissolved.

EXHIBIT 8   Little Sheep's Management Team after 3i's Investment

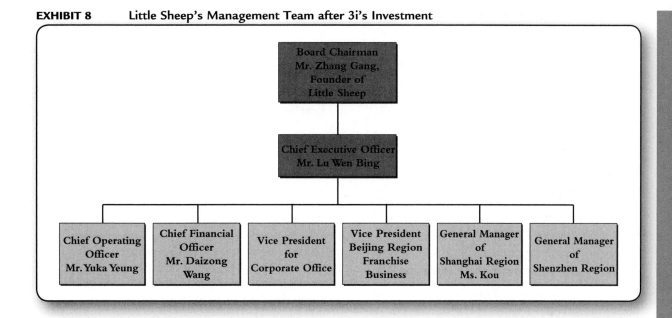

Creating and Executing a New Franchise Strategy

Although Little Sheep had taken the initiative to halt the awarding of new franchises in 2003, the existing sprawling network of over 500 franchises was not systematically addressed prior to 3i's involvement. Symptomatic of the problem was the fact that management had actually lost count of the exact number of stores in the Little Sheep network. Cleaning up the existing franchise system and designing a new franchise strategy thus became a top priority for the newly constituted board. Based on the insights from the Roland Berger report, the board came to the conclusion that the new strategy should focus on quality rather than quantity, and that the franchise system should become more centrally managed. Not only was this consistent with protecting and strengthening the Little Sheep brand, it was also made feasible by the strengthened management and headquarters capabilities. The following three-phased overhaul of the franchise system was agreed on and carried out:

- *Phase 1: Cleaning up the existing franchise system.*
  A systematic effort was taken to visit and catalogue every franchise in the country. These visits generated store-by-store information that was fed into a database created to track critical performance

indicators, and served as a basis for making decisions about the future status of each franchise. More than 200 franchises that had clearly violated the Franchise Agreement or did not meet Little Sheep's quality standards were closed. Others that were performing reasonably well had their franchise agreement renewed, and the best performing stores were bought back by Little Sheep to become directly owned as part of the new, more centralized strategy. This task was complete by the end of 2006.

- *Phase 2: Enhancing training and support to remaining franchise stores.* This phase involved stepping up the training for all franchise personnel through an elaborate new program consisting of various stages of training at headquarters, on site, and during regular national and regional franchisee meetings. In addition, headquarters staff continued to provide on-site training during their regular store visits.

- *Phase 3: Developing new franchise stores.* The final phase in the new franchise strategy was to proactively develop new stores and grow the franchise fee base. In contrast to the traditional passive expansion method of responding when potential franchisees called, Little Sheep's new active approach began with research into the local business environment, which then led to a choice of locations. The company then actively sought out restaurant operators with good reputations to run the franchise stores.

In little more than a year, this new proactive strategy transformed the profile of Little Sheep's franchise system. The company moved from having 40 directly owned stores versus over 500 franchises before the 3i investment to a more balanced mix of 101 to 260 by late 2007. Even with a dramatically decreased total store count, these fundamental changes resulted in a year-on-year revenue growth of close to 40%, about double the industry average.

Shelving the International Expansion Plan

Prior to 3i's investment, Little Sheep had an ambitious plan for international expansion. With successful restaurants already operating in Toronto and Hong Kong, management was eager to accelerate the pace of overseas growth and establish the Little Sheep brand name globally. Each regional VP was designated to lead expansion efforts in different overseas regions—North America, North Asia, and South East Asia—even though they were already stretched thin managing their domestic operations.

Little Sheep's overseas ambitions were quite common among the new generation of Chinese private enterprises. On this issue, however, 3i and Little Sheep management had different views. Even though 3i was well placed to provide introductions and on-the-ground support for an overseas expansion, it strongly recommended that Little Sheep initially focus on strengthening domestic operations rather than rushing into overseas expansion. "Given the vast and yet untapped opportunities in China's restaurant industry, it is strategically important for Little Sheep to leverage the leading market share and brand name it has already established to secure a dominant market position at home before expanding its operations overseas," Cheung explained.

Although management initially resisted this 3i recommendation, Zhang later conceded that this was a sensible approach. Looking back on the incident, one of the independent directors viewed the outcome as one more example of the company's fundamental

strength: "They [Little Sheep management] are open-minded, and very willing to listen," remarked Yuka Yeung, "which is really remarkable. It is a learning company."

Early Results

From the time of 3i's investment in mid-2006 until the end of 2007, Little Sheep opened 37 new stores and achieved a year-on-year revenue growth rate of 40%, far in excess of the 15%–20% average growth in China's food sector. The strong revenue growth was also fueled by the evolution of Little Sheep from a pure restaurant business into a more diversified food and beverages group with two meat-processing facilities, a packaged-seasoning plant, a logistics company, and a number of regional subsidiary companies. Little Sheep also completed its search for new senior executive talent: Daizong Wang validated his confidence in Little Sheep by resigning from 3i in October 2007 to become Little Sheep's new CFO, and Yuka Yeung, one of the independent directors and the former CEO of KFC's Hong Kong franchise, became the new COO.

Conclusions

At first glance, the pairing of 3i, a global private equity group with almost no track record in China, and a restaurant chain with origins in remote Inner Mongolia, might seem like an odd and unlikely match. But the story of their relationship conforms to many of the fundamental characteristics of successful private equity transactions, especially in emerging markets. First, the initial driver that allowed 3i to win the mandate after an intense contest with better-known competitors was chemistry, or the ability to make the founder comfortable with its industry expertise, commitment to the company, and approach to post-investment value creation. Money was secondary. Second, Little Sheep's founder had the foresight and self-confidence to recognize the value of accepting an *active* investor into his company. Even though he had never heard of 3i before meeting Daizong Wang, he and his senior management team exhibited an openness and eagerness to learn from outsiders, which is not always the case, especially with closely held family-run firms in emerging markets. Third, this is a textbook case of the positive results that stem from closely aligned interests between a private equity investor and the management of a portfolio company. From the beginning, the 3i team was exceptionally hands-on, working closely with the company's senior management team on a continuous basis to make significant changes in the company, always with an eye to building value and moving closer to the day when Little Sheep would be positioned to successfully execute an IPO. The combination of these three factors goes far to explain the ingredients required for successful private equity transactions in emerging markets, or anywhere.

Case Discussion Questions

1. From an industry-based view, identify some of the competitive forces affecting the Chinese restaurant industry.

2. What are the key factors that explain the success of Little Sheep? What are the main obstacles associated with its continued growth?

3. From a resource-based view, explain the nonfinancial benefits 3i can bring to Little Sheep. In other words, why did 3i win the competition against other private equity suitors such as Goldman Sachs and Morgan Stanley?

4. Compare and contrast the similarities and differences between the typical mid-sized private equity investment in the West and such investments in China (as captured by this case). If you were a manager working for a Western private equity firm (such as 3i), what lessons would you draw from this case?

5. If you were an entrepreneur at a firm in China (such as Little Sheep) or in emerging economies in general, what lessons would you draw from this case?

Building a Better Rat Trap[1]

Siri Terjesen

Texas Christian University and *Queensland University of Technology*

A better rat trap is being developed and commercialized for the Irula tribe in rural India.

Sethu Sethunarayanan, director of the nonprofit nongovernmental organization (NGO) Center for Development of Disadvantaged People (CDDP), beamed as World Bank President James Wolfensohn presented him with the prestigious Global Development Marketplace award for using innovative technologies to alleviate poverty. At the podium, Sethu provided a brief overview of his winning project:

> "There are three million poor Irula indigenous tribal people of untouchable status in India who make their income by catching rats in agricultural fields. They use a clay pot filled with burning straw to smoke these rats out of their burrows. Their mouths and hands touch the pot, and they are severely affected by heart, skin, eye, and respiratory problems. They are only successful 40% of the time and are in poverty and unable to send their children to schools. We developed a new hand-operated steel rat trap which eliminates the health hazards completely and enables the Irula to double their income. We have an integrated self-help plan to empower them. Thank you for this award. With it, we can implement our project and make a complete socioeconomic change in the lives of millions."

As Sethu returned to his seat in the World Bank auditorium, he thought about how this journey began, on a morning walk through the impoverished Irula villages in Tamil Nadu, India.

Introduction

On a sticky morning in January 2003, Sethu walked briskly, anxious to check on the progress of a new drinking-water pump well installed in a remote Thiruvallar district village. Sethu wanted to make sure the new pump was installed properly so the Irula people who live in this village no longer had to bring water from a few miles away.

Seeing Sethu, the Irula villagers greeted him eagerly and escorted him to the well. Sethu was pleased to see that the pump worked perfectly, but was exhausted from his two-mile hike. He asked a lady villager for some water to drink. While she went inside her mud hut to retrieve a cup, Sethu glanced at a clay pot in front of the hut door and noticed a similar pot in front of most of the huts. Thinking he might be able to drink out of this pot, he picked it up, but noticed that, in addition to the top opening, there was a small hole at the base of the pot. He put the pot down and picked up a neighbor's pot which also had an extra hole. Sethu recalled the subsequent conversation,

> "I asked the lady, 'How will you carry water in the holed pot?' She replied with a sarcastic smile, 'This is not for carrying water, but for killing rats.' I knew that Irula income is derived, in large

[1] This case was written by Siri Terjesen (Texas Christian University and Queensland University of Technology) and originally published as "Building a Better Rat Trap: Technological Innovation, Human Capital, and the Irula" in *Entrepreneurship Theory and Practice,* Volume 31, Issue 13. November 2007: 953-963. © Baylor University. Reprinted with permission. The author is grateful for the hospitality of Sethu, Karthick and the Irula villagers during her visit. The case has benefited from many conversations with Sethu, Karthick and other CDDP team members, as well as Dr. Rachel Golden, representatives of the World Bank, and leaders of local and international NGOs operating in the region.

part, from farmers' payments for catching and killing rats in their agricultural fields. The rats and the grains found in their burrows are part of the rat catchers and their families' diets. But I wanted to know how they could possibly use this pot to kill the rats. So she explained, holding the pot close to her lips and kneeling down on the dirt path, 'My husband carries this pot when he goes rat catching. He looks for a rat burrow and places the pot at its entrance. He then stuffs wet straw into the hole and lights it, creating smoke. On this little hole at the bottom, he places his mouth and blows air through, pushing the smoke out the other side of the pot and into the rat's burrow. The smoke traps the rat. Then my husband digs into the earth and gets the trapped rat. He brings it home and I cook it for dinner. But sometimes he also comes home with burned lips and hands from handling the pot when the straw is burning . . . He doesn't always catch a rat.' "

Sethu handed the pot back to the woman, but he did not stop thinking about the inefficiency of this pot and the resulting health problems. As he walked back the dirt path, he contemplated this latest challenge to help the Irula. Sethu had 25 years of experience in developing innovative solutions to improve the quality of life for poor and disadvantaged rural people. From a young age, Sethu admired Mahatma Gandhi's efforts to alleviate poverty, liberate women, create economic self-sufficiency, and end untouchability and caste discrimination in India. Sethu decided to study at India's only Gandhian university, focusing on Gandhi's methods for developing and unleashing human potential, resolving conflict, and introducing new ideas. Upon completion of his studies, Sethu was offered the opportunity to teach school or work at an NGO. Considering Gandhi's philosophy of generating the greater good and the potential impact Sethu could have on so many lives, he chose the latter. At the NGO, he specialized in developing collective self-help, needs-based ventures. In 1998, then 38-year-old Sethu established his own NGO, the CDDP, in Tamil Nadu, India.

Negotiating the Byzantine maze of philanthropic management regulations in India is not easy (Sidel,

2001). However, CDDP is one of only a handful of Indian NGOs to be recognized by the United Nations and World Bank. The organization has 23 employees and 56 volunteers. CDDP's mission is "to develop those who are disadvantaged educationally, economically, socially, and culturally through self-help and self-governing collective development activities." Or as Sethu says, "In short, to help them to help themselves." The activities are undertaken on Gandhian lines of organizing constructive development actions through mobilization of human and local resources. CDDP develops and harnesses human capital through technological innovation and entrepreneurship. CDDP's target areas are 80 villages in the Thiruvallur and Kancheepuram districts of the Tamil Nadu state and five villages in the Andhra Pradesh state of India. The programs are aimed at helping women and children belonging to socially and economically weak sectors, unorganized agriculture labor, small and marginal farmers, youth (especially those who are disorganized and misdirected), destitutes, orphans, and physically challenged and other socially and economically disadvantaged people. CDDP received the best rural development organization award from the Indian government in the year 1998. CDDP's objectives are listed in Exhibit 1.

The CDDP has several other key employees. Sethu's 26-year-old son, Karthick Sethunarayanan, has been involved in organizing and training the Irula people for five years and is an expert in the effective use of information technology for the rural poor. He holds a bachelor's degree in business administration from Madras University and a master's degree in information and communication from Bharathidasan University. In addition to his CDDP work, Karthick runs his own IT company, which has an alliance with Microsoft as well as clients in India and abroad. When driving to the villages, Karthick uses a wireless card in his laptop to access the Internet, providing a striking contrast to the road outside, populated by beggars, wandering cows, and women selling giant baskets of produce. A dynamic and engaging spirit, Karthick is keenly aware of the role of technology in transforming the world around him, and the great potential for the world's poor. He is also a talented classical Tamil singer and the villagers often ask him to sing for them.

EXHIBIT 1   CDDP Objectives

1. To promote people's organizations, especially for women/youth/village folk belonging to weaker sections and to strengthen them as self-reliant and self-governing development groups.

2. To initiate need-based training and development programs for eradicating illiteracy, ignorance, poverty, disease, and disunity among the rural poor.

3. To undertake life education activities through non-formal and Gandhian basic education systems.

4. To conduct problem-based community health activities and to regenerate faith and knowledge on indigenous systems of medicine.

5. To organize special activities for eradicating specific problems of children.

6. To implement activities aimed at environment preservation and ecological balance.

7. To propagate sustainable indigenous non-chemical agriculture activities.

8. To coordinate and cooperate with various government departments, national and international agencies, and interested individuals or groups for organizing various need-based training and development activities on the basis of the aforesaid objectives.

9. To provide other voluntary organizations with needed training, consultancy, and evaluation services.

10. To undertake necessary applied research programs on rural/urban development.

11. To organize such other activities, which will help in utilizing constructively the untapped human and natural resources available in the society.

National, Local, and Community Context

India

A recent global survey revealed that India is the world's second most entrepreneurially active country with 17.9% of the adult population involved in some type of entrepreneurship (Reynolds et al., 2002), although this activity is largely confined to members of certain castes and ethnic groups (Dana, 2006). Tamil Nadu is one of the most industrialized states in India (mostly due to the success of its capital, Chennai, India's fourth largest city and the world's 34th largest metropolitan area). However, the rural areas that the Irula populate are extremely impoverished (TNG, 2002).

The Irula

An estimated three million Irula people live in India, including 150,000 in Tamil Nadu and 250,000 in the bordering Andhra Pradesh state. The term "Irula," used for centuries, is thought to refer to either the dark complexions of the people or to their spotting in forests as silhouettes. The Irula people are considered

indigenous, and DNA tests reveal their close ancestry to African populations (Watkins et al., 2005). Until recently, the Irula people lived in forests and eked out a living by bartering or selling honey, wax, and firewood to local villages in exchange for village products. They obtained food by hunting for vegetation and wild animals in the forests. The 1976 Forest Protection Bill made the Irula lifestyle illegal, forcing moves into villages of huts with straw roofs and dirt floors. Most Irula people do not have the official right to occupy their lands, and the villages do not have electricity or roads. Sethu described the situation,

> "Irula are tribals and considered to be untouchables and unequal in society. For example, they are not allowed to use the wells of upper castes. They live in interior locations from which it is hard to reach towns and cities, and they do not interact with the community outside . . . They speak the local languages Tamil and Telegu . . . and are Hindus."

The Irula have a life expectancy of approximately 45 years. Only 5% of Irula children under 15 attend school and as a community they are 99% illiterate. They have access to government schools; however, a manager from a visiting international charity shared:

> "Even though . . . there was a panchayat [government] school close by, I could completely understand why the children would not go there—they needed to work, they seemed to be Irulas and there was not much precedent in that particular Irula community of much learning."

Today, the Irula in Thirinvallur and other districts make a living by performing physical labor for land owners. For example, men, widows, and destitute women catch rats in agricultural fields. The farmers pay the rat catchers per rat and the rat catcher's average income varies from $15–$30 per month. The rat may be the Irula's only source of meat and grains, usually consumed as one meal per day. In the past, some Irula people have starved.

Building a Better Rat Trap

Back in the office, Sethu contemplated solutions. With the help of a local mechanical engineer, Sethu fashioned a steel cylinder and hand-crank to generate air for pushing smoke into the burrow. The cylinder had a door for the straw. A wooden handle eliminated direct contact with the hot areas of the trap. He gave sample traps to 15 Irula rat catchers. Sethu met regularly with the rat catchers in order to obtain their feedback and subsequently made improvements to the trap. After six iterations over an eight-month period, Sethu was satisfied that the trap met the villagers' rat catching and safety needs.

The rat catchers brought Sethu to the fields. He remembers watching the men:

> "I asked the catcher, 'How do you find the rat?' He said 'The rat keeps his house like my wife does—very tidy, including the area outside the door. So I know when I come across a burrow hole with a clean entrance, there is a rat inside.'"

Sethu observed as the rat catchers filled the steel trap with straw. The men located a hole on the bank between two fields, and another two holes about five feet away, which they covered with dirt to prevent the rat's escape and to cause its suffocation. The lead rat catcher dug a larger entrance to the first hole, and put the trap's pipe inside. The other two men guarded the covered holes and watched as the lead rat catcher opened the trap's door, lit the straw and cranked the handle. The trap chortled as smoke filtered down the hole, emerging from another hole in the earth, which was then quickly covered. It became clear that if there was a rat inside the hole, it had been deprived of oxygen. The lead rat catcher then removed the trap and began to dig on the side of the hole, following the winding burrow. He reached down the hole and pulled out a dazed rat, stunned by smoke. The rat was then humanely killed with a blow to its head. Sethu and the rat catchers were excited—the trap was a success!

Sethu realized that he had identified a suitable technology for this opportunity and decided to seek funding for its commercialization. From past experience, Sethu knew that he would need to convince outside organizations of the merits of such an investment. He outlined the problems with the traditional pot method and the advantages of the steel trap (see Exhibits 2 and 3).

Sethu applied for a grant from the World Bank's Development Marketplace. Since 1988, the World Bank has distributed over $40 million to 1,100 projects in more than 60 countries. Sethu presented the rat trap project at the marketplace in December 2003 and received a grant for $98,500, enabling him to implement the project.

Implementation

The rat trap project was undertaken from January to December 2004 and incorporated the following key components: site visits to identify beneficiaries, health checks and treatment, preparatory workshops, factory establishment, factory training, production, establishment of women's micro-credit collectives, distribution, and project evaluation.

Site Visits to Identify Beneficiaries

Sethu and a large team of volunteers began by visiting 170 Irula villages in order to identify the most needy

EXHIBIT 2   Disadvantages of Traditional Fumigation Method

Occupational health: As the rat catcher uses his mouth to blow air through the hole of the pot, he inhales heavy amounts of smoke, leading to severe respiratory, heart, eye, and other occupational health problems. CDDP studied the rat catchers, finding that 40% have one or many of these health complications. In particular, they burn their lips, hands, and fingers.

Poor efficiency and limited income: The method is only effective in 40 of 100 attempts due to the limited air pressure from mouth blowing and the lack of constant (or even) distribution of smoke. Thus, the rat is more liable to escape. The Irula are paid per rat, and income ranges from $15 to $30 a month. The rat catchers need at least $35 a month to meet their family's minimum requirements in food, shelter, medicine, and education, and many of these basic needs are unmet.

Mud pot breaks: In the course of their work, the Irula carry the pot over long distances. The pot breaks about once every two months and a new pot costs 50¢.

Drudgery of work: The rat catcher's lack of success makes work a drudgery, leading to disinterest in the work, which in turn leaves him impoverished.

Rat menace in agriculture fields: Fewer kills lead to a greater rat menace. Rats destroy about 25% of grains in agricultural fields. This is economically devastating in a country where 85% of the population are involved in agriculture. One estimate indicates that if the rat menace were alleviated, India would be able to feed its entire population thrice a day.

individuals. The visits were conducted simultaneously every day in order to reach the target deadline. However, the visits were not without their problems. As Sethu explained:

> "We needed to take extra time and effort to explain the project to the villagers. The Irula are especially sensitive to political matters, and

at first they thought the CDDP volunteers were politicians . . . We encountered this problem in every new village we approached."

The selection criteria were health and socioeconomic need, with priority given those suffering health problems from the old pot fumigation method and whose entire income is based on rat catching.

EXHIBIT 3   Advantages of New Trap Technology

Complete elimination of occupational health hazards: The hand-operated wooden-handled trap eliminates burns to the lips and hands. There are no problems with smoke inhalation.

Doubled work efficiency: CDDP research shows that the rat catchers achieve 95% success due to the sufficient, constant, and even distribution of pressure. The rat is instantly stunned and unable to escape. Furthermore, the trap is easier to operate, enabling older men and also widowed and destitute women who did not have the stamina for mouth blowing to participate.

Doubled income: The success rate improvement more than doubles the rat catchers' income to $30 to $60. With this additional funding, the Irula can send their children to school and attend to health care needs.

No breakage: The steel trap is impossible to break.

Release from work drudgery: The rat catcher is able to undertake his work with ease, comfort, and efficacy. The Irula also take pride in working with a machine, rather than a dirty pot. They are willing to work and earn more.

Social and educational change: The additional income enables the Irula to send their children regularly to school. Members of higher castes in neighboring communities may develop respect due to the decent professional type of device.

Reduction of rat menace: The rat menace is reduced, although it is impossible to eliminate it entirely since each female rat produces up to 1,000 offspring in her lifetime.

Affordable cost: The new trap costs just $25 and is affordable for the rat catcher.

Destitute, deserted, and widowed women were also a priority and comprised 15% of beneficiaries. The selectors included members of the local government and community and farmer groups. A total of 1,500 beneficiaries were identified. One volunteer reported:

> "The enthusiasm and interest among the beneficiaries is more than we had expected. They are very much looking forward to involving themselves fully in the project activities. They feel this device is going to be a turning point in their impoverished life conditions. The response was really exemplary, so we added 278 more beneficiaries in our reserves in case the others dropped out."

Health Check and Treatment

A basic health check was completed for 1,500 beneficiaries. In some cases, special tests for tuberculosis and diabetes, as well as ECG, X-ray, and optometry exams were conducted. Treatment was begun for all affected villagers.

Preparation Workshops

Individual and collective meetings were held at both the villages and CDDP's field office. From his experience working on the water pump and other projects, Sethu knew that he would need to work closely with the Irula to elicit interest in the new technology. As he explained:

> "In the past, the Irulas have been given things by other NGOs and the government, but these things have basically been useless. So they do not like to get things for free. The only things they consider useful are those that they work for. Irula want to be involved. They have to express their needs . . . We asked about their health. We tried to find out if the pot fumigation method was causing problems and to get them to see the link between the old method and their health troubles. We ask them if they would like to solve these problems. We talk

about how important it is to be healthy and how the new technology can help them. Sometimes it takes weeks to reach a level of understanding and commitment."

Factory Establishment

A factory was established in a 60-square-foot building adjacent to CDDP's field office in the Nedumbaran village. Sethu ordered the equipment, including a welding torch and steel marking, cutting, and shaping machines. He also purchased materials for three months of production and paid other factory costs such as electricity, maintenance, wastage, tools, and labor. Based on 50 workers who work 8 hours a day, the factory has a monthly output of 400 traps, but can easily be expanded. Sethu calculated that each trap would cost $30 to produce, including $25 for raw materials and $5 for labor. Karthick negotiated wholesale prices from Tata Steel, lowering costs by $3, a savings which was then reinvested in the factory. The factory was also equipped to produce other steel products to be sold to farmers, such as knives, sickles, ploughs, grill gates, chairs, and benches. These products would be produced in the event of a drop in demand for the traps.

Factory Training

Sethu faced an important decision regarding the manufacturing of the traps: What village group should run the factory? Rat catching is predominantly undertaken by men, sometimes accompanied by their sons, while wives and older women have a historical role as domestic and productive members of the family. Selecting men, boys, or wives for factory work would upset traditional tribal roles and create friction in the community. Sethu opted to create new opportunities for young unmarried women who were unemployed. Fifty young women were invited to work in the factory. The women organized themselves into the "Tribal Women Technotrapper Producers Society" and registered as a small industries cooperative. They appointed officers and took responsibility for the factory's daily operations. CDDP transferred whole ownership of the factory to the workers so that the women could control the profits. CDDP hired two technical people to provide three months of training in manufacturing, marketing, and finance. The young Irula women, who did not have any business or manufacturing training, took great delight in their new roles. They were paid $35–$70 a month, very high for village standards and were able to provide for their siblings and parents. Sethu shared the following in a progress report:

> "To our surprise, the tribal women who were illiterates and totally new to industrial type of work grasped the industrial techniques very quickly . . . It is a source of great pride among all the villagers that the devices are made by their own women. The villagers are able to go to the factory anytime to watch them make traps."

Production

To make the trap, the young women first trace the design on the sheet metal, beginning with a long rectangle. A compass and chalk were then used to mark a circle 15 inches in diameter. From the same piece of metal, a few long rectangular strips were marked for the handle and other components. Next, a team of women pulled a heavy handle to cut the metal and drilled holes for smoke ventilation. The rectangular piece of steel was rolled through a machine to make it cylindrical. From here, two women worked together to weld the cylindrical rectangle to the circle. Finally, the door for the straw and the hand crank were added.

Women's Micro-credit Collectives

In parallel, CDDP launched a number of women micro-credit funds, each comprised of 12 to 15 women. The fund enabled the women to obtain small loans for urgent household needs or to begin self-employment activities. The fund reduced the women's dependence on exploitative moneylenders and helped the women become economically independent. Each micro-credit group had a revolving fund collected from their monthly savings and also from the interest accrued from the loan given through

their micro-credit fund. Each woman's initial contribution was $1–$2. Fund availability ranged from $200–$500, depending on each group's prerogative. The micro-credit groups were often used to purchase the new trap. Once a woman raised 50% of the payment for the trap ($12.50), she was given the trap and paid the remaining half in loan installments according to a timeline agreed to by the group.

Distribution

The trap was distributed in special village ceremonies. Since most Irula are illiterate, Sethu began by reading a ten commitment pledge. This pledge included a promise that their families will use the rat trap, or else give it back to CDDP for distribution to other families. One by one, villagers' names were read and they came forward, signing the pledge with a thumbprint and receiving the new rat trap.

Project Evaluation

An evaluation committee, composed of local World Bank employees, government officials, and development experts, met with beneficiaries, staff, and concerned communities to ascertain the impact of the project. The committee learned that many families are now able to send their children to school. The survey included indicators for improvements in health and socioeconomic standards. Based on the evaluations, the World Bank considers CDDP's rat trap initiative to be a success and has used the Knowledge Exchange to share lessons learned with other projects and suggest appropriate policy responses (total project expenses are provided in Exhibit 4). In the final progress report to the World Bank, Sethu shared:

> "We estimated that the income of the tribal rat catchers would be more than doubled when they would use the new device. To our surprise, the income is more than tripled. There is great enthusiasm among the families. Another important unexpected positive development is that the rat catchers could use the trap for catching rabbits, foxes, and other small animals which live in burrows. This fetches very high income for them."

EXHIBIT 4   Project Expenses for January through December 2004 (in US$)

Materials and Equipment: Including the purchase of factory machines and raw materials to make 1,500 traps	$67,197
Training: The making of traps and other steel items to be sold to farmers	$9,435
Health and Self-Help Groups: The identification and treatment of health problems, the formation of micro-credit and self-help groups, societies, and workshops	$7,529
Personnel	$7,053
General Administration	$2,930
Travel	$2,300
Information Dissemination	$2,056
Total Expenses	$98,500

Conclusion

Driving back from an Irula village visit with the case author, Sethu and Karthick discussed the future challenges for the rat trap project and their development work. Quoting Gandhi, Sethu said, "I do not wish to study history, I wish to make it." Sethu and Karthick identified the following major challenges: factory expansion, NGO alliances, micro-credit developments, providing support for special projects, continuing to develop technology-based solutions, fundraising, and spreading Gandhi's message.

With over 100 million small farmers in the Tamil Nadu and Andhra Pradesh states seeking the Irula rat catchers' help, the trap is in great demand. CDDP has taken orders for over 2,000 devices. Sethu considered the factory expansion options:

"We could expand the factory to more than 50 employees, but then it would need to be registered under the Big Industries Act and we would incur enormous taxes and other bureaucratic problems. Instead, we could create a number of small factories across the villages. Each could cater to the needs of people in those locations. We would also reduce transportation costs and the local people would be employed . . . If the demand for traps ever falls,

these small factories can produce steel products for farmers instead . . . We also need to figure out a way to lower our overall costs to make the traps so we can have more profit."

CDDP has received requests for assistance and alliances from over a dozen NGOs, based locally and as far afield as Sri Lanka. Sethu contemplated the best way forward:

"This technology is the best available to control rats, and the project will boost agricultural community living anywhere. But we want to make sure that we identify and train good partners. It is not easy to organize . . . We want to be able to visit those NGOs and their villages to monitor progress."

A third challenge is to determine the best loan structure that will enable the Irula to buy new traps and repay their loans. Relatedly, Sethu is eager to explore other possibilities with the micro-credit. People from other villages have also approached CDDP for help in launching collectives.

Fourth, CDDP would like to continue to devote resources towards special projects such as the release of children who are bonded laborers in other villages. CDDP has already helped some children attain their freedom. These children now attend special programs and holiday camps, including competitions in literature, dance, drama, and sports. CDDP identifies highly talented children in particular fields and sends them to specialized training institutions. CDDP also organizes special classes for children with learning disabilities and community-based education programs for orphans, destitutes, and physically challenged children. In December 2004, when the tsunami devastated the oceanfront villages in Tamil Nadu, Sethu immediately organized CDDP assistance in the form of food, shelter, grief counseling, and self-help collectives.

Sethu and his team continue to use technology to create innovative solutions for the poor, including a smokeless oven and a natural water purification system that uses materials, such as indigenous plants, which are easily found in impoverished areas. Karthick noted the need to attract fundraising to expand the projects:

> "We are thankful to all those who are helping our ventures for the upliftment of the most disadvantaged sections of people in the society. However, what we have achieved is very little. The demand on us is so heavy that we have to continuously seek patronage from various quarters."

CDDP has received other international funding. In November 2004, Karthick accepted the $50,000 San Jose Tech Museum Innovation Award for the expansion of the rat trap project to other districts. CDDP received funding for other villages from the Rachel Golden Foundation. A trained economist, Dr. Rachel Golden is a member of a World Bank special committee to the United Nations and is deeply interested in rural development. In November 2006, CDDP won another $50,000 Tech Museum award, this time for its innovative water purification system.

This case concludes with comments from the villagers whom the author interviewed, using a Tamil translator, during her site visit 18 months after the completion of the World Bank initiative:

- "As a man living with severe respiratory problems due to mouth-blowing for rat catching, I found the new device to be a God-sent property. I wish this device to be given to more people of our community."

- "My husband brings more rats home, which I skin and cook. It tastes very good. The grains that the rat kept in its hole also taste very good. Because the rat has chewed on them a little, they have a special taste which is better than ordinary grains. Would you like to come to my house for dinner with me and my family?"

- "My son and daughter now go to school in the evening. When they come home, sometimes we learn something from them."

Case Discussion Questions

1. What makes Sethu's new trap an appropriate technology?

2. What are some examples of societal problems and market failures that present an opportunity for entrepreneurs?

3. What technologies and entrepreneurial efforts could help the disadvantaged in your community?

4. What characteristics of Sethu, CDDP, and the Irula villagers enabled their success?

5. What skills did the Irula villagers develop from their training in health awareness, manufacturing, and business?

6. What might be the implications of this training on other aspects of the Irula's lives?

7. Why was micro-credit so effective for the Irula village women?

8. What other needs could micro-credit collectives fulfill?

9. How could micro-credit activities be expanded to other parts of the economy?

10. How can poverty alleviation programs evolve from charity to building local, durable self-reliance?

11. How can NGOs work in villages without weakening or replacing local conventions?

12. Think of a community you belong to. What entrepreneurial activities could your community initiate to improve itself?

References

L. P. Dana, 2006, *Asian Models of Entrepreneurship,* Singapore: World Scientific.

P. Reynolds, W. D. Bygrave, E. Autio, & M. Hay, 2002, *Global Entrepreneurship Monitor Report.*

M. Sidel, 2001, Recent research on philanthropy and the nonprofit sector in India and South Asia. *Voluntas: International Journal of Voluntary and Nonprofit Organizations,* 12(2): 171–180.

Tamil Nadu Government (TNG), 2002, *Tamil Nadu Human Development Report.* New Delhi: Social Science Press.

United Nations Human Development (UNDP), 2006, Human Development Index.

W. S. Watkins et al., 2005, Diversity and divergence among the tribal populations of India, *Annals of Human Genetics,* 69: 680–692.

Have You Offset Your Own Carbon Emissions?[1]

Mike W. Peng
University of Texas at Dallas

As more countries join the Kyoto Protocol, it seems necessary for every manager and company to be prepared to answer this question: "Have you offset your own carbon emissions?"

No longer only referring to a Japanese city, Kyoto has now become a new buzzword. The 1997 Kyoto Protocol (hereafter "Kyoto" in short) was a global initiative to reduce emissions of greenhouse gases linked to global warming. Kyoto was a hard-fought attempt to do something immensely difficult: Create a worldwide mechanism for solving a long-term problem. Under Kyoto, developed countries pledge to cut emissions by 6% from 1990 levels by 2012. Each country is permitted to emit a certain quantity of carbon dioxide. Governments issue emission "allowances" (permits) to polluting firms within their borders, and such allowances (essentially rights to pollute) can be bought and sold by firms worldwide. Through this carbon trading system, polluting firms in developed countries can pay someone else (at home or abroad) to cut emissions and claim credit.

The EU has taken Kyoto most seriously. The British economy grew by 36% between 1990 and 2002, while greenhouse emissions fell by 15%, thus already exceeding Kyoto. In comparison, the United States did not ratify Kyoto, and Australia only ratified Kyoto in late 2007. Canada and Japan, both presently running at 25% *above* 1990 levels, may fail to comply. China, India, and many developing countries essentially argue: "Sorry, we have to develop our economy first—and must forget about Kyoto for now."

Effective as of February 2005, the market for emissions allowances has soared. Most of the action has taken place on the Amsterdam-based European Climate Exchange (ECX). Such trading is literally "selling hot air." The British government, Bank of Tokyo-Mitsubishi, Swiss Re, HSBC, and many others have pledged to go "carbon neutral" by reducing their own emissions and buying offsets to compensate for what they cannot eliminate. Swiss Re, a major reinsurance firm, says it wants to fight global warming because global warming causes extreme weather and more devastating claims on its policies (think of Hurricane Katrina in 2005). By going "carbon neutral," HSBC tries to establish credibility for its new carbon-finance business.

Interestingly, while the US federal government has refused to ratify Kyoto, numerous states, industries, firms, and NGOs have joined forces to combat climate change. America's leading Kyoto crusader is Al Gore, the former vice president turned alarmist filmmaker. His documentary film on global warming, *An Inconvenient Truth*, won an Oscar in 2007. Al Gore flies commercial most of the time to generate less CO_2 and purchases offsets to maintain a carbon-neutral life. Although he drives a sports utility vehicle (SUV), it is a Mercury *hybrid*. In part, due to Gore's campaign, a dozen or so states—in the absence of federal action—have moved to restrict CO_2 emissions. More encouragingly, the Chicago Climate Exchange (CCX) was set up in 2003, with its membership growing from 23 firms to over 200 currently, including DuPont, Ford, and Motorola.

CSR advocates (advocates for corporate social responsibility) argue that voluntary offsets, while small at the moment, can in time help slow global warming. However, close scrutiny by *BusinessWeek* revealed that

[1]This case was written by Mike W. Peng (University of Texas at Dallas) and supported by a National Science Foundation CAREER Grant (SES 0552089). It was entirely based on published sources. All views expressed are those of the author and not necessarily those of the NSF. © Mike W. Peng. Reprinted with permission.

some deals amounted to little more than "feel-good hype." For instance, in 2005, Seattle City Light made an astounding announcement that it had eliminated its share of contributing to global warming. Of course, it still puffed out some 200,000 tons of greenhouse gases annually, but Seattle City Light claimed to have paid other organizations to reduce more than 200,000 tons of emissions. Such buying and selling offsets have now gone global. The sellers are often developing countries—China may soon beat the United States in being the largest greenhouse gas emitter by 2015. At the Carbon Fair in Cologne, Germany, organized by the World Bank, the Chinese state planning committee distributed a glossy 200-page book crammed with projects. Since developed countries that ratified Kyoto are expected to produce 3.5 billion tons of carbon above their targets by 2012, the sellers have excellent prospects. While paying someone else to do the (less) dirty work is nice, it reduces the incentive for firms in developed countries to bite off the more challenging task of reducing their own emissions.

Another issue is the lack of standards and oversight. Buying and selling offsets has rapidly become an industry itself, with a number of for-profit intermediaries. For example, the for-profit, two-year-old TerraPass issued every 2007 Oscar performer and presenter (including Gore) a "carbon-neutral" certificate, by using funds from the Oscar organizers to pay for emission-reduction projects, primarily at Waste Management landfill facilities in Arkansas. However, *BusinessWeek* found that the Waste Management projects in Arkansas had been launched long *before* any carbon-offsets deals. In other words, the offsets had nothing to do with emission reduction at the particular facilities. The main effects of the offsets were "to salve guilty celebrity consciences and provide Waste Management, a $13 billion company, with some extra revenue." According to *BusinessWeek*, this was another "inconvenient truth." Overall, although Kyoto may be flawed, it seems better than nothing.

Sources: Based on (1) T. Blair, 2005, A year of huge challenges, *The Economist*, January 1: 44–46; (2) *BusinessWeek*, 2007, Another inconvenient truth, March 26: 96–102; (3) *The Economist*, 2006, Upset about offsets, August 5: 53–54; (4) *The Economist*, 2007, Selling hot air, September 9: 17–18; (5) *Time*, 2007, The last temptation of Al Gore, May 28: 30–39.

Case Discussion Questions

1. From an institution-based view, explain why some firms in countries such as the United States, whose governments did *not* ratify Kyoto, are interested in participating in carbon offsets.

2. From a resource-based view, identify potential first-mover advantages in carbon offsets.

3. As the CEO of a coal-fired utility in Canada, how can your firm reduce greenhouse gas emissions? As CEO of a similar utility in China, what are your options?

A

absorptive capacity The ability to absorb new knowledge by recognizing the value of new information, assimilating it, and applying it.

accommodative strategy A strategy that tries to accommodate corporate social responsibility considerations into decision making.

acquisition The transfer of control of assets, operations, and management from one firm (target) to another (acquirer); the former becomes a unit of the latter.

acquisition premium The difference between the acquisition price and the market value of target firms.

agency costs The costs associated with principal-agent relationships. They are the sum of (1) principals' costs of monitoring and controlling agents, (2) agents' costs of bonding, and (3) the residual loss because the interests of the principals and the agents do not align.

agency relationship The relationship between principals and agents.

agency theory The theory about principal-agent relationships (or agency relationships in short). It focuses on principal-agent conflicts.

agents Persons (such as managers) to whom authority is delegated.

agglomeration Clustering economic activities in certain locations.

anchored replicators Companies that seek to replicate a set of activities in related industries in a small number of countries anchored by the home country.

antidumping laws Laws that punish foreign companies that engage in dumping in a domestic market.

antitrust laws Laws that attempt to curtail anticompetitive business practices such as cartels and trusts.

antitrust policy Competition policy designed to combat monopolies, cartels, and trusts.

arm's-length transactions Transactions in which parties keep a distance (see also formal, rule-based, impersonal exchange).

attack An initial set of actions to gain competitive advantage.

B

backward integration Acquiring and owning upstream assets.

bargaining power of suppliers The ability of suppliers to raise prices and/or reduce the quality of goods and services.

base of the pyramid The vast majority of humanity, about four billion people, who make less than $2,000 a year.

benchmarking Examination as to whether a firm has resources and capabilities to perform a particular activity in a manner superior to competitors.

born global Start-up companies that attempt to do business abroad from inception.

BRIC Brazil, Russia, India, and China.

build-operate-transfer (BOT) agreements A special kind of turnkey project in which contractors first build facilities, then operate them for a period of time, and then transfer back to clients.

bureaucratic costs The additional costs associated with a larger, more diversified organization, such as more employees and more expensive information systems.

business group A term to describe a conglomerate, which is often used in emerging economies.

business-level strategy Strategy which builds competitive advantage in a discrete and identifiable market.

C

capabilities The tangible and intangible assets a firm uses to choose and implement its strategies.

capacity to punish Having sufficient resources to deter and combat defection.

captive sourcing Setting up subsidiaries to perform in-house work in foreign location. Conceptually identical to foreign direct investment (FDI).

cartel An entity that engages in output- and price-fixing, involving multiple competitors. Also known as a trust.

causal ambiguity The difficulty of identifying the causal determinants of successful firm performance.

centers of excellence MNE subsidiaries explicitly recognized as a source of important capabilities, with the intention that these capabilities be leveraged by and/or disseminated to other subsidiaries.

473

CEO duality When the board is led by the CEO, who doubles as a chairman.

chief executive officer (CEO) The top executive in charge of the strategy and operations of a firm.

classic conglomerate A company that engage in product-unrelated diversification within a small set of countries centered on the home country.

code of conduct (code of ethics) Written policies and standards for corporate conduct and ethics.

cognitive pillar The internalized, taken-for-granted values and beliefs that guide individual and firm behavior.

collectivism The perspective that the identity of an individual is most fundamentally based on the identity of his or her collective group (such as family, village, or company).

collusion Collective attempts between competing firms to reduce competition.

collusive price setting Monopolists or collusion parties setting prices at a level higher than the competitive level.

 co-marketing Agreements among a number of firms to jointly market their products and services.

commoditization A process of market competition through which unique products that command high prices and high margins generally lose their ability to do so—these products thus become "commodities."

competition policy Policy governing the rules of the game in competition, which determine the institutional mix of competition and cooperation that gives rise to the market system.

competitive dynamics Actions and responses undertaken by competing firms.

competitor analysis The process of anticipating rivals' actions in order to both revise a firm's plan and prepare to deal with rivals' responses.

complementary assets Numerous noncore assets that complement and support the value-adding activities of core assets.

complementors A firm that sells products that add value to the products of a focal industry.

concentrated ownership and control Ownership and control rights concentrated in the hands of owners.

concentration ratio The percentage of total industry sales accounted for by the top four, eight, or twenty firms.

conduct Firm actions such as product differentiation.

conglomerate M&As M&A deals involving firms in product-unrelated industries.

conglomerates Product-unrelated diversifiers.

conglomeration A strategy of product-unrelated diversification.

constellations Multipartner strategic alliances (also known as strategic networks).

contender A strategy that centers on rapid learning and then expanding overseas.

contractual (non-equity-based) alliances Alliances which are based on contracts and which do not involve the sharing of equity.

corporate governance The relationship among various participants in determining the direction and performance of corporations.

corporate social responsibility (CSR) The social responsibility of corporations. It pertains to consideration of, and response to, issues beyond the narrow economic, technical, and legal requirements of the firm to accomplish social benefits along with the traditional economic gains that the firm seeks.

corporate-level strategy (also known as corporate strategy) Strategy about how a firm creates value through the configuration and coordination of its multimarket activities.

corruption The abuse of public power for private benefit usually in the form of bribery.

cost leadership A competitive strategy that centers on competing on low cost and prices.

counterattack A set of actions in response to attacks.

country (regional) manager The business leader in charge of a specific country (or region) for an MNE.

country-of-origin effect The positive or negative perception of firms and products from a certain country.

cross-listing Firms list their shares on foreign stock exchanges.

cross-market retaliation Retaliation in other markets when one market is attacked by rivals.

cross-shareholding Both partners invest in each other to become cross-shareholders.

cultural distance The difference between two cultures along some identifiable dimensions.

culture The collective programming of the mind that distinguishes the members of one group or category of people from another.

currency risks Risks stemming from exposure to unfavorable movements of the currencies.

D

defender A strategy that leverages local assets in areas which MNEs are weak

defensive strategy A strategy that is defensive in nature. Firms admit responsibility, but often fight it.

differentiation A strategy that focuses on how to deliver products that customers perceive as valuable and different.

diffused ownership An ownership pattern involving numerous small shareholders, none of which has a dominant level of control.

direct exports Directly selling products made in the home country to customers in other countries.

dissemination risks The risks associated with the unauthorized diffusion of firm-specific assets.

diversification Adding new businesses to the firm that are distinct from its existing operations.

diversification discount Reduced levels of performance because of association with a product-diversified firm (also known as conglomerate discount).

diversification premium Increased levels of performance because of association with a product-diversified firm (also known as conglomerate advantage).

dodger A strategy that centers on cooperating through joint ventures with MNEs and/or sell-offs to MNEs.

domestic demand Demand for products and services within a domestic economy.

dominance A situation whereby the market leader has a very large market share.

dominant logic A common underlying theme that connects various businesses in a diversified firm.

downscoping Reducing the scope of the firm through divestitures and spin-offs.

downsizing Reducing the number of employees through lay-offs, early retirements, and outsourcing.

downstream vertical alliances Alliances with firms in distribution (downstream).

dumping An exporter selling below cost abroad and planning to raise prices after eliminating local rivals.

duopoly A special case of oligopoly that has only two players.

E

economic benefits Benefits brought by the various forms of synergy in the context of diversification.

economies of scale Reduction in per unit costs by increasing the scale of production.

efficiency seeking Firms going after certain locations in search of efficiency gains.

emerging economies (emerging markets) A label which describes fast-growing developing economies since the 1990s.

emerging strategy A strategy based on the outcome of a stream of smaller decisions from the "bottom up."

entrepreneurs Individuals who identify and explore previously unexplored opportunities.

entrepreneurship The identification and exploitation of previously unexplored opportunities.

entry barriers The industry structures that increase the costs of entry.

equity modes Modes of foreign market entry which involve the use of equity.

equity-based alliances Strategic alliances which involve the use of equity.

ethical imperialism The imperialistic thinking that one's own ethical standards should be applied universally around the world.

ethical relativism The relative thinking that ethical standards vary significantly around the world and that there are no universally agreed upon ethical and unethical behaviors.

ethics The norms, principles, and standards of conduct governing individual and firm behavior.

excess capacity Additional production capacity currently underutilized or not utilized.

exit-based mechanisms Corporate governance mechanisms which focus on exit, indicating that shareholders no longer have patience and are willing to "exit" by selling their shares.

explicit collusion Firms directly negotiate output, fix pricing, and divide markets.

explicit knowledge Knowledge that is codifiable (that is, it can be written down and transferred without losing much of its richness).

exploitation Actions captured by terms such as refinement, choice, production, efficiency, selection, and execution.

exploration Actions captured by terms such as search, variation, risk taking, experimentation, play, flexibility, discovery, and innovation.

expropriation (1) of foreign assets: Confiscation of foreign assets invested in one country. (2) of minority shareholders: Activities which enrich the controlling shareholders at the expense of minority shareholders.

extender A strategy that centers on leveraging homegrown competencies abroad by expanding into similar markets.

extraterritoriality The reach of one country's laws to other countries.

F

factor endowments The endowments of production factors such as land, water, and people in one country.

far-flung conglomerates Conglomerate firms which pursue both extensive product-unrelated diversification and extensive geographic diversification.

feint A firm's attack on a focal arena important to a competitor, but not the attacker's true target area.

femininity A relatively weak form of societal-level sex role differentiation whereby more women occupy positions that reward assertiveness and more men work in caring professions.

financial control (or output control) Controlling subsidiary/unit operations strictly based on whether they meet financial/output criteria.

financial synergy The increase in competitiveness for each individual unit that is financially controlled by the corporate headquarters beyond what can be achieved by each unit competing independently as standalone firms.

firm strategy, structure, and rivalry How industry structure and firm strategy interact to affect interfirm rivalry.

first mover advantages The advantages that first movers enjoy and later movers do not.

five forces framework A framework governing the competitiveness of an industry proposed by Michael Porter. The five forces are (1) the intensity of rivalry among competitors, (2) the threat of potential entry, (3) the bargaining power of suppliers, (4) the bargaining power of buyers, and (5) the threat of substitutes.

flexible manufacturing technology Modern manufacturing technology that enables firms to produce differentiated products at low costs (usually on a smaller batch basis than the large batch typically produced by cost leaders).

focus A strategy that serves the needs of a particular segment or niche of an industry.

foreign direct investment (FDI) A firm's direct investment in production and/or service activities abroad.

foreign portfolio investment (FPI) Foreigners' purchase of stocks and bonds in one country. They do not directly manage operations.

formal institutions Institutions represented by laws, regulations, and rules.

formal, rule-based, impersonal exchange A way of economic exchange based on formal transactions in which parties keep a distance (*see also* arm's-length transactions).

forward integration Acquiring and owning downstream assets.

friendly M&As Mergers and acquisitions in which the board and management of a target firm agree to the transaction (although they may initially resist).

G

gambit A firm's withdrawal from a low-value market to attract rival firms to divert resources into the low-value market so that the original withdrawing firm can capture a high-value market.

game theory A theory which focuses on competitive and cooperative interaction (such as in a prisoners' dilemma situation).

generic strategies Strategies intended to strengthen the focal firm's position relative to the five competitive forces, including (1) cost leadership, (2) differentiation, and (3) focus.

geographic area structure An organizational structure which organizes the MNE according to different countries and regions, and is the most appropriate structure for a multidomestic strategy.

geographic diversification Entries into new geographic markets.

global account structure A customer-focused structure that supplies customers (often other MNEs) in a coordinated and consistent way across various countries.

global matrix An organizational structure often used to alleviate the disadvantages associated with both geographic area and global product division structures, especially for MNEs adopting a transnational strategy.

global product division An organizational structure which assigns global responsibilities to each product division.

global standardization strategy An MNE strategy that relies on the development and distribution of standardized products worldwide to reap the maximum benefits from low-cost advantages.

global strategy (1) Strategy of firms around the globe. (2) A particular form of international strategy, characterized by the production and distribution of standardized products and services on a worldwide basis.

global sustainability The ability to meet the needs of the present without compromising the ability of future generations to meet their needs.

global virtual teams Teams whose members are physically dispersed in multiple locations in the world. They cooperate on a virtual basis.

globalization The close integration of countries and peoples of the world.

greenfield operations Building factories and offices from scratch (on a proverbial piece of "greenfield" formerly used for agricultural purposes).

H

hedging Spreading out activities in a number of countries in different currency zones to offset the currency losses in certain regions through gains in other regions.

home replication strategy A strategy which emphasizes the international replication of home country–based competencies such as production scales, distribution efficiencies, and brand power.

horizontal alliances Strategic alliances formed by competitors.

horizontal M&As Merger and acquisition deals involving competing firms in the same industry.

hostile M&As (also known as hostile takeovers) Mergers and acquisitions undertaken against the wishes of the target firm's board and management, who reject M&A offers.

hubris Managers' overconfidence in their capabilities.

hypercompetition A way of competition centered on dynamic maneuvering intended to unleash a series of small, unpredictable but powerful, actions to erode the rival's competitive advantage.

I

incumbents Current members of an industry that compete against each other.

indirect exports Exporting indirectly through domestic-based export intermediaries.

individualism The perspective that the identity of an individual is most fundamentally based on his or her own individual attributes (rather than the attributes of a group).

industrial organization (IO) economics A branch of economics that seeks to better understand how firms in an industry compete and then how to regulate them.

industry A group of firms producing products (goods and/or services) that are similar to each other.

industry positioning Ways to position a firm within an industry in order to minimize the threats presented by the five forces.

informal institutions Institutions represented by norms, cultures, and ethics.

informal, relationship-based, personalized exchange A way of economic exchange based on informal relationships among transaction parties. Also known as relational contracting.

information asymmetries Asymmetric distribution of information between two sides. For example, in principal-agent relationships, agents almost always know more about the property they manage than principals do.

information overload Too much information to process.

in-group Individuals and firms regarded as part of "us."

initial public offering (IPO) The first round of public trading of company stock.

innovation seeking Firms targeting countries and regions renowned for generating world-class.

inshoring Domestic outsourcing.

inside directors Directors serving on corporate boards who are also full-time managers of these companies.

institution Humanly devised constraints that structure human interaction—informally known as the "rules of the game."

institution-based view A leading perspective of strategy that argues that in addition to industry- and firm-level conditions, firms also need to take into account wider influences from sources such as the state and society when crafting strategy.

institutional distance The extent of similarity or dissimilarity between the regulatory, normative, and cognitive institutions of two countries.

institutional framework A framework of formal and informal institutions governing individual and firm behavior.

institutional relatedness A firm's informal linkages with dominant institutions in the environment that confer resources and legitimacy.

institutional transitions Fundamental and comprehensive changes introduced to the formal and informal rules of the game that affect organizations as players.

intangible resources and capabilities Hard-to-observe and difficult-to-codify resources and capabilities.

integration-responsiveness framework A framework of MNE management on how to simultaneously deal with two sets of pressures for global integration and local responsiveness.

intended strategy A strategy that is deliberately planned for.

interlocking directorate A situation whereby two or more firms share one director affiliated with one firm who serves on multiple boards.

internal capital market A term used to describe the internal management mechanisms of a product-unrelated diversified firm (conglomerate) which operate as a capital market inside the firm.

internalization The process of replacing a market relationship with a single multinational organization spanning both countries.

internalization advantage The advantage associated with internalization, which is one of the three key advantages of being a multinational enterprise (the other two are ownership and location advantages).

international diversification The number and diversity of countries in which a firm competes.

international division A structure typically set up when firms initially expand abroad, often engaging in a home replication strategy.

international entrepreneurship A combination of innovative, proactive, and risk-seeking behavior that crosses national borders and is intended to create wealth in organizations.

J

joint venture (JV) A "corporate child" that is a new entity given birth and jointly owned by two or more parent companies.

K

knowledge management The structures, processes, and systems that actively develop, leverage, and transfer knowledge.

L

late mover advantages Advantages associated with being a later mover (also known as first mover disadvantages).

learning by doing A way of learning not by reading books but by engaging in hands-on activities.

learning race A race in which alliance partners aim to outrun each other by learning the "tricks" from the other side as fast as possible.

leveraged buyout (LBO) A means by which private investors, often in partnership with incumbent managers, issue bonds and use the cash raised to buy the firm's stock.

liability of foreignness The inherent disadvantage foreign firms experience in host countries because of their nonnative status.

liability of newness The inherent disadvantage that entrepreneurial firms experience as new entrants.

licensing/franchising agreements Agreements according to which the licensor/franchiser sells the rights to intellectual property, such as patents and know-how, to the licensee/franchisee for a royalty fee.

local content requirements Government requirements that certain products be subject to higher import tariffs and taxes unless a given percentage of their value is produced domestically.

local responsiveness The necessity to be responsive to different customer preferences around the world.

localization (multidomestic) strategy An MNE strategy which focuses on a number of foreign countries/regions, each of which is regarded as a standalone local (domestic) market worthy of significant attention and adaptation.

location-specific advantages Advantages associated with operating in a specific location.

long-term orientation A perspective that emphasizes perseverance and savings for future betterment.

M

managerial human capital The skills and abilities acquired by top managers.

marginal bureaucratic costs (MBC) The bureaucratic costs of the last unit of organizational expansion (such as the last subsidiary established).

marginal economic benefits (MEB) The economic benefits of the last unit of growth (such as the last acquisition).

market commonality The degree that two competitors' markets overlap.

market seeking Firms going after the most lucrative markets for their products and services.

masculinity A relatively strong form of societal-level sex role differentiation whereby men tend to have occupations that reward assertiveness and women tend to work in caring professions.

mass customization Mass produced but customized products.

merger The combination of assets, operations, and management of two firms to establish a new legal entity.

mergers and acquisitions (M&As) Firms either merging with or acquiring other firms.

micro-macro link Micro, informal interpersonal relationships among managers of various units may greatly facilitate macro, interorganizational cooperation among various units.

mobility barriers Within-industry differences that inhibit the movement between strategic groups.

monopoly A situation whereby only one firm provides the goods and/or services for an industry.

multimarket competition Firms engage the same rivals in multiple markets.

multinational enterprise (MNE) A firm that engages in foreign direct investment (FDI) by directly controlling and managing value-adding activities in other countries.

multinational replicators Firms which engage in product-related diversification on one hand and far-flung multinational expansion on the other hand.

mutual forbearance Multimarket firms respect their rivals' spheres of influence in certain markets and their rivals reciprocate, leading to tacit collusion.

N

natural resource seeking Firms entering foreign markets in search of natural resources.

network centrality The extent to which a firm's position is pivotal with respect to others in the interfirm network.

network externalities The value a user derives from a product increases with the number (or the network) of other users of the same product.

non-equity modes Modes of foreign market entries which do not involve the use of equity.

nongovernmental organization (NGO) Organization advocating causes such as the environment, human rights, and consumer rights that are not affiliated with government.

non-scale-based advantages Low-cost advantages that are not derived from the economies of scale.

nontariff barriers Trade and investment barriers which do not entail tariffs.

norm The prevailing practice of relevant players that affect the focal individuals and firms.

normative pillar How the values, beliefs, and norms of other relevant players influence the behavior of individuals and firms.

O

obsolescing bargain The deals struck by MNEs and host governments, which change their requirements after the entry of MNEs.

offshoring International/foreign outsourcing.

OLI advantages Ownership, location, and internalization advantages which are typically associated with MNEs.

oligopoly A situation whereby a few firms control an industry.

operational synergy Synergy derived by having shared activities, personnel, and technologies.

opportunism Self-interest seeking with guile.

organizational fit The complementarity of partner firms' "soft" organizational traits, such as goals, experiences, and behaviors, that facilitate cooperation.

out-group Individuals and firms not regarded as part of "us."

outside directors Non-management members of the board.

outsourcing Turning over all or part of an activity to an outside supplier to improve the performance of the focal firm.

ownership advantage Advantage associated with directly owning assets overseas, which is one of the three key advantages of being a multinational enterprise (the other two are location and internalization advantages).

P

partner rarity The difficulty to locate partners with certain desirable attributes.

perfect competition A competitive situation in which price is set by the "market," all firms are price takers, and entries and exits are relatively easy.

performance The result of firm conduct.

power distance The degree of social inequality.

predatory pricing (1) Setting prices below costs in the short run to destroy rivals and (2) intending to raise prices to cover losses in the long run after eliminating rivals.

price leader A firm that has a dominant market share and sets "acceptable" prices and margins in the industry.

primary stakeholder groups Constituents on which the firm relies for its continuous survival and prosperity.

principal-agent conflicts Conflicts of interests between principals (such as shareholders) and agents (such as professional managers).

principal-principal conflicts Conflicts of interests between two classes of principals: controlling shareholders and minority shareholders.

principals Persons (such as owners) who delegate authority.

prisoners' dilemma In game theory, a type of game in which the outcome depends on two parties deciding whether to cooperate or to defect.

private equity Equity capital invested in private (non-public) companies.

proactive strategy A strategy that focuses on proactive engagement in corporate social responsibility.

product differentiation The uniqueness of products that customers value.

product diversification Entries into new product markets and/or business activities that are related to a firm's existing markets and/or activities.

product proliferation Efforts to fill product space in a manner that leaves little "unmet demand" for potential entrants.

product-related diversification Entries into new product markets and/or business activities that are related to a firm's existing markets and/or activities.

product-unrelated diversification Entries into industries that have no obvious product-related connections to the firm's current lines of business.

R

R&D contracts Outsourcing agreements in R&D between firms (that is, firm A agrees to perform certain R&D work for firm B).

reactive strategy A strategy that is passive about corporate social responsibility. Firms do not act in the absence of disasters and outcries. When problems arise, denial is usually the first line of defense.

real option An option investment in real operations as opposed to financial capital.

refocusing Narrowing the scope of the firm to focus on a few areas.

regulatory pillar How formal rules, laws, and regulations influence the behavior of individuals and firms.

related and supporting industries Industries that are related to and/or support the focal industry.

related transactions Controlling owners sell firm assets to another firm they own at below-market prices or spin off the most profitable part of a public firm and merge it with another of their private firms.

relational (collaborative) capabilities The capabilities to successfully manage interfirm relationships.

relational contracting Contracting based on informal relationships (*see also* informal, relationship-based, personalized exchange).

replication Repeated testing of theory under a variety of conditions to establish its applicable boundaries.

resource similarity The extent to which a given competitor possesses strategic endowments comparable to those of the focal firm.

resource-based view A leading perspective of strategy which suggests that differences in firm performance are most fundamentally driven by differences in firm resources and capabilities.

resources The tangible and intangible assets a firm uses to choose and implement its strategies.

restructuring (1) Adjusting firm size and scope through either diversification (expansion or entry), divestiture (contraction or exit), or both. (2) Reducing firm size and scope.

S

scale economies (economies of scale) Reductions in per unit costs by increasing the scale of production.

scale of entry The amount of resources committed to foreign market entry.

scale-based advantages Advantages derived from economies of scale (the more a firm produces some products, the lower the unit costs become).

scope economies (economies of scope) Reduction in per unit costs and increases in competitiveness by enlarging the scope of the firm.

secondary stakeholder groups Stakeholders who influence or affect, or are influenced or affected by, the corporation, but they are not engaged in transactions with the corporation and are not essential for its survival.

semiglobalization A perspective that suggests that barriers to market integration at borders are high but not high enough to completely insulate countries from each other.

separation of ownership and control The dispersal of ownership among many small shareholders, and control of the firm is largely concentrated in the hands of salaried, professional managers who own little or no equity.

serial entrepreneurs People who start, grow, and sell several businesses throughout their careers.

shareholder capitalism A view of capitalism which suggests that the most fundamental purpose for firms to exist is to serve the economic interests of shareholders (also known as capitalists).

single business strategy A strategy which focuses on a single product or service with little diversification.

small and medium-sized enterprises (SMEs) Firms with less than 500 employees.

social capital The informal benefits individuals and organizations derive from their social structures and networks.

social complexity The socially complex ways of organizing typical of many firms.

social issue participation Firms' participation in social causes not directly related to managing primary stakeholders.

solutions-based structure An MNE organization structure which caters to the needs of providing solutions for customers' problems.

speculation Making bets on currency movements by committing to stable currencies.

stage models Models which suggest firms internationalize by going through predictable stages from simple steps to complex operations.

stakeholder Any group or individual who can affect or is affected by the achievement of the organization's objectives.

state-owned enterprises (SOE) Firms owned and controlled by the state (government).

stewardship theory A theory which suggests that managers should be regarded as stewards of owners' interests.

strategic alliances Voluntary agreements between firms involving exchanging, sharing, or co-developing of products, technologies, or services.

strategic control (or behavior control) Controlling subsidiary/unit operations based on whether they engage in desirable strategic behavior (such as cooperation).

strategic fit The complementarity of partner firms' "hard" skills and resources, such as technology, capital, and distribution channels.

strategic groups Groups of firms within a broad industry.

strategic investment One partner invests in another as a strategic investor.

strategic management A way of managing the firm from a strategic, "big picture" perspective.

strategic networks Strategic alliances formed by multiple firms to compete against other such groups and against traditional single firms (also known as constellations).

strategy A firm's theory about how to compete successfully.

strategy as action A perspective that suggests that strategy is most fundamentally reflected by firms' pattern of actions.

strategy as integration A perspective that suggests that strategy is neither solely about plan nor action and that strategy integrates elements of both schools of thought.

strategy as plan A perspective that suggests that strategy is most fundamentally embodied in explicit, rigorous formal planning as in the military.

strategy formulation The crafting of a firm's strategy.

strategy implementation The actions undertaken to carry out a firm's strategy.

strategy tripod A framework that suggests that strategy as a discipline has three "legs" or key perspectives: industry-, resource-, and institution-based views.

strong ties More durable, reliable, and trustworthy relationships cultivated over a long period of time.

structure Structural attributes of an industry such as the costs of entry/exit.

structure-conduct-performance (SCP) model An industrial organization economics model that suggests industry structure determines firm conduct (strategy), which in turn determines firm performance.

subsidiary initiative The proactive and deliberate pursuit of new business opportunities by an MNE's subsidiary to expand its scope of responsibility.

substitutes Products of different industries that satisfy customer needs currently met by the focal industry.

sunk costs Irrevocable costs incurred and investments made.

SWOT analysis A strategic analysis of a firm's internal strengths (S) and weaknesses (W) and the opportunities (O) and threats (T) in the environment.

T

tacit collusion Firms indirectly coordinate actions to reduce competition by signaling to others their intention to reduce output and maintain pricing above competitive levels.

tacit knowledge Knowledge that is not codifiable (that is, hard to be written down and transmitted without losing much of its richness).

tangible resources and capabilities Assets that are observable and more easily quantified.

tariff barriers Taxes levied on imports.

thrust The classic frontal attack with brute force.

top management team (TMT) The team consisting of the highest level of executives of a firm led by the CEO.

trade barriers Barriers blocking international trade.

transaction costs Costs associated with economic transaction—or more broadly, costs of doing business.

transnational strategy An MNE strategy which endeavors to be cost efficient, locally responsive, and learning driven simultaneously.

triad Three primary regions of developed economies: North America, Europe, and Japan.

triple bottom line A performance yardstick consisting of economic, social, and environmental performance.

tunneling Activities of managers from the controlling family of a corporation to divert resources from the firm for personal or family use.

turnkey projects Projects in which clients pay contractors to design and construct new facilities and train personnel.

U

uncertainty avoidance The extent to which members in different cultures accept ambiguous situations and tolerate uncertainty.

upstream vertical alliances Alliances with firms on the supply side (upstream).

V

value chain Goods and services produced through a chain of vertical activities that add value.

vertical M&As Merger and acquisition deals involving suppliers (upstream) and/or buyers (downstream).

voice-based mechanisms Corporate governance mechanisms which focus on shareholders' willingness to work with managers, usually through the board of directors, by "voicing" their concerns.

VRIO framework A resource-based framework that focuses on the value (V), rarity (R), imitability (I), and organizational (O) aspects of resources and capabilities.

W

weak ties Relationships that are characterized by infrequent interaction and low intimacy.

wholly owned subsidiaries (WOS) Subsidiaries located in foreign countries which are entirely owned by the MNE.

worldwide mandate The charter to be responsible for one MNE function throughout the world.